EVOLO
SKYSCRAPERS 2

150 NEW PROJECTS REDEFINE BUILDING HIGH

eVolo

CREDITS

CREDITS

CREDITS

CREDITS

EDITOR-IN-CHIEF

CARLO AIELLO

EDITORS

PAUL ALDRIDGE

NOÉMIE DEVILLE

ANNA SOLT

JUNG SU LEE

CONTRIBUTING EDITORS

CARLOS ARZATE

JOSEPH COHAN

DANIELLE DEL SOL

JESSICA ESCOBEDO

Library of Congress Cataloging-in-Publication Data Available.

ISBN: 978-1-938740-05-3

Manufactured in China

Evolo, Inc.
6363 Wilshire Blvd. #311
Los Angeles, CA 90048

www.evolo.us

CONTENTS
CONTENTS

CONTENTS

CONTENTS

5

MORPHOTECTONIC AESTHETICS

INTRODUCTION

INTRODUCTION
INTRODUCTION
INTRODUCTION

THESE SUPER-TALL STRUCTURES TAKE INTO CONSIDERATION THE ADVANCES IN TECHNOLOGY, THE EXPLORATION OF SUSTAINABLE SYSTEMS, AND THE ESTABLISHMENT OF NEW URBAN AND ARCHITECTURAL METHODS TO SOLVE ECONOMIC, SOCIAL, AND CULTURAL PROBLEMS OF THE CONTEMPORARY CITY.

The year 2014 marks the tenth anniversary of *eVolo*. What started a decade ago as a modest publishing house has grown into one of the leading architecture and design publishers in the world. In the same fashion, the annual *eVolo Skyscraper Competition*, inaugurated in 2006, is one of the world's most important architecture awards and without a question the most popular architecture competition, with more than 1200 annual submissions from almost every country. The award challenges architects and designers' creativity and explores the future of building high through the use of new technologies, materials, programs, aesthetics, and spatial organizations.

This publication is the follow-up to the highly acclaimed book *eVolo Skyscrapers* in which 150 new skyscrapers submitted to the competition are categorized and examined. These super-tall structures take into consideration the advances in technology, the exploration of sustainable systems, and the establishment of new urban and architectural methods to solve economic, social, and cultural problems of the contemporary city; including the scarcity of natural resources and infrastructure and the exponential increase of inhabitants, pollution, economic division, and unplanned urban sprawl.

The projects have been placed in six distinct chapters including: *Technological Advances, Ecological Urbanism, New Frontiers, Social Solutions, Morphotectonic Aesthetics,* and *Urban Theories.* Although many of the projects could have been included in more than one chapter, we gave more importance to the predominant area of research of each concept.

The core of the competition is the expertise of the world-renowned Jury whose talent and dedication make this endeavor possible. The Jury included: Maria Aiolova, Chris Bosse, Gaël Brulé, Julien Combes, Giacomo Costa, Julien De Smedt, Hernan Diaz Alonso, Marc Fornes, Matthias Holwich, Florian Idenburg, Minnie Jan, Mitchell Joachim, Edward Keller, Marc Kushner, François Lepeytre, Jing Liu, Daisuke Nagatomo, François Roche, Alexander Rieck, Roland Snooks, Kivi Sotamaa, Tuuli Sotamaa, Michael Szivos, Tobias Wallisser, Tom Wiscombe, and Ma Yansong

Over the last five years eVolo has been invited to universities, events, and festivals to talk about the completion's winning entries. At every lecture there is always a mixed sentiment of excitement and disbelief when the audience is confronted by the audacious proposals. Many believe that these projects belong to science fiction, that they would never be built, let alone solve any of our current habitation problems. We usually finish our presentations with conceptual sketches by *Futurists* like Arne Hosek, Piero Portaluppi, and Sergei Lopatin, whose "out of this world" projects published in the 1900's by *Lacerba* in Italy and *Le Figaro* in France have become a reality 100 years later. It is our mission to enter the ranks of such inspiring publications through stimulating and promoting bold architectural and urban concepts. We can only hope to see these ideas as built projects in the years to come.

eVolo – to study, to develop, to evolve, to fly away...

JURORS

Maria Aiolova

MARIA AIOLOVA is an educator, architect, and urban designer in New York City. Her work focuses on the theory, science and application of ecological design. She is the founding Co-President of Terreform ONE. Presently, Maria chairs the ONE Lab NY School for Design and Science and the One Prize Design and Science Award. She is an adviser to New Lab at the Brooklyn Navy Yard and an academic adviser to CIEE (Council on International Educational Exchange). She won the 2013 AIA NY Award for Urban Design. Maria is currently a visiting faculty at University of Applied Arts Vienna. She taught at Pratt Institute and Parsons the New School for Design. Maria has been a visiting lecturer at Harvard GSD, Columbia University, Cornell University, CUNY, Washington University, The Cooper Union, University of Toronto, and Rhode Island School of Design. She served as Vice President and Chief Scientific Officer of ETEX Corporation, a bio-tech company in Cambridge, MA. Maria is an inventor, holding 18 technology patents. Maria received her M.Arch. in Urban Design from Harvard University, B.Arch. from Wentworth IT with Honors, and Dipl.-Ing. from the Technical University of Vienna, Austria and Sofia, Bulgaria.

CHRIS BOSSE co-founded LAVA with Tobias Wallisser and Alexander Rieck in 2007 as a network of creative minds with a research and design focus. LAVA explores frontiers that merge future technologies with the patterns of organization found in nature and believes this will result in a smarter, friendlier, more socially and environmentally responsible future. Chris is director of LAVA Asia Pacific based in Sydney, Australia, and Adjunct Professor at the University of Technology, Sydney. Educated in Germany and Switzerland, he worked with several high-profile European architects before moving to Sydney. Whilst Associate Architect at PTW Architects in Sydney he completed many projects in Asia and the Middle East. His work on the Watercube Olympic Swimming Centre in Beijing received the Atmosphere Award at the 9th Venice Architecture Biennale; he won an Emerging Architect Award from RIBA in 2008 and a Perspective 40 Under 40 Award in 2012. Bosse bases his work on the computerized study of organic structures and resulting spatial conceptions.

Chris Bosse

Gaël Brulé

GAËL BRULÉ was trained as an engineer in sustainability; after experience in different fields (transportation, energy production, life cycle analysis), he found a particular interest in architecture and urbanism, in which he decided to develop his environmental knowledge. He cofounded the Paris-based company Atelier CMJN, and participated in a few calls for ideas and open competitions that lead to a few prizes (eVolo, Arqfutura, Cityvision, New Italian Blood). For the past two years, Atelier CMJN has been developing projects related to urbanism, education and cultural centers, while combining sustainability and architecture. Brulé is now interested in incorporating the sciences of well-being, in which he is doing so by working on his PhD in architecture, with a particular interest in buildings related to education.

VINCENT CALLEBAUT is the lead architect of Vincent Callebaut Architectures. In 2000, Callebaut graduated with the Great Architecture Prize René Serrure awarded to the best diploma project at the Institute Victor Horta in Brussels for the Parisian project, Metamuseum of Arts and Civilisations. The year after, he won the Grand Architecture Prize Napoléon Godecharle of the Académie Royale des Beaux-Arts of Brussels. In 2008, he published his second monograph "Archibiotic" in Chinese with the support of the United Asia Art & Design Cooperation at Beijing. In 2010, Vincent Callebaut Architectures SARL won first prize for the design and consturction of a luxurious residential tower at the bottom of the Tower 101 in Taipei, Taiwan. Recently, Callebaut has participated in lectures in Paris, Bucharest, Bratislava, Moscow, Singapore, etc. in order to exhibit all the prospective and positive visions for up and coming green lifestyles. Vincent Callebaut Architectures was nominated for the Design German Awards 2014 for the project "Asian Cairns, Sustainable Farmscrapers."

Vincent Callebaut

Julien Combes

JULIEN COMBES established Julien Combes Architecture in 2012. Combes designs with Delphine Bourgouin, developing projects ranging from furniture design to urban development strategies. His education includes earning a diploma and HMONP from ENSA Paris La Vilette in 2008 and 2009 respectively as well as completing the Master 2 program at the Royal Institute of Technology (KTH) in Stockholm. His work experience includes co-managing the Workshop CMYK and working for Herzog & de Meuron in Basel as well as Ateliers Jean Nouvel.

JURORS

ACOMO COSTA was born in 1970 in Florence. He left education after the first years of high school to devote time to otorcycles and later to become a mountaineer by which he began to cultivate his interest in photography. He returned Florence in 1994 and met the critic Maria Luisa Frisa who introduced him to the art world. His collaboration with the llery Arezzo Marsilio Margiacchi began in 1996 but it is in 1998 that he made a strong working relationship with the anese gallerist David Faccioli of Photology who exhibits his work in Milan and London. In 2009 he published the book e *Chronicles of Time* which reviews all his works from 1996 to 2008. The volume is introduced by architect Norman ster and the Italian critic Luca Beatrice. In 2009 he was invited to the 53rd Venice Biennale. His work is featured in CNO (Contemporary Arts Center of New Orleans), the Contemporary Arts Museum in Houston, Centre Pompidou in ris and the Center for Contemporary Art Luigi Pecci in Prato.

Giacomo Costa

JULIEN DE SMEDT is the founder and director of JDS Architects based in Brussels, Copenhagen, Belo Horizonte and Shanghai. Julien's commitment to the exploration of contemporary architecture has helped to re-energize the discussion of the practice with projects such as the VM Housing Complex, the Mountain Dwellings, the Maritime Youth House and the Holmenkollen Ski Jump. Prior to founding JDS Architects, he worked with Rem Koolhaas and OMA and co-founded and directed with Bjarke Ingels the architecture firm PLOT in Copenhagen. Julien received the Henning Larsen Prize in 2003 and an Eckersberg medal in 2005. In 2004 the Stavanger Concert Hall was appointed World's Best Concert Hall at the Venice Biennale, and the Maritime Youth House won the AR+D award in London and was nominated for the Mies van der Rohe award. In 2009, De Smedt received the Maaskant prize of Architecture, and in 2011 he received the WAN-World Architecture News "21 for 21" Award. His academic contributions include visiting professorships in Rice and Lexington University. JDS Architects released two monographs entitled *PIXL to XL* and *Agenda* which are distributed worldwide.

Julien De Smedt

ERNAN DIAZ ALONSO is principal and founder of Xefirotarch, a Los Angeles-based design practice. Before coming the Graduate Program's Chair at SCI-Arc, Diaz Alonso has served for the past several years as Distinguished ofessor of Architecture and the Graduate Thesis Coordinator at SCI-Arc. He has taught as a design studio professor Columbia University GSAPP and was the head studio professor in the "Excessive" post-graduate program at the niversitat fur angewandte Kunst in Wien, Austria. He was recently honored by Yale University with the Louis I. Kahn siting Assistant Professorship of Architectural Design for fall 2010 and by the American Institute of Architects as the ucator of the Year in 2012. His designs have been displayed in architecture and art museum exhibitions, such as w York MoMa, San Francisco MoMa, Art Institute of Chicago, and Artist Space in New York. His work has been blished in periodicals and multiple books, including the "*Excessive*" monograph and an upcoming monograph by ames and Hudson. His work is part of the permanent collections of the FRAC Center, the San Francisco MoMa, New rk MoMa, Thyssen Bornamiza Collection in Vienna, MAK Museum in Vienna and the Art Institute of Chicago.

Hernan Diaz Alonso

MARC FORNES is a registered "Architect DPLG." As a connoisseur in computer science, he designs through writing text files, or codes. Under his long time label THEVERYMANY™ he is a recognized figure in the development of computational protocols applied to the field of design and fabrication. His research on ways to describe complex curvilinear surfaces into a series of flat elements has defined a field of Computational Skinning for architecture. Marc has designed over the last 10 years an extensive body of experimental, highly organic, large scale and self-supported structures. His prototypical work has been displayed as part of the permanent collection of the Centre Pompidou in Paris, the FRAC Centre in Orleans and the CNAP. He has exhibited work at the Guggenheim and Miami Art Basel. In 2012 he was the recipient of the Artist Residency at the Atelier Calder and his studio was awarded the New Practices New York 2012 by the American Institute of Architects. Involved in academia, Marc, with Francois Roche, started "(n) Certainties," a graduate studio at Columbia University, with visiting semesters at the University of Southern California and at Die Angewandte in Vienna. He taught at Princeton, Harvard GSD and the University of Michigan.

arc Fornes

ATTHIAS HOLWICH, SBA, is a registered European Architect, co-founder and principal of Hollwich Kushner (HWKN), New York Based design office, and cofounder of Architizer.com. Before starting his own enterprises he worked at MA in Rotterdam, Eisenman Architects and Diller+Scofidio in New York City. He is currently a visiting professor at the niversity of Pennsylvania, where he has been the creator of an international conference on aging and architecture: w Aging, held in the fall of 2010 at UPenn. In 2004, Matthias finished editing his first book with Rainer Weisbach at e Bauhaus: UmBauhaus – Updating Modernism. His work has been featured in *Wallpaper**, *New York Times*, *Bauwelt*, vell, and *Architectural Digest*. He has been a speaker at TEDx East, TEDx Atlanta and the PICNIC conference in nsterdam.

Matthias Holwich

JURORS

FLORIAN IDENBURG is a Dutch architect and co-founder of the award-winning SO - IL architecture firm in New York City. Idenburg studied architecture at the Delft University of Technology in the Netherlands, receiving a masters degree in 1999. In 2000, he became a senior associate with SANAA, his major assignment being the New Museum of Contemporary Art in New York. In 2008, he, with his wife Jing Liu, set up SO - IL (Solid Objectives – Idenburg Liu). In 2010, the firm won the MoMA PS1 Young Architects Program. They went on to design a residence for Ivan Chermayeff in upstate New York, a wedding chapel in Nanjing, China, the Flockr outdoor exhibition space in Beijing, and a project space for the Kukje Gallery in Seoul. They currently have a commission to design tent facilities for the Frieze fair in New York. Idenburg teaches at Harvard and Columbia Universities. He has held the Brown-Forman Chair in Urban Design at the University of Kentucky and has been a visiting lecturer at Princeton University. In 2010, Idenburg won the Dutch Charlotte Köhler Award.

Florian Idenburg

MINNIE JAN is the codirector of MisoSoupDesign, the multi-disciplinary design studio she founded with Daisuke Nagatomo based in Taipei. MisoSoupDesign is known for innovative architecture and product design, and won several international design awards including Far Eastern International Digital Architectural Design Award, Green Dot Award, and A'design Golden Award. Jan received her Bachelor of Architecture from University of Southern California and Master of Science in Advanced Architectural Design from Columbia University. Jan was also the invited researcher at Institute for Advanced Architecture of Catalonia. She is the assistant professor at National Chiao Tung University in Taiwan.

Minnie Jan

MITCHELL JOACHIM, PhD, Assoc. AIA, is the founding co-president of Terreform ONE. Mitchell is an Associate Professor at NYU and EGS in Switzerland. Previously he was the Frank Gehry Chair at University of Toronto and faculty at Pratt, Columbia, Syracuse, Washington, and Parsons. He was formerly an architect at Gehry Partners, and Pei Cobb Freed. He is a 2011 TED Senior Fellow and has been awarded fellowships with Moshe Safdie and Martin Society for Sustainability, MIT. He won the Zumtobel Group Award for Sustainability and Humanity, History Channel and Infiniti Award for City of the Future, and Time Magazine Best Invention of 2007 with MIT Smart Cities Car. Mitchell is also a Partner at Planetary ONE. He was chosen by Wired magazine for "The 2008 Smart List: 15 People the Next President Should Listen To." *Rolling Stone* magazine honored Mitchell in "The 100 People Who Are Changing America." Mitchell was the Winner of the Victor Papanek Social Design Award sponsored by the University of Applied Arts Vienna, the Austrian Cultural Forum, and the Museum of Arts and Design in 2011. He earned a Ph.D. at Massachusetts Institute of Technology, MAUD Harvard University, M.Arch. Columbia University, and BPS SUNY at Buffalo with Honors.

Mitchell Joachim

EDWARD KELLER is the Director of the Center for Transformative Media at The New School, and Associate Professor at Parsons The New School for Design. He is a designer, professor, writer, musician and multimedia artist. Prior to joining Parsons, he taught at Columbia University GSAPP from 1998 to 2010 and SCIArc in Los Angeles from 2004 to 2009. With Carla Leitao he co-founded AUM Studio, an architecture and new media firm that has produced residential projects, competitions, and new media installations in Europe and the US. His work and writing has appeared in *Punctum*, *Praxis*, *ANY*, *AD*, *Arquine*, *Leonardo Electronic Almanac*, *Architecture*, *Parpaings*, *Precis*, *Wired*, *Metropolis*, *Assemblage*, *Ottagono*, and *Progressive Architecture*. *Chronomorphology: Active Time in Architecture*, a survey of his graduate design studios at the Columbia GSAPP, was published in 2004 by CBA. He has spoken on architecture, film, technology and ecology internationally.

Edward Keller

MARC KUSHNER, AIA, is co-founder and CEO of Architizer.com and partner at Hollwich Kushner (HWKN), a New York based design office. After graduating from Harvard's Graduate School of Design he spent time working at J Mayer H Architects in Berlin and Lewis Tsurumaki Lewis (LTL) in New York City. Marc teaches at Columbia University's Graduate School of Architecture, Planning and Preservation and lectures on the topic of social media and architecture across the country and sits on the boards of Storefront for Art and Architecture and Goods for Good.

Marc Kushner

François Lepeytre

ᴿANÇOIS LEPEYTRE is a licensed architect from Paris. He has experience is working for Jourda Architects and ᴶMA Nicolas Michelin in Paris as well as Soriano & Asos in Madrid. He has extensive training including receiving his ᴹONP from ENSA Paris Belleville as well a diploma from there as well. He hold a Master 2 from ETSA Madrid and ᵉvious attended ENSA Marseille Luminy. He is a member of Paris-based company Atelier CMJN. For the past two ᵃrs, Atelier CMJN has been developing projects related to urbanism, education and cultural centers, while combining ᵗstainability and architecture.

ng Liu

JING LIU is a Chinese architect and co-founder of the award-winning SO - IL architecture firm in New York City. Liu studied in China, Japan, the United Kingdom and the United States before receiving a Master of Architecture degree from Tulane School of Architecture in New Orleans. She interned with SANAA in Japan and has worked for Kohn Pedorcon Fox and the Starwood Group. In 2008, she, with her husband Florian Idenburg, set up SO – IL (Solid Objectives – Idenburg Liu). In 2010, the firm won the MoMA PS1 Young Architects Program. They went on to design a residence for Ivan Chermayeff in upstate New York, a wedding chapel in Nanjing, China, the Flockr outdoor exhibition space in Beijing, and a project space for the Kukje Gallery in Seoul. They currently have a commission to design tent facilities for the Frieze fair in New York. Liu has taught at Columbia University's GSAPP and at Parsons The New School for Design.

ᴰAISUKE NAGATOMO is the codirector of MisoSoupDesign, the multi-disciplinary design studio he founded with ᵃnnie Jan based in Taipei. MisoSoupDesign is known for innovative architecture and product design, and won several ᵗernational design awards including Far Eastern International Digital Architectural Design Award, Green Dot Award, ᵈ A'design Golden Award. Nagatomo graduated from Meiji University with a degree in Bachelor of Engineering in ᵗchitecture and Columbia University with Master of Science in Advanced Architectural Design. In 2010, Nagatomo ᵃs the visiting researcher at the Institute for Advanced Architecture of Catalonia. He has taught several universities ᶜluding Pratt Institute, Keio University, Tokyo University of Science and Tokyo Denki University. He is currently the ᵃssistant professor at National Chiao Tung University in Taiwan.

Daisuke Nagatomo

rançois Roche

FRANÇOIS ROCHE is a French architect. He studied in Chalon-sur-Saône, and afterwards entered scientific preparatory school in Lyon. He left that school prior to graduating, and enrolled at the School of Architecture of Versailles. He graduated in 1988. He founded an organization, the name of which changed several times between 1989 and 2001: BoyeRoche (1989); Roche (1990); Roche & François (1991); Roche, Francois, Lewis, Huber, Roubaud, Perrin (1992); Roche, DSV & Sie (1993–97); R, DSV & Sie. P (1998); R & Sie. D/B: L (1999–2001); R&Sie(n) (2001 to present), adding a new one, titled [elf/bt/c] since 2011. This transformation of his firm name over time serves to illustrate its hybrid character, to destabilize the figure of the architect. He is Visiting Professor at Columbia University GSAPP. He was also a Visiting Professor at the University of Southern California in Los Angeles. Roche is a guest editor of LOG#25, NY Critic Review.

ᴸEXANDER RIECK co-founded LAVA with Chris Bosse and Tobias Wallisser in 2007 as a network of creative ᵐinds with a research and design focus. LAVA explores frontiers that merge future technologies with the patterns ᵒⁱ organization found in nature. Rieck is a co-director of LAVA, based in Stuttgart, Germany. He works as a senior ᵉsearcher at the renowned Fraunhofer Institute for Occupational Economics and Organisation. He studied architecture ᵗ Stuttgart and Phoenix completing his doctoral thesis in 2012 and worked with well-known German architects ᶜluding Kauffmann-Theilig. He started his research career in the virtual reality environment. He has led many Office 21 ᵉsearch projects, is responsible for the coordination of international multidisciplinary projects, and is a renowned expert ᵗ innovations in the fields of office, hotel, living, and future construction, and an author of many publications about ᵒrking environments and building processes of the future.

Alexander Rieck

JURORS

ROLAND SNOOKS is a design Director and a founding partner of Kokkugia. He holds a masters degree in Advanced Architectural Design from Columbia University where he studied on a Fulbright scholarship and is a graduate of RMIT University (B.Arch). He teaches graduate studios and seminars at the University of Pennsylvania, Columbia University and is the George Isaac Distinguished Fellow at the University of Southern California in Los Angeles. Roland has previously directed design studios and seminars at UCLA, SCI-Arc, Pratt Institute, RMIT, and the Victorian College of the Arts. Roland has considerable experience in the design and construction of high profile projects while working in the offices of Reiser + Umemoto, Ashton Raggatt McDougall and Minifie Nixon, prior to founding Kokkugia. Roland's design research is focused on emergent design methodologies involving agent-based techniques.

Roland Snooks

KIVI SOTAMAA is an international designer based in Helsinki & Los Angeles. Kivi Sotamaa's creative work is widely published and exhibited. His work has been exhibited by MoMA, the Wexner Centre for the Arts, Kiasma Museum of Contemporary Art, Fondazione Trussardi, and the 21st Century Museum of Contemporary Art Kanazawa. Publications featuring his work include the *New York Times*, Phaidon's *10×10 Architects* (1&2), *New Scandinavian Design*, *Forum Sweden*, *AD*, *Praxis*, *Kenhiku Bunka*, *L'Arca*, and *Domus*. In addition to heading Sotamaa Design, Kivi is the Director of ADD LAB, Aalto University Digital Design Laboratory, and an associate professor at UCLA Department of Architecture and Urban Design. Previously he has held positions at the Ohio State University and the Universität für Angewandte Kunst, Institut für Architektur in Vienna. He holds a masters degree from the University of Art and Design in Helsinki (TAIK) and in addition has studied at the Helsinki University of Technology and the Royal College of Art in London.

Kivi Sotamaa

TUULI SOTAMAA is a designer based in Helsinki with particular expertise in product design, ceramic and glass. Tuuli holds a masters degree in design from the University of Art and Design Helsinki and has also studied industrial design at the Central Saint Martins College of Graphic and Industrial Design in London. Tuuli has previously worked for University of Art and Design Helsinki, Aalto University and Alessi FAO s.p.a. in Italy. Tuuli's portfolio includes artworks, installation design, exhibition architecture, industrial design, and design research. Her individual and collaborative work has been exhibited in various galleries, museum, and exhibitions in Europe, the U.S., and Asia. She has taught in various schools in Finland, Oslo School of Architecture, and Architectural Association in London and lectured in various seminars in Europe and Asia. In addition to design Tuuli has an extensive experience on curating and producing events, seminars and exhibitions as a means for fostering discourse and supporting design innovation. She has been responsible in creating the Masters of Arts Festival for Aalto University and has initiated and produced over 50 international seminars relating to architecture, design, and visual culture.

Tuuli Sotamaa

MICHAEL SZIVOS is the principal and founder of SOFTlab, a design studio based in New York City. The studio has been involved in the design and production of projects across almost every medium, from digitally fabricated large-scale sculpture, to interactive design, to immersive digital video installations. In 2012 SOFTlab was awarded the Architectural League Prize for Young Architects & Designers and previously in 2010 the studio was selected for the New Practices New York award by the American Institute of Architecture Chapter of New York along with seven other young studios. Michael is also an assistant adjunct professor at the Graduate School of Architecture, Planning and Preservation at Columbia University and a visiting adjunct professor at the School of Architecture at the Pratt Institute.

Michael Szivos

TOBIAS WALLISSER co-founded LAVA with Chris Bosse and Alexander Rieck in 2007 as a network of creative minds with a research and design focus. LAVA explores frontiers that merge future technologies with the patterns of organisation found in nature. Wallisser is a co-director of LAVA, based in Berlin, Germany. He is professor of Innovative Construction and Spatial Concepts and vice-president at the State Academy of Fine Arts in Stuttgart. His expertise lies in the exploration of spatial effects based on new technology and parametric design. As associate architect at UN-Studio in Amsterdam for ten years he was responsible for the Mercedes-Benz Museum. He received a post-graduate degree from Columbia University and has worked for Asymptote Architecture and for German firm KTP. He won the 2005 Schreuders Award and 1997 Hugo Häring Prize and was a finalist in the 2007 Mies van der Rohe Prize.

Tobias Wallisser

OM WISCOMBE is an architect living in Los Angeles. He is founder and principal of Tom Wiscombe Design, an ernationally recognized contemporary architecture office. Wiscombe has developed an international reputation rough winning competition entries, exhibitions of work at major cultural institutions, and publications worldwide. In)12, Wiscombe, working in a design consortium led by Thom Mayne, won second place for the Chinese University Hong Kong in Shenzhen. In 2011, he won first place in two competitions for the 2013 Chinese National Games. His ork is part of the permanent collection of the FRAC Centre Paris, the Art Institute of Chicago, MoMA San Francisco, d MoMA New York. ICON Magazine, in its May 2009 issue, named Wiscombe one of the "top 20 architects in the orld who are making the future and transforming the way we work." Wiscombe is a senior faculty member at the outhern California Institute of Architecture. He is also visiting professor at PennDesign, and held the Louis I. Kahn siting Assistant Professorship at Yale University in 2012. Wiscombe has worked for Coop Himmelb(l)au for over 10 ars. Notably, he was chief designer for BMW Welt, Munich, and the UFA Cinema Center, Dresden.

Tom Wiscombe

MA YANSONG is the founder of MAD. Since its founding in 2004, his works in architecture and art have been widely published and exhibited. He graduated from the Beijing Institute of Civil Engineering and Architecture. Ma attended Yale University after receiving the American Institute of Architects Scholarship for Advanced Architecture Research in 2001 and holds a masters degree in architecture from Yale. He has since taught architecture at the Central Academy of Fine Arts in Beijing. Yansong was awarded the 2006 Architecture League Young Architects Award. In 2008 he was selected as one of the "twenty most influential young architects today" by ICON magazine and Fast Company named him one of the ten most creative people in architecture in 2009. In 2010 he became the first architect from China to receive a RIBA fellowship.

Ia Yansong

ENTRY DEMOGRAPHICS

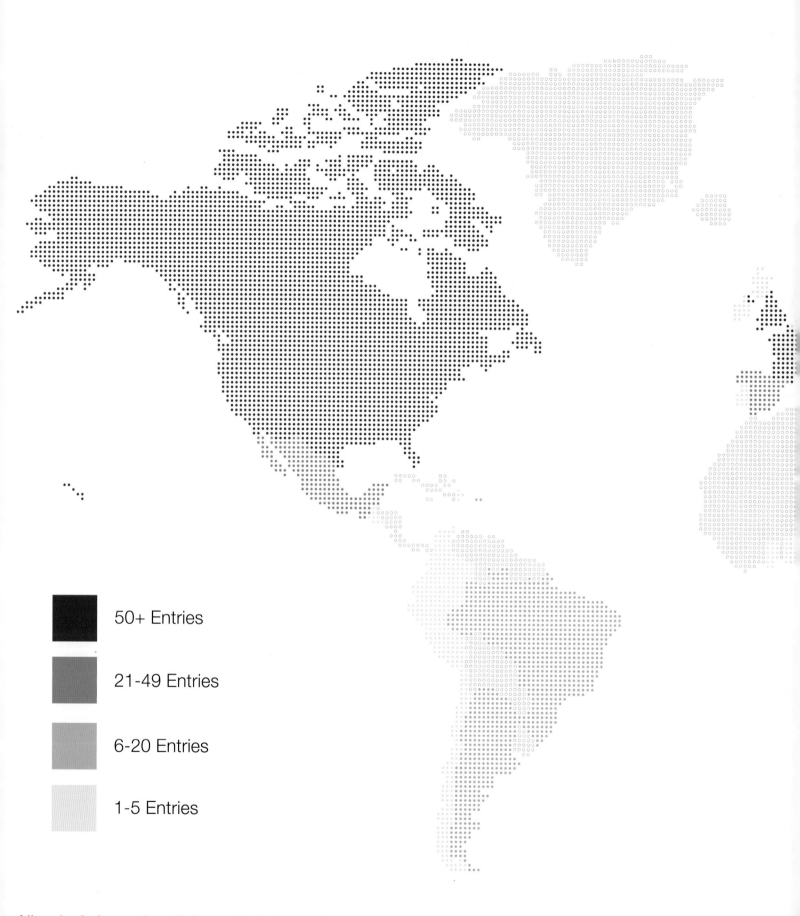

50+ Entries

21-49 Entries

6-20 Entries

1-5 Entries

Albania 2 Argentina 8 Armenia 2 Australia 41 Austria 12 Azerbaijan 1 Bahrain 1 Belarus 1 Belgium 2
Columbia 5 Croatia 1 Cyprus 5 Czech Republic 10 Denmark 2 Dominican Republic 1 Ecuador 4 Egy
Hong Kong 31 India 26 Indonesia 15 Iran 21 Iraq 1 Ireland 3 Israel 5 Italy 60 Japan 9 Jordan 4 Kc
Netherlands 13 New Zealand 12 Nigeria 1 Pakistan 2 Peru 1 Philippines 1 Poland 37 Portugal 5 Pu
Slovenia 1 South Africa 2 South Korea 69 Spain 38 Sweden 5 Switzerland 3 Taiwan 15 Thailand 1

Bermuda 1 Bosnia and Herzegovina 2 Brazil 18 Bulgaria 7 Burma 1 Canada 62 Chile 2 China 137
Salvador 2 Finland 1 France 54 Georgia 1 Germany 25 Ghana 1 Greece 12 Grenada 1 Guatemala 1
Kuwait 5 Latvia 3 Lebanon 7 Lithuania 1 Macau 1 Macedonia 1 Malaysia 12 Mexico 37 Moldova 1
o 10 Qatar 2 Romania 20 Russia 36 Saudi Arabia 5 Scotland 2 Serbia 11 Singapore 13 Slovakia 3
a 1 Turkey 16 Ukraine 16 United Arab Emirates 6 United Kingdom 78 United States 288 Vietnam 6

1 TECHNOLOGICAL ADVANCES

THE USE OF TECHNOLOGY INVOLVES THE RESEARCH OF NEW MATERIALS AS WELL AS THE ADOPTION OF NOVEL STRUCTURAL AND FABRICATION SYSTEMS. THE ARCHITECTS ARE NOT ACTUALLY DESIGNING THE FINAL FORM OF THE STRUCTURE BUT WRITING A SERIES OF RULES OF INTERACTION BETWEEN THE COMPONENTS AND THEIR SURROUNDINGS.

The projects featured in this chapter explore current and future technologies to re-imagine high-rise architecture. The use of technology involves the research of new materials as well as the adoption of novel structural and fabrication systems. The use of the most advanced software in their conception, visualization, and construction is also evident. Parametric design and algorithmic architecture paired with automated building machines operated by robots is increasingly popular. What it is interesting is that architects are not actually designing the final form of the structure but writing a series of rules of interaction between the components and their surroundings. These are examples that could potentially grow and shrink according to current habitation necessities and the availability of natural resources.

Some ideas go beyond the design of a single building and propose the reconfiguration of entire urban habitats. A common topic was the use of super light and strong materials such as carbon fiber to construct precast housing units of different sizes that plug into open frame structures. Such modules are placed according to an urban and environmental analysis. New material exploration includes high tensile and high compression Kevlar cables used as load bearing columns – hair-like filaments capable of supporting a super tall structure with column free open floor plans.

Other proposals recognize that modern society is highly mobile and that people rarely live for extended periods of time in the same location. The solutions to this new way of life range from "migrant buildings" that are literally capable of rolling to different locations, to inhabitable vessels that navigate around the world, or floating buildings that fly across cities and countries.

With the recent wave of natural disasters such as volcanic eruptions, tsunamis, earthquakes, and flooding, some participants have been studying the possibility of harvesting the natural energy released during these events while protecting the urban areas at risk. One example is the "Volcano Mask" skyscraper designed to extract the geothermal energy of active volcanoes and prevent sudden eruptions.

The revitalization of existing cities is the main goal of other projects. The variety of ideas is incredible – from buildings covered by nano-materials that filter polluted air to the creation of solar and wind power plants in typical buildings.

There is also the exploration of augmented reality, which is the technology to integrate the physical elements with the virtual ones – in other words, to enhance the visual experience of reality through virtual connections.

UNIT FUSION

Yam Sai Tung Tony

Hong Kong

UNITfusion
A NEW ALTERNATIVE HIGH-RISE RESIDENTIAL TYPOLOGY

Under rapid housing developments in the past years, Hong Kong has benefited much in terms of economy, however important values such as sense of community and individual identity were lost. This thesis hereby critically reviews current and past housing projects in Hong Kong, attacking the notion of verticality as the only solution. The ambition is a new alternative high-rise residential typology, in which its inhabitants are given unique units and allocations in accordance to specific zoning strategy within a tower structure, thus creates a phenomenal living experience through bonding and acquiring needs by each and every single individual. It is a re-interpretation of the balance between genericity and specificity aiming at formulating an extraordinary democratic living concept.

project data
project: high-rise residential prototype
location: WKCD, hong kong
building Type: tower
number of units: 1940 [90%]
unit types: XS, S, M, L, XL [18 types]
date Built: work in progress
dwelling Types: studio, 1, 2 & 3 BR
building height: 427.5m
floor to floor : 5.7m
no. Floors: 75
section Type: plug-in unit
exterior Finish Materials: prefab. concrete
construction Type: reinforced concrete
ancillary Services: 5 floors for public programs

XS4
S6a
S6b
S7a
S7b
S8a
S8b
M10a
M10b
M11
M12a
M12b
L14
L15a
L15b
L16
XL17
XL20

ceiling / roof system
facade
bath
kitchen
wall system
bath
structural system
balcony
floor system

unit type: L16
exploded axonometric drawing detailing major prefabricated component systems

unit floor plan [type L16]

L16: entry facade

L6: balcony

L16: sectional perspective interior view

L16: showing structural components

In accommodating the massive new housing needs, in recent decades, of Hong Kong's booming population, faceless public housing communities have sprung up and have stripped residential areas of their sense of community. What the city's inhabitants need is a redefinition of the high-rise, urban, residential typology: one that allows for individual identity to play a prominent role.

This alternative tower has taken shape as a 75-floor skyscraper that allows for pre-fabricated, concrete units to be plugged in after they are purchased and customized by residents. There is a catalog of 1,960 unique residential units that UNITfusion's dwellers can choose from: from a studio to a three-bedroom, the extra-small to extra-large options allow people to customize their apartments to their needs, with extra options specifically available in the kitchen,

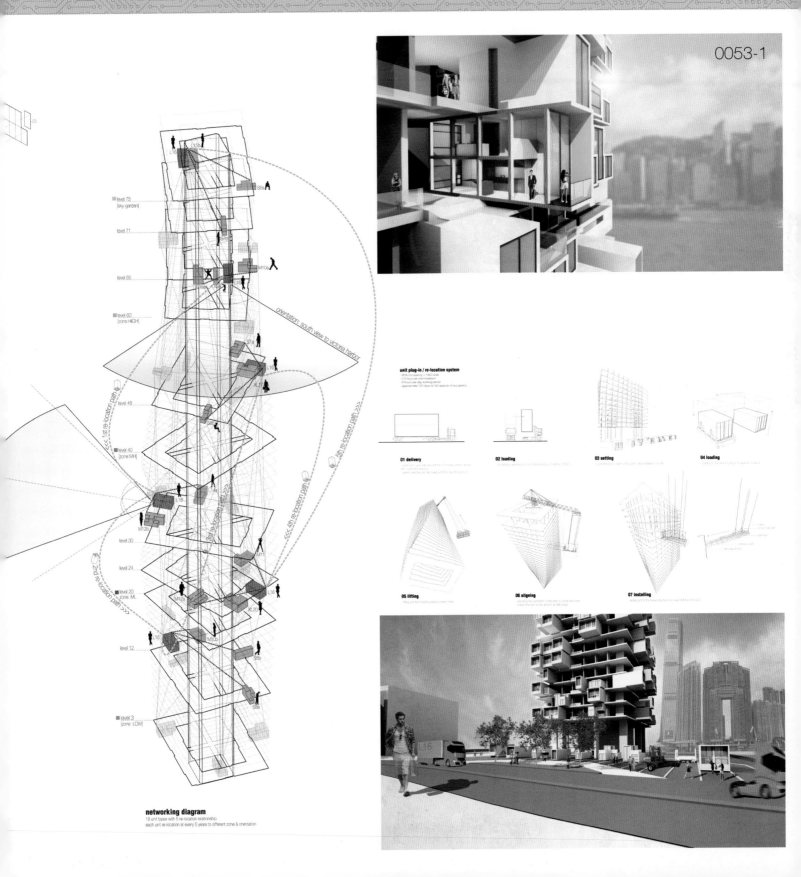

0053-1

networking diagram
18 unit types with 5 re-location relationship
each unit re-location at every 5 years to different zone & orientation

unit plug-in / re-location system

01 delivery

02 loading

03 setting

04 loading

05 lifting

06 aligning

07 installing

bathroom, closet, balcony and entryway.

Units are lifted into the building's twisted concrete core via crane and plugged in to its systems. Where each unit is located is dictated according to a zoning strategy within the tower that is largely defined by the surrounding environment (the sun's angle, wind direction and more); the building can hold 1,940 units, each of which has an estimated life cycle of 30 years. Every five years, each unit is relocated within the building to contribute to the ever-expanding networking and social growth that happens within the residence.

A diverse range of public, social programs within UNITfusion also contributes to the sense of community. Each floor has a sky garden, and there is a sky lobby located on every fifth floor. An additional special zone is located on

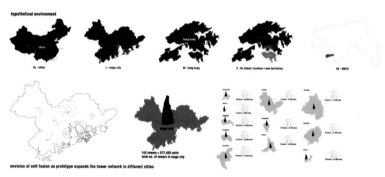

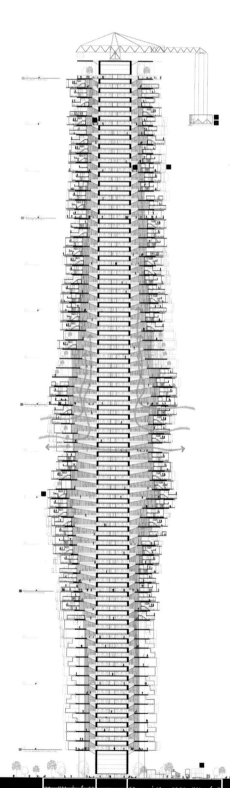

65th floor plan [typical]

floors 3, 20, 40, 60 and 75 to provide public services and pedestrian connections between levels.

Under rapid housing developments in the past years, Hong Kong has benefited in terms of economy but has lost important values of identity. UNITfusion is a re-interpretation of the balance between genericity and specificity aiming at formulating an extraordinary democratic living concept.

0053-2

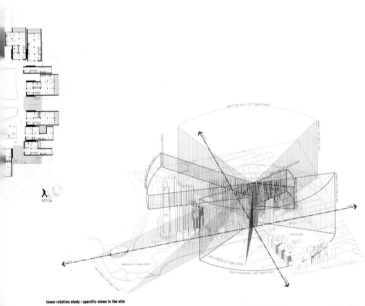
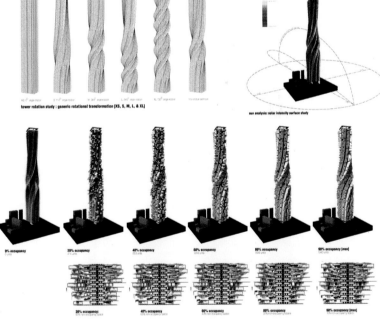

MIGRANT SKYSCRAPER

Damian Przybyła
Rafał Przybyła

Poland

MOBILITY AS A BASIC NEED NOWADAYS

Current world's condition indicates the necessity of rebinding the basic aspects of architecture with the smallest social groups. *Firmitas, utilitas* and *venustas* evolve into self-sufficiency, as the sum and, simultaneously - an expansion of each one.

Migrant skyscraper starts from a single user and their basic needs - this assumption is the concept's moral core. Nowadays, durability engages reusing of resources; usability is to be extended with mobility; beauty includes morality.

We believe that there are just few specific aspects (the most important and beneficial at the same time) where potential solutions should be directed. Increasingly important aim of architecture comes from actual social and natural dynamics of the world. Reality becoming dramatically less predictable and more improbable nowadays than any time before. These circumstances regard self-sufficiency, provided for each individual, as well as new dynamics within spatial solutions. Architecture has to assure a possibility of act in response to social and natural disasters. We also trust that new architecture

needs these possibilities as tools for exposing personal freedom, independence and precious opportunity to live.

Each society consists of different social volumes which are related to the wholeness, a single person is a *quantum* of this structure. Migrant skyscraper aspires to be its analogy - *quantum of porous structure*, which has the ability of living independently or in vast spectrum of relation with different ones - as a part of wholeness. *Migrant skyscraper* is to assure self-sufficient live and respect an individual's freedom to decide. Nowadays, a crucial paradox is becoming more visible - when some nations suffer from inability of satisfying basic needs, others suffer from exaggerated consumption and phony freedom. Both realities are deliberated, condemned to outer dependencies (social, economical).

Migrant skyscraper exposes such reality as a strict relation between developed and developing countries by exchanging resources and experiences, and redefining the social development as a common value and responsibility.

NATURAL AND SOCIAL DISASTERS: INTENSITY DIAGRAM

5 years backwards

number of casualties:
○ 100 - 1000
○ 1000 - 40 000
○ 40 000 +

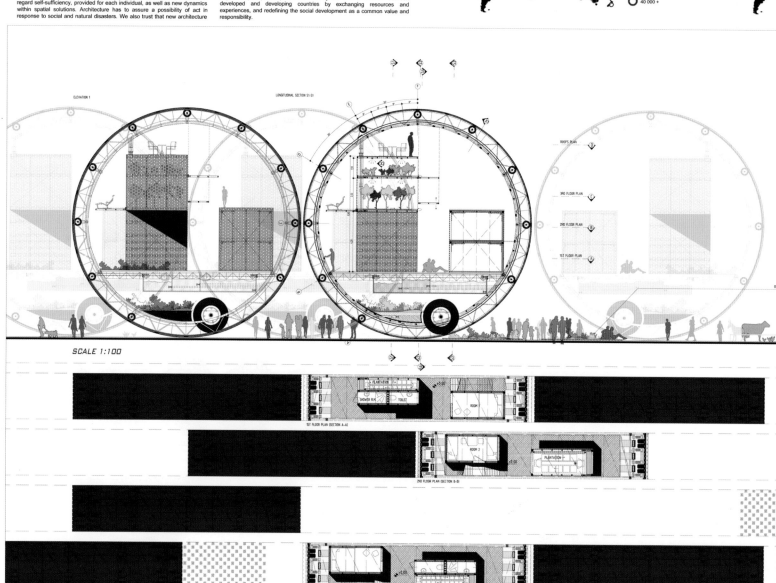

ELEVATION 1   LONGITUDINAL SECTION S1-S1   ROOFS PLAN

3RD FLOOR PLAN

2ND FLOOR PLAN

1ST FLOOR PLAN

SCALE 1:100

1ST FLOOR PLAN (SECTION A-A)

2ND FLOOR PLAN (SECTION B-B)

1ST FLOOR PLAN (SECTION A-A)

1ST FLOOR PLAN (SECTION A-A)

The "Migrant Skyscraper" is literally mobile: A giant, thin tire with a building and green space in the center. This skyscraper is ready to roll.

By constructing a safe haven for residents to live in that ensures they will have food to eat and water to drink, the Migrant Skyscraper affords people freedom despite what natural and social disasters may come. The building-inside-

The concept behind this structure is that in an unstable world, people need the stability of self-sufficiency to truly be free, and the future of the architectural field can help provide that to people. Architecture has to assure a possibility of acting in response to social and natural disasters. New architecture needs these possibilities as tools for exposing personal freedom, independence, and precious opportunity to live.

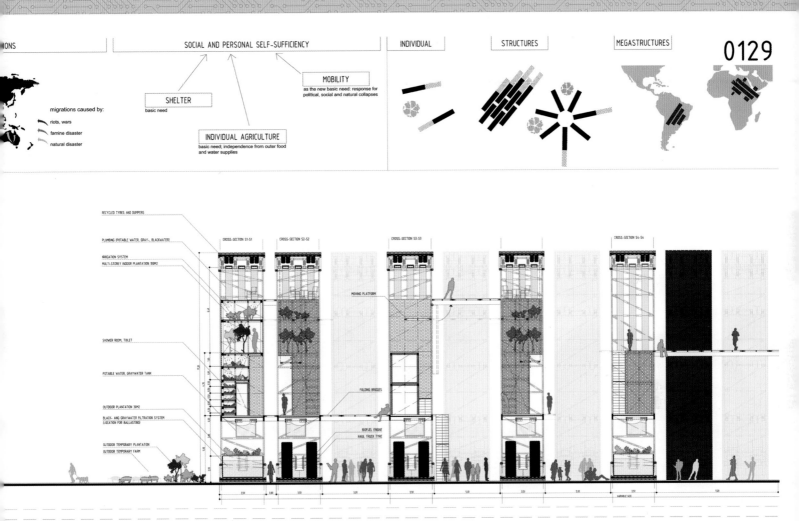

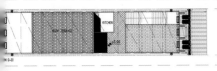

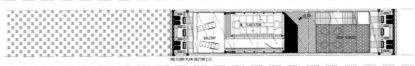

a-wheel can stay stationary for however long residents please, but, for example, if political upheaval destabilizes a region, residents can fire up the biofuel-powered engine and cruise to a new location.

The structure's exterior tire is clad in recycled rubber. Inside it, two buildings and surrounding green space provide everything residents need to survive while inhabitation the tire, making the tire-encapsulated unit completely self-sufficient. Outside of the buildings there is space for agriculture, including crops and livestock; within the tire, plumbing systems circulate potable, gray and black water for drinking, waste facilities, and irrigation.

Each tire holds facilities for one family; layouts show two buildings next to each other within the tire. The first is three stories tall, with restroom facilities on the ground floor, indoor agriculture space on the second, and a balcony

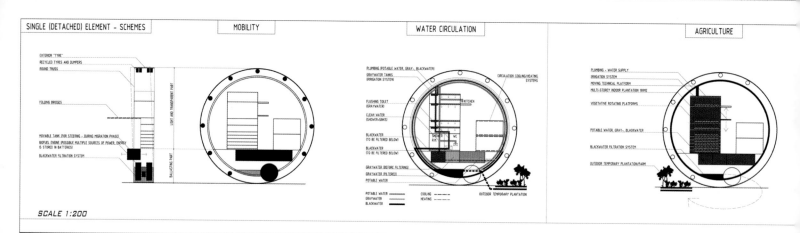

MIGRANT SKYSCRAPER: THE NEW DYNAMICS OF A SOCIETY

and kitchen on the third. Next door, both floors of the two-story building hold bedrooms for residents.

   Unique features within the buildings include rolling platforms for indoor and outdoor agriculture as well as bridges that fold up for stability when the tire structures are on the move. When stationary, the designers envision the tires grouping around public green spaces to form communities, or parking in tight spaces to create density.

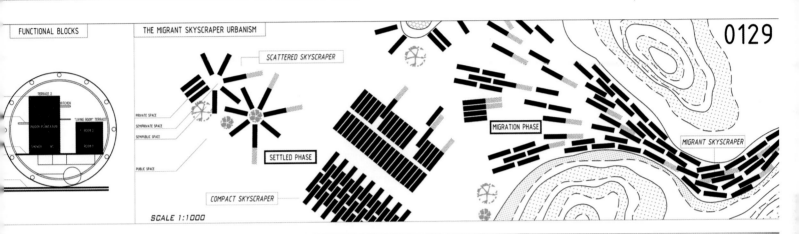

PSUDOBERG

Khairul Izzuddin Bin Mohd Hiffni
Sayed A. Bin Sayed Abul Khair
Muhammad Q. Bin Norhisham
Yasmin Binti Abdul Rahman
Muhammad Fawwaz Zullkefle

Malaysia

PSEUDOBERG
FAKE ICEBERGS THAT CAN SAVE THE WORL

GLOBAL WARMING REFERS TO THE RISING AVERAGE TEMPERATURE OF EARTH'S ATMOSPHERE AND OCEANS AS WELL AS ITS PROJECTED CONTINUATION. AN INCREASE IN GLOBAL TEMPERATURE WILL NOT ONLY CAUSE SEA LEVELS TO RISE AS IT MELTS THE POLAR ICE CAPS, BUT IT WILL AFFECT THE OCEAN'S UNDERWATER CURRENT. THIS PHENOMENA IS A THERMOHALINE CIRCULATION, BETTER KNOWN AS THE GREAT OCEAN CONVEYER BELT.

THIS 'CONVEYOR BELT' IS A SIMPLE CONCEPT DRIVEN BY THE DENSITY DIFFERENCES IN THE OCEAN FLOW. TEMPERATURE AND SALINITY DETERMINE THE DENSITY OF OCEAN WATER WITH COLDER AND SALTIER WATER BEING DENSER THAN WARMER WATER AND FRESHER WATER.

OXYGEN GETS MIXED INTO THE OCEAN BY THE TURNING ACTION OF WAVES, CURRENTS AND TIDES ON THE SURFACE, BUT IT IS THE GREAT OCEAN CONVEYOR THAT TAKES OXYGEN TO THE DEEPEST OCEAN DEPTHS. THE CONVEYOR MOVES SURFACE WATER WARMED AT THE EQUATOR TOWARDS THE POLES. AS THE WATER COOLS IT BECOMES DENSER AND SINKS TO THE DEEP OCEAN TAKING LIFE SUSTAINING OXYGEN WITH IT.

AS GLOBAL WARMING WARMS UP THE POLES, IT MOVES THE DIFFERENCE IN TEMPERATURE TWEEN THE POLES AND THE TROPICS AND WIL TOMATICALLY STOP THE CONVEYOR WHIC DRIVEN BY HEAT DIFFERENCES. THESE EFFECTS PROFOUND AS THE ARCTIC OCEAN COULD B FREE IN THE SUMMER BY THE END OF THE CEN WHEN THIS CONVEYOR STOPS, WE LOSE OXYGE THE BOTTOM OF THE OCEAN AND WE START MECHANISM OF MASS EXTINCTION.

PSEUDOBERG IS A VESSEL SKYSCRAPER THAT BE DEPLOYED IN THE ICY WATERS OF ANTARC WITH INTERNAL HEAT TRANSFER MECHANISM, TOWERS REGENERATE THE LOST ICY SHOREL AND RESTORE THE FROZEN LAND DURING THE 6 MONTHS OF SOUTH POLE NIGHT SKY. THE P DOBERGS WILL HELP THE EARTH CONVEYOR BE REMAIN IN MOTION AS IT HAS BEEN FOR THOUS. OF YEARS. SKYSCRAPERS ONCE KNOWN AS ON MAN'S LARGEST CONTRIBUTOR TO THE PRODUC OF CARBON DIOXIDE, MAY NOW BE THE ONLY S TION TO REVERSE THEIR CAUSE GLOBAL WARMI. A LAND AT THE BOTTOM OF THE WORLD WHERE SUN RISES AND SETS ONLY ONCE A YEAR.

In the "Pseudoberg" project, a vessel skyscraper regenerates the icy shores of the Antarctic amidst a global warming epidemic. Skyscrapers, once known as one of man's largest contributor to the production of carbon dioxide, may now be the only solution to reverse their cause of global warming in a land at the bottom of the world where the sun rises and sets only once within a year," say Psuedoberg's designers.

The south pole's perils lie not just in excess water and rising sea levels as icebergs melt: the implications are global as the imbalance of cold water, which is denser than warm tropical waters, messes up the flow of the Great Ocean Conveyer Belt, a global system of underwater currents driven by thermohaline circulation. As the ocean warms hotter than usual in the tropics due to global warming and the icebergs, all disappearing, fail to provide the adequate

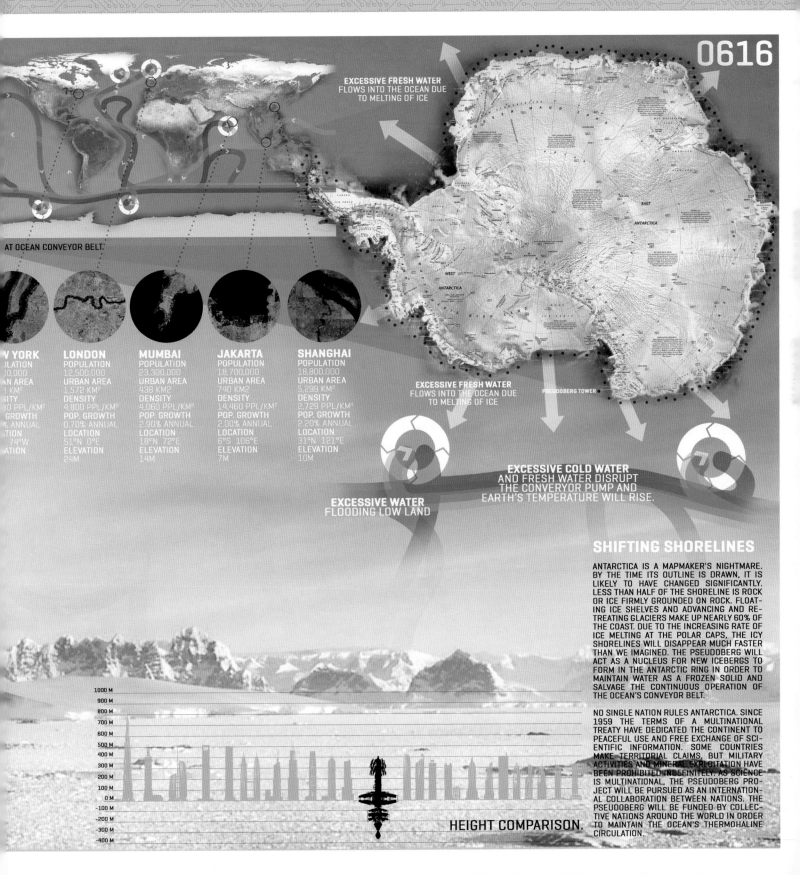

0616

EXCESSIVE FRESH WATER
FLOWS INTO THE OCEAN DUE
TO MELTING OF ICE

AT OCEAN CONVEYOR BELT.

V YORK	LONDON	MUMBAI	JAKARTA	SHANGHAI
JLATION 0,000	POPULATION 12,500,000	POPULATION 23,300,000	POPULATION 18,700,000	POPULATION 18,800,000
AN AREA 1 KM²	URBAN AREA 1,572 KM²	URBAN AREA 438 KM2	URBAN AREA 740 KM2	URBAN AREA 5,299 KM²
SITY 10 PPL/KM²	DENSITY 4,800 PPL/KM²	DENSITY 4,060 PPL/KM²	DENSITY 14,460 PPL/KM²	DENSITY 2,729 PPL/KM²
GROWTH % ANNUAL	POP. GROWTH 0.70% ANNUAL	POP. GROWTH 2.90% ANNUAL	POP. GROWTH 2.00% ANNUAL	POP. GROWTH 2.20% ANNUAL
TION 74°W	LOCATION 51°N 0°E	LOCATION 18°N 72°E	LOCATION 6°S 106°E	LOCATION 31°N 121°E
ATION	ELEVATION 24M	ELEVATION 14M	ELEVATION 7M	ELEVATION 10M

EXCESSIVE FRESH WATER
FLOWS INTO THE OCEAN DUE
TO MELTING OF ICE

PSEUDOBERG TOWER

EXCESSIVE COLD WATER
AND FRESH WATER DISRUPT
THE CONVERYOR PUMP AND
EARTH'S TEMPERATURE WILL RISE.

EXCESSIVE WATER
FLOODING LOW LAND

SHIFTING SHORELINES

ANTARCTICA IS A MAPMAKER'S NIGHTMARE. BY THE TIME ITS OUTLINE IS DRAWN, IT IS LIKELY TO HAVE CHANGED SIGNIFICANTLY. LESS THAN HALF OF THE SHORELINE IS ROCK OR ICE FIRMLY GROUNDED ON ROCK. FLOATING ICE SHELVES AND ADVANCING AND RETREATING GLACIERS MAKE UP NEARLY 60% OF THE COAST. DUE TO THE INCREASING RATE OF ICE MELTING AT THE POLAR CAPS, THE ICY SHORELINES WILL DISAPPEAR MUCH FASTER THAN WE IMAGINED. THE PSEUDOBERG WILL ACT AS A NUCLEUS FOR NEW ICEBERGS TO FORM IN THE ANTARCTIC RING IN ORDER TO MAINTAIN WATER AS A FROZEN SOLID AND SALVAGE THE CONTINUOUS OPERATION OF THE OCEAN'S CONVEYOR BELT.

NO SINGLE NATION RULES ANTARCTICA. SINCE 1959 THE TERMS OF A MULTINATIONAL TREATY HAVE DEDICATED THE CONTINENT TO PEACEFUL USE AND FREE EXCHANGE OF SCIENTIFIC INFORMATION. SOME COUNTRIES MAKE TERRITORIAL CLAIMS, BUT MILITARY ACTIVITIES AND MINERAL EXPLOITATION HAVE BEEN PROHIBITED INDEFINITELY. AS SCIENCE IS MULTINATIONAL, THE PSEUDOBERG PROJECT WILL BE PURSUED AS AN INTERNATIONAL COLLABORATION BETWEEN NATIONS. THE PSEUDOBERG WILL BE FUNDED BY COLLECTIVE NATIONS AROUND THE WORLD IN ORDER TO MAINTAIN THE OCEAN'S THERMOHALINE CIRCULATION.

1000 M
900 M
800 M
700 M
600 M
500 M
400 M
300 M
200 M
100 M
0 M
-100 M
-200 M
-300 M
-400 M

HEIGHT COMPARISON.

balance of cold currents, a cycle begins where the conveyer belt ceases to run and oxygen, captured into the water from churning surface waves and pulled down in dense, cold waters to sustain marine life below, fails to be pulled deep below, causing mass extinctions of ocean life.

Enter the Pseudobergs, which act as nuclei for icebergs to form in the Antarctic ring to salvage the continuous operation of the ocean's conveyor belt. The vessels arrive on site by propelling themselves like a surface submarine using mega-pumps on their tails. When it reaches its desired destination, the vessel's crews open the ballast tank and water fills the vessel's tail, lifting the top of the tower upright as the tail sinks. It is closed when a balance is reached and the tower is upright at 90 degrees. It is then anchored, and the heliopad high on the tower is unfurled, allowing the

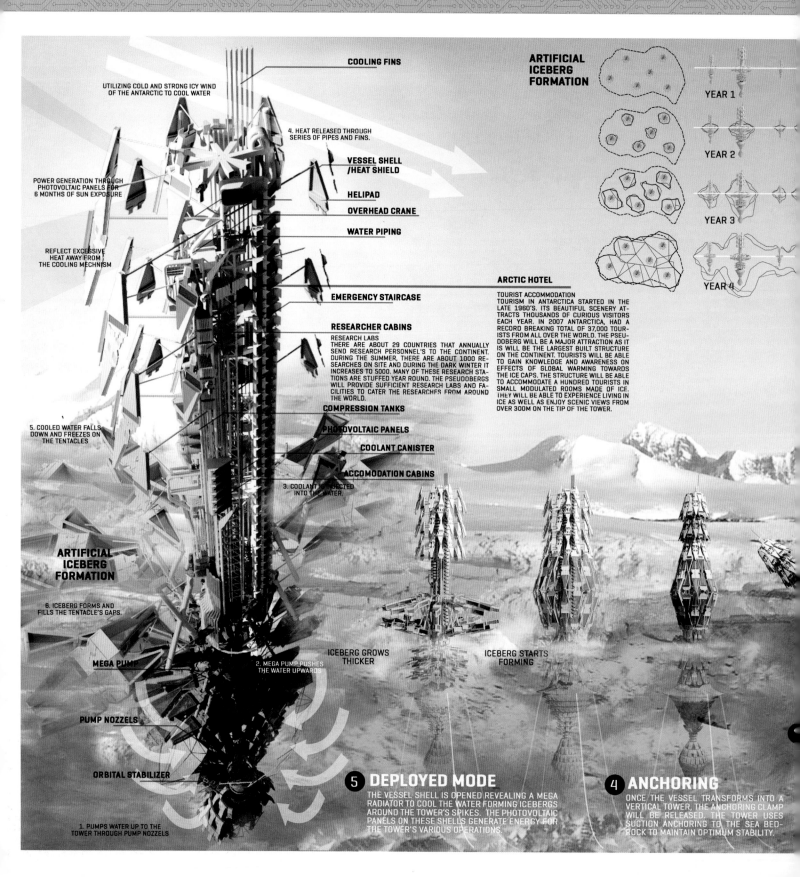

COOLING FINS

UTILIZING COLD AND STRONG ICY WIND OF THE ANTARCTIC TO COOL WATER

4. HEAT RELEASED THROUGH SERIES OF PIPES AND FINS.

POWER GENERATION THROUGH PHOTOVOLTAIC PANELS FOR 6 MONTHS OF SUN EXPOSURE

VESSEL SHELL /HEAT SHIELD

HELIPAD

OVERHEAD CRANE

WATER PIPING

REFLECT EXCESSIVE HEAT AWAY FROM THE COOLING MECHNISM

EMERGENCY STAIRCASE

RESEARCHER CABINS

RESEARCH LABS
THERE ARE ABOUT 29 COUNTRIES THAT ANNUALLY SEND RESEARCH PERSONNEL'S TO THE CONTINENT. DURING THE SUMMER, THERE ARE ABOUT 1000 RESEARCHES ON SITE AND DURING THE DARK WINTER IT INCREASES TO 5000. MANY OF THESE RESEARCH STATIONS ARE STUFFED YEAR ROUND. THE PSEUDOBERGS WILL PROVIDE SUFFICIENT RESEARCH LABS AND FACILITIES TO CATER THE RESEARCHES FROM AROUND THE WORLD.

COMPRESSION TANKS

PHOTOVOLTAIC PANELS

COOLANT CANISTER

ACCOMODATION CABINS

3. COOLANT IS INJECTED INTO THE WATER.

5. COOLED WATER FALLS DOWN AND FREEZES ON THE TENTACLES

ARTIFICIAL ICEBERG FORMATION

6. ICEBERG FORMS AND FILLS THE TENTACLE'S GAPS.

MEGA PUMP

2. MEGA PUMP PUSHES THE WATER UPWARDS

PUMP NOZZELS

ORBITAL STABILIZER

1. PUMPS WATER UP TO THE TOWER THROUGH PUMP NOZZELS

ARTIFICIAL ICEBERG FORMATION

YEAR 1

YEAR 2

YEAR 3

YEAR 4

ARCTIC HOTEL

TOURIST ACCOMMODATION
TOURISM IN ANTARCTICA STARTED IN THE LATE 1960'S. ITS BEAUTIFUL SCENERY ATTRACTS THOUSANDS OF CURIOUS VISITORS EACH YEAR. IN 2007 ANTARCTICA, HAD A RECORD BREAKING TOTAL OF 37,000 TOURISTS FROM ALL OVER THE WORLD. THE PSEUDOBERG WILL BE A MAJOR ATTRACTION AS IT IS WILL BE THE LARGEST BUILT STRUCTURE ON THE CONTINENT. TOURISTS WILL BE ABLE TO GAIN KNOWLEDGE AND AWARENESS ON EFFECTS OF GLOBAL WARMING TOWARDS THE ICE CAPS. THE STRUCTURE WILL BE ABLE TO ACCOMMODATE A HUNDRED TOURISTS IN SMALL MODULATED ROOMS MADE OF ICE. THEY WILL BE ABLE TO EXPERIENCE LIVING IN ICE AS WELL AS ENJOY SCENIC VIEWS FROM OVER 300M ON THE TIP OF THE TOWER.

ICEBERG GROWS THICKER

ICEBERG STARTS FORMING

5 DEPLOYED MODE
THE VESSEL SHELL IS OPENED REVEALING A MEGA RADIATOR TO COOL THE WATER FORMING ICEBERGS AROUND THE TOWER'S SPIKES. THE PHOTOVOLTAIC PANELS ON THESE SHELLS GENERATE ENERGY FOR THE TOWER'S VARIOUS OPERATIONS.

4 ANCHORING
ONCE THE VESSEL TRANSFORMS INTO A VERTICAL TOWER, THE ANCHORING CLAMP WILL BE RELEASED. THE TOWER USES SUCTION ANCHORING TO THE SEA BEDROCK TO MAINTAIN OPTIMUM STABILITY.

vessel to be controlled remotely by operators in helicopters.

As the vessel's shell opens, a major radiator is revealed which is used to cool the surrounding water. The radiator is powered by photovoltaic panels on the shell's surface, as are the freezing operations as a whole: Nozzles pump warm water into the tower and up its base to its midsection, where it is injected with coolant. (The heat is released at the top of the building.) The water is then moved through the building's outer tentacles, where it is sufficiently cold to freeze and begin the formation of an iceberg.

The vessel also houses residential and lab areas for up to 1,000 researchers, and a hotel to accommodate tourists wanting to visit the site.

0616

SEED BANK
EXISTING SEED ARCHIVES MAINTAIN BELOW FREEZ-ING TEMPERATURE BY THE USE OF REFRIGERATING UNITS, WHICH NEED SEVERAL BACKUP SYSTEMS TO AVOID EVENTUAL THAWING OF THE STORAGE. A SEED BANK WILL BE PRESENT IN EACH PSEUDOBERG TO TAKE ADVANTAGE OF THE ALREADY EXISTING CONDI-TION OF THE ENVIRONMENT.

ARCTIC ANIMAL RESEARCH
THERE ARE MANY ENDANGERED SPECIES HOME TO THE SOUTH POLE. RESEARCHES KEEP TRACK OF THESE ANIMALS FROM A MODERATE DISTANCE AND BAR-CODED TAGS HELPS THEM TO INVESTIGATE MORE ABOUT THEIR WHEREABOUTS AND MIGRATION DISTANCE. EMERGENCY VET CLINICS ARE HOSTED IN EACH PSEUDOBERG EQUIPPED WITH NECESSARY MEDICINE AND SURGICAL TOOLS.

KING THE TAIL

G MODE
ALLAST TANK WILL BE ATER WILL SLOWLY SINK TAIL. OPTIMUM VOLUME . BE FILLED INSIDE THE DER TO GET THE RIGHT

2 STILL MODE
WHEN THE VESSEL STOPS, ITS CREW PREPARES THE SHIP FOR ITS SINKING PROCEDURE. THE CRAFT THAT IS SOON TO BE A TOWER IS CONTROLLED FROM A DISTANCE BY A CREW ON A HELICOPTER LAUNCHED FROM THE VESSEL.

1 VESSEL MODE
THE TOWER TRANSPORTS ITSELF TO A CRITICAL SITE FROM AN INTERNATIONAL HARBOUR . BY USING MEGA PUMPS ON ITS TAIL, THE VESSEL PROPELS ITSELF FOR-WARD IN A VERY SIMILAR MANNER OF A SUBMARINE.

THE EPIPHYTE TOWER

Donald Dzidzor Kwaku

United Kingdom

With rising climate changes, the future of Britain's environmental health is at risk. A recent study concluded that the most dangerous climate change linked to Britain's public health could result in vector borne diseases. If factors such as immigration and population growth remain constant, the World Health Organization predicts that an additional 2 billion people could be exposed to malaria and dengue fever by the year 2080.

In attempts to combat a potential malaria or dengue fever outbreak, the Epiphyte Tower by Donald D. Kwaku introduces a new ecology in the London urbanscape that integrates parasitic structures that live on the sides of the building. Inside these structures will live a range of bat species, which are natural predators of the influx of the malaria. A lightweight frame structure covered by a tensile, permeable membrane allows bats to fly in and out to do

The Epiphyte Tower

Climate change spreads infectious diseases

0878

When we think of global climate change, we imagine melting ice caps, dying polar bears, hotter summers, and more erratic weather patterns. However, nine times out of ten we do not take into account of the higher risk of certain infectious diseases. The World Health Organization, the International Panel on Climate Change, and the Environmental Protection Agency have all issued reports on how climate change could impact human health. All specifically warn that climate change could impact infectious diseases. There are several ways this could happen. One of the main concerns centers on the so-called "vector-borne" diseases—that is, diseases like West Nile virus and malaria that are spread not directly by humans, but rather are transmitted to humans by other species, such as mosquitoes, ticks and rats.

Changing weather patterns due to climate change will provide an opportunity for the insects and animals that transmit infectious diseases to change their geographic range. As these creatures change their locations, they may introduce the diseases into areas where they aren't currently found. Climate change can also amplify the prevalence of a disease in places where it already exists. Warmer weather and longer, frost-free seasons can expand both the sheer number of individual disease carriers, as well as the time period during which people are vulnerable to bites. In addition, warmer weather may help the pathogens within infected carriers multiply more quickly. "Climate change also brings new challenges to the control of infectious diseases," the World Health Organization stated in a recent report, adding ominously: "Many of the major killers are highly climate sensitive to temperature and rainfall, including cholera and the diarrheal diseases, as well as vector-borne diseases such as malaria and dengue. In sum, climate change threatens to slow, halt or reverse the progress that the global public health community is now making against many of these diseases. Warmer temperatures are now allowing mosquitoes to carry the diseases farther north. The UK is by no means an exception to this trend and a recent study by the university of Plymouth concluded that, the most dangerous climate change linked to Britain's environmental health could be vector borne diseases. If all factors such as, immigration and population growth remain constant, the World Health Organisation predict that an additional 2 billion people could be exposed to Malaria and Dengue fever by the year 2080.

Given the fact that the UK has not had to combat infectious diseases such as, Malaria and Dengue Fever on a larger scale, the resources to combat this future threat are simply not sufficient. The intention of the Epiphytes is to combat the future threat by introducing a new ecology into the urban scape. The introduction of bats as a natural predator to the growing influx of diseases such as Malaria will be combated by parasitic structures, which live on the side of buildings. This is intended to expose unexpected readings of the built environment in the future, if we do not take more drastic steps to combat climate change. Set in London by Tower Bridge, cantilevered by the iconic Guy's hospital, the Epiphyte tower houses different bat species within the structure. The internal core serves as a vast repository of mankind's most valuable asset; knowledge. The architecture is a knowledge arch, which protects research material on infectious diseases.

In the past, London's East India docks were famous for importing exotic herbs and spices from the four corners of the globe. The bygone era of importing exotic products has now paradoxically become an influx of potential tropical hosts. Large cities, such as London, will be in future, a perfect breeding ground for infectious diseases. Given the vast amount of roof spaces that could hold stagnant water, old or inefficient drainage systems. This presents a new problem for a society, which has never had to combat issues such as the growth of malaria on a large scale and the intervention of the Epiphytes will allow for the control of the growing threat. The bat being the natural predator, of insects such as mosquitoes, can eat up to 3000 insects in a night. Making them the new guardians and protectors of the city.

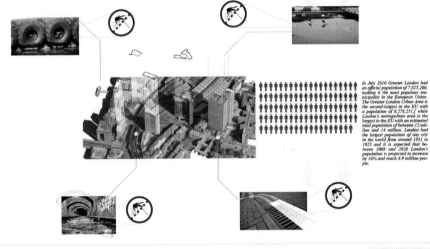

In July 2010 Greater London had an official population of 7,825,200, making it the most populous municipality in the European Union. The Greater London Urban Area is the second-largest in the EU with a population of 8,278,251,[while London's metropolitan area is the largest in the EU with an estimated total population of between 12 million and 14 million. London had the largest population of any city in the world from around 1831 to 1925 and it is expected that between 2008 and 2028 London's population is projected to increase by 16% and reach 8.9 million people.

A single pipistrelle can consume up to 3,000 insects in one night!

their hunting. Additionally, this structure will adhere to climatic conditions for bat colonies, keeping the structure warm and humid in the summer and cold during the winter by parasitically siphoning air conditioner exhaust in the height of summer and shutting down in the winter.

Encased in the internal core of the tower is a research center comprised of researchers, scientists, students, and leaders who would step up in such an event with an abundant amount of material on infectious diseases. A "knowledge arch" is created and cantilevers over London's Guy Hospital near the London Bridge. With a study by the World Health Organization predicting an influx of malaria and dengue fever, a city like London, which has never had to worry about combating such diseases, will need to utilize the natural resources of innovative complexity. As the future

Plan:

Detailed Plan
scale 1:200

A. frame structur
B. walkway
C. Track
D. structural an
E. Waste air ext
F. Pressurised
G. permeable n
H. Repository
I. storage units
J. re- trackable
K. steel frame
L. Guys Hospital
O. Bat Habhita

The Great Bat Hall

temperature changes allow for insects and wildlife to migrate to more suitable geographical locations, the Epiphyte Tower will serve as a solution to this challenge and illuminate the new guardians. The bat being the natural predator of insects such as mosquitoes can eat up to 3000 insects in a night, making them the protectors of the city.

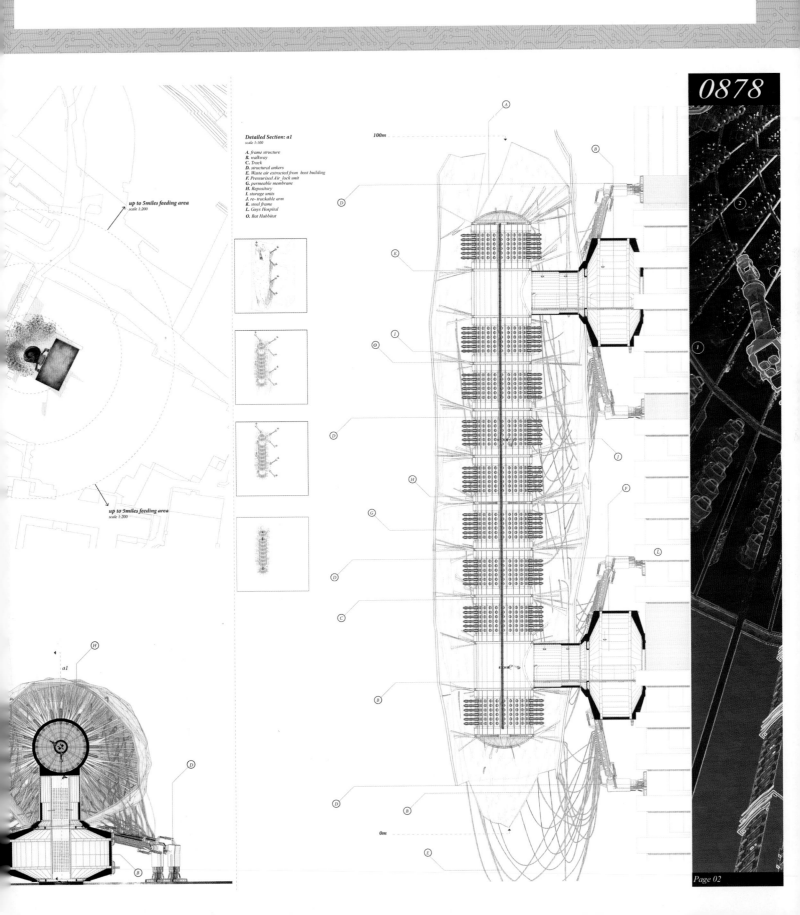

up to 5miles feeding area
scale 1:200

up to 5miles feeding area
scale 1:200

Detailed Section: a1
scale 1:100

A. frame structure
B. walkway
C. Track
D. structural ankers
E. Waste air extracted from host building
F. Pressurised Air_lock unit
G. permeable membrane
H. Repository
I. storage units
J. re- trackable arm
K. steel frame
L. Guys Hospital
O. Bat Habbitat

100m

0m

0878

GOD BLESS AFRICA

Son In-sung
Park Myoung-jin
Jo Sung-yong
Hwang Youn-seok

Republic of Korea

G.B.A God Blass Africa

Global Warming & Desertification

From the beginning of civilization mankind need the energy, and the energy requirement has been growing according the development of civilization. So fossil fuel, an energy source easy to get, has been consumed indiscreetly by mankind, and that caused the alteration of climate system. Global Warming is due to the decrease of radiant heat from the earth to the space. Global Warming triggered abnormal climates, i.e. flood, torrential rain, desertification, typhoon, and the natural disaster, caused by these abnormal climates, is now treating mankind's survival.

As of Global Warming problem the desertification is now on the rise. The desert is defined the arid region, where evaporation loss is higher than rainfall, and growing plants is difficult because of dry climate. So far 1/3 of land area is either the desert or semiarid region, and every year 60km² of land area is changed to desert. The main reasons of the desertification are expected as decrease of rainfall by weakened monsoon, ruined surface of the earth by excessive graze and destroy forest, and soil salinization.

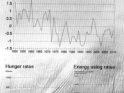

Tears of Africa

The annual average temperature of Earth has been periodically changed up and down within the range of 1.5°C with the cycle of 4~500 years. During the period of the 15'th to 19'th century the temperature has been relatively lower, and since the 20'th century the temperature has been gradually increased. Especially it is Africa, directly damaged by Global Warming. The desertification has mainly been appearedon Sahel region, south of Sahara desert in Africa, Chile in South America, North America, Asia and Australia, and so far 19% of total land area, 30 million km² is now regarded as desert region, and is the risk to mankind survival. Especially the Sahel region in Africa has been directly influenced by this desertification. Sahel region is located in the southern region of Sahara desert withdistance of 190 ~ 290 km by north to south, east from Sudan, Ethiopia, west to Senegal, Mali, Mauritania, Niger.

The recent drought, the largest one during last 60 years, has made an intense shortage of rainfall in Sahel region and East African region, Ethiopia, Somalia and Kenya, created over 10 million refugees so far, and over 2 million children are suffering from malnutrition. Though there are so many people living in Africa, the specific characters are insufficient natural resources in many areas and no technology to overcome this weak point. So the deforestation, impractical expansion of farmland and nomad have been done, but practically these are the main reasons of accelerating desertification and difficulties of their life. These Africans, lost their base of life by drought and famine, have become environmental refugee, to secure daily food for living, and under international aid program.

CONCEPT_GOD BLESS AFRICA(G.B.A) : "The intention of this project is to Bless Africa."

The climate change has been caused by the Global Warming, and it is rapidlyspread tothe desertification. Above all the recent drought in Africa is accelerating desertification of arid region. The target of this project is to make rainfall to the arid region, under way of desertification, and to grow plants by supplying water. Restore the base of living for Africans, environmental refugee currently, and let them back to their original life, growing crops and grazing cattle. Solve the fundamental factors of Global Warming by expansion of forest resource, presently decreasing, through fertilizing land by supplying water.

Mass concept process

Mass structure process

Construct a Mega-structure with a slope to respond the wind direction of land under desertification.

To support Mega-structure construct supporting space in both front and back side.

001

As a result of global warming, desertification has quickly risen, as a decrease of rainfall and weakened monsoons has ruined the surface of the earth by excessive grazing, deforestation, and soil salinization. The Sahel is no exception to the rising desertification of land, creating almost 10 million refugees and 2 million children suffering of malnutrition. The intent of God Bless Africa (GBA), designed by Son In-sung, Park Myoung-jin, Jo Sung-yong, and Hwang Youn-seok is to restore the base of living of Africans in the Sahel region through the production of water, and re-establishing means of shelter, agricultural and recreational restoration. GBA proposes the construction of a megastructure that is sloped in response to the wind direction, and distributes space and water from the front to the backside. By providing ample rainfall both naturally and artificially, the megastructure will solve the fundamental factors of global warming by

0889

expanding forest resources through fertilization. Integral to the self-generative power system is the ecosystem, which provides fundamental resources for the solar system, wind system, and methane (CH4) system and reduces the creation of wasteland.

The program of the GBA megastructure consists of module units of shelter, a centrally located farm, and restored grasslands that will provide a safe haven for wild species of flora and fauna previously undergoing extermination to flourish. This afforestation will prevent soil erosion and desertification of the land, and provide a solution to the food crisis through the growth of crops in a secured agricultural hub found both centrally or in the back of the megastructure.

Generating water

Water creating process by Natural wind (Ordinary case)

---Waste land of African region by drought and desertification.
---Build a massive GBA to induce ascending air current to make rainfall.

---As ascending air current through the structure surface, the air temperature is decreasing, and condensing water vapor.

---Condensed water vapor become rain drops, and flow through the structure surface, and create massive water.
---This massive water makes a water pond in front of the structure, and this water periodically flows to the backside of the structure.

---Flowing water through the stream makes the land fertilizing and create meadow of rich plantation.

1. The air is ascending through the slope.
2. The temperature of ascending air has been gradually decreased, 1℃/100m, by dry and adiabatic expansion till reach condensing altitude.
3. Water vapor starts Condensing when reaching saturation point, and cloud created.
4. High density water vapor in the cloud becomes rain drop and fall down to the slope.

Artificial water creating process (Dry season)

Animal feces and mankind feces store in the vacuum system, and ferment Methane gas at low, middle and high temperature.

Separate Hydrogen from Methane gas and collect pure Hydrogen.

Produce water by bonding Oxygen and Hydrogen, using electricity generated from Solar and Wind energy.

Store water in storage tank and flow it during dry season.

Synthesize algorithm_generation of water

The intention of this project is to "bless Africa" according to its designers. The climate change caused by global warming is rapidly spreading to the desertification already present in the Sahel. Above all, the recent drought in Africa is accelerating the desertification of the arid region. This project aims to restore the base of living for Africans, currently environmental refugees, and lead them back to their original lives, growing crops and grazing cattle. GBA would hopefully solve the fundamental factors of global warming by expansion of forest resource, presently decreasing, through fertilizing land by supplying water.

0889

Self-Power Generation System

Eco system to produce energy is necessary to prevent the deforestationfor energy source and becoming waste land. By GBA self-sufficient energy system the required energy can be provided to Africans without destroying environment.

Solar system

The Building Integrated Photovoltaic (BIPV) system on the surface of GBA structure converts Solar energy to electricity. The strong African Solar light would be useful for Solar power system, and the BIPV system, located at higher altitude, could generated electricity more efficiently.

Wind system

Install wind power generation system on top of GBA, and generate electricity powered by wind blowing through the slope. As wind velocity is getting higher according to the altitude, electricity generated at higher altitude is higher than that from ground level. Eco energy system, wind power, replaced fossil fuel in power generation, will produce much electricity.

Program

Africans, loose their base of living by draught and desertification, come to the refugee camp for food and water. This refugee camp is a solution at the present, but cannot be a permanent solution in the future. It is the purpose of this project, to provide the environment for Africans to survive their own living independently.

Shelter

These shelters are consisted of modular unit, so that each tribe can live separately as a unit. This big modular type open-space can be specialized by each tribe's characteristics. Stable and healthy life living can be available by supplied water and food.

Farm

Secure agricultural land by reclamation of ruined land, such as destroyed eco-system, eroded soil, sedimentation of sand, and deteriorated soil, by desertification. Give vitality to the ruined soil by supplying water, and growing plants there. By the crops from this secured agricultural land, solve the food crisis of Africans as well the Global food crisis. The farm is located at the center of GBA, butalso the crops can be grown from prepared grass land at the back side of GBA.

AFRICA 50 years hence

The North-Eastern region of Africa has recovered its original environment. The wild animals maintain their eco-system and enjoy their life on the wide green meadow. Africans maintain own tribal life, keeping its characteristics, safely through GBA system. Now this is an important place to solve the Global food crisis, massive production of crops by Africans. Now Africans are no more refugees of environment, under starvationas in the past, Africans are the guard responsible for Global food. The land, under desertification, is now turned to green, and its starting point is GBA, water producing system. GBA, supplying water to Africa, is the starting point of Blessing Africa.

SANCTUM

Rachel Janzen
Emily Kirwan
Joseph Varholick

United States

Modernity, Urbanism, along with all implicit expectations and impositions of lifestyle and culture have suppressed modes of human existence which are arguably most essential to our nature and happiness. "Our civilization is, generally-speaking, founded on the suppression of our instincts." The well-established urban center seems to have its inhabitant's lives well planed out, predetermined by a regulating infrastructure of steel and concrete. One occupies a 'generic' apartment complex, walks down a grid of streets, orthogonal movement only, 'works' in a tidy box, a cubicle in an office tower, staring at a screen, knowing what to and what not to do at any moment, knowing what is appropriate, knowing what is right and what is wrong, knowing the rules, knowing their place. Is it not easy to see many individuals afflicted by the increasing nervousness perpetuated by modern civilized life? "The man who in consequence cannot comply with the required suppression of his instincts, becomes a criminal, an outlaw. It was then found that men become neurotic because they cannot tolerate the degree of privation that society imposes upon them in virtue of its cultural ideals."

We wonder why we subject ourselves to an environment that seems to have little intrinsic reward. "Our so-called civilization itself is to blame for a great part of our misery, and we should be much happier if we were to give it up and go back to primitive conditions." We imagine a time before, what it must have been like before one had to live up to such expectations, when the world was simply the world, without symbols, without labels, before the greatest illusionist drew a line in the sand, called attention to the area and convinced the greatest fool that it was property. Should we not return to a lifestyle which perpetuates our happiness?

Yet our knowledge of to-day disables us. We are fascinated by our technology and infatuated with the convenience it affords us. We see this concept of ours as an anchor preventing our escape, our salvation. However the machine is not in direct conflict with the practice of an essential or naturalistic life, rather its historical utilization is to blame. In fact, we must now rely on the correct application of technology to deliver ourselves from the implications of modernity. We will raise ourselves above the cities. Let it be called an allegorical 'afterlife.' Here

we rely on techno[...] the earth. This new[...] nomadic; it feeds [...] grows, evolves opp[...] will of its liberated [...] in a greater harmo[...] analogous to prim[...] resources as natur[...] afforded by limited[...] implies carrying co[...] opportunity for a r[...] each of their own [...] 'nervousness of mo[...]

Rachel Janzen, Emily Kirwan, and Joseph Varholick wonder why we subject ourselves to an environment that seems to have little intrinsic reward. Our so-called civilization itself is to blame for a great part of our misery, and we would be much happier if we were to give it up and go back to primitive conditions. They imagine a time before, what it must have been like before one had to live up to such expectations, when the world was simply the world, without symbols, without labels, before the greatest illusionist drew a line in the sand, called attention to the area and convinced the greatest fool that it was property. Should we not return to a lifestyle that perpetuates our happiness?

Yet our knowledge of today disables us, they state. Modernity, urbanism, along with all implicit expectations and impositions of lifestyle and culture have suppressed modes of human existence which are arguably the most essential

1017

...han relied on
...d sustainable,
...y below and
...ng only to the
...munities live
...cooperation,
...es, treating
...n can be
...s and in turn
...chism, and the
...ent infrastructures.
...pe the
...Salvation.

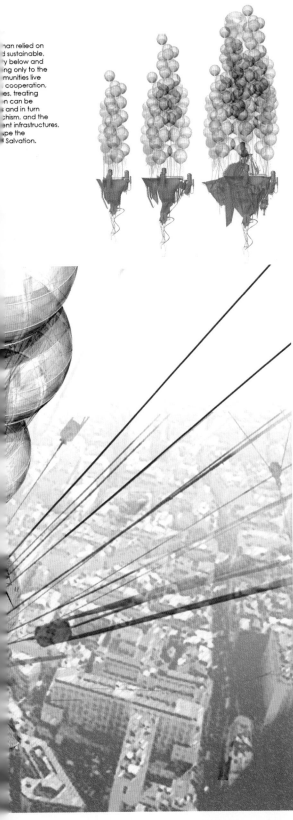

to out nature and happiness. We are fascinated by our technology and infatuated with the convenience it affords us. We see this concept of ours as an anchor preventing our escape, our salvation. However the machine is not in direct conflict with the practice of an essential or naturalistic life, rather its historical utilization is to blame. In fact, we must now rely on the correct application of technology to deliver ourselves from the implications of modernity. We will raise ourselves above the cities. Let it be called an allegorical "afterlife."

Here we rely on technology only as primitive man relied on the earth. This new place is separate and sustainable, nomadic; it feeds on the scraps of society below and grows, evolves opportunistically, according only to the will of its liberated inhabitants. Here communities live in a greater harmony, in closer care and cooperation, analogous

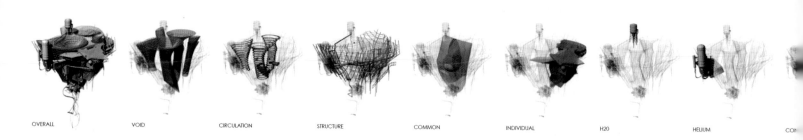

OVERALL   VOID   CIRCULATION   STRUCTURE   COMMON   INDIVIDUAL   H2O   HELIUM   CON

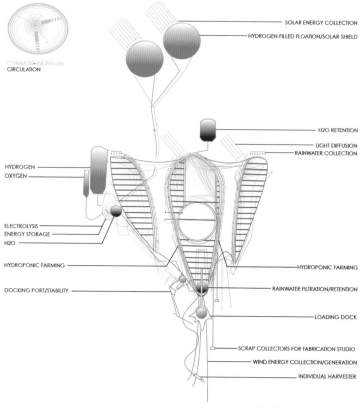

COMMON-INDIVIDUAL
CIRCULATION

SOLAR ENERGY COLLECTION
HYDROGEN FILLED FLOATION/SOLAR SHIELD

H2O RETENTION
LIGHT DIFFUSION
RAINWATER COLLECTION

HYDROGEN
OXYGEN

ELECTROLYSIS
ENERGY STORAGE
H2O

HYDROPONIC FARMING

DOCKING PORT/STABILITY

HYDROPONIC FARMING
RAINWATER FILTRATION/RETENTION

LOADING DOCK

SCRAP COLLECTORS FOR FABRICATION STUDIO
WIND ENERGY COLLECTION/GENERATION
INDIVIDUAL HARVESTER

to primitive tribes or communes, treating resources as natural commons. This notion can be afforded by limited, isolated populations and in turn implies carrying capacity, a necessary schism, and the opportunity for a multitude of independent infrastructures, each of their own identity. Here we escape the "nervousness of modernity." Here we find salvation.

1017

300'

0'

VOLCANELECTRIC MASK

Xingyue Chen
Jiangyue Han
Jing Hao
Zhanou Zhang
Shuo Zhou

China

VOLCANELECTRIC MASK I

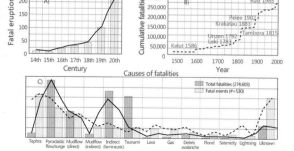

Background

According to the records, though the volcanic eruption is caused by magma and volcanic ash together, often the volcanic ash will bring greater harm once reaches a certain height. It will influence more of the affected area with the airflow movement spread. Once the volcanic ash whereabouts, it would cause serious harm to crops, cities, as well as the human respiratory tract. On the other hand, according to the survey, the volcanic ash owns certain benefits in building materials, grinding industry, daily chemical, petrochemical and thermal insulation materials. Since we cannot control the disaster, why not take advantage of it.

Fig. A) Fatal volcanic eruptions per century. It is revealing an increase in the global population living in the vicinity of active volcanoes. B) Cumulative documented fatalities caused by volcanic eruptions. The seven named eruptions claimed more than 10,000 victims. C) Cause of fatalities in volcanic eruptions. In some eruptions, fatalities result from mostly volcano ash (modified after Simkin et al., 2001).

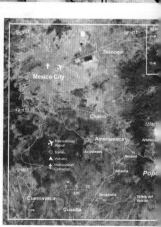

Fig. Main towns surrounding Popocatépetl volcano. Mexic located 40 km from the volcano. Inset depicts the volcano at

From the suffocation of Pompeii to the air traffic gridlock suffered in Iceland in 2010, the tephra that is expelled during volcanic eruptions has long posed grave threats to civilization. Since volcanic eruptions cannot be controlled, the designers of the VolcanElectric Mask propose constructing an industrial structure over a volcano that can collect tephra during an eruption, keeping it out of the skies and away from cities and villages below, and also harness the power from the volcano's heat in calm periods to provide clean electric power to surrounding areas.

For the prototype, the designers imagine locating the structure on the Popocatepetl Volcano, which is 70 km from Mexico City. It is one of the ten most active volcanoes in the developed world and has 500,000 people living within 10 to 30 km from its crater.

0130

AD 79, Mount Vesuvius erupted and buried Pompeii in volcanic ash overnight.
1991, Mount Pinatubo's volcanic eruption, so wet and heavy ash landed to the densely populated area, about 200 people died under the collapsed roof.
2006, Tungurahua volcano eruption, five villages were buried under volcanic ash.
2010, Iceland's Eyjafjallajokull volcano eruption, the greatest impact on aviation safety, volcanic ash caused the majority of European air traffic gridlock.
2011, Junction of Kagoshima and Miyazaki Prefecture active volcano Kirishima continuous eruption, causing Local traffic chaos, crop damage, and affected the daily lives.
2011, Argentina Chile puyehue's volcano eruption, thousands of sorties of flights were canceled due to the ash, causing serious economic losses.

Location

We select the volcano of a small amount of high frequency type as the main object of study and Popocatépetl Volcano (19.02° N, 98.62° W, located in central Mexico, just 70 km from downtown Mexico City) is suited, Popocatépetl is one of the 10 most populated active volcanoes in the world (Small and Naumann, 2001). Presently ~ 500,000 people live within 10–30 km from the crater and nearly 1.3 million within 40 km (De la Cruz-Reyna and Tilling, 2008). Moreover, within 40-80 km from the vent, more than 20 million inhabitants may be exposed to the effects of a large-magnitude explosive eruption.

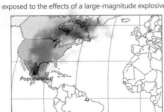

and Cuautla are can Volcanic Belt.
Fig. The influence of the tephra of Popocatépetl volcano. Based on the air flow,it can be seen obviously that North America and some part of Europe are suffered from tephra.

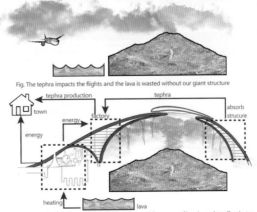

Fig. The tephra impacts the flights and the lava is wasted without our giant structure

Fig. The tephra is collected by the shell and is reused,the energy of lava is used to offer electriv to the towns surrounding volcano.And the production from tephra is put into people's life.

Concept

We imagine a bold vision, , set the giant industral structures around the volcano to collect volcanic ash and prevent the spread of tephra to cause great harm, then we use it. And the energy of the volcano is also used to support the industries and towns around it.There are two key points of concept.

First, the giant shell collect and utilize of volcano ash.

1, The temperature sensing switch set on the tentacles constantly monitoring the temperature changes, absorbing carbon dioxide and compress them into dry ice for storage.

2, The shell's surface contains layers of filter absorb, separate and transport the absorbent product.

Second, the giant shell is used as thermal power plants supplying energy when the volcano is calm.

1, With the rainwater collection, the shell use lava to supply Thermal Power Plant power.

2, Changing the negative volcanic heat into positive energy which could be used to supply people daily lives.

48

The VolcanElectric Mask is a multi-layered skin that covers the volcano, perched above its surface. The skin is comprised of the adjoining tops of tentacles, which are shaped like screws, that are relatively flat on top—this is what is visible when one looks at the volcano—but are long and sharpen to a point at the bottom. This long, sharp bottom allows each tentacle to burrow into the volcano itself to monitor its temperature, helping to predict eruptions, and also allows each one to capture carbon dioxide that is used to create and store dry ice.

In periods of tranquility, each tentacle operates as a power station. The top layers of the tentacles, the screw head-like areas, which are above the ground, have ample openings allowing the volcano's surface to be ecologically undisturbed, with access to rain and fresh air. To create thermal energy, the top level of each tentacle acts as a

VOLCANELECTRIC MASK II

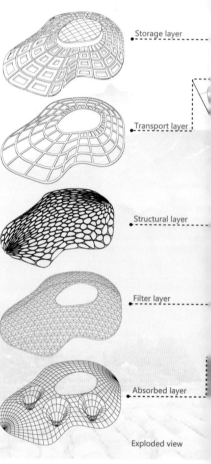

Storage layer

Transport layer

Structural layer

Filter layer

Absorbed layer

Exploded view

Working principle

collecting rain

factory

heating and power plant

energy storage

push turbine get energy

steam out   water in

deliver to towns

heating

movable roof

sightseeing layer

internal tentacles

study lab

closing roof

spray dry ice

Section (A)

Section (B)

(A) When the volcano is calm (General State)

1. The top lid should be kept open when the volcano is calm, exposing the volcano to natural elements. Rainwater collected from the basin at the surface of Main body, will be sent into the thermal cycle system after processed.

2. Thermal Power Plant then injects the water to the sub layer; steam is then produced by using high temperature of the lava which is then turns the turbines, to produce electricity of which is sent to the surrounding villages and towns.

(B) The stage of eruption

1. When the sensors senses an impending eruption the internal tentacles swit switches and spray dry ice which then closes building roof.

2. The volcanic eruptions' temperature is reduced by the dry ice to an accepta surface material, and then be aborted and separated by the layers.

rainwater collector. After it rains, water is transported to a sub-layer of the tentacle, where it comes into contact with lava. The resulting steam turns turbines in the middle of the tentacle, where the top meets the long, pointed bottom portion, and this creates clean thermal power.

When the tentacles sense an impending eruption, they activate shields that close the openings on the top layers of the tentacles. This keeps the lava, tephra and debris that erupts from actually being dispelled into the air or flowing into nearby towns. The tentacles then shoot the stored dry ice into the volcano's core to cool the lava down so when the volcano does erupts and coat the tentacles in lava, the temperature will not be so high as to ruin the tentacles' machinery. When the volcano does finally erupt, the outside world is shielded.

0130

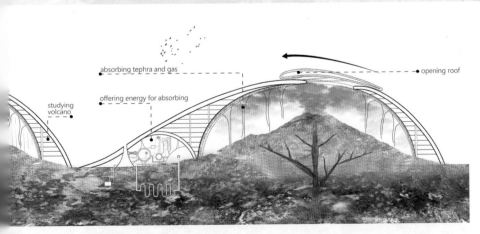

rain in
rain in   rain in   tephra storage
fresh air out

water

holes adsorption
macroporous adsorption

suction turbine

skin

Detail of storage and transport layer

CO2

dry ice

brain

Detail of suction turbine

tephra and gas

storage

pump

high voltage
transmission area

CO2

tephra and gas

temperature sensing
switch

the first layer screen

neuron

Detail of temperature sensing switch

Section of internal tentacle

Main transport layer

The giant shell surface is covered with transport tracks, constitute a comprehensive transportation system of the volcanic ash to a recycling facility. When the layer filters and collects a certain amount of ash it is then accumulated and shipped out along the surface of the transport rail.

Turbine suction

There's a suction turbine in the top of each tentacle, whose electric power is supplied by the cogeneration plants. The high speed rotation of the turbine make the tentacles upper into a negative pressure zone so that under the action of the pressure difference inside and outside, the ejected ash tentacles, is forced to flow to the main building along the internal pipe branch after adsorption, and then enter the main building lateral separation system.

Temperature sensing switch

There is a temperature sensing chip on each synaptic. These chips are covered with a huge case forming a system assembled with the Nervous system of human body, reflecting the relationship between Neurons and the brain. When the temperature sensing chips (Neuron) senses a heat signal, they will pass on the signal to the Control device on the top of the case (Brain) which can switch the cover and spray dry ice. The wires are made of Optical fiber which allows for immediate response to the eruptions.

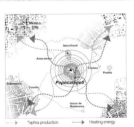

Regional impact

This giant structure can protect surrounding villages from being destroyed by the volcano eruptions. and reduce the impact on the aviation system and the environment at the same time. And it can also provide energy to the neighborhood using thermal power beneath the Lava layer when the volcano is quiescence.

absorbing tephra and gas

opening roof

offering energy for absorbing

studying
volcano

Section (C)

Long-term development

(C) The end of the eruption

1. Upon sensing the drop of the open surface temperature, the internal tentacles close, using the electricity supplied by the thermal power plants to compress the carbon dioxide aborted into dry ice in order to prepare for the next eruption. Linkage building roof again open.

2. The byproduct of an eruption is collected by the building filter and shipped out along the transport rail into the processing plant for in ustrial products.

This structure located on the Popocatépetl Volcano can also be a pre-fabricated module using on other volcanoes which can create a new type of architecture---volcano architecture. Meanwhile, the use of underground magma can maintain the temperature of the magma on a stable value and reduce the number of volcanic eruptions.

50

TINDEO

Hu Jiayuan
Zhu Meng
Li Moyu
Zhang Xinxing

Taiwan

The fire Prometheus stole from Zeus and gave to humanity is called Tindeo in Greek. As the name suggests, our proposal aims at providing human kind the power and shelter to continue our civilization and sustainable development. In the past 7 million years, our planet has experienced 7 ice ages. Though human activities (such as CO2 emission) have impact on global temperature to some extent, the decline of average temperature of the earth is being accepted by more and more scientists.. The earth has spent much of its history moving from one ice age to another which is separated by short periods of warm weather. These periods of warm weather are considered to be around 12,000 years. It seems that the earth is approching the end of one of those warm periods and a shift to a colder climate may be on the horizon. Even if it will take decades for the climate to turn to be unbearable to us, we should be well-prepared to the up-coming ice age. To establish a reliable energy supply system and basic construction of living space for mankind ahead of time, and to ensure the continuation of human civilization, well-being of mankind and long-term development is the main goal of our proposal.

The usage of wind power, solar power and other forms of energy failed to solve the current energy crisis fundamentally, most human activities still rely on traditional non-renewable energy resources such as fuel and coal. The shortage of traditional energy restrains the development of many countries and regions, and the economic systems of some countries even sink into stagnation. Geothermal energy as an unlimited renewable energy resource should catch enough attention. Earth as a huge energy reservoir contained 1.05x10^26 J in a single layer 10 km underground, as much as energy released by 3.58x10^15 ton standard coal. Based on condition mentioned above, our proposal makes full use of geothermal energy in 1st period.

In a near future Ice Age scenario Tindeo aims to provide new reliable energy supply and construction strategies to ensure the continuation of human civilization, based on geothermal energy as an unlimited renewable and reliable energy resource. Tindeo tower will be constructed in a volcanic vent left by a dead volcano. Nonmetallic mineral resources such as volcanic rock and cinerite are perfect building insulation materials for housing and shelters.

The proposal aims to provide humankind the power and shelter to continue sustainable development. Tindeo towers will dispose large amount of waste produced by every day life. Garbage will be sorted into different categories (organic/inorganic/non-recyclable). Organic waste will be turned into fertilizer and used in crops and planting. Recyclable garbage will be processed and non-recycled garbage will be smashed, burned and disposed in deep

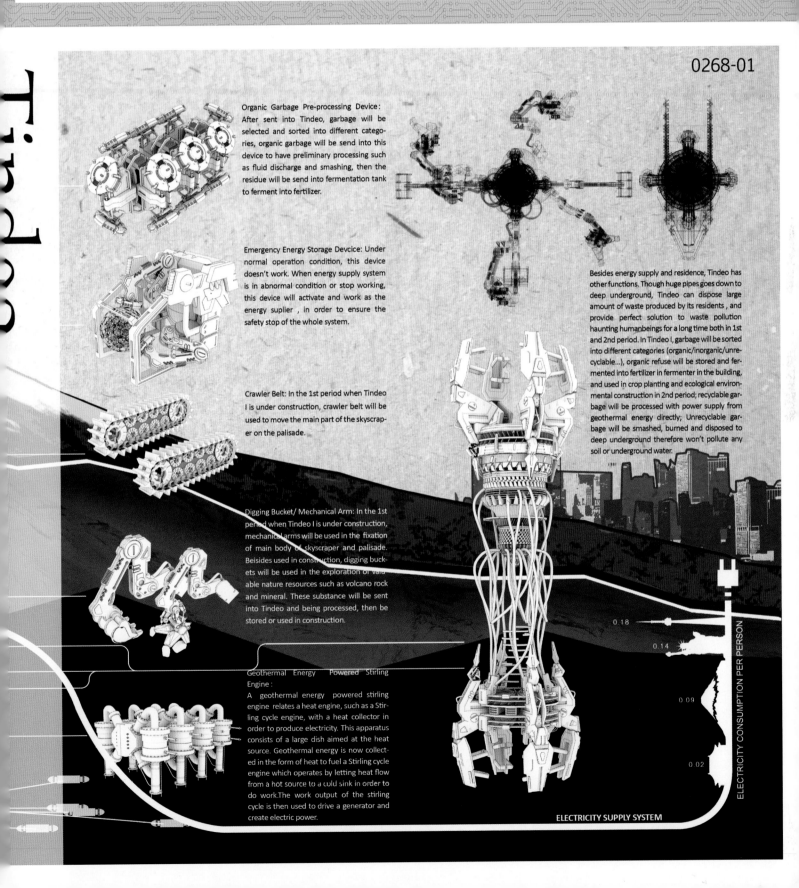

Tindeo

0268-01

Organic Garbage Pre-processing Device: After sent into Tindeo, garbage will be selected and sorted into different categories, organic garbage will be send into this device to have preliminary processing such as fluid discharge and smashing, then the residue will be send into fermentation tank to ferment into fertilizer.

Emergency Energy Storage Devcice: Under normal operation condition, this device doesn't work. When energy supply system is in abnormal condition or stop working, this device will activate and work as the energy suplier , in order to ensure the safety stop of the whole system.

Crawler Belt: In the 1st period when Tindeo I is under construction, crawler belt will be used to move the main part of the skyscraper on the palisade.

Digging Bucket/ Mechanical Arm: In the 1st period when Tindeo I is under construction, mechanical arms will be used in the fixation of main body of skyscraper and palisade. Beisides used in construction, digging buckets will be used in the exploration of valuable nature resources such as volcano rock and mineral. These substance will be sent into Tindeo and being processed, then be stored or used in construction.

Geothermal Energy Powered Stirling Engine :
A geothermal energy powered stirling engine relates a heat engine, such as a Stirling cycle engine, with a heat collector in order to produce electricity. This apparatus consists of a large dish aimed at the heat source. Geothermal energy is now collected in the form of heat to fuel a Stirling cycle engine which operates by letting heat flow from a hot source to a cold sink in order to do work.The work output of the stirling cycle is then used to drive a generator and create electric power.

Besides energy supply and residence, Tindeo has other functions. Though huge pipes goes down to deep underground, Tindeo can dispose large amount of waste produced by its residents , and provide perfect solution to waste pollution haunting humanbeings for a long time both in 1st and 2nd period. In Tindeo I, garbage will be sorted into different categories (organic/inorganic/unrecyclable...), organic refuse will be stored and fermented into fertilizer in fermenter in the building, and used in crop planting and ecological environmental construction in 2nd period; recyclable garbage will be processed with power supply from geothermal energy directly; Unrecyclable garbage will be smashed, burned and disposed to deep underground therefore won't pollute any soil or underground water.

ELECTRICITY CONSUMPTION PER PERSON

0.18

0.14

0.09

0.02

ELECTRICITY SUPPLY SYSTEM

underground facilities therefore will not pollute any soil or underground water.

In the design, Tindeo focuses on changing our perception and utilization pattern of natural resources. In ancient times, human beings maintained a harmonious relationship with nature. Nature provided habitat for human beings such as cave structures. This provided the inspiration for the design of Tindeo. The proposal of constructing Tindeo in a volcanic vent left by a dead volcano is based on the idea that we should go back to a natural way of life with a maintained living temperature from using nature.

Tindeo construction will be faced in 2 phases. Tindeo I will begin in 2014 and will focus on facing the energy crisis by constructing foundlings for the next phase. Tindeo II will focus on turning geothermal energy into electricity through

Tindeo

a Stirling engine.

Divided by time range, the construction and utilization of Tindeo are separated into two periods. The priority of the first period will be giving attention to the energy crisis while basic constructions will be conducted to prepare for the second period. By transfering unlimited geothermal energy into electricity through mechanisms such as the Stirling engine, Tindeo I can provide electricity to a medium sized city for domestic and industrial purposes. In the second period, Tindeo II (a reformed version of Tindeo I), serving as a microcirculation ecological environment, will provide stable energy supply and living space for mankind in extreme cold weather, and ensure the normal operation of society as a whole.

0268-02

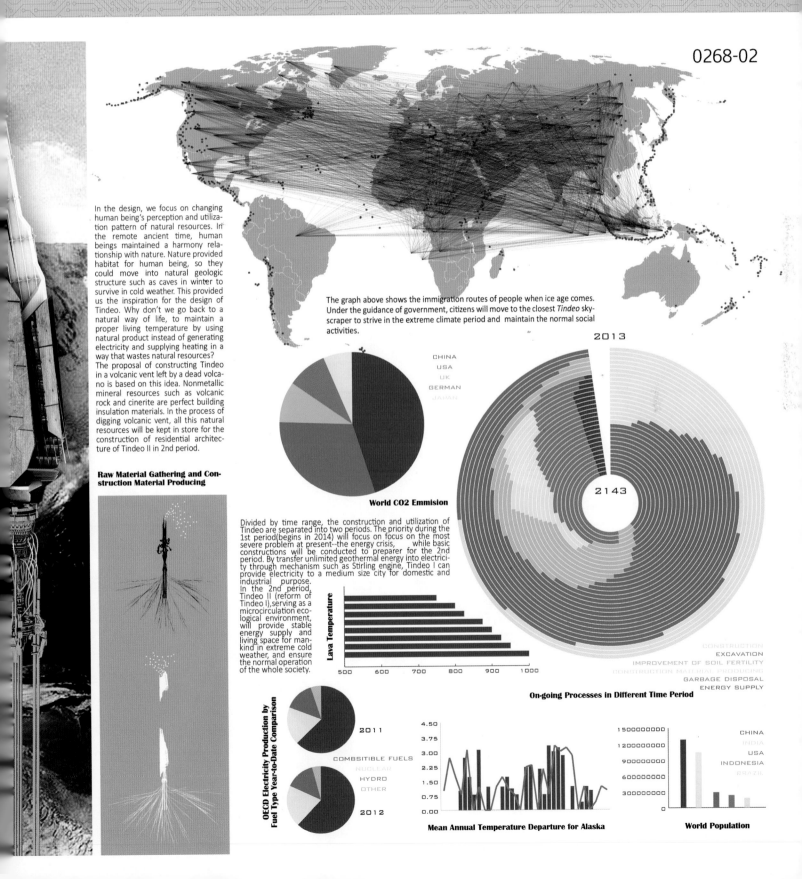

In the design, we focus on changing human being's perception and utilization pattern of natural resources. In the remote ancient time, human beings maintained a harmony relationship with nature. Nature provided habitat for human being, so they could move into natural geologic structure such as caves in winter to survive in cold weather. This provided us the inspiration for the design of Tindeo. Why don't we go back to a natural way of life, to maintain a proper living temperature by using natural product instead of generating electricity and supplying heating in a way that wastes natural resources? The proposal of constructing Tindeo in a volcanic vent left by a dead volcano is based on this idea. Nonmetallic mineral resources such as volcanic rock and cinerite are perfect building insulation materials. In the process of digging volcanic vent, all this natural resources will be kept in store for the construction of residential architecture of Tindeo II in 2nd period.

Raw Material Gathering and Construction Material Producing

The graph above shows the immigration routes of people when ice age comes. Under the guidance of government, citizens will move to the closest *Tindeo* skyscraper to strive in the extreme climate period and maintain the normal social activities.

CHINA
USA
UK
GERMAN
JAPAN

World CO2 Emmision

2013

2143

Divided by time range, the construction and utilization of Tindeo are separated into two periods. The priority during the 1st period(begins in 2014) will focus on focus on the most severe problem at present--the energy crisis, while basic constructions will be conducted to preparer for the 2nd period. By transfer unlimited geothermal energy into electricity through mechanism such as Stirling engine, Tindeo I can provide electricity to a medium size city for domestic and industrial purpose.
In the 2nd period, Tindeo II (reform of Tindeo I),serving as a microcirculation ecological environment, will provide stable energy supply and living space for mankind in extreme cold weather, and ensure the normal operation of the whole society.

Lava Temperature

500 600 700 800 900 1000

CONSTRUCTION
EXCAVATION
IMPROVEMENT OF SOIL FERTILITY
CONSTRUCTION MATERIAL PRODUCING
GARBAGE DISPOSAL
ENERGY SUPPLY

On-going Processes in Different Time Period

OECD Electricity Production by Fuel Type Year-to-Date Comparison

2011

COMBSITIBLE FUELS
NUCLEAR
HYDRO
OTHER

2012

4.50
3.75
3.00
2.25
1.50
0.75
0.00

Mean Annual Temperature Departure for Alaska

1 500000000
1 200000000
900000000
600000000
300000000
0

CHINA
INDIA
USA
INDONESIA
BRAZIL

World Population

SOUNDSCRAPER

Julien Bourgeois
Olivier Colliez
Savinien De Pizzol
Cédric Dounval
Romain Grouselle

France

(((SOUNDSCRAPER)))
NOISE POLLUTION CONVERTER

Energy is one of the major concerns of our current society. Today sustainable architecture seeks to minimize the negative environmental impact of buildings by enhancing efficiency and moderation in the use of materials. Noise is part of our urban environment and everyday life and it is one of the most prevalent pollution form in cities, but it is also an important source of energy not valued yet.

The soundscraper takes advantage of city noise pollution by capturing airborne sound and converting it into usable energy. One of the most abundant energy sources is ambient motion. Vibrations can provide plentiful energy and can be transferred through many media, making this form of kinetic energy very useful.

The Soundscraper is located next to main transport infrastructures, mostly outside city centers where noise

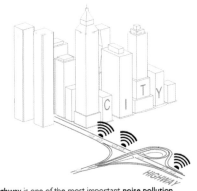

Highway is one of the most important noise pollution

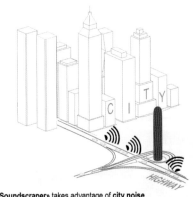

«Soundscraper» takes advantage of city noise

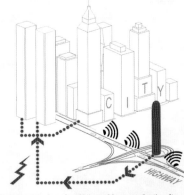

«Soundscraper» turn sound into usable power for the city

Highway exchanger are the highest noise pollution in the city

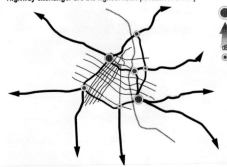

Capture and **convert** city noise pollution to create **usable energy** for the city 150 MW with one **«soundscraper»** tower.

City noise pollution captured to create usable energy

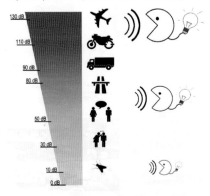

Energy is one of the major concerns of our current society. Scientific researches and technological progress had led architecture to **sustainable architecture**. In the broad context, sustainable architecture seeks to minimize the negative environmental impact of buildings by enhancing efficiency and moderation in the use of materials, energy, and development space to ensure that our actions and decisions today do not inhibit the opportunities of future generations. Energy efficiency is the most important goal of sustainable architecture. Designers use differents techniques to reduce the energy needs of buildings and increase their ability to capture or generate their own energy. **We use sun, wind and water but what about noise ?**

Noise is part of our urban environment and our everyday life. It surrounds us, puts us under stress, even oppresses us. It is one of the most prevalent pollution form in cities but it is also an important source of energy not valued yet. **The soundscraper tower takes advantage of city noise pollution by capturing airborne sound and converting it into usable energy.** One of the most abundant energy sources is ambient motion. Vibrations can provide plentiful energy, and can be transferred through many media, making this form of kinetic energy very useful.

The « Soundscraper » tower is located next to main **transport infrastructures**, mostly outside city centers where noise pollution is at it maximum. Motorway junction, railway hub represent no man's land in the urban territory and areas of greatest efficiency to produce energy . The energetic tower is a **signal**. It creates a new interaction between neglected peripheric spaces and global cityscape by giving a new function to huge interstitial spaces. It could symbolize **new comtenporary entrances for 21th century metroplitan cities**. Each motorway junction could welcome a « soundscraper » tower to generate enough power to provide electrical needs of a whole city.

«Soundscraper» as a **landmark** and an **efficient converter** to create energy

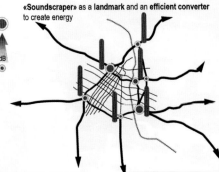

pollution is at its maximum. Motorway junction and railway hubs represent no man's land in the urban territory yet are areas where this type of energy can be harnessed efficiently.

The skyscraper's façade is evolutive; it vibrates depending on intensity and direction of urban noises. As the skyscraper's skin, the electro active lashes supported by a light metallic structure, form the exterior of the building, they provide maximum exposure to city noise. Covering a wide spectrum of frequencies, this noise includes vehicular traffic, pedestrians, train, building inhabitants, and even aircrafts passing overhead. 84,000 electro-active lashes are integrated throughout the 100-meter-high tower. The lashes are covered with sound sensors called P.F.I.G (Parametric Frequency Increased Generators). A specialized PFIG energy harvester converts sound vibrations caused

(((SOUNDSCRAPER))) NOISE POLL

by surrounding noises to capture kinetic energy, after which an array of transducer cells employing a novel actuation method are used to convert the mechanical energy into electricity. The electrical current is then transferred to a main storage compartment to be redistributed to the city. Based on scientifically researched results, one tower could produce up to 150 MW/h representing 10% of the urban lighting consumption of Los Angeles. At the same time, this renewable energy could participate in reducing CO_2 emissions.

The tower will be a landmark, creating a new interaction between neglected peripheric spaces and global cityscape, by giving a new function to huge interstitial spaces. Each motorway junction could welcome a soundscraper tower to generate enough power to provide electrical needs of a whole city.

Noise pollution due to high traffic

Electrical needs of the city

CONVERTER

The moving skin tower reflecting the surrounding sound environnement

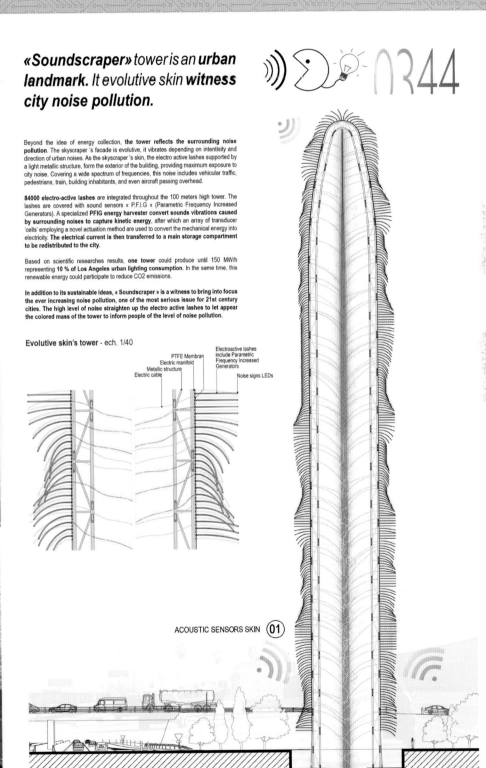

«Soundscraper» tower is an urban landmark. It evolutive skin witness city noise pollution.

Beyond the idea of energy collection, **the tower reflects the surrounding noise pollution**. The skyscraper 's facade is evolutive, it vibrates depending on intentisity and direction of urban noises. As the skyscraper 's skin, the electro active lashes supported by a light metallic structure, form the exterior of the building, providing maximum exposure to city noise. Covering a wide spectrum of frequencies, this noise includes vehicular traffic, pedestrians, train, building inhabitants, and even aircraft passing overhead.

84000 electro-active lashes are integrated throughout the 100 meters high tower. The lashes are covered with sound sensors « P.F.I.G « (Parametric Frequency Increased Generators). A specialized **PFIG energy harvester convert sounds vibrations caused by surrounding noises to capture kinetic energy**, after which an array of transducer 'cells' employing a novel actuation method are used to convert the mechanical energy into electricity. **The electrical current is then transferred to a main storage compartment to be redistributed to the city.**

Based on scientific researches results, **one tower** could produce until 150 MW/h representing 10 % of Los Angeles urban lighting consumption. In the same time, this renewable energy could participate to reduce CO2 emissions.

In addition to its sustainable ideas, « Soundscraper » is a witness to bring into focus the ever increasing noise pollution, one of the most serious issue for 21st century cities. The high level of noise straighten up the electro active lashes to let appear the colored mass of the tower to inform people of the level of noise pollution.

Evolutive skin's tower - ech. 1/40

PTFE Membran
Electric manifold
Metallic structure
Electric cable

Electroactive lashes include Parametric Frequency Increased Generators

Noise signs LEDs

ACOUSTIC SENSORS SKIN (01)

ENERGY TOWARD THE CITY (03)

(02) BATTERY

MAGNETIC CLOUD

Li Hanwei   Pei Zhao
Zhong Mengdie   Chu Ziyuan
Wang Moze
Zhang Wenjie
Yang Xiaodan

China

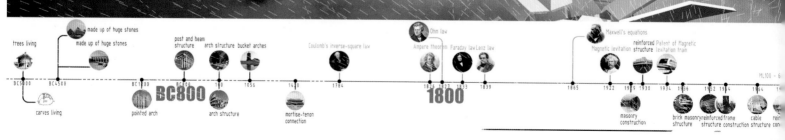

Hurricane Katrina was the largest Atlantic hurricane in American history, causing great damage to the country and ruining the infrastructure of many cities.

This project proposes a design for a man-made shield to protect the building from the attacks of hurricanes, and at the same time make use of the wind energy. This design will make a building out of the effects of gravity and load leveling by magnetic levitation, a building implanted elements with magnetic poles, and a building which is almost limitless in the height.

This design is first going to store the electrical energy converted by daily wind, tidal, and solar power. In ordinary state, the electromagnetic generator absorbs tidal energy and charges for the electromagnetic units. The units can

Hurricane Sandy made a historic landfall on the New Jersey coast during the night of Oct.29

Impact of Hurricane Sandy

The rain that the storm dropped along the U.S. eastern seaboard since Sandy's birth.

Sandy's wind speed is very fast and impact is broad.

Let Sandy rage like this?

New York City

Section of Sandy Hurricane

If we creat mountains...
Mountains enough high can promote part of the hurricane into eddy current and form rainfall so as to reduce the impact of the hurricane on city

Or Megnetic CLoud can be the shield

Hurricane

Megnetic Cloud

American Continent

Schematic diagram for DEFENCE

Background
Hurricane Sandy was a Category 1 storm, which made landfall and hit such Carribean areas as Cuba, Dominica, Jamaica, the Bahamas and Haiti from October 24 to 26. The storm then became the largest Atlantic hurricane in American history in the following 5 days, causing great losses to the country and its people. The hurricane killed at least 113 Americans along the path of the storm, and ruined many city infrastructure. Buildings of important agencies such as the head quarters of the United Nations and Wall Street were destroyed. Therefore, it's time to release the great impacts of natural disasters on our cities through smarter building design in such a day that the greenhouse effect are getting more and more serious, and disasters like Sandy becoming more and more frequent.

Concepts
The humid monsoon will be weakened by the mountain ranges and furtherformed monsoon rains, so the effects of monsoon on the plain are significantly reduced. Enlightened by the above natural phenomena, this design is going to made a building with a man-shield which can protect the building from the attacts of hurricanes, and at the same time make use of the wind energy.
This design is first going to store the electrical energy converted by daily wind, tidal power, and solar power. Then in face of the disasters like Hurricane Sandy, it will push forward the electromagnetic transformation system with the help of the wind, and convert the wind power into electricities which would be possibly cut off due to the damage of infrastructure. Therefore, the design can significantly reduce the impacts of disasters on the city.

Revolution
More and more skyscrapers come out due to the improvement of the building structure. However, factors such as gravity and load leveling should still be taken into account. This design is going to make a building out of the effects of gravity and load leveling by magnetic levitation, a building implanted elements with magnetic poles, and a building which is almost limitless in the height. What is more important, our society will reap more benefits from this design. For example, people can put different sections together as they wish, and they can better deal with the possible coming disasters.

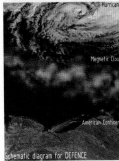

Gravity Form
Vertical skyscraper

Inform
Twisted skyscraper   Horizontal skyscraper

Anti-Gravity Anti-form
Magnet levitating skyscraper

Electromagnetic Technology shall give birth to Construction Revolution

2000

MLT Linimo train

building integrated PV

reinforced monolithic concrete construction

steel ribs structure

2025

MAGNETIC CLOUD MAGIC SHIELD

also absorb solar energy to ensure the basic energy of the magnetic cloud shield.

Then when facing a natural disaster like hurricanes, it will push forward the electromagnetic energy transformation system, and convert the wind power into electricity for an emergency scenario. The electromagnetic generators are arranged along the coastline. Each unit is prefabricated and transported to the sea. At the same time the rest of the units get together in a certain range, based by distribution rules applied on magnetic fields lines connected to the main generator. When the magnetic field enhances, the magnetic plate of each block begins to interact with the generators field in order to make itself levitate.

In a disaster scenario the magnetic cloud emerges gradually according to the magnetic field lines and expands in

a large scale. This activates the propulsion system in each unit in order to resist the displacement during the storm. In hurricane state, the propellers on the electromagnetic unit begin to rotate and cut magnetic field lines when hurricanes push them and this process will transform the Hurricane's kinetic energy into the magnetic cloud shield's power. In the meantime the Lorentz force can resist the units' displacement and make sure that the magnetic cloud shield can keep its configuration during the disaster. After the storm the magnetic cloud shield gradually returns to the original position and some units will recombine while others will fall to the sea.

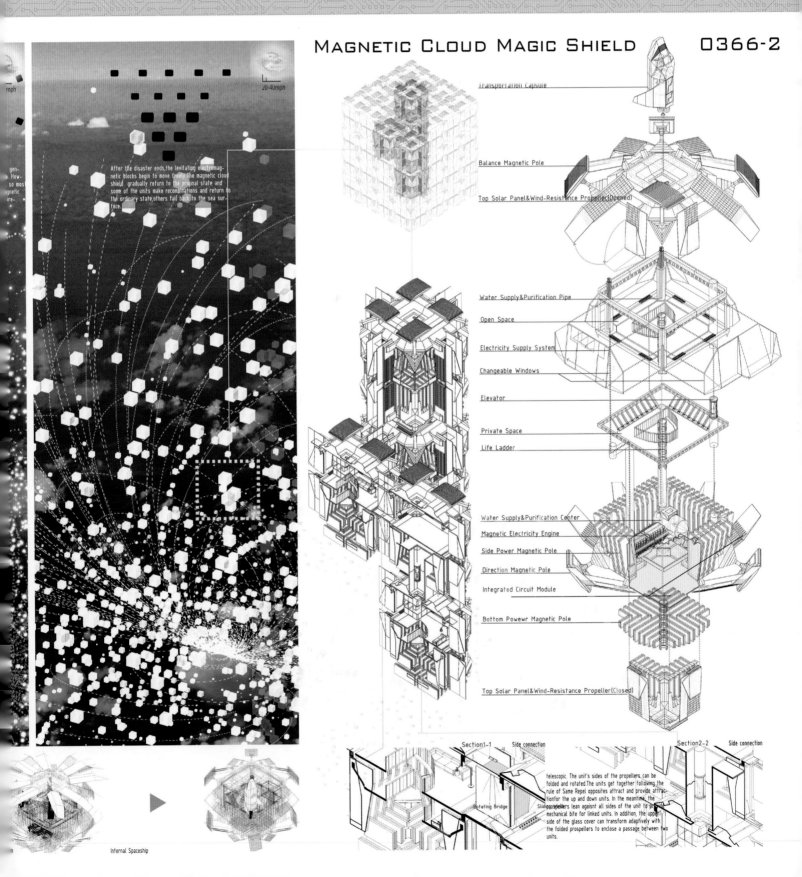

MAGNETIC CLOUD MAGIC SHIELD   0366-2

After the disaster ends,the levitating electromagnetic blocks begin to move freely.The magnetic cloud shield gradually return to the original state and some of the units make recombinations and return to the ordinary state,others fall back to the sea surface.

Transportation Capsule

Balance Magnetic Pole

Top Solar Panel&Wind-Resistance Propeller(Opened)

Water Supply&Purification Pipe

Open Space

Electricity Supply System

Changeable Windows

Elevator

Private Space

Life Ladder

Water Supply&Purification Center

Magnetic Electricity Engine

Side Power Magnetic Pole

Direction Magnetic Pole

Integrated Circuit Module

Bottom Powewr Magnetic Pole

Top Solar Panel&Wind-Resistance Propeller(Closed)

Section1-1   Side connection

Section2-2   Side connection

Rotating Bridge

telescopic. The unit's sides of the propellers can be folded and rotated.The units get together following the rule of Same Repel opposites attract and provide attraction for the up and down units. In the meantime the Sliding propellers lean against all sides of the unit to provide mechanical bite for linked units. In addition, the upper side of the glass cover can transform adaptively with the folded prospellers to enclose a passage between two units.

Internal Spaceship

BREAK BREATHE TOWER

Li Lei
Lyu Shengze
Lyu Tianyi
Huang Yumeng

China

BREAK· BREATHE
AIR PURIFICATION TOWER

Urban air pollution is one of the most problematic issues facing big cities in developing countries today. This skyscraper is a ventilator and a lung for the whole city which cooperates with the underground polluted air collecting pipe network to operate as an air purifying system.

This skyscraper is an air purification tower, operating based on the buoyancy-driven natural ventilation caused by its height, utilizing the temperature differences between the top and bottom of the tower for the air ventilation process. The skyscraper purifies the air by firstly collecting the polluted air near surface, and then undertaking the purification through the process of raising warm air in it, and finally, releasing the clear air to the outer atmosphere. By driving the airflow up and down, the tower upgrades the regular two-dimensional air-exchanging mode into a three-dimensional

0393

SITUATION

As we all know, urban air pollution is one of the most problematic issues facing big cities in developing countries today. Taking the case of Beijing as an example, As a consequence of city expansion, more suburban factories have become parts of the city. The surging number of car ownership is causing severe traffic jam and discharging a large amount of exhaust gas. Moreover, the city is consuming an increasing amount of energy owing to the expanding coverage of central heating system in Northern part of China. Under the control of the weak atmospheric pressure, there forms the 'cap' of polluted air hanging over the city of Beijing which hinders the air exchange between the urban areas and the suburban green zones.

Air pollutants, in accordance with the components of the contaminants, can be classified into tiny solid particles of pollutants (scientific name PM2.5, the tiny pollution particles can penetrate deep into the lungs), biological contaminants (bacteria, viruses, and other pathogenic microorganisms) and gaseous pollutants (sulfur and nitrogen oxides and other harmful gases). In the urban atmosphere, these pollutants are distributed hierarchically according to different density to air. From the bottom to the top of the atmosphere, they are: small particles of pollutants → biological pollutants →gaseous pollutants of which the diameters of particles are different from the biggest to the smallest respectively.

ANALYSIS

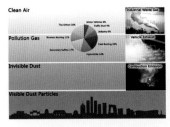

Clean Air

Pollution Gas

Invisible Dust

Visible Dust Particles

Unfortunately, despite the fact that the hazardous air pollutant has exerted a negative impact on the residents' health in the city, no effective measures have been taken to tackle this problem. That is where we want to make a difference, to design a particular air purifying tower which can function as an artificial ventilator and lung for the city so that we can get the air quality improved.

CONCEPT

close

Break

Breathe

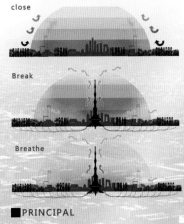

Our skyscraper is a ventilator and a lung for t he whole city, which cooperates with the underground polluted air collecting pipe network to operate as an air purifying system. The system will BREAK the 'cap' of the polluted air above the city, and let the purified air to participate in the nature's circulation and to BREATHE by the nature. The skyscraper, which is an air purification tower, operates based on the buoyancy-driven natural ventilation caused by its height, namely, utilizing the temperature differences between the top and bottom of the tower to realize the air ventilation. The skyscraper purifies the air by firstly collecting the polluted air near surface, and then undertaking the purification through the raising process of warm air in it, and finally, releases the clear air to the outer atmosphere. With driving the air flow up and down, the tower upgrades the regular two-dimensional air exchanging mode into a three-dimensional air exchanging mode. And the process will take the suburbs green area as a natural lung to BREATHE. In order to collect polluted air most effectively, we plan to dispose the pipe network system underground throughout the city to absorb polluted air near the ground, such as car exhaust, industrial production emissions and fossil fuel combustion exhaust. We can use a new-built pipe network in combination with one or more air purifying towers in order to form an air purification system covering the whole city. By altering the dimension of the tower and collecting the systemic coverage, it can be highly applicable to metropolitans worldwide.

PRINCIPAL

solar

hot-press   air pressure   mechanical power

Benefited from the unique hyperbolic exterior shape, the skyscraper increases the airflow velocity. By utilizing the greenhouse shed, the bottom air is heated with the temperature gradient increased. In addition, with a number of turbines installed to pump the air, the chimney effect is given rise to further increase the airflow speed. As an environmentally friendly design, the entire operation power of the tower is provided by the solar photovoltaic panels attached to the exterior wall.

air-exchanging mode.

In order to collect polluted air most effectively, it will use the pipe network system underground throughout the city to absorb polluted air near the ground, such as car exhaust, industrial production emissions and fossil fuel combustion exhaust. It can use a new-built pipe network in combination with one or more air purifying towers in order to form an air purification system covering the whole city. Altering the dimension of the tower and collecting the systemic coverage can help this design be reproduced in other metropolitan areas around the world.

Benefiting from the hyperbolic exterior shape, the skyscraper increases the airflow velocity utilizing the greenhouse shed. In addition, with a number of turbines installed to pump the air, the chimney effect is given rise to further increase

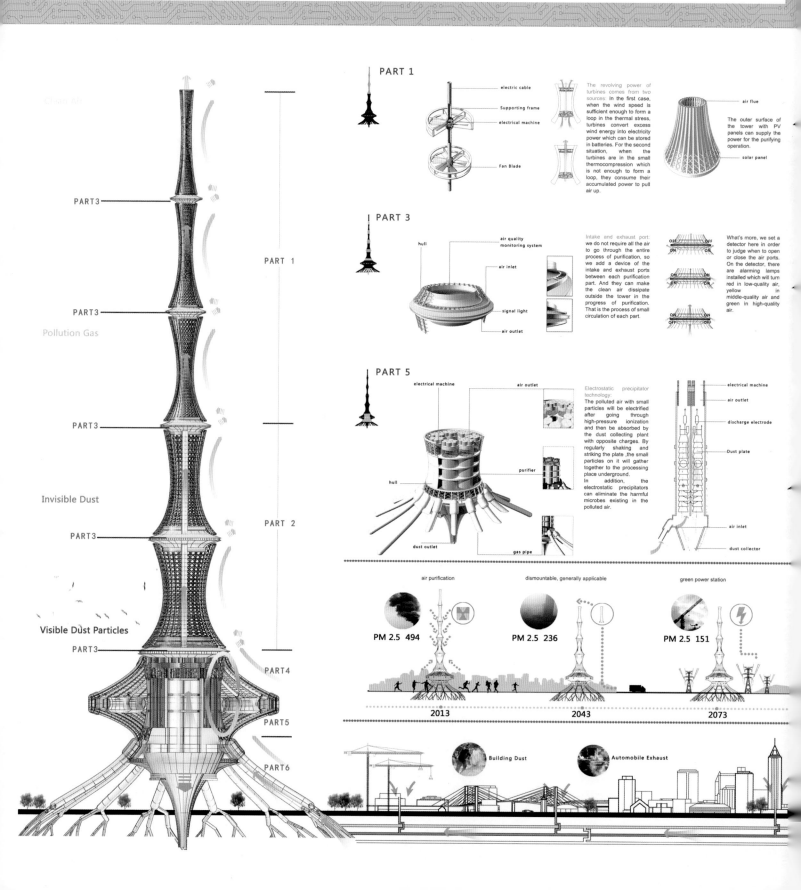

the airflow speed. As an environmentally friendly design, the tower will generate power using the solar photovoltaic panels attached to the facade.

The collected small particles can be made into renewables such as building materials. The oxygen and ionic state of sulfur and nitrogen compounds through the application of photocatalyst technology will be collected and used for industrial manufacturing.

light pipe

Photocatalyst Filter

O2 NO3-

NO2 SO2

Photocatalyst technology: the gaseous pollutants, such as sulfur oxides and nitrogen oxides are converted to oxygen and ionic state of sulfur application of Photocatalyst technology. Many of these converted materials can be used in industrial manufacturing.

BREAK • BREATHE
AIR PURIFICATION TOWER

0393

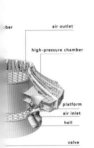

air outlet

high-pressure chamber

platform
air inlet
hell

valve

Adjustable pressure chamber:
A greenhouse which can generate greenhouse effect by absorbing solar radiation helps to increase the temperature at the bottom of the tower. Not only because it is scenery platform for visitors, but the heat formed by greenhouse effect will further assist natural ventilation.

Once the polluted air are up to standard after going through the first electrostatic precipitation, the middle valves will close and the upper valves open, directly discharging the air into the next air cleaning facility or the atmosphere.

Nevertheless, if the polluted air still includes many small particles after going by the first air cleaning facility, the middle valves will open while the upper valves close, guiding the air back to the electrostatic precipitators for a second cleaning.

collection system:
The collected small particles can be made into renewables such as building materials. The oxygen and ionic state of sulfur, nitrogen compounds through the application of photocatalyst technology will be collected and used for industrial manufacturing.

air inlet

Dust Outlet

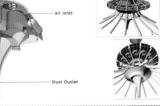

ilable for visit

commemorative architectures

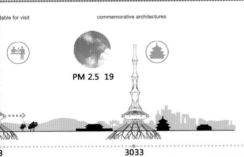

PM 2.5 19

3033

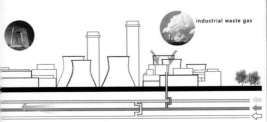

industrial waste gas

BIG WOOD

Michael Charters

United States

big wood

622 South Wells
Chicago, IL

Big Wood is a prototype on mass timber construction that offers the possibility to build more responsibly while actively sequestering pollutants from our cities. Sited in Chicago, Big Wood aims to write a new chapter in high-rise construction.

Steel and concrete structural systems have been the primary materials of choice in skyscrapers construction over the years. Unfortunately, these materials have a high energy production and recycle costs considering the entire life of a structure.

Understanding that the construction industry accounts for 39% of man-made carbon emissions, it's imperative that we develop more intelligent and less environmentally destructive strategies for construction. Recent studies had

0397

The high-rise is tired.

The birth of the skyscraper inspired ambitious visions of the future and necessary technological innovation, quickly followed developmental plateau due to an establishment of standards and an abundance of resources. This complacency has engendered a century of minute, incremental changes, improving upon existing building systems for the sole purpose of achieving greater heights. Concurrently, mounting data renders an irrefutable understanding of the detrimental impact our urban developments have on the natural environment. "Big Wood" is a prototype in mass timber construction offering the opportunity to build more responsibly while actively sequestering pollutants from our cities. Sited in Chicago; "Big Wood" aims to write the next chapter in high-rise construction.

Steel and Concrete

The majority of new, large-scale construction projects implement steel and concrete structural systems. The big two have been the primary materials of choice in skyscraper construction due to their availability, strength properties, and fire resistance (concrete). Unfortunately, these materials are extremely energy intensive in their production and nearly impossible to recycle when considering the entire lifecycle of a structure. Understanding that the building industry accounts for 39% of man-made carbon emissions, it is imperative that we develop more intelligent and less environmentally destructive means of construction.

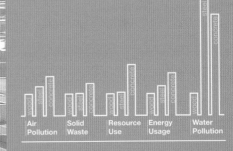

| Air Pollution | Solid Waste | Resource Use | Energy Usage | Water Pollution |

Wood; so hot right now.

Recent breakthroughs in the engineering of laminated wood products have made wood a viable primary material for mid-rise and high-rise construction. When sustainably farmed, wood is exponentially less energy intensive and polluting than both steel and concrete. Additionally, tree farms have the ability to pull carbon dioxide from the atmosphere and embed it within the lumber, making the elusive "carbon neutral" project a realistic pursuit. Recent studies have proven the success of 20-30 story mass timber structures with the potential to go higher using hybridized systems. The studies have also shown mass timber structures to be environmentally superior without sacrificing economy or life-safety standards. Contrary to the conventional perception of wood, the structures are feasible in seismically active areas as well as fire-resistant due to the massive density of the building components (In the case of a fire, only the exterior is charred, while the member core maintains its structural integrity).

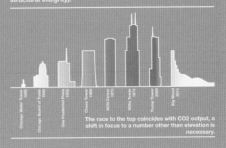

The race to the top coincides with CO2 output, a shift in focus to a number other than elevation is necessary.

proved the success of 20-30 story mass timber structures with the potential to go higher using hybrid systems.

Big Wood is a mixed-use university complex located in Chicago's South Loop neighborhood. The structure consists of a mass timber system utilizing lumber grown and manufactured on a brown-field site in South Chicago. Known as "South Works", the tree farm site was once home of a steel mill, where raw materials were brought in via barge on Lake Michigan. A majority of the steel used to build Chicago's famous towers (including Willis and John Hancock) came through the South Works steel mill. Implementing a tree farm will extract toxins from the soil as well as carbon dioxide from Chicago's air. While there is a future master plan for a sustainable housing development on the site, politics have stalled the project and are likely to do so for the foreseeable future. The university complex consists

Proposal

"Big Wood" is a mixed-use university complex sited in Chicago's South Loop neighborhood. The structure consists of a mass timber system utilizing lumber grown and manufactured on a brown-field site in South Chicago. Known as "South Works", the tree farm site was once home to a steel mill where raw materials were brought in via barge on lake Michigan. A majority of the steel used to build Chicago's famous towers (including Willis and John Hancock) came through the South Works steel mill. Implementing a tree farm will extract toxins from the soil as well as carbon dioxide from Chicago's air. While there is a future master-plan for a sustainable housing development on the site, politics and funding have stalled the project and are likely to do so for the foreseeable future.

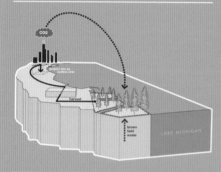

The South works steel mill site (now vacant) is an optimal tree farm location for its ample open space and adjacency to the city. Additionally, the farm inherits an ironic relationship with the site, reversing the damage incurred from past projects to create future ones.

Trees take 8-12 years to reach structural maturity for use in laminated products.

Program

Over the last decade, many of Chicago's academic institutions (DePaul, Columbia, and Roosevelt University) have been planting downtown campuses in the South Loop neighborhood. A Large, mixed-use development would fulfill the increasing demands of the growing downtown campuses. The university complex consists of three different housing types, retail, a library and media hub, sports complex, parking, as well as a community park and garden.

As the birthplace of the skyscraper, Chicago is an optimal location for a prototype in mass timber construction. Similar to the rapid innovation in building technology that occurred in the early 1900s,

Big Wood is positioned to be a catalyst for a new renaissance in high-rise construction, forever changing the shape of our cities.

of three different housing types, retail, a library, a media hub, sports complex, parking, as well as a community park and garden.

Known as the birthplace of the skyscraper, Chicago is an optimal location for a prototype in mass timber construction. Similar to the rapid innovation in building technology that occurred in the early 1900s, Big Wood is positioned to be a catalyst for a new renaissance in high-rise construction, forever changing the shape of our cities.

Big Wood under construction.
Engineered lumber has the ability to act structurally for all components of the building; including the elevator core.

0397

a
condo / apartment

b
lofts

c
family / townhome

Longitudinal section indicating the circulatory systems used to access different levels of the project. The structure's varied topography creates the opportunity for various housing types resulting in a diverse population make up with localized communities and neighborhoods.

Plaza and community garden at the Southeast corner of the site.
A diverse program results in a highly active community during all hours of the day.

ZERO

Ekkaphon Puekpaiboon

Thailand

ZERO.

WHEN THE WORLD ENDS, ZERO BEGINS

ZERO is a radical skyscraper, designed to ensure mankind's survival after global devastation. Like an emergency toolbox, it will be the starting point, the core, to the reestablishment of social order and human civilizations through digital communication and information exchange. The survival of mankind will always be the most important thing to us. The truth is that it is us, and only us, who has the power to restore what is lost, and to make better of what we may have left. ZERO will provide the crucial elements to support life and to rebuild our existence, even if we had to start from zero.

" WHEN WE HAVE TO START FROM ZERO, WE HAVE TO START AT ZERO. "

It's 2013, after more than two hundred thousand years of human evolution but we still cannot tell when the end of the world would come. Our way of life has darkened the future of our planet and even if we are able to recover from global destruction caused by our won hands, there is still possibility of unpredictable natural disasters that might end our future. Every predicted dates of apocalypse had frightened us. This fear is within all of us, the fear of dying. Despite any disbelief or skepticism about the apocalypse, one certain thing is that all of us hold dear to our own survival. Although we may not be able to predict when the world will end or when we will lose everything we take for granted but there is one thing we know for sure, that is we can over come our fear and prepare ourselves for the worst.

We live in the digital age. We are where we are today because of the knowledge we developed. It is our most important resources today. It is the age of information where our communication, knowledge, memories, and many more are translated into digital form. We learn and develop at an exponential rate because we can access this collective information. But most importantly, information is a record of what had happened, a historical cataloguing in its own right. Without it, we will be lost along with the record of our existence.

DIGITAL INTELLIGENCE

Information is the key to reestablishing our civilization. ZERO gathers, connects and shares the information such as to the survivors, allowing them to learn and maximize their contribution as a citizen in the new society. Each skyscraper contains hundreds of living pods. Each pod can be detached and relocated elsewhere to encourage urban sprawl. By creating a global network of people and invaluable information, we create hope and chance that we will get up on our feet again.

ZERO's architecture is dedicated to gathering information at present time; an online data vault to make sure human knowledge is not lost. Government, institute, organization, and every citizen around the world are able to upload information to ZERO data vault. Anything considered important from architectural construction, agricultural planning, scientific records, language translation, or even family photos are stored within this data vaults. When something happen, ZERO will be activated and the uploaded information will be made accessible. If a ZERO is destroyed, the data will not be lost as they are duplicated and shared around the world among other ZERO units.

PERSPECTIVE SCENE AFTER WORLD APOLCALYPSE

ACTIVATION

ZERO IS WHERE THE LINK BEGINS

DIGITAL INFORMATION AND COMMUNICATION TRAFFIC

FINDING ENERGY

Geothermal power is theoretically more than adequate to supply humanity's energy needs. ZERO accesses this source of energy using its powerful drill. Deeper the drill goes, higher the temperature and therefore more energy is generated using the steam deep from underground to spin the turbines, which generate electricity. It is a very simple from of power generation and produces only a fraction of carbon dioxide produced by fossil fuel.

GEOT

Mankind has always faced the threat of extinction from an extreme natural disaster. Zero is a radical skyscraper, designed to ensure mankind's survival after global devastation. Like an emergency toolbox, it will be the starting point to re-establish social order through digital communication and information exchange.

Zero will provide the crucial elements to support life and to rebuild our existence, even if we had to start from zero. The key element to ensure that humanity is not lost is information. We live in the digital age. Communication and knowledge are our most important resources today.

Zero is dedicated to gathering information; it serves like an online data vault to make sure human knowledge is not lost. Government, institutes, and organizations around the globe are able to upload information to Zero's data

0478

EARTHQUAKE RESISTANT PLATFORM

Designed to withstand extreme seismic activities, the platforms are positioned in a triangular arrangement to maximize stability. Massive hydraulics and free-moving shear plates allow the tower to move in the event on an earthquake to ensure the safety of the building's integrity.

LIGHTNING HARVESTOR

In addition to geothermal energy, ZERO captures lightning and stores as much power as it can to power the towers. With the height of over 950 meters tall, ZERO will be the tallest standing structures for kilometers. It will attract significant lightning activities. A single strike of lighting contains over 5 billion joules, enough to power a house for a month. This may not be much but ZERO is all about utilizing every resource as it could so that we can go on.

FINDING WATER

The main priority in any survival resolution is to find shelter and ZERO has provided that. The second priority is to find food and water. After a global disaster, clean water would be contaminated or inaccessible, therefore it is necessary to be able to reach the source of potable water. Located at the base of ZERO is an industrial drilling platform, capable of reaching the depths of the ground water level. Water is then channeled to a purification level where water is filtered and stored for ZERO's inhabitant. This water will also be used in other operations within ZERO such as the agriculture level.

The purification facility also has the ability to turn salt water into fresh water through the process of desalination. The byproduct of the desalination process is salt, which will be used for making boring mud, a crucial element for deep-core drilling.

DRILLING RIG

PERSPECTIVE SCENE AFTER WORLD APOLCALYPSE

FOUNDATION / DRILLING RIG

vault. Anything considered important from architectural construction, agricultural planning, scientific records, language translation, or even family photos can be stored within the data vault. If a "Zero" is destroyed, the data will not be lost as the information is duplicated and shared around the world among other Zero units.

The skyscraper is designed to be situated in strategic locations across the globe. Once the tower is activated, data will be accessible and shared among the survivors to rebuild our society. With the right knowledge and the right guidance, anything is achievable. The building is self-sufficient and capable to support life by providing it with all the necessary resources including energy, shelter, food, water, and information.

Geothermal power is theoretically more than adequate to supply humanity's energy needs. Zero accesses this

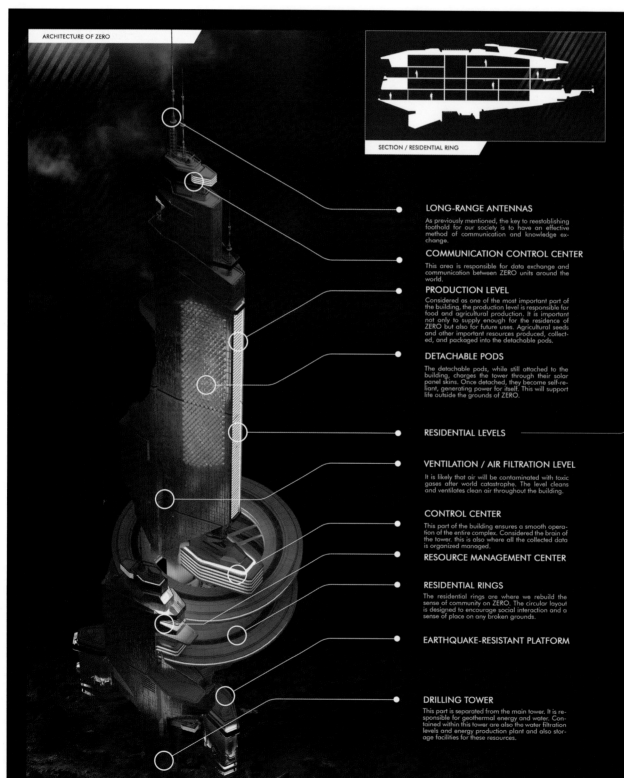

ARCHITECTURE OF ZERO

SECTION / RESIDENTIAL RING

INTERIOR PERSPECTIVE / RESIDENTIAL RING

LONG-RANGE ANTENNAS
As previously mentioned, the key to reestablishing foothold for our society is to have an effective method of communication and knowledge exchange.

COMMUNICATION CONTROL CENTER
This area is responsible for data exchange and communication between ZERO units around the world.

PRODUCTION LEVEL
Considered as one of the most important part of the building, the production level is responsible for food and agricultural production. It is important not only to supply enough for the residence of ZERO but also for future uses. Agricultural seeds and other important resources produced, collected, and packaged into the detachable pods.

DETACHABLE PODS
The detachable pods, while still attached to the building, charges the tower through their solar panel skins. Once detached, they become self-reliant, generating power for itself. This will support life outside the grounds of ZERO.

RESIDENTIAL LEVELS

VENTILATION / AIR FILTRATION LEVEL
It is likely that air will be contaminated with toxic gases after world catastrophe. This level cleans and ventilates clean air throughout the building.

CONTROL CENTER
This part of the building ensures a smooth operation of the entire complex. Considered the brain of the tower, this is also where all the collected data is organized managed.

RESOURCE MANAGEMENT CENTER

RESIDENTIAL RINGS
The residential rings are where we rebuild the sense of community on ZERO. The circular layout is designed to encourage social interaction and a sense of place on any broken grounds.

EARTHQUAKE-RESISTANT PLATFORM

DRILLING TOWER
This part is separated from the main tower. It is responsible for geothermal energy and water. Contained within this tower are also the water filtration levels and energy production plant and also storage facilities for these resources.

"BIG THINGS HAVE SM

DETACHABLE

source of energy using its powerful drill. The deeper the drill goes, the higher the temperature gets and therefore more energy is generated using the steam deep from underground to spin the turbines, which generate electricity. It is a very simple form of power generation and produces only a fraction of carbon dioxide produced by fossil fuel.

The skyscraper also has detachable pods that contain essential materials for establishing a settlement elsewhere outside of Zero ground. Equipped with communication tools and other important devices, the pods remain in contact with its mother tower and encourage urban sprawl.

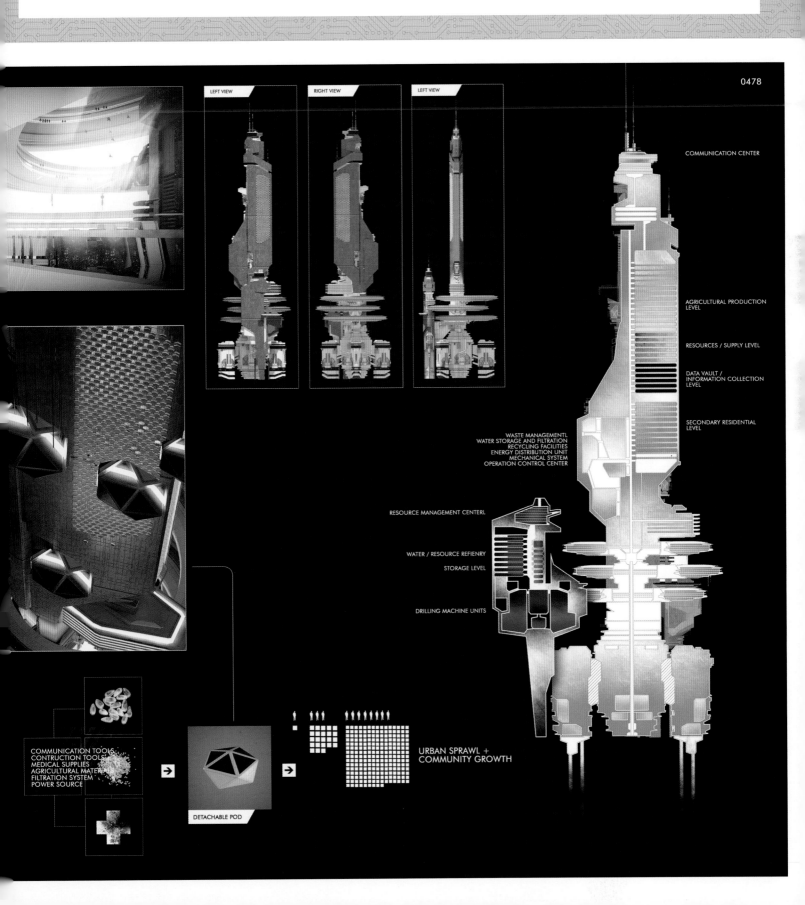

0478

LEFT VIEW   RIGHT VIEW   LEFT VIEW

COMMUNICATION CENTER

AGRICULTURAL PRODUCTION LEVEL

RESOURCES / SUPPLY LEVEL

DATA VAULT / INFORMATION COLLECTION LEVEL

SECONDARY RESIDENTIAL LEVEL

WASTE MANAGEMENTL
WATER STORAGE AND FILTRATION
RECYCLING FACILITIES
ENERGY DISTRIBUTION UNIT
MECHANICAL SYSTEM
OPERATION CONTROL CENTER

RESOURCE MANAGEMENT CENTERL

WATER / RESOURCE REFIENRY

STORAGE LEVEL

DRILLING MACHINE UNITS

COMMUNICATION TOOLS
CONTRUCTION TOOLS
MEDICAL SUPPLIES
AGRICULTURAL MATERIAL
FILTRATION SYSTEM
POWER SOURCE

DETACHABLE POD

URBAN SPRAWL + COMMUNITY GROWTH

POLAR UMBRELLA

Derek Pirozzi

1ST PLACE - 2013   United States

POLAR UMBRELLA

IDENTIFYING AND CREATING A IMMEDIATE ASSISTANCE TO THE WORLD'S ARCTIC ENVIRONMENT

ARCTIC IDENTITY

The world's polar ice caps are experiencing an accelerated rise in their average annual temperature. The Northern and Southern ice shelves are becoming thinner causing the ice to fracture, split and melt into the ocean. Recent images from NASA satellites illustrate a contraction of the permanent ice coverage at a rate of 9 percent each decade. This depletion is accelerating the earths already prevalent global warming issue. Acting as a protective layer, the polar ice caps provide an effective insulation between the frigid Antarctic atmosphere and the relatively warm ocean below.

1980   **2012**

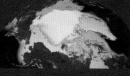

Illustrated NASA images above show the change in the Northern ice caps ove the past 3 decades.

By 2050, the earths temperature will rise by 2 degrees Celsius and 3 degrees by 2070. When this protective layer of ice and snow melts, the earth begins to absorb more solar radiation. This in return effects the far reaching global climate change. Rising temperatures and melting conditions have already begun to affect native people, wildlife and ecological habitats. Polar bears, whales, walrus and seals are changing their feeding and migration patterns in return effecting food sources for native inhabitants. The rising sea levels begin to also threaten low lying areas such through beach erosion, coastal flooding and contamination of freshwater supplies. These warmer arctic conditions begin to disrupt food production and weather patterns around the world.

AN IMMEDIATE RESPONSE

It has become undeniable that cutting down on carbon emissions and create a strategy to quell long term effects of global warming is imminent. Many goals presented in the scientific community today deal with long term solutions such as the elimination of burning fossil fuels and the containment of CFC's and Halocarbons. These vital propositions must be created, however these leading initiatives need to be accompanied by a **more immediate solution to help stop more immediate dangers** such as the polar ice caps melting. We must provide assistance today to help achieve our long term goals of tomorrow. If we do not conceive a method of prevention now, our concepts of cutting down on CO2 will not be given enough time to come to fruition.

Rebuilding our protective Northern and Southern layers must become a primary objective. We must begin to help cool the earths surface once again by reducing heat gain in our vulnerable arctic regions. With the increase of methane gases comes a larger depletion of our protective ozone, with the most destructive consequences over the earths ice shelves. Through the creation of a prompt respite to the melting ice, we can again begin to further repress imminent heat gain. By producing large amounts of ice and through the thickening of our current arctic shelf, we can begin to rejuvenate the current ice packs and help attack the problem creating a more prosperous and available future.

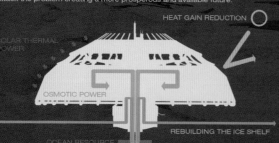

HEAT GAIN REDUCTION

SOLAR THERMAL POWER

OSMOTIC POWER

OCEAN RESOURCE

REBUILDING THE ICE SHELF

The architectural concept begins to provide a system of rejuvenation of the polar ice fields through the recycling of our vast aquatic resource, the ocean. The systems harvest the abundant supply of sea water, in return processing a regenerated ice field condition which helps begin to thicken and rebuild this earth's protective film. At the same time these large structures begin to alleviate the ice fields from direct ultra violet exposure, absorbing these harmful rays and in return producing usable thermal energy.

During the past few decades of global warming, the polar ice caps have experienced a severe rise in temperature causing the northern and southern ice shelves to become thin, fractured, and melt into the ocean. Rebuilding the arctic layers is the primary objective of this proposal which cools down the Earth's surface by reducing heat gain in vulnerable arctic regions.

The Polar Umbrella's buoyant superstructure becomes a statement for the prevention of future depletion of our protective arctic region. Through its desalinization and power facilities, this arctic skyscraper becomes a floating metropolis equipped with NOAA (National Oceanic and Atmospheric Administration) research laboratories, renewable power stations, dormitory-style housing units, eco-tourist attractions, and ecological habitats for wildlife.

Salt water is used to produce a renewable source of energy through an osmotic (salinity gradient power) power facility housed within the building's core. In addition, the structure's immense canopy allows for the reduction of heat gain on the arctic surface while harvesting solar energy. The umbrella's thermal skin boasts a series of modules that are composed of a polyethylene piping system that pumps brackish water. Finally, the Polar Umbrella also regenerates the ice caps using harvest chambers that freeze the ocean water.

The architectural concept begins to provide a system of rejuvenation of the polar ice fields through the recycling of our vast aquatic resource, the ocean. The systems harvest the abundant supply of sea water, in return processing a regerated ice field condition which helps begin to thicken and rebuild the Earth's protective film. At the same time

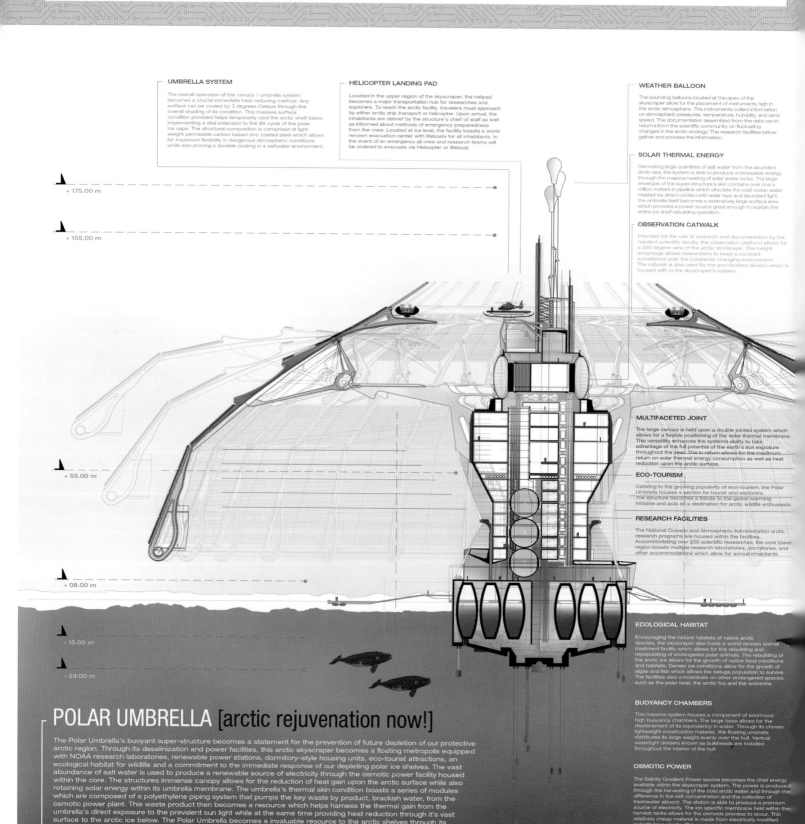

UMBRELLA SYSTEM

The overall operation of the canopy / umbrella system becomes a crucial immediate heat reducing method. Any surface can be cooled by 3 degrees Celsius through the overall shading of its condition. This massive surface condition provided helps temporarily cool the arctic shelf below implementing a vital extension to the life cycle of the polar ice caps. The structural composition is comprised of light weight permeable carbon based zinc coated steel which allows for maximum flexibility in dangerous atmospheric conditions while also proving a durable coating in a saltwater environment.

HELICOPTER LANDING PAD

Located in the upper region of the skyscraper, the helipad becomes a major transportation hub for researches and explorers. To reach the arctic facility, travelers must approach by either arctic ship transport or helicopter. Upon arrival, the inhabitants are debrief by the structure's chief of staff as well as informed about methods of emergency preparedness from the crew. Located at ice level, the facility boasts a world renown evacuation center with lifeboats for all inhabitants. In the event of an emergency all crew and research teams will be ordered to evacuate via Helicopter or lifeboat.

WEATHER BALLOON

The sounding balloons located at the apex of the skyscraper allow for the placement of instruments high in the arctic atmosphere. This instruments collect information on atmospheric pressures, temperature, humidity, and wind speed. The documentation assembled from the data can in return inform the scientific community on fluctuating changes in the arctic ecology. The research facilities below gather and process the information.

SOLAR THERMAL ENERGY

Harvesting large quantities of salt water from the abundant arctic sea, the system is able to produce a renewable energy through the massive heating of solar water tanks. The large envelope of the super-structure's skin contains over one a million meters in pipeline which circulate the cold ocean water. Heated via direct contact with solar rays and abundant light, the umbrella itself becomes a extensively large surface area which provides a power source great enough to sustain the entire ice shelf rebuilding operation.

OBSERVATION CATWALK

Intended for the use of research and documentation by the resident scientific faculty, the observation platform allows for a 360 degree view of the arctic landscape. This height advantage allows researchers to keep a constant surveillance over the constantly changing environment. The catwalk is also used for the eco-tourism division which is housed with in the skyscraper's system.

+ 175.00 m

+ 155.00 m

MULTIFACETED JOINT

The large canopy is held upon a double jointed system which allows for a flexible positioning of the solar thermal membrane. This versatility enhances the systems ability to take advantage of the full potential of the earth's sun exposure throughout the year. This in return allows for the maximum return on solar thermal energy consumption as well as heat reduction upon the arctic surface.

ECO-TOURISM

Catering to the growing popularity of eco-tourism, the Polar Umbrella houses a section for tourist and explorers. The structure becomes a tribute to the global warming initiative and acts as a destination for arctic wildlife enthusiasts.

+ 55.00 m

RESEARCH FACILITIES

The National Oceanic and Atmospheric Administration arctic research programs are housed within the facilities. Accommodating over 200 scientific researches, the core tower region boasts multiple research laboratories, dormitories, and other accommodations which allow for annual inhabitants.

+ 08.00 m

- 15.00 m

ECOLOGICAL HABITAT

Encouraging the natural habitats of native arctic species, the skyscraper also holds a world renown animal treatment facility which allows for the rebuilding and repopulating of endangered polar animals. The rebuilding of the arctic ice allows for the growth of native food conditions and habitats. Denser ice conditions allow for the growth of algae and fish which allows the beluga population to survive. The facilities also concentrate on other endangered species such as the polar bear, the arctic fox and the wolverine.

- 29.00 m

BUOYANCY CHAMBERS

This massive system houses a component of enormous high buoyancy chambers. The large base allows for the displacement of its equivalency in water. Through its chosen lightweight construction material, the floating umbrella distributes its large weight evenly over the hull. Vertical watertight dividers known as bulkheads are installed throughout the interior of the hull.

POLAR UMBRELLA [arctic rejuvenation now!]

The Polar Umbrella's buoyant super-structure becomes a statement for the prevention of future depletion of our protective arctic region. Through its desalinization and power facilities, this arctic skyscraper becomes a floating metropolis equipped with NOAA research laboratories, renewable power stations, dormitory-style housing units, eco-tourist attractions, an ecological habitat for wildlife and a commitment to the immediate response of our depleting polar ice caps. The vast abundance of salt water is used to produce a renewable source of electricity through the osmotic power facility housed within the core. The structures immense canopy allows for the reduction of heat gain upon the arctic surface while also retaining solar energy within its umbrella membrane. The umbrella's thermal skin condition boasts a series of modules which are composed of a polyethylene piping system that pumps the key waste by product, brackish water, from the osmotic power plant. This waste product then becomes a resource which helps harness the thermal gain from the umbrella's direct exposure to the prevalent sun light while at the same time providing heat reduction through it's vast surface to the arctic ice below. The Polar Umbrella becomes a invaluable resource to the arctic shelves through its regeneration of the ice caps via harvest chambers which freeze the dredged arctic ocean water, then returning the frozen by product to the thickening ice caps around the structures base.

OSMOTIC POWER

The Salinity Gradient Power source becomes the chief energy available within the skyscraper system. The power is produced through the harvesting of the cold arctic water and through the difference in the salt concentration and the collection of freshwater aboard. The station is able to produce a premium source of electricity. The ion specific membrane held within the harvest tanks allows for the osmosis process to occur. This relatively cheap material is made from electrically modified polyethylene plastic. This process does not contaminate or release CO2 emissions. The osmotic power used in this super-structure has become a research laboratory itself for the study of this modern method of electricity.

these large structures begin to alleviate the ice fields from direct ultra violet exposure, absorbing these harmful rays and in return producing usable thermal energy.

Through the creation of a prompt respite to the melting ice, we can again begin to further repress imminent heat gain. By producing large amounts of ice and through the thickening of our current arctic shelf, we can begin to rejuvenate the current ice packs and help attack the problem creating a more prosperous and available future.

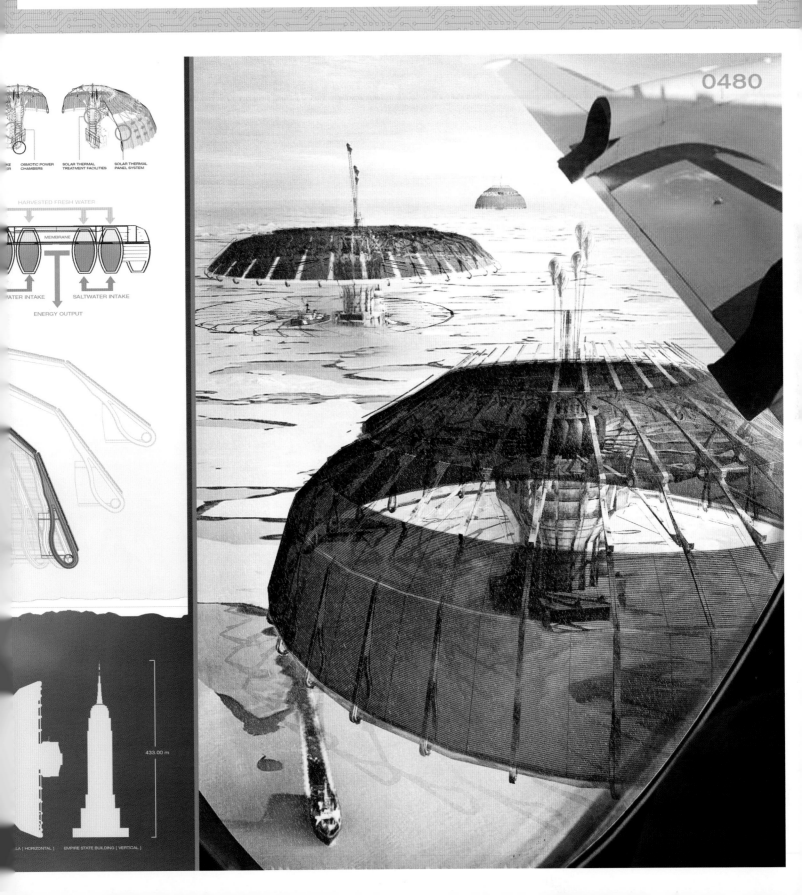

OSMOTIC POWER CHAMBERS | SOLAR THERMAL TREATMENT FACILITIES | SOLAR THERMAL PANEL SYSTEM

HARVESTED FRESH WATER

MEMBRANE

WATER INTAKE | SALTWATER INTAKE

ENERGY OUTPUT

433.00 m

[HORIZONTAL] | EMPIRE STATE BUILDING [VERTICAL]

0480

ARCTIC
DATASCRAPER

Ivan Reyes Almaraz
Juan Ruben Esparza
Ulises Zuniga Garcia
Graciela Lopez Gonzalez
Laura Helen Rojas

Mexico

ARCTIC DATASCRA

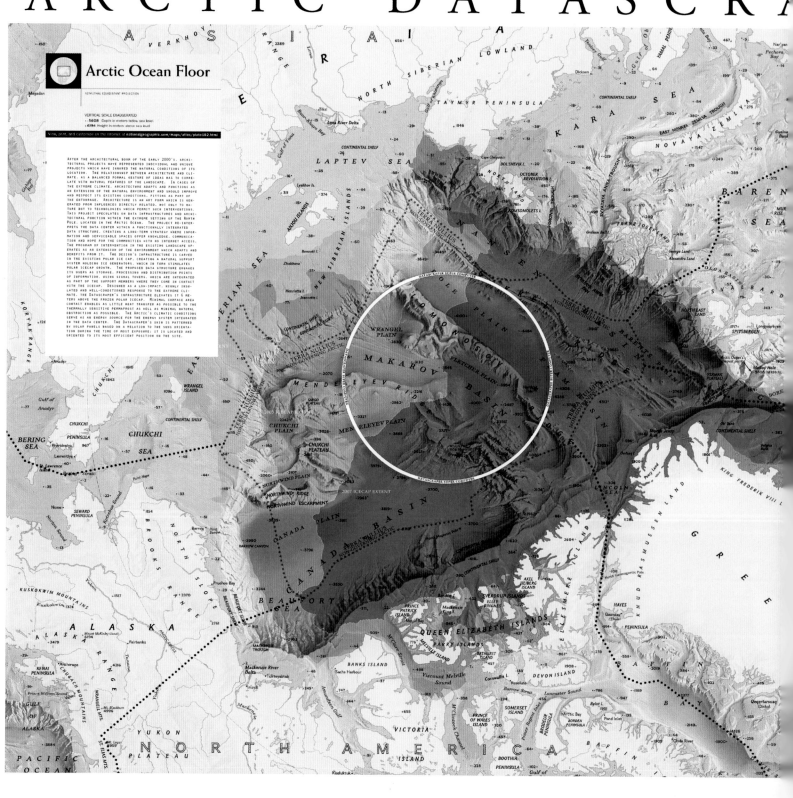

AFTER THE ARCHITECTURAL BOOM OF THE EARLY 2000'S, ARCHI-
TECTURAL PROJECTS HAVE REPRESENTED INDIVIDUAL AND UNIQUE
PROJECTS WHICH HAVE IGNORED THE NATURAL CONDITIONS OF ITS
LOCATION. THE RELATIONSHIP BETWEEN ARCHITECTURE AND CLI-
MATE, AS A BALANCED FORMAL GESTURE OF IDEAS HAS TO CORRE-
LATE WITH NATURAL FEATURES OF THE LANDSCAPE. IN CASES OF
THE EXTREME CLIMATE, ARCHITECTURE ADAPTS AND FUNCTIONS AS
AN EXTENSION OF THE NATURAL ENVIRONMENT AND SHOULD IMPROVE
AND RESPECT ITS EXISTING CONDITIONS, FITTING AS PART OF
THE ENTOURAGE. ARCHITECTURE IS AN ART FORM WHICH IS GEN-
ERATED FROM INFLUENCES DIRECTLY RELATED, NOT ONLY TO NA-
TURE BUT TO TECHNOLOGIES WHICH PERMIT SUCH INTERVENTIONS.
THIS PROJECT SPECULATES ON DATA INFRASTRUCTURE AND ARCHI-
TECTURAL FUNCTION WITHIN THE EXTREME SETTING OF THE NORTH
POLE, LOCATED IN THE ARCTIC OCEAN. THE PROJECT RE-INTER-
PRETS THE DATA CENTER WITHIN A FUNCTIONALLY INTEGRATED
DATA STRUCTURE, CREATING A LONG-TERM STRATEGY WHERE INFOR-
MATION AND SERVICEABLE SPACES OFFER KNOWLEDGE, COMMUNICA-
TION AND HOPE FOR THE COMMUNITIES WITH NO INTERNET ACCESS.
THE PROGRAM OF INTERVENTION IN THE EXISTING LANDSCAPE OP-
ERATES AS AN EXTENSION OF THE ENVIRONMENT WHICH ADAPTS AND
BENEFITS FROM IT. THE DESIGN'S INFRASTRUCTURE IS CARVED
IN THE EXISTING POLAR ICE CAP, CREATING A NATURAL SUPPORT
SYSTEM HOLDING ICE GENERATORS, WHICH IN TURN STIMULATES
POLAR ICECAP GROWTH. THE PROPOSED DATA STRUCTURE ENGAGES
ITS USERS AS STORAGE, PROCESSING AND DISTRIBUTION POINTS
OF INFORMATION, USING SIGNAL TOWERS, WHICH ARE INTEGRATED
AS PART OF THE SUPPORT MEMBERS WHERE THEY COME IN CONTACT
WITH THE ICECAP. DESIGNED AS A LOW-IMPACT, HIGHLY INSU-
LATED AND WELL-CONDITIONED RESPONSE TO THE EXTREME CLI-
MATE, THE DATASCRAPER'S INFRASTRUCTURE ELEVATES IT 6 ME-
TERS ABOVE THE FROZEN POLAR ICECAP. MINIMAL SURFACE AREA
CONTACT ENABLES AS LITTLE HEAT TRANSFER AS POSSIBLE TO THE
THERMALLY SENSITIVE PERMAFROST AS WELL AS MINIMAL NATURAL
OBSTRUCTION AS POSSIBLE. THE ARCTIC'S CLIMATIC CONDITIONS
SERVE AS AN ENERGY SOURCE FOR THE ENERGY SYSTEM INTEGRATED
IN THE DATA CENTER. THE DATASCRAPER'S SKIN IS PATTERNED
BY SOLAR PANELS BASED ON A RELATION TO THE SUNS ORIENTA-
TION DURING THE TIME OF MOST EXPOSURE. IT IS LOCATED AND
ORIENTED TO ITS MOST EFFICIENT POSITION ON THE SITE.

Throughout the history of architecture, many projects have been developed without consideration of the natural environment. The rapid urbanization of the last decade has increased the number of such projects. The relationship between architecture and climate, as a balanced formal gesture of ideas has to correlate with natural features of the landscape. In cases of extreme climate conditions, architecture adapts and functions as an extension of the natural environment with the goal of improving and respecting the existing conditions.

This project speculates on data infrastructures and architectural function within the extreme setting of the North Pole and the Arctic Ocean. The project re-interprets a data center within a functionally integrated data structure that creates a long-term strategy where information and support spaces offer knowledge, communication, and hope for

E R

0531

communities without Internet access.

The program of intervention in the existing landscape operates as an extension of the environment, which adapts and benefits from it. The design's infrastructure is carved in the existing polar ice cap, creating a natural support system holding ice generators, which in turn stimulate the polar icecap growth. The proposed data structure engages its users as storage, processing, and distribution points of information, using signal towers, which are integrated as part of the supporting structures, which come in contact with the icecap.

Designed as a low-impact, highly insulated and well-conditioned response to the extreme climate, the Datascraper elevates only 6 meters above the frozen polar icecap. Minimal surface contact enables as little heat transfer as

ARCTIC DATASCRA

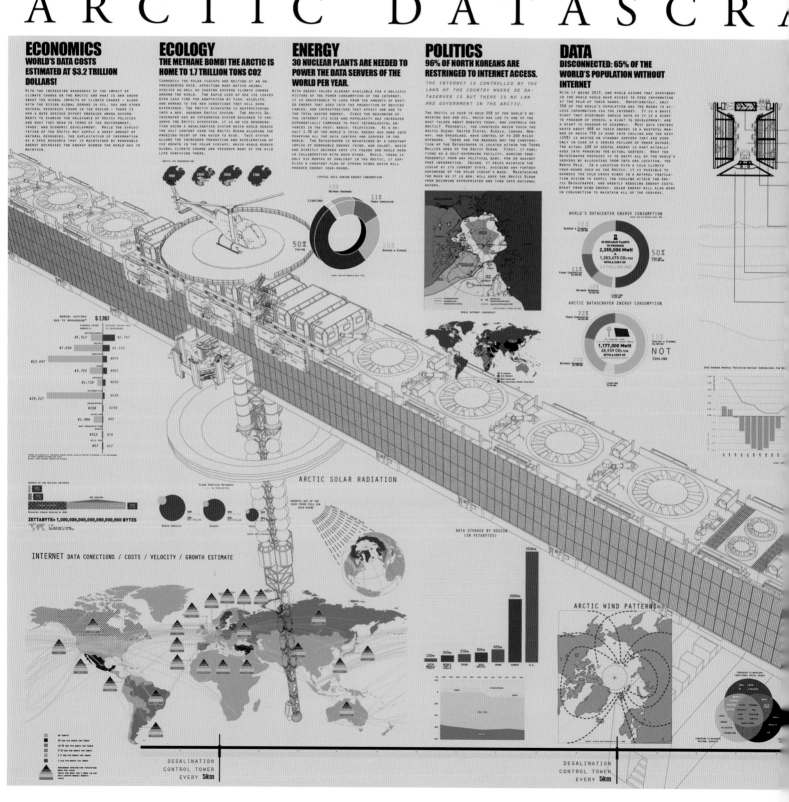

ECONOMICS
WORLD'S DATA COSTS ESTIMATED AT $3.2 TRILLION DOLLARS!

ECOLOGY
THE METHANE BOMB! THE ARCTIC IS HOME TO 1.7 TRILLION TONS CO2.

ENERGY
30 NUCLEAR PLANTS ARE NEEDED TO POWER THE DATA SERVERS OF THE WORLD PER YEAR.

POLITICS
96% OF NORTH KOREANS ARE RESTRINGED TO INTERNET ACCESS.

DATA
DISCONNECTED: 65% OF THE WORLD'S POPULATION WITHOUT INTERNET

possible to the thermally sensitive permafrost as well as minimal natural obstruction. The Arctic's climatic conditions serve as an energy source for the structure; the Datascraper's skin is patterned by solar panels based on its position relative to the best solar exposure.

ER

0531

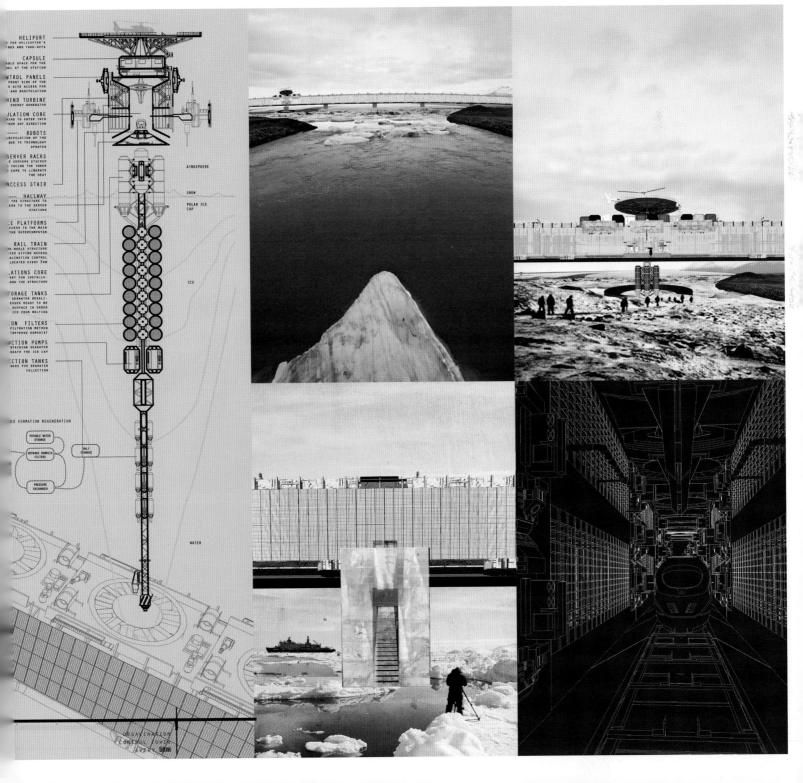

IN CHARYBDIS WATERSCARPER

Nam Il Joe
Laura E. Lo
Mark T. Nicol

United States

in charybdis

Generative Strands: 38N 148W, North Pacific

By extending the ethos of reuse to the aqueous environment, In Charybdis reconsiders the plastic detritus in the world's oceans as building material. Harnessing the complex, dynamic system of forces of the oceans and its intensive gradients, this project coalesces plastic particulates into a self-limiting, dynamically formed, yet chemically inert, super-tall building structure that plunges deep into the ocean's depths.

Utilizing advanced material technologies, it provides scaffolding for deep-sea research vessels. These vessels navigate through the water column, over time converging and dispersing within the structure, forming and disbanding spontaneous research communities as they venture to the depths and slowly return to air. By utilizing an existing material condition to build a research facility in the Great Pacific Garbage Patch, this project leverages cleanup and

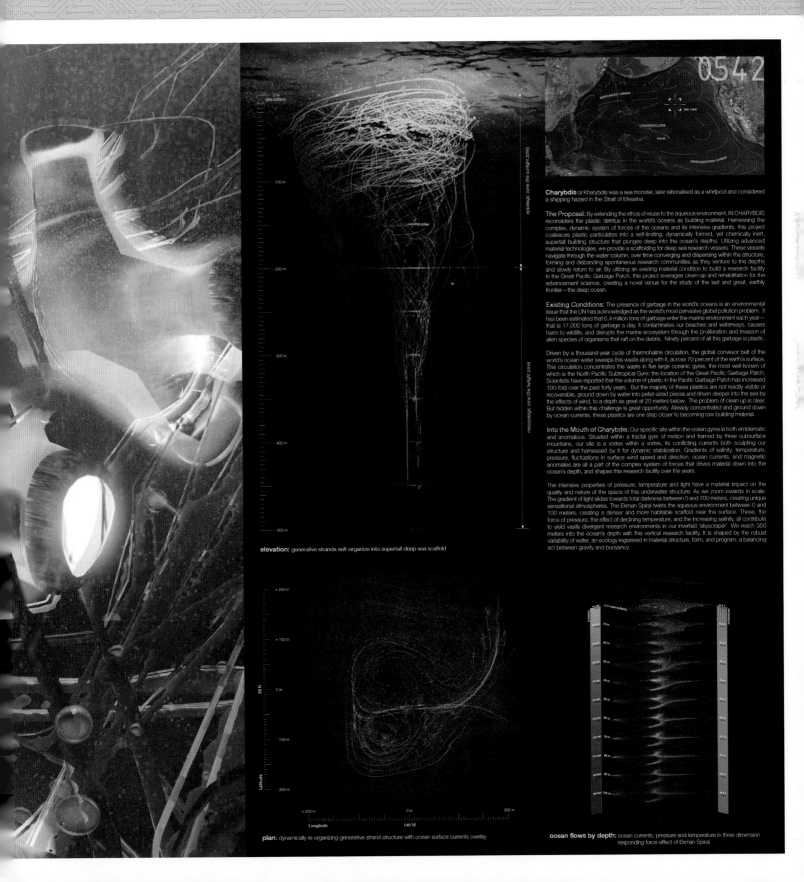

0542

Charybdis or Kharybdis was a sea monster, later rationalised as a whirlpool and considered a shipping hazard in the Strait of Messina.

The Proposal: By extending the ethos of reuse to the aqueous environment, IN CHARYBDIS reconsiders the plastic detritus in the world's oceans as building material. Harnessing the complex, dynamic system of forces of the oceans and its intensive gradients, this project coalesces plastic particulates into a self-limiting, dynamically formed, yet chemically inert, supertall building structure that plunges deep into the ocean's depths. Utilizing advanced material technologies, we provide a scaffolding for deep sea research vessels. These vessels navigate through the water column, over time converging and dispersing within the structure, forming and disbanding spontaneous research communities as they venture to the depths and slowly return to air. By utilizing an existing material condition to build a research facility in the Great Pacific Garbage Patch, this project leverages clean-up and rehabilitation for the advancement science, creating a novel venue for the study of the last and great, earthly frontier—the deep ocean.

Existing Conditions: The presence of garbage in the world's oceans is an environmental issue that the UN has acknowledged as the world's most pervasive global pollution problem. It has been estimated that 6.4 million tons of garbage enter the marine environment each year—that is 17,000 tons of garbage a day. It contaminates our beaches and waterways, causes harm to wildlife, and disrupts the marine ecosystem through the proliferation and invasion of alien species of organisms that raft on the debris. Ninety percent of all this garbage is plastic.

Driven by a thousand-year cycle of thermohaline circulation, the global conveyor belt of the world's ocean water sweeps this waste along with it, across 70 percent of the earth's surface. This circulation concentrates the waste in five large oceanic gyres, the most well-known of which is the North Pacific Subtropical Gyre: the location of the Great Pacific Garbage Patch. Scientists have reported that the volume of plastic in the Pacific Garbage Patch has increased 100-fold over the past forty years. But the majority of these plastics are not readily visible or recoverable, ground down by water into pellet-sized pieces and driven deeper into the sea by the effects of wind, to a depth as great at 20 meters below. The problem of clean up is clear. But hidden within this challenge is great opportunity. Already concentrated and ground down by ocean currents, these plastics are one step closer to becoming raw building material.

Into the Mouth of Charybdis: Our specific site within the ocean gyres is both emblematic and anomalous. Situated within a fractal gyre of motion and framed by three subsurface mountains, our site is a vortex within a vortex, its conflicting currents both sculpting our structure and harnessed by it for dynamic stabilization. Gradients of salinity, temperature, pressure, fluctuations in surface wind speed and direction, ocean currents, and magnetic anomalies are all a part of the complex system of forces that drives material down into the ocean's depth, and shapes this research facility over the years.

The intensive properties of pressure, temperature and light have a material impact on the quality and nature of the space of this underwater structure. As we zoom inwards in scale: The gradient of light slides towards total darkness between 0 and 700 meters, creating unique sensational atmospheres. The Ekman Spiral twists the aqueous environment between 0 and 100 meters, creating a denser and more habitable scaffold near the surface. These, the force of pressure, the effect of declining temperature, and the increasing salinity, all contribute to yield vastly divergent research environments in our inverted 'skyscraper'. We reach 350 meters into the ocean's depth with this vertical research facility. It is shaped by the robust variability of water, an ecology registered in material structure, form, and program. a balancing act between gravity and buoyancy.

elevation: generative strands self-organize into supertall deep sea scaffold

plan: dynamically re-organizing generative strand structure with ocean surface currents overlay

ocean flows by depth: ocean currents, pressure and temperature in three dimension responding force-effect of Ekman Spiral

rehabilitation for the advancement science, creating a novel venue for the study of the last and great, earthly frontier—the deep ocean.

The project's specific site within the ocean gyres is both emblematic and anomalous. Situated within a fractal gyre of motion and framed by three subsurface mountains, the site is a vortex within a vortex, its conflicting currents both sculpting our structure and harnessed by it for dynamic stabilization. Gradients of salinity, temperature, pressure, fluctuations in surface wind speed and direction, ocean currents, and magnetic anomalies are all a part of the complex system of forces that drives material down into the ocean's depth, and shapes this research facility over the years.

The intensive properties of pressure, temperature and light have a material impact on the quality and nature of the

Material Systems

extrusion · cohesion · calcification · shaping of plastic strands · membrane inflation · crystallization

Elevational Time-Line: self-limiting growth based on plastic collection

time: 0 year / collectn: 0 ton
time: 1 year / collectn: 2 tons
time: 2 years / collectn: 4 tons
time: 3 years / collectn: 8 tons
time: 5 years / collectn: 17 tons
time: 10 years / collectn: 20 tons

time: 17 years / collectn: 35 tons
time: 19 years / collectn: 40 tons
time: 21 years / collectn: 45 tons
time: 25 years / collectn: 50 tons
time: 30 years / collectn: 60 tons

section

Building Process

pacific ocean gire: garbage patches

machine: collecting plastic gabages

4 nozzles of a machine: extrusion and cohesion of plastic strands from machine into generative strand scaffold

ocean flows by depth: shaping generative strand scaffold and calcification

prefabrication: distribution of research vessel on generative strand scaffold

Machine Generating Strands

robot arm
GPS
solar panel + wave power generator
top view

turbine
nozzle
outlet
intake
bottom view

GPS
solar panel
wave power generator
turbine
outlet
intake
turbine
nozzle
perspective view

ocean surface: population of machines

deep

space of this underwater structure. The gradient of light slides towards total darkness between 0 and 700 meters, creating unique sensational atmospheres. The Ekman Spiral twists the aqueous environment between 0 and 100 meters, creating a denser and more habitable scaffold near the surface. These, the force of pressure, the effect of declining temperature, and the increasing salinity, all contribute to yield vastly divergent research environments in this inverted 'skyscraper'. The project reaches 350 meters into the ocean's depth with this vertical research facility. It is shaped by the robust variability of water, an ecology registered in material structure, form, and program, a balancing act between gravity and buoyancy.

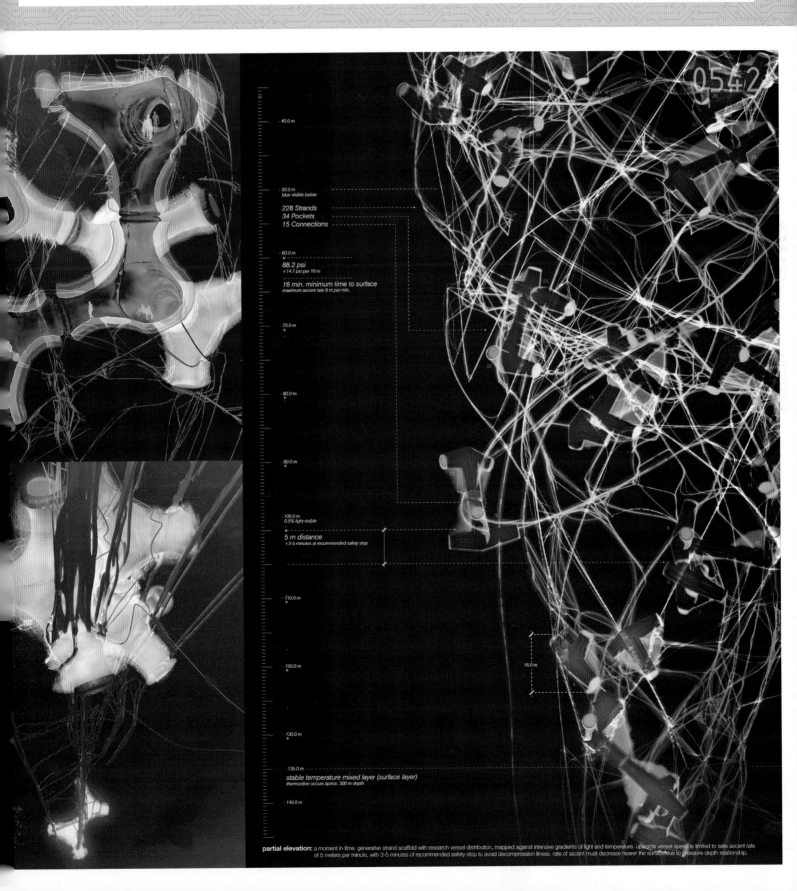

- 40.0 m

- 50.0 m
blue visible below

228 Strands
34 Pockets
15 Connections

- 60.0 m

88.2 psi
+14.7 psi per 10 m

16 min. minimum time to surface
maximum ascent rate 9 m per min.

- 70.0 m

- 80.0 m

- 90.0 m

- 100.0 m
0.5% light visible

5 m distance
+3-5 minutes at recommended safety stop

- 110.0 m

- 120.0 m

16.0 m

- 130.0 m

- 135.0 m
stable temperature mixed layer (surface layer)
thermocline occurs approx. 300 m depth

- 140.0 m

0542

partial elevation: a moment in time. generative strand scaffold with research vessel distribution, mapped against intensive gradients of light and temperature. upwards vessel speed is limited to safe ascent rate of 5 meters per minute, with 3-5 minutes of recommended safety stop to avoid decompression illness. rate of ascent must decrease nearer the surface due to pressure-depth relationship.

THE BEIJING HAZE-SCRAPER

Wang Fengying
Liu Jingyang
Zhou Qian
Yang Ye
Gao Yiwei

China

THE BEIJING HAZE-SCRAPER
FOG AND HAZE FILTER

The air quality of the city of Beijing in China has gradually deteriorated in the last couple of decades. Today it is recognized as one of the most polluted cities in the world because of the ever-increasing number of vehicles and factories. The risks of heart disease, cancer, respiratory illness, and birth defects have also risen to alarming levels. Many proposals to revert this condition have failed because the rapid urbanization of the city and the continuous exodus from rural to urban areas—a phenomenon that is unstoppable. It is now the time for architects, engineers, and urban planners to offer an innovative solution.

The Haze-Scraper is a novel building that seeks to purify Beijing's air through flying devices that absorb monoxide carbon and suspended particles and release oxygen. The main concept is to have series main structures carefully

0661

1.CITY ISSUE

BEIJING

PM 2.5 CONCENTRATION(ug/m³)

Global PM 2.5 Map By NASA

BEIJING Anual PM2.5 Diagram

The serious condition of densely polluted air in Beijing has caught great attention recently, on the top of Beijing laid the grey and dark sky, which is filled with haze and fog. The small particles, named as PM 2.5, reaches its high in Beijing for many days. The particles in the haze can cause heart disease, stroke, respiratory illness, birth defects and cancer.

2.The Cause of Haze

Resources of PM 2.5

Components of PM 2.5

Haze is traditionally an atmospheric phenomenon where dust, smoke and other dry particles obscure the clarity of the sky. The World Meteorological Organization manual of codes includes a classification of horizontal obscuration into categories of fog, ice fog, steam fog, mist, haze, smoke, volcanic ash, dust, sand and snow.[1] Sources for haze particles include farming (ploughing in dry weather), traffic, industry, and wildfires.

Seen from afar (e.g. approaching airplane) and depending upon the direction of view with respect to the sun, haze may appear brownish or bluish, while mist tends to be bluish-grey. Whereas haze often is thought of as a phenomenon of dry air, mist formation is a phenomenon of humid air. However, haze particles may act as condensation nuclei for the subsequent formation of mist droplets; such forms of haze are known as "wet haze."

3.The Danger of Haze

The increase of death rate(in percentage) due to angiocardiopathy and in Beijing,Shanghai and Shenyang as the combustion of PM2.5 increases 10mg/m3

The danger of PM2.5 pollution (particulate matter less than 2.5 microns) is widely acknowledged. A study conducted by Peking University and environmental NGO Greenpeace published last month says air pollution led to 2,349 deaths in Beijing in 2010, and the authors, Pan included, expect deaths in 2012 to reach 2,589.

Greenpeace has also published tips on their official website, urging people to protect themselves from the dangers of PM2.5.

Arccoding to the table, due to the haze pollution, the death rate of Beijing Shanghai and ShengYang is much higher than before. There is a word --"Beijing Caugh", which just describes the respiratory disease that is caused by Beijing Haze.

4.Concept

Haze often occurs when dust and smoke particles accumulate in relatively dry air. Because at this time the ground is affected by cold anticyclone, the temperature of the ground is much lower than the atmosphere high above, this temperature difference results in a temperature inversion layer, it blocks the dispersal of smoke and other pollutants, they concentrate and form a usually low-hanging shroud that impairs visibility and may become a respiratory health threat.

We proposed a suspending skyscraper which goes through the temperature inversion layer. The skyscraper will absorb the haze and fog, then the membrane filter in the skyscraper will remove the particles in the air. The TiO_2 will turn the NO_x and SO_x into oxide. All the waste in the scraper will be collected and recycled to produce bricks and other chemicals.

distributed throughout the city. The flying devices would attach to these buildings for maintenance and storage. These machines would be capable of flying over the inversion layer to open pockets for cross ventilation and gradual air purification.

Haze often occurs when dust and smoke particles accumulate in relatively dry air. Because at this time the ground is affect by cold anticyclone, the temperature of the ground is much lower than the atmosphere high above; this temperature difference results in a temperature inversion layer which blocks the dispersal of smoke and other pollutants. They concentrate and form a low-hanging shroud that impairs visibility and may become a respiratory health threat.

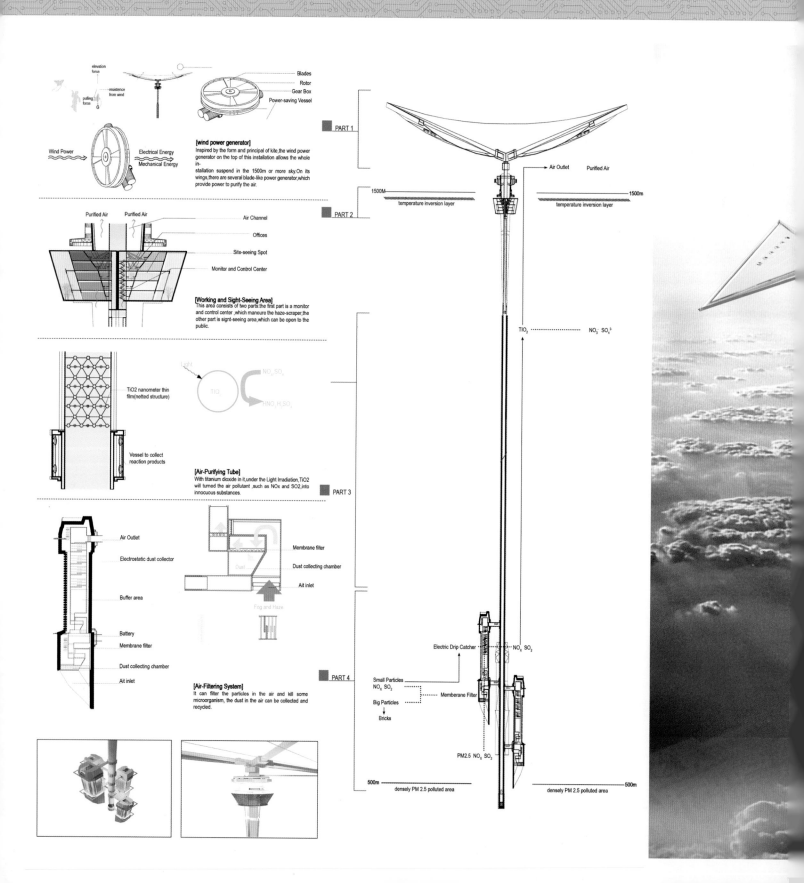

elevation force

resistence from wind

pulling force

G

Wind Power   Electrical Energy
                    Mechanical Energy

Blades
Rotor
Gear Box
Power-saving Vessel

PART 1

[wind power generator]
Inspired by the form and principal of kite,the wind power generator on the top of this installation allows the whole in-stallation suspend in the 1500m or more sky.On its wings,there are several blade-like power generator,which provide power to purify the air.

Air Outlet   Purified Air

1500M
temperature inversion layer   1500m
                                               temperature inversion layer

PART 2

Purified Air   Purified Air

Air Channel
Offices
Site-seeing Spot
Monitor and Control Center

[Working and Sight-Seeing Area]
This area consists of two parts:the first part is a monitor and control center ,which maneure the haze-scraper,the other part is signt-seeing area,which can be open to the public.

TiO2 nanometer thin film(netted structure)

Light
$NO_x SO_2$
TiO_2
$HNO_3 H_2SO_4$

TiO_2 .... $NO_3^- SO_4^{2-}$

Vessel to collect reaction products

[Air-Purifying Tube]
With titanium dioxide in it,under the Light Irradiation,TiO2 will turned the air pollutant ,such as NOx and SO2,into innocuous substances.

PART 3

Air Outlet
Electrostatic dust collector

Buffer area

Battery
Membrane filter

Dust collecting chamber

Ait inlet

Membrane filter
Dust collecting chamber
Ait inlet

Dust
Fog and Haze

PART 4

Electric Drip Catcher $NO_x SO_2$

Small Particles
$NO_x SO_2$
                    Memberane Filter
Big Particles

Bricks

[Air-Filtering System]
It can filter the particles in the air and kill some microorganism, the dust in the air can be collected and recycled.

PM2.5 $NO_x SO_2$

500m
densely PM 2.5 polluted area   500m
                                               densely PM 2.5 polluted area

This design proposes a suspending skyscraper which goes through the temperature inversion layer. The skyscraper will absorb the haze and fog, then the membrane filter in the skyscraper will remove the particles in the air. The TiO_2 will turn the NO_x and SO_2 into oxide. All the waste in the scraper will be collected and recycled to produce bricks and other needed chemicals.

0661
THE BEIJING HAZE-SCRAPER
FOG AND HAZE FILTER

BIOTIC-TECH
SKYSCRAPER CITY

Ruifeng Liu
Adela Manea
Anna Reznik

France

The skyscraper of the future adjusts to different environmental conditions by using advanced sustainable technology to generate energy and natural resources for its inhabitants. With the increase of population growth and the need for functional and spatial diversity, cities have grown higher and higher. Functional zoning of Skyscraper City is to be continued the same way with planned cities nowadays, including all essential components such as habitats, public, green, and work spaces.

This proposal is inspired by some ocean creatures including the octopus, jellyfish, and sea sponge because of their adaptive mechanism to new environments. The main structure is based specifically on the sea sponge for its unique ability to use water flow as food. The skyscraper is shaped like a wind tunnel to use airflow as power

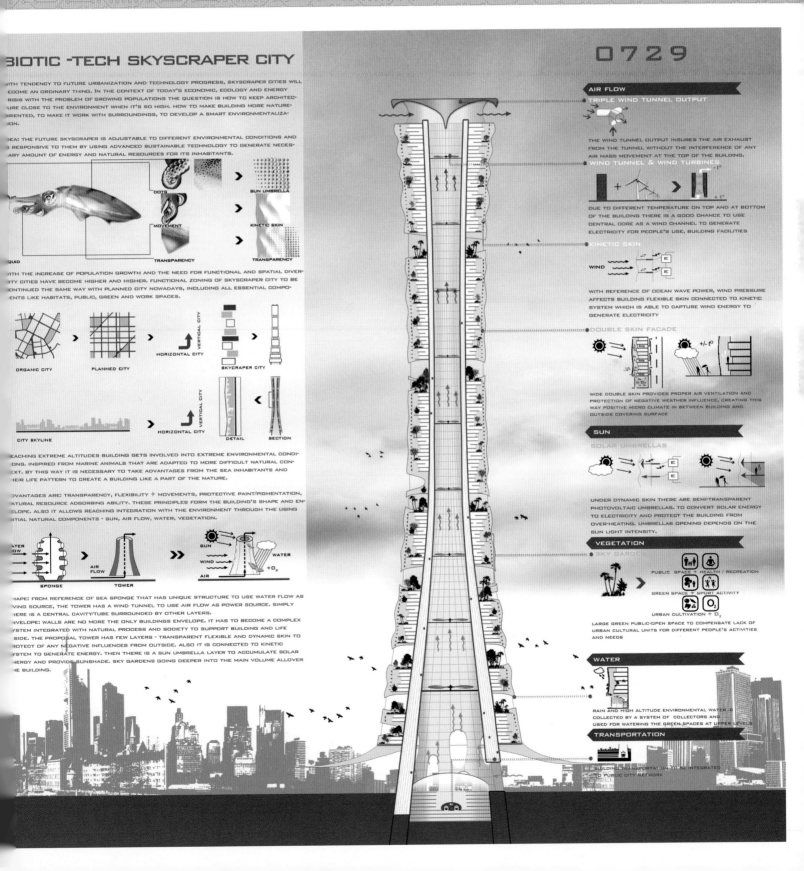

source—a central tube is surrounded by other layers for circulation, living, and working. The shape of the building, being a huge wind tunnel, is used for its height and consequently the environmental conditions to create air flow efficiently.

The first layer of the skyscraper consists of a transparent, flexible, and dynamic skin that allows proper transmission of sunlight and adequate protection from the environment. Another characteristic of this layer is the integration of a kinetic system that produces energy. Under wind pressure the polymer membrane pushes double-acting pistons integrated into the structural grid that transforms mechanical energy into electricity.

The second layer is the sun umbrella layer covered with photovoltaic cells and sensors that respond to different

CONCEPT / FACADE TECHNOLOGY

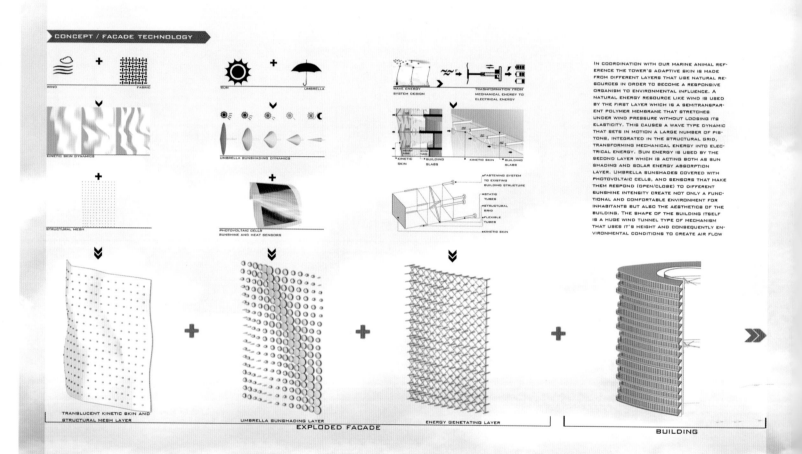

In coordination with our marine animal reference the tower's adaptive skin is made from different layers that use natural resources in order to become a responsive organism to environmental influence. A natural energy resource like wind is used by the first layer which is a semitransparent polymer membrane that stretches under wind pressure without loosing its elasticity. This causes a wave type dynamic that sets in motion a large number of pistons, integrated in the structural grid, transforming mechanical energy into electrical energy. Sun energy is used by the second layer which is acting both as sun shading and solar energy absorption layer. Umbrella sunshades covered with photovoltaic cells, and sensors that make them respond (open/close) to different sunshine intensity create not only a functional and comfortable environment for inhabitants but also the aesthetics of the building. The shape of the building itself is a huge wind tunnel type of mechanism that uses it's height and consequently environmental conditions to create air flow

WIND + FABRIC

KINETIC SKIN DYNAMICS

SUN + UMBRELLA

UMBRELLA SUNSHADING DYNAMICS

WAVE ENERGY SYSTEM DESIGN   TRANSFORMATION FROM MECHANICAL ENERGY TO ELECTRICAL ENERGY

STRUCTURAL MESH

PHOTOVOLTAIC CELLS SUNSHINE AND HEAT SENSORS

KINETIC SKIN   BUILDING SLABS   KINETIC SKIN   BUILDING SLABS

FASTENING SYSTEM TO EXISTING BUILDING STRUCTURE

STATIC TUBES
STRUCTURAL GRID
FLEXIBLE TUBES
KINETIC SKIN

TRANSLUCENT KINETIC SKIN AND STRUCTURAL MESH LAYER   +   UMBRELLA SUNSHADING LAYER   +   ENERGY GENERATING LAYER   +   BUILDING

EXPLODED FACADE

FACADE TRANSFORMATION

KINETIC SKIN DYNAMICS UNDER DIFFERENT WIND CONDITIONS

SUNSHADING UNDER DIFFERENT SUNLIGHT CONDITIONS

sunshine conditions. This layer does not only provide a significant portion of the necessary energy but it is also a crucial aesthetic part of the project. Finally, an inner layer of green pockets fragments the volume for different cultural and recreational activities.

Advantages to this project are transparency, flexibility and movement, protective paint, and natural resource absorbing ability. These principles form the building's shape and envelope. Also they allow it to reach integration with the environment through the use of natural components: sun, air flow, water, and vegetation.

0729

HOUSING
THE CLOUD

Mark Paz
Eleftheria Xanthouli

United States

Housing The Cloud is an investigation into the infrastructure and architecture that can be implemented to create new data centers that will reduce energy consumption to near carbon zero.

Historically, data centers consume as much wattage to cool down the servers as they do to run them; as a solution to this problem the "cloud" is to be strategically located in areas of the far northern hemisphere which have freezing bodies of water. The most efficient means of cooling a server will be carried out on a large scale via a hydro-coil cooling system tied directly to cold lake or ocean water.

The water of the lake will serve as a means for cooling the servers, but will also power them. The lake water will be converted to hydrogen fuel by using extremely concentrated solar energy collected by heliostats mirrors. The

HOUSING THE CLOUD: 0751-1
CARBON ZERO DATA CENTER

CURRENT ISSUE

There currently exist 3 million data centers worldwide, these data centers process the unseen trillions of gigabytes of digital information for everything from drug companies, military contractors, banks, media companies and the growing amount of pc users. The cloud is constantly growing, the number of servers in the US nearly quadrupled from 1997-2007 and from 2000-2005 the aggregate electricity used by data centers doubled; as it stands today digital warehouses use 30 billion watts of electricity. This amount of energy consumption is equal to the output of 30 nuclear power plants more than the entire country of Sweden. A single data center can take more power than a medium size town, and the cloud is growing without anyone ever seeing it. Internet use globally has surged dramatically in the past 10 years and will continue to rise in the future globally as technology becomes more affordable and efficient. Federal data centers alone grew from 432 in 1998 to 2,094 in 2010, this growth does not account for the amount of facebook, amazon, google and yahoo users. Google's data centers consume up to 300 million watts, facebook's consumes up to 60 million. All data from the internet is processed in enormous data centers composed of stacks of servers, miles of cables, diesel generators and back up batteries. Due to their nature and use, data centers can often run at up to 90% in-efficiency to ensure protection against lost data, and spikes in use. As the cloud continues to grow, it must be re-imagined and redesigned as it is quickly becoming the most stealth and unseen detriments to the environment.

GROWTH OF THE INTERNET

NORTH AMERICA	EUROPE	ASIA
+ 59%	+ 78%	+ 86%

LATIN AMERICA/ CARRIBEAN	AFRICA	MIDDLE EAST	OCEANIA/ AUSTRALIA
+ 91%	+ 95%	+ 95%	+ 62%

INTERNET USERS IN THE WORLD

INTERNET USERS IN THE WORLD
GROWTH 1995- 2010

MILLIONS OF USERS

YEAR

CONCEPT

Housing the cloud is an investigation into the infrastructure and architecture that can be implemented to create new data centers that will reduce energy consumption to near carbon zero. Historically, data centers consume as much wattage to cool the servers as it does to run them, as a solution to this problem the 'cloud' is to be strategically located in areas of the far northern hemisphere which have freezing bodies of water to cool the servers. The most efficient means of cooling a server will be carried out on a large scale via a hydro-coil cooling sytem tied directly to cold lake or ocean water. The water of the lake will serve as a means for cooling the servers, but also providing power for them. The lake water is to also be converted to hydrogen fuel using extremely concentrated solar energy collected using mirrors called heliostats. The condensed solar energy produced by the heliostats is then used to split water into hydrogen and oxygen using a two step water splitting process called 'hydrosol'. The water splitting process is performed on monolithic honeycomb reactors coated with active redox material capable of creating pure hydrogen fuel.   The resulting hydrogen fuel is then stored in high capacity fuel cells to power the data center around the clock, thereby replacing the need for all batteries, carbon energy, and back up diesel generators. Once the hydrogen fuel and cold water of the lake have been used to cool and power the data center/cloud, the resulting steam is released back into the environment to return to the lake. New high performance cloud servers will constantly be flown onto the site as pre-packaged modules allowing for a 'plug and play' system; once inserted into the infrastructure, they will instantly light up and sync into the cloud. The process of growth into the future is accommodated in an architectural module of hexagonal components capable of adaption as the cloud continues to grow into the future.

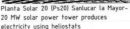

Planta Solar 20 (Ps20) Sanlucar la Mayor-
20 MW solar power tower produces
electricity using heliostats

Google server farm

condensed solar energy produced by the heliostats is then used to split water into hydrogen and oxygen using a two-step water splitting process called "hydrosol."

The water splitting process is performed on monolithic honeycomb reactors coated with active redox material capable of creating pure hydrogen fuel. The resulting hydrogen fuel is then stored in high capacity fuel cells to power the data center around the clock, thereby replacing the need for all batteries, carbon energy, and back up diesel generators. Once the hydrogen fuel and cold water of the lake have been used to cool and power the data center/cloud, the resulting steam is released back into the environment.

New high performance cloud servers will constantly be flown onto the site as pre-packaged modules allowing for

a "plug and play" system; once inserted into the infrastructure, they will instantly light up and sync into the cloud. The process of growth into the future is accommodated in an architectural module of hexagonal components capable of adaption as the cloud continues to grow into the future.

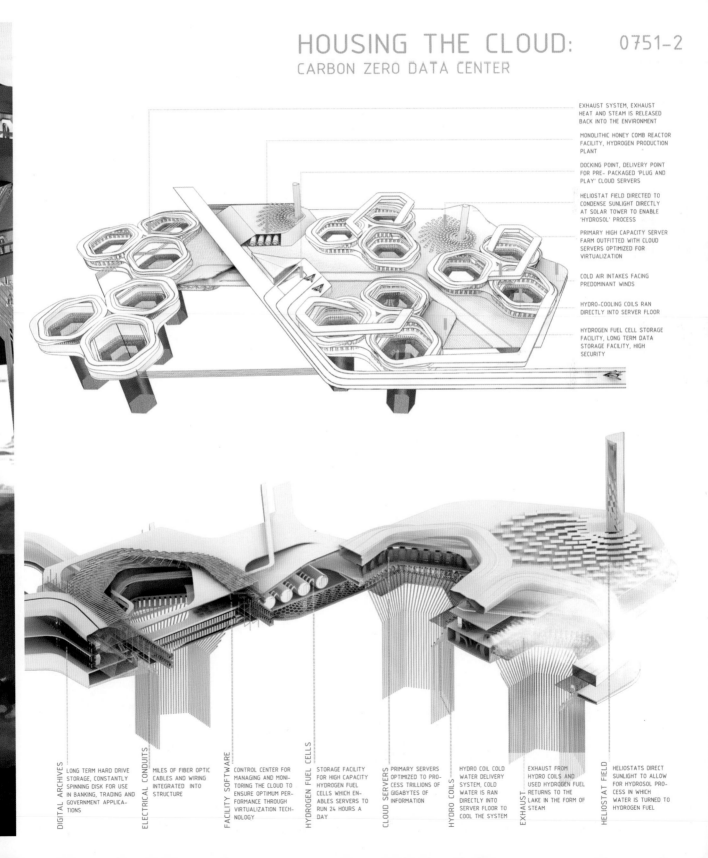

HOUSING THE CLOUD: 0751-2
CARBON ZERO DATA CENTER

EXHAUST SYSTEM, EXHAUST HEAT AND STEAM IS RELEASED BACK INTO THE ENVIRONMENT

MONOLITHIC HONEY COMB REACTOR FACILITY, HYDROGEN PRODUCTION PLANT

DOCKING POINT, DELIVERY POINT FOR PRE-PACKAGED 'PLUG AND PLAY' CLOUD SERVERS

HELIOSTAT FIELD DIRECTED TO CONDENSE SUNLIGHT DIRECTLY AT SOLAR TOWER TO ENABLE 'HYDROSOL' PROCESS

PRIMARY HIGH CAPACITY SERVER FARM OUTFITTED WITH CLOUD SERVERS OPTIMIZED FOR VIRTUALIZATION

COLD AIR INTAKES FACING PREDOMINANT WINDS

HYDRO-COOLING COILS RAN DIRECTLY INTO SERVER FLOOR

HYDROGEN FUEL CELL STORAGE FACILITY, LONG TERM DATA STORAGE FACILITY, HIGH SECURITY

DIGITAL ARCHIVES — LONG TERM HARD DRIVE STORAGE, CONSTANTLY SPINNING DISK FOR USE IN BANKING, TRADING AND GOVERNMENT APPLICATIONS

ELECTRICAL CONDUITS — MILES OF FIBER OPTIC CABLES AND WIRING INTEGRATED INTO STRUCTURE

FACILITY SOFTWARE — CONTROL CENTER FOR MANAGING AND MONITORING THE CLOUD TO ENSURE OPTIMUM PERFORMANCE THROUGH VIRTUALIZATION TECHNOLOGY

HYDROGEN FUEL CELLS — STORAGE FACILITY FOR HIGH CAPACITY HYDROGEN FUEL CELLS WHICH ENABLES SERVERS TO RUN 24 HOURS A DAY

CLOUD SERVERS — PRIMARY SERVERS OPTIMIZED TO PROCESS TRILLIONS OF GIGABYTES OF INFORMATION

HYDRO COILS — HYDRO COIL COLD WATER DELIVERY SYSTEM, COLD WATER IS RAN DIRECTLY INTO SERVER FLOOR TO COOL THE SYSTEM

EXHAUST — EXHAUST FROM HYDRO COILS AND USED HYDROGEN FUEL RETURNS TO THE LAKE IN THE FORM OF STEAM

HELIOSTAT FIELD — HELIOSTATS DIRECT LIGHT TO ALLOW FOR HYDROSOL PROCESS IN WHICH WATER IS TURNED TO HYDROGEN FUEL

CRYSTALLIZE

Fadil Foondun
Timothee Genty
Ludovic Gouche
Gabriel Guisen
Christophe Rouard
Arthur Vergne

France

CRYSTALLIZE
PERENNIAL DATA STORAGE FOR THE FUTURE

The volume of data being created worldwide everyday is exploding at an exponential rate. Virtual information, whether about scientific knowledge, culture, cinema or music is being created in hundreds of different languages every minute. Storing this information for future use or as a heritage is a very important issue in today's world where unlimited access to information is the norm.

The volume of data created may have exploded in recent times, but we have not necessarily improved our method of storing it since the days we inscribed things on stones in the form of hieroglyphs. CD-ROMs, tapes or hard disks have life expectancies of up to hundreds of years whilst hieroglyphs have stood the test of time far better. Now that we are immersed in an infinite ocean of data, the possibility of losing information may actually have increased as

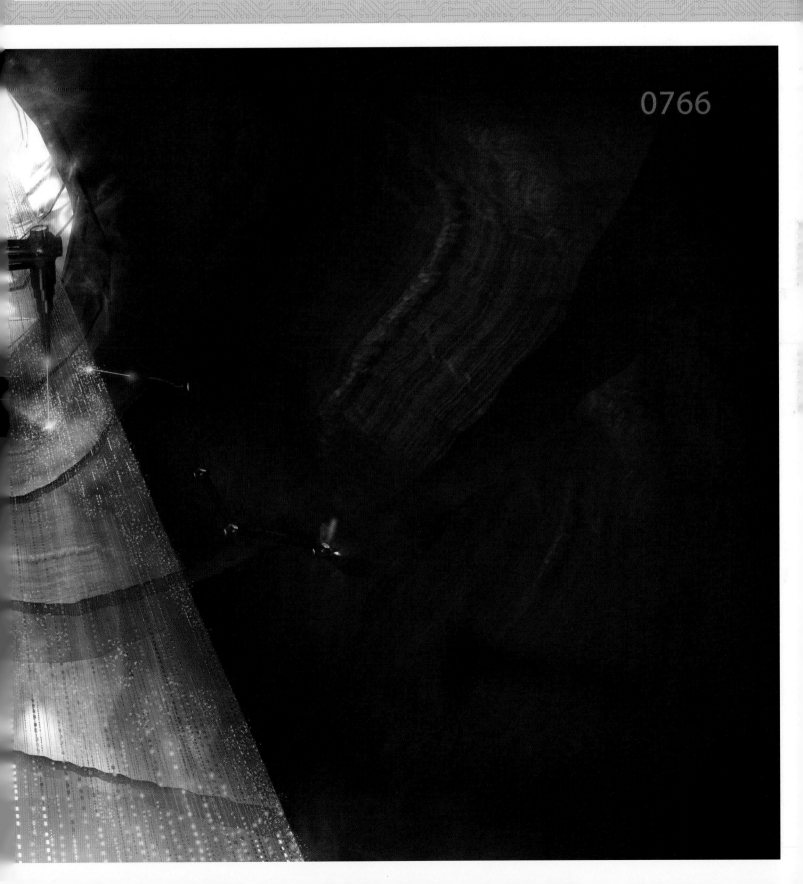

0766

compared to the hieroglyphs of ancient Egyptians.

The technology for storing data in a more perennial way actually exists, even though it is not yet commercialized. Japanese firms have developed in recent years a Quartz-glass data storage technology capable of lasting for millions of years. Small glass cubes 10 centimeters wide are engraved by binary laser beams creating thousands of tiny dots inside each cube. Using this method, data is crystallized within the glass cubes and can be read using an ordinary optical microscope. Each cube can store up to 1 tera-byte of information that can be stored without risks of being altered. Indeed Quartz-glass is a highly stable material that can withstand extreme heat up to 1832° Fahrenheit and is waterproof, being thus able to resist natural calamities such as tsunamis and fires.

CRYSTAL
PERENNIAL DATA STORAGE FOR THE FUTURE

PLANET EARTH   DATA NETWORK   FREE LAND

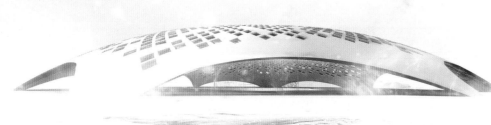

SOUTH POLE MAP

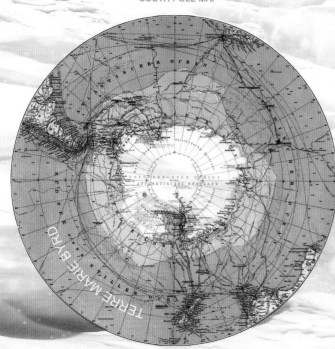

TERRE MARIE BYRD

CONCEPT

- CRYSTALLIZE -
PERENNIAL DATA STORAGE FOR THE FUTURE

The volume of data being created world-wide everyday is exploding at an exponential rate.

Virtual information, whether about scientific knowledge, culture, cinema or music is being created in hundreds of different languages every minute. Storing this information for future use or as a heritage is a very important issue in today's world where unlimited access to information is the norm.

The volume of data created may have exploded in recent times, but we have not necessarily improved our method of storing it since the days we inscribed things on stones in the form of hieroglyphs. Cd-ROMs, tapes or hard-disks have life-expectancies of up to hundreds of years whilst hieroglyphs have stood the test of time far better. Now that we are immersed in an infinite ocean of data, the possibility of losing information may actually have increased as compared to the hieroglyphs of ancient Egyptians.

The technology for storing data in a more perennial way actually exists, even though it is not yet commercialized. Japanese firms such as Hitachi have developed in recent years a Quartz-glass data storage technology capable of lasting for millions of years. Small glass cubes 10 centimeters wide are engraved by binary laser beams creating thousands of tiny dots inside each cube. Using this method, data is crystallized within the glass cubes and can be read using an ordinary optical microscope. Each cube can store up to 1 tera-byte of information that can be stored without risks of being altered. Indeed Quartz-glass is a highly stable material that can withstand extreme heat up to 1832 Fahrenheit and is waterproof, being thus able to resist natural calamities such as tsunamis and fires. It is also unaffected by chemicals and radio-waves.

Being able to collect data world-wide and crystallize it in a safe haven where it can stay preserved for future generations and as a heritage of our civilization can be an effective solution to keep hard-copies of the virtual earth in a similar way to the Sval-bard global seed vault in the North-Pole. This project aims at preserving plant biodiversity in the form of a seed bank. We aim to create a place which can be the 21st century equivalent of the ancient library of Alexandria. Our proposal is situated in 'Terre Marie Byrd' situated in Antarctica and which is the only place on Earth that does not actually belong to any country or any government.

A vaulted structure is the only visible part of this safe haven and is used to suspend a series of cables on which are mounted a significant number of Quartz-glass cubes. The cables hang from the ceiling of the vault into a gigantic hole which constitute the core of the project where data is crystallized to be preserved as hard-copies capable of lasting forever. Specifically designed armed-robots mounted on swirling tracks are used to crystallize data using binary laser beams.

To illustrate the method in which the crystallization process occurs, we will take the example of a piece of music composed by Mozart centuries ago. This piece of music has existed for centu-ries on vinyls, Cd-ROMs as well as on paper in the form of musical tablatures. All these media will preserve information for a limited period of a few months to several years. However, if the digital data available on this piece of music or on the whole of Mozart's discography were to be harvested by satellites, transmitted to 'Terre Marie Byrd', and engraved in Quartz-glass, then Mozart's music may really become ETERNAL.

Being able to collect data worldwide and crystallize it in a safe haven where it can stay preserved for future generations can be an effective solution to keep hard copies of the virtual earth in a similar way to the Svalbard global seed vault in the North Pole. This project aims at preserving plant biodiversity in the form of a seed bank comparable to a 21st century equivalent of the ancient library of Alexandria. The proposal is situated in "Terre Marie Byrd" in Antarctica, the only place on Earth that does not actually belong to any country or any government.

A vaulted structure is the only visible part of the safe haven and is used to suspend a series of cables on which are mounted a number of Quartz-glass cubes. The cables hang from the ceiling of the vault into a gigantic hole, which constitute the core of the project where data is crystallized to be preserved as hard copies capable of lasting forever.

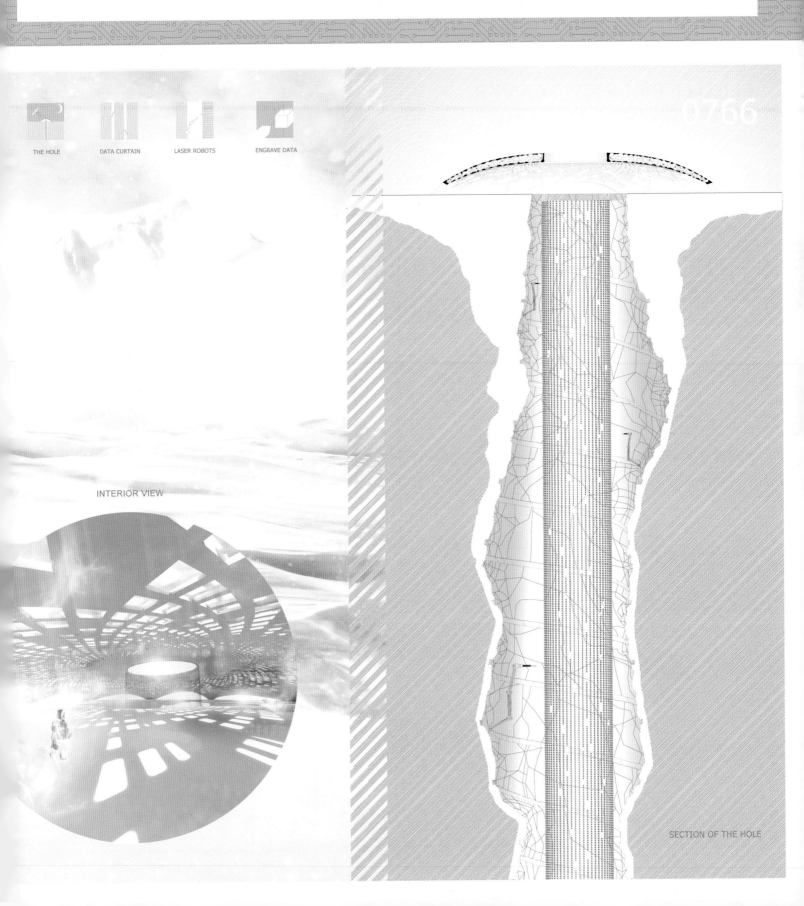

THE HOLE   DATA CURTAIN   LASER ROBOTS   ENGRAVE DATA

0766

INTERIOR VIEW

SECTION OF THE HOLE

FLIGHT ENERGY TOWER

Xingyun Peng

China

FLIGHT ENERGY TOWER
RECYCLE NATURAL LIGHTNING GLOBALLY

BACKGROUND

Energy Transition

The notion of a "alternative energy economy" is moving beyond the realm of scientists and engineers and into the lexicon of political and business leaders. The reality of an eventual transition to alternative energy becomes more evident when one takes an atomic view of energy use. Since the mid-19th century, **the world has been slowly shifting from one form of energy to another– from solids to liquids to gases**, as Robert Hefner of the GHK company has illustrated. For the sake of environment and limited natural resources, any innovative methods for alternative energy is under investigation every generation.

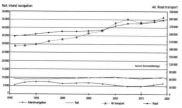
Global Energy Systems Transition, 1850–2150

Consumption Status

Fossil fuels are dominant in the global energy mix, supported by 6523 billion subsidies in 2011, up almost 30% on 2010 and six times more than subsidies to renewables. And **Air transport was the second largest consumer** after road transport. In addition, **Energy consumption grew fastest in air transport.** According to IEA (2012) the climate goal of limiting warming to 2 °C is becoming more difficult and costly with each year that passes. If action is not taken before 2017, all the allowable CO2 emissions would be locked-in by energy infrastructure existing in 2017. Thus, a question raised: how to largely reduce the consumption for air transport?

Consumption Comparision for transportation, 1990–2020

Environment Impact

In our modernized world, approximately 90% of the world's electricity demand is generated from the use of fossil fuels. On the other hand, Carbon dioxide is considered the most prominent contributor to the global warming issue due to the **Ozone depletion.** And Air pollution is another problem arising from the use of fossil fuels, and can result in the formation of smog. What is more, offshore oil exploitation causes **marine pollution** in large areas.

Ozone Hole   Marine Pollution
Low   High

CONCEPT

Harvesting Lightning Energy

Since the late 1960s, there have been several attempts to investigate the possibility of harvesting energy from lightning. It has been proposed that the energy contained in lightning be used to generate hydrogen from water, or to harness the energy from rapid heating of water due to lightning. The rate of lightning is 100 flashes per second all over the globe. One flash equals a strokes. **Each stroke has 10^{12} Watt.** This means that when human beings succeed to get one flash and transfrom it to electricity, that it is equal to **a power station of 20MW working for 50 hours continuously.**

Lightning Distribution and Airplane Routes

Lightning is not distributed evenly around the planet. About 70% of lightning occurs on land in the tropics, where most thunderstorms occur. The north and south poles and the areas over the oceans have the fewest lightning strikes. Obviously, a lightning capturing power would only be practical in regions with **frequent thunderstorms**, such as Florida. This indicates the **possible site** for flight tower at the airplane routes in frequent lightning distribution area.

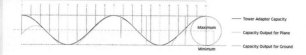
Average Strikes Per Square Kilometers Per Year
0.1   0.2   0.5   1   2   5   10   20   30   50   100   200

Capacity Control Scheme

The tower I proposed has a working program to control capacity flexibly. The adapter can regulate the capacity within an interval between the maximum of tower battery load and minimum of tower everyday running needs. Specially designed **buffer and transformer** could be used to safely **capture and harness** the massive amounts of electricity generated during a lighting strike, and transfer it to **large storage device** for later use and extra capacity could be **transported downward to power the ground.**

Maximum — Tower Adapter Capacity
— Capacity Output for Plane
Minimum — Capacity Output for Ground

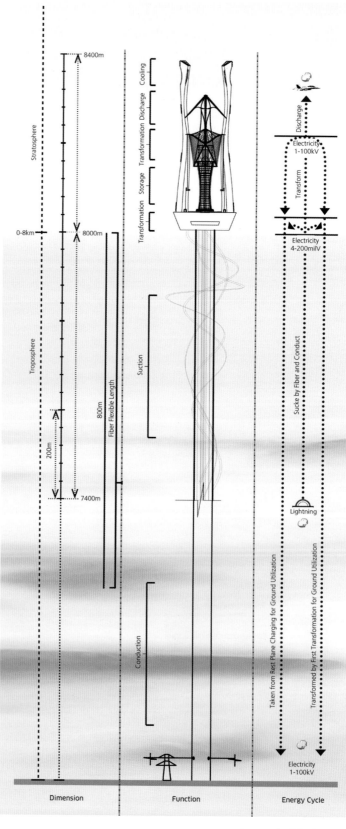

Dimension   Function   Energy Cycle

The notion of an "alternative energy economy" is moving beyond the realm of scientists and engineers and into the lexicon of political and business leaders. Since the mid-19th century, the world has been shifting from one form of energy to another—from solids to liquids to gases. For the sake of the environment and limited natural resources, any and every innovative method for alternative energy is researched.

Since the late 1980s, there have been several attempts to investigate the possibility of harvesting energy from lightning. The rate of lightning is 100 flashes per second. One flash equals 4 strokes. Each stroke has 1012 Watts. This means that when we succeed to capture one flash, its energy equals a power station of 20MW working for 50 hours.

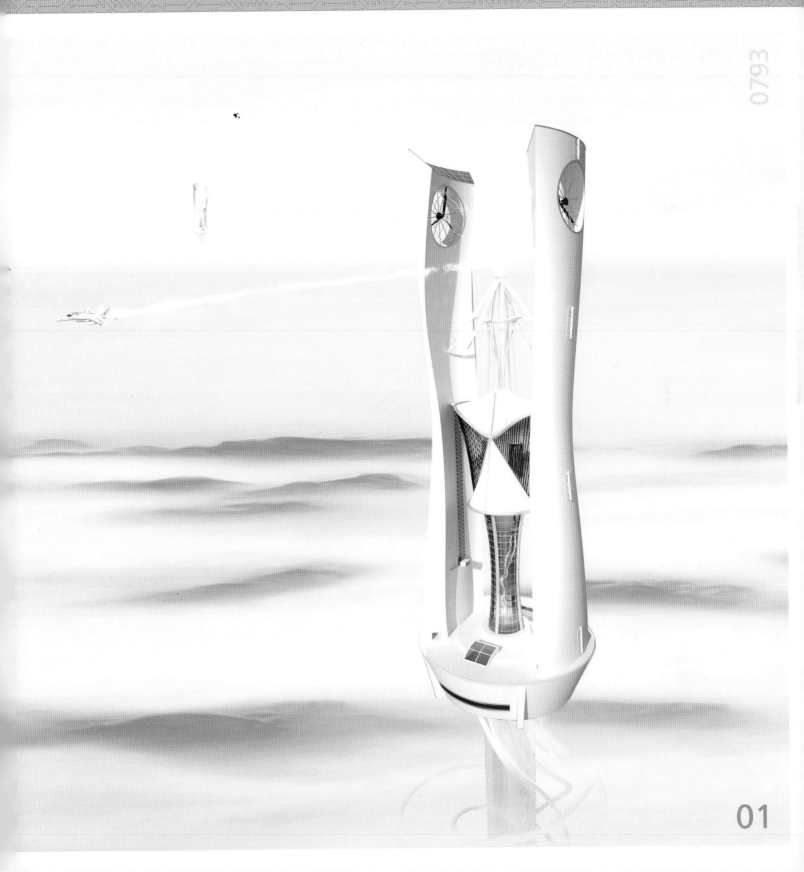

0793

01

Lightning is not distributed evenly around the plant. About 70% of lightning occurs on land in the tropics where most thunderstorms occur. The north and south poles and the areas over the oceans have the fewest lightning strikes, obviously a lightning capturing power would only be practical in regions with frequent thunderstorms, such as Florida. This indicates the possible site for flight tower at the airplane routes in frequent lightning distribution area.

The lower part of the proposed tower consists of 5 tubes connected to the ground, undertaking the task of transporting people, resources and energy. The upper part of the tower is mainly separated in parts. First comes the prime transformation system, which captures and transforms lightning to a medium level voltage of electricity. Second, the battery serves as a storage component, which provides a buffer for charging and discharging. Finally, the electricity

FLIGHT ENERGY TOWER
RECYCLE NATURAL LIGHTNING GLOBALLY

is treated by the secondary transformer and converted into suitable electricity.

Besides these fixed components, the tower has a flexible attachment, which aims at sucking lightning power whenever thunder is around. The maneuverability of these soft components adapts well to the changing condition of nature and fully recycle the lightning energy.

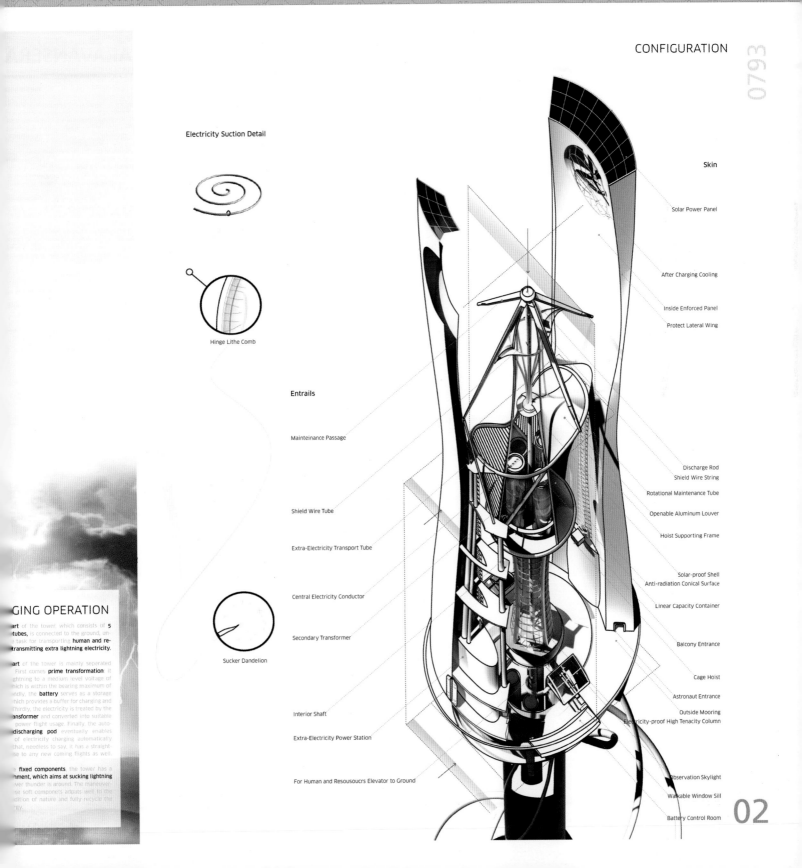

CONFIGURATION

0793

Electricity Suction Detail

Hinge Lithe Comb

Entrails

Maninteinance Passage

Shield Wire Tube

Extra-Electricity Transport Tube

Central Electricity Conductor

Secondary Transformer

Sucker Dandelion

Interior Shaft

Extra-Electricity Power Station

For Human and Resousoucrs Elevator to Ground

Skin

Solar Power Panel

After Charging Cooling

Inside Enforced Panel
Protect Lateral Wing

Discharge Rod
Shield Wire String
Rotational Maintenance Tube
Openable Aluminum Louver
Hoist Supporting Frame

Solar-proof Shell
Anti-radiation Conical Surface
Linear Capacity Container

Balcony Entrance

Cage Hoist
Astronaut Entrance
Outside Mooring
Electricity-proof High Tenacity Column

Observation Skylight

Walkable Window Sill

Battery Control Room

GING OPERATION

art of the tower, which consists of **5**
tubes, is connected to the ground, un-
a task for transporting **human and re-**
transmitting extra lightning electricity.

art of the tower is mainly seperated
First comes **prime transformation**. It
ghtning to a medium level voltage of
hich is within the bearing maximum of
ndly, the **battery** serves as a storage,
hich provides a buffer for charging and
Thirdly, the electricity is treated by the
ansformer and converted into suitable
power flight usage. Finally, the auto
discharging pod eventually enables
of electricity charging automatically
that, needless to say, it has a straight
se to any new coming flights as well.

e fixed components, the tower has a
hment, which aims at sucking lightning
ver thunder is around. The maneuver-
se soft components adapts well to the
dition of nature and fully recycle the
gy.

02

SAHARAN CARAVANSERAI

Richard John Andrews

United Kingdom

SAHARAN CARAVANSERA

CREATING A SUSTAINABLE POWER SOURCE TO MODERNISE THE AFRICAN CONTINENT COMMUNICATIONS NETWORKS

Concept

This Device is conceived as a contemporary Caravanserai. The conventional definition a caravanserai is can rest and recuperate after a long days travel. In turn it supports the flow of commerce and informati along the trade routes of Asia, North Africa and south eastern Europe they have been a vital part of tra continent as weather conditions can often be harsh and unpredictable particularly within areas of the S offer welcome and essential respite.

The Contemporary Caravanserai would supply amenities similar to the traditional one, but would also h harness the immense amount of solar power within the Sahara desert. The program itself would includ Communications. In terms of water there are 15mm of water per cubic inch which can be condensed fr Sahara desert. Traditionally water is supplied by an oasis which can't be manipulated by humans, they from underground aquifers push up closer to the surface of the desert. The device being able to extrac that it could create fresh drinkable water in any location: producing an evolutionary change in tradition remain encumbered by geology.

The power and communications program of the device runs side by side, the heliostat farm with an arr would produce an excess of energy, 21% of which would return into the running of the plant itself 79% elsewhere. The 21% is converted and fed directly from the vertical steam turbine into the device, with by the heliostat tower being directed into compressed air batteries at its base. This strategy is employe firstly to allow energy to be stored in smaller compressed air containers which are used in the construc communication nodes, which make up the complete network. (See 03. Antenna Communications Node be stored at the tower hub and released proportionally to power the individual nodes which spread ac turn creates the self-sustainable communications network needed in Africa to help the Tuareg and othe sustain themselves and in the future, to grow.

This device is conceived as a contemporary Caravanserai. The conventional definition a caravanserai is a place where travellers can rest and recuperate after a long day's travel. In turn it supports the flow of commerce and information. Historically located along the trade routes of Asia, North Africa and south eastern Europe they have been a vital part of trade routes throughout the continent as weather conditions can often be harsh and unpredictable particularly within areas of the Sahara, where caravanserai offer welcome and essential respite.

The Contemporary Caravanserai would supply amenities similar to the traditional one, but would also have the capability to harness the immense amount of solar power within the Sahara desert. The program itself would include power, water and communications. In terms of water there are 15mm of water per cubic inch, which can

Phase 01_Construct
Phase 02_Construct
Phase 03_Construct
Phase 04_Construct
Phase 05_Construct

1:400 Scale

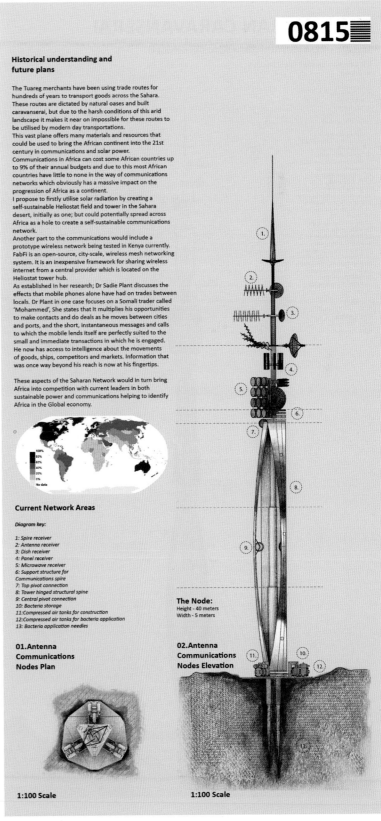

0815

Historical understanding and future plans

The Tuareg merchants have been using trade routes for hundreds of years to transport goods across the Sahara. These routes are dictated by natural oases and built caravanserai, but due to the harsh conditions of this arid landscape it makes it near on impossible for these routes to be utilised by modern day transportations.

This vast plane offers many materials and resources that could be used to bring the African continent into the 21st century in communications and solar power.

Communications in Africa can cost some African countries up to 9% of their annual budgets and due to this most African countries have little to none in the way of communications networks which obviously has a massive impact on the progression of Africa as a continent.

I propose to firstly utilise solar radiation by creating a self-sustainable Heliostat field and tower in the Sahara desert, initially as one; but could potentially spread across Africa as a hole to create a self-sustainable communications network.

Another part to the communications would include a prototype wireless network being tested in Kenya currently. FabFi is an open-source, city-scale, wireless mesh networking system. It is an inexpensive framework for sharing wireless internet from a central provider which is located on the Heliostat tower hub.

As established in her research; Dr Sadie Plant discusses the effects that mobile phones alone have had on trades between locals. Dr Plant in one case focuses on a Somali trader called 'Mohammed', She states that It multiplies his opportunities to make contacts and do deals as he moves between cities and ports, and the short, instantaneous messages and calls to which the mobile lends itself are perfectly suited to the small and immediate transactions in which he is engaged. He now has access to intelligence about the movements of goods, ships, competitors and markets. Information that was once way beyond his reach is now at his fingertips.

These aspects of the Saharan Network would in turn bring Africa into competition with current leaders in both sustainable power and communications helping to identify Africa in the Global economy.

Current Network Areas

Diagram key:

1: Spire receiver
2: Antenna receiver
3: Dish receiver
4: Panel receiver
5: Microwave receiver
6: Support structure for Communications spire
7: Top pivot connection
8: Tower hinged structural spine
9: Central pivot connection
10: Bacteria storage
11: Compressed air tanks for construction
12: Compressed air tanks for bacteria application
13: Bacteria application needles

The Node:
Height - 40 meters
Width - 5 meters

01.Antenna Communications Nodes Plan

1:100 Scale

02.Antenna Communications Nodes Elevation

1:100 Scale

be condensed from the humid air in the Sahara desert. Traditionally water is supplied by an oasis that cannot be manipulated by humans; they are located where water from underground aquifers push up closer to the surface of the desert. The device being able to extract water from air means that it could create fresh drinkable water in any location: producing an evolutionary change in traditional trade routes which remain encumbered by geology.

The power and communications program of the device runs side by side, the heliostat farm with an array of roughly 300 panels would produce an excess of energy, 21% of which would return into the running of the plant itself 79% that could be used elsewhere. The 21% is converted and fed directly from the vertical steam turbine into the device, with the excess steam created by the heliostat tower being directed into compressed air batteries at its base.

SAHARAN CARAVANSERAI
CREATING A SUSTAINABLE POWER SOURCE TO MODERNISE THE AFRICAN CONTINENT COMMUNICATIONS NETWORKS

01: Communications Tower Section

Diagram key:

1: Spire receiver
2: Antenna receiver
3: Dish receiver
4: Panel receiver
5: Support structure for Communications spire
6: Molten salt
7: Heat reflector cup
8: Service/Observation gantry 01
9: Preasure release valve
10: Salt transition tanks
11: Heat exchanger exchange vents
12: Vapour release vents
13: Steam turbine system
14: Electrical cable
15: Service/Observation gantry 02
16: Pleated air condensing facade
17: External facade framework
18: Internal facade support system
19: Tension cables
20: Water collection system
21: Water storage tanks
22: Water application pumps
23: Bacteria storage tanks
24: Bacteria application pumps
25: Tri-Forma base structural system
26: Base structural ground anchor
27: Bacteria application pipes
28: Solidified sand after Bacillus Pasteuri application
29: Lose sand

The Device:
Height - 150 meters
Width - 65 meters

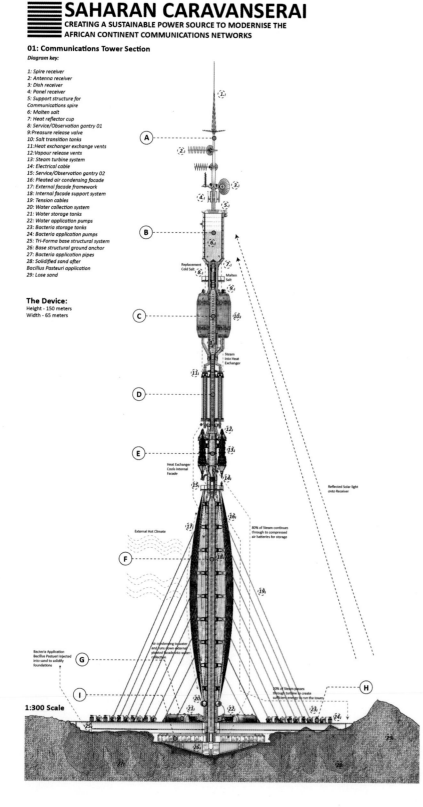

1:300 Scale

02: Vertical Inline Heliostat Tower

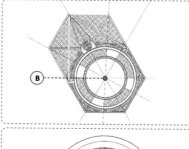
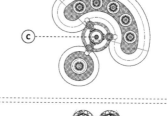
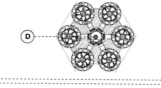
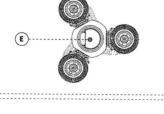
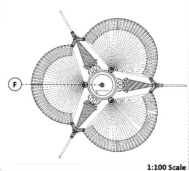

1:100 Scale

Diagram key:

A: Telecommunications spire
B: Molten salt boiler/Heliostat receiver
C: Hot and Cold salt storage tanks
D: Heat exchanger
E: Steam turbines
F: Central access/Air condensing facade
G: Water filtration/storage and application system
H: Bacteria storage and pumping system
I: Compressed air battery storage

04. Initial deployment of both Heliostat individual communications nodes

Site location is Timbuktu, situated traditionally on a to the Niger River for water resources. Due to the in River this is an ideal location to deploy not only a se tower, but also with an air condensing system to su and trade.

Map showing the range of the initial deployment of Heliostat tower and also showing distance covered trade route by individual communications nodes.

03: Communications Tower and He

This strategy is employed for two reasons; firstly this allows energy to be stored in smaller compressed air containers, used in the construction of the individual self-constructing pressurized communication nodes, which make up the complete network. The compressed air is released into the inner core structure of the node similar to hydraulics, which in turn pumps up the structure to its pre-set height. Once the structure is fully extended the trifoliate outer structure locks into place creating a stronger antenna tower that can deal with extreme conditions of the Sahara.

Secondly, energy is to be stored at the tower hub and released proportionally to power the individual nodes, which spread across the desert. This in turn creates the self-sustainable communications network needed in Africa to help the Tuareg and other local micro economies sustain themselves and in the future, to grow.

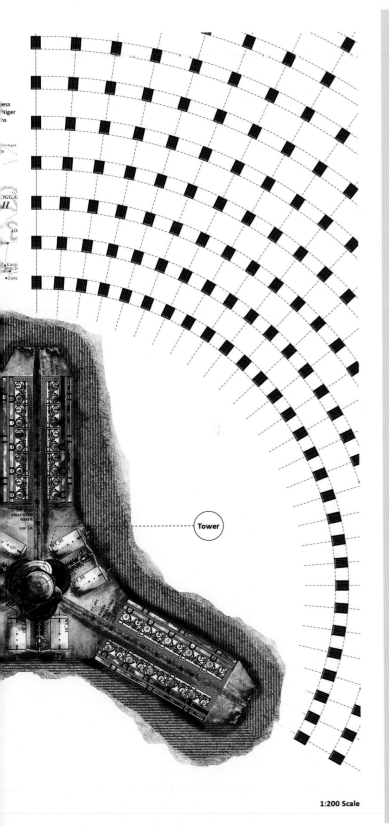

Tower

1:200 Scale

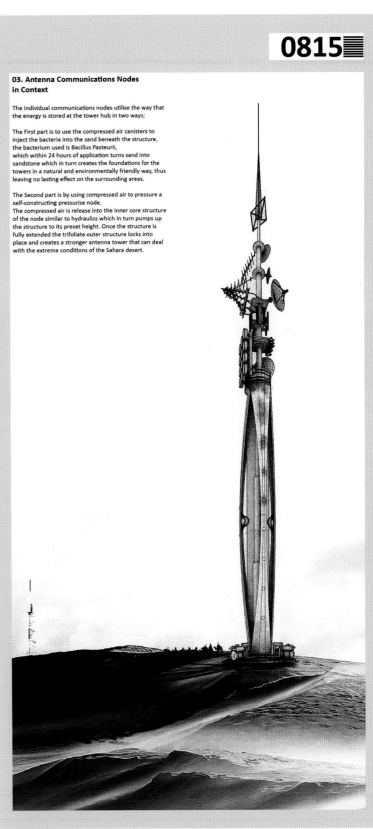

0815

03. Antenna Communications Nodes in Context

The Individual communications nodes utilise the way that the energy is stored at the tower hub in two ways;

The First part is to use the compressed air canisters to inject the bacteria into the sand beneath the structure, the bacterium used is Bacillus Pasteurii, which within 24 hours of application turns sand into sandstone which in turn creates the foundations for the towers in a natural and environmentally friendly way, thus leaving no lasting effect on the surrounding areas.

The Second part is by using compressed air to pressure a self-constructing pressurise node. The compressed air is release into the inner core structure of the node similar to hydraulics which in turn pumps up the structure to its preset height. Once the structure is fully extended the trifoliate outer structure locks into place and creates a stronger antenna tower that can deal with the extreme conditions of the Sahara desert.

HPV ARCHITECTURE PROJECT

Jung-Jun Moon

Republic of Korea

HPV Architecture Project
Hybrid of Physical Elements and Virtual Object

HPV architecture project is the project to re-design the design of the existing high-rise buildings around the world using augmented reality, which is the technology to integrate the physical elements and the virtual object. The most characteristic part of augmented reality is to conduct the augmented visual experience of reality and virtuality at the same time. The virtuality that can be seen in real space is the space that is set to maximize the perc a user artificially. It may appear to be present in real space; however, it is a relative concept rather than absolute as to a specific real space. Thus, users could perceive virtual objet, which would be visually perceived in real area, the physical properties.

There is a heterogeneous problem in terms of designing the physical elements and establishing the shape in order to build high-rise buildings. It is imperative to have the architecture that gives inspiration users want, capitals, envir infrastructure, time and technological competency in order to form an ideal space. If any of those is missing, it will probably be hard to establish an ideal high-rise building.
However, realistically these four conditions will hardly be satisfied. In particular, if it is to be conducted under the condition in which the capital strength is not met, the space will be very different from the initial plan and far from space. The space in which only the physical elements are established should meet the four conditions of capital, infrastructure, time and technology. However, when using virtual object, the physical space in which people can walk will likely be generated in a minimal form, and otherwise the virtual object will be able to perform a role of the part that can create an aesthetic morphological ideal type.
It is possible for virtual object to allow the form to eliminate the basic physical law. The base in which a shape can be formed is able to utilize the virtual objet as a visual satisfaction to allow the control through the program of c instead of the physical law of nature.

HPV Architecture Project is a project to re-design the existing high-rise buildings around the world using augmented reality, which is the technology to integrate the physical elements and the virtual object.

The most characteristic part of augmented reality is to conduct the augmented visual experience of reality and virtuality at the same time. The virtuality that can be seen in real space is the space that is set to maximize the perception of a user artificially. It may appear to be present in real space; however, it is a relative concept rather than absolute as to a specific real space. Thus, users could perceive virtual objet, which would be visually perceived in real area, as one of the physical properties.

There is a heterogeneous problem in terms of designing the physical elements and establishing the shape in

63 Building. Seoul. South Korea

1034

INTRO

While expansion by the use of a space in previous times produced spaces in the unit of village due to a horizontal expansion by individual entities, the range of territory has changed to a vertical expansion from the horizontal one due to the reduction of place and the expansion of territory through developed construction technology in the contemporary society. With the development in construction technology, a gigantic trend has begun due to users' desires wanting a variety of forms and higher places that couldn't be seen before.
Thus the users became desirous of a variety of forms as they were marveled at the pressure caused by visual forms and enormousness perceived by users for the high-rise buildings that naturally came into being.

HPV Architecture Project

Currently , each country is showing an active movement to build the high-rise buildings , which happen to be a good example that can demonstrate status economy and technological competence for a city for a small end of the scale or a country for a large end of the scale. However, several problems came to light with respect to the high-rise buildings that sprang up all at the same time.

1. supply failing to catch up with a sudden increase in the spatial demands
2. economical waste involving astronomical construction costs
3. issues related to safety facilities against fire, earthquake, disaster, etc.
4. influence of erratic winds generated by high buildings(aeronautics area)
5. traffic congestion in the neighborhood

CONCEPT

The modern society has gained a morphological and spatial freedom due to the rapid development of technology. In the ancient times, materials that could be obtained from nature such as wood, stone, etc. were utilized to make a space; however, it is now possible to generate even a space of the form in which even the characteristics of the morphological beauty is granted in addition to the shapes that were impossible in the earlier era, high space, various media and the user perspectives of space through cutting edge technologies.

At the time of digital age, a space is no longer a space that exists only in real world; rather, it is possible to generate a space in an artificial way by users. This is since people started reaching out their hands to the virtual area as well as the real space.

Since the human environment has been becoming networked and intelligent, a space got to operate as a contact point of virtual space and physical space, and perform the role of mutually communicating through embracing users and programs internally and the human shape in a space externally as integrating with new media that was born by digital technologies. As humans and space trade information between them, humans who had been passive to the already established space are influencing the space and leading the circumstantial changes through actively experiencing and communicating in a space that became an interface.

HPV architecture project can be regarded as a very different new method and a new architecture style rather than the architecture method that integrates visual shape and functionality. It is possible to achieve the visual increase of space through integrating the physical elements with the virtual elements of augmented reality when generating a space. In addition, the virtual elements can be utilized for the elements that has the purpose of beauty other than the space required for users when making a physical space.

The hint for the generation method of a space in the next era of the space that gained the morphological freedom may not be augmented reality. The physical elements would be generated as a minimal spatial area, and the virtual elements will be otherwise utilized as a spatial expressive element. In other words, the virtual elements are regarded as a kind of elements of real space using augmented reality and a space that integrates reality and virtuality will be generated.

order to build high-rise buildings. It is imperative to have the architecture that gives inspiration users want, capitals, environmental infrastructure, time and technological competency in order to form an ideal space. If any of those is missing, it will probably be hard to establish an ideal high-rise building.

However, realistically these four conditions will hardly be satisfied. In particular, if it is to be conducted under the condition in which the capital strength is not met, the space will be very different from the initial plan and far from the ideal space. The space in which only the physical elements are established should meet the four conditions of capital, infrastructure, time and technology. However, when using virtual object, the physical space in which people can walk and touch will likely be generated in a minimal form, and otherwise the virtual object will be able to perform a role of the

part that can create an aesthetic morphological ideal type.

It is possible for virtual object to allow the form to eliminate the basic physical law. The base in which a shape can be formed is able to utilize the virtual object as a visual satisfaction to allow the control through the program of coordinator instead of the physical law of nature.

1034

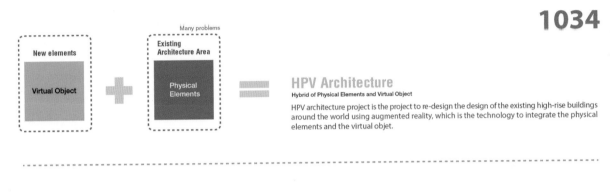

HPV Architecture
Hybrid of Physical Elements and Virtual Object

HPV architecture project is the project to re-design the design of the existing high-rise buildings around the world using augmented reality, which is the technology to integrate the physical elements and the virtual objet.

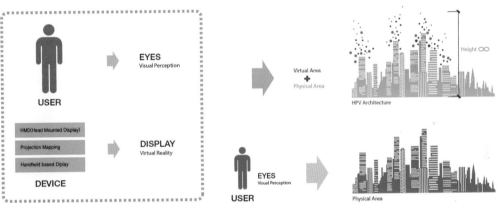

It is not possible for a user to experience augmented reality only with the function of body that a user has. Thus, it is necessary to have a device that performs a role of interface in the middle. Most devices are available as products of various types that are implemented by display format to improve the vision among human organs in order to perceive virtual object and reality at the same time since it is possible to perceive only objects of reality with the human eye in general.

The basic form of HPV architecture project is to be designed by the method in which the particles of virtual object that correspond to point among the most basic elements of a form such as point, line and area are gathered and perceived as a huge form. In order for HPV architecture project to be implemented, the controller of morphological deformation should be nature rather than humans when humans establish methodological design.

It is to determine as to the form of particles of virtual object through converting the physical impacts of nature such as wind, temperature, humidity, gravity, etc. into data by the sensor installed at the existing buildings. Since the form is not fixed and displays visually the physical flow of nature that cannot be seen by the eye, the height of high-rise buildings change all the time and it is possible to experience almost infinite height, which allows visual perception as for the height.

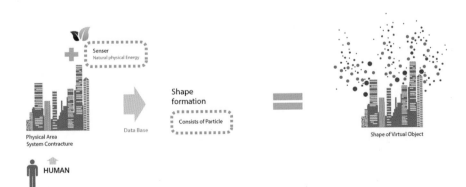

114

SUI TOWER

Jeffrey Adjei

United Kingdom

Sui Tower seeks to connect key aspects of Japanese culture using the flow of water. The proposal uniquely looks at Japan within the next 30 years with regards to future energy requirements, demands in digital technologies, declining local traditions, and earthquake technologies in Tokyo. The project is located in Asakusa, a more traditional area of Tokyo where modern technology blends successfully with traditional culture. With many young people leaving for the bigger cities where they can connect with pop culture, there has been a growing decline in old traditions due to the lack of interest. The project tries to preserve some of these traditions by modifying them to fit round developing technologies.

Considering current trends in digital technologies, particularly the growth of cloud storage, there will be huge

1071

demands for data centers, but there are anxieties concerning the handling and ownership of data as most are held in the hands of private companies, resulting in restricted availability for most people. By unifying and making this data completely accessible to the public, we can put it to greater use.

The Sui Tower allows people to donate aspects of their digital footprint. Much like a public library, this data archive will be completely owned and available to the public for research. Housing this data will pose the same problems that every data center experiences, the consumption of vast amounts of energy. The building works by recycling grey water from the community and feeding it via injection wells deep underground. Water vapor is brought to the surface via extraction wells and electricity is generated as the water vapor is forced through a series of steam turbines. During

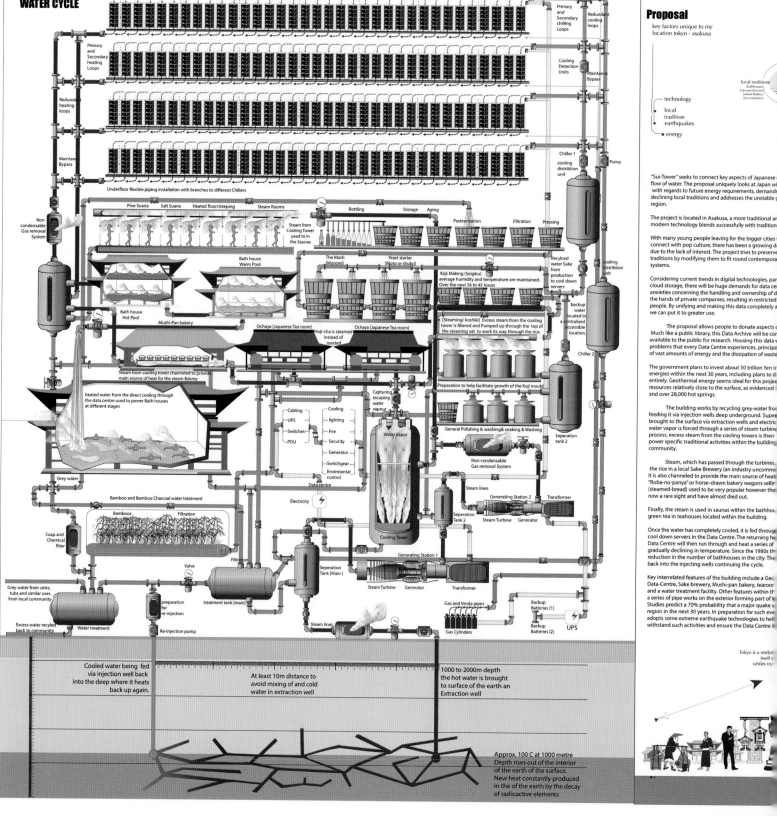

WATER CYCLE

Layout drawing of data center with flexible piping overhead

Primary and Secondary chilling Loops — Redundant cooling loops

Primary and Secondary heating Loops

Cooling Detection Units — Maintance Bypass

Redundant heating loops

Maintan Bypass

Chiller 1 cooling distribution unit — Pump

Underfloor flexible piping installation with branches to different Chillers

Pine Suana · Salt Suana · Heated floor/sleeping · Steam Rooms — Bottling · Storage · Aging — Pasteurization · Filtration · Pressing

Steam from Cooling Tower used to in the Saunas

Non condensable Gas removal System

The Mash [Moromi] · Yeast starter [Moto or shubo]

Bath house Warm Pool

Koji Making (Seigiku) average humidity and temperature are maintained. Over the next 36 to 45 hours

Recylced water Sake from production to cool down servers

cooling distribution unit

Bath house Hot Pool — Mushi-Pan bakery

Ochaya [Japanese Tea room] · Hoji-cha is steamed instead of roasted · Ochaya [Japanese Tea room]

[Steaming/ koshiki] Excess steam from the cooling tower is filtered and Pumped up through the top of the steaming vat to work its way through the rice.

backup water located in a centralized accessible location.

Chiller 2

Steam from cooling tower channeled to provide main source of heat for the steam Bakrey

heated water from the direct cooling through the data centre used to power Bath houses at different stages

Capturing escaping water vapour

Preparation to help facilitate growth of the Koji mould

Cabling · Cooling
UPS · lighting
Switches · Fire
PDU · Security
· Generator
· Switchgear
· Enviromental control

Data centre

Water Vapor

General Polishing & washing& soaking & Washing

Seperation tank 2

Non condensable Gas removal System

Bamboo and Bamboo Charcoal water treatment

Bamboos · Filtration

Soap and Chemical filter

Steam lines

Generating Station 2 — Transformer

Seperation Tank 2 — Steam Turbine · Generator

Electricity

Cooling Tower

Generating Station 1

Filtration

Valve

Seperation Tank [Main] — Steam Turbine · Generator — Transformer

treatment tank [main]

Grey water from sinks, tubs and similar uses from local community

preparation for re-injection

Gas and Vesda pipes

Backup Batteries [1]

Backup Batteries [2] — UPS

Excess water recyled back to community — Water treatment — Re-injection pump

Grey water

Gas Cylinders

Steam lines

Cooled water being fed via injection well back into the deep where it heats back up again.

At least 10m distance to avoid mixing of and cold water in extraction well

1000 to 2000m depth the hot water is brought to surface of the earth an Extraction well

Approx. 100 C at 1000 metre Depth rises out of the interior of the earth of the surface. New heat constantly produced in the of the earth by the decay of radioactive elements

Proposal

key factors unique to my location tokyo - asakusa

local traditions [Bathhouses] [sake production] [steam Bakery] [tea ceremony]

— technology
— local tradition earthquakes
— energy

"Sui-Tower" seeks to connect key aspects of Japanese c flow of water. The proposal uniquely looks at Japan wit with regards to future energy requirements, demands declining local traditions and addresses the unstable g region.

The project is located in Asakusa, a more traditional are modern technology blends successfully with traditiona

With many young people leaving for the bigger cities connect with pop culture, there has been a growing de due to the lack of interest. The project tries to preserve traditions by modifying them to fit round contempora systems.

Considering current trends in digital technologies, par cloud storage, there will be huge demands for data cen anxieties concerning the handling and ownership of d the hands of private companies, resulting in restricted people. By unifying and making this data completely a we can put it to greater use.

The proposal allows people to donate aspects o Much like a public library, this Data Archive will be co available to the public for research. Housing this data problems that every Data Centre experiences, principa of vast amounts of energy and the dissipation of wast

The government plans to invest about 50 trillion Yen i energies within the next 30 years, including plans to d entirely. Geothermal energy seems ideal for this proje resources relatively close to the surface, as evidenced and over 28,000 hot springs.

The building works by recycling grey-water fro feeding it via injection wells deep underground. Super brought to the surface via extraction wells and electric water vapor is forced through a series of steam turbine process, excess steam from the cooling towers is then power specific traditional activities within the building community.

Steam, which has passed through the turbines, the rice in a local Sake Brewery (an industry uncomme It is also channeled to provide the main source of heat "Roba-no-panya" or horse-drawn bakery wagons sellin [steamed-bread] used to be very popular however the now a rare sight and have almost died out.

Finally, the steam is used in saunas within the bathhou green tea in teahouses located within the building.

Once the water has completely cooled, it is fed throug cool down servers in the Data Centre. The returning he Data Centre will then run through and heat a series of gradually declining in temperature. Since the 1980s th reduction in the number of bathhouses in the city. The back into the injecting wells continuing the cycle.

Key interrelated features of the building include a Geo Data-Centre, Sake brewery, Mushi-pan bakery, tearoom and a water treatment facility. Other features within th a series of pipe works on the exterior forming part of t Studies predict a 70% probability that a major quake w region in the next 30 years. In preparation for such eve adopts some extreme earthquake technologies to hel withstand such activities and ensure the Data Centre

Tokyo is a restles itself r whiles try

the cooling process, excess steam from the cooling towers is then filtered and used as a catalyst to power specific traditional activities within the building and the local community. Once the water has completely cooled, it will be fed through pipes and used to cool down servers in the data center. The returning heated water from the data center will then run through and heat a series of bathhouses gradually declining in temperature. The water would be fed back into the injecting wells again continuing the cycle.

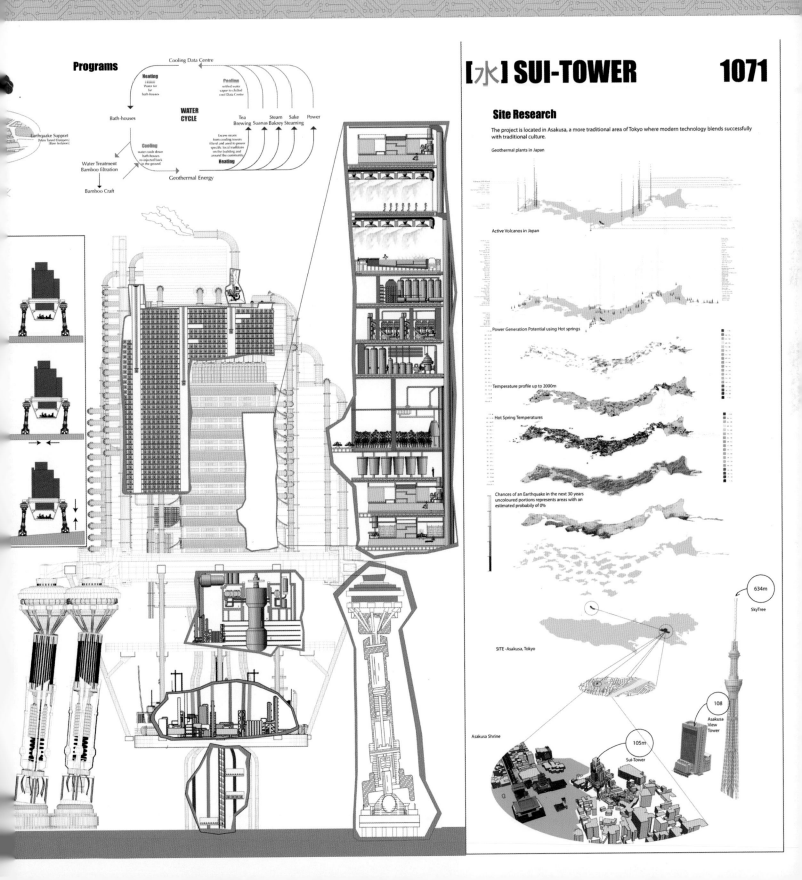

Programs

Cooling Data Centre

Heating
Water for bath-houses

Cooling
water cools down bath-houses re-injected back in the ground

Penline
settled water vapor to chilled cool Data Centre

WATER CYCLE

Tea Brewing   Suanas   Bakrey   Steam   Sake   Steaming   Power

Excess steam from cooling towers filtered and used to power specific local traditions on the building and around the community

Heating

Bath-houses

Earthquake Support
[Mass Tuned Dampers]
[Base Isolaion]

Water Treatment
Bamboo filtration

Bamboo Craft

Geothermal Energy

[水] SUI-TOWER 1071

Site Research

The project is located in Asakusa, a more traditional area of Tokyo where modern technology blends successfully with traditional culture.

Geothermal plants in Japan

Active Volcanos in Japan

Power Generation Potential using Hot springs

Temperature profile up to 2000m

Hot Spring Temperatures

Chances of an Earthquake in the next 30 years uncoloured portions represents areas with an estimated probably of 0%

634m
SkyTree

SITE -Asakusa, Tokyo

108
Asakusa View Tower

105m
Sui-Tower

Asakusa Shrine

It is no surprise that architects, designers, and urban planners are working on sustainable solutions for our cities. We have reached a point in which it is fundamental to be aware of the potential implications of our designs for the planet. Although the projects presented in this chapter mainly focus on green technologies for high-rise architecture, the concepts and ideas could be replicated in other architectural genres.

The main question asked is whether we continue migrating to urban centers or return to rural areas. Although these are two very distinct paths, both share similarities including the need to design net-zero structures that maximize their energy production and minimize their energy consumption. Some examples include the harness of solar, wind, geothermal and kinetic energy while making use of passive heating and cooling systems. Mathematical algorithms are also used to control every appliance and fixture at its best performance level with minimum energy requirement.

Transportation is another key area of research. How do we reduce transportation time and distance in a hyper-mobile era? Is it possible to create self-sufficient cities that do not rely on outside products and energy? A series of projects provide a solution when proposing vertical farms within city centers. Other proposals investigate the use of oscillating filaments on facades that would harness the kinetic energy of sound in cities like Los Angeles where noise exists at high levels.

ALTHOUGH THE PROJECTS PRESENTED IN THIS CHAPTER MAINLY FOCUS ON GREEN TECHNOLOGIES FOR HIGH-RISE ARCHITECTURE, THE CONCEPTS AND IDEAS COULD BE REPLICATED IN OTHER ARCHITECTURAL GENRES.

ECOLOGICAL URBANISM 2

THE HIMALAYAN WATER TOWER

1ST PLACE - 2012

Dongbai Song
Hongchuan Zhao
Zhi Zheng

China

THE HIMALAYAN WATER TOWER
SAVING WATER FOR THE FUTURE

Housed within 55,000 glaciers in the Himalayan Mountains sits 40 percent of the world's fresh water. The massive ice sheets are melting at a faster-than-ever pace due to climate change, posing possible dire consequences for the continent of Asia and the entire world, and especially for the villages and cities that sit on the seven rivers that are fed from the Himalayas' runoff as they respond with erratic flooding or drought.

The Himalayan Water Tower is a skyscraper located high in the mountain range that serves to store water and helps regulate its dispersal to the land below as the mountains range's natural supply dries up. The skyscraper, which can be replicated en masse, will collect water in the rainy season, purify it, freeze it into ice and store it for future use. The water distribution schedule will evolve with the needs of residents below; while it can be used to help in times of

0084

Case

In 2007, when climbing the Mount Everest, Mountaineer Dawa Steven Sherpa realized that the ice and glaciers were disappearing right before his eyes, and said: "This is the treasure for us, but it is also vital necessity for billions of people who depend upon these glaciers for water."t

Containing 40% of the world's fresh water, The Himalayas are the tallest mountains on earth, home to 55000 glaciers, and source to 7 of Asia's greatest rivers. The mountain glaciers at the highest Himalayas are the lifeblood of the Asia. The glaciers expand enormous geographic region, from Pakistan, through India, Nepal, Bhutan, Bangladesh and China. They are the source of water for some of the world's greatest rivers. The Indus, Ganges, Mekong, Yangtze and Yellow rivers all flow from the Himalayan Mountains, to the seas of Asia.

Glacier Volume Change Forecasts
Normalized volume variation

Glacier Lake Outburst Floods
Cumulative frequency of events

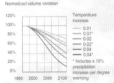

Average
Source: Oedemans et al., Climate Dynamics.

Source: reproduced from Richardson and Reynolds, An overview of glacial hazards in the Himalayas. Quaternary International, 65-86, 31-47.

However, our most precious resource is disappearing one drop at a time. Climate change is causing significant mass loss of glaciers in Himalayas. The Himalayas are the water towers of Asia. Once the water tower dries out, 2 billion people's life will be affected, and there is going to be serious problem.

The people of Asia face an uncertain future. From Nepal to the Tibet Plateau, Bhutan to India and the Bay of Bengal, their way of life is under threat. The climate is changing, and life as we know it, from the mountains to sea, is falling out of balance. Glacier lakes can burst anytime, droughts threaten once lush farmlands. Weather patterns become unpredictable. Thousands of miles downstream, sea level rise, forcing coastal villagers into crowded inner cities.

Concept

The inconvenient truth is that the high mountain glaciers are decreasing while the global climate is becoming warmer. Therefore, future adaptations need to be planned to the Himalayan Meltdown.

We conceive the skyscraper located in Himalayas to store water for the future and to regulate future water supply. We know that solid ice is convenient to store and ice can be a part of load-bearing structures. Thus, the project's proposal is to collect water in rainy season, we purify it, freeze it into ice and store it for the future.

It mainly consists of four parts. The lower part which has stem-like structures is for water collection during the rainy season. The upper part above the snow line is the place to store the ice cube. What's between the two parts is the cooling equipment, it freeze the water into ice by natural and mechanical means. The transport system is responsible for regulating the supply of water, it's down to the ground and can solve traffic problems of local people as well.

Meanwhile, by observing the storage of ice in the tower can generally realize the surplus of the fresh water. It can be a warning to the world as well.

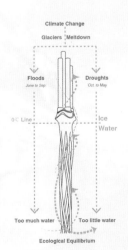

current drought, it is also meant to store plentiful water for future generations.

The lower part of the Himalayan Water Tower is comprised of six stem-like pipes that curve and wind together and collect and store water. Like the stem of a plant, these pipes grow strong as they absorb their maximum water capacity. In each of the six stems, a core tube is flanked by levels and levels of cells, which hold the water.

The upper part of the building, which is visible above the snow line, is used for frozen storage. Four massive cores support steel cylindrical frames that, like the stems below, hold levels that radiate out, creating four steel tubes filled with ice. In between the two sections are mechanical systems that help freeze the water when the climatic conditions are not able to do so, purify the water, and regulate the distribution of water and ice throughout the structure.

THE HIMALAYAS WATER TOWER
SAVING WATER FOR THE FUTURE

At the bottom of the structure, surrounding the six intertwined water tubes is a transport system that regulates fresh water distribution to the towns and cities below. The curving channels connect the mountains to the villages, and also hold within them a railway for the transportation of people and goods.

0084

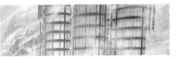

Single Level Perspective

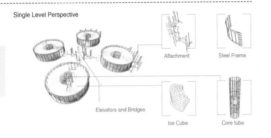

[Ice Cube Storage] The ice container is built above the 0℃ line. It's the place to store the ice cube. It consists of three parts: the core, the frame and the attachment. There are several layers in the core tube, so it can convey the ice in an energy saving way. The frame can hold the ice cubes frozen in the freezing center. The attachments offer places for vapor in the air to condense.

The very geographical environment in himalayan area forms the great gap of climate patterns between the two sides of the mountains. And people in different area are suffering from flood and drought. Addressing this problem, the water towers will redistribution part of the water resource and Improve quality of local people's life.

Area of Influence

Components

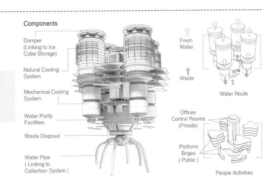

[Water Treatment Center] It's the main part of the tower. On one hand, it purifies the water, freeze it into ice; on the other hand, it's the control center of the whole tower and offers an extremely wide field of vision to people. The cooling equipment has two systems: Natural cooling system and mechanical cooling system. Only when the outside temperature is above 0 C ,the mechanical cooling system will begin to work.

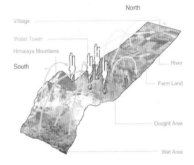

Meanwhile, the water towers are storing water for the next generations. The water collection and distribution strategy is adjusted base on time periods. We consider the worse possible situation in which the glaciers are completely disappeared.

Sectional Perspective

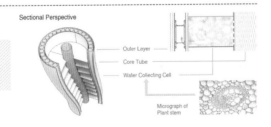

[Collection System] Six bent pipes are the main support structure of the tower. It's also the place for water collection and storage. Similar to plant stems, when the material is saturated with water, it gets a high toughness and a large weight capacity.

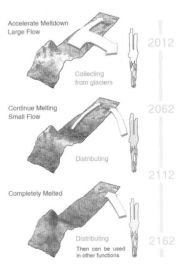

Sectional Perspective

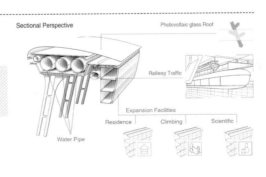

[Water Transportation System] For conveying the fresh water, it connects the glaciers, the towers and the villages together as a net. It's also equipped railway to transport people and goods. Space of expansion facilities are reserved in to add extra function in the future,

DETOXCITY

Ellen Ward

United Kingdom

DETOXCITY

VERTICALLY INTEGRATED WASTE REPROCESSING

LONDON'S MODERN DEVELOPMENT NEEDS

In 2000/01, London's municipal waste recycling rate was 8%, up from 5% in 1996/9. In 2006/07, the municipal waste recycling rate in London was up to 20%, somewhat short of the targets set in The Municipal Waste Management Strategy (MWMS) but a significant improvement all the same. As for the rest, 57% was buried in landfill sites and 22% was burnt in incinerators. Although recycling has now gathered a momentum, education and improvement in services is still required. Above all however London needs its own localised facilities to sort, manage and process these materials.

The London Plan published in 2004 set a self sufficiency target for managing all of London's waste of 85% by 2020. Currently it is estimated that 60% of London's waste (19m tonnes) is managed inside London. The construction and demolition industry are by far the best performers managing nearly 95% in London of which 85% is recycled. It is the household, commercial and industrial waste streams that require the most facilities. It is increasingly evident that existing waste management facilities need to become a means of focusing communal responsibility.

WASTE MANAGEMENT: 2050

There is an increasing desire to confront traditional preconceptions of waste and waste treatment. New waste treatment processes need to be brought into the city and, through thoughtful design, find an appropriate place in London, where waste is turned into energy for the benefit of the community. A local facility on a restricted inner city site would give waste management in London the context of the processes of infrastructure that the community needs. A proposal is sought for a coherent and integrated waste strategy for the city which can ultimately become this active focus of communal responsibility.

In order to create a waste management system for the future, new and emerging technologies need to be considered: anaerobic digestion and advanced thermal treatment technologies, which recover energy as part of the waste treatment process, are fundamental strategies to meet this aim. These technologies can be successfully integrated into London's infrastructure in order to achieve a complementary waste treatment facility to meet current and future needs. Through the twin prongs of it's central urban location and the prominent design, this facility has the ability to raise awareness of the waste treatment process in a grander context.

PROPOSAL

The concept is a multi-waste treatment facility which is integrated into the urban fabric of the capital which treats and processes the entire spectrum of waste including industrial, hazardous, municipal, water and e-waste. In essence, a localised reclamation facility which acts metabolically, detoxing and purifying waste in the heart of the city. It is at a specific existing advantageous location along the river Thames in terms of access to the site. Waste barges carrying municipal waste up and down the Thames already have access to the site as this is currently a waste transfer station. It has rail access adjacent to the East, road access to the North of the site and lastly it lies directly above the Victorian sewerage network.

By avoiding the transportation of waste disposal over long distances (predominantly to Essex,) this enables reintegration close to the site of consumption and waste production, thus becoming an efficient adjunct to the cities core processes. The net effect is that the process is generally marginalised as the peripheral is centralised.

While 2006-2007 estimates put London's recycling rate at 20 percent, 57 percent of the city's trash was still buried in landfill sites and the other 22 percent burnt in incinerators. The London Plan published in 2004 set a self-sufficiency target for managing 85 percent of London's waste by 2020 within the city; currently it is estimated that 60 percent of London's waste is managed inside London.

In order to reach this ambitious goal, new and emerging technologies need to be utilized: anaerobic digestion and advanced thermal treatment technologies, which recover energy as part of the waste treatment process, must be integrated into new facilities that are within the city. By stylizing London's infrastructure and waste treatment facilities, such structures could be didactic and useful not just because of their central location but also by using prominent

design to raise awareness of the waste treatment process in a grander context.

The design for Detoxcity proposes the construction of one such facility: a multi-waste treatment facility that is integrated into the urban fabric of the capital. This tower can treat and process the entire spectrum of waste: industrial, hazardous, municipal, water and e-waste. Such a localized reclamation facility would act metabolically, purifying waste in the heart of the city. It would also generate heat as the waste is processed, which would be captured and processed to put energy back on the city's grid. Its appearance is unabashedly industrial: a core aeration tube flanked by varying material processing compartments, all sitting atop a base with flared legs for support.

The tower is proposed for an existing site at an advantageous location along the river Thames: waste barges

carrying municipal waste up and down the river already have access to the site (it is currently a waste transfer station). The site also has rail access adjacent to the East, road access to the North of the site and lies directly above the Victorian sewerage network.

By avoiding the transportation of waste disposal over long distances (predominantly to Essex), this enables reintegration close to the site of consumption and waste production, thus becoming an efficient adjunct to the city's core processes. The net effect is that the process is generally marginalized as the peripheral is centralized.

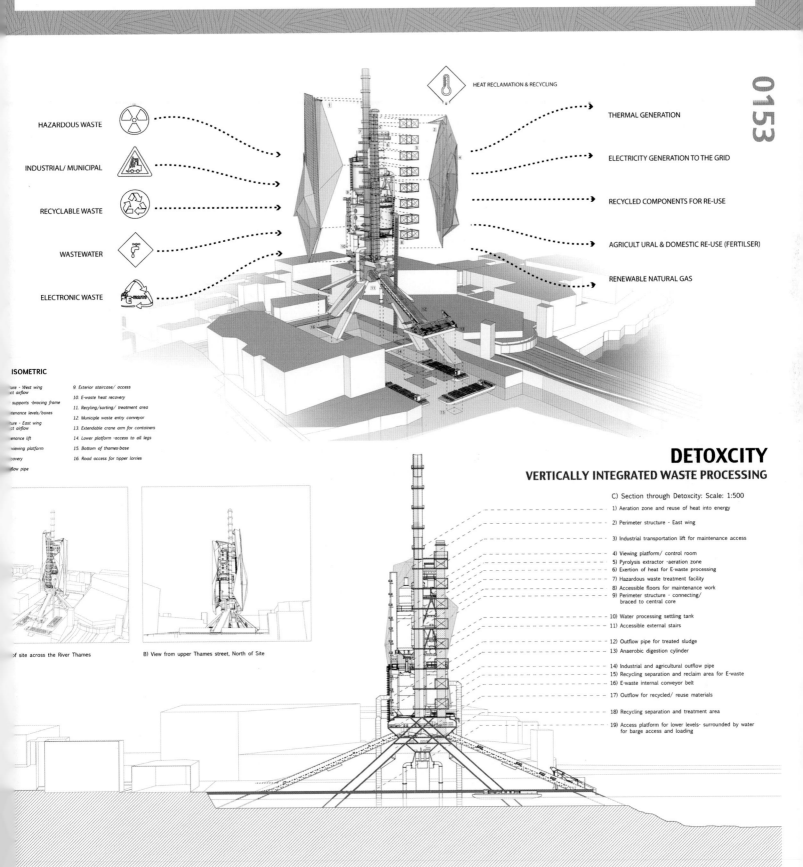

0153

HEAT RECLAMATION & RECYCLING

HAZARDOUS WASTE

INDUSTRIAL/ MUNICIPAL

RECYCLABLE WASTE

WASTEWATER

ELECTRONIC WASTE

THERMAL GENERATION

ELECTRICITY GENERATION TO THE GRID

RECYCLED COMPONENTS FOR RE-USE

AGRICULTURAL & DOMESTIC RE-USE (FERTILSER)

RENEWABLE NATURAL GAS

ISOMETRIC

...ure - West wing   9. Exterior staircase/ access
...ct airflow   10. E-waste heat recovery
... supports -bracing frame 11. Recyling/sorting/ treatment area
...tenance levels/boxes   12. Municiple waste entry conveyor
...ure - East wing   13. Extendable crane arm for containers
...ct airflow   14. Lower platform -access to all legs
...enance lift   15. Bottom of thames-base
...viewing platform   16. Road access for tipper lorries
...covery
...flow pipe

...f site across the River Thames   B) View from upper Thames street, North of Site

DETOXCITY
VERTICALLY INTEGRATED WASTE PROCESSING

C) Section through Detoxcity: Scale: 1:500

1) Aeration zone and reuse of heat into energy
2) Perimeter structure - East wing
3) Industrial transportation lift for maintenance access
4) Viewing platform/ control room
5) Pyrolysis extractor -aeration zone
6) Exertion of heat for E-waste processing
7) Hazardous waste treatment facility
8) Accessible floors for maintenance work
9) Perimeter structure - connecting/ braced to central core
10) Water processing settling tank
11) Accessible external stairs
12) Outflow pipe for treated sludge
13) Anaerobic digestion cylinder
14) Industrial and agricultural outflow pipe
15) Recycling separation and reclaim area for E-waste
16) E-waste internal conveyor belt
17) Outflow for recycled/ reuse materials
18) Recycling separation and treatment area
19) Access platform for lower levels- surrounded by water for barge access and loading

THE DUTCH DEFENDER

Tugrul Avuclu
Abdessamed Azarfane
Milad Pallesh
Ramon Scharff
Christiaan Schuit
Pim Van Tol
Frank Van Zuilekom

Netherlands

THE DUTCH DEFENDER

The Afsluitdijk is one of the most important dykes and well known landmarks in the Netherlands and plays a vital role in the evergoing struggle between the Dutch and the water. Dating from the year 1932, The dyke has a strong cultural and historical value, and regulates the amount of water in the IJsselmeer. The dyke was an end to the flooding situations which often struck the netherlands from the Zuiderzee and made it possible to lay dry new land which is known as the Flevopolders. The dyke has therefore become a world famous tourist attraction. Next to its landmark status it also has the very important task. Heavy rainfall causes rivers to flood. To overcome flooding this the excessive water is pumped in to the IJsselmeer and from there the dyke serves as the a draining system for the Netherlands to pump excessive water from the IJsselmeer

in to the Waddenzee. In 2006 the government announced that the dyke and its drainage system do not meet the required standards for water safety. Therefor restoration is urgent to ensure the future safety levels. Under future Dutch water law, the safety standards for the Afsluitdijk and its drainage system need to guarantee a protection from storms with strengths which occur once every 10.000 years. Currently, this minimum protection against storms, is 1000 years. By the damage of such storms the dyke's function is no longer guaranteed, the drainage system and locks for ships could be heavily damaged and this way salt water will stream in to the IJsselmeer and threaten its fresh water supply. In order to keep the Netherlands safe we will have to act and reinforce The Afsluitdijk..

THE NEW METROPOLIS

The prediction for the future is that the movement from rural areas towards the city will take a rapid flight. In Netherlands living along water is believed to be a quality. Especially living on the water is and will be enormously popular. Anticipating on the future, the Dutch defender is set up as a new metropolis on the water. Living and working on the water has never been implemented so greatly in a city. The Dutch defender can accommodate a population between 500,000 and 1,000,000 inhabitants, a density equal to that of Amsterdam. By linking mixed-use clusters with different densities a dynamic living-environment is created.

The Afsluitdijk, one of the most important dykes in the Netherlands, is an aging dam, one whose job as a defense wall protecting the shore from sea surges cannot be assured for much longer. The Dutch Defender project proposes, instead of restoring the 1932 dyke, building a massive structure around it that can not only take on the task of protecting the Netherlands from flooding but to also be a metropolis of equal density itself.

The dyke was an end to the flooding situations, which often struck the Netherlands from the Zuiderzee and made it possible to lay dry new land, which is known as the Flevopolders. The dyke has therefore become a world famous tourist attraction. Next to its landmark status it also has the a very important task. Heavy rainfall causes rivers to flood. To overcome flooding the excessive water is pumped into the IJsselmeer and from there the dyke serves as the

0166-1

draining system for the Netherlands to pump excessive water from the IJsselmeer into the Waddenzee. However the government announced in 2006 that the dyke and its drainage system do not meet the required standards for water safety. Therefore restoration is a must to ensure the future safety levels.

The Dutch Defender skyscraper can accommodate a population of between 500,000 to 1,000,000 people with a density equal to that of Amsterdam. Located in the sea, the structure has wind and water readily accessible for easy energy generation: windmills dot the structure and "blue energy" electro-dialysis is used to create energy from the seawater by combining fresh and salt water (and having the pressure caused from the concentration push water through turbines). The Afsluitdijk's use as a roadway is reinforced as improvements are made to better facilitate sea

A1

A2

A3

B1

B2

B3

B4

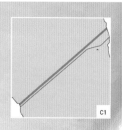
C1

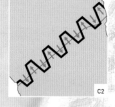
C2

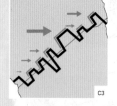
C3

C4

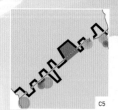
C5

C6

C7

C8

C9

C10

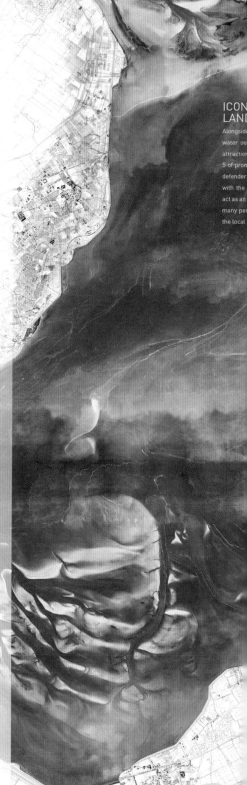

LOCATION

A1 The Netherlands is located in the North-Western part of Europe. On the north and west side the country borders to the Northsea which flows over the Waddenzee land inwards .

A2 The Netherlands is a small country with approximately 17.000.000 inhabitants. The biggest part of the Netherlands is located under sea level. The Dutch are famous for their dykes and other waterworks.

A3 The Afsluitdijk is a dyke in the northern part of the Netherlands which separates the IJselmeer from the Waddenzee. With it's length of 32 km it's also the direct connection between the provinces North-Holland and Friesland.

WATER THREAT

B1 This is an overview of the Netherlands when the waterlevel is 85 cm above sea level.

B2 The waterlevel is 150 cm above sea level.

B3 The waterlevel is 250 cm above sea level.

B4 To prevent a worst-case scenario of the Netherlands being under water, the Dutch defender can be placed along the whole coastline.

CONCEPT SHAPE

C1 First priority is to create an object that protects the existing Afsluitdijk.

C2 To improve the view of both sides of the Afsluitdijk, the shape of the Dutch defender swipes over the Afsluitdijk. This creates different atmospheres on the dyke.

C3 Based on the direction of the waterflow from the west, the dutch defender acts as a breakwater towards it.

C4 The Afsluitdijk will retain it's function as a traffic route and is reinforced with two naviducts to the improve the mobilty of road- and watertraffic.

C5 These ecological areas on land and water provide housing and breeding grounds for birds and waterlife.

C6 A new harbour for recreation and boating and introducing naviducts for easy passing through the Afsluitdijk.

C7 To improve the mobility, a fast transportation system will be added.

C8 The routing is divided in a fast transport route for destination and a recreational route to experience the context.

C9 Using the local quality of two different watertypes, energy can be generated using the blue energy technology.

C10 Integration of windturbines in the Dutch defender, wind energy can be generated without affecting views into open sea.

ICON
LAND

Alongside
water out
attraction.
5 of prom
defender
with the l
act as an
many peo
the local

and car traffic.

As a whole, the structure links mixed-use clusters of different densities to create a dynamic living-environment. Living in such a structure would be tremendously successful in attracting residents; in the Netherlands, living along the water is believed to be a quality. Living on the water is, and will be, enormously popular. It will be a self-sufficient metropolis and an enduring landmark that protects and provides.

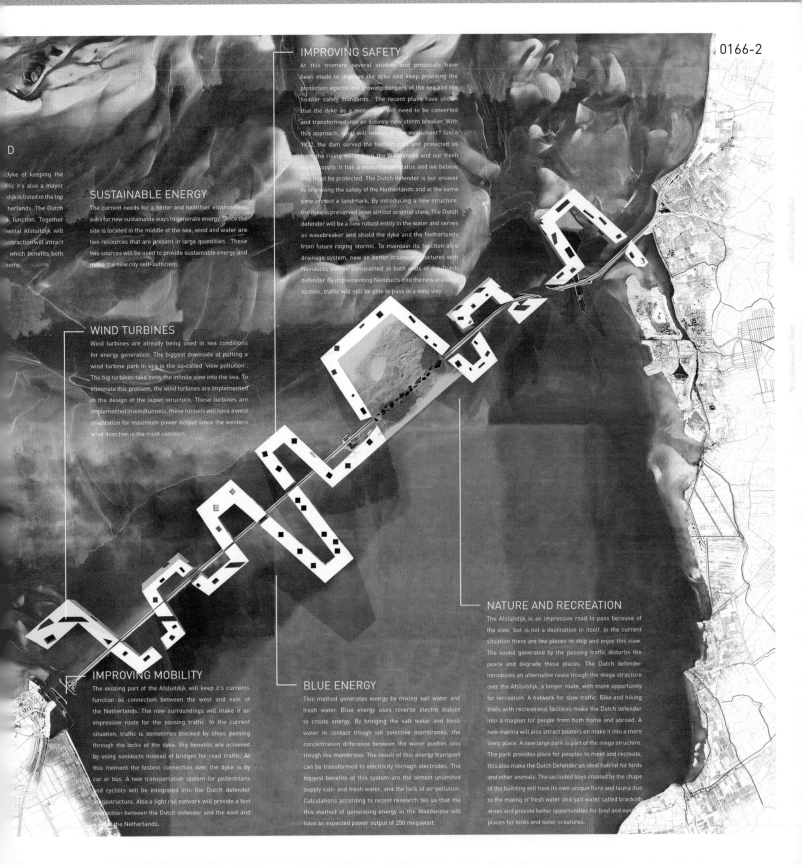

0166-2

IMPROVING SAFETY

At this moment several studies and proposals have been made to improve the dyke and keep providing the protection against the growing dangers of the sea and the heavier safety standards. The recent plans have shown that the dyke as a monument will need to be converted and transformed into an entirely new storm breaker. With this approach, what will remain of the monument? Since 1932, the dam served the Netherlands and protected us from the rising water from the Waddenzee and our fresh water supply. It has a monumental status and we believe this must be protected. The Dutch defender is our answer to improving the safety of the Netherlands and at the same time protect a landmark. By introducing a new structure, the dyke is preserved in an almost original state. The Dutch defender will be a new robust entity in the water and serves as wavebreaker and shield the dyke and the Netherlands from future raging storms. To maintain its function as a drainage system, new an better drainage structures with Naviducts will be constructed at both ends of the Dutch defender. By implementing Naviducts into the new drainage system, traffic will still be able to pass in a easy way.

SUSTAINABLE ENERGY

The current needs for a better and healthier environment asks for new sustainable ways to generate energy. Since the site is located in the middle of the sea, wind and water are two resources that are present in large quantities. These two sources will be used to provide sustainable energy and make the new city self-sufficient.

WIND TURBINES

Wind turbines are already being used in sea conditions for energy generation. The biggest downside of putting a wind turbine park in sea is the so-called 'view pollution'. The big turbines take away the infinite view into the sea. To eliminate this problem, the wind turbines are implemented in the design of the super structure. These turbines are implemented in windtunnels, these tunnels will have a west orientation for maximum power output since the western wind direction is the most common.

IMPROVING MOBILITY

The existing part of the Afsluitdijk will keep it's currents function as connection between the west and east of the Netherlands. The new surroundings will make it an impressive route for the passing traffic. In the current situation, traffic is sometimes blocked by ships passing through the locks of the dyke. Big benefits are achieved by using naviducts instead of bridges for road traffic. At this moment the fastest connection over the dyke is by car or bus. A new transportation system for pedestrians and cyclists will be integrated into the Dutch defender megastructure. Also a light rail network will provide a fast connection between the Dutch defender and the east and west of the Netherlands.

BLUE ENERGY

This method generates energy by mixing salt water and fresh water. Blue energy uses reverse electro dialyze to create energy. By bringing the salt water and fresh water in contact trough ion selective membranes, the concentration difference between the water pushes ions trough the membrane. The result of this energy transport can be transformed to electricity through electrodes. The biggest benefits of this system are the almost unlimited supply salt- and fresh water, and the lack of air pollution. Calculations according to recent research tell us that the this method of generating energy in the Waddenzee will have an expected power output of 250 megawatt.

NATURE AND RECREATION

The Afsluitdijk is an impressive road to pass because of the view, but is not a destination in itself. In the current situation there are few places to stop and enjoy this view. The sound generated by the passing traffic disturbs the peace and degrade these places. The Dutch defender introduces an alternative route trough the mega structure over the Afsluitdijk, a longer route, with more opportunity for recreation. A network for slow traffic. Bike and hiking trails with recreational facilities make the Dutch defender into a magnet for people from both home and abroad. A new marina will also attract boaters en make it into a more lively place. A new large park is part of the mega structure. The park provides place for peoples to meet and recreate, this also make the Dutch Defender an ideal habitat for birds and other animals. The secluded bays created by the shape of the building will have its own unique flora and fauna due to the mixing of fresh water and salt water called brackish areas and provide better opportunities for food and nesting places for birds and water creatures.

EARTH-SHAPED CITY

Charly Duchosal

Switzerland

EARTH-SHAPED CITY 0318

1. RELATIONSHIP BETWEEN CITY AND NATURE

With today's weight of cities in the landscape, we tend to lose our original relationship with nature. The cities are getting bigger, larger, and higher as the population is increasing and our visual connection to natural landscape is disappearing. Urban planners and architects have been trying to put parts of nature in cities, such as drawing parks and putting trees in the streets. I believe that the implementation of these "green parts" in cities have nothing to do with nature in its original state, because they are designed and constructed just like classic buildings. The cities are disconnected from nature and so are the human beings living in them.

2. CONCEPT

Instead of trying to put nature in the city, I believe that we should put the city into nature in a way that wouldn't affect it. Living inside the earth allows us to preserve most of its surface. We know that oblique and verticality permits cities to face the increasing needs for density but topography could also be as a vertical weft.

I like to envision a city that is set in a wild landscape digged in rock to preserve the development of nature around, it and where all the spaces needing natural light will benefit from a constant visual connection with the surrounding site. That is, a city that wouldn't be shaped by humans but by Earth itself.

A geothermic system, which doesn't have to be visually connected to the landscape, is the logical solution to provide energetics needs to this city. The main condition for this is that the city should be located in a geographic zone with high abnormal geothermal gradients (active tectonic and volcanic areas).

The advantages of geothermal stations is that they do not emit CO2, but also they do not use or waste fossil fuels and they protect us from audio and visual pollution with the help of cooling towers.

3. CONTEXT

Iceland is a state which has significant energy resources provided by its unique geology and its abundant hydrography. In 2007, statistics showed that 66% of the primary energy of this country came from geothermal energy.

On Monday 7th of March 2011, the spokesman of the public energy group Landsvirkjun announced a study for the construction of the world's longest electrical submarine cable, connecting Iceland to Europe, in order to sell electricity made out of volcanic origins to European countries.

Therefore, implanted in Iceland, "Earth-shaped city" benefits from the geological advantages of the land to insure its energetic needs. This city would also participate in Landsvirkjun's project by selling the surplus of produced electricity.

ICELAND

HIGH TEMPRATURE AREA BEDROCK AGE

4. VISION

In a general matter, the constant progress of technologies keeps taking us further away from nature, and therefore from our natural needs. Earth-shaped city highlights the fact that technology could be used to recover our relationship with nature if exploited in an efficient way, and thus participate to the well-being of each of us.'

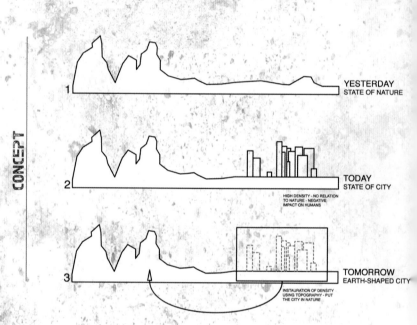

CONCEPT

1 YESTERDAY
STATE OF NATURE

2 TODAY
STATE OF CITY
HIGH DENSITY - NO RELATION TO NATURE - NEGATIVE IMPACT ON HUMANS

3 TOMORROW
EARTH-SHAPED CITY
INSTAURATION OF DENSITY USING TOPOGRAPHY - PUT THE CITY IN NATURE

PROCESS

1 - NATURAL LANDSCAPE   2 - DIG - CREATE SPACES   3 - GET SUSTAINBLE ENERGY   4 - EARTH SHAPED CITY

ELEVATION   SECTION   SECTION   ELEVATION

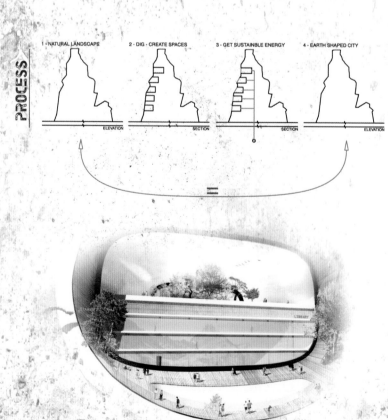

With today's weight of cities on the landscape, we tend to lose our original relationship with nature. The cities are getting bigger, larger, and higher as the population increases and our connection to natural landscape is disappearing. Urban planners and architects have been trying to recreate nature in cities by drawing parks and planting trees on streets. The implementation of these "green parts" in cities has nothing to do with nature in its original state.

Instead of trying to force nature into the city, we should adapt the city to nature. For example, living underneath the earth allows us to preserve most of its surface. We know that verticality allows cities to face the increasing needs for density.

The design for this city is set in a wild landscape inside a mountain to preserve the development of nature around

it. A geothermic plant is the logical solution to provide energy to the city. The main condition for this is that the city should simply be located in a geographic zone with high geothermal gradients: active tectonic and volcanic areas for energy use.

Iceland is the ideal location for this city because the country has significant energy resources provided by its unique geology. In 2007, statistics showed that 66% of the primary electricity of this country came from geothermal energy. Implanted in Iceland, Earth-Shaped City benefits from the geological advantages of the land to insure its energy needs. This city would also in turn participate in Landsvirkjun's project by selling the surplus of produced electricity.

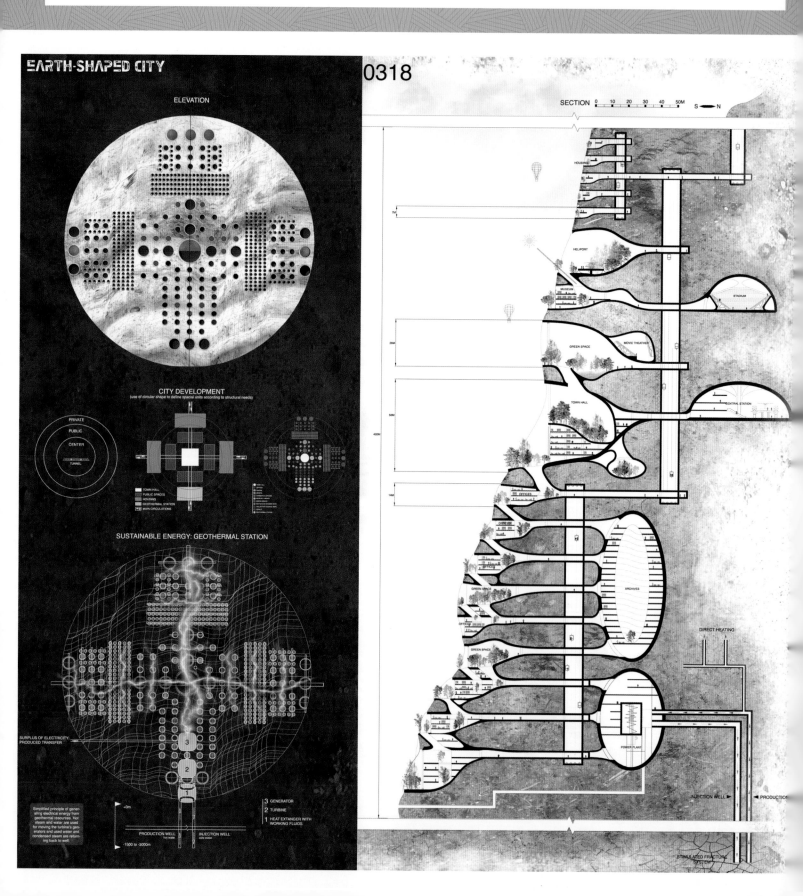

What this project encapsulates is a city envisioned to be set in a wild landscape dug in rock to preserve the development of nature around it where all the spaces needing natural light benefit from a constant visual connection with the surround site. This city would not be shaped by humans but by Earth itself.

MOUNTAIN BAND-AID

2ND PLACE - 2012

Yiting Shen
Nanjue Wang
Zihan Wang
Ji Xia

China

MOUNTAIN DISRUPTION

The original village settled at the mountain side with their farmland nearby on lower lines.

With the exhausive exploitation, the village was damaged and vegetation line fell back. And the mountain was deprived of its natural surface.

The natives were transit to other places, in modern buildings that no longer provide spaces for the original life mode.

CONCEPT

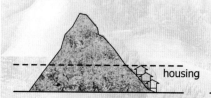

Industrialization and mining are destroying China's natural settings, especially mountains, which are excavated to the point of destruction in man's search for minerals. These processes do not just devastate the region's ecologies; they also displace whole populations of people, separating them from their homes and also their means of living, as many in these rural areas work as farmers. The Mountain Band-Aid project seeks to simultaneously restore the displaced Hmong mountain people to their homes and work as it restores the mountain ecology of the Yunnan mountain range.

This is achieved with a two-layer construction project. The outer layer is a skyscraper that is built into and stretched across the mountain. By building the structure into, and as part of, the mountain, the skyscraper helps the Hmong people recover their original lifestyle. It is organized internally by the villagers to replicate the traditional village

BACKGROUND

0350

Today **the deterioration of mountain has become the main disaster** for both natural environment and human settlement in Southwestern China.
Nowadays, the overwhelming industrialization in China has resulted in overexploitation of mineral resources. This is especially the case in Southwestern China like **Yunnan**, where heavy industry plays the major role in its economy and mountains are excavated in the search of minerals. Mining exploitation have imposed increasingly harm on ecological environment, including occupation of plowland, initiating geologic hazards, destroying water equilibrium, physiognomy and vegetation.
Moreover, in such mountainous provinces, many local residents like the **Hmong people,** who settled there for generations, have to move from damaged mountain site to block buildings, separating themselves from their previous living pattern.

CONCEPT

Now government has been aware of the seriousness of the deterioration of mountains and some ongoing projects are designed to offer an opportunity to save the situation. But in such projects , the ideas of recovering human settlement and natural environment are always considered separately. Is there a way to **recover both Hmong people's living tradition and mountain environment**? In our opinion ,the answer is YES .
One important issue in our task is to build a skyscraper on the mountain in order to help Hmong people recover mountain environment and their original lifestyle. This is difficult because the steep slope of damaged mountains is sometimes hard for people to live on. However, in our design where **the skyscraper leans on the mountain**, this question is fixed easily because people can build their house standing on the surface of mountain. Beyond that, the steepness of the slope even become an advantage. Since the height of our skyscraper is mainly determined by the height of the mountain, we have more freedom in our design, therefore **strengthening the adaptation of our skyscraper.**
Our design is also efficient for the **'dual recovery'** . On one hand, when Hmong people return to the mountain, their motherland, they can keep the unique organization of space in their formal village. On the other hand, the Hmong people living on the damaged mountain can take part in the environment restoration by, as an example, recycling domestic water for mountain irrigation. In sum, our proposed project creates **a win-win relationship, benefiting both human community and the natural environment.**
Based on this win-win relationship ,we are trying to translate skyscraper into a structural system to recover the damaged mountain.

SYSTEM

In order to create the possibility of the interaction between the mountain and the newly built society, our project has established the double layer green surface of the mountain--- **the "outer layer" and the "inner layer".**
The outer layer provides the Hmong people with a new inhabited environment .Our design, which stretches a modern high-rise building along the surface of the mountain, ensembles the space organization of traditional Hmong village. This incorporation of original mountain village pattern helps keep the Hmong people's **'mountain lifestyle'**.
At the same time, the inner layer irrigates the mountain. This inner layer is formed of **irrigation system** for stabilization of soil and growth of plants. With the help of this inner layer, we would have chances to green the destroyed region.

CONSTRUCTION

Constructed in the traditional Chinese Southern building philosophy known as Chuan Dou style, the big **framework** that our project provides is focusing on the local construction technique. In this framework, Hmong people could remain their village planning strategy and expand or organize the area freely as if the exploitation had never happened.
For easy construction, we use **the little residential blocks** in the framework. The blocks are freely organized as they were in the original village, while our framework controls the organization of blocks into different floors, acting as the contour line in traditional Hmong village. Therefore, the philosophy is re-organized and returned to the native mountain Hmong village mode

Mountain Band-Aid

PROGRAM RESULT

The concept and strategy was bonded together to create new life pattern in the damaged mountain area. The native Hmong people was driven away from their village for an overwhelming power and this skyscraper provided a solution, a possible life mode for these Hmong people.

Irrigation was brought to the system to revive the vegetation implanted onto the mountain surface. This was realized by the design of a drip irrigation system that flows along the mountain.

This grid holds the arable soil in their position to maintain an adequate condition for the plants. This also stabilized the soil and water system in the whole mountain.

mountain

mountain

NATURE   HUMAN

SELF-BUILT HOUSING

design they utilized before they were displaced. The building's placement on the mountain means that its height is mainly determined by the height of the mountain. The design as a whole is one of "dual recovery": the Hmong people living on the damaged mountain can keep the unique organization of space in their village, recreating it within the skyscraper, but they will not be contributing to the mountain's degradation. Instead, they help the mountain's environmental restoration by recycling domestic water for mountain irrigation. It is this irrigation system that comprises the project's inner layer: an irrigation system is constructed to stabilize the mountain's soil and grow plants.

The skyscraper is constructed in the traditional Chinese Southern building style known as Chuan Dou. Small residential blocks are used as the framework: the blocks are freely organized as they were in the original village, but

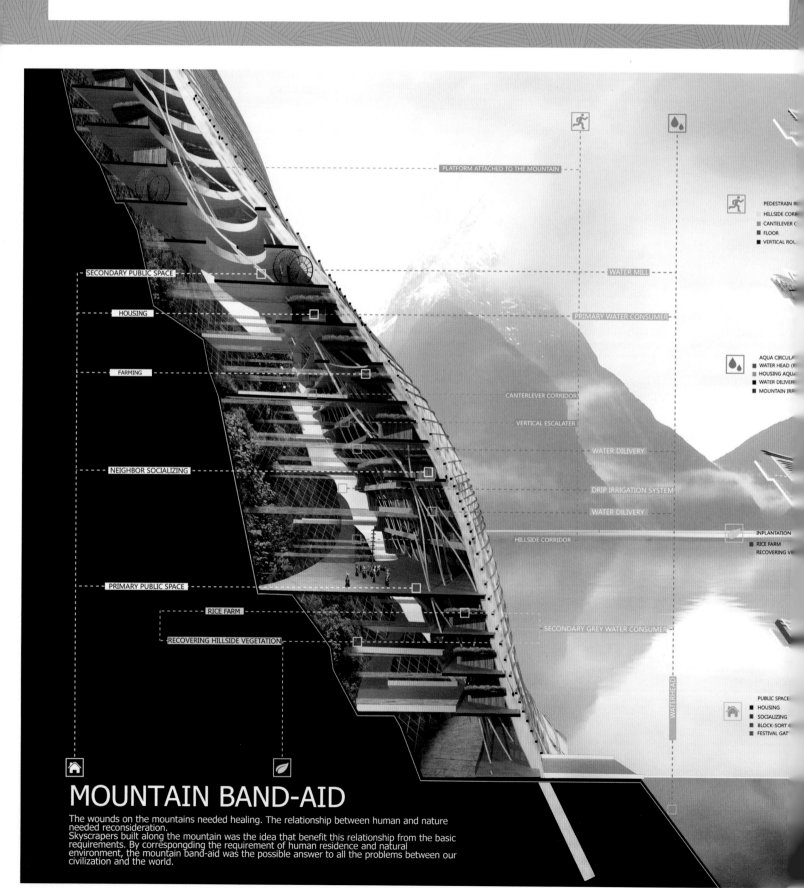

MOUNTAIN BAND-AID

The wounds on the mountains needed healing. The relationship between human and nature needed reconsideration.
Skyscrapers built along the mountain was the idea that benefit this relationship from the basic requirements. By correspongding the requirement of human residence and natural environment, the mountain band-aid was the possible answer to all the problems between our civilization and the world.

the framework controls this organization of blocks into different floors, acting as the contour line in traditional Hmong village.

The concept and strategy was bonded together to create a new life pattern in the damaged mountain area. The native Hmong people were driven away from their village for an overwhelming power and this skyscraper provides a solution, a possible alternate lifestyle for these people.

FARMING

SECONDARY PUBLIC SPACE

PRIMARY PUBLIC SPACE

0350

• WATER TRANSITION SYSTERM

the basic water transition systerm in a housing unit

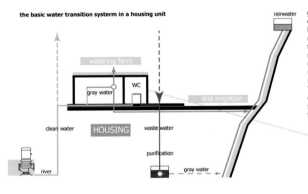

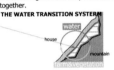

The water transition system was generated on the idea that water in this consumption structure was a circulation between the mountain and the community. Clean water were pumped up in the outer parts of the secondary S-shaped strucure, and used by the residents. The result as grey water could be purified and reused for purposes like mountain surface recovery, toilet usage and farm irrigation. The black water was seperated and drained down the building in the middle strut weaving the secondary structure unit together.

THE WATER TRANSITION SYSTERM

• CONSTRUCTION STRATAGIES

This project followed the historical lineage and renewed the system to fit into a new constructural system following the arranged functions. The traditional Chinese architecture was consisted of components of modulus and connected by tenon and mortise works. Struts acting as pillars for plane buildings was nailed into the rocks and perpendicular [vertical] components worked as beams could be attached to them by handwork. Secondary structure, shaped in S, connected the system as additional crossing beams of the traditional architecture. This layer of strucutre carried the drainage system to the top of the vertical village and enabled the wholesystem to be flexible to reduce the effect of possible earthquakes. The floor plane were finally fit into the system supported by the three levels of structure.

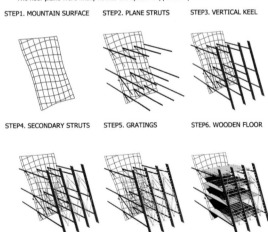

STEP1. MOUNTAIN SURFACE STEP2. PLANE STRUTS STEP3. VERTICAL KEEL

STEP4. SECONDARY STRUTS STEP5. GRATINGS STEP6. WOODEN FLOOR

Structure and water

Clean water
Waste water
Grey water+struts

MATERAIL SELECTION

The local materail,woods and bamboo,were firm and flexible for construction. The residents could be able to build their houses in an rather free and easy mode comparring to using glass, steel or concrete.The mortise and tenon joinery in the traditional Chinese architectureprocess can be employed to bear the characteristics of variability and sustainability.When the architectural form is changed, slight walls, roofs and beams can be dismantied to installate unto other palces for recycling.

• Plan

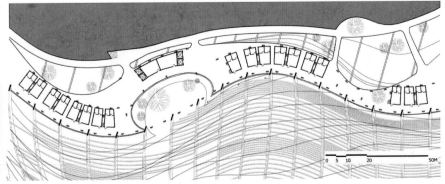
0 5 10   20   50M

140

THE ANTI-BUILDING

Chana Haouzi
Hedvig Skjerdingstad

Canada

the anti-building
manhattan reshift

another skyscraper?

When approaching Manhattan as the site for a new skyscraper, we ask ourselves the question of whether our intentions should lay in the pursuit for the biggest and most spectacular building. Instead, should we challenge this current tendency, and try to rethink the way we understand and perceive the skyscraper today?

Does the 'Capitol of Skyscrapers' really need yet another conventional skyscraper, or would the most spectacular actually be the anti-building?

By blurring the conventional systems for the skyscraper, the anti-building reflects on contained space, boundaries between interior/exterior and the expected embodiment of program. In order to achieve this, water is used as the key element and generator for special perceptions and experiences.

In considering the task of designing a new skyscraper for Manhattan, the creators of the Anti-Building wanted to avoid the typical architectural pursuit to build the biggest and most spectacular building. Instead, they pondered, wouldn't the most dramatic skyscraper in a city full of dramatic skyscrapers be an anti-skyscraper?

Their project makes a statement on the notions of contained space, boundaries between interior and exterior areas and the expected embodiment of a skyscraper. The designers' project seeks to do this by using water as the key element in their building, both in the structure itself and the surrounding landscape. To achieve the latter, Manhattan' 29th Street is transformed into a canal, creating a new urban environment beneficial to the city's inhabitants and bringing water as a main element back into the city. For the former, a structural grid gives the building

0531

manhattan as site

Water is also considered when it comes to the specific site and the urban scale. Currently, the relationship between land and water on Manhattan is never fully exploited, partly due to the highway enveloping the island forming a metropolitan inversion.

By investigation, this conjunction of land and water, we want to activate the edge and physically reintroduce water to the cityscape. This is done by transforming Manhattan' 29th street to a canal, thus creating a new urban environment beneficial to the city's inhabitants.

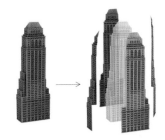

dematerialized structure

In order to maintain an impression of the anti-building, a structural grid is used to obtain the desired impression of transparency and lightness. From this moiré grid, voids are carved out creating spaces relating to the city.

1. conjunction of land and water
2. metropolitan introversion
3. city of skyscrapers
4. location of existing skyscrapers
5. highway surrounding and isolating the island for from its water.
6. rethinking the skyscraper
7. structural grid
8. effect of transparency

the desired impression of transparency and lightness. From this moiré grid, voids are carved out creating spaces relating to the city.

The water that travels through the building is essentially pumped from the Hudson River and onto the top of the tower, where it is then stored in a reservoir. Gravity powers the water down the building grid. This process is meant to engage each of the five senses of visitors, thereby creating unique curatorial spaces throughout the building as water is reflected and activated by the architecture.

Visitors travel through the building's core. The visitor's movement through the public building occurs in the core, mimicking the trajectory and behavior of the water as they travel up and slowly work their way down. This immersive

sensorial space

The spaces recognize and appreciate the innate qualities and ambiances of water and are therefore based on a range of sensorial spaces dealing and activating the visitor's five senses through water. Additionally, some of the sensorial spaces are in direct contact with the outside, allowing the environment and weather to affect the immediate perception of water in all of its states.

1. water descent trajectory
2. water cycle: path of travel
3. visitor's circulation

hydrokinetic energy

The water is pumped from the Hudson River and is pumped up to the top of the tower where it collects into a reservoir. Then, following Manhattan's existing water tower model, gravity powers the water as it travels through the grid until. This transfer of water offers the opportunity to create unique sensorial spaces throughout the building as it is collected in reflecting and activated by the architecture. The entire system is zero energy, as it follows the river's current and uses its nature flow to garner hydrokinetic energy through a system of underwater turbines.

placement of underwater turbines

reshift

The visitor's movement though the public building occurs in the core, mimicking the trajectory and behaviour of the water as they travel up and slowly work their way down. This immersive environment allows the visitor to experience a physical, visual and haptic interaction with water, ultimately reshifting the relationship between Manhattan as megacity and Manhattan as island.

1. ground plan
2. ground reflecting pool plan

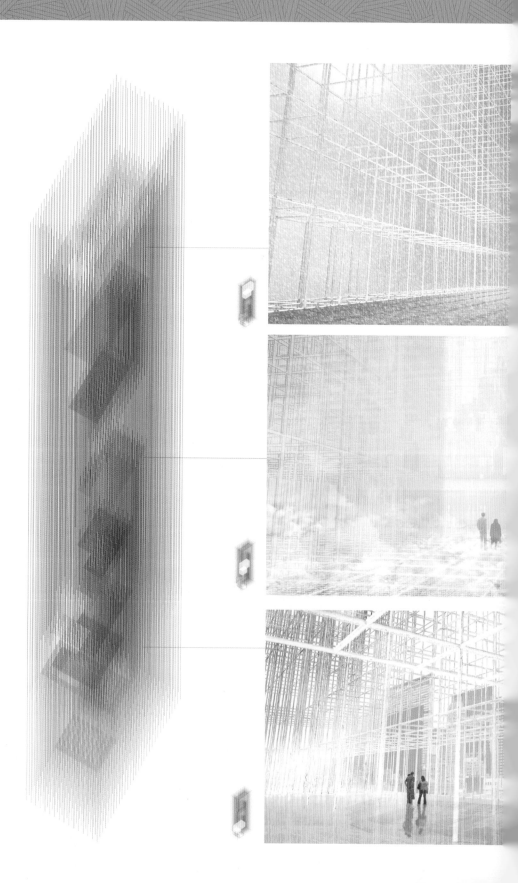

environment allows the visitor to experience a physical, visual and haptic interaction with water, ultimately ends up reshifting the relationship between Manhattan as a megacity and Manhattan as an island.

The building uses no energy, as the process of water flowing down the grid system and ending at a system of underwater turbines creates energy hydro-kinetically.

0531

LANDSCAPED INSERTION

Eric Israel Dorantes
Izbeth K. Mendoza Fragoso
Daniel Justino Rodríguez
Román J. Cordero Tovar

Mexico

LANDSCAPED INSERTION
A symbiotic sustainable structure for a vertical community experience

ARGUMENT

Is it possible to develop a cero foot print construction?
Is it possible to built being part of the landscape?

We have been developing thru the years unsustainable models that year after year are taking more territory to satisfy the necessity of grow. The typical skyscraper offered the chance to have a compact surface in ground in order to have more free horizontal space, but at the end, if we built a lot of them (as the current time) we will end in a sort of situation very linked with the previous one mentioned.
Let's think in the possibility to inhabit our natural vertical geographical territories.
The vertical plane with cero occupancy offers the possibility, with the help of the technology, to conquest the apparently inhospitable wall areas in order to preserve the green potential horizontal plane for an exclusively wild life.

Those are latencies waiting for think and to have a reflection in its surface. The cliffs are the new virgin territories to explore.

The follow research examples, attempts to look into the nature, art and history in order to learn how these concepts interact within the theme.

NATURE SHELTERS

In a way, this is back to the primitive refugees; the native fauna experience the vertical plane as an inhabiting surface. A surface that is, at the same time, protector and structural place.

The ants for example, develop vertical tunnels with chambers to live within the community, as well as birds, squirrels, etc

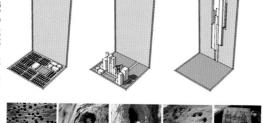

ART EXPLORATIONS

Many artists explore different techniques of low relief sculpture in its artwork, using it as a language to show the presence of the void.

It's interesting how the result show some cavities that can easily, in other scale, acts as program (activity spaces, circulation, etc.)

CLIFF DWELLINGS

This is not utopia, many civilization use this logic to settle, using techniques to erode the rock.

If at that time was possible, why we can't rethink the possibility to develop using actual building technology?

OPPORTUNITIES

The proposal explores the argument as a system that can be use in different location.

Our world geography shows many potential places to develop a vertical community in where the territorial occupation is radical but possible, living inside the landscape and being part of the view.

Is it possible to develop a zero footprint construction? Is it possible to build while being part of the landscape? Many artists explore different techniques of low relief sculpture in artwork, using it as a language to show the presence of the void. It is interesting how the result shows some cavities that can easily house program (activity spaces, circulation, etc.).

For many years we have been developing unsustainable models that year after year are taking more precious natural landscape and resources from the earth just to satisfy the necessity for grow. The typical skyscraper was appealing because it offered the chance to have a small footprint all of a sudden in order to have more free horizontal space. However in the end, if we continue to build a lot of them, we will end up with the same unsustainable model

0598

PANEL 1

and will eventually run out of free space.

The main idea behind this project is to inhabit the natural vertical geographical conditions. The vertical plane with zero occupancy offers the possibility, with the help of technology of course, to conquest the apparently inhospitable wall areas in order to preserve the green horizontal plane exclusively for wild life. The cliffs are the new virgin territories to explore.

In a way, this takes us back to the time of primitive refugees; the native fauna experience and the vertical plane were an inhabiting surface. This surface is, at the same time, becomes a protector and structural place. Ants for example develop vertical tunnels with chambers to live within the community. Our world geography shows many

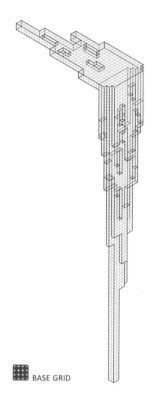

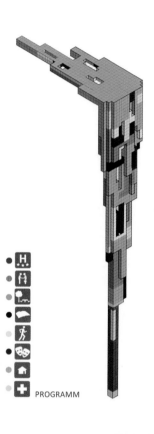

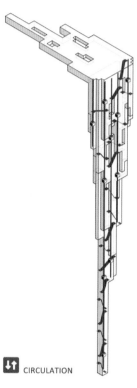

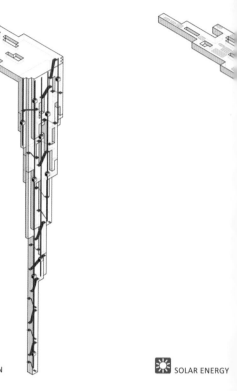

BASE GRID   PROGRAMM   CIRCULATION   SOLAR ENERGY

potential places to develop a vertical community in where the territorial occupation is radical but possible. This landscaped insertion is a symbiotic sustainable structure for a vertical community experience.

0598

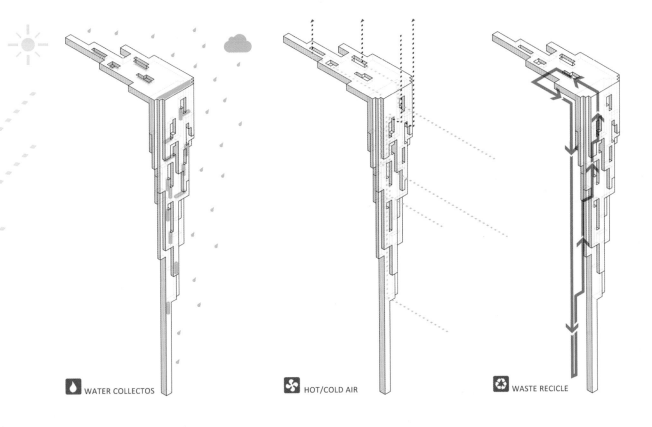

WATER COLLECTOS   HOT/COLD AIR   WASTE RECICLE

NOAH'S ARK

Aleksandar Joksimovic
Jelena Nikolic

Serbia

NOAH'S ARK

" Noah's Ark is a vessel appearing in the Book of Genesis and Quran. These narratives describe the construction of the ark by Patriarch Noah at God's command to save himself, his family, and the world's animal species from the worldwide deluge of the Great Flood. "

END OF THE WORLD ?

Since the beginning of the world, people and all living species have been fighting for their survivor. Natural disasters are something that is beyond our control and, naturally, it is something that we are most afraid of. Many great civilizations have had their predictions about the end of the world and one of the most popular is "Mayan end of the calendar" on 21.12.2012 which many interpret as a prediction of a series of major natural disasters. Despite all mentioned above, world shifts are obvious and hard rains, tsunamis and great earthquakes are more frequent than ever before.

OVERCROWDING

Overpopulation is the biggest environmental problem. It is directly followed by several different issues, such as: more pollution, less resources for the new demanding population, loss of habitat and environment. In the 60-year period, from 1900 - 1960 human population increased by a factor of 1.84 and in the 40-year period from 1960 - 2000 it increased by 3.04 wich makes it the biggest growing environmental problem. In addition to this, many researches revealed that, because of climate changes, by year 2090 megafloods could occur as frequently as every three to four years and that sea levels will rise by at least one to two feet and, if emissions of greenhouse gases remain unchecked and significant melting of the ice caps occurs, it is possible that rise will be from three to six feet wich would have significant negative consequences on all costal areas. Therefore, the lack of land and overpopulation combined together will make our present way of living and cities, as we know them, utopian and unsustainable.

CONCEPT

This project represents a "Noah's Ark" - self-sustainable city on the water which will inhabit all living species from fish, animals, humans to the trees and natural plants and provide them comfort and natural living, giving them, at the same time, shelter and structure that will resist all natural disasters. Moreover, this structure is architectural rethinking of the existing cities and conquest of the new territories in order to solve the overcrowding of the land. 72% of the earth's surface is already covered by water, therefore extend of urban city grid on water will be logical and, at the same time, very usefull because water has great bio and energy potential.

Noah's Ark is a self-sustainable city on the water that can support all living species, from humans to animals and fish to plants and trees, that have been evicted from land by natural disasters, warfare, and whatever disasters the end days may bring. In addition to providing protection from these disasters, the Ark concept also addresses overcrowding on land: 72% of the earth's surface is already covered by water, so extension of the urban city grid onto water is both logical and useful, as solar, wind and wave energies are easily captured at sea, and it is these natural energy sources that will power the development.

It is designed as part of a network consisting of other Arks, which connect with floating underwater tunnels and the main land. As the settlements grow, the Arks can attach to each other, creating one big artificial mainland from a series

0653

noah's ark | 01

of artificial islands.

A large number of flexible cables connect the island to the ocean's bottom, providing stability, and an external wall as tall as 64 meters protects the interior spaces of the island structure from hard sea winds and tsunamis. When emergencies of grave severity arise, residents can retreat to bubbles inside the depths of the islands for protection. The floating transportation tunnels do not overshadow the water surface and do not depend on weather conditions. The tunnels are filled with air and anchored to the ocean bottom therefore they float below the surface of the ocean. The anchors are flexible and can absorb hard hits and great movements; the anchors keep the structure in place and releases it if huge waves are coming. Therefore external influences do not affect the high-speed trains inside these

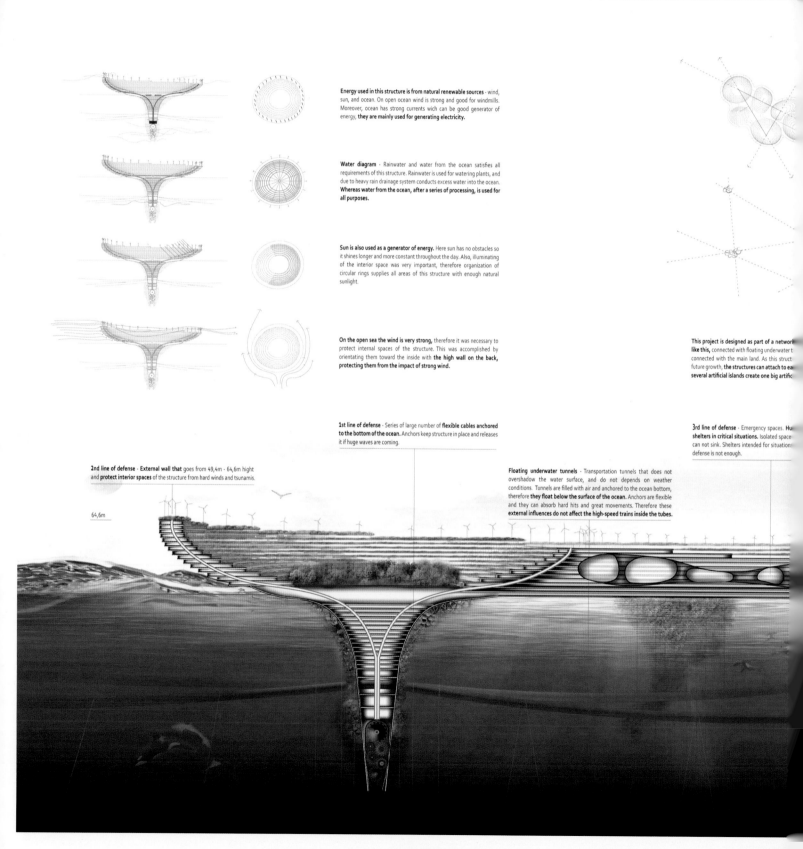

Energy used in this structure is from natural renewable sources - wind, sun, and ocean. On open ocean wind is strong and good for windmills. Moreover, ocean has strong currents wich can be good generator of energy, **they are mainly used for generating electricity.**

Water diagram - Rainwater and water from the ocean satisfies all requirements of this structure. Rainwater is used for watering plants, and due to heavy rain drainage system conducts excess water into the ocean. **Whereas water from the ocean, after a series of processing, is used for all purposes.**

Sun is also used as a generator of energy. Here sun has no obstacles so it shines longer and more constant throughout the day. Also, illuminating of the interior space was very important, therefore organization of circular rings supplies all areas of this structure with enough natural sunlight.

On the open sea the wind is very strong, therefore it was necessary to protect internal spaces of the structure. This was accomplished by orientating them toward the inside with **the high wall on the back, protecting them from the impact of strong wind.**

This project is designed as part of a network like this, connected with floating underwater t connected with the main land. As this struct future growth, **the structures can attach to ea** several artificial islands create one big artific

1st line of defense - Series of large number of **flexible cables** anchored to the bottom of the ocean. Anchors keep structure in place and releases it if huge waves are coming.

3rd line of defense - Emergency spaces. Hu shelters in critical situations. Isolated space can not sink. Shelters intended for situations defense is not enough.

2nd line of defense - **External wall** that goes from 49,4m - 64,6m hight and **protect interior spaces** of the structure from hard winds and tsunamis.

Floating underwater tunnels - Transportation tunnels that does not overshadow the water surface, and do not depends on weather conditions. Tunnels are filled with air and anchored to the ocean bottom, therefore **they float below the surface of the ocean.** Anchors are flexible and they can absorb hard hits and great movements. Therefore these **external influences do not affect the high-speed trains inside the tubes.**

64,6m

tubes.Underneath the island, great turbines attached to the bottom convert ocean currents to energy, and artificial coral coats the surfaces, encouraging the development of new ecosystems.
As a settlement, the Ark has everything inhabitants need for comfort: residences, offices, recreation areas, parks and forests, and beaches.

0653

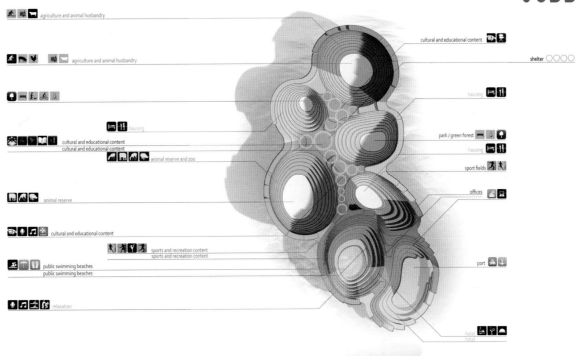

Underwater facades - These facades are covered with corals thus this structure is forming artificial coral islands and a natural environment for the water world.

Turbines that convert ocean current energy into electricity by forcing ocean water through them which then activate a generator.

Vertical communications

57m

section

O³ HEALER

Sang Jun Park

Republic of Korea

O³ HEALER
Ozone recover + Moving lab

OZONE WILL DEPLETE

Ozone layer is indispensable for protect nature from ultraviolet. Experts are warning and predicting that ozone layer will deplete 2/3 in 2065. It'll be cause to awful disaster for humankind and all of living creatures. It has been destroying by Chlorofluorocarbons and Nitro-oxide easily. There is no way to recover the ozone layer passively. Now is the time to be responsible for recover the ozone hole.

**Destruction of the ozone layer is creating awful aftereffects
How do we solve this problem?**
Recover Ozone layer from Antarctica

SITE ANALYSIS

Antarctica has a special condition that keep the night all day during April to September. On the contrary, white night* continues October to March. *White night : a night of the midnight sun on which it never gets completely dark. Min. temperature was recorded - 49˚C average wind velocity was 15 m/s and max. wind velocity was recoded 57 m/s . Antarctic wind power density is higher than any region in the world has the potential. Building or facility need to way of movement because of melting glaciers is to survive.

January   Feburary   March   October   November   December   Ratio of wind direction   Larsen Ice Antarctica 2010 (66)

MASS STUDY

Finding the form of a strong wind and gust from the computational fruid dynamics. Then Lower center of gravity to increase stand stability and I have focused on using wind turbines. Ducted wind turbine system can increase wind velocity and can regulate prevailing. Electricity used to produce ozone to heal the ozone layer and will operate the motor for move that need to avoid melting glacier.

Cylinder geometry for aerodynamic any direction

Meancurve shape 10% lower center of gravity

Revolve to three dimension

Turbine attach gravity center will improve stand stability

Subtract the air-turnel volume for wind turbine

Transform air-turnel to wind accelation

Make the air-turnel four directions for adaptation

Leg differentiation for mobility

Set the level of the legs

SKIN DEVELOPMENT

Can withstand very cold weather in Antarctica and movable light structure is membrane. This structure takes less time to build and Materials are lightweight, so it is easy to transport. For solid insulation and double-membrane structures thought to become regional interpretation of the system was L-shaped snowflake. It was from Sierpinski triangle and Koch snowflake I-system was developed using a strong structure.

Use a modified L-system (Koch snowflake) can be increased structural performance and can attach the membrane

To build and to aggregate three-dimensional surface with component. Choose the L-system (Sierpinski triangle) as a solution

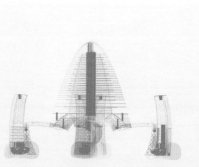

Strider's stance lowering your center of gravity position is extreme. At this time, using air sacs across the shallow sea, or it is advantageous to move faster.

Mobile position where the rugged terrain a disappear and power generation efficie

The ozone layer's depletion has posed a major threat to mankind for decades now, and O³ Healer in Antarctica can be seen as an ideal place to begin to restore the atmosphere, as the ozone layer is the thinnest over the south pole. It also has the highest wind density, which can be harnessed to provide ample energy to power this special skyscraper.

Missiles containing ozone particles are shot directly into the ozone hole from the skyscraper: the long, thin vessels are stored vertically in the center of the structure, and wind power helps propel them out the top, to an ultimate height of 25 km, whereupon the ozone particles are released. The building functions as "artillery" like a mounted electric rail gun. However the projectiles only use electricity without any chemical thrust powder and thus the ozone layer will be recovered with natural power.

0734

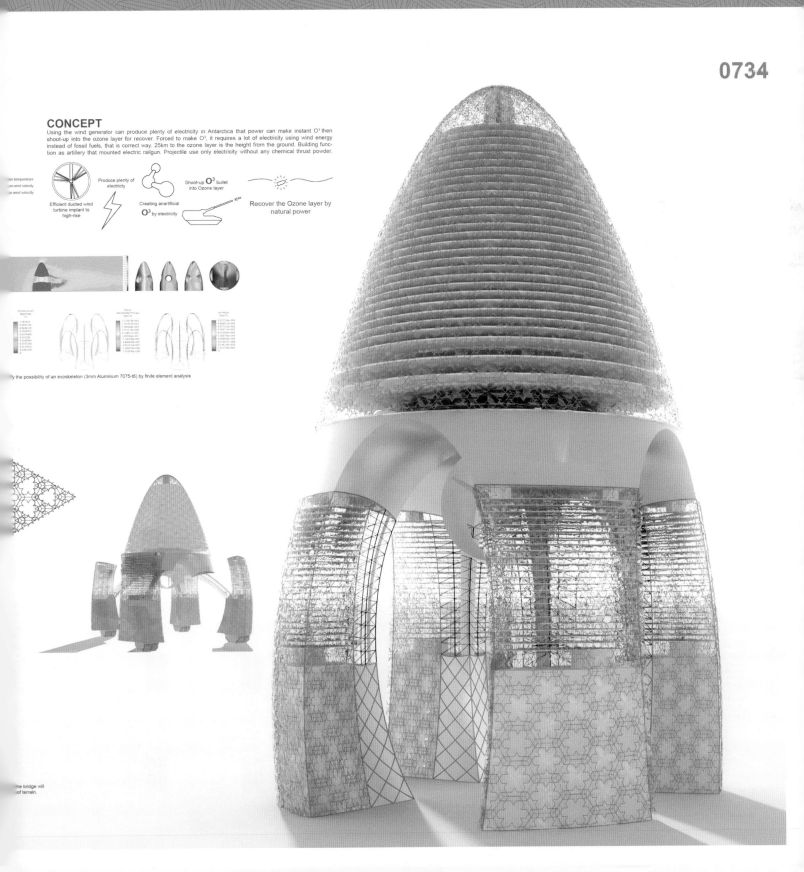

CONCEPT

Using the wind generator can produce plenty of electricity in Antarctica that power can make instant O³ then shoot-up into the ozone layer for recover. Forced to make O³, it requires a lot of electricity using wind energy instead of fossil fuels, that is correct way. 25km to the ozone layer is the height from the ground. Building function as artillery that mounted electric railgun. Projectile use only electricity without any chemical thrust powder.

Efficient ducted wind turbine implant to high-rise

Produce plenty of electricity

Creating an artificial O³ by electricity

Shoot-up O³ bullet into Ozone layer

Recover the Ozone layer by natural power

the possibility of an exoskeleton (3mm Aluminium 7075-t6) by finite element analysis

the bridge will of terrain.

In the middle of the bullet-shaped structure, which is supported by 3 arched legs, there are bisecting tunnels that are filled with turbines to generate energy from the wind. The building is covered in a "snowflake" skin of lightweight but solid material that coats the exterior in double HDPE membranes to keep in warmth but not weigh the structure down. Staying lightweight is important because the terrain in the Antarctic is rugged and icebergs melt, so the skyscraper needs to be mobile. The building's thick legs are put into place first so as to settle in the ground of the skyscraper's new location; only after the legs are stable is the top added.

The interior spaces of the building's major elements also support programs. For example, each leg of the building supports a 25-story research and lab facility. Up the main part of the structure, floors serve different purposes, but the

O³ HEALER
FLOOR PLAN - DETAIL - SECTION

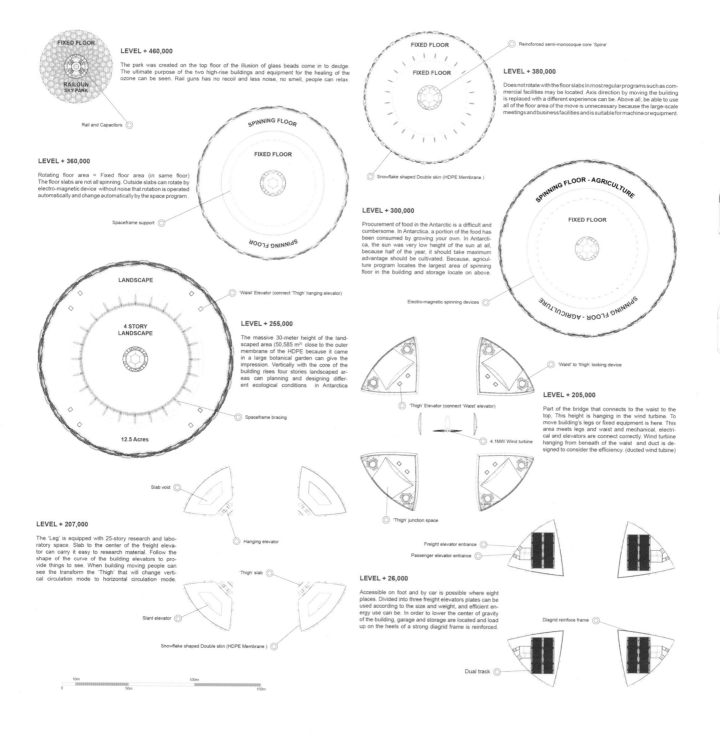

FIXED FLOOR
RAILGUN SKY PARK

Rail and Capacitors

LEVEL + 460,000

The park was created on the top floor of the illusion of glass beads come in to deulge. The ultimate purpose of the two high-rise buildings and equipment for the healing of the ozone can be seen. Rail guns has no recoil and less noise, no smell, people can relax.

SPINNING FLOOR
FIXED FLOOR
SPINNING FLOOR

Spaceframe support

LEVEL + 360,000

Rotating floor area = Fixed floor area (in same floor) The floor slabs are not all spinning. Outside slabs can rotate by electro-magnetic device without noise that rotation is operated automatically and change automatically by the space program .

LANDSCAPE
4 STORY LANDSCAPE
12.5 Acres

'Waist' Elevator (connect 'Thigh' hanging elevator)

Spaceframe bracing

LEVEL + 255,000

The massive 30-meter height of the land-scaped area (50,585 m²) close to the outer membrane of the HDPE because it came in a large botanical garden can give the impression. Vertically with the core of the building rises four stories landscaped areas can planning and designing different ecological conditions in Antarctica

Slab void

LEVEL + 207,000

The 'Leg' is equipped with 25-story research and laboratory space. Slab to the center of the freight elevator can carry it easy to research material. Follow the shape of the curve of the building elevators to provide things to see. When building moving people can see the transform the 'Thigh' that will change vertical circulation mode to horizontal circulation mode.

Hanging elevator

'Thigh' slab

Slant elevator

Snowflake shaped Double skin (HDPE Membrane)

FIXED FLOOR
FIXED FLOOR

Reincforced semi-monocoque core 'Spine'

LEVEL + 380,000

Does not rotate with the floor slabs In most regular programs such as commercial facilities may be located. Axis direction by moving the building is replaced with a different experience can be. Above all, be able to use all of the floor area of the move is unnecessary because the large-scale meetings and business facilities and is suitable for machine or equipment.

Snowflake shaped Double skin (HDPE Membrane)

LEVEL + 300,000

Procurement of food in the Antarctic is a difficult and cumbersome. In Antarctica, a portion of the food has been consumed by growing your own. In Antarctica, the sun was very low height of the sun at all, because half of the year, it should take maximum advantage should be cultivated. Because, agriculture program locates the largest area of spinning floor in the building and storage locate on above.

Electro-magnetic spinning devices

SPINNING FLOOR - AGRICULTURE
FIXED FLOOR
SPINNING FLOOR - AGRICULTURE

'Waist' to 'thigh' locking device

LEVEL + 205,000

Part of the bridge that connects to the waist to the top, This height is hanging in the wind turbine. To move building's legs or fixed equipment is here. This area meets legs and waist and mechanical, electrical and elevators are connect correctly. Wind turbine hanging from beneath of the waist and duct is designed to consider the efficiency. (ducted wind tubine)

'Thigh' Elevator (connect 'Waist' elevator)

4.1MW Wind turbine

'Thigh' junction space

Freight elevator entrance
Passenger elevator entrance

LEVEL + 26,000

Accessible on foot and by car is possible where eight places. Divided into three freight elevators plates can be used according to the size and weight, and efficient energy use can be. In order to lower the center of gravity of the building, garage and storage are located and load up on the heels of a strong diagrid frame is reinforced.

Diagrid reinfoce frame

Dual track

10m   100m
0   50m   150m

majority of spaces serve as agriculture floors that have an outer band that can spin and turn to face the weak South Pole sun, ensuring that food can be grown year-round for the researchers within. There are also floors that feature residences, control rooms and a sky lounge.

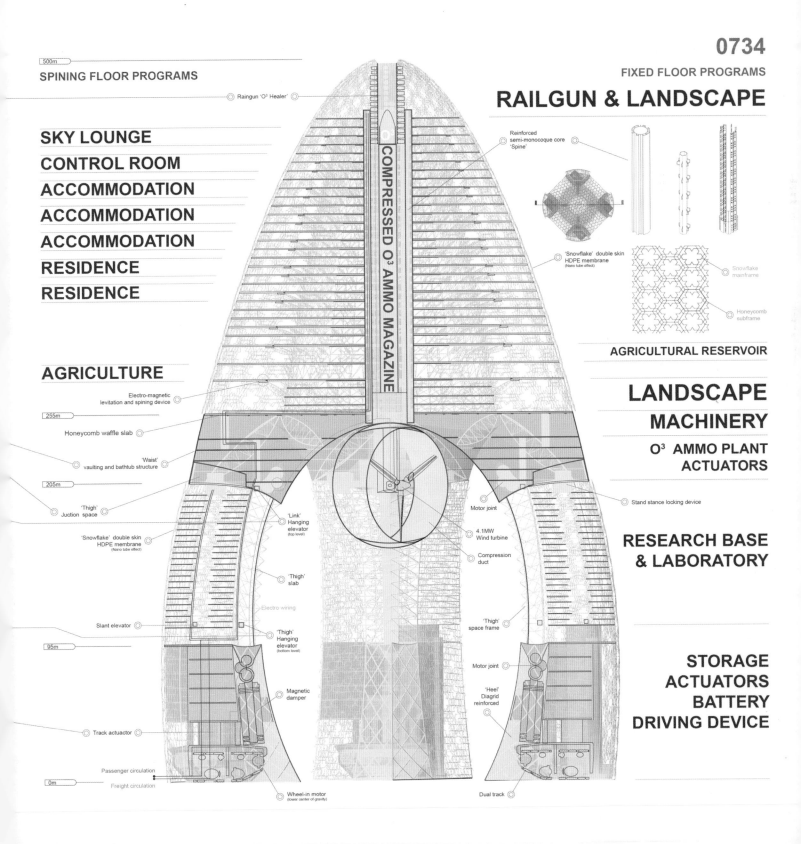

0734
FIXED FLOOR PROGRAMS

RAILGUN & LANDSCAPE

SPINING FLOOR PROGRAMS

SKY LOUNGE
CONTROL ROOM
ACCOMMODATION
ACCOMMODATION
ACCOMMODATION
RESIDENCE
RESIDENCE

AGRICULTURE

500m

Raingun 'O³ Healer'

COMPRESSED O³ AMMO MAGAZINE

Reinforced semi-monocoque core 'Spine'

'Snowflake' double skin HDPE membrane (Nano tube effect)

Snowflake mainframe

Honeycomb subframe

AGRICULTURAL RESERVOIR

LANDSCAPE
MACHINERY
O³ AMMO PLANT
ACTUATORS

Electro-magnetic levitation and spining device

255m

Honeycomb waffle slab

'Waist' vaulting and bathtub structure

205m

'Thigh' Juction space

'Snowflake' double skin HDPE membrane (Nano tube effect)

'Link' Hanging elevator (top level)

'Thigh' slab

Electro-wiring

Slant elevator

95m

'Thigh' Hanging elevator (bottom level)

Magnetic damper

Track actuactor

Passenger circulation

0m

Freight circulation

Wheel-in motor (lower center of gravity)

Motor joint

4.1MW Wind turbine

Compression duct

Stand stance locking device

RESEARCH BASE
& LABORATORY

'Thigh' space frame

Motor joint

'Heel' Diagrid reinforced

Dual track

STORAGE
ACTUATORS
BATTERY
DRIVING DEVICE

CONDENSATION CONSERVANCY

Yu Sung Eung
Bae Tae Goan

Republic of Korea

CHANGE
CONDENSATION
CONSERVANCY

Though humankind has strived for thousands of years to conquer nature, through technology and architecture and engineering, with the thought of securing comfort, the true result has been the onset of myriad natural disasters. One of these, desertification, has had a profound effect on land in Mongolia already due to climate change. This case study examines the tribes of nomad goat herders living in Mongolia, and a site in particular that is located next to a lake— land that was once fertile but is quickly becoming barren.

The area's nomads collect and herd goats to make cashmere, and as they breed more animals to make more money, the land is cleared at an accelerated rate as the growing number of goats graze and eat away the ground cover. In addition, the chlorine left in the plant roots spoils the ground, leading to an alarming rate of acceleration in the

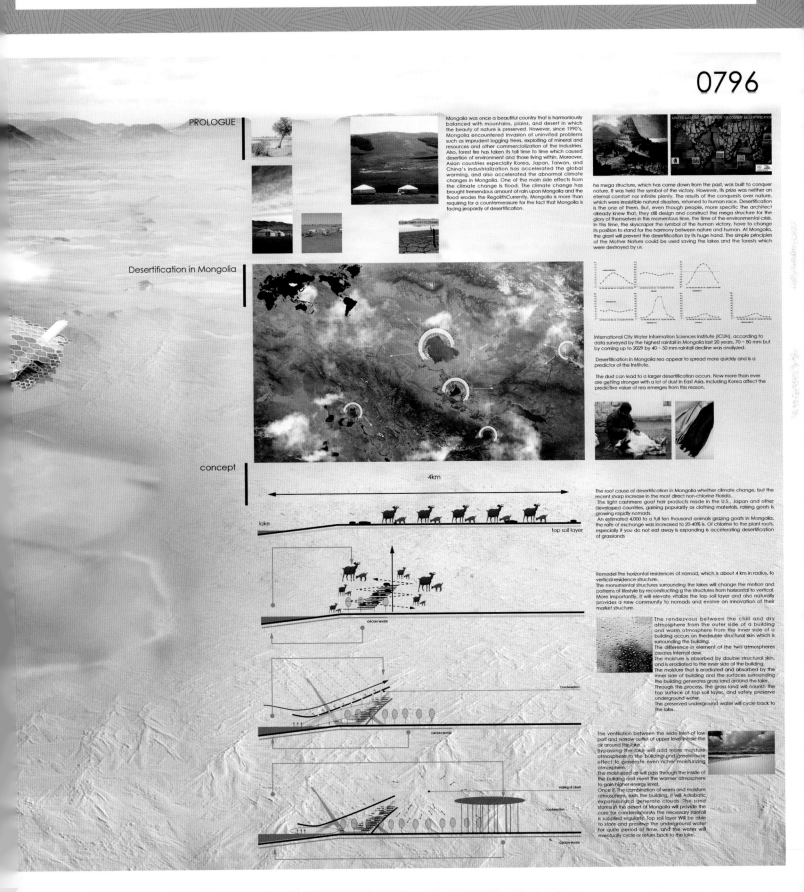

desertification effect in that region.

By relocating this tribe, which occupies an area with a 4 km radius, into vertical structures, the land's top layer of soil will be allowed to revitalize. The plan calls for the construction of an above ground, half-moon-shaped platform that is supported, like a large bridge, with towers and cables. It is located along the lake waterfront, and is completely coated with a double skin that traps heat; when the cool desert air interacts with the skin, which is warm from the building's interior, an internal dew is created inside of the skin. This fresh water flows down the skin to the ground, watering the parched surrounding land and helping further its regeneration.

The strategies this project uses include the double ETFE structural skin and its steel honeycombed structure

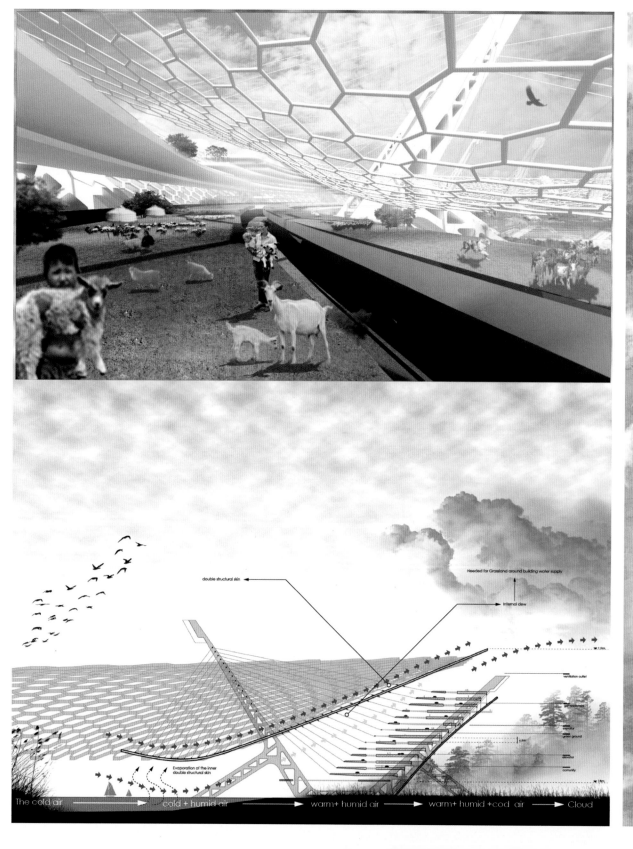

which combine strength and lightrness.The honeycombed grill leads to more contact surface which means more heat conductivity and more dew to be generated. The strategies used also include the convex ETFE membrane to further increase surface area and the insolation collecting surface for diffuse light to be harnessed.

   The lake's proximity and the natural humidity it creates aids in this process. As the top level of soil is replenished, excess water is able to be stored underground to feed the lake and further revitalize the ecology of the area as a whole.

160

TOWER 3
AGRÓPOLIS

Guiomar Contreras Ruiz

Spain

TOWER 3_ AGRÓPOLIS IN MADRID (San Chinarro)
FRESH LIVING VEGETABLE MARKET

TOWER 1   TOWER 2   TO

TOWER COOPERATION

- TOWER 1: PLANTS GERMINATION
- TOWER 2: PLANT MATURATION
- TOWER 3: **FRESH LIVING VEGETABLE MARKET**
- TOWER 4: SEED BANK AND LABORATORY

FROM HORIZONTAL TO VERTICAL: URBAN FARM PRINCIPLE

FOR ORGANIC VERTICAL FARMING:

FOR IRRIGATION: URBAN WATER RECYCLING SYSTEMS: PHYTOTECHNOLOGY
FOR LICUID AND SOLID ORGANIC NUTRIENT: WARMCULTURE
FOOD FOR WARMS: URBAN ORGANIC WASTE

HOUSING AND FARM COOPERATION   HOUSES — GREEN HOUSE

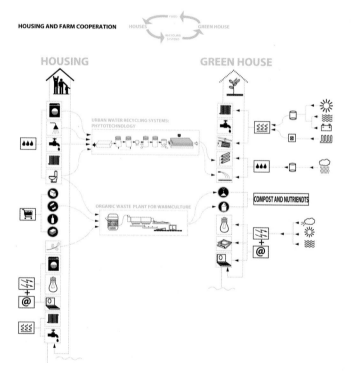

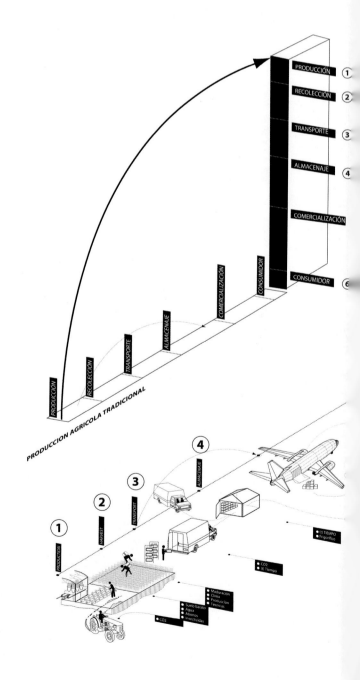

TOWER 3 PROGRAMME: FRESH LIVING VEGETABLE MARKET

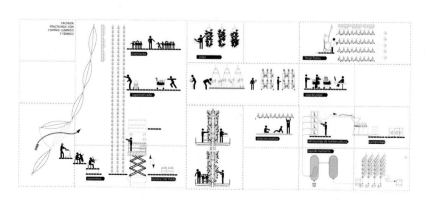

We are living in an agro-industrial era where production and consumption are growing apart from each other, and commercialization and distribution have become economic and power filters. Work and consumption feed each other the same way production and commercialization do. As this happens, distribution and transportation of these products become the main platforms for this system to work. At the same time we are entering a slow but profound climate change and because of that intensive agriculture will have to become more and more independent.

Intensive agriculture has to do directly with the city's food demand. While population increases, the direct

1057

PRODUCCIÓN

Implica una de las bases fijas de Agrópolis, y por lo tanto la que da en, en principio, sentido al concepto. Se trata de una agricultura intensiva vertical, aúnque ecológica y respeturosa con los recursos que la capacitan para desarrollarse, desde su formalización-construcción hasta su desarrollo.
Los diferentes aspectos tecnológicos se componen para maximizar el rendimiento de estos recursos. Tanto el agua como los residuos urbano se reciclan para dar alimento a los cultivos.
La forma de gestión de estos espacios sería a nivel de cooperativas-sociedades-consorcios, etc. Estas alquilarían los espacios de alto rendimiento, manteniendo una cuota mínima de productividad.

RECOLECCIÓN

La recolección se transforma en un aspecto más directo y cercano al consumidor, tanto, que el mismo puede recolectar su propia cesta de la compra o si lo prefiere hacer un pedido y el personal se lo corta en el momento.

TRANSPORTE

El transporte se reduce al mínimo. Son ascensores y grúas los que acercan el producto al consumidor. El producto siempre llega fresco y en tiempo de maduracion óptimo ya que no tiene que recorrer largas distancias.

ALMACENAJE

Así mismo el almacenaje se reduce en gran medida, ya que la planta se mantiene viva hasta el mismo momento de la consumición.

COMERCIALIZACIÓN

Se ahorra en intermediarios. El productor conectado directamente con el consumidor. La imágen del producto es el propio producto vivo. Aunque existen subastas para "exportar" a la propia ciudad.

CONSUMIDOR

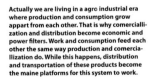

Actually we are living in a agro industrial era where production and consumption grow apart from each other. That is why comercialization and distribution become economic and power filters. Work and consumption feed each other the same way production and comercialization do. While this happens, distribution and transportation of these products become the maine platforms for this system to work.

At the same time whe are entering into an slow but profound climate change, and for that intensive agriculture will have to become more and more independent of this fact. This is happening already.

Intensive agriculture has to do directly with city´s food demand. So while population increases, the direct consequences of increasing agriculture land are not bearable.

Agrópolis is a general term that covers the concept of biological-ecological-organic urban agriculture in any part of the word. That means that the basic concepts will be applied depending of the place and the specific needs.

The basic concepts that able urban agriculture:
-Hidroponic ore low water consuming systems
-Recycle urban grey and black water for irrigation
-Recycle urban organic waste for nutrients
-Agricultural biodiversity

consequences of increasing agriculture land are unbearable. Agrópolis is a general term that covers the concept of biological-ecological-organic urban agriculture in any part of the word. Tower 3 Agrópolis includes the basic concepts that make up urban agriculture. In this project, hydroponic or low water consuming systems are implemented. Urban grey and black water is recycled for irrigation, and urban organic waste is used for nutrients.

   Tower 3 (the fresh living vegetable market) is part of a 4 tower system including Tower 1 (plant germination), Tower 2 (plant maturation) and Tower 4 (seed bank and laboratory). The towers support each

TOWER 3_ AGRÓPOLIS IN MADRID (San Chinarro)
FRESH LIVING VEGETABLE MARKET

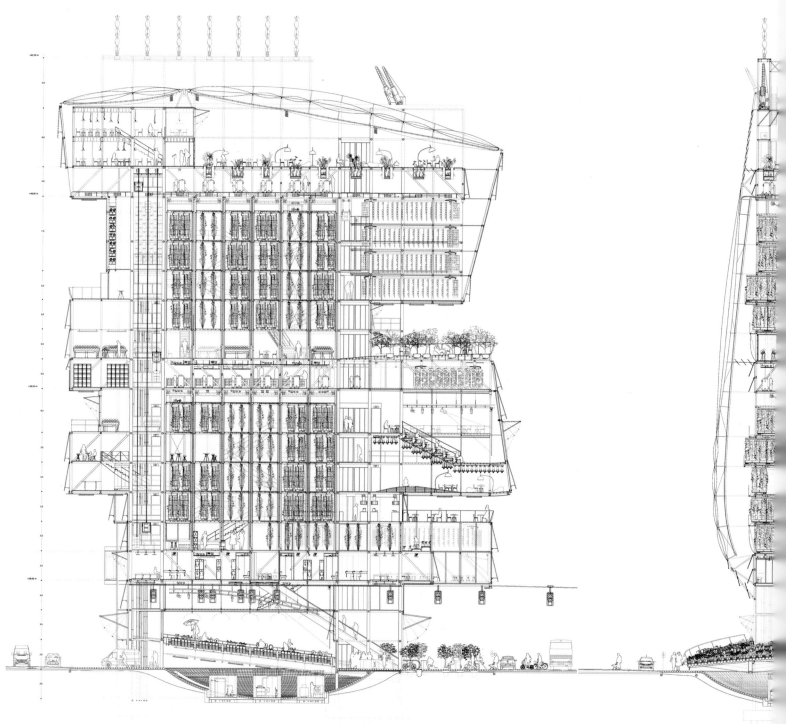

other in terms of research and functionality as well as for housing and farm cooperation. The process of agricultural production is thus put into a vertical program and includes all the necessary stages: consuming, commercializing, storing, transporting, recollecting, and production.

The basic concepts that enable this project and its urban agricultural characteristic include hydroponic ore low water consuming systems, recycling water for irrigation, recycling urban organic waste for nutrients and agricultural biodiversity. Transportation is kept to a minimum as products are consumed within the immediate area of where they are freshly cultivated and grown.

1057

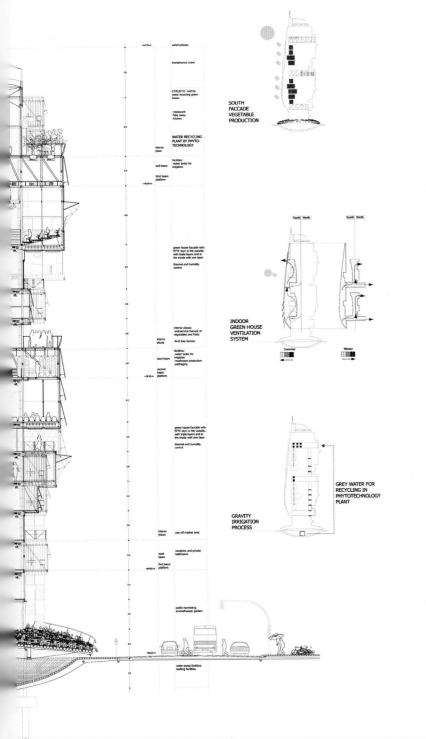

BUILDING PROCESS:

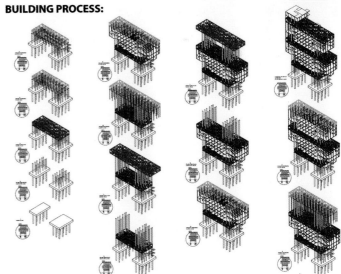

SOUTH FACCADE IRRIGATION SYSTEM:

TRADITIONAL AGRICULTURE PROCESS:

1_ROOF TOP WATER RECYCLING TANKS

2_IRRIGATION TANKS MIXT WITH NUTRIENTS

3_WARMOLOGY LIQUID FLUID PRODUCTION PLANT

4_AXIS ROTATION GROWING SYSTEM

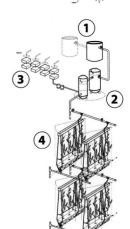

GAPLANT

Maya Ben Shmuel
Adi Cohen

Israel

A new city skyline is to be created in favor of the gaps. The urban void between buildings is to become the city's accelerator.

Tel Aviv, Israel, was planned in a semi-orthogonal grid while ensuring a consistent gap between every building. These gaps were initially planned in order to enable airflow from the nearby sea into the depths of the city. Today, these gaps, along with their original purpose, became unused empty places that inhabit mostly garbage and dirt. These are places that unfortunately lack urban activity.

This project creates an opportunity for inner growth and a platform to emerge positive urban density. A new city skyline is to be created in favor of the gaps. Urban density, like natural growth, wishes to grow in places where it is sometimes impossible.

The given urban situation in the world today, deals with an increasing need of building density and ongoing questions about the lack of potential building grounds. While at the same time emerges a deliberation about the existence of unexploited territories and the hunt after a proper way of using them in order to enable an inner urban growth of the city, using its existing grounds within. Combining both, the need of density and unexploited territories, might bring the solution for that inner growth and the capacity of the city to evolve and offer new urban situations in places where it seems impossible. Tel -aviv , located in Israel, like many other cities, deals with the same questions. The city was planned in a semi orthogonal grid while ensuring a consisting gap between all buildings. These gaps were initially planned in order to enable air flow from the nearby sea into the depth of the city. Today, these gaps, along with their original purpose , became unused and empty places that inhabit mostly garbage and dirt. Places that lack urban activity although existing in the heart of the city.

The project creates an opportunity for that inner growth and a platform to emerge positive urban density. A new city skyline is to be created in favor of the gaps. The urban void between buildings is to become the city's accelerator. Urban density, much like natural growth, wishes to grow in places where it is sometimes impossible. The project is inspired by the world of plants. Drawing principles of growing while maintaining minimal ground footprint due to the small space of the gap and due to its basic given character of which it is unable to stand as an urban functional place on its own. The minimal footprint does not decrease the original intent of the gap, but adds new urban contents into it. Urban contents that take place in a vertical scheme due to the dimensions of the gap. The project leans on the existing buildings but also exists as an individual unit. The project offers an extension to the existing commerce area located on the street and new dwelling units that rises above the existing buildings. The vertical scheme offers a new garden level which is located on the rooftops of the existing buildings for the use of residences from the new project as well as the inhabitants of the existing buildings.

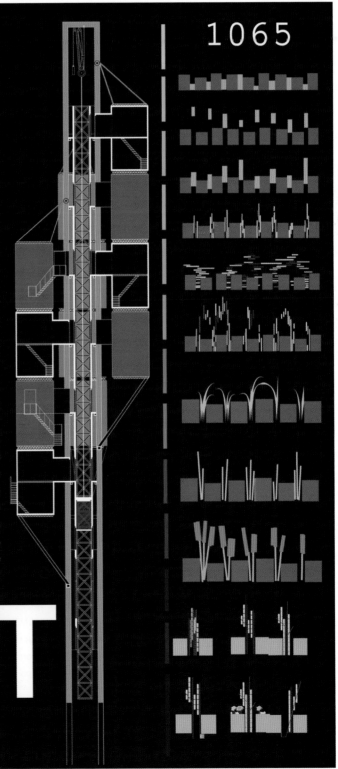

1065

GAPLANT

PLANT THE GAP

The project is inspired by the world of plants. Drawing principles from growing while maintaining minimal ground footprint due to the small space of the gap. The minimal footprint does not decrease the original intent of the gap, but adds new urban contents into it: urban contents taking place in a vertical scheme.

Offering an extension to the existing commerce area located on the street and new dwelling units that rise above the existing buildings, the vertical scheme features a new garden level located on the rooftops of the existing buildings for the use of residents from the new project as well as the inhabitants of the existing buildings. The air circulation of the existing buildings is not harmed due to maintaining airflow by a minimal

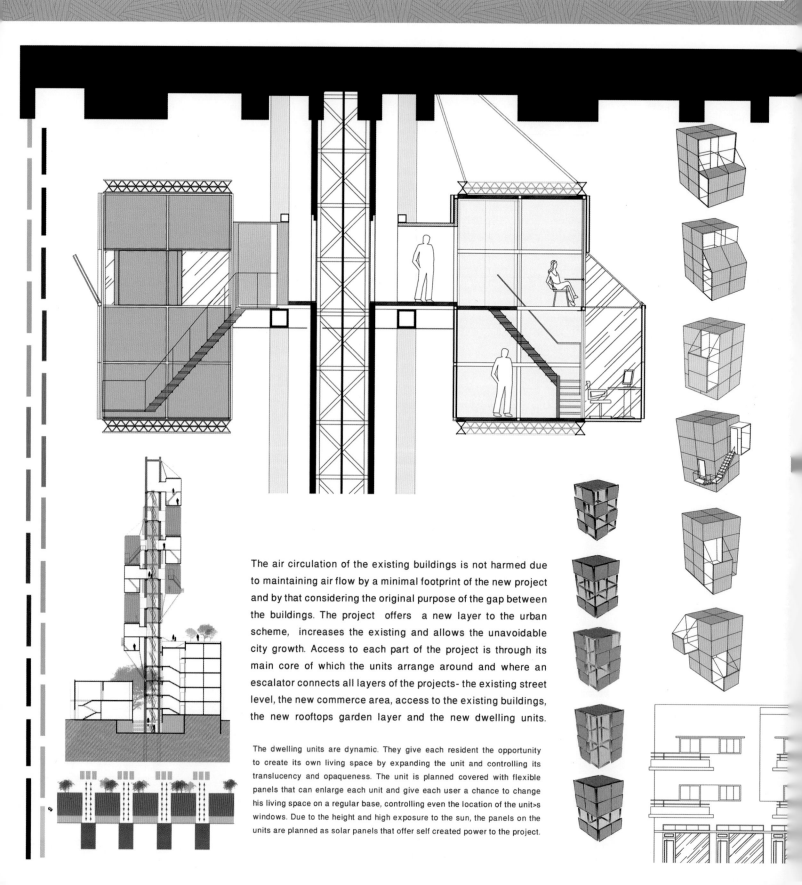

The air circulation of the existing buildings is not harmed due to maintaining air flow by a minimal footprint of the new project and by that considering the original purpose of the gap between the buildings. The project offers a new layer to the urban scheme, increases the existing and allows the unavoidable city growth. Access to each part of the project is through its main core of which the units arrange around and where an escalator connects all layers of the projects- the existing street level, the new commerce area, access to the existing buildings, the new rooftops garden layer and the new dwelling units.

The dwelling units are dynamic. They give each resident the opportunity to create its own living space by expanding the unit and controlling its translucency and opaqueness. The unit is planned covered with flexible panels that can enlarge each unit and give each user a chance to change his living space on a regular base, controlling even the location of the unit>s windows. Due to the height and high exposure to the sun, the panels on the units are planned as solar panels that offer self created power to the project.

footprint of the new project and by considering the original purpose of the gap between buildings.

Access to each part of the project is through the main core and where an escalator connects all layers of the project.The dwelling units are dynamic giving each resident the opportunity to create his or her own living space by expanding the unit and controlling its translucency and opaqueness.

The unit is covered with flexible panels that can enlarge each unit and give each user a chance to change his living space, and even the location of the unit's windows. Due to height and high exposure to the sun, the panels on the units are planned as solar panels that offer self-created power to the project.

1065

URBAN EARTH WORM

Lee Seungsoo

Republic of Korea

Urban Eearth Worm
penetration into the city

The pollution(air, soil), waste disposal and energy production, agricultural production is a big problem in modern cities. These problems are to be solved effectively in cramped cities. But In the city there are no site already can not afford.

Accordingly Urban Earth Warm consumes (charge) the (small scale) Energy Station in a city(high density) and solves several problems at once.

The Urban Earth Worm skyscraper uses one of the simplest of creatures as its inspiration. Just as earthworms clean the soil and solve pollution problems, promulgating life in thriving ecosystems, this skyscraper will clean air and soil pollution in cities and also feed cities—literally.

The structure is in fact even shaped like a worm, horizontally extending and curving throughout the city, cleaning the air, processing waste and providing food in not just one but many points.

The top part of the structure has growing tubes that are filled with soil and grow trees and plants. This green area cleans the city's air and also provides crops for the city's residents.

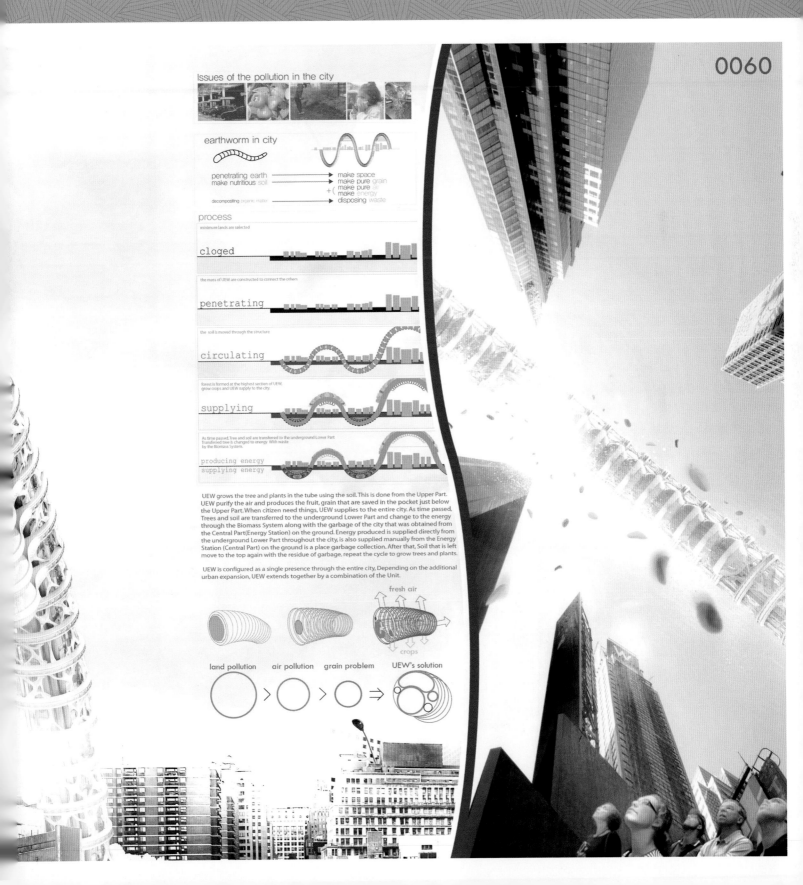

0060

Issues of the pollution in the city

earthworm in city

penetrating earth → make space
make nutritious soil → make pure grain
+ (make pure air
make energy
decompositing organic matter → disposing waste

process

minimum lands are selected

cloged

the mass of UEW are constructed to connect the others

penetrating

the soil is moved through the structure

circulating

forest is formed at the highest section of UEW, grow crops and UEW supply to the city.

supplying

As time passed, Tree and soil are transferred to the underground Lower Part. Transferred tree is changed to energy With waste by the Biomass System.

producing energy
supplying energy

UEW grows the tree and plants in the tube using the soil. This is done from the Upper Part. UEW purify the air and produces the fruit, grain that are saved in the pocket just below the Upper Part. When citizen need things, UEW supplies to the entire city. As time passed, Trees and soil are transferred to the underground Lower Part and change to the energy through the Biomass System along with the garbage of the city that was obtained from the Central Part(Energy Station) on the ground. Energy produced is supplied directly from the underground Lower Part throughout the city, is also supplied manually from the Energy Station (Central Part) on the ground is a place garbage collection. After that, Soil that is left move to the top again with the residue of garbage, repeat the cycle to grow trees and plants.

UEW is configured as a single presence through the entire city, Depending on the additional urban expansion, UEW extends together by a combination of the Unit.

fresh air

crops

land pollution   air pollution   grain problem   UEW's solution

An energy station near the ground (but still within the worm) takes the city's garbage and processes it into biomass from which energy can be generated. This energy fuels the skyscraper's own processes but also is sent back to the city.

The biomass is also used to replenish the soil that is used to grow the trees and crops in upper levels. Soil is periodically transported down to the energy station and mixed with biomass. It is left to sit for some time and replenish its nutrients. When that process is complete, it is transported back up to the growing levels, and the soil already up there is moved down to be regenerated.

section

city view

suck/spit part

Urban Earth Worm grows trees and plants in the tube with soil and is done from the upper part. It purifies the air and produces fruits and grains that are saved in the pocket just below the upper part. When citizens need resources, the project will supply it. As time passes trees and soil are transferred to the underground lower part and change to energy through the biomass system along with the garbage of the city that is obtained from the central part. Energy produced is supplied directly from the underground lower part throughout the city and is supplied manually from the energy station on the ground. After that, soil that is left is moved to the top again with the residue of garbage, where the cycle of growing plants is repeated.

0060

crop pocket

bimass plant

underground

Energy Station

WATER
RE-BALANCE

Liu Chunyao
Zhang Zhiyang

China

WATER RE-BALANCE

Shanghai's distribution of water resources is out of balance

CURRENT SUITATION

1.Lack of groundwater

Since 1860, people in Shanghai started to exploit underground water, Shanghai has drilled for so much water that land in the center of the city has sunk 1.7m in the past 40 years. Facing the problem of both land subsidence and sea level rise, shanghai will be submerged in sea water.

2. Lack of municipal water

Although Shanghai has rich water resources, after considering both upstream water and local water pollution, we consider Shanghai as a typical city of lacking quality water which has exacerbated water supply shortages.

3. Adequate rainfall

Shanghai's average annual rainfall in recent 5 years is 1178.2 mm, north of tropical monsoon climate, sufficient sunlight, adequate rainfall, three pluvials per year.

4. Suzhou river's high water level

Suzhou river's water level rises quickly during pluvial, the construction of the dams costs a lot, sometimes water can reach the street level.

STRATEGIES

Based on the situation, we want to build a water project, to rebalance the distribution of water.

We collect and purify rainwater and water in Suzhou river for daily water supply in the community, and injecting the recycled water underground at the same time. We can balance the amount of rainwater, underground water and river water. The re-balance and the co-ordination of the three can reduce the disasters. Moreover, we use the organic matter obtained by filtering water to develop farm, wetland, and to cultivate green alga. The flora contribute to our "clean air zones". The energy provided by green algae and hydraulic generator is utilized by the community.

THE FUTURE INFULUENCE

1. To recovery supplement groundwater resources, thus sloving the problem of land subsidence.

2. To purify Suzhou river and provide sufficient water supply for the city.

3. To ease the pressure of the flood controling and we can lower the water level of suzhou river.

4.To solve the high-density and high-population urban planning problems by forming a self-sufficiency and multi-function community.

5. To use the vertical eco-system to form "Clean air zones".

6. Wetlands along the river and vertical park provides public space for citizens.

7. Reorganize the special sceneries and form a new symbol of Shanghai.

This project begins with the premise that Shanghai's distribution of water resources is out of balance. The first problem is a lack of groundwater; the people of Shanghai, in the quest for clean water, have taken so much water from under the city since 1860 that the city itself has sunk 1.7 meters in the past 40 years. Additionally, the water supplies that do exist today are largely polluted. Despite that shortage, the city does experience flooding in monsoon season, and the Suzhou River's level can sometimes reach the city's streets.

By building towers that can collect and purify rainwater and also purify the water from the river, several

0094

advantageous things occur: clean, drinkable water is readily available for the city, rising river levels are mitigated before flooding occurs, and clean water can be pumped back under ground to fix the sinking subsidence problem the city is experiencing. Furthermore, the tower collects organic matter as it filters the water and uses that waste to develop and feed farmland, wetlands, and to grow green algae. The farm and wetlands purify the air, and the algae is cultivated and processed within the tower by a generator to create energy.

The tower is thin and is based underground, allowing the structure to pump collected and cleaned

rainwater into the underground water table. From this base it spirals up and flowers at the top with a large platform that holds a green roof that collects the rainwater. After it is collected on top, water filters as it flows down through the tower, and is clean by the time it reaches ground level. There, a pump either directs the water for use by the city, or it is sent underground. Grey water is also captured and used to irrigate the vertical gardens throughout the structure. Turbines are also placed through the spiraling tower to generate energy with the water flow. That energy, plus that generated by the algae, creates enough to both power the tower itself and send energy back into the city.

0094

1. When underground water is sufficient, water can go up to supply the community and river.

2. When the rainwater reserves is sufficient and quantity of underground water or river water is insufficient, water goes down to supply the underground

3. When the flood comes, accelerated water flow towards the vertical community and underground, thus easing the flood threats.

WORKING MECHANISM

VERTICAL COMMUNITY PLAN

VERTICAL FARM PLAN

ALGAE POWER PLANT PLAN

TICAL WETLAND PARK PLAN

DATA ANALYSIS

VERTICAL COMMUNITY

VERTICAL FARM

ALGAE POWER PLANT

VERTICAL WETLAND PARK

RECHARGE OF GROUND WATER

FLOOD

LEVEE

LAND SUBSIDENCE

MIGRATORY BIRD TOWER

Dongbo Han
Wente Pan
Yilei Xu
Chao Yue

United Kingdom

MIGRATORY BIRD TOWER

Today many metropolises on the world prove deadly for migratory birds, breaking down the route of migration and killing numerous birds with glass towers. In Toronto, one of the most deadly cities for migratory birds, it is estimated that one million to nine million birds die every year from impact with buildings in the Toronto area. To protect the birds from the urban skyscrapers, it is necessary to alter the traditional skyline of the city and create a bird habitat above the city.

We want to explore the use of wood in the building of skyscrapers. The wood sticks provide proper habitat for birds at the same time act as a structure for themselves. The architecture also combines bird research center and bird museum, acting as a educational place for people. It reminds people the importance of respecting nature and it is time to rethink the today's planning of most cities.

Window strikes estimated to kill 97 to 976 million birds/year – Millions of houses and buildings, with their billions of windows, pose a significant threat to birds. Birds see the natural habitat mirrored in the glass and fly directly into the window, causing injury and, in 50% or more of the cases, death. Simple steps can be taken to reduce the number of birds striking windows. Decals that stick to the glass are not very effective, but strips of tape on the outside of the glass, or strings or feathers hanging outside the window, each no more than 10 inches apart, are fairly effective. Decorative features like stained glass designs or window dividers can achieve the same result. Outside screens are very effective both to reduce the reflection and to cushion the impact. In short, anything that reduces or breaks up the window's reflection will reduce bird strikes.

A tragic consequence of urban development has been an increase in bird mortality. The construction of metropolises not only disrupts migratory patterns for birds, but has also led to an alarming number of bird deaths due to collisions with skyscrapers. It is estimated that between one and nine million birds die annually in Toronto alone as result of the impact of collisions with windows of glass towers, making the threat to the various species' survival more grave than any other predator or disease. This project proposes the creation of a bird haven above skyscraper skylines of the world's major cities in an effort to mitigate this problem.

The Migratory Bird Tower is comprised of a circular, enclosed metal core that is braced by a large-

0199

scale, angular metal mesh; both ascend high into the sky. The metal beams of the mesh support open-air platforms and also large planks of wood that extend into the surrounding airspace and stack and cross each other to resemble a bird nest. The wood beams, whose densities and lengths can be changed to serve particular species' needs, act as literal perches and temporary homes for migrating birds, and also permanently support plant life, as vertical vines grow and twist to fortify the structure. Some wood beams extend directly from the metal structure; others are joined to wood beams, creating a jumble of planks that indeed replicates, on a massive scale, the intertwined twigs that comprise a bird nest.

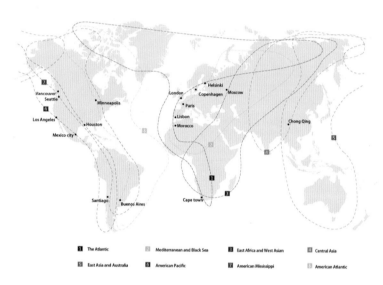

| 1 The Atlantic | 2 Mediterranean and Black Sea | 3 East Africa and West Asian | 4 Central Asia |
| 5 East Asia and Australia | 6 American Pacific | 7 American Mississippi | 8 American Atlantic |

Bird migration is the regular seasonal journey undertaken by many species of birds, which include those made in response to changes in food availability, habitat, or weather. Migration is marked by its annual seasonality. Approximately 1800 of the world's 10,000 bird species are long-distance migrants. This image shows thtere are eight major bird migration routes in the world: The Atlantic, Mediterranean, East Africa and West Asian, Central Asia, East Asia and Australia, American Pacific, American Mississippi, American Atlantic. When they migration, they will meet several large cities which may pose a threat to them. As a result, our tower will locate in these cities so they may provide a safety place for them.

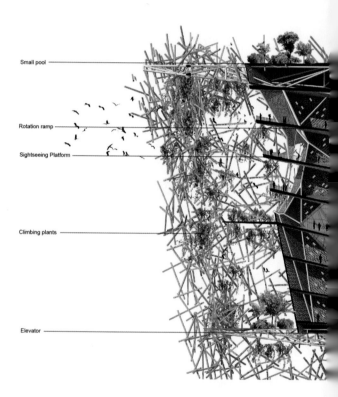

Small pool

Rotation ramp

Sightseeing Platform

Climbing plants

Elevator

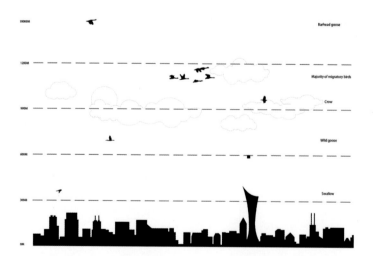

The flight altitude of bird migration is generally not more than 1000 meters. Small songbirds flying height is generally no more than 300 meters, some of the large birds are up to 3000-6300 meters, some large species (such as bar-head goose) are over Mount Everest whose altitude is 9000 meters. The height of the migration of the birds at night is often lower than during the day. Therefore, our tower height is nearly 400 meters which is almost the tallest building in the city so they can escape the dangerous from human being.

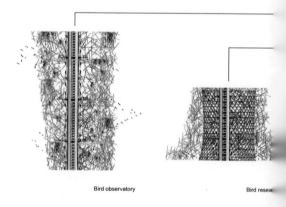

Bird observatory   Bird resea

The building's tall, narrow core, which uses an elevator to transport people, holds many uses specifically aimed at promulgating bird survival, including a bird research center and bird museum, which seeks to educate the public. The open-air platforms allow visitors great views of bird life and collectively operate as an observatory. Small pools are interspersed among the wooden beams of the "nest" to provide water for birds.

By strategically locating Migratory Bird Towers in metropolises across the globe and building them above the skylines that hold dangerous glass skyscrapers and other built dangers, birds can be guaranteed safe havens in at least these locations.

0199

Bird museum

...spiration from the formation of the bird nest. By repeating one piece ...can create a large structure. The wood stick is suitable for the perch ...the growth of climbing plants. By connecting every sticks, we can ...ial structure model. The density of the sticks can also be changed ...the need of the birds.

AQUAPONIC TOWER

Adiran Calitz
Minh-Khoi Nguyen-Thanh
Jian Yang

Germany

AQUAPONIC
FEEDING THE WORLD **TOWER**

As the world's population continues to rapidly swell, food scarcity becomes a problem at the fore of future crises. The world's current population of 6.8 billion is projected to grow to 9.1 billion by 2050, requiring a significant increase in food production. Despite this, urbanization continues to be the prominent residential trend globally, with UN estimates saying that 50 percent of people live in cities. Such growth patterns decrease acreage available for food production, and also further fuel a cycle where cities import most of their food, wasting vast amounts of fossil fuels and energy in the process.

The aquaponic tower inserts aquaponic ecosystems, or closed system growing tanks where different

0210

Case

This is not a Farming Tower - this is a concept for an idea, a solution to a problem that can be solved with the utilization of the technology we have readily at hand. We have chosen to address the fore casted rise in population and demand for food and clean air, to avoid the sharp rise in use of transport and to somehow provide our most basic needs.

Growth of Population

UN world population statistics indicate we have a 6.8 billion person population on the planet. This number is set to increase by 34% by 2050, giving us the massive task of providing for 9.1 Billion people. The statistics show that this increase will happen predominantly in developing countries. With malnutrition across the board with a population of 6.8 billion people an increase of 70% (minimum) in world food production is required, new techniques to provide to the bulging population will have to be incorporated.

Urbanization

The United Nations states that 50% of the total world population inhabit urban areas and this number is set to increase to 70% by 2050. Currently the level of food imported into the urban areas requires huge amounts of energy, fossil fuel energy that as of today is a pollutant harming the environment and those living beings that have to inhabit within it. As the city spreads out and the inhabitants become accustomed to a higher standard of living. The free space allowed for farming fish, fruit and meat will become more rare and a vertical approach to food growth will have to be undertaken.

Current

We require a paradigm shift in the concept of food production. Most developed cities import their food from across the planet, wasting countless amounts of energy in processing and transporting food. The means of production uses many chemicals and poisons to treat the plants and are harmful to the environment.

IN 2050 WE NEED TO PRODUCE MORE FOOD THAN WE DO NOW **70%**

THE WORLDS POPULATION WILL INCREASE FROM 6.8 BILLIION TO

9.1 BILLION

70% LIVING IN CITY

OUR ARABLE LAND WILL DECREASE DRAMATICALLY

BY FOOD AND AGRICULTURE ORGANIZATION

Concept

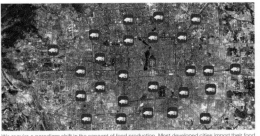

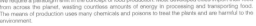

We require a paradigm shift in the concept of food production. Most developed cities import their food from across the planet, wasting countless amounts of energy in processing and transporting food. The means of production uses many chemicals and poisons to treat the plants and are harmful to the environment.

A common feature in all large metropolitan cities are large transport hubs hat connect the various circulation systems of the city. Beijing is no different. Currently the city has 25 major transport hubs and our plan is to place 25 towers on and around these transport hubs. This will use land that is not desirable for housing or office space and convert it into use for the population.

The tower has three components to it. Two of which are located on the southern side of the tower. There are assigned the to the concept of growing food and fish in an aquaponic system of growth. The floors are packaged up in groups of 6 and can rotate so that they catch the sun evenly as shown in diagram. These two towers bend and contract in size to create a slope in the facade. This slope allows more sunlight to flood into the grow areas.

On the north tower is located the 'wind machines' that catch the major winds. In Beijing for example the major winds blow from North West to South East. The 'Wind Machines' not only produce power but they also filter air from the surrounding, transferring carbon dioxide into the . Also located in these towers are grow areas for produce such as mushrooms that do not require much sunlight to grow.

These towers can work anywhere, in any city on any continent. They are quick to produce and are highly efficient at producing large amounts of food fort he population.

25 TOWER 35% FOOD PRODUCE IN 2050 **100%** MORE THAN NOW

Beijing 1980
population 9.2 mio.
arable land 52%

Beijing 2010
population 23 mio.
arable land 17%

Beijing 2050
population 40 mio.
arable land 0%

organisms work in a symbiotic relationship to provide for one another, near major transport hubs in cities, utilizing land that is undesirable for housing or other high uses. The towers grow tilapia fish, plants, and vegetables. The dissolved fish waste (nitrates) is absorbed by the plants, a process that both feeds the plants and cleans the water; this, in turn, prevents the potentially harmful material from entering the environment around and affecting the ecosystem.

Each tower is made of three vertical cores; two hold ecosystem activity, and the third is filled with "wind machines" that both generate energy and filter the city's polluted air. In the growing towers, the floors rotate,

AQUAPONIC TOWER
FEEDING THE WORLD

and the towers themselves can bend and contract, to capture the most sunlight possible. In the third tower, the air is filtered as carbon dioxide is sucked in and fed to plants. The process of photosynthesis that is fueled by this produces energy, causes the plants to grow and also emits clean oxygen back to the city's residents. These towers also have space for growing food, but restrict crops to those that don't require much sunlight, such as mushrooms.

Far more than just a "farming tower," the aquaponic tower provides a sustainable solution to population rise, food scarcity, excess energy use in transporting food and air pollution all at once.

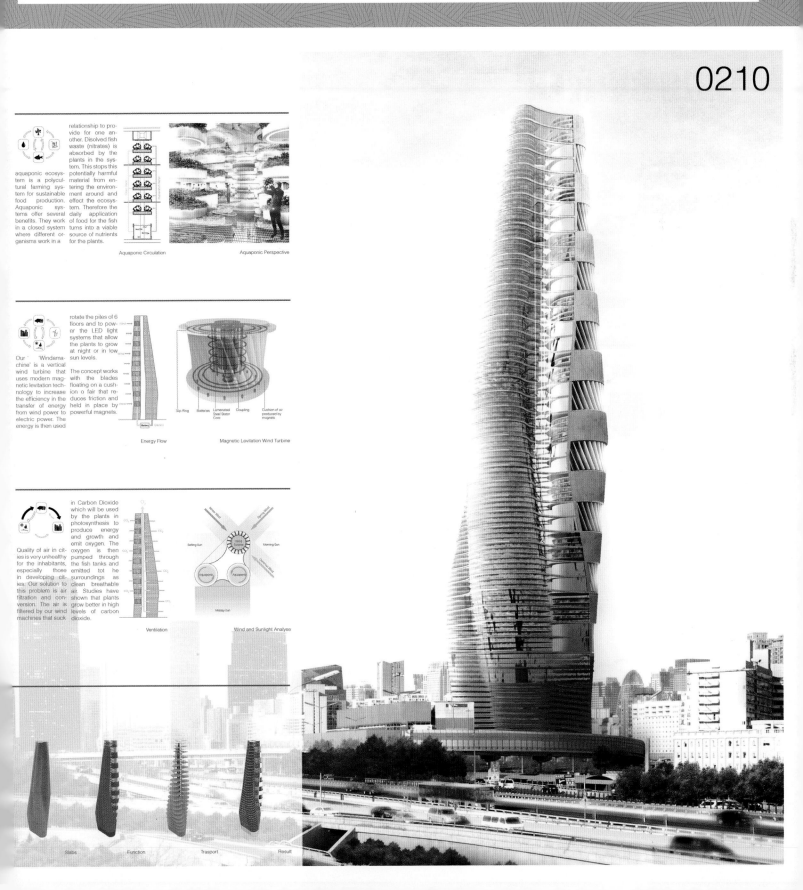

0210

aquaponic ecosystem is a polycultural farming system for sustainable food production. Aquaponic systems offer several benefits. They work in a closed system where different organisms work in a relationship to provide for one another. Disolved fish waste (nitrates) is absorbed by the plants in the system. This stops this potentially harmful material from entering the environment around and effect the ecosystem. Therefore the daily application of food for the fish turns into a viable source of nutrients for the plants.

Aquaponic Circulation

Aquaponic Perspective

Our 'Windamachine' is a vertical wind turbine that uses modern magnetic levitation technology to increase the efficiency in the transfer of energy from wind power to electric power. The energy is then used to rotate the piles of 6 floors and to power the LED light systems that allow the plants to grow at night or in low sun levels. The concept works with the blades floating on a cushion o fair that reduces friction and held in place by powerful magnets.

Energy Flow

Magnetic Levitation Wind Turbine

Quality of air in cities is very unhealthy for the inhabitants, especially those in developing cities. Our solution to this problem is air filtration and conversion. The air is filtered by our wind machines that suck in Carbon Dioxide which will be used by the plants in photosynthesis to produce energy and growth and emit oxygen. The oxygen is then pumped through the fish tanks and emitted tot he surroundings as clean breathable air. Studies have shown that plants grow better in high levels of carbon dioxide.

Ventilation

Wind and Sunlight Analyse

Slabs

Function

Trasport

Result

LAND BUOYER

Hu Jiandong

China

LAND BUOYER
SAVE LAND FROM THE RISING SEA LEVEL

ISSUE

As we all know, global warming is one of the major problems we face today. Triggered by global warming, negative effects such as the rising sea level have gradually began to break the earth's environmental balance.

However, according to a 2012 report from NCAR, research shows that even if greenhouse are brought under control, and the temperature of sea surface and deep sea water still have differences, deep sea temperatures will increase slowly. This will lead to the heating of the water and then make the water volume expand. This complicated phenomenon means that even if global temperatures stabilize it will still cause sea levels to continue to rise for hundreds of years.

Rising sea levels will trigger a global episode with low lands being submerged and coastal erosion etc. This will greatly damage the environment and exert a tremendous influence on a third of the world's coastal population and island residents' life.

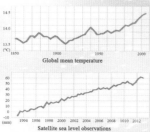

Global mean temperature

Satellite sea level observations

Melted ice shelf   Sea rising

CONCEPT

The idea we have come up with is to choose an appropriate place in the polar regions to establish a high performance snow jet spray tower. This will take advantage of the polar low temperature environment and use the salt in sea water as the snows core, turning the water into ice and spray snow on the ground. In the tower spray range, the mass of ice we control is greater than the mass of snow and ice melted, so part of the sea water is stored. This method will transfer the increased volume of the sea water back into frozen ice reducing the sea level and address global warming.

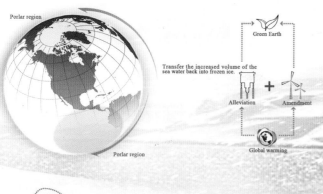

Porlar region

Green Earth

Transfer the increased volume of the sea water back into frozen ice.

Alleviation + Amendment

Global warming

Porlar region

Antarctic ice

Patching ice shelf

The tower "growth" = The tower will spray widely

Reflect sunshine

Reduce sea level

The sea   Patching ice shelf   Ice shelf

With the increased amount of sprayed snow, the snow cover will thicken. The spray tower will use its six pillars to maintain the space between the tower and snow cover. Then it will gradually become a skyscraper standing on the earth's polar region. Because of this "growth", the overall height of the tower will increase gradually and the tower will spray widely, so that the influence of the spray tower extends and this improves work efficiency.

Triggered by global warming, negative effects such as the rising sea level have gradually began to break the earth's environmental balance. NCAR research shows that even if greenhouse effect is under control, the temperature of sea surface and deep sea water still have differences; deep sea temperatures will increase slowly causing sea levels to continue to rise for hundreds of years.

The proposal chose an appropriate place in the polar regions to establish a high performance snow jet spray tower. This will take advantage of the polar low temperature environment and use the salt in seawater as a snow core, turning the water into ice and spraying snow on the ground. In the tower spray range, the

0297

mass of ice we control is bigger than the mass of snow and melted ice, so part of the seawater will be stored. This method will transfer the increased volume of the seawater back as frozen ice reducing the sea level and address global warming

With the increased amount of sprayed snow, the ice surface will thicken. The spray tower will use its six pillars to maintain the space between the tower and ice surface, only then it will gradually become a skyscraper standing on the earth's polar region. Because of this "growth", the overall height of the tower will increase gradually.

LAND BUOYER
SAVE LAND FROM THE RISING SEA LEVEL

Formation Illustration

Make water into ice terminal machine
Jet spray Machine

The machine can use the salt in sea water as the snows core to turn the water into ice and spray snow. It can also according to different environments to adjust the jet distance and volume of snow.

High speed

Low speed

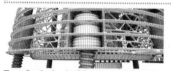

Transfer the load of the tower to the pillar and use it to make the tower climb up.
Climbing Apparatus

Pillar up   tower up

Separate the clutch   Engage the clutch

The aquaduct guide the sea water into the spray tower.
Aquaduct

There are turbines at regular intervals in the aquaduct to add to the water pressure.

Inner shell
Outer shell
Thermal insulation
Pressure boost turbine

Section of the aquaduct

Climbing of the tower

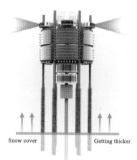

Snow cover   Getting thicker

The snow cover under the tower would be more and more thick with the spraying of the tower.

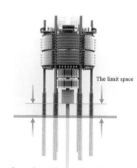

The limit space

In order to keep a necessary space between the tower and the snow cover, the tower needs to climbing up.

Step one: The
to rotate part
to lift them u
does' t break
is sustaining th
tower.

The climbing process will be by taking advantage of the inner ice surface below the tower, gradually the tower will rotate on its own pillars so it does not break the ice that sustains the load and then the constructed part of the tower will be pulled up by itself to a new altitude. In this way the high of the tower can change in order to its needs.

0297

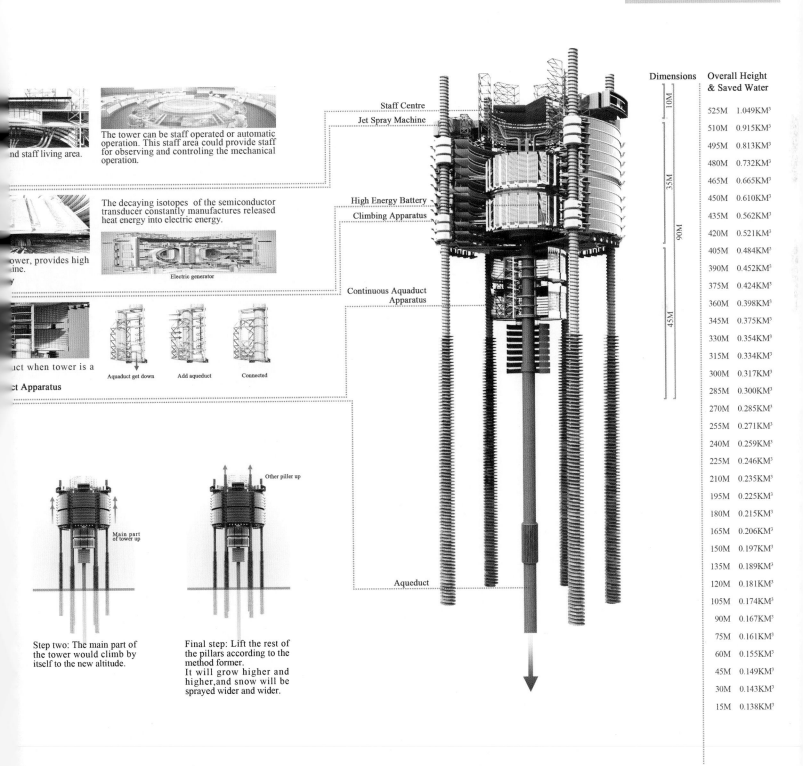

...nd staff living area.

The tower can be staff operated or automatic operation. This staff area could provide staff for observing and controling the mechanical operation.

The decaying isotopes of the semiconductor transducer constantly manufactures released heat energy into electric energy.

...ower, provides high ...ine.

Electric generator

...ct when tower is a

...ct Apparatus

Aquaduct get down   Add aqueduct   Connected

Main part of tower up

Other piller up

Step two: The main part of the tower would climb by itself to the new altitude.

Final step: Lift the rest of the pillars according to the method former.
It will grow higher and higher, and snow will be sprayed wider and wider.

Staff Centre
Jet Spray Machine

High Energy Battery
Climbing Apparatus

Continuous Aquaduct Apparatus

Aqueduct

Dimensions	Overall Height & Saved Water	
	525M	1.049KM³
	510M	0.915KM³
	495M	0.813KM³
	480M	0.732KM³
	465M	0.665KM³
	450M	0.610KM³
	435M	0.562KM³
	420M	0.521KM³
	405M	0.484KM³
	390M	0.452KM³
	375M	0.424KM³
	360M	0.398KM³
	345M	0.375KM³
	330M	0.354KM³
	315M	0.334KM³
	300M	0.317KM³
	285M	0.300KM³
	270M	0.285KM³
	255M	0.271KM³
	240M	0.259KM³
	225M	0.246KM³
	210M	0.235KM³
	195M	0.225KM³
	180M	0.215KM³
	165M	0.206KM³
	150M	0.197KM³
	135M	0.189KM³
	120M	0.181KM³
	105M	0.174KM³
	90M	0.167KM³
	75M	0.161KM³
	60M	0.155KM³
	45M	0.149KM³
	30M	0.143KM³
	15M	0.138KM³

10M   35M   90M   45M

PH CONDITIONER

Huang Haiyang
Shi Jianwei
Hao Tian

China

PH CONDITIONER
URBAN ACID DEPOSITION TREATMENT CENTER

BACKGROUND

The outbreak of the Industrial Revolution in Europe, since 1750s, has significantly promoted the pace of human civilization, while unavoidably brought severe environmental pollution at the same time. The most explicit consequence is the **Acid Deposition** caused by waste of large-scale industrial production.

With the development of the society, Acid Deposition became a worldwide environmental issue progressively. It first sprang up in European&North America, then placed emphasis on developing countries in Middle East, South America and Asia. In the predictable future, it has the trend to cover Africa and much broader range. So people have been, are and may continue to be **living in the atmospheric environment with the PH value less than 5.6.**

ACID DEPOSITION

"Acid Deposition" is a popular term referring to the deposition of wet (rain, snow, sleet, fog, cloudwater, and dew) and dry (acidifying particles and gases) acidic components. Brought by the fossil fuel people use in abundance, namely coal, oil, and gas, as well as the heavy traffic and industrial production, the **SO2&NOx drives the PH value of atmosphere under 5.6.**

Gradually precipitating to the surface of the earth where people live, these acidic materials have caused great harm to plant, architecture and humanbeing. **On the whole, Acid Deposition has become one of the most serious urban environmental issues.**

$$2SO_2(g)+O_2(g)=2SO_3(g) \qquad H_2O(l) + SO_3(g) =H_2SO_4(aq)$$

$$2NO(g)+O_2(g)=2NO_2(g) \qquad 3NO_2(g)+H_2O(l)=2HNO_3(aq)+NO(g)$$

ACID CITY—CHONGQING

First, the geographical position and the topographical condition of Chongqing make it to be a perfect breeding ground for Acid Deposition. Chongqing is embraced three sides by mountains and has hills and lower mountains in much of its areas—theses characteristics make up barriers for airflows on low levels, thus lead to the large gathering of pollutants and finally suspension form with high concentration.

Moreover, Chongqing, with a large populations and high density of heavy industry, is a **typical Asian city using coal as its chief energy**; all of the reasons mentioned above work together to provide the origin to Acid Deposition. As the forth pole of China's economy, we can expect a severer extent of acidification degree with the on-going urbanization process.

CONCEPT
OVERVIEW

This project is aiming at using a gentle way to manage Acid Deposition and eventually turn pollutants into available resources for cities where land is highly demanded by gradually **balancing the low PH value** in atmosphere.
Acidic pollutants will be transformed into **reclaimed water and nutrients** (chemical fertilizer) and **city will be heathier via the PH CONDITIONER!**

PROCESS

We set the main body of our architecture to be 200-300 meters high, producing a protective layer of human being from the layer where acidic pollutants gather. The aerocyst filled up with H2 is at the top of the building and will provide buoyancy to it. Besides, we can change the range of the coverage through adjusting the spatiality of the air bags. There are some porous membrane attached to the air bags, which can absorb the acidic materials, like acid fog, collect and put them into core purifier hanging under the aerocyst. **Neutralization can take place with alkaline substance produced by nitrogen-fixing microorganism** via biological action, which is stored in the processor.

MICROORGANISM ACTION:

$$6CO_2(g)+6H_2O(l) \to C_6H_{12}O_6(s)+6O_2(g) \qquad 2H_2O(l) \to 2H_2(g)+O_2(g)$$

$$N_2(g)+e+H^++ATP \to NH_3(g)+ADP+Pi$$

ACID NEUTRALIZATION:

$$2NH_3+2H^++SO_4^{2-}=2(NH_4)_2SO_4(aq) \qquad NH_3+H^++NO_3^-=NH_4NO_3(aq)$$

With a series of processing, acid pollutants can be transformed into neutral solution with ammonium salt which will be absorbed by plants attached to tentacle pipelines as green nutrients. The remained liquid will be delivered to every city terminal through tentacle as the source of reclaimed water.

MANIFESTO OF AIR QUALITY

PH Conditioner gives up the style of monument expressed in most traditional skyscraper, instead choosing a gentle, graceful poetic style with oriental aesthetic consciousness deeply embodied. It is an exploration and a challenge of skyscraper in multiple possibilities with functions, forms and structures.

Moreover, PH Conditioner has became rather **a living organism interacting with city**, than merely a architecture standing on the ground. At the beginning, the city is heavily polluted with a air PH value lower than 5.6; the living being shows slight vital signs. Later on, with acid pollutants transformed into water&nutrients, air is significantly improved so as the PH value; the living being start to prosper. As time passing by, PH value is verging to neutral and the color of life—green—spreads everywhere and makes itself integrated into the city; living being eventually becomes the organic composition of the urban public space. PH Conditioner will record and witness this whole process and at last as **a manifesto of living in a city with excellent quality of air.**

Nowadays, the speed of urbanization in developing countries keeps accelerating so that environmental pollutions become inevitable issues. PH Conditioner is more like a **manifesto of atmospheric environment**, WARNING people to pay close attention to the harmonious coexistence of human being, the city and the nature.

SHIFT
SHIFT OF ACID POLLUTION

18XX CITIES WITH ACID POLLUTION
19XX CITIES WITH ACID POLLUTION
NOWADAYS CITIES WITH ACID POLLUTION

ACID IMPACT
SEVERE IMPACT OF ACID DEPOSITION

Plants   Buildings   People

CURRENT SITUATION
STATISTICS OF ACID DEPOSITION IN CHONGQING

Density of Acid Pollutants in the Air   Developments of Acid Deposition

EVOLUTION
EVOLUTION OF PH CONDITIONER & CHONGQING

PH=3
Acid Deposition

PH=5
PH CONDITIONER Treatment

PH=7
Renewed Cityscape

PURIFICATION PROCESS
ACID DEPOSITOIN >>> WATER + PLANTS

PH
3.0

ACID DEPOSITION

Collecting

Purifying

H2O+ NUTRIENTS

Distributing

PLANTS+WATER

7.0

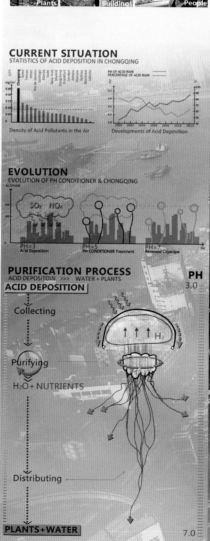

The outbreak of the Industrial Revolution in Europe in 1750 unavoidably brought severe environmental pollution. The most explicit consequence is the acid deposition caused by waste of large-scale industrial production.

Produced by the fossil fuel used in abundance, as well as the heavy traffic and industrial production, the SO_2 & NO_x drives the PH value of the atmosphere under 5.6. Gradually precipitating to the surface of the earth, these acidic materials have caused great harm to plants, architecture, and human beings.

The project aims to use a gentle way to manage acid deposition and eventually turn pollutants into

0342

available resources (reclaimed water & chemical fertilizer) for the region of Chongqing.

The project is set to be 200-300m high where acidic pollutants gather. The aerocyst filled up with H_2 at the top of the building provides buoyancy to it. The porous membrane attached to the air bags can absorb the acidic materials, like acid fog, collect and put them into the core purifier where neutralization takes place with alkaline substance produced by nitrogen-fixing microorganism via biological action, which is stored in the purifier center.

With neutralization, acid pollutants can be transformed into neutral liquid with ammonium salt, which

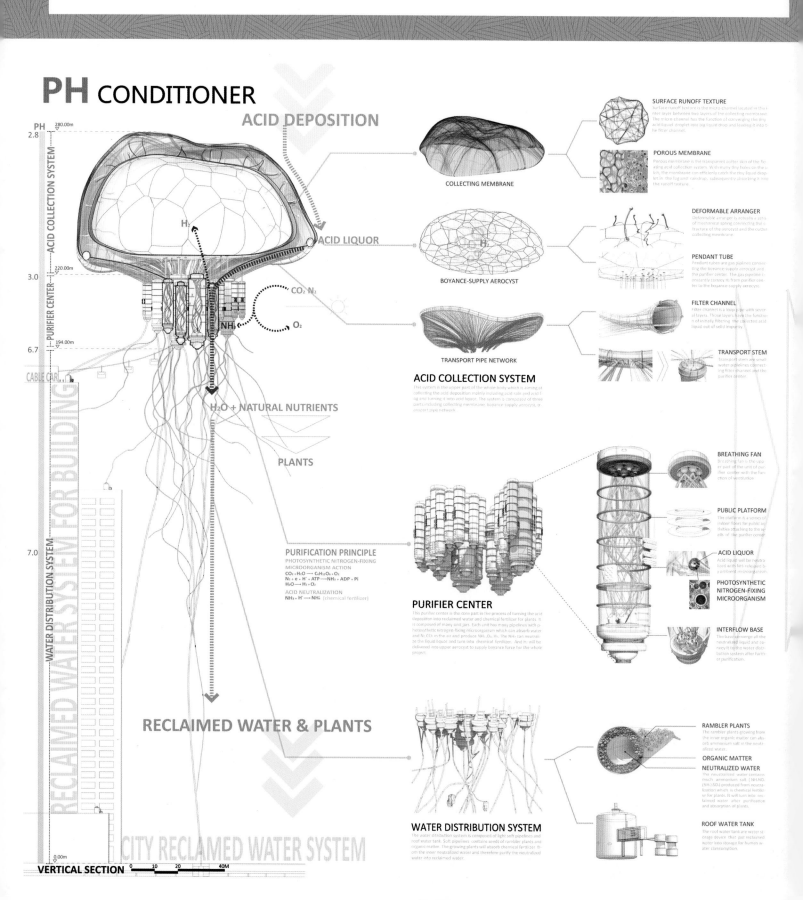

will be absorbed by plants attached on tentacle pipelines as green nutrients. The remained liquid will be delivered to the terminal tank as the source of reclaimed water.

The project will become a green urban landmark; by the time the air becomes significantly cleaner, the city will be witness to the improvement of their quality of life.

View of CHONGQING in 2053

INHABITED-LAYER

Mingxuan Dong
Xu Han
Yuchen Xiang
Aiwen Xie

China

3013 INHABITED-LAYER

Things will develop in the opposite direction when they become extreme.'

If the span is big enough within the scale of the earth, it seems that the unstableness brought by the size decreases inversely.
If an overhead bridge span covering the entire circumference of the earth, it will no longer need the support from the earth and can be suspended in the air, because the gravity can be balanced by their own . No need to be sticked to the ground, the elevated bridge can reach any height - only need to increase its perimeter- without worrying about overturning,earth-quakes, floods and any other natural disasters.

In the progress when people get along with the earth, ecological balance has been disturbed.

Earth starts to move restlessly, people continue to be selfish. The earth nowadays is tired out with scars, losing the balance and peace in the past.

EARTH CHANGING

Ecological earth	Harmony with nature	Resources over-used	Earth destroyed
At one time,the ecology of the earth is in great balance.	Since human beings exist on the earth,they began to make use of the resource to change nature.	As the resource is over used, the earth is overburdening and heavily damaged.	If human keep doing harm to the earth, the earth will be unsuitable for living sooner or later.

EARTH UNLIVABLE

Energy Burst	High density pressure	Pollution disaster	
In recent years, the energy in the inner core erupts, disasters break out in high frequency.	As everything develops rapidly , high-density-earth is not the livable space any more.	Pollution erodes the earth, also threatens the health and safety of human beings.	We need a solution!

THE SIN OF SKYSCRAPERS

How to be higher

Since the day of birth, the skycrappers have been pusuing a higher and larger volume. But they still need to rely on the support of the ground. So a higher height usually means greater unstableness and risk, as well as weaker capacity to resist disasters.

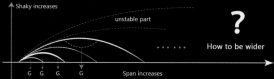

How to be wider

The larger the span is, the greater the scale is, the greater unstableness the structure will have. And risk there will be, as well as weaker capacity to resist disasters.

The skyscrapers around us

Pantheon Dome

Structural logic updating often brings the technology breakthrough. Stress from changes can sometimes make the Millennium immortal miracle.

REDEMPTION

When the span is large enough,the structure will circle around the earth under the action of gravity. It will form a new spherical shell without support.The height of architecture can increase with the distance between the shell and earth.
The outer shell grow into a layer for human beings, earth surface will recover to an ecology layer.

This great project unites people all over the world together. Only do people co-operate in harmony, can we create a new space for living.

Statement of design

Since the day of birth, the skycrappers have been pursuing to a higher, larger volume. But they still need to rely on the support of the ground. So a higher height usually means greater unstableness and risk, as well as weaker capacity to resist disasters.
If the span is big enough within the scale of the earth, it seems that the brought by the size decreases inversely. If an overhead bridge span covering the of the earth, it will no longer need the support from the earth and can be suspen gravity can be balanced by their own . No need to be sticked to the ground, the only need to increase its perimeter without worrying about overturning,earth-qu

As technologically innovative and higher the latest skyscrapers can be, they still need to rely on the support to the ground. So a higher height usually means more unstableness as well as a weaker capacity to resist disasters.

This project proposes a mega hexagonal grid that evolves around the earth's circumference at a stratosphere height; the principle that supports this hypothesis is that it seems to be that in a building the larger the span is, the scale and the unstableness will proportionally increase. But if the span is large enough within the scale of the earth, the unstableness brought by the size decreases inversely. In this case the

0353-01

THE CONCEPT

"a green earth"   +   human higher space   =   a new big green earth

y height -
atural disasters.

network of buildings and bridges connected to each other, covering the entire circumference of the earth, will no longer need structural ground support and can be suspended in the air by the effect of the earth's gravity. The elevated bridges and buildings that relate the grid can reach any height with out worrying about overturning, earthquakes, floods and any other natural disasters.

The earth needs to find an environmental balance. As humankind has overused resources, the earth is being heavily damaged, approaching to a point in which the earth will be unsuitable for human living.

The modern skyscraper has represented for years the modern urban ideal. But in a non-far future the

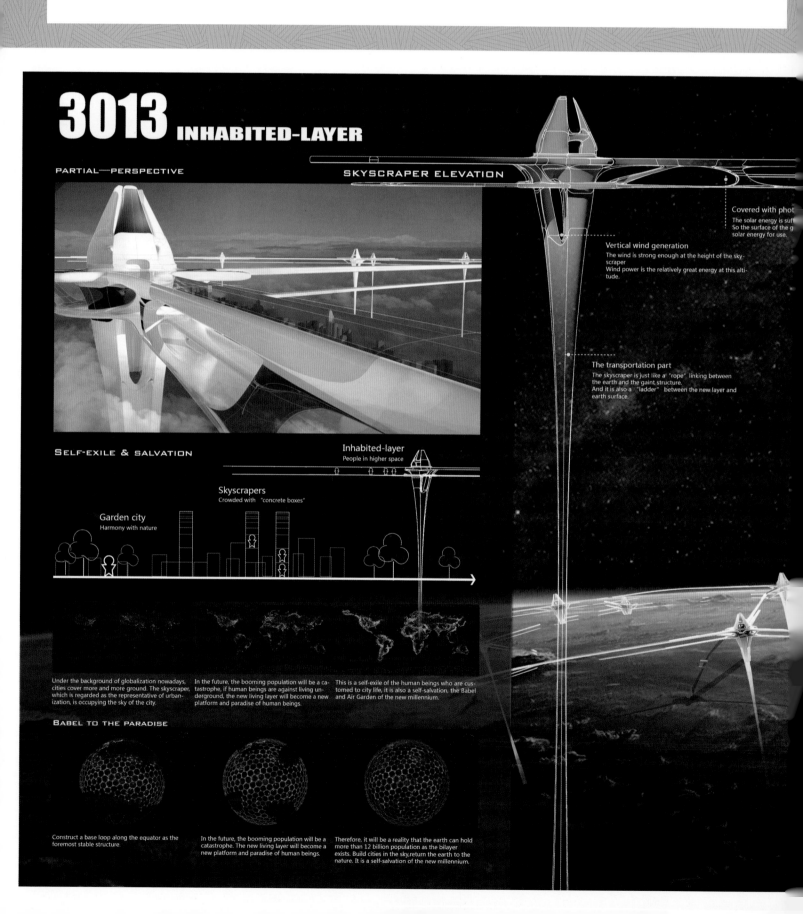

3013 INHABITED-LAYER

PARTIAL—PERSPECTIVE

SKYSCRAPER ELEVATION

Covered with phot
The solar energy is suff
So the surface of the g
solar energy for use.

Vertical wind generation
The wind is strong enough at the height of the sky-scraper
Wind power is the relatively great energy at this altitude.

The transportation part
The skyscraper is just like a "rope" linking between the earth and the gaint structure.
And it is also a "ladder" between the new layer and earth surface.

SELF-EXILE & SALVATION

Inhabited-layer
People in higher space

Skyscrapers
Crowded with "concrete boxes"

Garden city
Harmony with nature

Under the background of globalization nowadays, cities cover more and more ground. The skyscraper, which is regarded as the representative of urbanization, is occupying the sky of the city.

In the future, the booming population will be a catastrophe, if human beings are against living underground, the new living layer will become a new platform and paradise of human beings.

This is a self-exile of the human beings who are customed to city life, it is also a self-salvation, the Babel and Air Garden of the new millennium.

BABEL TO THE PARADISE

Construct a base loop along the equator as the foremost stable structure.

In the future, the booming population will be a catastrophe. The new living layer will become a new platform and paradise of human beings.

Therefore, it will be a reality that the earth can hold more than 12 billion population as the bilayer exists. Build cities in the sky, return the earth to the nature. It is a self-salvation of the new millennium.

booming population increase will be catastrophic, being the stratosphere grid the only platform for ensuring the continuity of human civilization.

Under the background of globalization nowadays, cities cover more and more ground. The skyscraper, which is regarded as the representation of urbanization, is occupying the sky of the city. In the future, the booming population with force the self-exile of the human beings who are accustomed to city life.

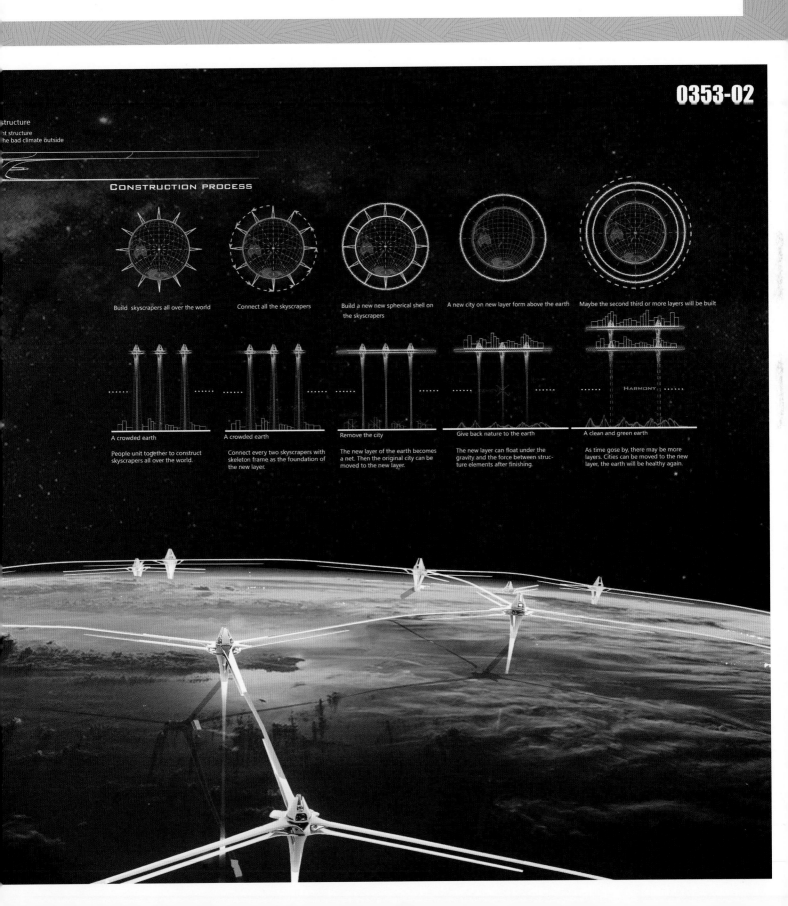

WORLDWIDE DAM

Damien Brau-Arnauty
Nicolas Podpovitny

France

73.8 Meters higher

Industrialization, excessive consuming and overproduction have resulted in a massive increase of greenhouse gas emissions causing a great rising of the sea water level. The rising of the sea level would force most of the population to inland exodus. The loss of urban and cultivated areas combined with a demographic growth would result in the overcrowding of the remaining land surface.

This project stands as an answer to these main issues by preserving the widely populated coastlines, leaving the continents' ground free of construction, allowing nature to regenerate. At the same time that creates new habitat and shelter for the growing new populations.

0375

Industrialization, excessive consuming and overproduction have resulted in a massive increase of greenhouse gas emissions. Nowadays, the prospect for the future looks pessimistic.

The sea level could ultimately tower above 73.8m. Explanations: 0.5m of increase corresponds to the melting of the glaciers and the ice cap, 7.2m for the melting of the Groenland inlandsis, 61.1m for the Antarctic inlandsis and 5.0 more meters for the melting down of the ice reserve locked inside the Antarctic inlandsis.

James Hansen/ Goddard Institute/ NASA

In all: 0.5+7.2+61.1+5.0= 73.8 meters(236 feet). The project takes this data as its starting point.

But the rising of water level is not the only issue. The population repartition and its worldwide growth is adding up.

In fact, 80% of the population is currently living at a distance of less than 200km from the coast. The remaining 20% have settled along the rivers (world map).

The rising of the sea level would force most of the population to inland exodus. The loss of urban and cultivated areas combined with a demographic growth would result in the overcrowding of the remaining land surface.

The project is an answer to three major issues:
-It aims at preserving the widely populated coasts.
-It leaves the old continents free of new constructions allowing nature to regenerate and absorb the major part of the CO2 emitted by human activities.
-It is giving shelter to the growing new populations and the migrant ones.

The project is a worldwide inhabited dam. It surrounds the continents and is built away from the coasts. This construction protects the lands from the excess of water but more than a barrier it becomes an exchange area between the ocean and the inner sea.

In red the world populations threatened by the rise of the sea level by 73.8 meters

The ocean is the place for logistic activities such as goods transport, the inner sea becomes a marina used for aqua culture and entertainment.

The building is designed as a linear structure composed of horizontal layers of functions each of them dedicated to a specific activity. The destination of each area would be flexible according to the geographic location and the specific needs of each population; we assume it would vary greatly depending on local climate and population density for instance.

Presently the displayed project is located in San Francisco bay (San Francisco map) where the dam is divided into three stratums: the top end for dwellings, the median area composed of public and working areas, and the lower part where the technical activities take place.

Industrial containers are recycled as accommodation modules supported by metallic beams plugged onto a mega structure. The color of the structure echoes back the Golden Gate which hue had been a subject for debate during its construction.

The wandering modules are connected to the tower through sanitary facilities already built in place. The containers are elevated thanks to cranes linked to the core of the tower. A warning light allows the travelers to know whether a location is available from the ocean (1).

In red the SF populations threatened by the rise of the sea level by 73.8 meters

The mega structure rotates around a mast, allowing to adapt its orientation to benefit from optimized sunlight (2) or to be protected from stormy winds like a flag (3). This core contains the vertical circulations leading into each of the sea wall levels (4). Staircases, elevators, networks and pipes are all gathered into this element running through the structure. It is dug deeply into the sea bed and enables to generate geothermal energy for heating (5).

The median part of the dam is composed of public areas and workplaces. On the top part of the structure a promenade links the five continents. It is a communication forum where the citizen gather and also a recreational area where all sorts of outdoor activities can be done. Underneath, a storage space for foodstuff arriving from the ocean or local peach is to be found.

At the same level workplaces and all sorts of public buildings are located on the continental side (schools, concert halls, sports halls..). On the floor below there are maintenance areas linked with the activities above. Water treatment plants treat organic wastes from the accommodations and transform them into fertilizer for the green areas and the floating agriculture.

These large spaces are also dedicated to other functions such as industrial activities, jails, animal storage. In this part of the sea wall large doors maintain exchanges between the ocean and the lower sea in order to manage the level of the inner sea and renew the water (6). Power is supplied through turbines along the course of the water.

The median area receives in its lower part a commercial mall and a covered market all along the inner sea and opened towards it. It is the meeting point of the goods arriving from the ocean and from the continent.

The lower part of the dam comprises the technical premises.

First, the underwater public transports associated with storage of continental goods.

Below, a filtering system of 60 meters high treats the water (7). A semipermeable membrane located upstream of the storage pond desalinates the water intended for consumption. An overflow system re-injects the water into the ocean before it is desalinated. This system presents two advantages: it produces fresh water becoming a rare and expensive product and also purifies and cleans the ocean.

Finally, this lower part is buried deeply inside the hard soil (rocks) on a depth of over 200 meters in order to anchor the structure.

This project is located in the San Francisco Bay, designed as an inhabitant dam, a linear structure composed of horizontal layers of functions each of them dedicated to a specific activity. The dam will surround the continents' coastlines, protecting the lands from the excess of water, and creating an exchange area between the ocean and the inner sea.

In this proposal the dam is divided into three stratums: the top end for dwellings, in the middle public and working areas, and in the lower layer where the technical activities will take place. The megastructure rotates around a mast, allowing it to adapt its orientation to benefit from optimized sunlight or to be protected from

stormy winds like a flag. This core contains the vertical circulations leading into each of the sea wall levels. Staircases, elevators, networks, and pipes are all gathered into this element running through the structure. It is dug deeply into the seabed and enables the generation of geothermal energy for heating.

The destination of each program will be flexible according to the geographic location and the specific needs of each population. The hypothesis is that it would vary greatly depending on local climate and population density.

PHOENIX

Karolina Studencka
Aneta Swiezak
Jakub Kafel

Poland

PHOENIX

THE HIGHER THE BUILDINGS WE BUILD THE MORE DIFFICULT IT IS TO MAKE THEM RESISTANT FOR ANY KIND OF DESTRUCTION. WITH REGARD FOR THE LATEST DISCUSSIONS ON THE END OF THE WORLD IT WOULD BE UNWISE NOT TO CONSIDER THE POSSIBILITY OF A SERIOUS DESTRUCTION HAPPENING TO OUR CIVILIZATION. IT CAN OCCUR AS A RESULT OF HUMAN ACTIONS AND DECISIONS, LIKE FOR EXAMPLE THE NUCLEAR WINTER OR FROM NATURAL DISASTERS LIKE METEORITE STRIKE, EARTHQUAKES OR TSUNAMI. TILL THIS DAY WE ARE NOT ABLE TO PREVENT MOST OF THOSE NATURAL CATASTROPHES BUT WE CAN THINK OF A WAY TO COPE WITH THE RESULTS IN ORDER TO ASSURE THE CONTINUOUS EXISTENCE OF HUMANITY.

'PHOENIX' IS A PROPOSAL OF HOW HUMANITY CAN PREPARE THEMSELVES FOR THIS SITUATION.
THE BUILDING PROVIDES SHELTER FOR PEOPLE DURING AS WELL AS SHORTLY AFTER THE CATOSTROPHE WHEN THE CONDITIONS OVERGROUND ARE NOT CONDUCTIVE OR EVEN UNPOSIBILITAR FOR LIVING ON THE SURFACE OF THE GROUND. THEN, EVEN MORE IMPORTANTLY, AFTER THIS PERIOD IT ALLOW TO REBUILD THE DESTROYED CIVILIZATION. AS A LOCALIZATION THE DESIGNERS OF 'PHOENIX' CHOSE THE BIGGEST AND THE MOST SIGNIFICANT CITIES OF THE WORLD, WHERE THE DISTRUCTION WOULD BE MOST FATAL.

WHEN THE CITY FUNCTIONS NORMALLY SOME OF THE PARTS OF 'PHOENIX' ARE PLACED ABOVE GROUND IN ORDER T ATED AS AN INDEPENDENT STRUCTURAL MODULE FIXED TO A STEEL CONSTRUCTION. IN TIME OF THREAT OR DANG EPING INFRASTRUCTURE IS SITUATED. THANKS TO THAT 'PHOENIX' WHEN ITS HIDDEN UNDERGROUND FUNCTIONS SYSTEM OF CONTAINERS WITH EDIBLE PLANTS AND CROPS WHICH ALLOWS PRODUCTION OF FRESH FOOD DURING T UND. APART FROM HOUSING UNITS THERE IS ALSO A CORE CONTAINING OFFICES, PUBLIC UTILITIES, RECREATIONAL UTI TIES. WHEN THE CATASTROPHE NO LONGER THREATENS PEOPLE'S LIFE 'PHOENIX' CAN RISE UP OVER THE RUINS OF TH WHILE THE BUILDING IS MOVING UP, FLOOR BY FLOOR, THE UNITS OF THE EXTERNAL STRUCTURE WITH CONTAINERS W TO AN HORIZONTAL POSITION AND MOVE APART FROM THE BUILDING. THAT ALLOWS TO CREATE A GREEN SURROU BACK. THE HOUSING MODULES CAN SLIDE OUT ON SPECIAL RAILS, AND SOME OF THEM CAN BE MOVED ONTO A NEW STORED IN THE BUILDING DURING ITS UNDERGROUND PHASE. THIS WAY THE FIRST ELEMENTS NECESSARY FOR THE N POSSIBLE.

BEFORE   DURING

Aware of a possible catastrophic scenario in which human, cities, and civilization face great risk of destruction by man-made pollution or by a natural disaster, Phoenix is proposed as a high-rise shelter, that would help cities evacuate and be prepared to overcome an environmentally hazardous situation as well as to rebuild it.

The design applies a modular principle in which various program modules are connected to a core creating a smart habitable system, which in a normal scenario will perform as a regular high-rise building. During a natural disaster, the tower system will perform as a self-intelligent structure dismounting modules

0412

DING. EVERY HOUSING UNIT IS CRE-
GROUND WHERE ALL THE LIFE-KE-
UIPPED 'BUNKER'. IT CONTAINS THE
NG THE CATASTROPHE UNDERGRO-
WER PLANTS, AND STORAGE FACILI-

EPARATE FROM THE BUILDING, SPIN
HE NATURAL GREENERY TO GROW
ND THE CORE WITH THE MATERIALS
O CITIES ARE CREATED AS SOON AS

AFTER

one by one, and orderly placing them on massive bunker located near the core founding.

It is equipped with modules that during the year produce and store crops, and food resources allowing the population to continue their normal activities underground. Modules contain different programs such as offices, public utilities, recreational utilities, health services, power plants, and storage facilities.

After the situation, the tower will rise up over the ruins of the old city, uploading module-by-module trough the core until the original height and external shape is completed.

The external structure will place the containers with growing plants and separate them from the building,

PHOENIX

THE BIGGEST CITIES ARE MOST LIKELY TO BE ENDANGERED BY HUMAN DESTRUCTION DUE TO THEIR LARGE POPULATION, AND IN CASE OF A NATURAL CATASTROPHY THE BIGGEST CASUALTIES WOULD BE IN THOSE LARGE CITIES. THAT IS WHY THE DESIGNERS PROPOSE TO PLACE PHOENIX BUILDINGS AT THOSE LOCATIONS.

THE CULTIVATION OF EDIBLE PLANTS PROVIDES FOOD FOR PEOPLE DURING THE HIDING PERIOD, WHEN PHOENIX IS UNDERGROUND. SPECIAL LAMPS FIXED TO THE EXTERNAL STRUCTURE ALLOW THE PHOTOSYNTHESIS PHENOMENON TO OCCUR AND IMITATE THE NATURAL RYTHM OF DAYLIGHT AND NIGHT TIME. WHEN THE BUILDING OPENS THE CONTAINERS WITH PLANTS REPLACE THE FIELDS FOR THE TIME NECESSARY FOR THE NATURAL FIELDS TO REGROW THEMSELVES.

THERE ARE MANY SCENARIOS IN WHICH PHEONIX WOULD BE HELPFUL IN THE PROCESS OF REBUILDING OUR DESTROYED CITIES. BOTH DURING AND JUST AFTER THE CATASTROPHE, IT WOULD PROVIDE SHELTER FOR PEOPLE AND NECESSARY FOOD AS WELL AS ALMOST EVERY OTHER FACILITY THAT WE CAN FIND IN A NORMAL CITY.

SYSTEM OF CONTAINERS WITH GROWING CROPS AND PLANTS

CORE WITH COMMUNICATION

INSTALATIONS

CORE

OFFICE

PUBLIC GARDENS

EDUCATION

HOUSING UNITS

PUBLIC UTILITIE

HEALTH SERVI

PRODUCTIC

POWER PLAN

STORAGE CONSTRUCTIC MATERIA

TSUNAMI
COUSED BY SUBMARIN EARTHQUAKES, EXPLOSIONS OR VOLCANO ERUPTIONS, TSUNAMI WAVES ON THE COASTAL WATERS CAN BE DOZENS OF METERS HIGH, AND REACH THE SPEED UP TO 900KM/H. IN 2004 THE INDIAN OCEAN TSUNAMI KILLED OVER 230 000 PEOPLE IN 14 COUNTRIES ADJACENT TO THE OCEAN, AND LEFT MANY MORE AS HOMELESS.

NUCLEAR WINTER
THE PHENOMENON OCCURING AFTER EXPLOSION OF MANY NUCLEAR BOMBS CAUSING HUGE CLOUDS OF SOOT PREVENTING THE SUNLIGHT FROM REACHING THE EARTH SURFACE, THE TEMPERATURE OF THE AIR WOULD GO DOWN AND AS A RESULT PLANTS WOULDN'T BE ABLE TO GROW ANY MORE. IT WOULD INDUCE ALSO SERIOUS CLIMATE CHANGES AND FINALLY THE MAJORITY OF HUMAN POPULATION WOULD DIE OF STARVATION.

METEORITE STRIKE
EACH YEAR THERE ARE HUNDRETS OF METEORS CROSSING ATMOSPHERE, MOST OF THEM, TOTALLY BURNING OUT BEFORE EVEN REACHING THE SURFACE OF THE EARTH. BUT THERE IS STILL A POSSIBILITY THAT SOME BIGER CELESTIAL BODY [LIKE THE ONE WHICH HAS ENDED THE DINOSAUR DOMINANCE, AND COUSED ICE AGE] WILL CROSS EARTH TRAJECTORY.

FOUR TYPES OF RESIDENTIAL UNITS FOR VARIED SOCIETY

FAMILY UNIT

2 x SINGLE UNIT

BIG FAMILY UNIT + SINGLE UNIT

CONFORTABLE UNIT

TO REBUILD OUR CIVILIZATION, AND ONLY WHEN THE SITUATION ABOVE GROUND BECOMES ACCEPTABLE AND DOESNT ENDANGER THE PEOPLE'S HEALTH OR LIFE, THE BUILDING RISES UP FROM UNDER THE SURFACE. PHEONIX USES THE PRESSURE CREATED BY THE UNDEGROUND WATERCOURSES. PROGRESSIVELY AND IN A CONTROLLED ENVIRONEMENT THE WATER PUSHES THE BUILDING UP WHILE REMAINING UNDERGROUND. THE BEARING FIXED TO THE OUTSIDE STRUCTURE MINIMALIZES THE FRICTION BETWEEN THE BUILDING AND THE RETAINING WALL.

CONCEPT
PHASE 1
NORMALLY FUNCTIONING CITY
PHOENIX IS ONE OF THE RESIDENTIAL BUILDINGS

PHASE 2
DESTRUCTION OF THE CITY - TIME AFTER DESTRUCTION
PHOENIX WORKING AS A SHELTER PROVIDING ALL MEANS NECESSARY FOR HUMAN SURVIVAL UNDERGROUND FOR LONG PERIOD OF TIME

and spin to a horizontal position away from the building. This allows the creation of a green surrounding while expecting the natural greenery to grow back. The housing modules can slide out on special rails, and some can be moved onto a new construction space built around the core.

0412

AROUND A VOID

Bertrand Chapus
Thomas Hostache

France

AROUND A VOID

Nowadays, every country faces rural flight. Over 50% of the World's six billion people now live in cities. By 2050 this figure will pass 80%; the future is urban.

In fact, cities keep growing and spreading. As they get denser and denser, they are meant to start evolving toward the sky; it is a historical fact. Towers are constructed to centralize the cities different organs to form its heart, and they often become the symbol of the city's economic power, a recognizable landmark, or even a country visual identification.

A lot of areas in developing countries are full with local richness, knowledge and potentials. They could benefit from better infrastructures to make their cities evolve in a positive way. A lot of radical changes have taken place in some regions, with the quick rising of Honk Kong, Shanghai or Dubaï for instance, that transformed the landscape and the attractiveness of the area.

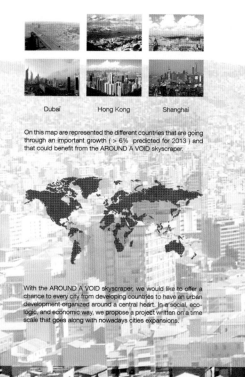

Dubaï   Hong Kong   Shanghai

On this map are represented the different countries that are going through an important growth (> 6% predicted for 2013) and that could benefit from the AROUND A VOID skyscraper.

With the AROUND A VOID skyscraper, we would like to offer a chance to every city from developing countries to have an urban development organized around a central heart. In a social, ecologic, and economic way, we propose a project written on a time scale that goes along with nowadays cities expansions.

Nowadays, every country faces rural immigration. Over 50% of the world's six billion people now live in cities. By 2050 this figure will pass 80%; the future is urban.

In fact, cities keep growing and spreading. As they get denser and denser, they are meant to start evolving toward the sky.

The project proposes a skyscraper as a solution to every city in emerging and developing countries for apply an urban model organized around local centricity.

The project is based on a diagnostic made for a programmatic building that takes consideration of public

0444

space, ecological repercussions and economical return.

The tower proposes a vertical public space to get out of the smothering, agitated ground activities, offering a refreshing and peaceful atmosphere. These various spaces are linked to each other and act like bits of urban spaces, such as parks, plazas, monument squares, and markets.

The spaces are disposed on different heights and are held by an exoskeleton made of a steel structural facade that also has photovoltaic glass. This 80% transparent energetic glass is the skin of a skyscraper. In the first years, the empty tower only works as an electric central for the nearby neighborhoods and provides

AROUND A VOID

New public space: the tower central plazza

New public space : market

New public space : a park over the city

SOCIAL ASPECT

The different aspects of the project are developed through three phases. First the social part established dealing with public spaces, then the ecological dimension coming from the façade, and finally the architectural concept with an economic feature introduced by the value of the resulted void.

A city needs public spaces to evolve with a sociable population. The areas where we'd like to see AROUND A VOID skyscraper grow are very dense, low rise neighborhoods. In that kind of district, the only public areas are generally the crowded streets along with their traffic issues. The tower proposes vertical open spaces to get out of the smothering agitated ground, and offers a new image of the city, with framings on the sky and the horizon. Those public spaces are linked to one another and act like bits of urban spaces, such as parks, plazas, monument squares, and markets.

ECOLOGIC FEATURES

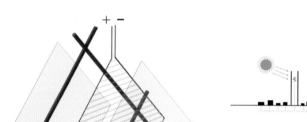

Photovoltaic glass detail

Energy

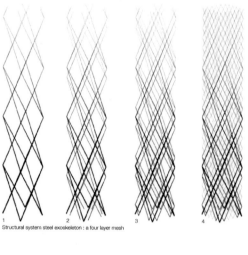

Structural system steel exoskeleton : a four layer mesh

The public spaces dis on different heights are he an exoskeleton, a steel structural façade. Beside a green-development pro the façade produces ener its surrounding by using a available technology: the p voltaic glass. Photovoltaic are sandwiched between glass squares, held by th dow structures. This 80% parent energetic glass is th of a skyscraper dimension punctuated with public spaces. For a while, the tower only works as an e central for the nearby nei rhood and provides wide areas.

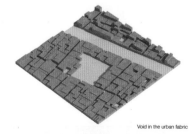

Void in the urban fabric

Extrude a volume from its surface

Distribute public spaces

Photovoltaic glas

wide-open public spaces. Over the years the emptiness eventually will become very valuable as a potential built environment.

Around A Void proposes to insert new programs in its emptiness. Every kind of program is welcomed to fulfill city needs. 20 percent of the void is dedicated to social housing; benefits of the project could be re-invested into another Around A Void Tower in another city performing again its social, ecological, and economical objectives.

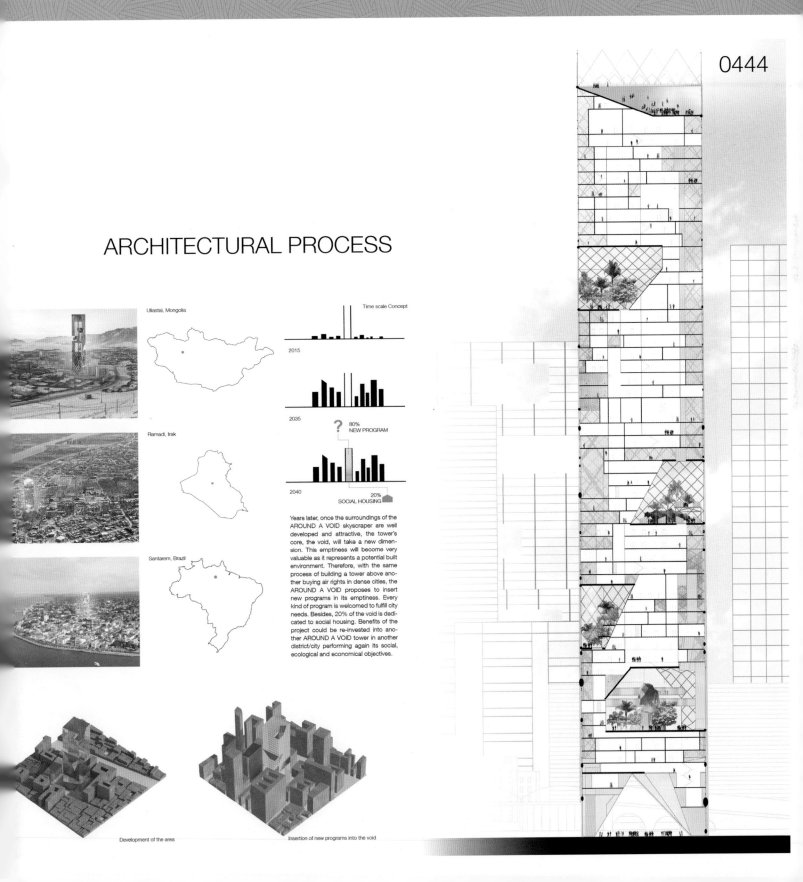

0444

ARCHITECTURAL PROCESS

Uliastai, Mongolia

Time scale Concept

2015

2035

? 80% NEW PROGRAM

Ramadi, Irak

2040   20% SOCIAL HOUSING

Santarem, Brazil

Years later, once the surroundings of the AROUND A VOID skyscraper are well developed and attractive, the tower's core, the void, will take a new dimension. This emptiness will become very valuable as it represents a potential built environment. Therefore, with the same process of building a tower above another buying air rights in dense cities, the AROUND A VOID proposes to insert new programs in its emptiness. Every kind of program is welcomed to fulfill city needs. Besides, 20% of the void is dedicated to social housing. Benefits of the project could be re-invested into another AROUND A VOID tower in another district/city performing again its social, ecological and economical objectives.

Development of the area

Insertion of new programs into the void

KAPLA-SKY

Francesco Colarossi
Rosamaria Faralli
Giovanna Saracino
Luisa Saracino
Francesca Silvi

Italy

Kapla-sky is a rapid assembly skyscraper based on the French wooden planks game Kapla. The unconventional high-rise is imagined as a modular system that can be easily transported and deployed in emergency areas. The system allows for different aggregation possibilities depending on the desired housing units and urban response.

A simple building block, the shipping container, allows for endless configurations from a rectangular aggregation with a central courtyard to a spiral tower or a hybrid with a courtyard inside a double spiral. For all configurations, an outer-structure, a steel wireframe, provides stability and creates a filter for sunlight and

wind. It is designed to accommodate private housing and community spaces such as meeting areas and playgrounds for children. Moreover, a series of skyscrapers could be interconnected and create a new urban fabric that will function as a temporal downtown for the city. The skyscraper could be equipped with solar panels, wind turbines to produce energy, or could be easily plugged into the existing infrastructure.

Kapla-sky permits not leaving the town center hit by a disaster and helps avoid many psychological issues caused by victims being removed from their living places. Moreover, it allows the continuation of life through a structure which at the end of the emergency, will remain inserted in the urban environment and

In an urban emergency like a flood, the horizontal connections decay due to the influx of water and the masses of mud blocking the streets, a system of vertical communication, and human life recreates an urban habitat would otherwise be impossible get inside a classic field of emergency. Kaplasky permits not to leave the town center hit by the flood and avoid many psychological problems caused by the removal of victims forced from their living places for the return to a normal situation. Moreover, it allows the continuation of life through a structure, which, at the end of the emergency, will remain inserted in the urban environment and reused as a housing tower for special accommodations or social housing.

Section Type 1

Section Type 2

reused as a housing tower for special accommodations or social housing.

Once the city has recovered from the disaster, the Kapla-sky could be transported to other cities in need or could also become permanent. In that case, students, young professionals and people in need would be able to use it.

0577-2

LONDON

NEW ORLEANS

ROME

VERTICAL FARMING

Jin Ho Kim

United Kingdom

VERTICAL FARMING HOUSE
MORE THAN A STAPLE FOOD FOR THE NATION

Nowadays approximately 3 billion people rely on rice as their major source of food. It is expected that the rice demand will continue to accelerate and by 2025 more than 4 billion people will rely on it. As a consequence, local governments in East Asia have established a total control on rice fields and production. This has been a disastrous event for the local farmers and has left the price of rice in absolute control of a handful of people. It is also expected that the price of rice will gradually increase to a point in which the majority of the Asian population will not be able to afford it.

In modern life, processing, packaging, transportation, and storage have enabled convenience of

Context

0758

Rice is one of major staple foods especially in East Asia. In the world, there are about 3 billion people who rely on rice as their major source of food. In 2025, the world's rice eaters are expected to hit 3.9 billion. It is the grain with the second-highest worldwide production.

In the Philippines, rice consumption has continuously increased. In a standard of 5 members-family, a single family consumes a half ton of rice. In terms of living cost rate, four-times bigger than any other Asian countries. 90% of Filipino falls into the poor class. The commodification of rice has accelerated the hardship to the poor. Monopolised and manipulated rice market by the government was emerged from distorted global rice market. Since rice became a commodity, everyone involved in the market invested on rice. In the case of Philippines, government had deal with rice producers and stored the rice until its price went up and earned the profit. The project agenda, vertical farming house will alleviate the hardship of living for the poor by cutting vicious restrain controlled by government's rice market monopoly and manipulation.

Metro Manila

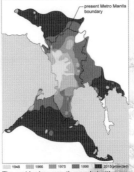

present Metro Manila boundary

1948 1966 1975 1996 2015(projected)

The rapid urban growth, coupled with an equally explosive population growth pretty much explains why Philippines went from the idyllic urban scenes of the 60s to the current chaos of Metro Manila. Greater Manila's population was about 1.5 million in 1948. It hit 10.8 million by 2000. Which meant we added about 180,000 people to the metropolis each year. The pace of growth also explains the housing crunch that Philippines currently face. To cope with that growth, Philippines would have had to build at the pace of nearly a hundred houses everyday for the last fifty years. If the projections are correct, the highly urbanized core will nearly double in size by 2015. This kind of growth though is par for the course of megacities worldwide and is a part of the global trend of rapid urbanization.

Aeroponic

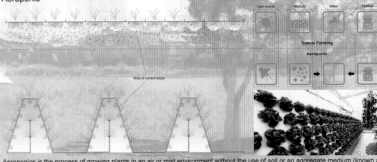

Light source   Medium   Water   Fertilizer

Typical Farming

Aeroponic

Area of nutrient scope

Aeroponics is the process of growing plants in an air or mist environment without the use of soil or an aggregate medium (known as geoponics). The basic principle of aeroponic growing is to grow plants suspended in a closed or semi-closed environment by spraying the plant's dangling roots and lower stem with an atomized, nutrient-rich water solution. Aeroponic growing is considered to be safe and ecologically friendly for producing natural, healthy plants and crops. The main ecological advantages of aeroponics are the conservation of water and energy. When compared to hydroponics, aeroponics offers lower water and energy inputs per square meter of growing area. When used commercially, aeroponics uses one-tenth of the water otherwise necessary to grow the crop but this can be reduced to as little as one-twentieth.

Basic Design Module

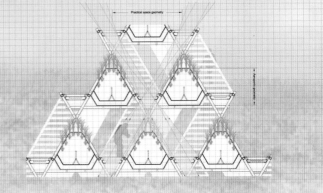

gaining food, saved time and reduced labor. However, the system has caused a disassociation between the food producer and product and between rural supplier and urban consumer. The consequence of this disassociation is that we, as consumers, are not seeing the clear effects of climate change and energy shortage on food production. Urban agriculture would result in food immediacy within cities, providing nutrition and health benefits. The community development would be facilitated and the city would benefit from urban greening

This project proposes the creation of decentralized aeroponic vertical farmlands that will be able

VERTICAL FARMING HOUSE
MORE THAN A STAPLE FOOD FOR THE NATION

to provide enough rice for future generations. The basic structure consists of an array of bamboo parallelograms that create stepping terraces of rice fields. It operates with a natural irrigation system in which its water gradually flows down with gravity through a network of irrigation paths.

In addition, the proposed skyscrapers will be located within the cities to avoid unnecessary processing, packaging, transportation, and storage. The facilities will also be operated by the local community providing countless jobs and opportunities for the inhabitants.

0758

Design Inspiration

Aeroponic ties up several complex typical farming process together, so it saves time, energy and money. Far more striking advantage of aeroponics that I am trying to apply on the project is vertical stacking farming. In average a single family in philippines cultivates 6724 square meters of rice paddy, meaning about 1.5 tons of rice production per a year and a family consumes 1/3 of their production. Applying multiple crops, aeroponics and if 8 levels vertical farming, comparing typical single crop method, about 98.5% of crop land will be saved meaning only 105 square meters is required. Based on existing aeroponic technique, I have implemented an irrigation logic of rice terrace, Natural irrigation system of the rice terrace is based on local topographic conditions. From top of the terrace, water is gathered and eventually flow down to the bottom.

In the design, aeroponic field creates a continuous branch-like design. In current aeroponics, one thing to be carefully considered for back up the system is its continuous irrigation path. If one part of irrigation system fails, the rest of it fails too. So multiple branch design that is stretched to different ends would prevent entire system fail. Also prefabricated design based on convenient frame structure would be good for quick and easy replacement of aeroponic containers.

Urban Farming

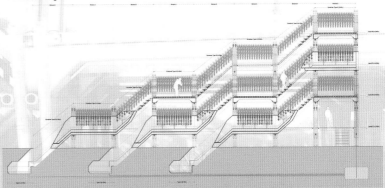

In modern life, processing, packaging, transportation and storage enabled convenience of gaining food, saved time and reduced labor. However the system caused a disassociation between the food producer and product, and between rural supplier and urban consumer. The consequence of this disassociation is that we, as consumers, are not seeing the clear effects of climate change and energy shortage on food production. Urban agriculture would result in food immediacy within cities, providing nutrition and health benefits. The community development would be facilitated and the city would benefit from urban greening.

Material

 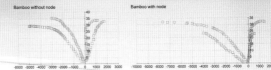

Bamboo without node   Bamboo with node

Compared to bigger tubes slim tubes have got in relation to their cross section a higher compressive strength parallel and vertical to their fibre. That relatively slimmer tubes possess better material conditions is caused by the fact that bigger tubes have got a minor part of the outer skin, which is very resistent in tension. Bamboo is able to resist more tensile than compression. Slim tubes are in this occasion superior, too. Inside the silificated outer skin you find axial-parallel extremly elastical fibres with a tensile strength up to 40kN/cm² As a comparison: extremly strong wood fibres can resist a tension up to 5 kN/cm² and steel St37 can resist as highest possible a tension of 37kN/cm²

COAL CITY

Anna Slimak

Poland

Poland is among the top ten countries in the world in regards to coal mining. The country's economy is based on coal mining due to the large share of energy production from coal. Silesia is a major mining region. Silesian cities were built near mines which resulted in their unique industrial personality. There are many active and closed mines. A major problem of mining areas is the deterioration of post-industrial areas and landscapes.

   Coal City is located in the industrialized region of Poland. It is an attempt at redefining the current structure of mining towns. The mission is to create a environmentally friendly life for people, neutralizing the

0819

01

dominants of spatial-industrial chimneys and developing a new form of landmark on the present chimneys in conjunction with the afforestation of mining dumps, and the utilization of ecological aspects in the process of energy consumption and generation.

Coal City includes all the program layers typical of a mid-size city, including public spaces, shops, cultural areas, offices, housing, etc., but they are all in the midst of green and connected by an internal and external system of communication. Skyscrapers are independent spatial structures where the higher layers are linked to the grid of underground mining tunnels, which are now used for recreational and cultural

activities. The skyscraper is crowned with three vertical axis wind turbines providing the town with sufficient green energy. Finally, the green tissue attached to the main structure is a natural filter for air pollution.

The core is divided into two parts: the green core and the urban core. Each of the cores has an assigned grid, corresponding to the proportion of its layers. By imposing those two layers, an abstracted vertical model of the redefined city was formed. The expression of Coal City involves constructing a skyscraper around the base of an industrial chimney.

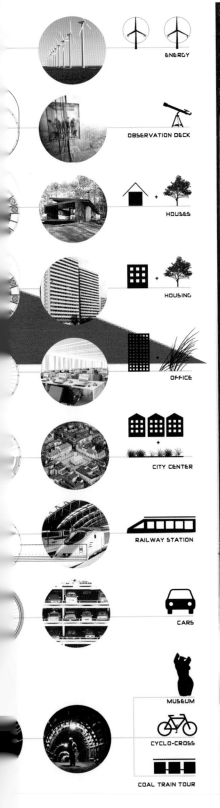

ENERGY

OBSERVATION DECK

HOUSES

HOUSING

OFFICE

CITY CENTER

RAILWAY STATION

CARS

MUSEUM

CYCLO-CROSS

COAL TRAIN TOUR

0819

SILO PARK

Ros Cheong
Adrian Vincent Kumar
Chuyan Qin
Yun Kong Sung

New Zealand

SILO PARK
A METHANE BIO-DIGESTER FOR COWS

Methane, a fundamental component of natural gas and arguably the most abundant organic compound on Earth, is hailed as an environmentally friendly and renewable fuel source. However, methane becomes a devastating greenhouse gas when released into the atmosphere. Silo Park proposes the construction of a methane bio-digester to harvest and store methane, offering more multifaceted benefits than current methods.

    With the understanding that the more agricultural methane that is successfully harvested and stored means phenomenal reductions in the amount of methane escaping into the atmosphere, the bio-digester

Methane (CH4), a fundamental component of natural gas and arguably the most abundant organic compound on Earth, is hailed as an environmentally-friendly and renewable fuel source. With a heat of combustion of about 891kj/mol, burning methane generates more energy per mass unit with less carbon dioxide produced for each unit of heat released compared to other hydrocarbon fuels. (GRAPH), as well as steadier output rates against other renewable energy sources.

On the other hand, methane becomes a devastating greenhouse gas when released into the atmosphere; in terms of its contribution to global warming, it is 23 times more powerful than carbon dioxide and projected to increase by 60 percent by 2030. A recent study in 2009 show that agricultural methane emissions are responsible for 51 percent of the world's methane emissions, primarily attributed to the 1.5 billion cows on the planet. Experts estimate this amount to be between 200 to 500 litres (70 and 120 kg of Methane per year) a day from one cow, comparable to the pollution produced by a car.

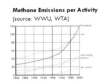

Atmospheric Methane Concentrations
(source: NOOA 2012)

Methane Emissions per Activity
(source: WWU, WTA)

Current efforts are underway to reduce ruminant methane production, such as attempting to breed cows that live longer and have better digestive systems, reshaping their diets, installing tubes (e.g. having a collection bag over each cow) and proposing flatulence tax. Within the context of commercial grazing such solutions are expensive and hard to monitor, and restricting the number of cows is unrealistic.

Our proposal to construct a methane bio-digester to harvest and store methane has multifaceted benefits. Not only will mankind be able to utilize an already-abundant, promising energy source that would replace the use of other non-renewable fuels, it also effectively control and mitigate pollution than other means of energy production, in the critical fight against climate change. Our design sheds a new light on cow farming beyond conventional food production schemes.

Methane Emissions from Animals
(source: NASA)

Methane Production for Fuel
(source: WWU, WTA)

Concept

The more agricultural methane that is successfully harvested and stored would mean phenomenal reductions in the amount of methane escaping into the atmosphere. Therefore, the bio-digester will be installed onsite on local dairy and beef farms for the direct convenience of harvesting methane. The building form is reminiscent of traditional grain silos, situated within a grain field which also provides feed for the buildings cow inhabitants.

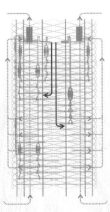

The Bio-Digester involves four key parts. The interior of the building housing the cows is continuously ventilated using a bladeless fan system integrated into the floor system; the ventilated air generated travels through an air filtration device which separates out the methane.

This methane is trapped between the semi-permeable membranes of the ETFE panels which inflates the membrane. Inflation of the membrane passively controls the amount of light that enters the building. These ETFE panels stores methane for a temporary period before it is being pumped to solid oxide fuel cells, an electrochemical conversion device that produces electricity directly from oxidizing methane. Advantages include high efficiency, long-term stability, fuel flexibility, low emissions, and relatively low cost. For general self-sustaining illumination, methane harvested is used to burn the biogas lights.

would be installed onsite on local dairy and beef farms for the direct convenience of harvesting methane. The building form is reminiscent of traditional grain silos, and pays homage to agricultural practices. The bio-digester involves four key parts. The interior of the building housing the cows is continuously ventilated using a bladeless fan system integrated into the floor system. The ventilated air generated travels through an air filtration device, which separates out the methane.

This methane is trapped between the semi-permeable membranes of the ETFE panels which inflate the membrane. Inflation of the membrane passively controls the amount of light that enters the building.

These ETFE panels stores methane for a temporary period before it is pumped to solid oxide fuel cells, an electrochemical conversion device that produces electricity directly from oxidizing methane. Advantages include high efficiency, long-term stability, fuel flexibility, low emissions, and relatively low cost. It is envisioned that each bio-digester will accommodate 2,500 cows, which would produce more than enough methane to power the entire building. It is an appropriate technology because of its low investment costs, ease of management, simple maintenance and accessibility to both small and large-scale producers.

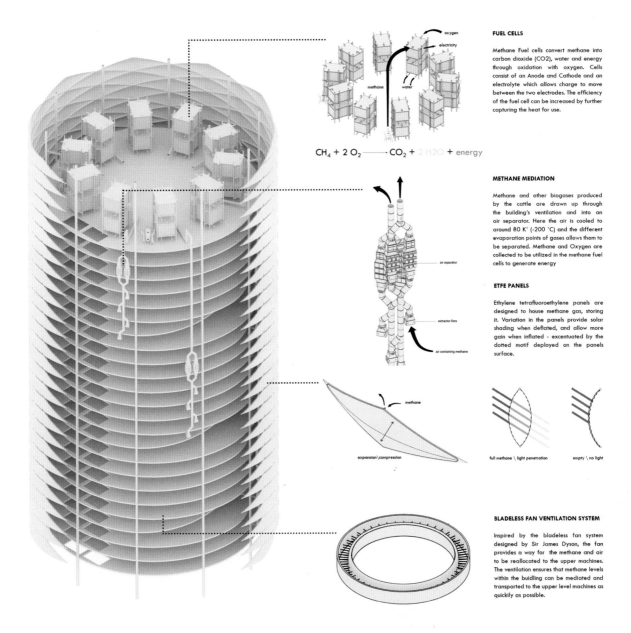

FUEL CELLS

Methane Fuel cells convert methane into carbon dioxide (CO2), water and energy through oxidation with oxygen. Cells consist of an Anode and Cathode and an electrolyte which allows charge to move between the two electrodes. The efficiency of the fuel cell can be increased by further capturing the heat for use.

$$CH_4 + 2\,O_2 \longrightarrow CO_2 + 2\,H_2O + energy$$

METHANE MEDIATION

Methane and other biogases produced by the cattle are drawn up through the building's ventilation and into an air separator. Here the air is cooled to around 80 K° (-200 °C) and the different evaporation points of gases allows them to be separated. Methane and Oxygen are collected to be utilized in the methane fuel cells to generate energy

ETFE PANELS

Ethylene tetrafluoroethylene panels are designed to house methane gas, storing it. Variation in the panels provide solar shading when deflated, and allow more gain when inflated - excentuated by the dotted motif deployed on the panels surface.

full methane \ light penetration   empty \ no light

BLADELESS FAN VENTILATION SYSTEM

Inspired by the bladeless fan system designed by Sir James Dyson, the fan provides a way for the methane and air to be reallocated to the upper machines. The ventilation ensures that methane levels within the buidling can be mediated and transported to the upper level machines as quickly as possible.

Through our proposal, methane becomes a renewable source of electricity that can be used on the farm or sold to the electricity distribution grid, substantially decreasing emission of methane to the environment, hence reducing methane taxes for countries, while catering to the future demand for beef. The ability for the bio-digester to adapt across variable beef farming contexts makes it a sustainable model on an international scale.

We envision each bio-digester to accommodate 2,500 cows, which would produce more than enough methane to power the entire building. It is an appropriate technology because of its low investment costs, easy management, simple maintenance and accessibility to both small and large-scale producers. Implementation of the bio-digester will also stimulate local and rural economies.

THIS CHAPTER IS DEDICATED TO OUR WISH TO EXPLORE AND COLONIZE. WOULD IT BE POSSIBLE TO BUILD INHABITABLE UNDERWATER ENVIRONMENTS? ARE FLOATING CITIES AND SPACE COLONIES THE NEXT FRONTIER? WHICH TECHNOLOGIES, MATERIALS, AND OTHER RESOURCES ARE NECESSARY TO ACHIEVE THESE GOALS?

NEW
FRONTIERS 3

The eVolo Skyscraper Competition was born as an architecture contest with few constraints with the intention of liberating the designers' imagination. Conceiving the future of our built environment is our core mission. We seek to enter the ranks of legendary publications such as the Italian journal Lacerba and French magazine Le Figaro, which envisioned the current state of architectural advancement in the 1910's – both published visionary ideas, which included the first imagined skyscrapers, that became a reality 75 years later. Similarly, several of the projects presented in the next few pages could become the reality of our built habitats down the line.

This chapter is dedicated to our wish to explore and colonize. Would it be possible to build inhabitable underwater environments? Are floating cities and space colonies the next frontier? Which technologies, materials, and other resources are necessary to achieve these goals?

The need to explore new territories also comes from the understanding of the fragile natural state of our planet – a time characterized by global warming and its disastrous consequences. If we foresee our darkest possible future we may be able to actually prevent it from happening.

Examples of the projects presented include underwater and floating cities that generate their own energy by harvesting solar, wind, and wave power. They also explore the production of their own food through studies of aquaculture and hydroponics and the use of halophytic vegetation to desalinate water. Other projects envision carving entire mountains for underground cities or even the colonization of Mars and its transformation into an inhabitable planet through CO_2 emissions.

OCEAN-SCRAPER

Hui Chen
Luying Guo

China

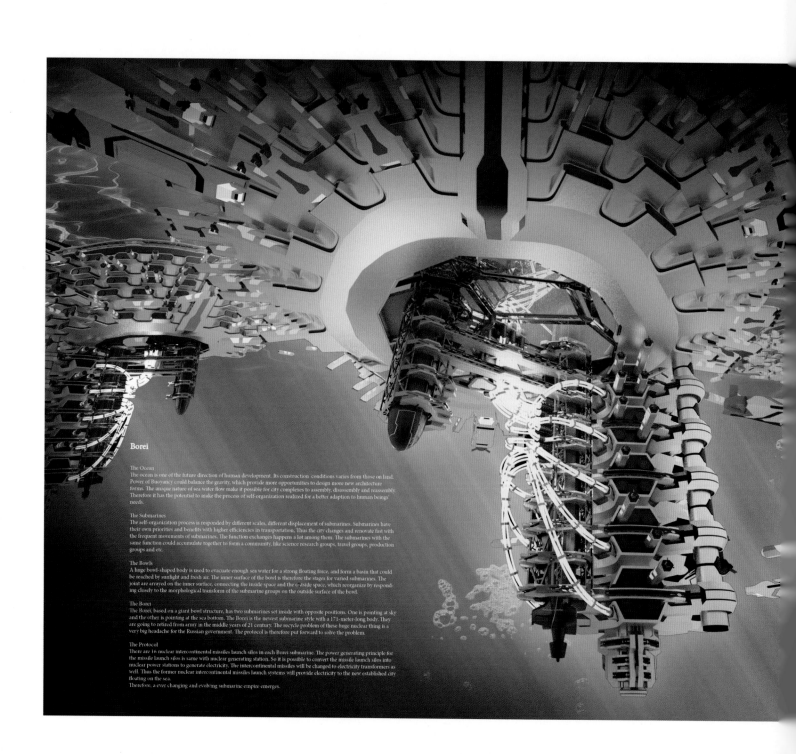

Borei

The Ocean
The ocean is one of the future direction of human development. Its construction conditions varies from those on land. Power of Buoyancy could balance the gravity, which provide more opportunities to design more new architecture forms. The unique nature of sea water flow make it possible for city complexes to assembly, disassembly and reassemble. Therefore it has the potential to make the process of self-organization realized for a better adaption to human beings' needs.

The Submarines
The self-organization process is responded by different scales, different displacement of submarines. Submarines have their own priorities and benefits with higher efficiencies in transportation. Thus the city changes and renovate fast with the frequent movements of submarines. The function exchanges happens a lot among them. The submarines with the same function could accumulate together to form a community, like science research groups, travel groups, production groups and etc.

The Bowls
A huge bowl-shaped body is used to evacuate enough sea water for a strong floating force, and form a basin that could be reached by sunlight and fresh air. The inner surface of the bowl is therefore the stages for varied submarines. The joint are arrayed on the inner surface, connecting the inside space and the outside space, which reorganize by responding closely to the morphological transform of the submarine groups on the outside surface of the bowl.

The Borei
The Borei, based on a giant bowl structure, has two submarines set inside with opposite positions. One is pointing at sky and the other is pointing at the sea bottom. The Borei is the newest submarine style with a 171-meter-long body. They are going to retired from army in the middle years of 21 century. The recycle problem of these huge nuclear thing is a very big headache for the Russian government. The protocol is therefore put forward to solve the problem.

The Protocol
There are 16 nuclear intercontinental missiles launch silos in each Borei submarine. The power generating principle for the missile launch silos is same with nuclear generating station. So it is possible to convert the missile launch silos into nuclear power stations to generate electricity. The intercontinental missiles will be changed to electricity transformers as well. Thus the former nuclear intercontinental missiles launch systems will provide electricity to the new established city floating on the sea.
Therefore, a ever changing and evolving submarine empire emerges.

Constructing a building that floats in the ocean has inherent benefits, the main boon being buoyancy. Locating a structure in the sea allows the possibility for massive complexes to be constructed without the restraints of gravity, opening possibilities for great architectural experimentation.

Enter Oceanscraper, a design for a cone-shaped underwater city complex. The Oceanscraper has a large "bowl" in the center to allow daylight to reach the depths; surrounding the bowl is a ring of living space. Submarines dock into the living space, and residents remain inside, creating a community of submarine apartments. This mobility affords freedom for residents and also allows each city complex to shift rapidly, if

Borei

0142

The Project 955, or Borei class, is a forth-generation nuclear-powered missile submarine. The Borei class will eventually replace ageing Russian Delta IV and Typhoon class ballistic missile submarines and would form a core of Russian naval deterrent.

But after the life pan, Boeris will have to be abandoned, which threaten the ocean environment.

However, the valubale nuclear energy has the potential to be recycled and reused.

The nuclear missile launch systems are generally set at the tail part of the Borei submarine.

They could be convered to nuclear power stations, which are used in the new submarine city.

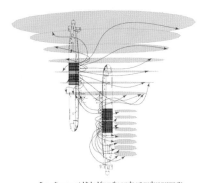

Power lines are established from the newly-set nuclear power stations and pluged into the city complex.

need be. Submarines are free to navigate both within the bowl and outside of the complex, and can dock collectively in themed groups, such as submarines that are performing research, or those that are hosting tourist groups, etc.

Each complex has two Borei nuclear submarines stationed at the bottom; one is positioned to face the sky, the other to face the sea floor. Borei submarines are the fourth-class nuclear subs used by the Russian Navy, but their life spans will only carry them through to the middle of the 21st century. After they are decommissioned, they must sit on the ocean floor with radioactive waste material inside, posing great

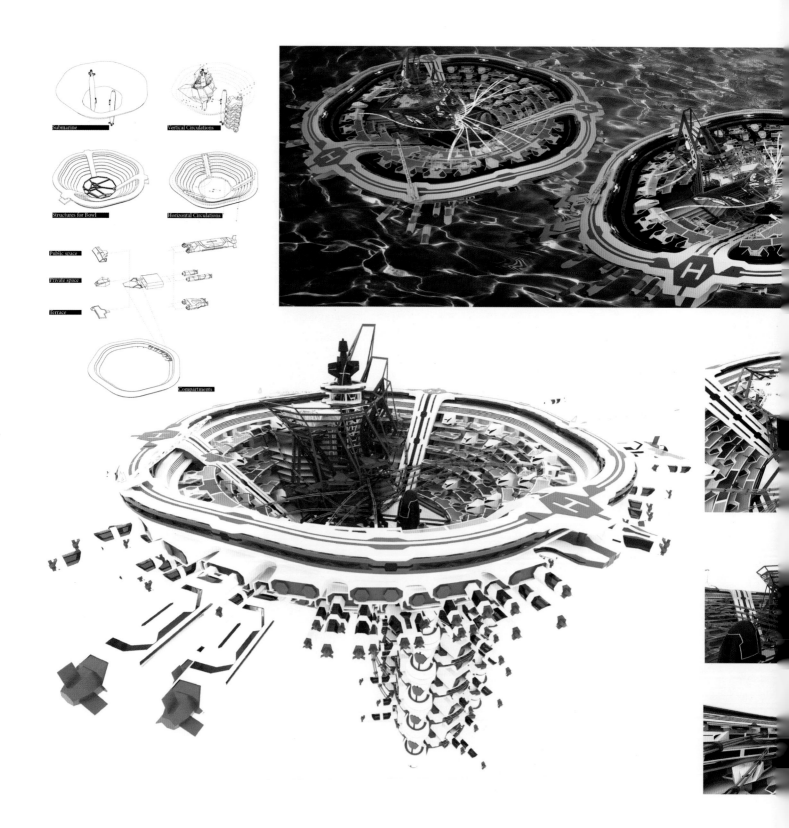

Submarine

Vertical Circulations

Structures for Bowl

Horizontal Circulations

Public space

Private space

Terrace

Compartments

potential threats to sea life. Instead of letting them rot, The Oceanscraper will commission these subs back into use, using them as nuclear power stations. Power lines from the submarines will connect directly to the city complexes to bring them energy. The power will be generated from the 16 intercontinental missile launch silos located inside each Borei submarine.

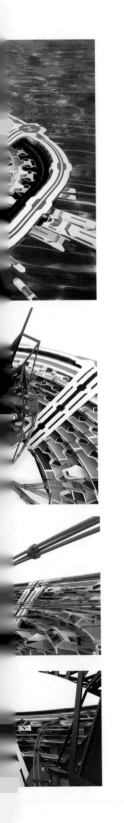

0142

Borei_0142

HOUSE OF BABEL

Nikita Asadov

Russia

HOUSE OF BABEL
the post-crisis skyscraper

The race between countries, cities, and corporations to construct the highest structure is a challenge of pride and power. Our technological advances allowed for the construction of super-tall buildings—the higher they are, the more space they lose and the harder the engineering challenge becomes. The global financial crisis was the last decisive argument against such structures. The skyscraper as an architectural typology, owes its appearance to Manhattan, where the height of the building has grown with the cost of the area. Altitude gradually became self-sufficient function, as the way of satisfying the ambitions of the customer.

The House of Babel offers a radical revision for the common method of building a traditional home.

0282

With the help of aerostatic construction we can eliminate extra floors and elevate the building to almost any desired height. The post-crisis skyscraper is the house consisting of two floors connected with a high-speed elevator on a thin heavy-duty cable.

    The first floor is located at ground level while the second floor is attached to the aerostatic bearing structure that holds it at a height of up to several kilometers. The upper floor has a fully sealed enclosure. For security purposes, the aerostatic dome has several compartments. The cable connecting the floors can shorten or lengthen, thus changing the height of the building. In normal mode, the house can be used as a

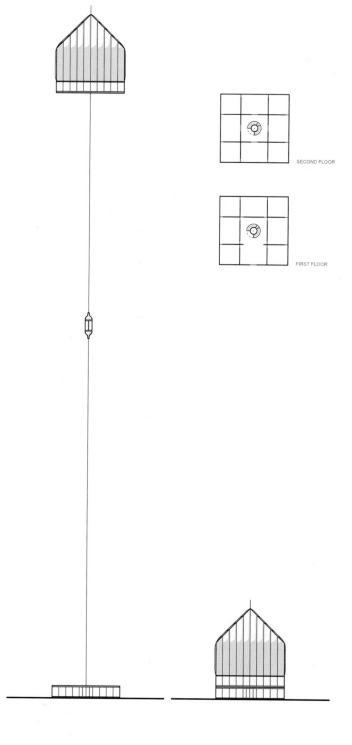

SECOND FLOOR

FIRST FLOOR

HOUSE OF BABEL
the post-crisis sky

Dream to reach out
nomenon throughou
Skyscraper as an a
appearance of Man
building has grown
titude gradually bec
the way of satisfying
To date, high-rise b
the race into an ind
in which has a symb
country, city, or corp
high building to get
Progress of constru
life the buildings of
become almost imp
the more space the
evators, the harder
Thus, the symbolic
cality.
The global financial
gument against suc
hardly serve as a d

Present design offe
tional method of co
ings. With the help
can refuse extra flo
almost any height.
Skyscraper of post-
sisting of two floors
elevator on a thin h
The first floor is loc
based on a tradition
is attached to the a
holds it at a height
upper floor has a fu
system of autonom
poses, aerostatic d
In the event of dam
slowly go down to
The cable connecti
shorten or lengther
building. In normal
a traditional two-sto
height can be incre
or simply enjoy the
If we compare this
advantage will be
rapid fabricated. Ar
than the tallest sky
loosen the rope. N
have the highest h

traditional two-story house.

If we compare this structure with the traditional skyscraper, the advantages will be obvious. It is way more economical and can be more rapidly fabricated. To become a couple feet taller than the tallest skyscraper, one would just need to slightly loosen the cable. Now, finally, anyone can afford to have the highest house in the world.

0282

er common phe-
mankind.
logy, owes its
e height of the
st of the site. Al-
ent function, as
of the customer.
ion has turned
line, the primacy
Almost every
eeking for ultra-
ity complex.
has brought to
life in them has
her they rise,
ruction and el-
gineer support.
y kills the practi-

st decisive ar-
ngs. But he
ay up..

ise for the tradi-
kind of build-
structions we
ouilding to

the house con-
the high-speed

vel, and is
he second floor
structure that
ilometers. The
ure and a
security pur-
compartments.
m, the house

flective. It can
he height of the
can be used as
ecessary, the
strate the power,

traditional, the
ty budget and
ouple feet taller
ld just slightly
e can afford to

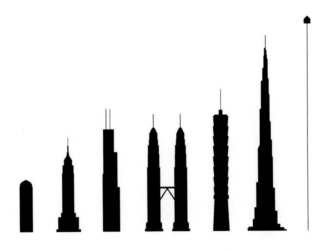

LITOGRAPH BY GUSTAVE DORE

PLASTIC FISH TOWER

Kim Hongseop
Cho Hyunbeom
Yoon Hyungsoo
Yoon Sunhee

Republic of Korea

In the middle of the Pacific Ocean sits a mass of garbage that is 8.1% the size of the entire sea. It is known as the Great Pacific Garbage Patch (GPGP), and is estimated to contain over 100 million tons of waste. The debris gathers in that particular location as ocean currents convene in the Subtropical Convergence Region, and is causing grave harm to the immediate ecosystem and those within a broad surrounding swath.

The Plastic Fish Tower, a circular structure floating on the ocean surface within the GPGP, will collect and reprocess plastic, which estimates say comprises 90% of the GPGP and is often ingested by birds and fish, causing their demise. A large fence will circle the structure underwater in a 1 km diameter to capture all the

0321

PLASTIC FISH TOWER

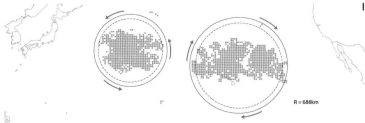

I

R = 688km

In the middle of the Pacific Ocean, There is a great garbage island which is not visible on the satellite photography. It is so called GPSP(Great Pacific Garbage Patch) which remind of a huge land because it reaches about 8.1% of the size of the Pacific Ocean. The marine debris gathered by oceanic current and wind gradually move to clockwise direction on the Flux of North Pacific, and it make a stock at the calm belt in Subtropical Convergence Region (STCZ), located roughly between 135°W to 155°W and 35°N to 42° N.

II

The estimated volumes of them reach about one hundred million ton and small broken plastic particles sized 1-2 mm hold over 90% of them. These are threating the lives of fishes and birds because they can easily eat them as a food. This may also cause a serious social problem because it can make harm to people's health.

III

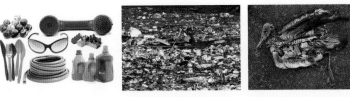

Plastics, not easily biodegrade in nature are being produced over 90 billion kg in a year and about 10% of them are thrown away in the sea. Among them, about three hundred million kg of them are concentrated in GPGP, and the volume of them is so huge that they are just laid aside without any control.

IV

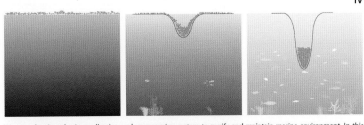

We are adopting plastic recollecting and reprocessing system to purify and maintain marine environment. In this system, recollected plastic patch will be used to make artificial fishing banks for the purpose of constructing marine farm and keeping healthy marine ecosystem. As the restored marine ecosystem also could have tourist's attractions, appropriate architectural program may also be choosen to provide people with wide information as to unrevealed seriousness of GPGP as well as the chances to reconsider about their egoistic mind for the nature.

plastic that floats its way. The plastic will be recycled within the structure and processed into plastic patches that can be assembled into fish farms to restore the ecosystem. In addition to helping mitigate the pollution, the fish farm will also have two added benefits: the buoyancy of the plastic fish farm elements will be enough to keep the entire structure afloat since plastic is in fact so buoyant, and it will position the structure as a tourist attraction.

Bringing tourists to the GPGP would greatly help in disseminating widely the reality of this manmade ecological catastrophe. The tourists will be transported to and from the site by ships that are fueled

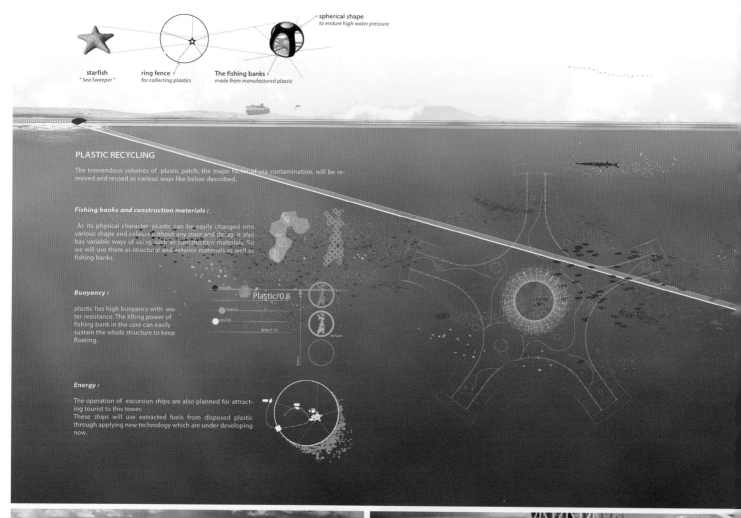

spherical shape
to endure high water pressure

starfish
" Sea Sweeper "

ring fence
for collecting plastics

The fishing banks
made from manufactured plastic

PLASTIC RECYCLING

The tremendous volumes of plastic patch, the major factor of sea contamination, will be re-moved and reused as various ways like below described.

Fishing banks and construction materials :

As its physical character, plastic can be easily changed into various shape and colours without any stain and decay, it also has variable ways of using such as construction materials. So we will use them as structural and exterior materials as well as fishing banks.

Buoyancy :

plastic has high buoyancy with wa-ter resistance. The lifting power of fishing bank in the core can easily sustain the whole structure to keep floating.

Energy :

The operation of excursion ships are also planned for attract-ing tourist to this tower.
These ships will use extracted fuels from disposed plastic through applying new technology which are under developing now.

Plastic/0.8

by chemicals that will be collected from the processed plastics within the skyscraper in an as-of-yet-undiscovered method of chemical extraction.

The structure itself is a ring that rises above the water and also goes below, but is largely hollow. The outer ring holds residential and leisure spaces, and is connected at intervals by bridges that are enclosed underwater (and one that is open on the water's surface). Fishing banks made from the recycled plastic funnel up through the middle of the ring, helping to keep the structure buoyant.

0321

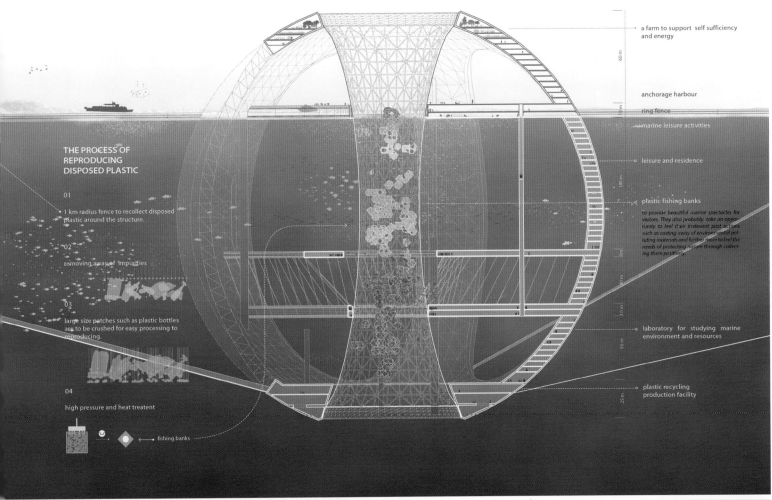

THE PROCESS OF
REPRODUCING
DISPOSED PLASTIC

01

1 km radius fence to recollect disposed plastic around the structure.

02

removing away of impurities

03

large size patches such as plastic bottles are to be crushed for easy processing to reproducing.

04

high pressure and heat treatent

fishing banks

a farm to support self sufficiency and energy

anchorage harbour

ring fence

marine leisure activities

leisure and residence

plastic fishing banks
to provide beautiful marine spectacles for visitors. They also probably take an opportunity to feel their irrelevant past actions such as casting away of environmental polluting materials and furthermore to feel the needs of protecting nature through collecting them positively.

laboratory for studying marine environment and resources

plastic recycling production facility

238

VOLCANIC-SCRAPER

Kim Beomjun
Heo Gyeongyoung
Jo Myeongseon

Republic of Korea

VOLCANICSCAPER

Scenario of the year 2312

Now year 2312, over the 70% of whole earth continent has been sunken under the water. Following disappearing of Tuvalu 300 years ago, Maldives, Japan, and Manhattan have been flooded one by one. Just sharp steeples show traces of sky-scraper cities, they were disappeared under the water. They are just one of evidences revealing the past glory. A number of people is sharing left 30% ground. This is very super high-density society. Our humanity is confusion itself. There are neither building materials for architecture, nor ground for building.

One day starting rising sea level 300 years ago, The grid system structure which has been located in the earth, function as one of the continent as well city for us. It has served various shape space to us. We can control position that we want to build. The depth is various, the minimum 15m the maximum 120m. Now, we are living in these cities together.

One of the most serious problems facing humanity is rising sea levels, which threaten to flood or outright swallow some of the world's most populous and important cities. One solution to this dire problem could be building a city out of a porous and buoyant material: lava.

The designers conceived the idea by imagining how lava that is spewed under water hardens into large masses and creates caves; perhaps, they thought, people could live within these holes. With the amount of lava that is released during an eruption, a whole city could be formed from the material, shaped and utilized like concrete.

0338

1. Inconvenient city in the future.

After industrial revolution, as concerning about greenhouse gases, sun cycle and volcanic eruptions which are caused by indiscreet consumption of fossil fuel, the government has noticed that surface of sea rise maximum 1.8 meter at 2100. In these days, the rising sea level is one of the most serious issue which is considered inconvenient truth. It is threatening earth that our livelihood and as a result, there is no land we can live in the earth. At just 1m rising sea levels is happened, The Venezia and Tokyo will be into the water. In case of 2m rising, Los Angeles and Amsterdam will be going down the sink and 3m rising, almost of world major cities will be sunken like Manhattan and San Francisco.

2012   2112   2312

A city grid made of tungsten (a metal that melts at over 6100 degrees Fahrenheit, far above lava's typical temperature of 1700 degrees Fahrenheit) is created using an urban plan. When a volcano erupts, the lava flows along the path of the grid system. Utilizing the pressure of the gasses that blow lava from a volcano, lava if pushed into the pipes of the grid system; some pipes create the main arteries of the city while others push lava underwater into large molds to form buildings.

Even if a city was inundated with floods from rising sea levels, a lava city could float. Imagine a futuristic situation where 70 percent of the continent is flooded, but thanks to the work of the lava grid, a whole

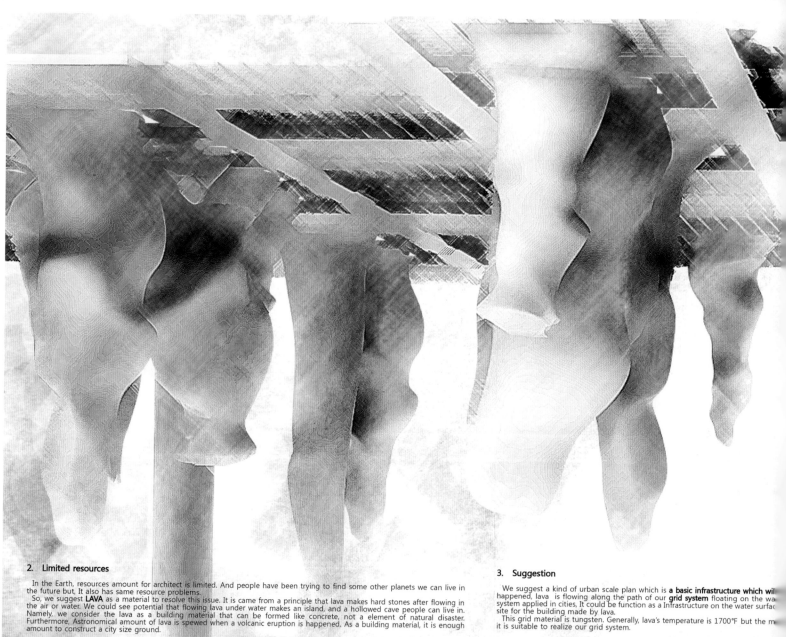

2. Limited resources

In the Earth, resources amount for architect is limited. And people have been trying to find some other planets we can live in the future but, It also has same resource problems.

So, we suggest **LAVA** as a material to resolve this issue. It is came from a principle that lava makes hard stones after flowing in the air or water. We could see potential that flowing lava under water makes an island, and a hollowed cave people can live in. Namely, we consider the lava as a building material that can be formed like concrete, not a element of natural disaster. Furthermore, Astronomical amount of lava is spewed when a volcanic eruption is happened. As a building material, it is enough amount to construct a city size ground.

 =   × 700,000,000

3. Suggestion

We suggest a kind of urban scale plan which is **a basic infrastructure which will** happened, lava is flowing along the path of our **grid system** floating on the wa system applied in cities, It could be function as a Infrastructure on the water surfac site for the building made by lava.

This grid material is tungsten. Generally, lava's temperature is 1700°F but the m it is suitable to realize our grid system.

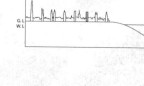

floating content has been formed, keeping life on earth possible.

As far as an urban scale plan goes, a basic infrastructure to make the city by itself is suggested. Once volcanic eruption has occurred, the lava that flows along the path of the grid system will be floating on the water surface by buoyancy. As a result of this the grid system applied in cities, it could function as infrastructure on the water surface as a vein. Each lava pocket would have its own depth and they would respond to various demands of program individually.

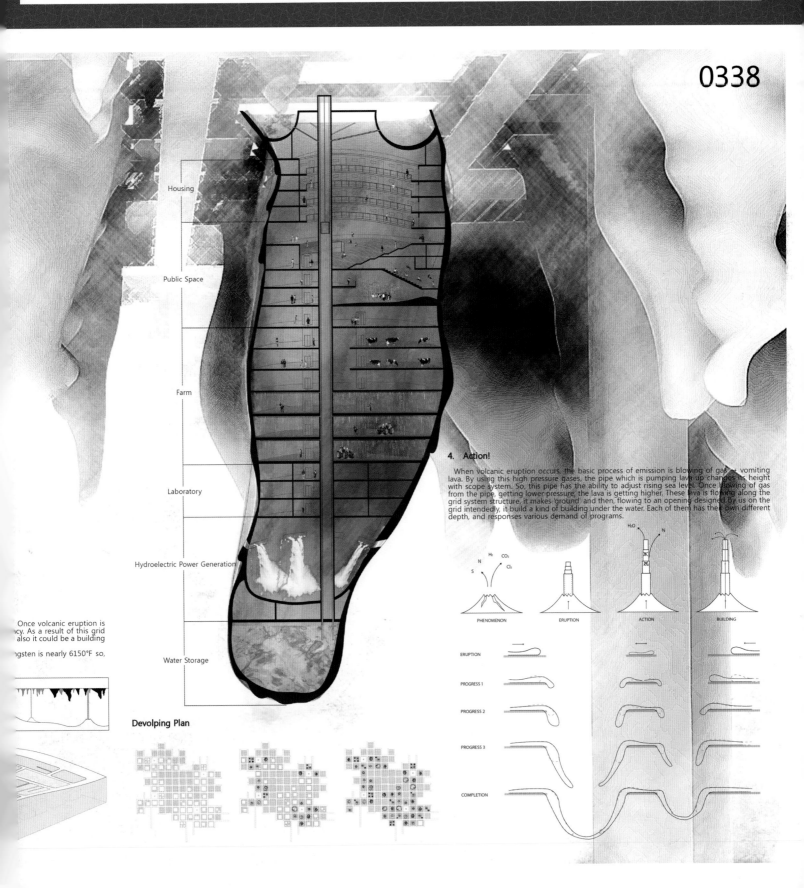

0338

Housing

Public Space

Farm

Laboratory

Hydroelectric Power Generation

Water Storage

4. Action!

When volcanic eruption occurs, the basic process of emission is blowing of gas or vomiting lava. By using this high pressure gases, the pipe which is pumping lava up changes its height with scope system. So, this pipe has the ability to adjust rising sea level. Once blowing of gas from the pipe, getting lower pressure, the lava is getting higher. These lava is flowing along the grid system structure, it makes 'ground' and then, flowing to an opening designed by us on the grid intendedly, it build a kind of building under the water. Each of them has their own different depth, and responses various demand of programs.

PHENOMENON | ERUPTION | ACTION | BUILDING

ERUPTION

PROGRESS 1

PROGRESS 2

PROGRESS 3

COMPLETION

Once volcanic eruption is
ncy. As a result of this grid
also it could be a building

ngsten is nearly 6150°F so,

Devolping Plan

SHIPBREAKING TOWER

Paul Lipan-Weber
Ioana Alexandra Mititelu
Victor-Ioan Pricop

Romania

There are two ways that ships die: - they become obsolete vessels
- they sink (shipwrecks)

SHIP LIFE. Ships have a normal lifespan of about 40 years after which any repair becomes uneconomical. These ships are then retired and sold for scrap to commercial ship breakers.

SHIPWRECKS. Throughout history, ships have been lost at sea due to war and severe weather. The total of WWII shipwrecks stands at 7807 vessels worldwide combining to over 34 million tons of shipping with 861 tankers and oilers. Each year that passes, because of corrosion, the vessels deteriorate more and the risk of significant oil release becomes more likely. The data collected identifies the South Asian-Pacific region as the area with the highest number of sunken potentially polluting tank vessels.
As the entire wreck represent itself a source of pollution, its recovery is considered the best option.

SHIPBREAKING is "green". At present, the global center of the ship breaking and recycling industry is in South Asia, specifically Bangladesh, India, and Pakistan. These three countries account for 70–80 percent of the international recycling market for ocean-going vessels. Almost everything on the ship and the ship itself is recycled.

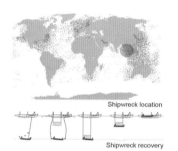

Shipwreck location

Shipwreck recovery

O **Preparatory operations:**
- wreck inspection using R.O.V.'s
- transfer oil and chemicals into tanks
O **Elimination of seafloor effects on the wreck:**
- pumping and removing silt and mud from the wreck
- breaking down the clay layers with a water jet or air lance
O **Heavy lift ship out** fitted with cranes allowing wrecks to be lifted and stowed inside the hold.

BANGLADESH/ CHITTAGONG
At present the ship breaking industry in Bangladesh is concentrated in Chittagong, one of the largest yards in the world and the busiest seaport here.

PROBLEMS
O Ship-breaking has contaminated the coastal soil and sea water environment with many hazards (asbestos, persistent organic pollutants, heavy metals, oil). Wastes of the scrapped ships are drained and dumped into the Bay of Bengal.
O Working conditions are poor for the majority of these workers and even the use of child labor is allowed. Over the last twenty years more than 400 workers have been killed and 6000 seriously injured.
O Environmental damages could worsen as result of sea level rise. The amount of infested sand that could be disturbed and washed out from the beaches could pose significant threats.
O The hazardous waste management (storage, transport, and disposal) facility is a costly requirement.
O Bangladesh has a serious power problem. Nearly half of its 162-million population does not have access to electricity.

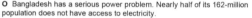

Preser

Located at the entrance of Chittagong's harbor in Bangladesh, the Shipbreaking Tower is a ship recycling facility that dismantles obsolete and wrecked sea vessels. Ships have a lifespan of about 40 years, after which they are too old to make repairs financially viable. When a ship has reached the end of its life cycle, it can be broken apart and its materials recycled. This self-sustaining skyscraper will complete that process, separating the dismantling process from the melting of steel and the production of bars through its architectural layout.

The building is meant to be more than utilitarian—though it is convenient and cost-effective for such a

city connection

tribution   ship dismantling   the coast
+

city gate   iron works
+

tower connection   transport

THE SHIPBREAKING TOWER

O ship dismantling (obsolete vessels + shipwrecks) > recycling steel > finished rods > storage > loading cargo > distribution

O a good management > producing faster and more efficient -> reducing the cost

O protection of the environment

O releasing the cost from shipbreaking > recovery of the ecosystem >tourism and fish restocking as first feeding source for poor people

O improvement of living and working conditions

O self-sufficient and energy power producer > solar panels exterior skin which harness on a massive scale Bangladesh's abundance of sunlight > reuses the heat from melting to recover energy

O an icon for the city > tourist attractor
>a gate to city's harbor
>signal for the ships

O send children to school instead of working in shipbreaking

0374

Shipbreaking tower plan

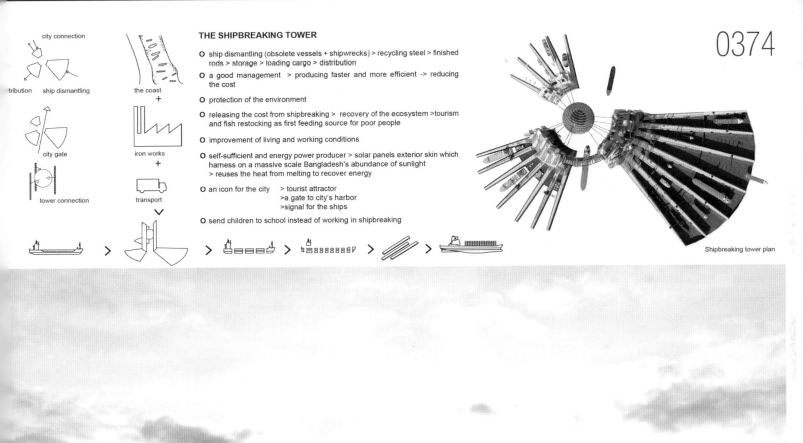

SHIPBREAKING TOWER

structure to be located at sea, taking away the need to move ships farther than usual—and instead can be seen as an icon for the city, and a tourist attraction.

But the fact that it was developed as a working tower to process materials still lies at the core of its mission. The structure's exterior skin is in fact a solar curtain, a surface covered in solar panels. Batteries that store energy collected from these panels are located within the building. Additional energy is created for the building thanks to a steam-powered turbine that spins when heat from the furnace boils water.

Large, finger-like docks fan from the base of the skyscraper to take in ships to be inspected for

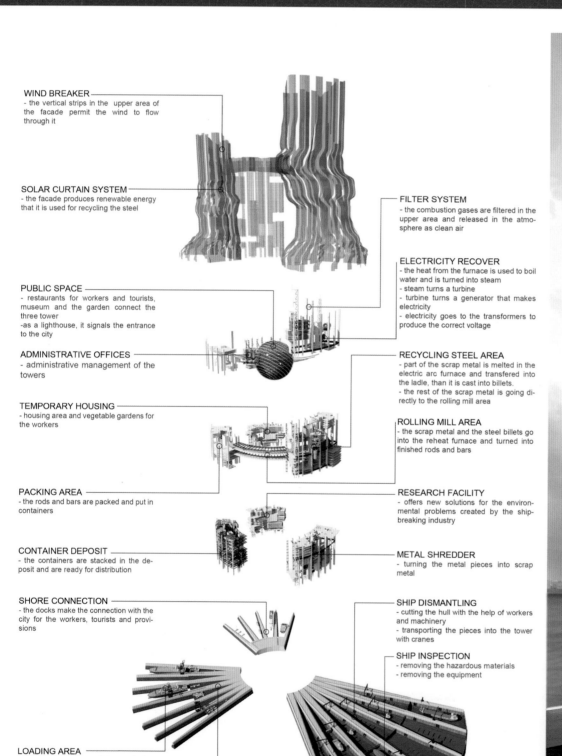

WIND BREAKER
- the vertical strips in the upper area of the facade permit the wind to flow through it

SOLAR CURTAIN SYSTEM
- the facade produces renewable energy that it is used for recycling the steel

PUBLIC SPACE
- restaurants for workers and tourists, museum and the garden connect the three tower
-as a lighthouse, it signals the entrance to the city

ADMINISTRATIVE OFFICES
- administrative management of the towers

TEMPORARY HOUSING
- housing area and vegetable gardens for the workers

PACKING AREA
- the rods and bars are packed and put in containers

CONTAINER DEPOSIT
- the containers are stacked in the deposit and are ready for distribution

SHORE CONNECTION
- the docks make the connection with the city for the workers, tourists and provisions

LOADING AREA
- the cranes load the containers onto the ships

CONTAINER HANDLING
- the forklifts move the containers to the loading area

FILTER SYSTEM
- the combustion gases are filtered in the upper area and released in the atmosphere as clean air

ELECTRICITY RECOVER
- the heat from the furnace is used to boil water and is turned into steam
- steam turns a turbine
- turbine turns a generator that makes electricity
- electricity goes to the transformers to produce the correct voltage

RECYCLING STEEL AREA
- part of the scrap metal is melted in the electric arc furnace and transfered into the ladle, than it is cast into billets.
- the rest of the scrap metal is going directly to the rolling mill area

ROLLING MILL AREA
- the scrap metal and the steel billets go into the reheat furnace and turned into finished rods and bars

RESEARCH FACILITY
- offers new solutions for the environmental problems created by the ship-breaking industry

METAL SHREDDER
- turning the metal pieces into scrap metal

SHIP DISMANTLING
- cutting the hull with the help of workers and machinery
- transporting the pieces into the tower with cranes

SHIP INSPECTION
- removing the hazardous materials
- removing the equipment

EXPLODED 3D SECTION

" We all know how ships a[...] a bottle of champagne. Bu[...] their death every year. Fror[...] with all their steel, their as[...] countries in the world, cou[...] here, until you see it. It cou[...] the fumes, and the heat. T[...] dirty, dangerous work, for l[...]

processing and also to welcome those holding workers and tourists. Each separate part of the dismantling and recycling process requires a different section within the building: there is a metal shredding room, a rolling mill area to turn recycled steel into rods and bars, a packing area and container storage area for the packaging and shipment of recycled products created from ship dismantling, a research facility, and even public spaces like restaurants for tourists who come to visit. A large light at the top allows the Shipbreaking Tower to also be a beacon, serving as the harbor's lighthouse. As the structure ages, its anchors in the seawater will come alive with sea life, allowing the structure to act as a living reef.

0374

stic vessels are nudged into the ocean with
how they die. And hundreds of ships meet
iners, to grubby freighters, literally dumped
s on the beaches of some of the poorest
lesh. You can't really believe how bad it is
you'll get to hell on earth, with the smoke,
here are the wretched of the earth, doing
a day."

(Bob Simon, CBS News)

HEAVEN AND EARTH

Wei Zhao

China

天上人間 (Tian-shan-ren-jian)

天上人間 is the physical manifesdation of the traditional shanshui painting which aims to reach the ideal lifestyle.

Earth, with 70 bilion population, is continuously increasing her load with three babies born per seond. With limited resources, the rapid growth of population has caused many problems. Earth is suffering from environmental degradation, ocean acidification, ozone holes, water consumption and the loss of biodiversity.

天上人間
is a solu
food, wa
consum

Tian-shan-ren-jian (Heaven and Earth) is the physical manifestation of the traditional Shanshui painting, which aims to reach the ideal lifestyle.

Earth, with 7 billion people, is continuously increasing her load with three new babies born every second. With limited resources, the rapid growth of population has caused many problems included environmental degradation, ocean acidification, ozone holes, lack of fresh water, and constant loss of biodiversity.

The Heaven and Earth project is a utopia wonderland residing in the air. There are mountains, rivers, lakes, forests, and animals. It solves the problems that exist on Earth, including food, water, and housing.

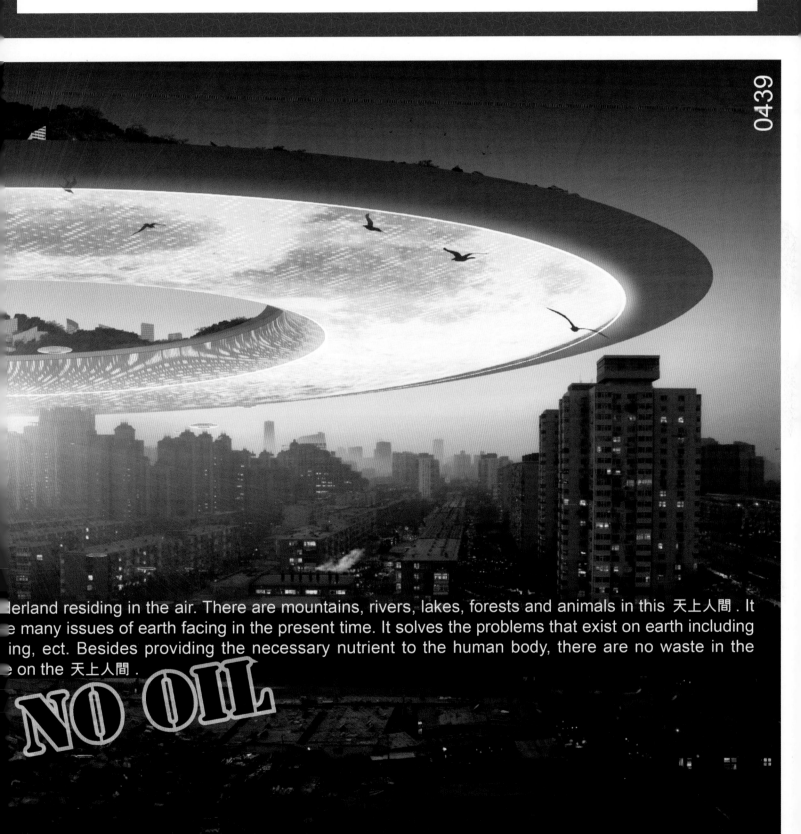

0439

...derland residing in the air. There are mountains, rivers, lakes, forests and animals in this 天上人間 . It ...e many issues of earth facing in the present time. It solves the problems that exist on earth including ...ing, ect. Besides providing the necessary nutrient to the human body, there are no waste in the ...e on the 天上人間 .

NO OIL

Heaven and Earth is operated by the Maglev Technology to allow it to float in the air. The repulsion caused by the aircraft's magnetic system and the Earth's magnetic field will control the floating city. There are a large number of molecular magnets distributed along the underside of the vessel. The rotation of the curved bottom can generate the power necessary for the city. This rotation could also maintain the balance of the flight.

Small, magnetic suspension aircrafts are used as the transport links between the vessel and Earth. They borrow the magnetic force from the land to reach the earth or the land. Food will be grown in different

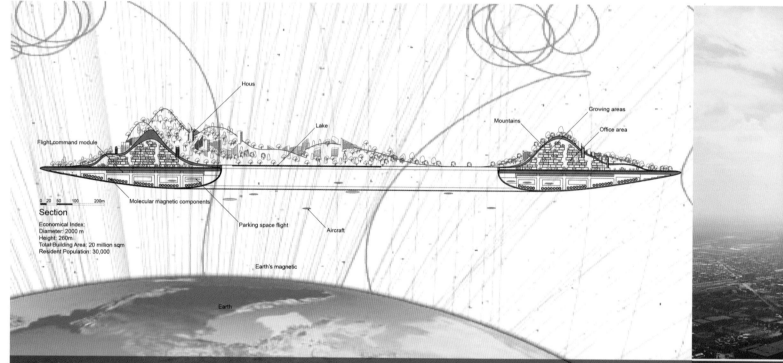

Hous

Growing areas

Mountains

Office area

Flight command module

Lake

Molecular magnetic components

Parking space flight

Aircraft

Section

Economical Index:
Diameter: 2000 m
Height: 260m.
Total Building Area: 20 million sqm
Resident Population: 30,000

0 20 50 100 200m

Earth's magnetic

Earth

天上人間 is operated by the maglev technology to allow it to float in the air. The repulsion caused by aircraft magnetism and the Earth's magnetic will control the magnetic floating in the air. There are a large number of molecular magnets distributed at the underside of the flight arc. Each molecule magnets combined with magnetic container, the container can be adjusted to capture the magnetic force from the earth's field. By changing the magnetic repulsion and attraction force between the container and earth, the land could float as smoothly as the wind in the air. The rotation of the curve bottom can generate the power to provide the living on the land. The rotation could also maintain the balance of the flight. Small, magnetic suspension aircrafts are used as the transport links between the land and earth. They borrow the magnetic force from the land to reach the earth or the land. Food will be grown in different cabins, 24 hours of light will be provided for the growth. Organic food without the pollution from chemicals could be produced. Surplus food could be distributed to the low incomes on the earth. The fabric from food plants could be made into cloth.

Elevation

Everything consumed could be recycled to realize the goal of zero emissions. The 天上人間 will, at the end, stop the damage from human to earth and give earth time to recover.

cabins, 24 hours of light will be provided for growth. Organic food without chemical pollution could be produced. Everything consumed could be recycled to realize the goal of zero emissions. Heaven and Earth will at the end stop the damage of humans on Earth and will give Earth time to recover.

AWAROA LIGHTHOUSE

Jansen Aui
Nick Roberts
Henry Stephens

Australia/New Zealand

[archival image] - Early Awaroa Settlement.

[fig i]. The landscape viewed as an idealised New Zealand image. The presence of the lighthouse offsets this calm, making visible an otherwise hidden tension of an impending earthquake or tsunami.

[fig ii]. The Lighthouse viewed in its fragile profile, overwhelmed by the atmosphere of the landscape.

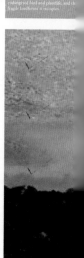

[fig iv]. The presence of the lighthouse from this strong profile creates a provocative counterpoint to the serene things of the day time context. The form gazes outward, protecting the endangered bird and plantlife, and its fragile landforms it occupies.

AWAROA LIGHTHOUSE

A Skyscraper for the New Zealand Landscape

The developer model for the skyscraper sees an initial reflection upon site in terms of a potential factor of multiplication of its footprint. In the thirst for yield, the point immediately within the tide boundary becomes absolute. What is achievable within these constraints? becomes the question, and the answer necessarily divorces the consideration of architecture from the point immediately outside of that title boundary.

We are interested in the tower as architecture and landscape; the tower and all the points naturally occurring in its immediate situation. More specifically, the skyscraper as forming a dramatic integration with the land. We turn to New Zealand as both a site and a model for thinking: a nation clouded by anxiety over vertically built form damaging its rugged, otherworldly beauty. We turn to the lighthouse as both an architectural typology for inquiry and for its imagistic quality. Historically pictured amidst precipitous coastline and shrouded by violent waters, its solidity, stability and reassuredness within its siting becomes the idyllic reference point for the vertical structure romanticised on shaky ground. The lighthouse is thus engaged with both the physical site beyond its formal boundary, and the metaphorical 'non-site' of the spatial and psychological relationship New Zealand has to its landscape [Smithson, 1979].

Within the Awaroa inlet of the South Island's Abel Tasman National Park, the Awaroa Lighthouse proposes a reinterpretation of the lighthouse's function for an increasingly precarious mental state. The historical processes of the lighthouse as a navigational, directive, and organisational structure are reimagined here as a symbol of foresight in the event of an earthquake or related natural disaster. The lighthouse thus needs to literally penetrate and understand the core of its site in order to protect it from harm.

Like lighthouses of old, the Awaroa Lighthouse oscillates between states of information flow both material (elemental site conditions) and immaterial (networking and co-ordination). The tip of the tower embraces the immaterial data flow of recent technological advances – an above earth recording of satellite photography from a global network of similar towers in similarly earthquake-prone sites. Materially, a network of telemetric rods radiating across the site, in conjunction with a primary drill at the base of the tower record beneath earth: tectonic and soil movement, seismic noise and electromagnetic waves. In-between, a single residence for a nominated 'keeper' is provided, where the streams of data from both sources can be consolidated into an anticipatory forecast for impending disaster.

In this scenario, the architectural system shifts from its passive, 'recording' state to its active, 'protective' state, through a dormant system within the telemetric rods that expand and direct tidal flow. This is achieved through the distribution of sand into a network of 'sand walls,' formed between the outermost rods, in a gesture towards the defence and preservation of its landscape in the event of a tsunami.

Formally, the geometric composition of the tower enfolds its functional concepts in exposing a play of opposites. It is invested in the tension generated between an image of stability, in a phenomenal sense, versus the reality of fragility, in a literal and tactile sense. At once austere, monolithic, even muscular when confronted in one elevation, upon rotation of one's viewline the tower is revealed as potentially fragile, susceptible to decay and weather. Within, traditionalist concepts of structure are inverted or emphasised in a play of anchors and cantilevers, interrupted and dislodged views, and disproportionate scale that is never easily absolved. These are purposeful absurdities, given our interest in anxiety as a headspace and more importantly, an activator for a designed architectural experience.

As day passes into night, the tower within the landscape fluctuates once more between functional and symbolic states. Illuminated from within as the darkest hours emerge, the structural exoskeleton is given an imagistic emphasis and weight. After Vidler [1992: 168], here we are referencing concepts of light as arcane as they are socio-culturally embedded in our nature, a skyscraper engaged in both its physical and metaphysical contexts. The lighthouse remains a beacon in the always-recurrent dark, as it always was, and with it all our internalised understandings of its symbolism: of foresight, and of knowledge, even where the endgame is most unwritten.

SMITHSON, R. ROBERT SMITHSON: THE COLLECTED WRITINGS, 2nd Edition, edited by Jack Flam, The University of California Press, Berkeley and Los Angeles, California; University of California Press, LTD. London, England; 1996, Originally published: The Writings of Robert Smithson, edited by Nancy Holt, New York, New York University Press, 1979.

VIDLER, A. THE ARCHITECTURAL UNCANNY: ESSAYS IN THE MODERN UNHOMELY, Massachusetts: The Massachusetts Institute of Technology Press, 1992.

[fig iii]. Entry into the lighthouse, sitting 6m above sea level is only accessible by boat during high tide.

[fig v]. The landscape at Awaroa is constantly reformed by the shifting tides. The telemetric rods relay vital information to the thread-like locate at the top of the lighthouse, creating virtual topography registering changes in the physical one.

The Awaroa Lighthouse skyscraper is a project that allows a building to form a dramatic integration with the land; located in the sand on the coast of the Awaroa inlet of New Zealand's South Island's Abel Tasman National Park, the lighthouse has specialized infrastructure to warn but also literally protect those on land from harm. Such reassurance is necessary for people such as the residents of New Zealand, as it is a nation clouded by anxiety over the vertically-built form damaging its rugged, otherworldly beauty and one where natural disasters such as earthquakes and tsunamis pose a huge threat.

As a historic architectural typology, the lighthouse is used as a navigational, directive, and organizational

0530 - 1

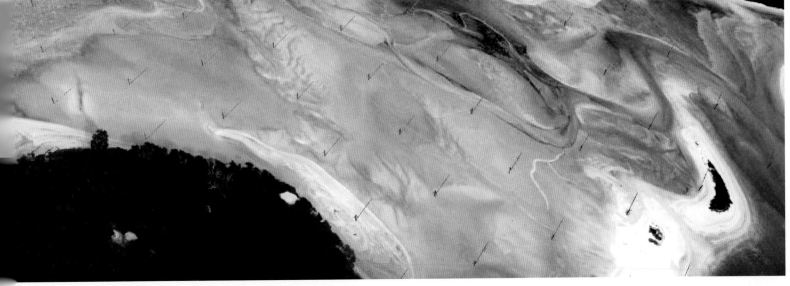

structure. However, its function here is reimagined and taken further, symbolizing to those on shore foresight and safety from natural disaster. The tip of the tower is a collector of data, receiving photography of the earth from above from satellites and data from a global network of similar towers in similar earthquake-prone sites. Additionally, a network of telemetric rods radiating across the site, in conjunction with a primary drill at the base of the tower, record tectonic and soil movement, seismic noise and electromagnetic waves below. These systems help predict earthquakes. Inside the lighthouse is a single residence for a "keeper;" this individual analyzes the incoming streams of data and sounds warning if conditions indicate impending

facade

structure

circulation

living & working spaces

telemetric needle

[fig vi]. The view to the illuminated lighthouse at night is a critical diurnal link the the fluctuation between the Awatoa Lighthouse's symbolid and functional states.

The fragile, thin profile as viewed during the day is inversely revealed as the structural core and primary telemetric needle - physically connecting the building to the landscape.

danger.

In addition to predicting danger, this lighthouse can also protect. The telemetric rods that radiate from the building can also expand and direct tidal flow. This is achieved through the distribution of sand into a network of "sand walls" formed between the outermost rods, which are meant to defend land in the case of a tsunami.

Come nighttime, the tower is illuminated from within, and the structural exoskeleton is given an imagistic emphasis and weight to remain a beacon in the always-recurrent dark and ease the fears of those on land.

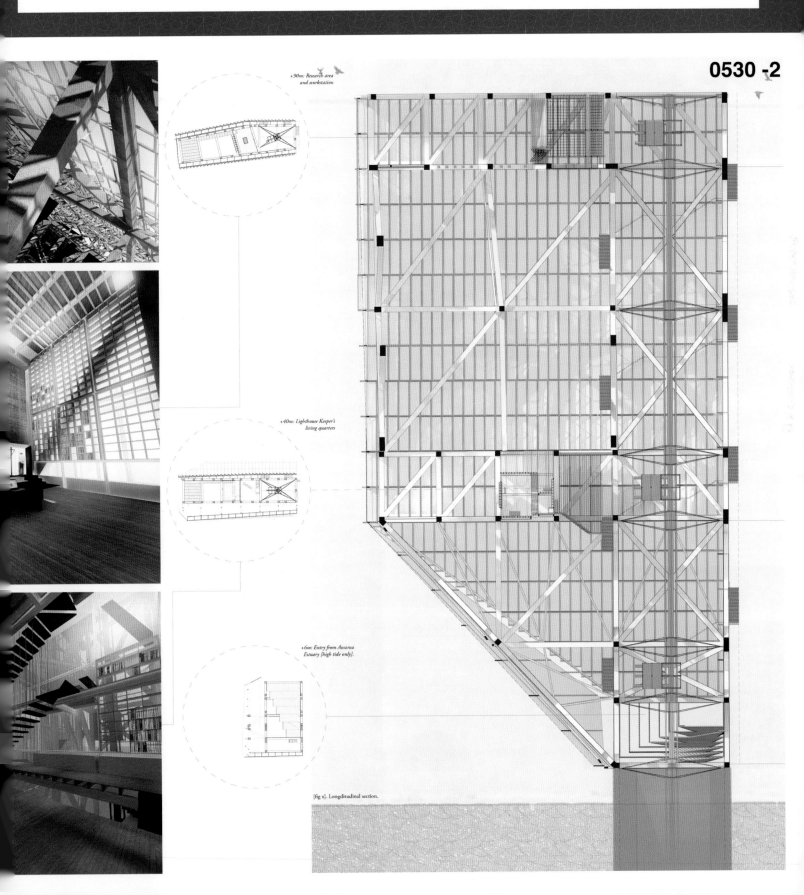

0530 -2

+90m: Research area
and workstation

+40m: Lighthouse Keeper's
living quarters

+6m: Entry from Awaroa
Estuary [high tide only].

[fig x]. Longditudinal section.

SED

Juan Pablo Accotto
Mauro Ivan Barrio
Matias Damian Martin

Argentina

SED

The Water Factory

{ "No shortage of water in the blue planet: Freshwater only" }

Karen E. Lange, National Geographic

The Proyect

There are changes that continuously demand certain adaptation; however, these opportunities to rethink reality have never been too many nor have they had such a global impact. We are witnesses to a cycle closing; we face a scenario of ecological, economic, and social crisis. ¿Which type of architecture do these new conditions demand? At this point, what is left is the action, being aware of the phenomena is no longer enough. If crisis means opportunity for change, what comes next is evolution, innovation in favor of more sustainable, flexible, diverse, and integrating architectures. SED is a typological essay developing in the interdisciplinary scope of ecology, landscape, urbanism, and architecture. It means renovation of energy infrastructure as well as formulation of new matter and energy management systems and their hybridization with other programs, suggesting a new definition of public sphere.

97.5% of water in our planet is salty, and only less than 1% is suitable for human consumption.

Today, one third of world population lives in areas with some kind of water shortage, and that proportion is expected to increase to two thirds in 2025 and to three thirds in 2050.

Desalinating seawater is one potential solution to drinking water shortage. Desalination plants, known as water factories, are seen as the new alternative to worldwide shortage problems. It is known that the employment of chemical methods to get it implies an excessive energy consumption increasing excessively production costs and producing saline residue, which alters coastal marine ecosystems.

SED explores desalination of water via natural methods. Energetically self-sufficing it will spread over maritime platforms of cities that require so as a constant manifestation of what is evident, as a new architecture that not only produces water but also raises awareness and educates through accessibility from manufacturing to domestic, public and egalitarian perspective.

SED innovative

SED is configured as a possible response to today social crisis. It tries out a typological innovation suggesting domestication and a new way of approaching infrastructures, getting them closer to society by creating a quiet factory where the production of freshwater by means of natural methods is experienced, appreciated, and understood, ultimately aiming at awareness.

SED is a flexible model starting from a unique prototype designed to allow adaptability to each well-established environment in its configuration as a system, it intends not only to contribute and provide a potential solution to global water crisis but also to incorporate programs suitable to critical problems of each particular area. Being, in this way, a global but singular architecture.

Factories are not only located on their main energy source, sea water, but also they appear as a new way of colonizing which is maybe the larger dessert in the world, the ocean, a common territory shared by all inhabitants. Concerning its applied technology, SED is built by adapting marine water line systems used in other typologies like oil rigs generating a honeycomb platform that configures a new soil over which structures are set up.

SED the investment

Maybe it's time for the bog oil companies begin to invest in equality projects.

There are protocols, such as Kyoto Protocol, that force companies to reduce water consumption and CO2 emissions or negotiate by investing in sustainable projects for power generation.

For this reason, SED suggests negotiating with the enemy: In order to continue extracting petroleum from natural territories, each oil company shall invest funds in the production of double the freshwater they consume.

{ "Thirst (SED) is necessary and makes us progress" }

Thirst (SED) is the need for water. This has stimulated the development of knowledge and experience in different societies.

70% the world is water

Salt water   Frozen Freshwater   Freshwater

Año 2000   Año 2050

Disponibilidad de Agua
Falta de Agua
Escasez de Agua

1 in 6

people have not access to fresh water

Whenever the temperature rises by 2%, 3 billion people lose access to freshwater.

2025

people
will live in regions with
absolute waters scarcity

1965   2011

The first desalination plant high production was installed in Spain.   13.869 desalination plants in the world.

> Disaster emerge

SED. Artificial Geography projected that opens the city to the sea as constructed nature becomes landscape and close everyday.

Find the dimension of the city outside the original plot represents an opportunity to think a strategy to meet dislocated fragments of city, seeking to build a coherent and continuous facing the sea.

In an era when one-third of the world's population lives in areas with some sort of water shortage, and 97.5% of the water on the planet is salty, desalination is a growing necessity. While it presents a solution to this ever-growing dilemma, the chemical processes used in desalination plants require excessive energy consumption, and their byproducts disrupt coastal marine ecosystems.

The SED project instead proposes to build a structure that can desalinate water through natural methods. 50% of the structure is built to grow halophytic vegetation, which is a type of plant group that can survive in water with high levels of salinity. Steam produced by these plants' photosynthesis is captured in

0556

Naval Sports
Public Space
Springs
Floating Gardens
Water Front
Quay Cruise
Freshwater Reserve
Beaches
Containers Islas
Floating Park
Pedestrian Walks
Breakwater

New ways of living.
> Health and social assistance.
> Large scale events.

SED
Ayuda a Haiti
SED 2016

SYSTEM

these facilities to power the desalination process. The other 50% of the site is covered with solar collectors that are also used to generate steam. This steam is retained, however, as the liquid to gas process separates the water particles from the salt, producing freshwater. This fresh water steam rises to the top of the tower, where it condenses and then causes rainfall in the building. This rain is captured for use, as the water is now salt free and potable.

The structure consists of a central tower with four outstretching arms, which reach up only as far as the tower's bottom third. Within the arms are halophytic vegetation chambers, and on top are solar collectors.

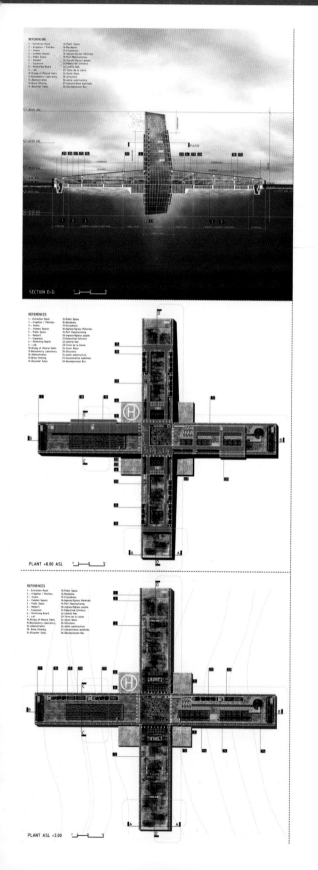

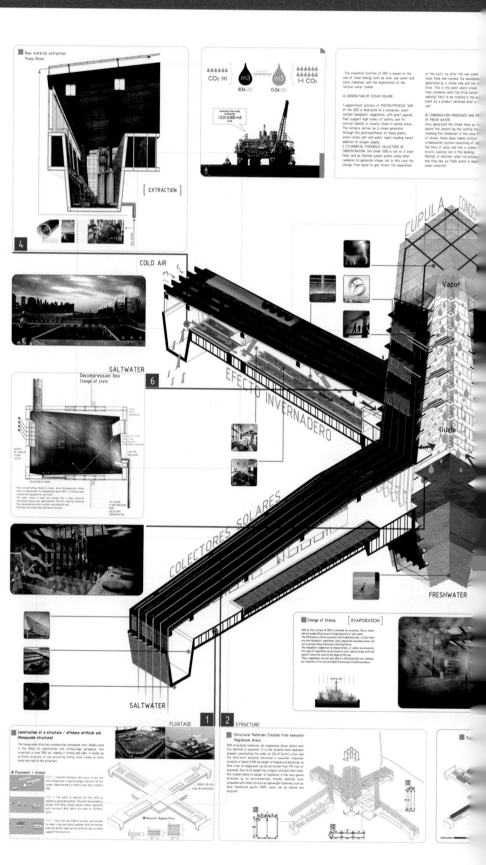

The structure is meant to be located at sea; however, to stay light, the designers mean for the SED platform and tower to attach to another entity instead of being alone at sea. They propose attached the SED tower to oil rig platforms. Also for the purposes of avoiding great weight, the structure is built from magnesium alloy, which is stronger than steel and doesn't risk deterioration at sea because its main raw material composition is ocean water.

Though the desalination process is powered by solar cells, the energy needed to power the facility as a whole is also collected naturally through solar cells and also through wind and sea waves.

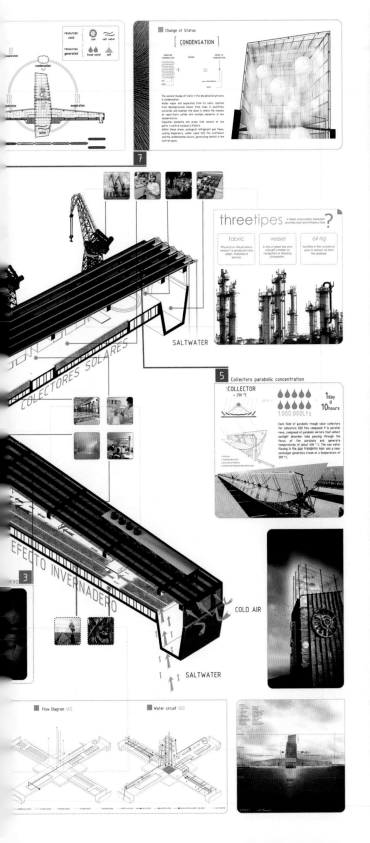

CITADEL SKYSCRAPER

Victor Kopieikin
Pavlo Zabotin

Ukraine

CITADEL SKYSCRAPER

GLOBAL CLIMATE CHANGE (WHICH PROVOKES NEGATIVE CONSEQUENCES IN THE FORM OF EARTHQUAKES, HURRICANES, FLOODS, TSUNAMIS), TECHNOLOGICAL CATASTROPHE OF GLOBAL SCALE, AS WELL AS THE PROBABILITY OF THREAT TO HUMANITY FROM SPACE INDICATE THE NEED TO DEVELOP NEW SYSTEMS OF TYPOLOGICAL UNITS IN THE STRUCTURE OF MODERN ENGINEERING AND DESIGN. RECENT EVENTS IN TURKEY, INDONESIA AND JAPAN ARE STRIKING AND UNAMBIGUOUS ILLUSTRATION OF THE URGENCY OF THE PROBLEM OF DEVELOPING STRATEGIC PROGRAMS OF HUMAN SURVIVAL ON EARTH.

AS OF TODAY, THE MOST AFFECTED BY THE DISASTER REGION IS JAPAN. ON THAT EXAMPLE WE SEE THAT EVEN THE MOST ECONOMICALLY AND TECHNOLOGICALLY DEVELOPED COUNTRIES OF THE WORLD ARE HELPLESS TOWARDS THE DESTRUCTIVE FORCES OF NATURE.

OUR VIEW ON THIS ISSUE IS FOCUSED ON THE DEVELOPMENT OF THE CONCEPT OF A PREVAILING TYPE OF ALTERNATIVE SETTLEMENT SYSTEM IN JAPAN. THE MAIN IDEA OF THE PROJECT IS A CREATION OF A "DEFENSIVE SHIELD" AROUND JAPAN, GRAPHICALLY RESEMBLING A FORTRESS. THE SO-CALLED "DEFENSIVE SHIELD" IS DESIGNED TO PROTECT THE ISLAND FROM THE INSIDE AGAINST EXTERNAL NATURAL AND ANTHROPOGENIC INFLUENCES. THE PROJECT PROVIDES CARRYING THE RESIDENTIAL FUNCTIONS OF CITIES IN THE LAND OUT TO SELF-SUPPORTING RESIDENTIAL UNITS LOCATED IN THE SEA (RESIDENTIAL SKYSCRAPERS, CITADELS).THESE CITADELS INTERACT WITH EACH OTHER ON THE SHORELINE, FORMING A SINGLE CLOSED DEFENSIVE CHAIN THAT OPERATES BOTH ON THE SURFACE AND UNDERGROUND. THEREBY PROCEEDS THE MASTERING OF NEW TERRITORIES.

THE PROJECT PROVIDES A SOLUTION OF THE DEMOGRAPHIC, FUNCTIONAL SATURATION OF THE CITIES BY CARRYING ECONOMICAL AND TECHNOLOGICAL FUNCTIONS OUT OF THE CITY. AND FAVORABLE CONDITIONS FOR THE RESTORATION OF NATURAL RESOURCES ARE FORMED AS A RESULT OF DEVELOPMENT OF NEW TERRITORIES FOR LIFE.

In response to Japan's vulnerability to damage from natural disasters, the Citadel Skyscraper was developed as a concept of a prevailing type of alternative settlement system. The main idea of the project is a creation of a "defensive shield" around Japan, graphically resembling a fortress. This defensive shield is designed to protect the island from external natural and anthropogenic influences. The project carries the residential functions of cities in the land out to self-supporting residential units located in the sea (residential skyscrapers, citadels). These citadels interact with each other on the shoreline, forming a single closed defensive chain that operates both on the surface and underground.

0970-1

It is proposed to create a single "sheet" of the planned skyscrapers across the shoreline at a distance of 2-3 km from the shore, which will serve as a protective function for the whole island. The skyscrapers themselves are connected by a system of breakwaters and drainage channels, able to withstand waves up to 50 meters that prevent the destructive waves to reach the shoreline.

The structural system of the building is a solid metal frame system. At the same time laying the foundation depth is 1,200 meters with a building height of 500 meters. In this form of the building it is almost impossible to influence seismically on it. A main feature of the building is the fact that it is completely self-

CITADEL SKYSCRAPER

IT IS PROPOSED TO CREATE A SINGLE "SHEET" OF THE PLANNED SKYSCRAPERS ACROSS THE SHORELINE AT A DISTANCE OF 2-3 KM FROM THE SHORE, WHICH WILL SERVE AS A PROTECTIVE FUNCTION FOR THE WHOLE ISLAND. SKYSCRAPERS THEMSELVES ARE CONNECTED BY A SYSTEM OF BREAKWATERS AND DRAINAGE CHANNELS, ABLE TO WITHSTAND WAVES UP TO 50 METERS THAT PREVENT THE DESTRUCTIVE WAVES TO REACH THE SHORELINE. IN OUR OPINION, INNOVATIVE DECISION OF THE PROBLEMS, ASSOCIATED WITH UNDERGROUND COASTAL SHOCKS, WOULD BE THE CREATION OF A SINGLE CHAIN "SAILS"-REFLECTORS OF SEISMIC WAVES. THE SYSTEM OF "SAILS", DUE TO OSCILLATIONS BETWEEN STRETCHED FIBERS, WOULD CREATE DISSONANCE WITH THE SEISMIC WAVE, GRADUALLY REDUCING IT TO NOTHING. SUCH CHAIN OF AN UNDERGROUND "SAILS" CLOSING THE RING, SURROUNDS THE ISLANDS OF JAPAN AT A DEPTH OF 1200 METERS.

sustaining in regards to electricity; the facilities use tidal wave energy.

The main function is residential; there are cells for families of 2 to 6 people. Every 50 meters of the building has a system of recreation (recreation areas, mini parks) and well-developed infrastructure: restaurants, cafes, shops, and cinemas. The central light atrium has a system of bridges and crossings. In case of complete closure of the outer shield, the building will be ventilated by a blower in every 100 meters and the system of niches filled with hydroponic algae, which in turn will produce oxygen by absorbing carbon dioxide, and the turbine at a lower level will enable the natural circulation of air around the building.

0970-2

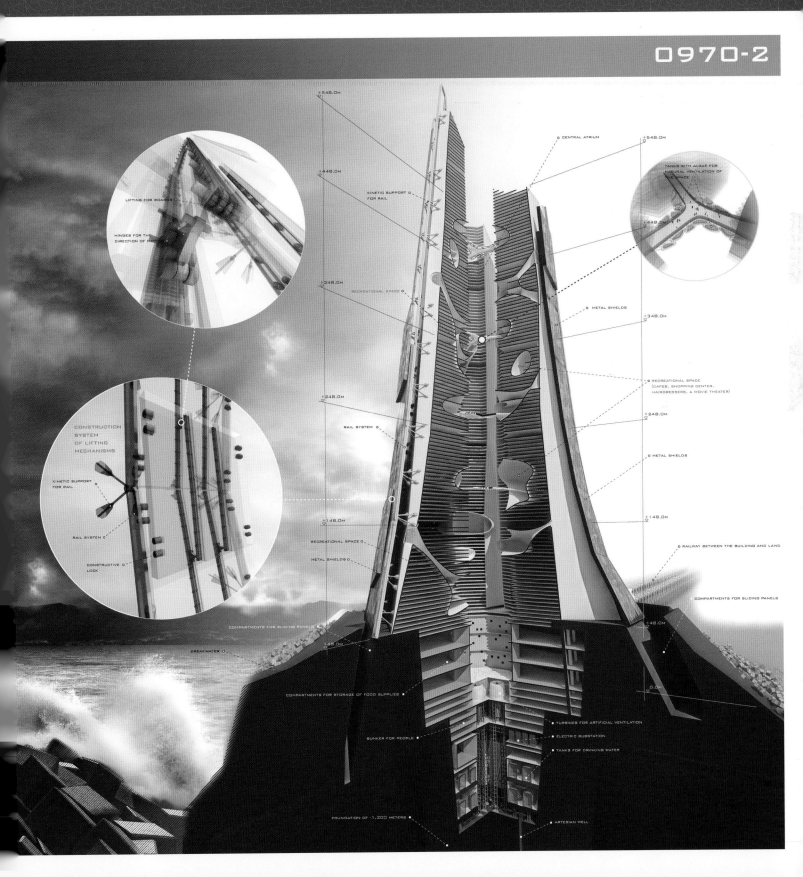

MAHAMERU PROJECT

Andre Pradiktha

Indonesia

MAHAMERU PROJECT

The island of Bali is small, being only 5,000 square miles, but supports a population of 5 million—and that number doubles during the high season of tourism. As a result, real estate prices have gone sky high, investment is largely done by foreigners, culture and traditions are degraded, and the land itself is depleted. The Mahameru Project proposes the construction of sustainable towers on the island's coast to orient holistic development vertically and move people off the island itself.

There are six problems in all this structure seeks to ameliorate: shortage of land, unceasing development, fresh water scarcity, threat of flooding, culture degradation, and overcrowding in urban areas.

The concept for the tower's shape comes from the traditional Balinese respect for the mountain (meru), which

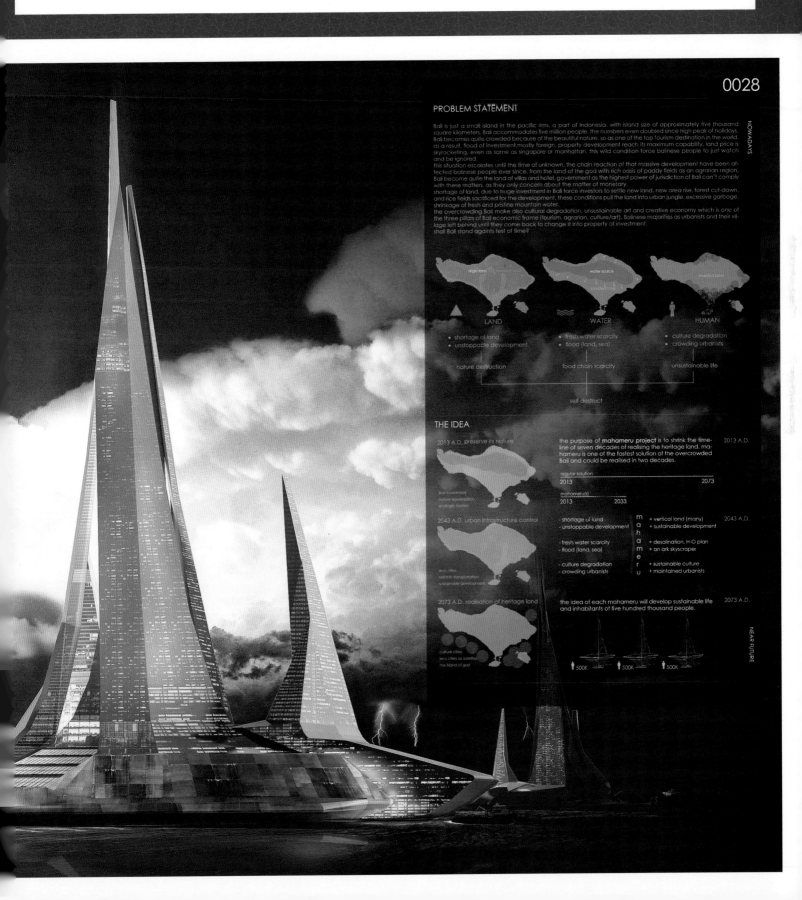

is sacred to the Balinese. Architecture inspired by mountains has a specific name in Bali, Tri Angga, and that means "three parts of the human body as a representation of a micro cosmos," says the designer. Using this as inspiration, one Mahameru tower rises to a peak of over 800 meters and holds over 100,000 units, meaning a mass exodus off the island and onto the Projects could occur and, essentially, save the island. Within 20 years, the designer says, overcrowding on the island would be under control, giving the land and island culture the ability to restore itself.

The base of each tower descends 200 meters into the water; the area below water holds the engine room, storage facilities, a hull and a balancing tank to steady the structure. On the water's surface, a desalination plant connected to the structure creates clean water; the levels ascending above hold every programmatic use needed in a

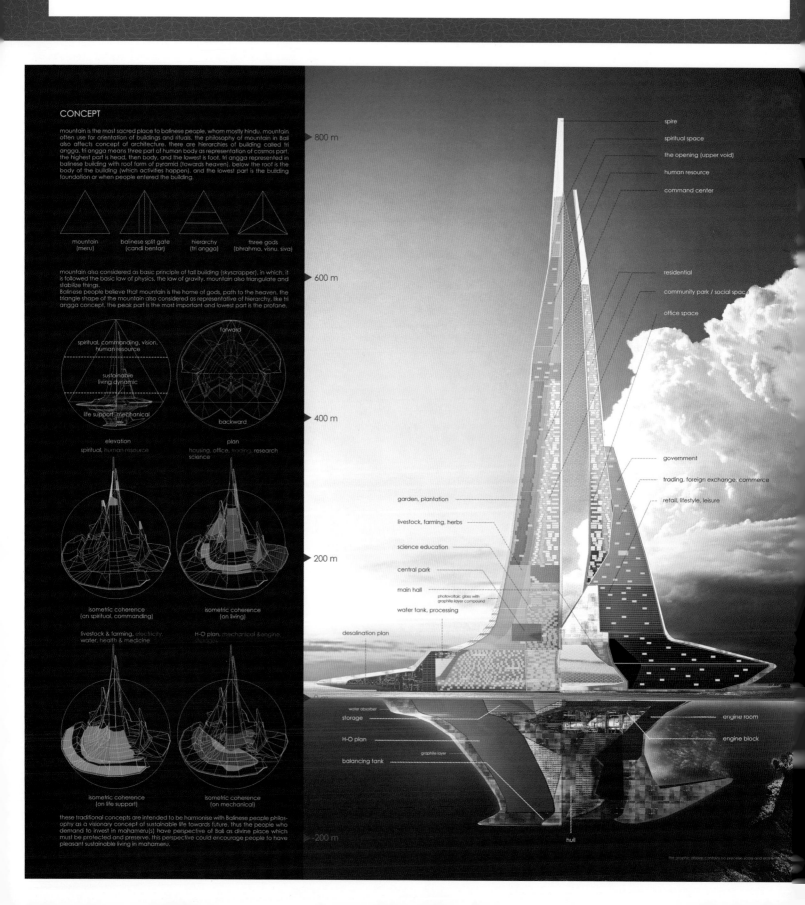

city, including schools, residences, hospitals, offices, commercial spaces and parks. Solar and wind power collectors provide green energy, and rainwater is captured for use in addition to the desalinated supplies.

The structure's mass, shape and location also protects its inhabitants from natural disaster. A tsunami less than 100 meters high could not fell the tower; its graphite compound material and photovoltaic panels protect it from solar flares; and its mountain-like shape helps protect against tornadoes and damaging winds.

Finally, within the structure, units are modular, meaning that residences and spaces for any use can be combined in a myriad of ways. They can exist singularly, be grouped into compounds, be stepped into terraces, etc. This structure gives residents flexible living conditions, all the amenities they would need and protection from the elements.

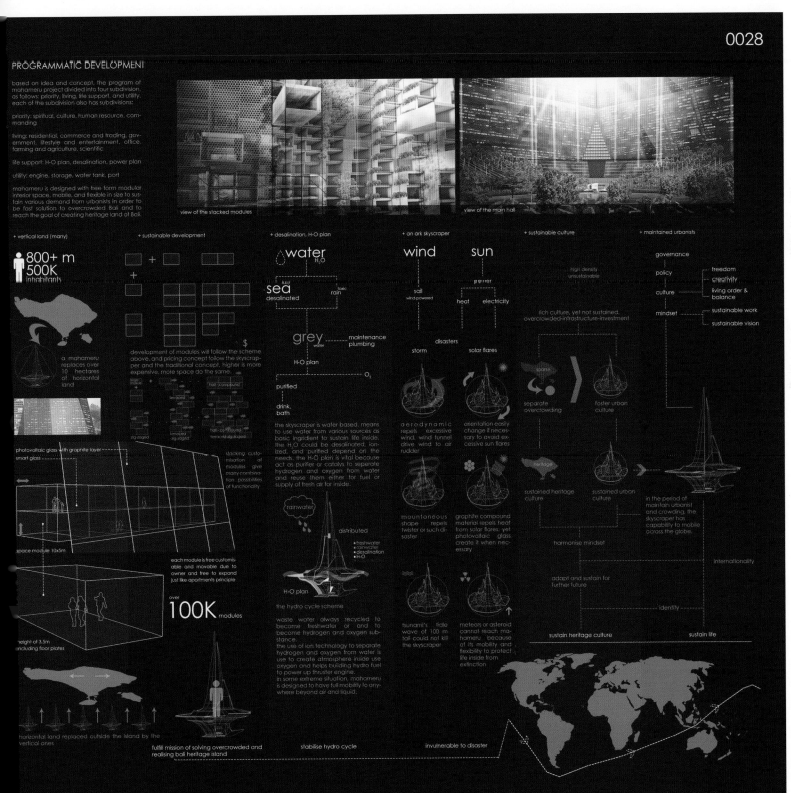

"MAHAMERU PROJECT INTENDED TO REALIZE A HERITAGE ISLAND OF BALI. VISIONARY CONCEPT TOWARDS FUTURE BALI SUSTAINABLITY" ■ MAHAMERU PROJECT

WATERFALL CITY

Longwei Wu

United States

Waterfall City

Waterfall City is a proposal for a multi-functional complex that literally is built around a waterfall, suspended from the cliff that the waterfall runs down, and houses malls, offices, hotels, apartments, farms, and a waste-water disposal system.

In addition to inspiring beauty, the complex utilizes its waterfall to harness hydropower (via generators located along the waterfall) and provide fresh water to those within. Because of this, it is completely self-sustaining, and has zero carbon emissions.

The structure is massive enough that it supports car traffic as the main means for transportation; however, because the city is oriented vertically, large elevators must be employed to transport cars between levels. These

0074

CONCEPT

God separated lands by creating precipices as monuments to honor the power of nature, and gave those stationary land-separators living souls – waterfalls.

This proposal "Waterfall City", is not only a building, but also a multi-functional complex - a complex that integrates malls, offices, hotels, apartments, farms, and a waste water disposal station. It consumes the product it produces, and disposes the waste it leaves, working as a cyclical system.

"Waterfall City" tries to get rid of the notion that a skyscraper should be a modern tower of Babel, which is arrogant and self-centered. Here, a skyscraper, "Waterfall City" is considered as a humble attachment to nature, creating human activities vertically along a waterfall. Also it is a metaphor of civilization development. A society normally starts from people gathering along a river to live together. To emphasize the concept of "attachment", "Waterfall City" is completely lifted off the ground by the frame embedded deeply into the precipices' rocky structure.

Unlike skyscrapers, which consume energy, waterfalls provide natural energy. When a waterfall, which is an unstoppable stream, is pouring down over a thousand feet, it is providing not just a spectacular view, but also an enormous amount of energy. For instance, if we drop one gallon of water from the top of Angel Falls, known as the highest waterfall in the world, the hydraulic energy generated by the water is more than four time the energy generated by dropping that from the top of Hoover Dam. There are at least 421 waterfalls known that are higher than Hoover Dam, however, most of them with their incredible power, are untouched by humans. In this proposal, the building generates clean, self-sufficient hydroelectricity from the waterfall, with zero carbon dioxide emission. Besides providing hydraulic energy, a waterfall also satisfies the demand for daily water consumption.

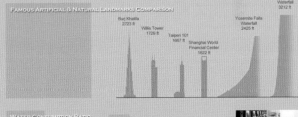

FAMOUS ARTIFICIAL & NATURAL LANDMARKS COMPARISON

Burj Khalifa 2723 ft — Willis Tower 1729 ft — Taipei 101 1667 ft — Shanghai World Financial Center 1622 ft — Yosemite Falls Waterfall 2425 ft — Angel Falls Waterfall 3212 ft

WATER CONSUMPTION RATIO

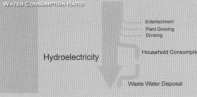

Hydroelectricity

Entertainment
Plant Growing
Drinking
Household Consumption

Waste Water Disposal

For many years, ground transportation has had to go all the way around a precipice just to deliver goods on the other side of the precipice, which is extremely inefficient and time-consuming. In order to solve that issue, "Waterfall City" provides a system which breaks through that geographic limitation and makes ground transportation easier. It is a set of huge elevators for moving vehicles and heavy objects up and down between the upper and lower lands, connecting the two sides of a precipice with a direct route.

—— Mountain Road
- - - - ShortCut Provided by "Waterfall City"

GROUND TRANSPORTATION PATTERN IN MOUNTAIN AREA

elevators move cars and heavy objects within the city and also connect it with the ground below. This giant elevator system hiding inside the precipice is designed to connect ground transportation between the upper and lower levels of the precipice by lifting and lowering vehicles. The influence of this system is enormous. It creates a shortcut for transportation and business. Before entering the elevator, the road splits into two lanes to separate the incoming traffic from the departing traffic. Then these two traffic flows are distributed to the two sides of the elevator system for loading and unloading. Separate elevators run parallel to transport people.

A wastewater disposal system is located at the bottom of the complex, purifying the gray and black water that is expelled throughout the city before it reenters the waterfall's flow. The complex as a whole is anchored by a horizontal

Waterfall City

WATERFALL

The waterfall is the core component of the building. It not only provides electricity, but also water for human activities: drinking, washing, entertaining, etc. At the same time, the existence of the waterfall solves the water pumping issue that a skyscraper normally will encounter, providing a more stable water supply system.

ELEVATOR FOR VEHICLES

This giant elevator system hiding inside the precipice is designed to connect ground transportation between the upper and lower areas of the precipice, by lifting or lowering vehicles. The influence of this system is enormous – it creates not only a shortcut for transportation, but also potential business. The elevator goes in one direction, functioning like an aerial tramway to keep traffic continuous all the way through. Before entering the elevator, the road splits into two lanes to separate the incoming from the departing traffic. Then these two traffic flows are distributed to the two sides of the elevator system for loading and unloading. Also, it can be used to lift heavy objects.

ELEVATOR FOR PERDESTRIANS

Besides the vehicle elevator, there are several ordinary elevators for pedestrians moving inside the building.

pipe array embedded deep within the cliff rock. If the complex needs to grow, more pipe can be added to fortify the structure.

Cars and pedestrians enter the structure from the top of the complex, which is flush with the ground at the top of the waterfall.

Office and mall levels are found towards the top, allowing easy access for visitors. Below that are residential levels, and apartments and hotels. Farm levels have ceiling heights twice as high as other levels to allow for clearance for large plants. It produces fresh food year round and also purifies the air within the complex, acting like its "lung."

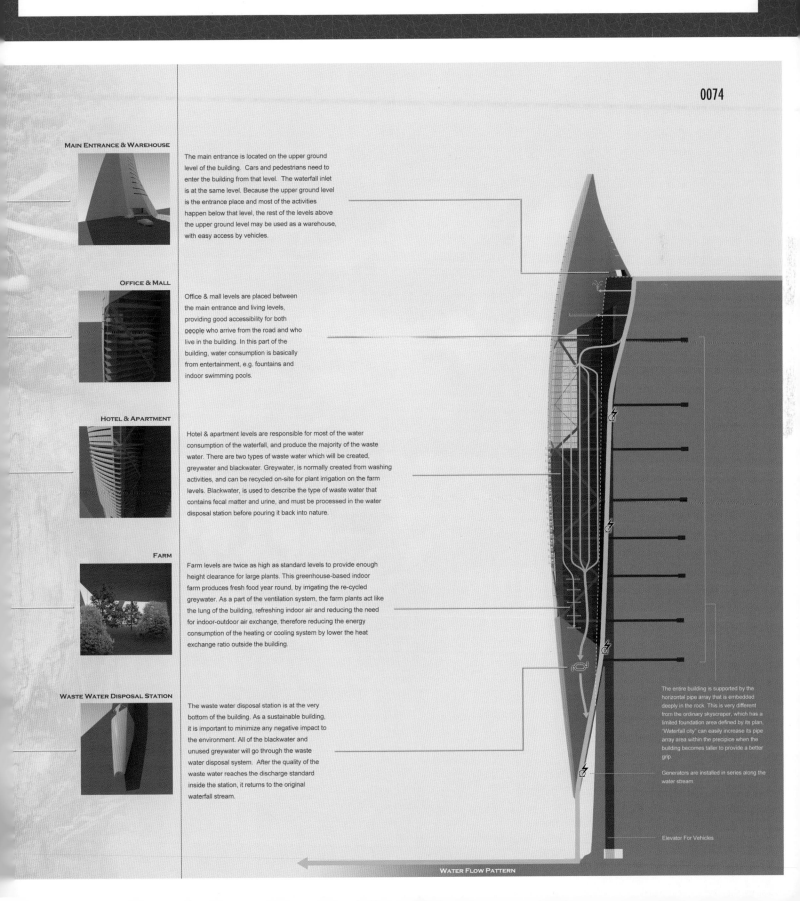

0074

MAIN ENTRANCE & WAREHOUSE

The main entrance is located on the upper ground level of the building. Cars and pedestrians need to enter the building from that level. The waterfall inlet is at the same level. Because the upper ground level is the entrance place and most of the activities happen below that level, the rest of the levels above the upper ground level may be used as a warehouse, with easy access by vehicles.

OFFICE & MALL

Office & mall levels are placed between the main entrance and living levels, providing good accessibility for both people who arrive from the road and who live in the building. In this part of the building, water consumption is basically from entertainment, e.g. fountains and indoor swimming pools.

HOTEL & APARTMENT

Hotel & apartment levels are responsible for most of the water consumption of the waterfall, and produce the majority of the waste water. There are two types of waste water which will be created, greywater and blackwater. Greywater, is normally created from washing activities, and can be recycled on-site for plant irrigation on the farm levels. Blackwater, is used to describe the type of waste water that contains fecal matter and urine, and must be processed in the water disposal station before pouring it back into nature.

FARM

Farm levels are twice as high as standard levels to provide enough height clearance for large plants. This greenhouse-based indoor farm produces fresh food year round, by irrigating the re-cycled greywater. As a part of the ventilation system, the farm plants act like the lung of the building, refreshing indoor air and reducing the need for indoor-outdoor air exchange, therefore reducing the energy consumption of the heating or cooling system by lower the heat exchange ratio outside the building.

WASTE WATER DISPOSAL STATION

The waste water disposal station is at the very bottom of the building. As a sustainable building, it is important to minimize any negative impact to the environment. All of the blackwater and unused greywater will go through the waste water disposal system. After the quality of the waste water reaches the discharge standard inside the station, it returns to the original waterfall stream.

The entire building is supported by the horizontal pipe array that is embedded deeply in the rock. This is very different from the ordinary skyscraper, which has a limited foundation area defined by its plan. "Waterfall city" can easily increase its pipe array area within the precipice when the building becomes taller to provide a better grip.

Generators are installed in series along the water stream.

Elevator For Vehicles

WATER FLOW PATTERN

HANG-RISE BUILDING

Boji Hu
Die Hu
Yang Zhao

China

HANG-RISE BUILDING

In the town of Yinxing, located in Wenchuan County in the Sichuan Province of China, townspeople live at the bottom of the Min River Valley. The valley experiences substantial amounts of rainfall throughout the year, and the threats of flooding and mudslides from the surrounding steep hills are constant, and dangerous. Though such catastrophic events have destroyed homes in the village and even washed away the rope bridge that allowed residents to cross the river, the villagers are reluctant to leave their home.

Hang Rise Building is a solution inspired by the rope that held the now-destroyed bridge together. By creating rope cables out of steel, instead of twine, and suspending the cables from the crags of the surrounding hills, residents will simply elevate their residences above ground, allowing them to keep their address but live above it, protecting them

BEFORE THE DEBRIS FLOW OCCURED

AFTER THE DEBRIS FLOW OCCURED

0138

HIGH INCIDENCE AREA OF DEBRIS FLOW

HIGH INCIDENCE AREA OF DEBRIS FLOW

WORLDWIDE   CHINA   SICHUAN

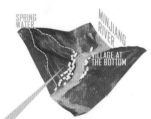

SPRING WATER / MINJIANG RIVER / VILLAGE AT THE BOTTOM

Event

In Yinxing Town, Wenchuan County, Sichuan Province in China, the hills are steep and valleys are long and narrow. Taking the water source and feasibility of construction, villages all locate along the bottom of the valley of Min River.

The amount of rain is pretty large all the year round. Heavy rain falls gather at the valley, forming flood. The flood usually scours the mountain, bringing away large amount of muds and causing the rocks to fall down, which brings violent debris flows. Local villagers are always living in danger.

RAIN WATER / DEBRIS FLOW / WATER AND SOIL LOSS

YINXING VILLAGE / SUPO INN / TAIPING POST / YINGXIU TOWN / BANGANG / MINJIANG RIVER

SPRING WATER / DISPERSE / VILLAGE ON THE MOORING ROPE

Many debris flows happened in a few years, inflicting heavy losses to this developing village. The villagers' houses were destroyed. Even the bridge which was built across the river couldn't survive. The dream to rebuild the bridge was shattered because the bridge was destroyed again and again. The ropeway which was built by the villagers on their own across the two mountains became the only way villagers could use, especially schoolchildren.

Therefore, we try to find a strategy, using the ropeway which is very common in the village, to bring about new territories beyond the space they currently have, reaching a harmonious state between people and the nature.

Concept

Designers will make a combination of these villages, moving them from the bottom of the valley to the space above their original address. This is a Ferris wheel skyscraper based on the Ropeway, complying with the feature of the valley, interacting with the nature and changing with people's needs. It can make the continuous disaster a discontinuous view, providing a totally new life mode and a platform to live for the local villagers.

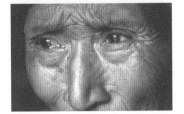

RAIN WATER / ASSEMBLE / CLOSURE

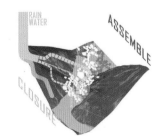

from flooding and mudslides.

The villagers themselves will construct their homes, which will hang from the steel cables, in a manner also inspired by local custom: as if they were making a giant basket, residents will create living units for themselves from bamboo and rattan. In individual residential units, the top level will serve as the residence, and the bottom level will be live or work space.

By grouping several units together, villagers can form markets, schools, theaters, even streetscapes—anything and everything they need to survive and rebuild their community in the sky.

In addition to holding these units, the steel cables also serve as vessels of fresh water. Pipes within the cables

HANG-RISE BUILD

NORMAL DAYS
WHEN THE DEBRIS FLOW OCURED

TO THEIR HOUSES

Water System Construction Detail

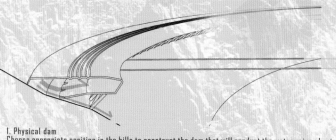

1. Physical dam
Choose approriate position in the hills to construct the dam that will conduct the water using physical effects. Leading the water to the storage layer of the cable.
Providing water for residence in their daily life, and dredging excessive water to prevent it to scour the mountain during the flood.

2. Water storage weight dropper
Under the weight difference between the amount of water and the weight of the water storage case, the case will be able to move.

3. Water storage case
Store water for daily use for the residence. By using th along the steel cable by adjusting the amount of wa bottom of the case. By opening it, the excessive water through the drainage opening to the river.

transport spring water from the hills to water storage units that are located on the top of each basket structure.

After an excessive amount of rainfall, the water collectors on top of each unit fill and weigh the units down, causing the units to slide down the cables and rest together further towards the ground. The heaviness that transports the units allows for lightness amongst the villagers, who, in closer proximity, are then able to weather bad storms together.

4. Cable The outside part is the sliding layer. The inside part is the water storage layer

E-SPIRE

Yuanmin Tao
Jiangwei Tian
Si Xiong

Australia/China

aspire to where energy ceases to expire

E-SPIRE

ENVIRONMENTAL INSTABILITY

New studies by the International Panel on Tectonic Implosion (iPTI) suggest that the increased use of non-renewable energies has lead to a rise in the number of earthquakes around the globe (Figure 2).

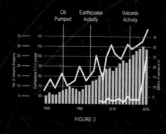

FIGURE 2

Inevitably, an increase in tectonic activity leads to a rise in volcanic eruptions. Statistics also indicate that 36% of worldwide media coverage on natural disasters focused on 'Earthquake' and 'Volcanic eruption', leading to speculation that global climate change may be a major factor in the rise of tectonic and volcanic activity.

Most notably, the 40,000km long 'the Pacific Ring of Fire' is home to over 450 volcanoes, and is also where 90% of the world's earthquakes occur (Figure 3). A direct result of plate tectonics, the region's volcanic ash clouds have impacted on countless urban and environmental issues, including water contamination, aircraft and flight safety, loss of telecommunication signals, building structural collapse, water acidification and oxygen deprivation, resulting in loss of aquatic ecosystems and horticultural damages.

FIGURE 3

ISSUES

ENERGY CRISIS

The International Energy Agency predicts 'World energy demand will rise by 45 percent between now and 2030 – an average rate of increase of 1.6 percent per year – with coal accounting for more than a third of the overall rise.' With fossil fuels predicted to account for 80 percent of the world's energy in the near future, CO_2 emissions and related environmental damages are likely to continue (Figure 1).

The likelihood of renewable sources, including solar, wind and geothermal, of substantially changing the mix of our energy supply is most unlikely. This is mostly due to the high investment costs and low, in-efficient returns. Moreover, solar and wind technologies are very unstable as they are too dependent on the surrounding environment. Nuclear energy investment is also unlikely due to high capital costs and resistance from society at large.

As the global community continues to be faced with energy-related problems, including the Fukushima nuclear disaster, Beijing's coal-related air pollution, and the Middle-East oil war, a new form of energy generation, whereby anyone can easily access it in the form of electricity, must be considered.

FIGURE 1

CONCEPT

THERMO-ELECTRIC EFFECT

Another example of sustainable energy practice is the 'Thermo-Electric Effect' – the direct conversion of temperature difference into electric voltage. Thermo-Electric devices use materials which respond to temperature differences. At the atomic scale, an applied temperature difference on the material, will cause charged carriers in the material to disperse from the hot side to the cold side of the material, inducing a thermo-electric voltage (Figure 4).

FIGURE 4

An increase in the temperature difference will also lead to an increase in the thermo-electric voltage.

Traditionally, thermo-electric devices are devised using alternating p-type and n-type semi-conductor elements connected by metallic connectors (Figure 5).

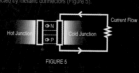

FIGURE 5

DESIGN

E-SPIRE

In response to the detrimental effects resulting from volcanic activities, as well as inefficiencies se renewable energy sources, the E-Spire establishe energy generation based on thermo-electric princip

Principles

Traditionally, thermo-electric generators are qu However, the E-Spire has opened new bounda structure which maximises and regulates a constall difference, hence producing a thermo-electric hyper-efficient, clean form of electricity (Figure 6).

The tower is mounted on top of a volcanic c micro-perforated Heat-Pipes are inserted into the magma chamber (the 'Hot Junction' – 3km unde 1000°C) via the volcanic conduit. At the high-performance Alloy-Pipes are wound togethe umbrella-like mesh which captures cool tempe Mesosphere (the 'Cold Junction' – 100km in the sk

Electric conductors are positioned at both ends of t are connected by an electric circuit that runs in th structure. Hence, a 'mega' thermal-electric conceived. The vast temperature difference cro 1000°C) as well as the use of high-performance from nanotechnology, maximises the efficiency of generation.

At the centre of the tower is the Electricity Trans (ETS). Using a sophisticated, highly integrated E-Transmission System, electricity is run throug transformers before being transmitted through E-worldwide use (Figure 7). The consumer, having E-WIFI device, can 'receive' electricity and charge wherever there is electrical signal, as the ETS is The entire system is controlled and maintained ofte

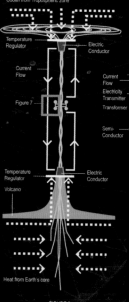

FIGURE 6

Based on thermo-electric principles, the E-Spire is a structure that proposes a non-traditional way to generate clean energy. It maximizes and regulates a constant temperature difference, hence producing a thermo-electric voltage (clean electricity) trough the use of the resulting energy effects from tectonic and volcanic activity.

The tower is mounted on top of a volcanic crater. Micro-perforated Heat-Pipes are inserted into the underground magma chamber via the volcanic conduit. At the other end, high performance Alloy-Pipes are wound together, creating a mesh that captures cool temperatures in the Mesosphere.

The tower core is fundamentally made from a Thermo-Electric Conduction material with a titanium diamond-cubic structure in the middle and an anti-magnetic field support as an external re-vestment. The Thermo-Electric Conduction

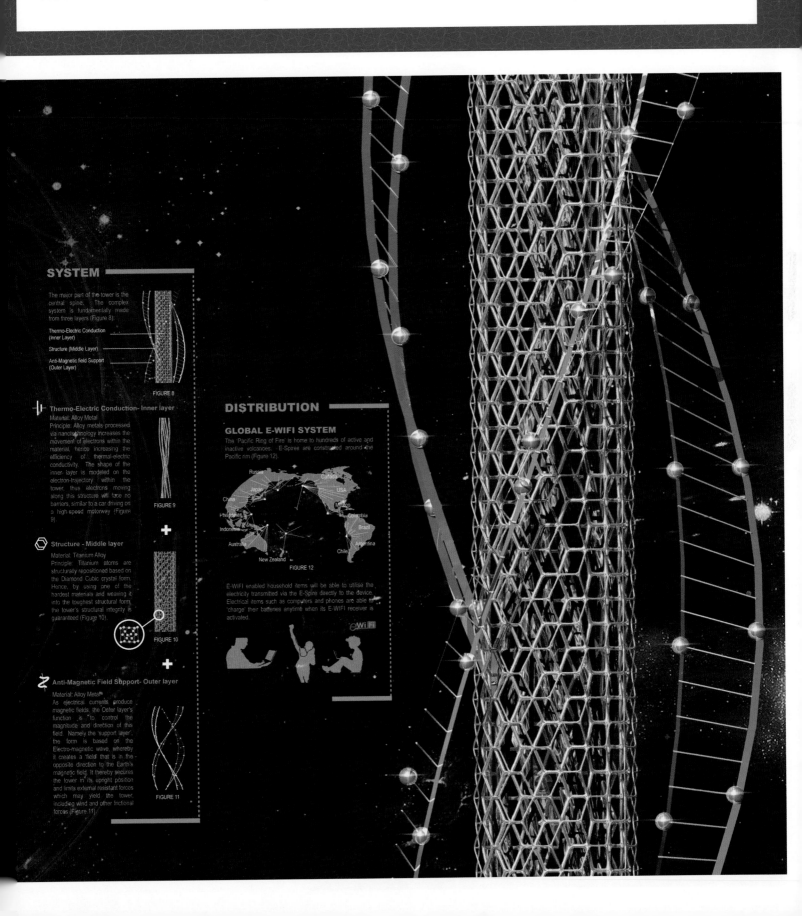

SYSTEM

The major part of the tower is the central spine. The complex system is fundamentally made from three layers (Figure 8):

Thermo-Electric Conduction (Inner Layer)

Structure (Middle Layer)

Anti-Magnetic field Support (Outer Layer)

FIGURE 8

Thermo-Electric Conduction- Inner layer

Material: Alloy Metal
Principle: Alloy metals processed via nanotechnology increases the movement of electrons within the material, hence increasing the efficiency of thermal-electric conductivity. The shape of the inner layer is modeled on the electron-trajectory within the tower, thus electrons moving along this structure will face no barriers, similar to a car driving on a high speed motorway (Figure 9).

FIGURE 9

Structure - Middle layer

Material: Titanium Alloy
Principle: Titanium atoms are structurally repositioned based on the Diamond Cubic crystal form. Hence, by using one of the hardest materials and weaving it into the toughest structural form, the tower's structural integrity is guaranteed (Figure 10).

FIGURE 10

Anti-Magnetic Field Support- Outer layer

Material: Alloy Metal
As electrical currents produce magnetic fields, the Outer layer's function is to control the magnitude and direction of this field. Namely the support layer, the form is based on the Electro-magnetic wave, whereby it creates a 'field' that is in the opposite direction to the Earth's magnetic field. It thereby secures the tower in its upright position and limits external resistant forces which may yield the tower, including wind and other frictional forces (Figure 11).

FIGURE 11

DISTRIBUTION

GLOBAL E-WIFI SYSTEM

The 'Pacific Ring of Fire' is home to hundreds of active and inactive volcanoes. E-Spires are constructed around the Pacific rim (Figure 12).

Russia
Canada
China
Japan
USA
Philippines
Mexico
Colombia
Indonesia
Brazil
Australia
Argentina
Chile
New Zealand

FIGURE 12

E-WIFI enabled household items will be able to utilise the electricity transmitted via the E-Spire directly to the device. Electrical items such as computers and phones are able to 'charge' their batteries anytime when its E-WIFI receiver is activated.

eWiFi

layer uses alloy metals processed via nanotechnology to increase the movement of electrons within the material, hence increasing the efficiency of thermal-electric conductivity. The shape of this later is modelled on the electron tractor within the tower, thus electrons moving along this structure will face no barriers. The middle later of structure is made of titanium alloy whose atoms are structurally repositioned based on the diamond cubic crystal form. Hence, by using one of the hardest materials and weaving it into the toughest structural form, the tower's structural integrity is guaranteed. Finally the anti-magnetic field support which is in the outer layer helps control the magnitude and direction of the magnetic fields created by the electrical currents. The form of this layer is based on the electro-magnetic wave, creative a field that is in the opposite direction to Earth's magnetic field. It thereby secures the tower in its upright

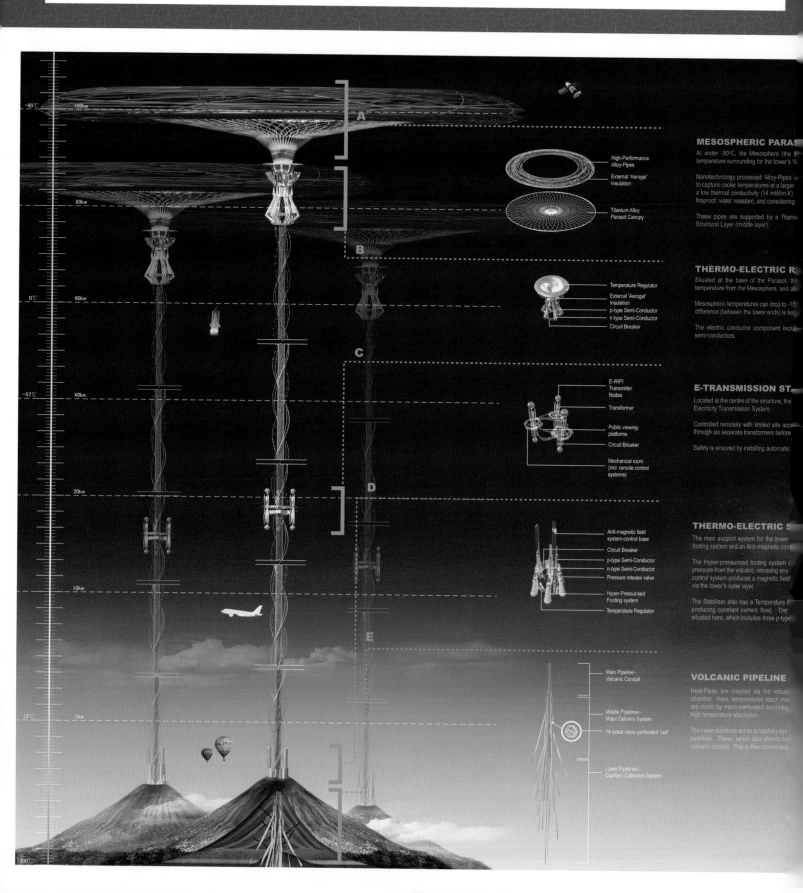

A

High-Performance Alloy-Pipes

External 'Aerogel' Insulation

Titanium Alloy Parasol Canopy

B

Temperature Regulator
External 'Aerogel' Insulation
p-type Semi-Conductor
n-type Semi-Conductor
Circuit Breaker

C

E-WIFI Transmitter Nodes
Transformer
Public viewing platforms
Circuit Breaker
Mechanical room (incl. remote control systems)

D

Anti-magnetic field system-control base
Circuit Breaker
p-type Semi-Conductor
n-type Semi-Conductor
Pressure release valve
Hyper-Pressurised Footing system
Temperature Regulator

E

Main Pipeline - Volcanic Conduit
Middle Pipelines - Major Delivery System
14-sided micro perforated 'cell'
Lower Pipelines - Capillary Collection System

MESOSPHERIC PARAS

At under -90ºC, the Mesosphere (the temperature surrounding for the tower's 't

Nanotechnology processed 'Alloy-Pipes' to capture cooler temperatures at a larger a low thermal conductivity (14 mW/m-K) fireproof, water resistant, and considering

These pipes are supported by a Titani Structural Layer (middle layer).

THERMO-ELECTRIC R

Situated at the base of the Parasol, th temperature from the Mesosphere, and al

Mesospheric temperatures can drop to -1 difference (between the tower ends) is ke

The electric conductor component inclu semi-conductors.

E-TRANSMISSION ST

Located at the centre of the structure, the Electricity Transmission System.

Controlled remotely with limited site acc through six separate transformers before

Safety is ensured by installing automatic

THERMO-ELECTRIC S

The main support system for the tower footing system and an Anti-magnetic con

The Hyper-pressurised footing system pressure from the volcano, releasing any control system produces a magnetic field via the tower's outer layer.

The Stabiliser also has a Temperature R producing constant current flow). The situated here, which includes three p-type

VOLCANIC PIPELINE

Heat-Pipes are inserted via the volcan chamber. Here, temperatures reach ove are made by micro-perforated technolo high temperature absorption.

The lower pipelines act as a capillary sys pipelines. These, which also absorb he volcanic conduit. This is then connected

position and limits external resistant forces.

Electric conductors are positioned at both ends of the tower, which are connected by an electric circuit that runs in the center of the structure. The vast temperature difference created (-90° C to 1000° C) as well as the use of high-performance materials made from nanotechnology, maximizes the efficiency of thermal-electric generation.

An electric transmission station is located at the center of the tower. Using an integrated E-WIFI System, electricity is run through transformers before being transmitted through E-WIFI nodes for worldwide use. E-WIFI enabled household items will be able to utilize the electricity transmitted via the E-Spire directly to the device. Items such computers and phones are able to charge their batteries anytime while their E-WIFI receiver is activated.

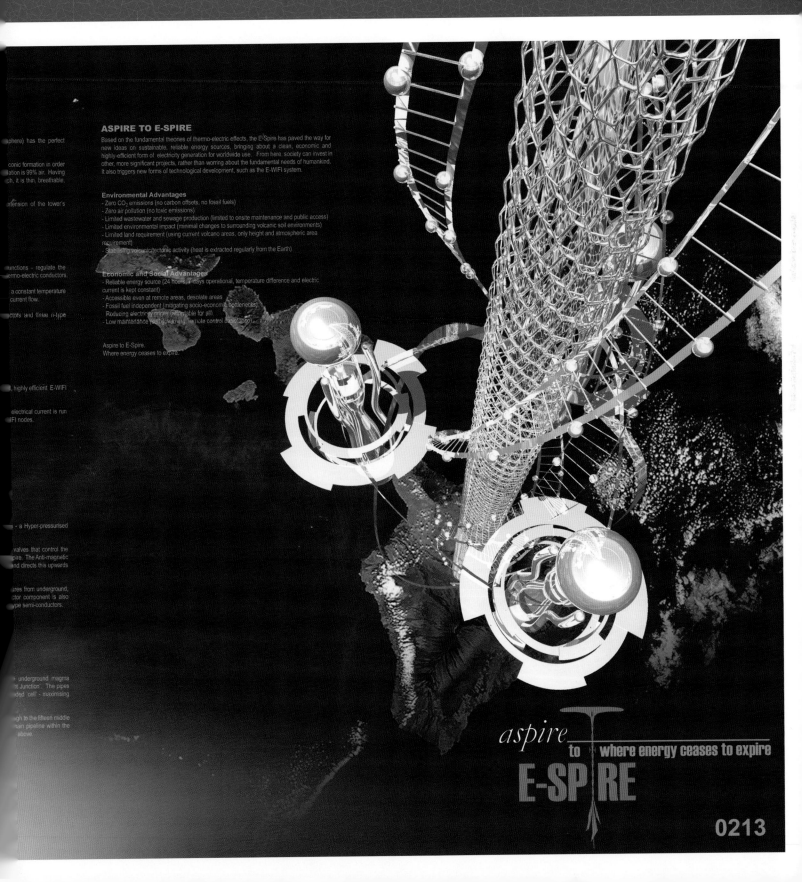

ASPIRE TO E-SPIRE

Based on the fundamental theories of thermo-electric effects, the E-Spire has paved the way for new ideas on sustainable, reliable energy sources, bringing about a clean, economic and highly-efficient form of electricity generation for worldwide use. From here, society can invest in other, more significant projects, rather than worring about the fundamental needs of humankind. It also triggers new forms of technological development, such as the E-WIFI system.

Environmental Advantages
- Zero CO_2 emissions (no carbon offsets, no fossil fuels)
- Zero air pollution (no toxic emissions)
- Limited wastewater and sewage production (limited to onsite maintenance and public access)
- Limited environmental impact (minimal changes to surrounding volcanic soil environments)
- Limited land requirement (using current volcano areas, only height and atmospheric area requirement)
- Stabilising volcanic/tectonic activity (heat is extracted regularly from the Earth)

Economic and Social Advantages
- Reliable energy source (24 hours, 7 days operational, temperature difference and electric current is kept constant)
- Accessible even at remote areas, desolate areas
- Fossil fuel independent (mitigating socio-economic bottlenecks)
- Reducing electricity prices (affordable for all)
- Low maintenance (self governing, remote control assistance)

Aspire to E-Spire.
Where energy ceases to expire.

aspire
to where energy ceases to expire
E-SPIRE

REPAIR GOAF

Liangpeng Chen
Yating Chen
Lida Huang
Gaoyan Wu
Lin Yuan

China

Shaanxi Provincial Department of Land data shows that Shaanxi had cumulatively produced about 10 billion tons of coal in the past 30 years, forming a coal goaf area of more than 5000 square kilometers. Hundreds of villages face the ground subsidence and landslides and other geological disasters of which 70% are caused by mining. More than 700 villages became unsuitable to live in Shaanxi and about 300 million people were affected.

The abandoned Shenfu Dongsheng coalfield was China's largest coal-producing base goaf. The goaf not only influenced the local soil and land, but also wasted the terrestrial heat at a large scale with many consequences including collapse, debris flow and soil erosion, destruction of buildings and cropland, atmosphere pollution etc.

This project proposes to reuse the goaf and part of the pipelines on the working platforms. The vertical pipelines

0318

Goaf
craper

CASE:

Shaanxi Provincial Department of Land data show that Shaanxi has cumulative produced about 10 billion tons of coal in 30 years, forming a coal goaf area more than 5000 square kilometers, hundreds of villages facing the ground subsidence and landslides and other geological disasters, 70% of geological disasters caused by mining determine the need to govern the subsidence area of 1100 square kilometers.

More than 700 villages become unsuitable to live in Shaanxi which caused by the coal goaf. About 300 million people were affected, the ground also continue to collapse.

SITE:

The Shenfu Dongsheng coalfield, China's largest coal-producing base, boosted its annual output to 205 million tons. Located on the borders between Shaanxi Provinces and Inner Mongolia Autonomous Region, the field covers an area of 1,136 square kilometers. The field started production in the 1980s and saw its annual coal output hit 100 million tons for the first time in 2005. The field is among the seven-largest coal-producing bases in the world.

The shenfu coalfield, one of the eight coal mines of the world.

Red Lake, the scenic area inside the shenfu coalfield.

Cave dwelling, The traditional architectural culture of Shaanxi.

PRESENT SITUATION:

Various geological hazards and environmental effects induced by coal mining are presented. Including ground subsidence, crack, landslides, collapse, debris flow, soil erosion, destruction of building and cropland, atmosphere pollution etc.

Like surface mining, requires large areas of land to be temporarily disturbed. This also raises a number of environmental challenges, including, dust, noise and water pollution, and impacts on local biodiversity. Steps are taken in modern mining operations to minimize impacts on all aspects of the environment. They lead to ecological degradation and environmental pollution in mining area and restrict regional sustainable development.

Besides, the waste from mountaintop mining pollutes the lakes and valleys where it is placed, causing floods, stream droughts, and fish poisoning. The toxic drainage from abandoned mines also causes runoff which can greatly impact soil quality, so much so that it can take up to 150 years to recover, according to an article on Associated Content.

will work as the chief transportation system. The main volumes are deposited in the site.

Applying principles used in mining, the horizontal skyscraper will use the existing vertical mining elevator systems as a way of transportation. The housing and habitable space will be underground, supported by a vertical tube that will bring fresh air. Water will be taken from the underground soil through advanced and explorative techniques and will be heated by geothermal processes. The terrestrial heat is used to cultivate the saplings and the grown trees are replanted on the mountains to renovate the worn-out land.

The whole complex will have different features and programs such as housing, offices, tourism, commercial, etc. each one located in a strategic place in the mountain. The infrastructure will have different routes available to different

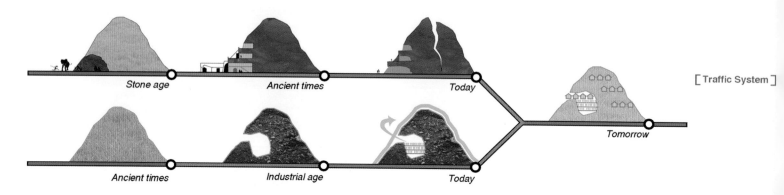

CONCEPT:

The resources of mine are spread all over the world. With the profits brought about by mining, the environment has been damaged, the rate of natural disaster turns high, and the miners have struggled with the rough life.

The shenfu coalfield in Shaanxi, China has been chosen as a site where was abandoned as a goaf because of mining. The goaf not only influenced the local soil and land, but also wasted the terrestrial heat at a large scale.

Hence, the site of the goaf will be reused and part of the pipelines on the working platforms will remain, and the vertical pipelines and the adits are worked as the chief transportation system. The main volumes are deposited in the site, so the living space in different sizes develop and are available for miners.

The terrestrial heat is used to cultivate the saplings and then the grown trees are replanted on the mountains to renovate the worn-out land.

In order to continue the life style in the cave which was lasted for thousands years, the local life style are imitated and taken advantage of outside the mountains. The residences are built along the surface of the mountains. In this way, the water and soil can be prevented from lossing.

■ Outside: continue the life style in the cave which was lasted for thousands years.

■ Inside: Fill the coal goaf and repair the environment .

● Exhibition: Show the coalminers' daliy life and coal mining process to visitors.

● Production: Cultivate saplings and raise fry.

● Public area: Open public area for coalminers and visitors.

Coal Mining System

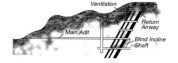

Transportation System of Coalface

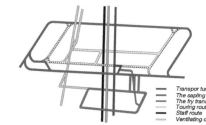

Transpor tunnel
The sapling transport channel
The fry transportation channel
Touring route
Staff route
Ventilating duct

Geothermal System

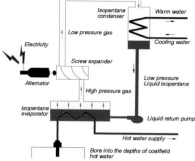

[Traffic System]

[Tourism, Exhibition Area]

[Living Area]

[Saplings Cultivating Area]

[Fry Raising Area]

Mountain Skyscraper R e p a i r G o a

operating sectors including a transport tunnel, a sapling transport channel, a fry transportation channel, a touring route, and a staff route.

In order to continue the lifestyle in caves, which has lasted thousands, years, the local lifestyle will take advantage of the mountain life. The residences are built along the surface of the mountains. In this way, the project takes the most advantage of local water and soil.

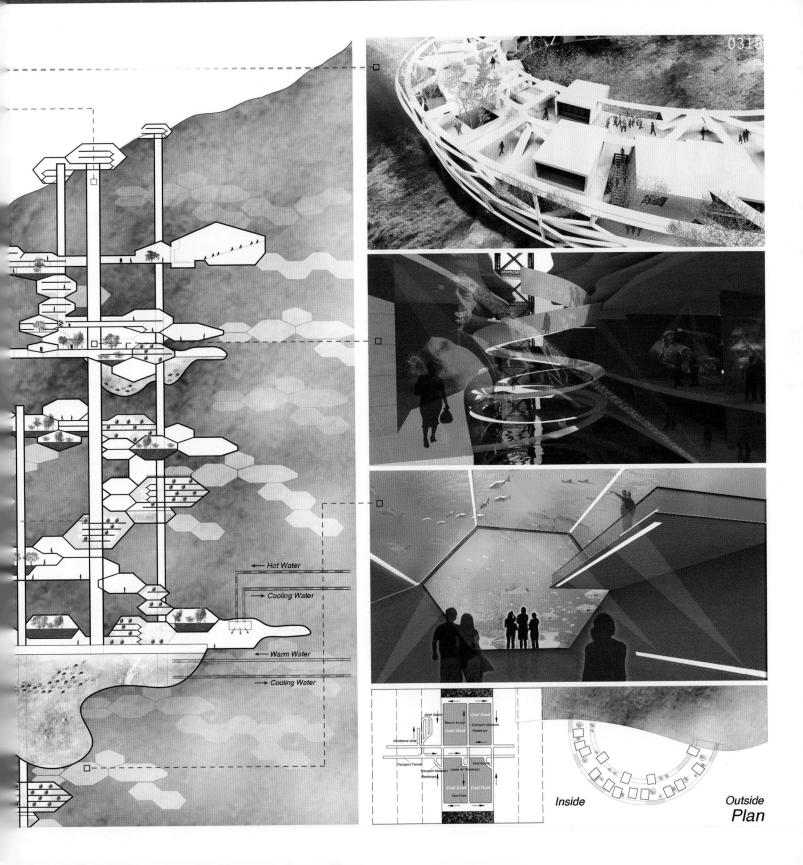

Hot Water

Cooling Water

Warm Water

Cooling Water

Inside

Outside
Plan

KINETIC ISLANDS

Park Sung-Hee
Na Hye Yeon

Republic of Korea

THE 7TH CONTINENT - KINETIC ISLANDS

WHERE IS WORLD'S TRASH COLLECTED?

Most of people might not know the seriousness of the Great Pacific Garbage Patch, But it definitely a tragedy for human being.

To solve this, the 7th Continent - Kinetic Islands, the architectural construction is a sollution for disposal huge-amount of plastic garbage patches in North-east Pacific Ocean, people can see the biggest farm and ocean resort that they have never seen before.

CASE

The quantity of small plastic fragments floating in the north-east Pacific Ocean has been increased a hundred times over the past 40 years.
We are all aware of the Great Pacific Garbage Patch, the humorous pile of plastics and other garbages that are floating under the waters of the Pacific Ocean.
However, most of us choose to ignore it, probably because we hardly ever see it and, it has very little effect on our daily lives.
Unfortunately, a recent study released by the Scripps Institution of Oceanography at University of California San Diego has revealed that the increasing amount of plastic debris may lead to a dramatic increase in the population of certain organisms and ocean animals, which in turn, will result in the demise of others, altering the eco balance that currently exists.
Also, while the study was done just on the plastic floating around in the largest underwater patch that scientists estimate to be twice the size of the US State of Texas.
Therefore, North-east Pacific Ocean is the best needed place for Kinetic Islands.

CONCEPT

A plenty of units in the Kinetic Islands can collect garbages that moving along Pacific Ocean current. When a plenty of garbage units connect and combine with the others, it can form a trash chain. By the time many chains floating in Pacific Ocean, they can be assembled like a Spiral Shape formed by ocean currents and centralized like a big island. That island can be covered by soil to plant mangrove tree.
When mangrove trees grow up, we can have a strongly solid base island in combined units to plant grass for farming crops like corn and wheat and cultivating domestic animals such as cattles and pigs.

The quantity of small plastic fragments floating in the north-east Pacific Ocean has increased a hundred times over the past 40 years, accumulating and forming what we know as the Great Pacific Garbage Patch, a great hazard to the earth's ecosystem balance. Studies estimate that the amount of plastic floating on the Pacific Ocean is twice the size of the US State of Texas. Studies have also revealed that the increasing amount of plastic debris may lead to a dramatic increase in the population of certain organisms and ocean animals which in turn will result in the demise of others due to the altering of the ecological balance that currently exists.

To solve this, Kinetic Islands, the architectural construction is a solution for the disposal of the huge amount of plastic garbage patches; people will witness the big farm and ocean resort become similar to a seventh continent.

0368

Kinetic Islands address this problem and propose a solution for disposal huge-amount of plastic and garbage patches in North-east Pacific Ocean, and take advantage of them as construction elements for a futuristic floating city.

The project proposes a modular study on floating elements. Each module or element works as a flotation device, using 3 floats that allow it to move through the Pacific Ocean's currents. Each module will recollect as much garbage as it is founding through its path. Then when it is full it will move to meet the nearest units to form a garbage chain. When a group of chains floating in Pacific Ocean meet each other, they can be assembled along a spiral shape formed by ocean currents and centralized like a big island. That island can be covered by soil in order to have a solid founding that will allow the development of farming crops.

The trash chains will be covered by soil to allow for the growth of the mangrove tree. Once the trees grow the islands' bases will be strong and the combined units will be used for planting, farming, and cultivating. The units in the island will work as an artificial land, and eventually can be steady enough to support agricultural activities, as well the possibility to use vacant units as building blocks for housing and resorts.

0368

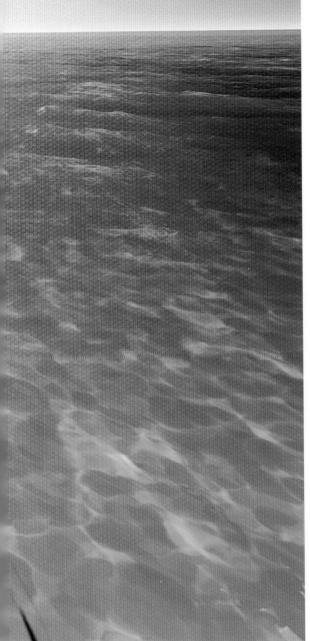

PROCESS

Unit allows the soil to sustain the role and collect garbage at the same time. Each unit with plastic floats along the Ocean Currents. Each units which have 3 parts float in opened with plastics along the Ocean Current.
The units are filled with the garbages and closed. They assembled together forming a chain. Then, chains are also combined. The combination of chains makes the Kinetic Island. On the Kinetic Islands, many vacant units are placed and have a role as buildings like shelthers and resorts.

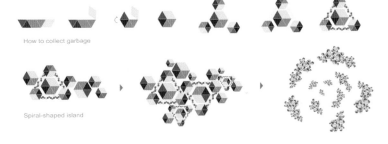

How to collect garbage

Spiral-shaped island

SECTION

Step 1: Unit collects garbage along the Ocean Currents.
Step 2 : When units are filled with the garbages, they assembled together.
Step 3 : Many mangrove trees make the ground firmly.
Step 4 : Various size of units can function as a resort and farm.
Step 5 : Many people can use residences and leisure facilities. Also, animals can move into a unit-shelters, whenever they need it.

FARM

On the Kinetic Island, there are many mangrove trees which make the ground firmly and function as a foundation of other creatures. It might solve the problems of grasslands and habitats for animals. In addition, when weather is harsh, the animals can move into a units-shelters.

RESORT

Ocean resort offer residences and leisure facilities. Also, it includes harbors which connect the island and ocean directly. People can go sailing yachts and cruising through them.

SEA-TY

Shinypark
Lyo Heng Liu
Liu Tang

China/South Korea

SEA-TY

Building an underwater city is the main goal of this project that responds to the sea level rise in the upcoming decades. The US National Research Council estimates that in this century alone, the sea level will rise between 50 and 200 centimeters, leaving some existing cities underwater.

This project is designed as a floating bowl with a massive atrium open to the sky where sunlight will be able to reach all the underwater levels. The geometry is composed as an array of boxes in different sizes that allow for very specific program delineation. The stepping and shifting of volumes create an intricate system of terraces and voids imagined as community and leisure areas.

The project also resembles a traditional hillside town with a network of stairs connecting the various levels.

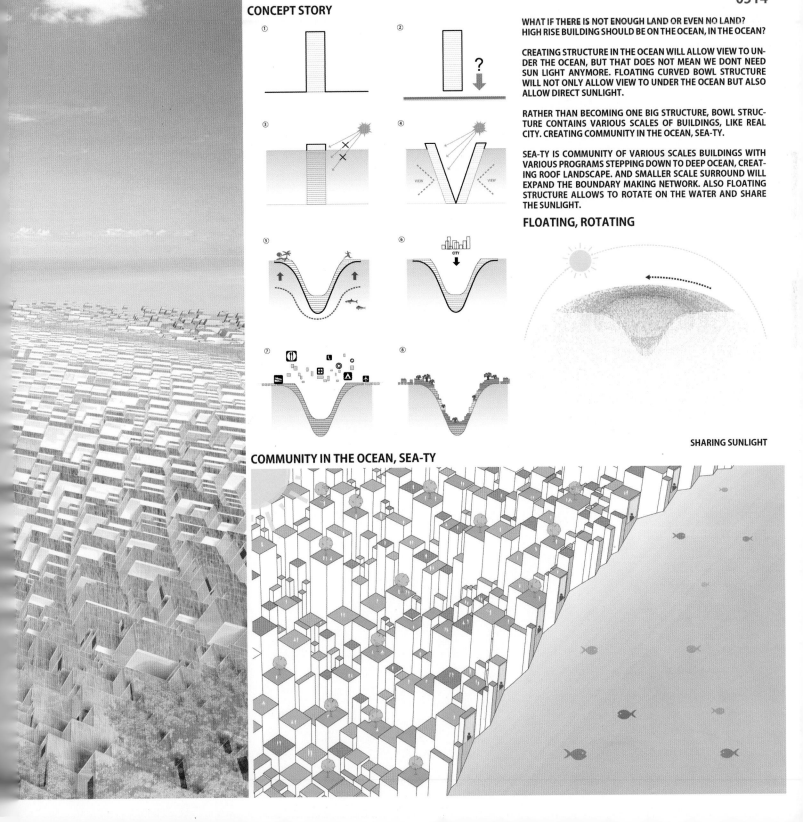

0514

CONCEPT STORY

WHAT IF THERE IS NOT ENOUGH LAND OR EVEN NO LAND?
HIGH RISE BUILDING SHOULD BE ON THE OCEAN, IN THE OCEAN?

CREATING STRUCTURE IN THE OCEAN WILL ALLOW VIEW TO UNDER THE OCEAN, BUT THAT DOES NOT MEAN WE DONT NEED SUN LIGHT ANYMORE. FLOATING CURVED BOWL STRUCTURE WILL NOT ONLY ALLOW VIEW TO UNDER THE OCEAN BUT ALSO ALLOW DIRECT SUNLIGHT.

RATHER THAN BECOMING ONE BIG STRUCTURE, BOWL STRUCTURE CONTAINS VARIOUS SCALES OF BUILDINGS, LIKE REAL CITY. CREATING COMMUNITY IN THE OCEAN, SEA-TY.

SEA-TY IS COMMUNITY OF VARIOUS SCALES BUILDINGS WITH VARIOUS PROGRAMS STEPPING DOWN TO DEEP OCEAN, CREATING ROOF LANDSCAPE. AND SMALLER SCALE SURROUND WILL EXPAND THE BOUNDARY MAKING NETWORK. ALSO FLOATING STRUCTURE ALLOWS TO ROTATE ON THE WATER AND SHARE THE SUNLIGHT.

FLOATING, ROTATING

SHARING SUNLIGHT

COMMUNITY IN THE OCEAN, SEA-TY

Providing views to the mysterious world beneath the water surface is a priority of the design while vegetation also plays an important role in the design as well. The idea is to provide as much green surface as possible for parks, farms, and oxygen generation.

In addition, the city has been designed to rotate according to light exposure and transported to different locations around the globe. This project will still require sunlight and so this floating curved bowl structure will allow direct sunlight. The stepping pattern created by the varying scales of the members helps the sharing of sunlight within the community, as each will have access to it.

Rather than becoming one big structure, Sea-ty's structure contains various scales of buildings, like an actual city's

ROOF PLAN

289

composition. Sea-ty is a community of various scales for buildings with various programs stepping down into the deep ocean, creating a roof landscape. The smaller scale for the surrounding members will expand the boundary to enforce the network of this floating and rotating community in the ocean.

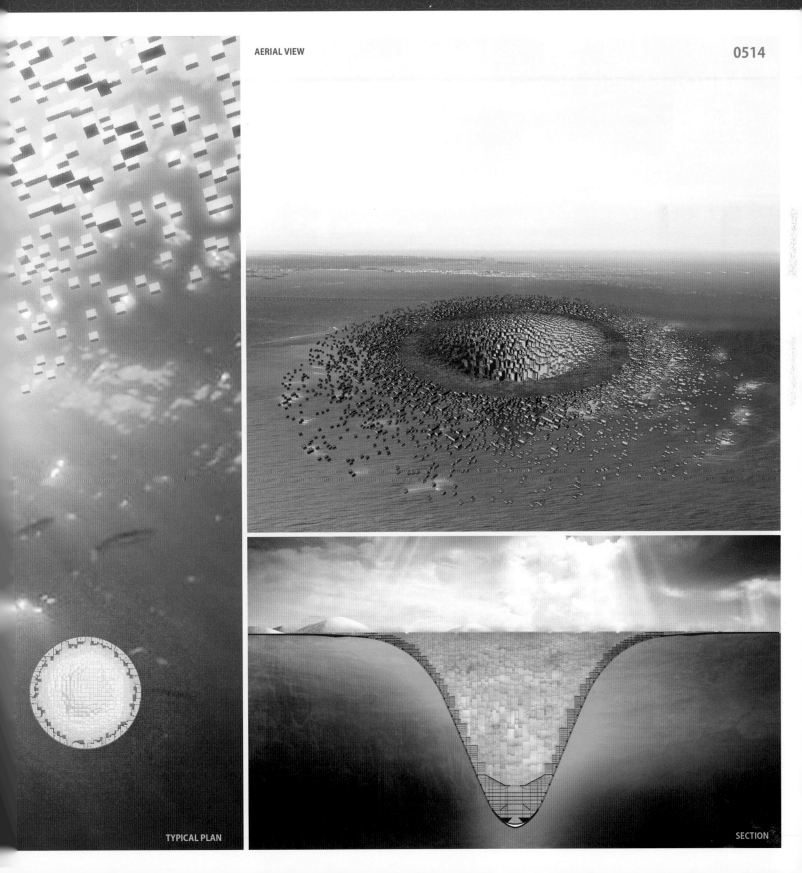

AERIAL VIEW

0514

TYPICAL PLAN

SECTION

AEROGENESIS

Alexandre Caussel
Julian Combes

France

AEROGENESIS

CONTEXT

The life condition on Earth is believed to have changed over the course of the planet's lifetime. Before being a cradle for life, Earth has been a very hostile environment. In a too soon future, it might become again inadequate for the life as we know it.

Today, the human activity contributes to accelerate the degradation of our environment. Climate anomalies become more and more frequent. They create serious and very unpredictable incident. Thus we should be prepared to live in an environment that is becoming more and more unfriendly.

The human metabolism is very fragile and relies on precise needs. If we follow the evolution process, we can suppose we'll mutate and adapt to our future environment. But, that's hypothetical and we don't know in which form. Although, something sure for now is that we master engineering machines. We must design specific devices that will help our environment instead of degrading it.

CONCEPT

AEROGENESIS is an environmental asset that understands and terraforms its hostile environment. It retrieves renewable resources vital to thrive and foster life within its surroundings.

Ultimately designed to be placed in other planets, it has a research laboratory that comprises an infrared telescope and atmospheric measure tools. Placed on different location, several entities will form a powerful network, essential for the exploration of our universe.

The height of a man, it is nevertheless a very complex facility. This is possible because of miniaturization. Nano machines can perform very complex operation with very low energy consumption. For a spatial mission, the AEROGENESIS is easy to launch outside our atmosphere while its system is still very advanced.

We first like to demonstrate that terraforming process is possible. But in a soon future, we'll be able to build and anchor AEROGENESIS at larger scale to produce in sound quantity.

EXPERIMENTATION

The tower is flexible and is designed to make the most of tough environments such as the atmosphere of an alien planet. Therefore, experiences and goals may vary regarding the place. For now, we will work on two locations that share close characteristics: The Atacama Desert in Chile and Mars.

THE ATACAMA DESERT

Commonly known as the driest place on Earth, it has been compared to Mars: In a region about 100 km south of Antofagasta city, which averages 3,000 meters height, we reach the dry limit for microbial life and we miss present signs of life in soil samples. The goal is to introduce basic form of life such as cyanobacteria but also cultivate plants.

The Atacama Desert is rich in metallic mineral resources such as copper, gold, silver and iron as well as non-metallic minerals including important deposits of boron, lithium, sodium nitrate and potassium salt.

This place is also well-fitted for astronomical observation. There is a minimum of 330 clear days a year and there is absolutely no light pollution.

MARS

Unlike Earth, the atmosphere doesn't protect from UV and isn't breathable. For now, we can't expect to make it earthlike. Although, we can transform its composition in order to make it more suitable for life.

The goal is to protect the planet from the solar radiation, warm the planet with greenhouse gases, introduce mars-resistant form of microorganisms and cultivate plants under controlled atmosphere.

Also, we can't miss the chance to observe and study the universe from Mars.

MAIN ASSETS

It is supplied by renewable energies: An integrated windmill and PV panels on the façade produce electricity for the building and its equipment. The extra production is stored in batteries, located in the core. Thus the building may continuously function.

The skin of the building is crystalline and contains several gas layers that filter and protect from the aggression of the outside. (Thermal insulation and UV)

The Aeroponic culture is a technique for growing plants without soil or hydroponic media. The plants are withdraw from the ground and are held above a system that constantly mists the roots with nutrient-laden water. Therefore, with good nutrients, we can consider cultivating anywhere since the soil fertility is no more a sine qua non condition.

The fractional distillation is the separation of a mixture into its component parts by their boiling point by heating them to a temperature at which one or more fractions of the compound will vaporize. There are two fractional distillation towers in our building: One is engineer to separate liquid air at very low temperature (-200°C). The other is designed to separate liquids or distilled materials at very high temperature (+400°C). Extracted elements are used for the building operation and to create nutrients for the aeroponic culture.

SPATIAL OBSERVATORY

VITAL RESOURCES ▷▷▷ ▷▷▷ MICROORGANISM AND/OR GASES TO TERRAFORM ITS HOSTILE ENVIRONMENT PLANTS

	ATACAMA DESERT	MARS
Atmosphere composition	N2 (78%), O2 (21%), Ar (0.9%), others (< 0.1%)	CO2 (95.3%), N2 (2.7%), Ar (1.6%), O2 (0.13%), CO (0.07%) H2O (0.03%)
Soil components	NaNO3, KNO3, Au, I, B, Li & no trace of live in soil samples	Na2O, MgO, Al2O3, SiO2, P2O5, SO3, Cl, K2O, CaO, TiO2, Cr2O3, MnO, FeO, Ni, Zn, Br & no trace of live in soil samples
Temperature range	-25°C to +45°C	-143°C to +27°C
Wind speed range	5 m/s to 25 m/s	10 m/s to 30 m/s
Pressure	101.3 kPa (14.9psi) at sea level	0.6 kPa (0.08 psi)
Gravity	9.81 m.s-2	3.71 m.s-2
Electricity production	windmill & PV panels	windmill & PV panels
H2O manufacturing	air condensation, no rainfall	CO2 electrolysis (Sabatier reaction)
O2, O3 synthesis	fractional distillation	fractional distillation & CO2 electrolysis

GOALS	SPREAD LIFE	ENHANCE LIFE CONDITION
	Microorganism and plants are spread into the land.	The atmosphere is terraformed and organisms are cultivated within controlled environment.

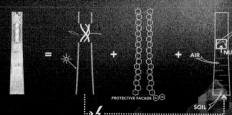

TERRAFORMING OPERATORS

AEROPONIC CULTURE

NUTRIENTS

FRACTIONAL DISTILLATION

PROTECTIVE FAÇADE

AIR

SOIL

RENEWABLE ELECTRICITY

Earth's life conditions are believed to have changed over the course of the planet's lifetime. Before being a cradle for life, Earth was a very hostile environment. In a too soon future, it might become inadequate for life again. Today, human activities contribute to accelerate the degradation of our environment. As climate anomalies become more and more frequent we should be prepared to live in a new environment.

Aerogenesis is an environmental asset that understands and terra-forms its hostile environment. It retrieves renewable resources vital to thrive and foster life within its surroundings. Ultimately designed to be placed in other planets, it has a research laboratory that comprises an infrared telescope and atmospheric measure tools. Placed in different locations, several entities will form a powerful network for the exploration of our universe.

SODIUM NITRATE (NaNO3) & POTASSIUM SALT (KNO3)
The Atacama Desert is the world's largest natural supply of sodium nitrate, well known as Chile saltpeter. Sodium nitrate is a white solid which is very soluble in water. It may be used as a constituent of fertilizers, pyrotechnics, glass, as a food preservative and a solid rocket propellant.

01

WITHIN ATACAMA DESERT

The tower is flexible and is designed to make the most of hostile environments such as the atmosphere of an alien planet. Therefore, experiences and goals may vary regarding the place. For now the project is conceived for two locations that share common characteristics: The Atacama Desert in Chile and the planet Mars.

An integrated windmill and PV panels on the façade produce electricity for the building while excess is stored in batteries located in the core. The skin of the building is crystalline and contains several gas layers that filter and protect it from outside forces, including UV rays and temperature.

The Aeroponic culture is a technique for growing plants without soil or hydroponic media. The plants are withdrawn from the ground and are held above a system that constantly mists the roots with nutrient-laden water. Therefore, with

AEROGENESIS

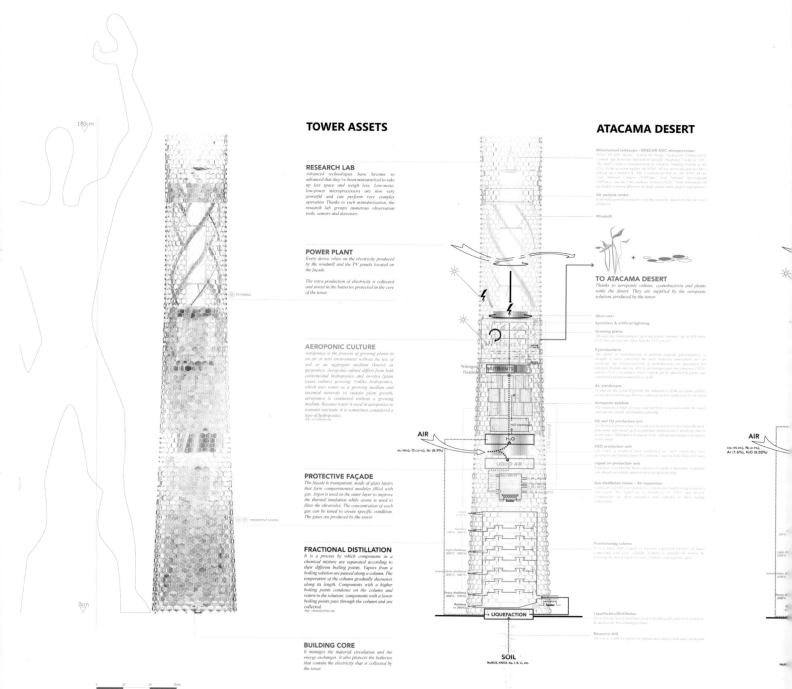

TOWER ASSETS

RESEARCH LAB
Advanced technologies have become so advanced that they've been miniaturized to take up less space and weigh less. Low-noise, low-power microprocessors are now very powerful and can perform very complex operation. Thanks to such miniaturization, the research lab groups numerous observation tools, sensors and detectors.

POWER PLANT
Every device relies on the electricity produced by the windmill and the PV panels located on the façade.

The extra production of electricity is collected and stored in the batteries protected in the core of the tower.

AEROPONIC CULTURE
Aeroponics is the process of growing plants in an air or mist environment without the use of soil or an aggregate medium (known as geoponics). Aeroponic culture differs from both conventional hydroponics and in-vitro (plant tissue culture) growing. Unlike hydroponics, which uses water as a growing medium and essential minerals to sustain plant growth, aeroponics is conducted without a growing medium. Because water is used in aeroponics to transmit nutrients, it is sometimes considered a type of hydroponics.
http://en.wikipedia.org

PROTECTIVE FAÇADE
The façade is transparent, made of glass layers that form compartmented modules filled with gas. Argon is used on the outer layer to improve the thermal insulation while ozone is used to filter the ultraviolet. The concentration of each gas can be tuned to create specific condition. The gases are produced by the tower.

FRACTIONAL DISTILLATION
It is a process by which components in a chemical mixture are separated according to their different boiling points. Vapors from a boiling solution are passed along a column. The temperature of the column gradually decreases along its length. Components with a higher boiling points condense on the column and return to the solution; components with a lower boiling points pass through the column and are collected.
http://chemistry.about.com

BUILDING CORE
It manages the material circulation and the energy exchanges. It also protects the batteries that contain the electricity that is collected by the tower.

ATACAMA DESERT

TO ATACAMA DESERT
Thanks to aeroponic culture, cyanobacteria and plants settle the desert. They are supplied by the aeroponic solution, produced by the tower.

good nutrients, we can consider cultivating anywhere without soil.

Fractional distillation is the separation of a mixture into its component parts by their boiling point by heating them to a temperature at which one or more fractions of the compound will vaporize. There are two fractional distillation towers in the building. One is engineered to separate liquid air at very low temperature (-200°C). The other is designed to separate liquids or distilled materials at very high temperature (400°C). Extracted elements are used for building operation and to create nutrients for the Aeroponic culture.

MARS

Mars telescope
The most noticeable advantage is the saved atmosphere between compared to earth atmosphere masters. Another advantage is that it doesn't have to deal with light that is reduced to the atmosphere. This telescope alone is deal with light pollution. They can more easily observe different wavelengths of light than are harder to work with from earth.

TO MARS SOIL

Only cyanobacteria can survive and thrive within the atmosphere of mars. The goal is to engage a global oxygenic photosynthesis that will convert the CO2 massively present in the atmosphere of Mars.

Plants remain cultivated within closed and controlled atmosphere. For now, a colony will have to live in such hermetic environment.

H2 & N2 extra tanks
Many hydrogen and nitrogen are to be a part material on the building structure to bring extra gas tanks from earth. Ammonia is several airships are power elements between the different plants.

H2O synthesis
The H2O is produced through the Sabatier process that involves the reaction of hydrogen with carbon dioxide at elevated temperatures (approved 300-400°C) and pressure in the presence of a nickel catalyst to produce methane and water: CO2 + 4H2 → CH4 + 2H2O. The H2O is used within the tower while the greenhouse gas CH4 is released is also the atmosphere of Mars.

CH4

GREENHOUSE GASES

O3
O2

TO MARS ATMOSPHERE

To terraform Mars, the first step is to warm the planet. Only few degrees would increase the atmospheric pressure to 300 mbar (30kPa), comparable to the altitude of the peak of Mount Everest where it is 337 mbar. While this would not be comfortably breathable by humans, it would eliminate the present need for pressure suits.

The tower release CH4 which is known to be a powerful greenhouse gas.

The CO2 is electrolyzed and turned into O3. Ozone blocks harmful ultraviolet sunlight but it is also three thousand times stronger as a greenhouse gas than CO2. Therefore, to warm the planet and also protect it from the sun radiation, the tower will massively produce ozone.

MnO, FeO, Ni, Zn, Br

0573

VISION

It may, however, be ultimately impossible to fine tune Mars' climate to support human life as we currently know it on Earth. In the centuries it would take for us to get to this point, it might just be easier to engineer humans to tolerate the "better" conditions that we can produce on Mars. For instance, it is now conceivable to warm up Mars atmosphere and remove the necessity of pressurized suit. But to make it breathable is another story... In the end, humans do not just terraform Mars, Mars aeroform us....

02

WITHIN MARS

NOMAD

Joaquin Rodriguez Nuñez
Konstantino Tousidonis Rial
Antonio Ares Sainz

Spain

location
MARS

year
2020

average temperature
-63⁰

atmospheric pressure
7.5 Mbar

In the 21st century, the transformation of Mars to the conditions of life on earth was like the greatest adventure of mankind and its greatest challenge. Gradually, this became a distant epic legend ...

PROJECT

NOMAD

@eVoloMagazine #OverPopulation #GlobalWarming #Mars #ProjectNomad #Factories #Terraforming

"In the beginning there was nothing but rocks and dust ... Lost in the great space, where life could not venture, the red world was resting in a deep and glacial sleep. But it all changed with the Project NOMAD"

...

Mars planet, year 2020

One day, the nomad factories tore the sky apart!

The air grew warmer and warmer
The clouds filled the sky
The ground shook over and over again
then the blue waters came

The global increase in population, its concentration in cities, and the development of emerging countries lead to a big increase in energy need. Earth has undergone dramatic climatic changes, which have been linked, by a large consensus, to greenhouse gases (GHG).

The concentration of GHG in the atmosphere directly affects the global temperature, with potentially dramatic global consequences. Without any doubt, it is indispensable to define an objective of maximum emissions, in order to limit problems in the future in the Earth.

The Project Nomad goal is to change the atmospheric and soil chemistry of Mars to make it hospitable for human colonization. The concept is to build nomad factories that use Martian minerals to create complex carbon greenhouse

0703

THE PROBLEM

A significant increase in the population

The global increase in population (Fig. 1), its concentration in cities, and the development of emerging countries lead to a big increase in energy needs. Although oil, gas and coal will be available for many years still, resources are limited.

Climate change in Earth [negative consecuences]

The planet is know to have undergone dramatic climatic changes (Fig. 2) which have been linked, by a large consensus, to greenhouse gases (GHG). The concentration of GHG in the atmosphere directly affects the global temperature, with potentially global, dramatic consequences. Without any doubt, it is indispensable to define an objective of maximum emissions, in order to limit problems in the future in the earth.

Fig. 1 World Population (Thousands of People)   Fig. 2 Global Warming

TURNING TWO MAJOR PROBLEMS INTO A GREATEST CHALLENGE FOR HUMANITY

Terraforming Mars

The Project Nomad goal is change the atmospheric and soil chemistry of the planet to make it more hospitable for human colonization (Fig. 3). The concept is build nomad factories that use martian minerals to create complex carbon greenhouse gases (GHG) in the atmosphere (Fig. 4).

Mars   Phase 1: Blue Mars   Phase 2: Green Mars

Fig. 3 Terraforming Mars Phases

Mars' Poles   Nomad Factory   Mars' New Atmosphere

Fig. 4 Terraforming Mars Concept

Climate change in Mars [positive consecuences]

We know to warm planets, our goal is terraform Mars from a cold, dead planet into a warm, vital planet with green forests, blue oceans and a sustainable ecosystem.

1. WARMING   Artificial radiactive forcing

CO_2 CAP   Regolith CO_2 CAP

2. OUTGASSING   3. WARMING

Thickening of atmosphere   Increased greenhouse effect

Sublimation and degassing of CO_2

CO_2 CAP   Regolith CO_2 CAP CO_2 CAP   Regolith CO_2 CAP

gases (GHG) in the atmosphere. The project has two main phases: Blue Mars and Green Mars. Project Nomad has been designed to complete Phase One.

The terraformer's movement is made possible by a vehicle called a crawler transporter that has an estimate load capacity of 12,600,000 pounds. While the terraformer progresses, the digger and collector which sits on the crawler is in charge of collecting the regolith for further processing. Resting on the digger is the atmosphere processor. Mars regolith undergoes the atmospheric distillation process here.

The material is transferred to the combustion chamber where it is decomposed by a heater. Greenhouse gases obtained from this process will be driven to the Martian atmosphere increasing its average temperature. The vertical

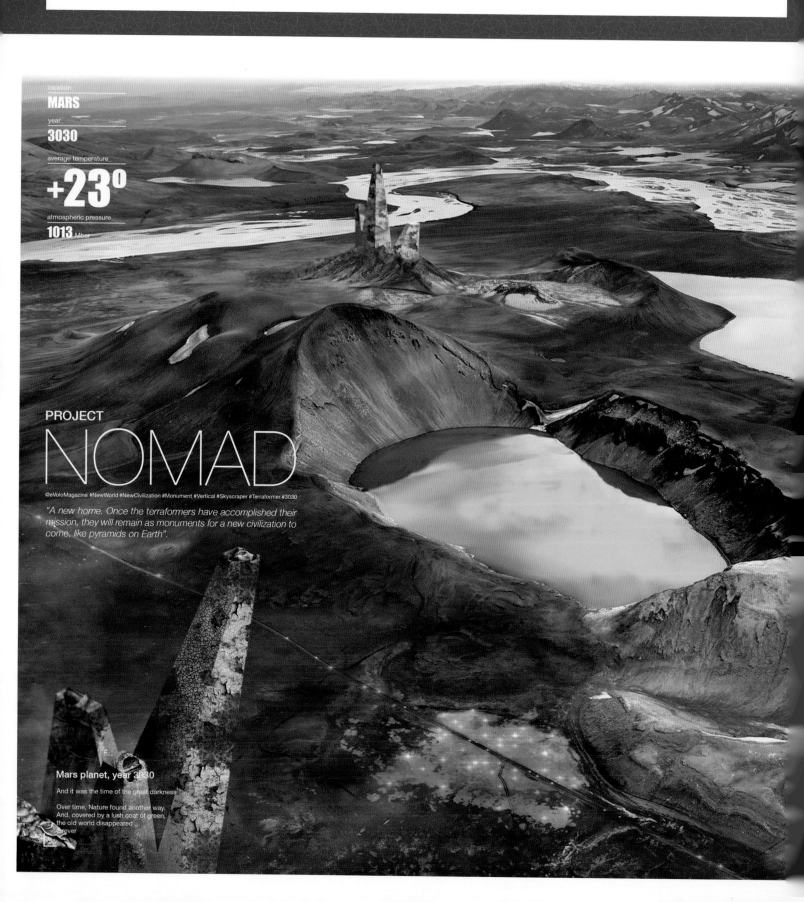

location
MARS

year
3030

average temperature
+23⁰

atmospheric pressure
1013 Mbar

PROJECT
NOMAD

@eVoloMagazine #NewWorld #NewCivilization #Monument #Vertical #Skyscraper #Terraformer #3030

"A new home. Once the terraformers have accomplished their mission, they will remain as monuments for a new civilization to come, like pyramids on Earth".

Mars planet, year 3030

And it was the time of the great darkness

Over time, Nature found another way.
And, covered by a lush coat of green,
the old world disappeared ...
forever

structure through which combustion product gases are exhausted to the outside is the flue gas stack.

The main goal is terraforming Mars from a cold, dead planet into a warm, vital planet with green forests, blue oceans and a sustainable ecosystem. We will use what we know about warming a planet to bring climate change to Mars for a positive outcome.

0703

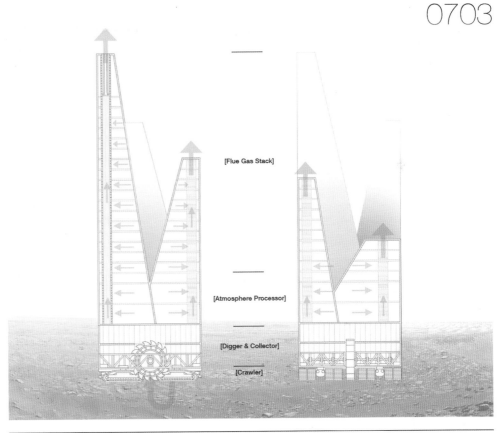

[Flue Gas Stack]

[Atmosphere Processor]

[Digger & Collector]

[Crawler]

[Crawler]
Load capacity 12,600,000 pounds. The crawler transporter is a crawler vehicle that makes possible the terraformer's movement.

[Digger & Colector]
While the terraformer progresses, the digger is in charge of collecting the regolith for further processing.

[Atmosphere Processor]
Mars regolith undergoes atmospheric distillation process. The material is transferred to the combustion chamber where it is decomposed by a heater. Greenhouse gases obtained from this process will be driven to the Martian atmosphere increasing its average temperature.

[Flue Gas Stack]
Vertical structure through wich combustion product gases are exhausted to the outside air.

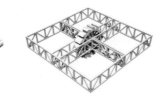

RED MARS   BLUE MARS   GREEN MARS

MOSES

Vuk Djordjevic
Milos Jovanovic
Darki Markovic
Milos Vlastic

Serbia

MOSES
HABITACULUM FUTURAE

The existing ratio of 29% of land to 71% of water on Earth is slowly changing as a result of negative human impact on the planet. This has triggered the processes of global warming together with the thermal expansion of the world's oceans. Also, the rapid increase of the number of people substantially affects the density of the population on the mainland. Research shows that the sea level will rise, decreasing land surface which will affect agricultural yields.

Moses is a decentralized, self-sustaining city unit, populated by approximately 25,000 inhabitants, which offers the transition of men from land to sea, so that the land could be used for food production and the Earth could start its process of self-regeneration from the negative human impact. It functions independently as a city-unit, as well as a cluster of units, which share information, energy, and goods.

0735

FACTS

The existing ratio of 29% of land and 71% of water tends to change, as a result of negative human impact on the planet, which has triggered the processes of global warming, together with the thermal expansion of the world oceans.

Also, the rapid increase of people number substantially affects the density of the population on the mainland, which gets reduced on a daily basis as a result of the sea level increase. Statistics and scientific research state that the sea level is going to rise more than two meters until the end of the 21st century, decreasing the land surface by another 1%, which has the important role of feeding the population by giving an agricultural yields.

These circumstances have brought the civilisation to the point when it has to engage in serious research and exploration to solve the existing global issues in order to preserve population and make the civilisation sustainable.

CONCEPT

Moses is a decentralised, self sustaining city unit, populated by approximately 25000 inhabitants, which offers the transition from land to sea, so the land could be used for food production and earth could start the process of regeneration from the negative human impact. It functions independently as a city unit, as well as the system of city units which share the information, energy and goods among themselves. Each city unit is placed upon the intersection of perpendicular traffic lines, which form the grid that serves as a connection between the cities, as well as the connection of the cities to the land, in order to enable the transport of energy, goods and people.

In terms of energy production, Moses takes the maximum advantage of its offshore location and uses strong wind and water streams as renewable resources to generate electricity.

It consists of two structures that can rotate independently in order to suck in the air or water flow, depending on their position: upper part uses the wind energy and the lower one uses the energy of water stream.These structures are connected by the ring structure which allows them independent full circle rotation, and enables circular movement of the trains coming from four directions of the traffic lines.

Worldwide "grid" system could connect continents

Energy transfer is applied through the connection rods between buildings and cities. This system compensates excess and shortage of energy in each building and city; therefore the energy system is stable and provides an uninterruptible power supply.

The upper part of the building is always positioned following the wind flows.. The lower part of the building is always positioned following sea currents. Independent positioning is enabled by the toroid basis which floats on water.

Each city-unit is placed on the intersection of perpendicular traffic lanes, which form the grid that serves as a connection between cities and land through a network of ultra fast trains. The square transport grid connects cities. The quadratic shape provides the shortest distances between the cities. Ultra fast maglev trains will pass through the large cross section.

The upper and lower parts of the building can be rotated around the toroid base of the building using the uniquely developed system. The torus base is used as bogie—a revolving platform for 360-degree rotation. The upper part of the building is continuously positioned to use the maximum wind power i.e. to steer it towards the propeller generators. The same system has been applied to the lower part of the building, converting the available water

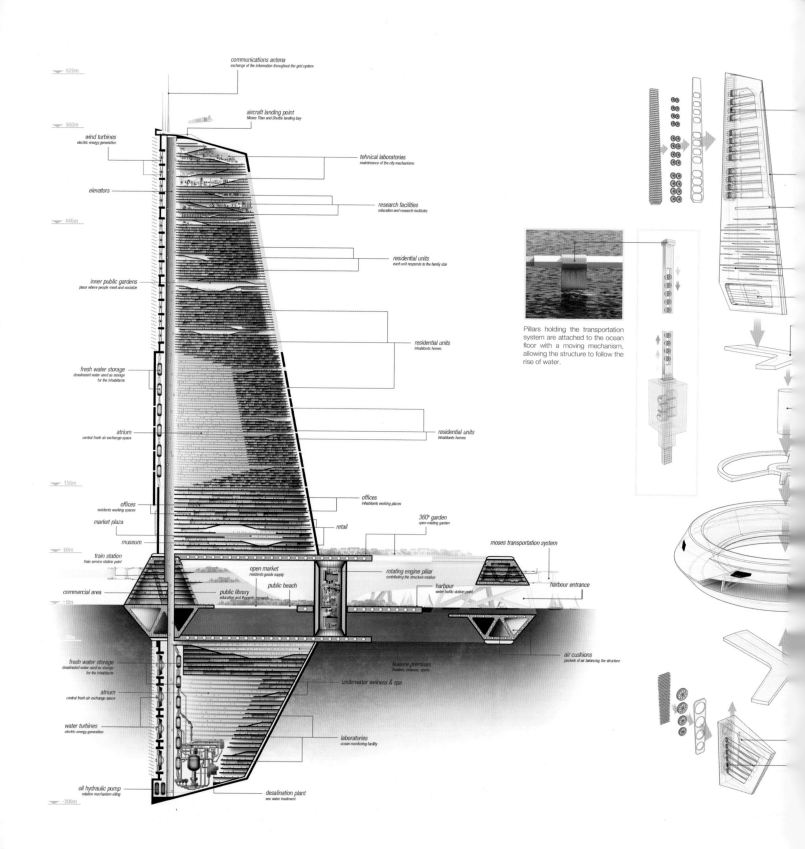

Pillars holding the transportation system are attached to the ocean floor with a moving mechanism, allowing the structure to follow the rise of water.

currents into energy for use.

Each Moses city has a runway for aircrafts. The runway is within the building construction and equipped for takeoff and landing in all weather conditions. Moses Titan is an aircraft for mass transportation (about 400 passengers). It moves through the use of propellers and is adjusted to maintain reduced power and fuel consumption once Moses Titan reaches the set altitude. Moses Shuttle is a personal aircraft for not more than four persons.

Moses takes maximum advantage of its offshore location to produce renewable energy by two main systems. It consists of two structures that can rotate independently to utilize wind and water flow energy.

intakes
...eling air flow to wind turbines

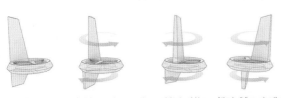

Upper and lower part of the building can be rotated around the toroid base of the building using the specially developed system. Torus base is used as bogie - a revolving platform for 360 degrees rotation. Upper part of the building is continuously positioned to use the maximum wind power i.e. to steer it towards the propeller generators. The same system has been applied to the lower part of the building, converting the available water currents into energy.

...oramic screen

...gation center
...illumination that allows ships to navigate during night

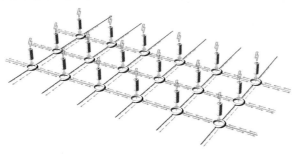

...dential windows
...al light source for the housing units

...ic balconies

... platform
...ng the rotation of the upper building part

Generated energy is continuously shared between the buildings and cities connected by the transportation grid. Excess energy can be stored in each building and can be used as energy source whenever and wherever necessary throughout the network system.

...r engine
...and rotates the platform where the upper structure stands

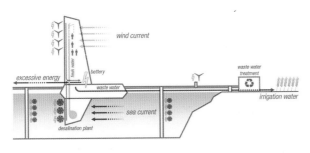
wind current
excessive energy
battery
waste water
waste water treatment
irrigation water
sea current
desalination plant

...our

...d base
...ne that separates the 2 structures

"Moses Titan"   "Moses Shuttle"

AIR TRAFFIC

Each "Moses" city has a runway for aircrafts. Runway is within building construction and equipped for take-off and landing in all weather conditions. Within the building are hangars and aprons. "Moses" Titan is an aircraft for the mass transportation (about 400 passengers). It is moved around using propellers and it is adjtusted to maintain reduced power and fuel consumption once Moses Titan reaches the set altitude.

"Moses shuttle" is a personal aircraft for not more than four persons.

platform
...the rotation of the lower building part

LAND TRAFFIC

The square transport grid connects cities. Quadratic shape provides the shortest distances between the cities. Ultra fast maglev trains will pass through the large cross section.

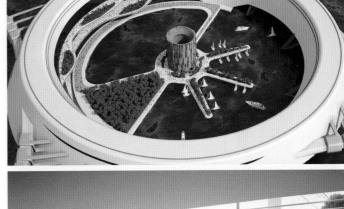

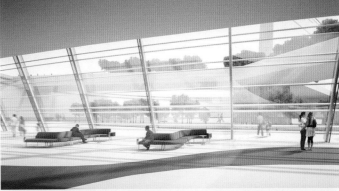

THE SCRAPER

Gyoeng Hwan Kim
Jae Chung Ko
Jong Hyuk Lim
Sung Wha Na
Seung Jun Park
Ho Young Yeo

Republic of Korea

Ocean, Sky and Universe- THE SCRAPER

Prologue

This is a part of the sky-scraper that is taller than any others that exist in the world. This is beyond the definition of a sky-scraper. because it is a universe-scraper starting at the ocean and passing through the sky facing the universe.

This idea started from something about whether human-civilization is expanding that territory somewhere. The territorial activities of humans aren't limited as much now inside of the earth, and it is facing the universe, going beyond the earth. Because of that, currently, the ocean is contaminated from the ocean arriving at the universe from the selfishness of civilization.

At the Pacific, the waste which is thrown away by humans has made huge trash-islands floating on the ocean under the influence of ocean currents and about 60,000 satellites Debris having run out threaten the earth.

It is reported that the ocean life mistakes a part of the trash-island floating on the ocean as food and eats it, athen dies and has a bad influence on the ocean's environment. Also, the trash of the universe rotates around the earth's orbit, then falls to the earth and damages residential areas and airliners.

First of all, because the universe is a territory that we should pioneer in the future and currently, the trash surrounding the earth always has danger of colliding with projectiles launched up in the future, there is much concern about this harmful situation.

Following this, methods for removing this trash in each country has become the greatest issue related with the universe industry.

Now, through the scraper that picks up the trash of the universe and the earth, we try to suggest a sky-scraper of a new type, wanting to serve the environment.

The massive amount of waste and debris accumulated in the Pacific Ocean is known as the Great Pacific Garbage Patch. Through a skyscraper that picks up the trash of the universe and Earth, this design strives to serve the environment. The Scraper is a floating building designed to collect and compact the garbage into cubes with the use of automated robots.

These cubes will later be burned by two different actions. The first system burns the cubes using space rockets exhausts during launch. The second is the transportation of the cubes to outer space and let them re-enter the Earth's atmosphere to burn down. The skyscraper can float by buoyancy and the shape of the form is flexible and can be changed, as the packing cube combination methods of the scraper are easy to edit.

0811

Concept

1. Scraper gathers ocean trash and puts that into PACKING CUBE that removes trash and is on-board the units.

2. Then, that PACKING CUBE is piled up on the ocean, and the scraper divides the trash piled up.

3. And it is docked on the rocket being loaded in the units when the movable launcher comes.

4. When the rocket is launched, the scraper opens PACKING CUBE, combusts the trash, using frictional heat of the rocket launched, and then it is removed.

5. In the universe, by using metal wires, the trash is gathered,

6. falls to the earth, and is combusted by the atmosphere's frictional heat.

Through this repetitive process, the trash from the earth and the universe is removed.

Scrap

Satellites
Debris

Universe

Combusts the Debris
using frictional heat of

Atmosphere

Earth

Ocean
Trash

Scrap   Combine   Docking

The concept begins with the Scraper gathering ocean trash and placing it into the packing cube that removes trash and is on-board the units. Then that packing cube is piled up on the ocean and scraper divides the trash piled and it is docked on the rocket being loaded in the units when the movable launcher arrives.

When the rocket is launched the scraper opens the packing cube, combusts the trash using the frictional heat of the rocket that launches and then it is removed. In space, the trash is gathered by using metal wires, falls to Earth and combusted by the atmosphere's frictional heat. The magnetic field of Earth draws the debris when currents are flowing through metal wires of the Scraper. Through this repetitive process, the trash from the earth is removed. This method of removing satellite debris is the way suggested by many scientists based on research to be efficient.

Location

The tower's location is near the equator of the Pacific. The logic of the set-up of the tower's location is the following:

1. Because of the fast rotating velocity, the ocean near the equator is advantageous to rocket launches, in case of failure, the example of launching a rocket after people send the movable universe launcher near the equator is increasing since it can minimize damage as it falls onto the ocean.

2. Under the influence of the ocean current, ocean trash from all countries of the world goes to the Pacific, and then it makes trash islands.

The units defined as 'Scraper' spread out, remove ocean trash and pile them up near the Pacific's equator.

Sky-scarper

The sky-scarper can be floated on the ocean by the buoyancy, and shape of the form can be flexibly changed as the packing cube combination methods of the scraper.

The Scraper Detail

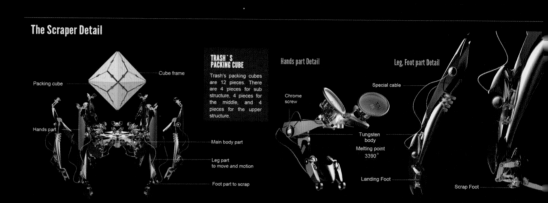

TRASH'S PACKING CUBE
Trash's packing cubes are 12 pieces. There are 4 pieces for sub structure, 4 pieces for the middle, and 4 pieces for the upper structure.

The Scraper Activity Route

PHASE # 01   PHASE # 02   PHASE # 03   PHASE # 04   PHASE # 05   PHASE # 05

Ocean Trash Pickup   Combine   Move to universe

Metal wire detail

Indium selenide skin thermoelectric genera-tion used frictional heat.

Copper coil

Magnetic fields of the Earth draw the debris when currents are flowing through metal wires of the SCRAPER And frictional heat is generated and it burns out the debris. This method removing the satellite debris is the way suggested by many scientists through a real study, based on scientific basis.

Packing Cube Assembly

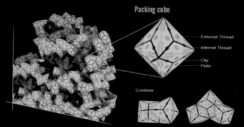

Packing cube
External Thread
Internal Thread
Clip
Plate
Combine

Combination principle

THE COMBINE OF PACKING CUBE.
Grooves on the packing frames are combined, and each packing frame becomes stan-dard structure to be combined. Each tower is finished with a combi-nation of other joint

Rocket docking

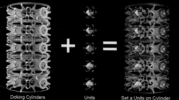

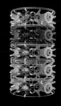

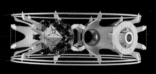

Doking Cylinders   Units   Set a Units on Cylinder

Docking Cylinders
As cylinders to be able to dock on the rocket are added, The scrapers loaded with packing cubes are docked outside, and the ocean trash combusts as it is rubbing against the air when the packing cube opens going to the universe.

The tower's location is near the equator of the Pacific. The logic of the set-up of the tower's location is firstly that because of the fast rotating velocity, the ocean near the equator is advantageous to rocket launches. In case of failures of launching a rocket, danger of human fatality is minimalized as the movable launcher is sent to the middle of the ocean. Also, under the influence of the ocean current, ocean trash from all countries of the world goes to the Pacific and makes "trash islands." The ideal location for this project would be the source of the problem.

Sky-scraper's Growth

SCRAP 4800 ton
SCRAP 3600 ton
SCRAP 2400 ton
SCRAP 1200 ton
SCRAP 600 ton

0811

HORIZONTAL SKYSCRAPER

Yan Jieming
Mingyang Li
Danjing Zhu
Ning Zong

China

BACKGROUND

CHINA IS A MOUNTAINOUS COUNTRY. ACCORDING TO STATISTICS, 69% OF THE LAND IS COVERED BY MOUNTAINS, HILLS AND HIGHLAND.

DUE TO THE RAPID URBANIZATION THROUGHOUT THIS COUNTRY, URBAN POPULATION AND CITY SCALE ARE INFLATING BEYOND IMAGINATION, WHILE THE ARABLE LAND IS SHRINKING.

BECAUSE OF THE LIMITED AVAILABLE LAND AND POOR TRANSPORTATION, THE CAPACITY OF MOUNTAINOUS AREA FOR HOLDING PEOPLE IS ALWAYS RESTRICTED.
IN ORDER TO CREATE A HIGH-DENSITY LIVING MODE AND HIGH-SPEED TRANSPORTATION NETWORK, WE TRY TO FIND A WAY OUT, WITHIN THE PROTOTYPE OF SKYSCRAPER.

CHINA   SICHUAN   MA PING CUN

SITE

MA PING CUN IS A VILLAGE LOCATED IN SICHUAN PROVINCE, IN THE SOUTHWESTERN OF CHINA. IT HAS THE TYPICAL MOUNTAINOUS LANDSCAPE OF THE REGION. THE LOCAL PEOPLE MAINLY DEPEND ON TRADITIONAL AGRICULTURE TO MAKE A LIVING. BECAUSE OF THE STEEP TERRAIN, THE AMOUNT OF HOUSING AND FIELD IS LIMITED. IN SOME OTHER PARTS OF MOUNTAINOUS AREAS, TERRACED FIELDS ARE APPLIED, BUT MOST OF THE VILLAGE HAS THE SAME SITUATION WITH MA PING CUN, OR EVEN WORSE.

POOR TRANSPORTATION IS ANOTHER PROBLEM FOR THE VILLAGERS. PEOPLE HAVE TO WALK FOR HOURS TO THE TOWNS DOWNHILL BECAUSE THE ROAD IS TOO STEEP AND NARROW TO LET VEHICLES PASS.

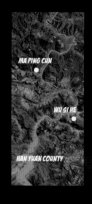
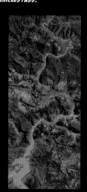
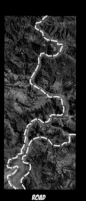
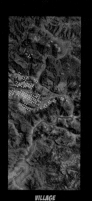

MA PING CUN   WU SI HE   HAN YUAN COUNTY

DA DU RIVER   ROAD   VILLAGE

CONCEPT

OUR PROPOSAL IS TO DESIGN A HUGE STRUCTURE WHICH LOOKS LIKE A 'COLLAPSED SKYSCRAPER', AS A CONTAINER FOR FUTURE DEVELOPMENT OF THIS VILLAGE.

FOR THE VERY FEW AMOUNT OF AVAILABLE LAND IN THE MOUNTAINOUS AREA, THE 'COLLAPSCRAPER' IS ORIGINALLY DESIGNED AS A SMALL-SCALE URBAN SYNTHESIS CONTAINER, WHICH CAN PROVIDE MUCH SPACE.

GENERALLY, THE SPECIFIC ARRANGEMENT OF BUILDING IS NOT DEFINED BY DESIGNER BUT THE NATIVE PEOPLE. WHAT WE DO IS ONLY TO OFFER THE GIANT STRUCTURE WITH SUGGESTIONS, LIKE TUTORIALS.

FIELD COULD BE LAID ON THE EACH LAYER TO MAKE THE STRUCTURE INTO A CROPS MACHINE.
WIND TURBINE COULD BE SETTLED TO MAKE IT LIKE A CLEAN ENERGY PRODUCER.
IF POPULATION STARTED TO INCREASE, 'COLLAPSCRAPER' MAY ALSO TAKE THE RESPONSIBILITY OF HOUSING DISTRIBUTOR.
OF COURSE, USERS CAN COMBINE VARIOUS FUNCTIONS, TURNING IT INTO A MINI BUT COMPLEX CITY.

IN THE ASPECT OF STRUCTURE, THE FORM OF LIFT SHAFT IS KEPT AND CHANGED INTO ANOTHER FORM — TUNNELS.
IT ALSO PLAYS THE ROLE OF A LONG SPAN BRIDGE, CONNECTING MOUNTAINS RIGHT OVER THE VALLEYS, IMPROVING THE TRANSPORTATION FROM MOUNTAINS TO MOUNTAINS.

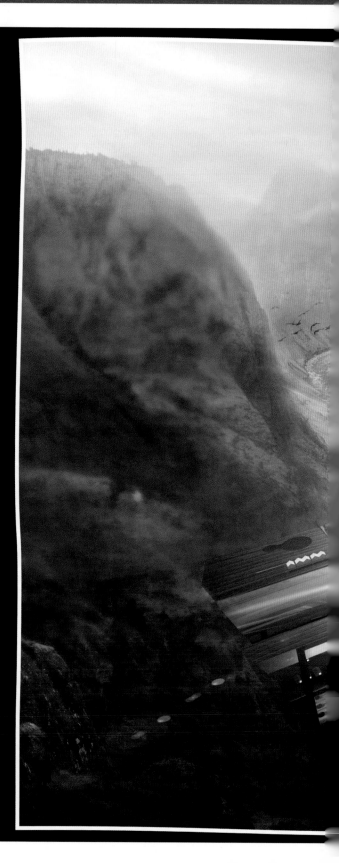

Seventy percent of the land in China lies within mountain ranges. Although some of these regions are sparsely populated, they do not account for a significant portion of the country's entire population. Due to the rapid urbanization, the majority of the existing urban areas lack the necessary infrastructure for the inhabitants. Because of the limited available land and poor quality of transportation, the capacity of mountainous area for holding people is always restricted. In order to create a high-density living and high-speed transportation network, architecture in that area must try to find a way out within the prototype of a skyscraper.

   Ma Ping Cun is a village located in the Sichuan province in southwestern China. It has the typical mountainous landscape of the region. The local people mainly depend on traditional agriculture to make a living. Because of the

0835-1

COLLAPSCRAPER ?

steep terrain, the amount of housing and field is limited. In some other parts of mountainous areas, terraced fields are applied, but most of the other villages are in the same situation as Ma Ping Cun, or even worse. Poor transportation is another problem for the villagers. People have to walk for hours to the towns because the road is too steep and narrow to let vehicles pass.

The Horizontal Skyscraper is a proposal to create a network of horizontal skyscrapers between the mountains of China. The structure is conceived as an inhabitable mega bridge equipped with a variety of programs and the latest green technologies. The main idea is to develop self-sufficient cities that will be interconnected by a secondary network of bridges.

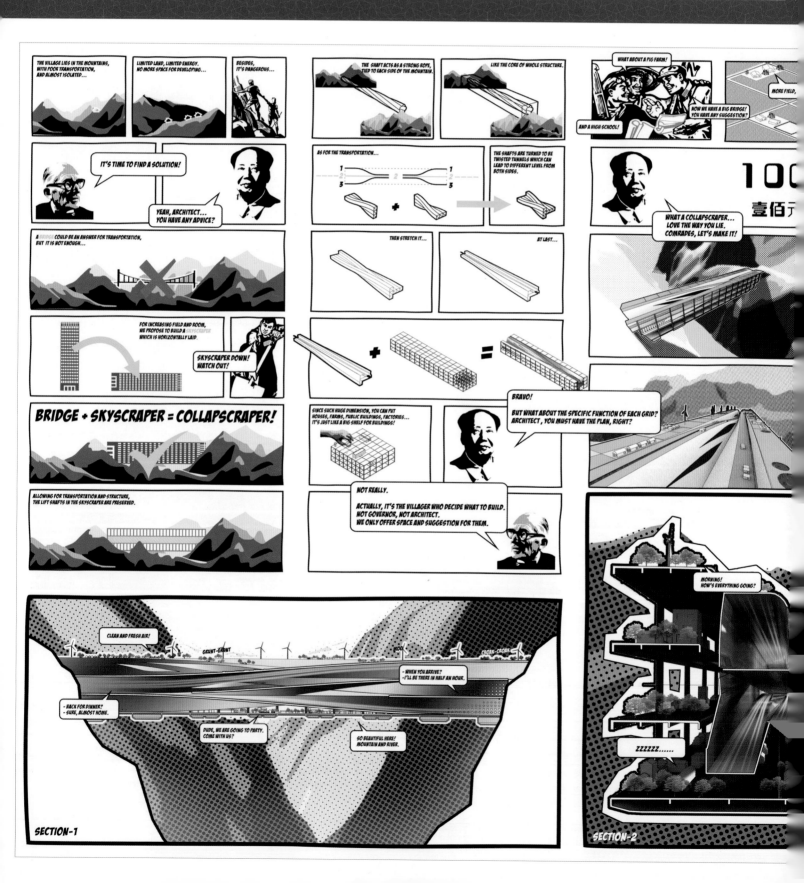

The city-like structures are designed to minimize their contact with the ground and conserve the natural environment. These are modular cities where program units could be interchanged and systematically grow according to demand.

The project is not designed as a finished product, but as an idea in which the residents will create their own city according to their needs in a specific point in time.

MARTIAN RING

Mamon Alexander
Tyutyunnik Artem

Ukraine

The basis of this concept is a progressive broadening of human habitation boundaries due to exploration of space. As it is difficult to imagine human life without its natural environment, plants and animals will occupy other planets after people. In the future, life will be able to prosper in place where it could not before.

In the years to come the first people will set foot on the surface of Mars as a research expedition. That will hopefully be the beginning of a new era in the history of mankind, where the period of cosmic exploration will begin. This first experimental colony is nothing but one of the stages of our preparation for creation of the human colony outside of our native home, Earth.

Why should we inhabit Mars? NASA scientists confirmed the theory that water in liquid state had previously existed

on Mars and even complicated life forms had probably existed. But owing to the excursion of the planet orbit all water available on Martin surface went from liquid state to solid, crystalline.

The Martian Ring is a closed, self-sufficient off-line mega-structure, which contains all functions for comfortable existence and development of all life forms. The ring is designed on the model of linear cities, a circular system for comfortable connection of all parts of the structure as single agglomerate.

The structural element includes residential units and public space. The program for public space is varied to house shops, theaters, cafes, museum, libraries, recreation space, and premises for living cell maintenance. Living cells can accommodate up to 30 people. This is an automatically piloted aircraft launched form Earth which serves as home.

The ring is conventionally subdivided in zones, a residential zone and a green zone. The residential zone contains accommodation modules, i.e. houses being automatically man-carrying aircrafts, in which people arrive for settling in the ring. The green zone includes simulations of Earth's habitats such as forests, fields, meadows, rivers, and lakes.

COLUMBARIUM SKYSCRAPER

Ganna Kosharna
Andrian Sokolovkiy
Vladislav Tyminski

Ukraine

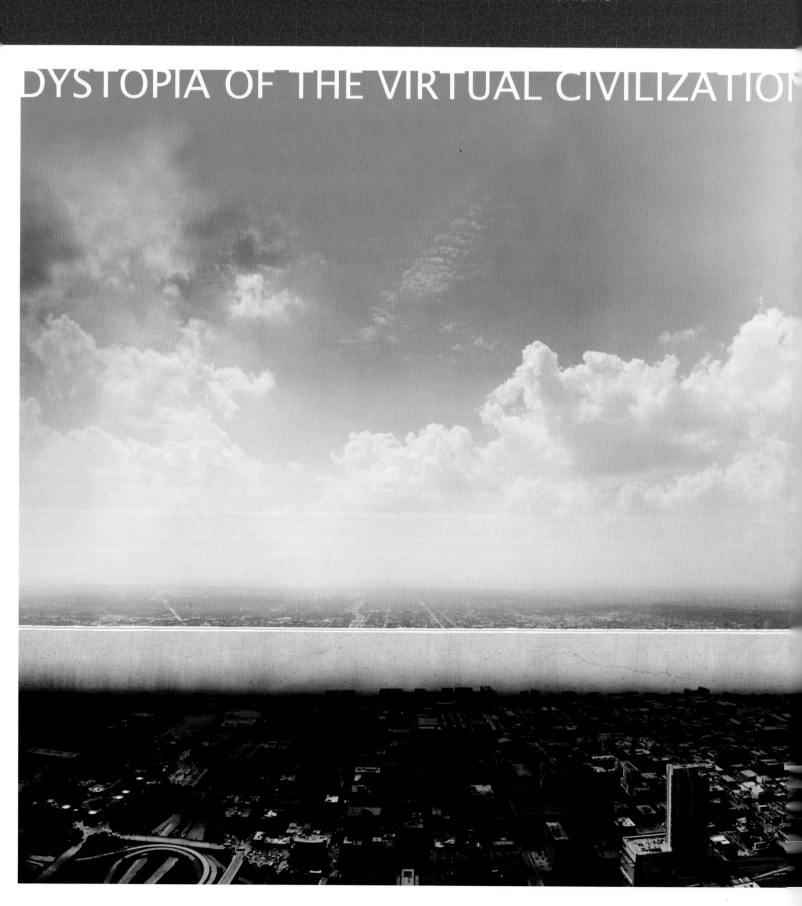

DYSTOPIA OF THE VIRTUAL CIVILIZATION

A rapid technological progression and total modernization of the 20th century erased the previously existing borders between countries and continents. A whole new world, created by the modern human, has become a global infrastructure network. After overcoming the physical limitations, a human of the late industrial era made the first step to go beyond the limits of the classical time-space model to the new type of reality—the virtual reality.

   After denying out biological mother we have created a new one, the machine. Soon machines will become not just tools for the intensification of our physical labor. They will gradually begin to master our minds. All dreams about beauty, success, strength, and courage will become a new reality.

   Columbarium Skyscraper is the final tangible embodiment of the architectural typology. It has emerged when the

1057-01

last physical barrier to the permanent immersion of the human in the virtual reality was his body. The main task of architects of the virtual era is the creation of the network of mega-structures that save humans bodies, whose minds exist in the virtual reality.

The skyscraper spans across the present city as a long enclosed capsule of 300 meters in height, spanning the length required to eventually store the city's population, serving as a preparation vault space for sending humans off to a virtual reality. The skyscraper is not vertically erect, but encloses several box-shaped containers with gel capsules where human bodies remain, kept alive on life support during their time in the virtual reality. The conflict between the natural and anthropogenic has been resolved forever; everyone can now become the creator of another reality.

In ancient times our world was like a wonder. A nature - the womb from which the first humans had come - was a primary source for the search of meanings. The identity with the outside world compelled the ancient humans to a harmonic living with the nature.

But soon the human person began to understand its fundamental difference from the animal world. The ability to the consciously thinking and socialization process determined all further development of the mankind. Family fireplace has become a symbol of the unity with the nature, concured by the man of the industrial era.

After denying our biological mother we have created a new one - the machine. Soon machines have become not just tools for the intensification of our physical labor. They gradually began to master our minds. All dreams about beauty, success, strength, courage, became a new reality – the artificial reality.

We have made the final choice in favor of Mind, recognizing the negligibility of our bodies. People began to leave the real world more and more often. Local connections to the global virtual network acquired a global character.

The last physical barrier to the permanent immersion of the human in the virtual reality was his body. The man finally refused the real world and chosen the another type of reality. The conflict between the Natural and Anthropogenic has been resolved forever. Everyone now become the Creator of his own virtual world .

TOKYO population 13.050.000
height 300 m;
lenght 38 km

SEOUL population 10.464.000
height 300 m;
lenght 32 km

MEXICO population 8.851,000
height 300 m;
lenght 27 km

CHICAGO population 2.862.000
height 300 m;
length 8 km

For the mantaining of the most omportant vital functions, the human body is immersed in a gel capsule

Gel capsule is placed in the container-box

Hermetically sealed box is connected to the distribution blockof life support

FUNCTIONAL DIAGRAM

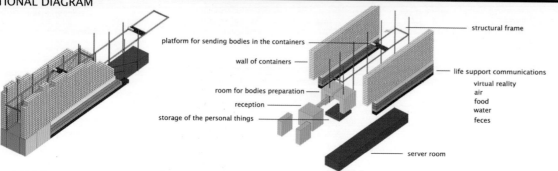
structural frame
platform for sending bodies in the containers
wall of containers
life support communications
room for bodies preparation
virtual reality
air
reception
food
water
storage of the personal things
feces

server room

Four container-boxes are grouped into a single module

The post-virtual world is full of absence. At one point humans left the material reality, forever leaving nature. A few centuries later, dense forests and prairies will cover the planet; it has been stuffed by flocks of wild animals and birds. Oceans, seas, and rivers become clean and habitable again. There are no more any roar of cars, stench of exhaust gases and flickering of the neon advertising. The new world has become a giant cemetery of the voluntarily abandoned humans' bodies, whose souls and minds are wandered somewhere in the virtual spaces.

1057-02

when we have made the final choice in favor of Mind, recognizing the negligibility of our bodies. All the countless wealth of the industrial and post-industrial civilizations – luxury homes and hotels, sterile office towers, nightclubs, endless ... even ... cities – became unnecessary extravagances for the human of the virtual civilization. People began to leave the real world more and more often. Local connections to the global virtual network acquired a global character. In the ... – a giant cyber network – all of the most pressing problems (ecological, social, political, economic, ethic) were completed. A new era of the total rebirth of the nature, thrown by humans, has come. The long-awaited eco-utopia has become a ...um-skyscraper – is the final tangible embodiment of the architectural typology. It has emerged when the last physical barrier to the permanent immersion of the human in the virtual reality was his body. The main task of architects of the ...reation of the network of mega-structures that saving humans bodies, whose minds are existed in the virtual reality. The conflict between the Natural and Anthropogenic has been resolved forever. Everyone now become the Creator of the ...st-virtual world is full of absence. At one time humans left the material reality, forever leaving the nature. A few centuries later, the planet was covered by a dense forests and prairies; it has been stuffed by the flocks of wild animals and ...s and rivers became clean and habitable again. There are no more any roar of cars, stench of exhaust gases and flickering of the neon advertising. The new world has become a giant cemetery of the voluntarily abandoned humans' bodies, ...minds are wandered somewhere in the virtual spaces.

MIST TREE

Kwon Han
Hojeong Lim
Hyeyeon Kwon
Yeonkyu Park

United States

Mist Tree in Atacama Desert

ANDES MOUNTAIN RANGE

PACIFIC

ATACAMA RELATIVE HUMIDITY

75%–95%   5%–10%

Desertification is the process of land degradation which is caused by various reasons, including climatic variation and human activities. Affecting millions of people, desertification has emerged as an environmental crisis of global proportions which currently threatens the lives and livelihoods of people around the whole world.

Located in the Republic of Chile, Atacama Desert is one of the oldest and driest places on Earth. This desert is fenced by the Andes Mountains on one side and the Chilean Coast Range on the other. The moisture which comes from the Pacific Ocean cannot get through either side and creates a "rain shadow effect". The "rain shadow effect" is an area of relatively little precipitation due to the effect of a barrier such as a mountain range. This causes prevailing winds to lose their moisture before reaching the area. Due to this geographic situation, Atacama Desert is constantly dried even though it is located near the Pacific Ocean. People living in Atacama are at risk and degradation is spreading rapidly.

Despite degradation being a serious issue, there is hope which can potentially end the desertification of the Atacama region. That hope is found in a dense fog known as "Camanchaca." Coming from the Pacific Ocean, this fog has the potential to nourish plants and other living things in the desert. If there were a way to collect the fog and carry the moisture over the high range of the mountains, the water would bring hope to life in Atacama.

"Mist-Tree" is a skyscraper which can bring the hope of new life to Atacama, Chile. It proposes a simple solution to end the drought coming from the high ranges of the mountains. The skyscraper penetrates through the Andes mountain range and captures fog from the sky of the Pacific Ocean. The building façade is a "net structure" which attracts condensation to form on the building itself. It promotes this condensation by gaining heat on the interior, harvesting sunlight though its large glass structure. As the moisture from the fog is captured, the gathered water is brought down to the Atacama area to nourish life. Inside of "Mist-Tree" is no different; the water collected also gives life to a variety of plants throughout interior green spaces. This building becomes a node in the mountains, a starting point for anti-desertification reaching out to make further green lands. "Mist-Tree" skyscraper would provide numerous benefits for promoting a high quality of life in and around Atacama.

Located in the Republic of Chile, the Atacama Desert is one of the oldest and driest places on Earth. This desert is fenced by the Andes Mountains on one side and the Chilean Coast Range on the other. The moisture which comes from the Pacific Ocean cannot get through either side and creates a "rain shadow effect." Due to this geographic situation, Atacama Desert is constantly dry even though it is located near the Pacific Ocean. People living in Atacama are at risk and degradation is spreading rapidly.

However, a dense fog known as "Camanchaca" could potentially end desertification in the Atacama Desert. Sourced from the Pacific Ocean, this fog has the potential to nourish plants and other living organisms.

Mist Tree is a skyscraper that can bring new life to this area of Chile. It proposes a simple solution to end the

1086

drought coming from the high ranges of the mountains. The skyscraper penetrates through the Andes mountain range and captures fog from the sky of the Pacific Ocean.

The building façade is a "net structure" which attracts condensation to form on the building itself. It promotes this condensation by gaining heat on the interior and harvesting sunlight though its large glass structure. As the moisture from the fog is captured, the gathered water is brought down to the Atacama area to nourish life. Inside of Mist Tree is no different; the water collected also gives life to a variety of plants throughout interior green spaces.

In the side of the body of Mist Tree's structure, water not only runs down but there are spaces for plant life to inhabit. The Mist Tree has three different types of plants. Inside the upper part of the building there are sun plants,

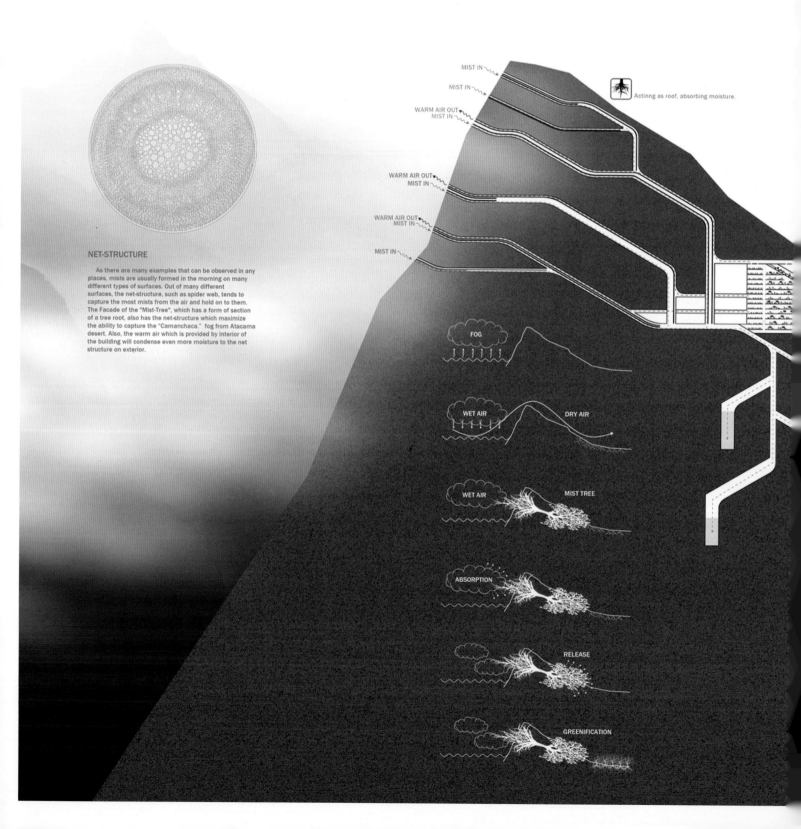

NET-STRUCTURE

As there are many examples that can be observed in any places, mists are usually formed in the morning on many different types of surfaces. Out of many different surfaces, the net-structure, such as spider web, tends to capture the most mists from the air and hold on to them. The Facade of the "Mist-Tree", which has a form of section of a tree root, also has the net-structure which maximize the ability to capture the "Camanchaca." fog from Atacama desert. Also, the warm air which is provided by interior of the building will condense even more moisture to the net structure on exterior.

MIST IN
MIST IN
WARM AIR OUT
MIST IN
WARM AIR OUT
MIST IN
WARM AIR OUT
MIST IN
MIST IN

Actinng as roof, absorbing moisture.

FOG

WET AIR   DRY AIR

WET AIR   MIST TREE

ABSORPTION

RELEASE

GREENIFICATION

which require full or at least partial sun to grow and thrive. In the middle part, half-shade plants grow since they require less sunlight and a cooler condition. Finally at the bottom there are shade plants that require shaded conditions for growth.

This building becomes a node in the mountains, a starting point for anti-desertification reaching out to make further green lands. Mist Tree skyscraper would provide numerous benefits for promoting a high quality of life in and around the Atacama.

1086

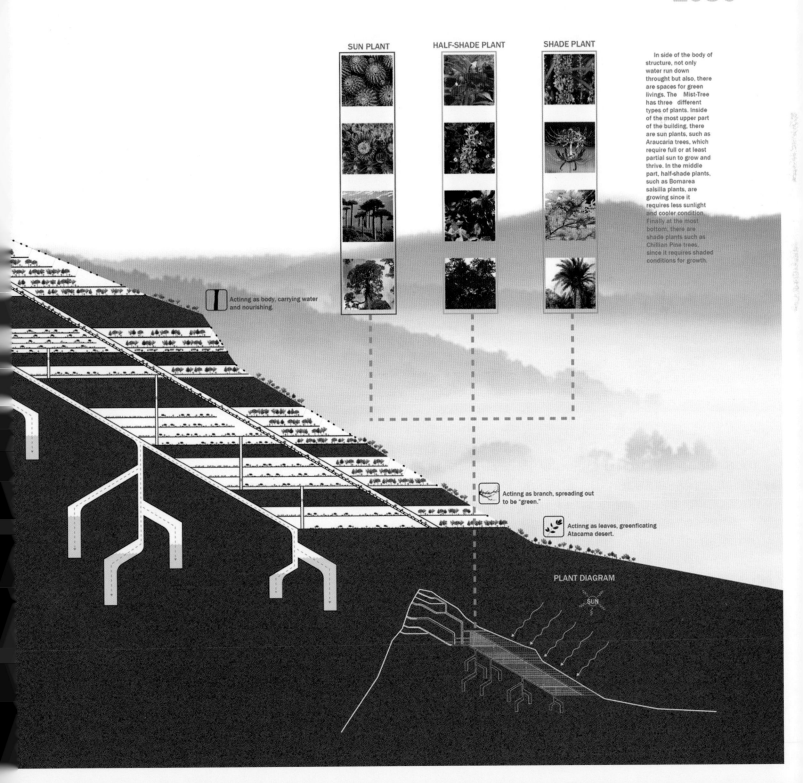

SUN PLANT   HALF-SHADE PLANT   SHADE PLANT

In side of the body of structure, not only water run down throught but also, there are spaces for green livings. The Mist-Tree has three different types of plants. Inside of the most upper part of the building, there are sun plants, such as Araucaria trees, which require full or at least partial sun to grow and thrive. In the middle part, half-shade plants, such as Bomarea salsilla plants, are growing since it requires less sunlight and cooler condition. Finally at the most bottom, there are shade plants such as Chillian Pine trees, since it requires shaded conditions for growth.

Actinng as body, carrying water and nourishing.

Acting as branch, spreading out to be "green."

Actinng as leaves, greenficating Atacama desert.

PLANT DIAGRAM

SUN

4 SOCIAL SOLUTIONS

Can architecture respond to and solve social problems? If we live in a society characterized by social imbalance, how can architecture alleviate this situation? These are the questions investigated by the projects presented in this chapter. Proposals include super-tall structures that respond to social, economic, and cultural problems through the use of technological advances and new materials.

A few of the proposals include, a trashscraper in the middle of New York City that serves as a reminder of the amount of waste produced every day – the structure is equipped with recycling and energy production plants. Other submissions acknowledge the pros and cons of informal housing, like the Favelas in Brazil or the Hutongs in China, while investigating a multi-layered system that provides the necessary infrastructure (water, energy, circulation) to the settlements while allowing for a controlled vertical expansion that works in conjunction with the existing structures.

Another group proposes expandable, inflatable skyscrapers to be used during emergencies such as earthquakes, flooding, or fire, through the research of new materials that allow for the desired flexibility and ease of transportation without compromising the structural integrity.

Finally, other ideas serve as a social statement. Included in this category there are projects that attach to existing skyscrapers to provide temporal refuge for homeless people or a new set of buildings designed to inject more social programs into the city.

CAN ARCHITECTURE RESPOND TO AND SOLVE SOCIAL PROBLEMS? IF WE LIVE IN A SOCIETY CHARACTERIZED BY SOCIAL IMBALANCE, HOW CAN ARCHITECTURE ALLEVIATE THIS SITUATION? THESE ARE THE QUESTIONS INVESTIGATED BY THE PROJECTS PRESENTED IN THIS CHAPTER. PROPOSALS INCLUDE SUPER-TALL STRUCTURES THAT RESPOND TO SOCIAL, ECONOMIC, AND CULTURAL PROBLEMS.

OCCUPY
SKYSCRAPER

Ying Xiao
Shengchen Yang

China

Moved by the economic disparity in the United States brought to light by the 2011 Occupy Wall Street movement, the Occupy Skyscraper is a proposal to create a building that can further empower protesters and accelerate the Occupy movement. The temporary Occupy skyscraper can be erected on any protest site to provide shelter and meeting spaces for dissenters. By providing a means for protesters to take their movement from a horizontal plane to a 3D vertical reality, the Occupy skyscraper strengthens and bolsters the event as a whole, but amazingly, it does so only using hemp rope and canvas.

The skyscraper's construction begins as soon as a protest takes place: Ropes are woven into a vertical web by attaching to and climbing nearby buildings. The webs are woven thicker and thicker until they form nets that can

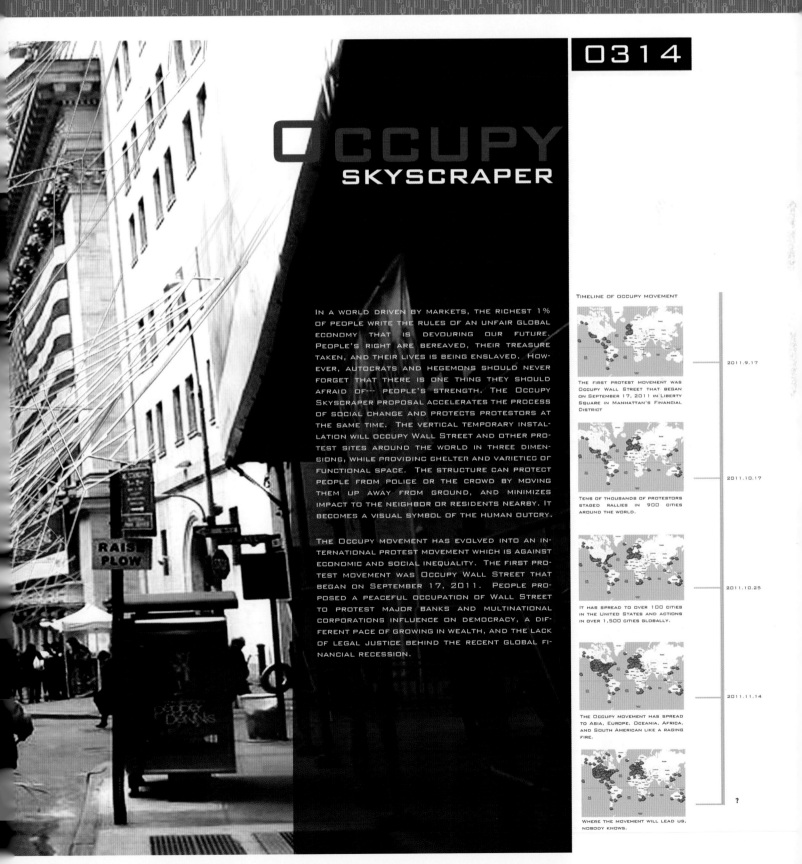

0314

OCCUPY
SKYSCRAPER

IN A WORLD DRIVEN BY MARKETS, THE RICHEST 1% OF PEOPLE WRITE THE RULES OF AN UNFAIR GLOBAL ECONOMY THAT IS DEVOURING OUR FUTURE. PEOPLE'S RIGHT ARE BEREAVED, THEIR TREASURE TAKEN, AND THEIR LIVES IS BEING ENSLAVED. HOWEVER, AUTOCRATS AND HEGEMONS SHOULD NEVER FORGET THAT THERE IS ONE THING THEY SHOULD AFRAID OF--- PEOPLE'S STRENGTH. THE OCCUPY SKYSCRAPER PROPOSAL ACCELERATES THE PROCESS OF SOCIAL CHANGE AND PROTECTS PROTESTORS AT THE SAME TIME. THE VERTICAL TEMPORARY INSTALLATION WILL OCCUPY WALL STREET AND OTHER PROTEST SITES AROUND THE WORLD IN THREE DIMENSIONS, WHILE PROVIDING SHELTER AND VARIETIES OF FUNCTIONAL SPACE. THE STRUCTURE CAN PROTECT PEOPLE FROM POLICE OR THE CROWD BY MOVING THEM UP AWAY FROM GROUND, AND MINIMIZES IMPACT TO THE NEIGHBOR OR RESIDENTS NEARBY. IT BECOMES A VISUAL SYMBOL OF THE HUMAN OUTCRY.

THE OCCUPY MOVEMENT HAS EVOLVED INTO AN INTERNATIONAL PROTEST MOVEMENT WHICH IS AGAINST ECONOMIC AND SOCIAL INEQUALITY. THE FIRST PROTEST MOVEMENT WAS OCCUPY WALL STREET THAT BEGAN ON SEPTEMBER 17, 2011. PEOPLE PROPOSED A PEACEFUL OCCUPATION OF WALL STREET TO PROTEST MAJOR BANKS AND MULTINATIONAL CORPORATIONS INFLUENCE ON DEMOCRACY, A DIFFERENT PACE OF GROWING IN WEALTH, AND THE LACK OF LEGAL JUSTICE BEHIND THE RECENT GLOBAL FINANCIAL RECESSION.

TIMELINE OF OCCUPY MOVEMENT

2011.9.17

THE FIRST PROTEST MOVEMENT WAS OCCUPY WALL STREET THAT BEGAN ON SEPTEMBER 17, 2011 IN LIBERTY SQUARE IN MANHATTAN'S FINANCIAL DISTRICT

2011.10.17

TENS OF THOUSANDS OF PROTESTORS STAGED RALLIES IN 900 CITIES AROUND THE WORLD.

2011.10.25

IT HAS SPREAD TO OVER 100 CITIES IN THE UNITED STATES AND ACTIONS IN OVER 1,500 CITIES GLOBALLY.

2011.11.14

THE OCCUPY MOVEMENT HAS SPREAD TO ASIA, EUROPE, OCEANIA, AFRICA, AND SOUTH AMERICAN LIKE A RAGING FIRE.

?

WHERE THE MOVEMENT WILL LEAD US, NOBODY KNOWS.

RAISE PLOW

support weight. At this stage, the "building" can be used for climbing, hanging flags and supporting sleeping bags in the vertical spaces, and can be used for gatherings on the horizontal plane. Canvas is then attached to create solid paneling to segregate space uses within the building itself. The designers envision several designated areas within the structure: orientation spaces, and other spots for recreation, sleeping, workshops, conferences, rallies, and large meetings.

    The web and panel systems provide the opportunity for different types of spaces to be created for different uses such as resting areas, large meeting spaces for protestors to gather, rally spaces where subgroups can start protests, conference spaces for leaders to discuss strategies and plans, and workshop spaces for people to make their various

VERTICAL OCCUPY

THE PROPOSAL IS OCCUPYING SPACE ARCHITEC-
TURALLY AND CONSTRUCTS A TOWER FOR DE-
MOCRACY. IT CHANGE ORIGINAL HORIZONTAL
PROTEST TO VERTICAL PROTEST AND FINALLY
3-D OCCUPATION.

HORIZONTAL PROTEST

VERTICAL PROTEST

CONSTRUCTION:

PEOPLE START TO CONSTRUCT WEB
SYSTEM WHEN THE EVENT HAPPENS.
BY USING THE EXISTING BUILDING ON
BOTH SIDES AS STRUCTURE, ROPES
CAN BE USED TO CREATE NETS
BETWEEN THE BUILDINGS.

2011.9.17

CONSTRUCT WEB AND PANEL SYSTEM.
USING CANVAS OR OTHER FABRIC TO
TIE WITH ROPES. DIFFERENT FUNCTION
OF SPACE IS CREATED.

2011.10.17

AS PROTESTING BECOMES INCREAS-
INGLY FIERCE, MORE AND MORE
PEOPLE WILL JOIN THE EVENT. PEOPLE
WILL BUILD THIS SKYSCRAPER HIGHER
AND HIGHER FOR THE GROWING NEED
AND SYMBOLIZE OF PEOPLE'S POWER.

2011.10.25

VERTICAL WEB SYSTEM IS USED FOR
CLIMBING HIGHER, HANGING FLAGS
AND SLEEPING BAGS. HORIZONTAL
WEB SYSTEMS BOUNDING WITH PANEL
SYSTEMS CREATE A LARGER SPACE FOR
A LOT OF DIFFERENT FUNCTION SUCH
AS MEETING AND GATHERING.

2011.11.6

THE HEIGHT OF OCCUPY SKYSCRAPER
REACHES ITS PEAK WHEN THE STRUC-
TURE REACHES THE HEIGHT OF THE
EXISTING BUILDINGS.

2011.12.3

THE OCCUPY SKYSCRAPER MAY GET
SMALLER WHEN THE EVENT COMES TO
THE END, ONLY PARTS OF THEM
REMAIN FOR MEMORY AND MEMORI-
ALS.

?

MATERIAL:

HEMP ROPE
CANVAS
TENT
CARABINER

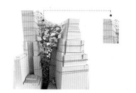

SYSTEM:

TWO GROWING SYSTEMS:
WEB SYSTEM
PANEL SYSTEM

●VERTICAL WEB SYSTEM

VERTICAL WEB SYSTEM IS USED
FOR CLIMBING HIGHER, HANGING
FLAGS AND SLEEPING BAGS.

●HORIZONTAL WEB SYSTEM

HORIZONTAL WEB SYSTEMS CREATE
A LARGER SPACE MEETING AND GATH-
ERING.

ORIENTATION SPACE ❶

ORIENTATION SPACE IS ALSO A STAGE. IT IS
WHERE PROTEST ORGANIZER CAN GIVE SPEECHES
OR ORIENTATIONS. IT SET VERY CLOSE TO THE
GROUND SO THAT THEY CAN ALSO GUIDE THE
PROTEST ON THE GROUND LEVEL.

WORKSHOP SPACE ❷

WORK SHOP IS THE SPACE FOR PEOPLE TO MAKE
PLACARDS AND FLAGS. IT IS SET NEAR TO
GROUND SO PEOPLE DON'T HAVE TO CARRY EQUIP-
MENT WHILE CLIMBING THE INSTALLATION.

LARGE MEETING SPACE ❸

MEETING SPACE IS A LARGE SPACE PROVIDED
FOR PROTESTORS TO GATHER. THEY CAN
SHOUT OUT THEIR SLOGAN OR SIT-DOWN WITH-
OUT WORRY ABOUT POLICE AND CRUSHING
CROWDS. THE PROTEST IS FUELED BY DISCUS-
SIONS ELEVATED ABOVE WALL STREET.

RALLY SPACE ❹

RALLY SPACES ARE MEETING SPACES, THE
POINTS WHERE SUBGROUPS CAN GATHER IN
ORDER TO START PROTESTS WITHIN THE OVER-
ALL EVENT. RALLY SPACES ARE FLEXIBLE IN
TERMS OF SUBGROUP SIZE AND PURPOSE.

RECREATION SPACE ❺

RECREATION SPACE IS WHERE PEOPLE DO SOME
CASUAL EVENTS TO RELAX THEMSELVES. BE-
SIDES PROTEST, PEOPLE ALSO CAN FIND A
PLACE TO GET SOME RELAX, LIKE WATCHING TV,
PLAY CARDS AND HAVING SOME FUN.

SLEEP/RES

SLEEPING AREA IS
CAN REST. SEVER
REST AREA ARE LO
ING AREAS IN ORD
VENIENCE FOR PRO

LARGE MEE

CONFRENC

CONFERENCE ROOM
OTHER SPACES IN C
AND BE SAFE. THE
ERS OF PROTEST TO
MAKE PLANS FOR PE

placards and flags for protesting.

As the movement gains in strength and more people join, the masses will continue to build out the skyscraper, adding space as needed. The height of the skyscraper reaches its peak, however, when the heights of the surrounding buildings that are supporting the ropes are met. As the protest dies down the building is deconstructed, and after it is over, its remains can be removed completely, restoring the urban fabric to what it was before the event.

0314

OCCUPY
SKYSCRAPER

STRUCTURE OF HUMAN RIGHTS

Luo Jing
Kang Jun
Ren Tianhang

China

A STRUCTURE OF HUMAN RIGHTS IN BEIJING

Illegal acquisition of land by local Chinese government entities has caused thousands of residents incredible grief and even death recently, plus social instability. Though private property does not really exist in China (and buying a property only ensures its use for 70 years), the designers of this structure feel that land use needs to be re-examined in China, as a private home is a basic human right.

Their proposal to bring every person a place to live takes into account the country's exploding population and need for dense development, and thus is oriented vertically.

Unlike European residences, the famous traditional Chinese housing type, *Siheyuan*, the quadrangle courtyard formed in the Ming and Qing Dynasty is usually rectangular and closed for more privacy and is popular in Beijing. One

0392

family shares a ***siheyuan*** and all of them are organized to have the same size and they together form the grid lines in the city plan of Beijing. These elements of Chinese residence and housing planning definitely show the emphasis of land distribution and the pursuit of equal rights in ancient China. Influenced by the traditional way of housing planning, the designers which that the distribution of land in this modern city can guarantee every citizen's rights and freedom to own land.

Inspired by the Chinese character for farmland, ***Hanzi***, the traditional ***siheyuan*** residence, and ancient Chinese urban planning, the Structure of Human Rights is designed as a giant reinforced concrete structure that serves more as infrastructure than a building. It is "land" for housing, instead of the housing itself —a 3D checkerboard that houses

A STRUCTURE OF HUMAN RIGHTS IN BEIJING

China`s List of Violent&Forced Demolition and Eviction Cases Grows Longer

A man **set himself on fire in protest** in Northeast China and another man in North China was **beaten to death after he refused to move out** on November 02, 2010, making China's list of violent and forced demolition cases grows even longer.

Cui Dexi, a 56-year-old man from Mishan city of Heilongjiang province, set himself alight in the morning during a conflict with about 100 local officials, policemen and housing developers who wanted to demolish Cui's house for a real estate project.
Cui's son-in-law, Hou Jinlong, said more than 100 people, most not in uniform, burst into their house on Saturday morning as ambulances and fire engines waited outside."It was about 7 am, we found the house was filled with people. They even set a police cordon around the nine houses not demolished yet in the neighborhood," Hou told China Daily on Monday over the phone. "They came to demolish the house."However, the local city government said the people went to negotiate with the Cui family, not to demolish the house. The government said nine households have refused to move out because they are not satisfied with the compensation deal, which for Cui's family is 600,000 yuan ($89,800).

A similar case happened the same day in Shanxi province, where a man was beaten to death and another seriously injured by about 10 attackers who demolished their homes, according to local police.At about 2 am on Saturday, Meng Fugui and Wu Wenyuan, neighbors of Guzhai village of the provincial capital, Taiyuan, were sleeping in Wu's house when more than 10 people broke in.The group beat them, left them in the street, and later demolished their homes. Meng died in the attack, and Wu was later sent to hospital.The local government announced on Sunday that it was a case of violent demolition.

Actually,the number of similar cases are shockingly increasing in recent years.

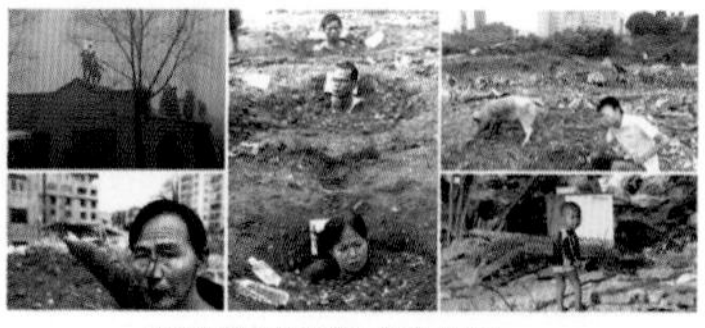

1|3|4 / 2|5
1.Cui Dexi set himself on fire in protest.
2.A chinese man got hurt when he refused to move out.
3.Several Chinese residents buried themselves in protest.
4.A young man was crying because the housing developers tore down his house when he wasn`t at home.
5.A child standing in front of his distroyed house,didn`t know what to do.

Forced Demolition Standoff in Guangzhou

In Guangzhou's Yuexiu district lie the remains of what Chinese people colloquially call "villages within a city" – clusters of decrepit old housing bordered by colorful office buildings and towering housing complexes. While the land under these towns is wholly government-owned, residents must sign contracts to give their homes over for demolition and receive compensation.On September 6, a standoff with police ensued at the top of a building in the urban "village" of Yangji, when a husband and wife refused to comply with a court ruling forcing them to relocate. **The husband stood at the top of his home, threatening to immolate himself with gasoline, as demolition crews waited nearby to receive the go-ahead to tear down his home.**
Yao Run-Zhen and his wife were not the last remaining residents here. There are still a handful remaining and they will fight just as Yao did before they leave. Basically many of the other remaining residents were trying to film the process to make sure if anything went down, they'd have it on film. Those that were spotted by the police were confronted, their cams taken and they were carried off out of sight.the locals (the OTHERS that have not yet given up the fight and moved out)could not contact Yao and are worried about his and his wife's safety, as the last thing they heard they had been taken into police custody.

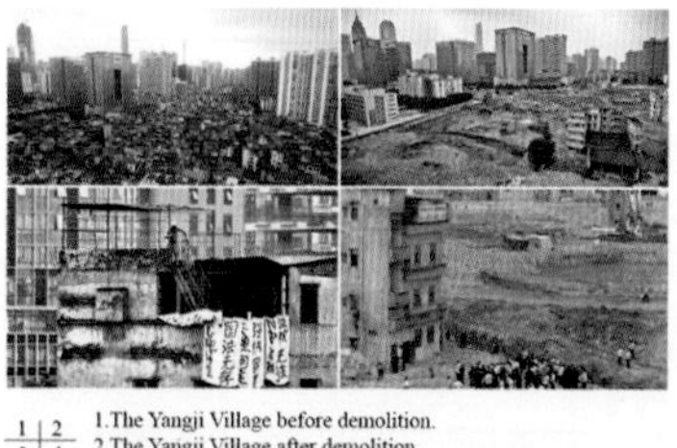

1|2 / 3|4
1.The Yangji Village before demolition.
2.The Yangji Village after demolition.
3.The husband stood at the top of his home, threatening to immolate himself with gasoline.The banner said "**the laws have been dead,and even the court doesn`t respect them** ",etc.
4.Officers,policemen were negotiating with the couple.The banner said"**the officers of this villige do not have any conscience, forcing us to sign the contract to destroy our houses.The house can only be tore down over my dead body!**"

The Bloody Map

An anonymous Chinese blogger devoted to charting incidents of violent eviction throughout China on a "Bloody Map" (xuefang ditu, 血房地图.) His motive is to inform the public and encourage new home buyers to boycott any property stained by violent acquisition. From his Sina account:
The goal of Bloody Map is to collect and list cases of violent eviction which have, or will, already faded from public view; some cases going back 2-3 years I had to dig up myself, but with your support, it'll be much easier. When I say that new housing is being built right now on land covered in blood, people know what I mean.

There are forceful evictions taking place now which need more media attention, Bloody Map on its own isn't an appropriate platform to that end. People can't expect that an effort like this will create enough attention to put an end to current forced evictions. The goal of this site is to present evidence allowing consumers to make decisions. **If a day comes when this tiny map is able to make people within the interest chain of a particular eviction reconsider their actions, then it will have achieved its goal.**

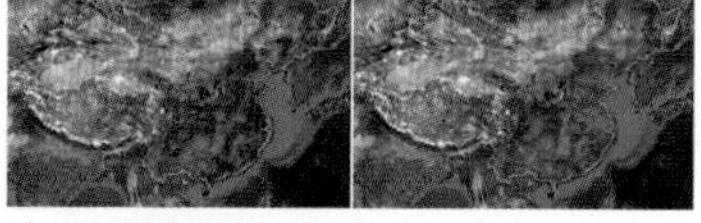

1|2 1.the Bloody Map
- **Where the forced demolitions happen**
- **Self-immolation by fire**
- **Incident involving a death**

2.The Map of China`s fast developing areas
In the fast developing areas of China,the force demolitions are more likely to happen because the cities' populations are increasing and there are more needs for lands for new high densed buildings rather than the old-fashioned houses with low capacities.

The Ugly Truth of Bloody Demolitions in China

In recent years, forced demolitions carried out by local governments have been a root cause of social instability and led to various violent social conflicts. To stop this situation, earlier in 2011, the Chinese regime introduced new laws and regulations regarding forced demolition.The Bureau of Land and Resources released an emergency notice; **the Ministry of Public Security claimed a 'zero tolerance' on forced demolition, but cases of forced demolition continue to happen.In the first quarter of 2011 alone, there were almost 10,000 cases of illegal land acquisition, a 2.3 percent increase compared to the first quarter of 2010**. Regarding this, the Bureau of Land and Resources released an emergency notice requiring that local governments employ strict management to prevent forced demolition, but this still has had no effect.

What caused these local officials and law enforcement officers to neglect the public interest and resort to violent methods to demolish people's homes? What is the real reason?
Cheng Xiaonong, (an economist and Chinese affairs expert)gives an analysis.

Truth 1 privately owned land does NOT exist in China

Cheng: Before 1978, for thousands of years, land in China was privately owned. No matter whether it was during the era of emperors, during the Nationalist Government era after feudalism ended in the early 20th century, or during Communist rule before 1978, it has always been so.

In rural areas, the land was collectively owned by the villagers, but collective ownership is still private, not public—not owned by the government. In cities, except for streets and government buildings, all residential buildings were the property of the house owners, which means they were private possessions. However, all this suddenly changed in 1978.
In 1978, some farmers in rural areas started what was called the Contract Responsibility System (household responsibility system). The idea was that farmers were to be given quotas of land by the government.
The general public did not know about this. Also, the government did not compensate anyone after making this change. For many house owners, such as those in the countryside whose families had held the house for generations, suddenly they only owned the building, the land underneath was no longer theirs anymore.
Since that time, all land in China has been state owned. However, that so--called "state-owned" does not allude to the central government, but specifically to the local governments. This means all land within the jurisdiction of the local government is owned by the local government, which also means that the local governments can freely allocate land.**Even if you buy a house in mainland China today, the land underneath is NOT yours.**

This is a phenomenon unique to China, that for the first time in the world, buying the house doesn't come with the land underneath.
During the 1990s, the conflicts were not so large because the local governments did not forcibly demolish homes on a large scale. Forced demolitions actually started in the late 1990s and have continued until now. Now, the problem is getting even worse.

Truth 2 Buying a house in China only means having the right of usage of the land for 70 years.
Chinese regulations state that when a resident buys a house, he has the right to use the land, but not ownership rights, and **there is a due date associated with the usage rights.This time limit is 70 years,** according to the regulations **but the government doesn't really respect this time limit.** Last year, an official from the Ministry of Construction said to the public media that all houses in China constructed before 1995 are of bad quality and all of them should be torn down.
This means, if this statement was implemented, then for those who bought the house before 1995, while still within 70 years, the government might still demolish the house. **In other words, this 70 year usage limit is an empty promise.** If the government doesn't respect it, then the 70 years disappears into thin air.
Suppose someone built a house before 1995, but the government wants to reacquire this land for other purposes, then the government has the right to demolish the house. This means the money that this person spent to buy the 70 years of usage rights is out the window.

Let's say **the government builds a new residential building on the same land and this person wants to continue living there, then he has to buy the land for the second time; paying for the land use for a second time.** We know that the value of the building is limited, usually only less than 40 percent of the purchase price, the rest is mainly for the land. **So, if the government wants to, it can reacquire the land many times to take money from the building owner.**

Truth 3 Not only the real estate agents ,But local governments are behind the demolitions.local governments depend on forced demolition of houses to acquire land and sell land to make profits.

From the cases reported of violently demolishing houses, we see the violence of the demolitions is not only done by the real estate agents, but local governments and law enforcement officers are involved in many cases.
Media in China reported that though some of the forced demolitions are done by the real estate agents, if there hasn't been the local government behind the demolitions, they could not have happened.

For example, in the case of the self-immolation related to a forced demolition that happened in Jiangxi Province on Sept. 10, 2010, the law enforcement officers had threatened the owner, "If you don't tear down the house, you might not know how you die tomorrow."
From these cases, we can see the government and law enforcement officers manipulate things behind the scenes. It is practiced mainly by the collusion of local governments and real estate companies. Of course, sometimes, local governments will directly do it under the name of establishing a development zone or constructing public facilities, and then choose some lands they want to develop.
They first send the people employed by real estate companies to demolish houses. If that doesn't work, they send the police to force the demolition of the houses, such as the Jiangxi case we just mentioned. The typical cases involve policemen.
After they demolish the residents' houses and seize the land, the local governments will give some compensation to the house owners, but they will only give a little compensation.

The reason is that **the local governments don't use the lands directly, but sell them to real estate companies**. They have to earn a large amount of money from selling the lands to the real estate companies. That is, **if the local governments can bring down the compensation as low as possible and raise the land price as high as they can, they can earn the most money.**
As a result, in the past few years—take the Beijing and Shanghai governments as examples—about 50-60 percent of their financial revenue came from selling land. We can imagine if a government disregards its own interests, and sells the land at the price it buys them, the price of the land will be much lower, and the price of houses will not be so expensive.
Precisely speaking, what the government earns is what the house owners lose. it might be a few trillion yuan per year [one trillion yuan equals approximately US$157 billion].

Cheng Xiaonong, Ph.D., trained as an economist. He is a former aide to ousted Party leader Zhao Ziyang and former editor-in-chief of the journal Modern China Studies. He currently lives in the United States.

We Just Want a House,and a Land

We are not politicians.,or economists.We are people.We just want a house,and a land.
In ancient China,people owned lands ,cultivated them and relied on them for the harvests.People and lands were tied up closely.Owning a land seems a fundamental right of human beings.Now,the lands under our feet are not even private owned anymore,which basically means that we have lost a significant human right.Now we just want it back.

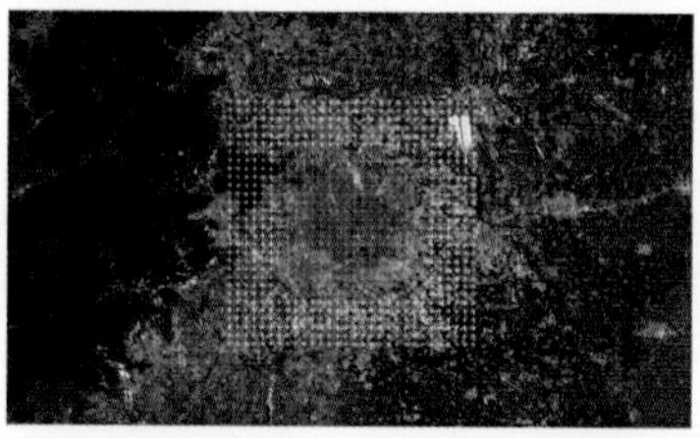

There is a simple picture which shows how much land Beijing needs if the citizens are all living in houses in American way.
The gray crossings represent the present urban area of Beijing.The white crossings represent the extra area needed if residents live an American way.

Besides the political factors,an another important reason that stops chinese people from owning their owe lands&villas is the high density of population,which makes the metropolises in China like Beijing,Shanghai and Shenzhen open their minds to the realities of vertical living. In Shanghai the statistics are hard to get your head around – 19.21 million people, very nearly the population of Australia, in one city. It gets you thinking about the future of cities. And as urbanisation rates explode around the globe, governments and urban planners increasingly see more high-rise as the answer to reducing urban sprawl and creating more sustainable cities.
Frankly,the American housing&urban planning isn`t an appropriate way for most of the cities of China,the high-rise do exist for a reason.However,should we give up our fight for freedom&rights just because of the realities and the authorities?

A Rising Structure of Human Rights and Freedom

Just like the American Dream,if there is no secured policies to protect our basic rights and freedom,then maybe we should build it practically in solid.

The inspiration of this structure is from a Chinese character "田"."田" means "farmland". As we know,written Chinese is a kind of hieroglyphs.The character "田" looks squared and divided evenly.It perfectly explains an old Chinese idiom:one person,one land,showing the idea of equal rights in ancient China.
The landscape of farmland near Minot,North Dakota,US,looks just like "田".

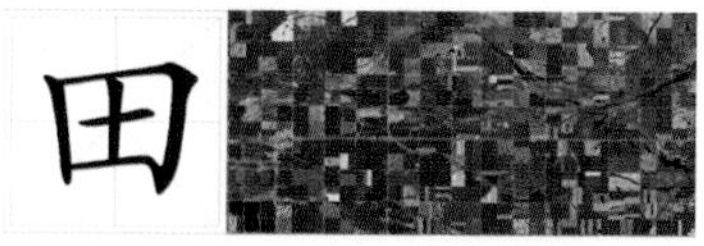

The character "田" and the form behind it definitely have a great influence on anciant China`s urban planning.We can see this idea in the city plan of Chang`an.the capital of ancient China in Tang Dynasty in 7th century,which is highly organized in many rectangular areas with different functions.And according to the historical documents,this city plan actually worked very well and became so popular as **to be the prototype of many famous asian cities` urban plans** such as Heian-kyo(平安京, now as Kyoto) and Heijo-kyo(平城京, now as Nara)in Japan.

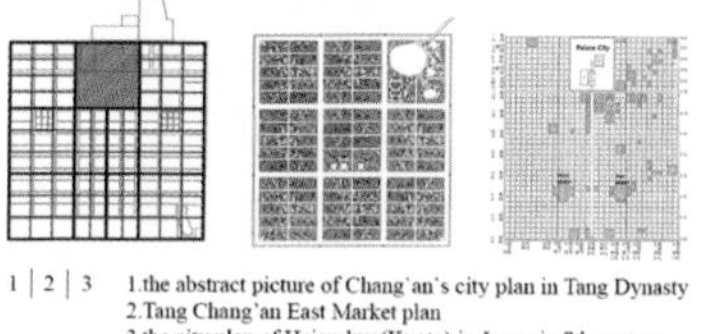

1|2|3 1.the abstract picture of Chang`an`s city plan in Tang Dynasty
2.Tang Chang'an East Market plan
3.the city plan of Heian-kyo(Kyoto) in Japan in 7th century

Unlike European residence,the famous traditional Chinese housing type "siheyuan"(quadrangle countyard)which was formed in Ming and Qing Dynasty,is usually rectangular,closed for more privacies and especially popular in Beijing.One family shares a "siheyuan".And **all the "siheyuans" are arranged in a very organized way because they almost have the same size.And they together form the grids in the city plan of Beijing.**
These elements of Chinese residence and housing planning definitely shows the emphasis of land distribution and the pursue of equal rights in ancient China.

Influenced by the traditional way of housing planning,we wish that the distribution of land in modern city can guarantee every citizen`s rights and freedom.**All men are created equal,which means everyone should have the same rights and freedom of having a land.**

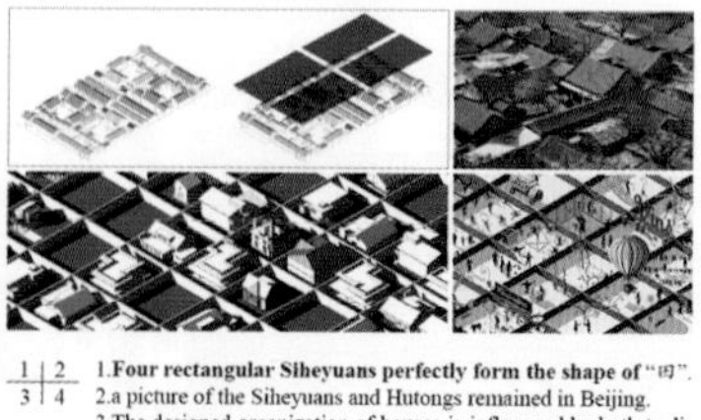

1|2 / 3|4
1.**Four rectangular Siheyuans perfectly form the shape of "田".**
2.a picture of the Siheyuans and Hutongs remained in Beijing.
3.The designed organization of houses is influenced by both traditional Chinese housing plan and the piece of artwork by western artist Adam Simpson.
4.Boundary-by Adam Simpson.**Actually boundaries are not always negative**.Sometimes we need boundaries to clearify the space and protect privacies,just like the Great Wall.

units within each cell. Living spaces within the structure measure 25 by 30 by 25 meters.

The structure is the same length as the Forbidden City, and is located directly to the east of it. Ironically, it confronts the Forbidden City, the symbol of the superpower of despotism, emphasizing the priority of human rights in a dramatic and symbolic way.

0392

a Metaphor, a Symbol and a Monument

When it comes to the whole image of the structure, we all agree that it should be giant reinforced concrete solid with extremely large size. To some extent, it is never just about the functions any more, the visual image makes our point of view even more strong and sound by looking like a symbolic monument with metaphor. Just like Hoover Dam, it did not only provide irrigation water and produce hydroelectric power, but also became the symbol of American spirit in that difficult Great Depression time.

We developed a structure that has the same length as the Forbidden City, and it is located right on the east side of Forbidden City. If we lay the structure flat, it creates a series of living spaces of 25m*30m*25m. Then we put it vertically, it becomes a huge structure that creates spaces in 3 dimensions, and ironically confronts the Forbidden City, the symbol of the superpower of despotism, emphasizing the Priority of Human Rights in a dramatic and symbolic way.

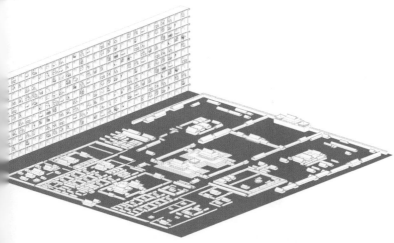

Actually, the structure itself is never a "building". It functions more like railways, highways, dams or airports, which are the basic infrastructures of a city or a country. The structure will redefine so many words such as "property" and "real estate", and make people rethink about the "land distribution" issue. Because it creates the "land" for housing, instead of creating housing. It produces more "lands" for people who are in metropolises with high density of populations, making their dreams of having their own "lands" and "villas" in big cities come true.

INTERVENTION

Jay Campbell
Ryan Duval
Alex Ilten
Moodie Yunis

United States

DEPL

intervention @ the 38th parallel

Future Political Timeline of Korea:

February 2012: In a nationally televised address, South Korean president Lee Myung-bak announces his intention to place the maritime border under a naval blockade. Citing recent incidents and North Korean failure to make amends for the 2010 sinking of the Cheonan, Lee authorizes ROK forces to fire upon any vessels attempting to illegally to cross the designated boundary. Liberal lawmakers within the National Assembly are quick to criticize Lee for warmongering and using a dangerous situation to distract from increasing domestic dissatisfaction with the ruling Grand National Party.

June 2012: Officials from the South Korean Ministry of Labor announce a temporary freeze on new participation with the Kaesong Industrial Region, which will levy a fine on any southern company which opens additional facilities in the region. Modeled on the special economic zones within China, Kaesong is a zone on the northern side of the DMZ, which allows southern companies to build factories and employ northerners. The announcement comes as a major blow, as the region was popular with South Korean businesses and a promising sign for the northern economy.

September 2012: While not released the western press, elements within the CIA and DIA receive a report prepared by the South Korean National Intelligence Service which describes the events preparing for the succession of Kim Jong-il. The report cites the growing influence Jang Song Taek, Kim's brother in law and a crucial member of the National Defense Commission. The National Intelligence Service (NIS) report speculates that Jang will be a senior overseer in the transition of power to Kim Jong-Un, the youngest of Kim's sons.

October 2013: Citing violations of the National Security Law, the South Korean government shuts down a major television broadcaster. In the joint order issued by the ministries of justice and national defense, the station is said to have revealed information about the exact location of ROK military maneuvers near the DMZ, compromising their tactical security. In an interview, the chairman of the company announces that no such security breach occurred and that the government actions were retaliation for a report alleging that President Lee had illegally steered military contracts to Hyundai Heavy Industries Group. Prior to his election as mayor of Seoul, Lee was a major executive within the construction branch of the Hyundai group.

April 2012: In a widely publicized set of maneuvers, the North Korean navy carries out several exercises in defensive surface warfare. Of particular concern is the test of Chinese manufactured Sik-worm anti-ship missiles. US naval units in the region refuse to confirm detection of numerous submarine exercises as well.

August 2012: In what appears to be a sudden crackdown, special teams from the Seoul Metropolitan Police Agency launch several simultaneous raids throughout the capital that result in the arrest of almost 20 South Koreans deemed to be in violation of the National Security Law. While several are charged with espionage for the north, the accused represent prominent leftist opposition to the Lee presidency, sparking questions of the political use of the national police force.

April 2013: Northern officials announce an invitation to southern diplomats and business-men to a joint commission on economic unification. The purpose of the commission would be to explore greater southern investment in northern infrastructure and manufacturing, as well the renewal of transportation routes between the two nations. In an attempt to show regional cooperation, the north also announces Chinese participation in the commission and invites Japan or other regional powers to participate. This move is the greatest showing of pragmatism since the death of Kim Il-Sung. The commission is to be headed

February 2015: In meetings with high level South Korean diplomats, former President and informal envoy Bill Clinton pushes for a resumption of negotiations with the north, placing an emphasis on exchanging economic cooperation for guarantees of disarmament. Despite reports of heated argument between the former American president and President Lee, the summit produces a joint statement which announces that the ROK is willing to prepare a significant economic aid package if IAEA inspectors are allowed to resume inspections of the Yongbyon facilities and the north is willing to reduce its conventional arms by 15 percent over the next five years.

May 2015: In his first major appearance in several years, an obviously ailing Kim Jong-il presides over the announcement allowing IAEA inspectors to return to a designated list of inspection sites, including the nuclear plant at Yongbyon. Secretary of State Hillary Clinton is quick to praise the act as a step on the road to the resumption of six-party talks. Congressional Republicans criticize the ongoing negotiations as validating northern attempts to blackmail the West with its nuclear program.

June 2015: In their first report, IAEA inspectors at Yongbyon announce that samples and records from the last 10 years suggest that Pyongyang has enriched enough uranium for several tactical weapons. However, the investigation also claims that serious economic and logistical woes have challenged the program, speculating that most of the weapons grade material was produced prior to 2010. An additional side note on the continued development of northern missile tests is expanding the list of sites authorized for inspection.

March 2016: Citing the rapid progress being made in disarmament negotiations, President Lee receives approval from the national legislature to postpone the scheduled presidential election until the end of the year, in order to preserve "continuity of diplomatic perspective."

October 2016: Conferring in Moscow, the US agrees to renew shipments of fuel oil halted in the early 2000s as a guarantee of the pilots' release. The pilots are escorted onto the southern side of the DMZ on the final day of the month. While the nature of the agreement is not released to the public, Congressional Republicans are quick to accuse the Obama administration of appeasement.

January 2016: Conducting routine exercises with the South Korean navy over the Yellow Sea, a US Navy SH-60 Seahawk helicopter is hit with an anti-aircraft missile fired from the North Korean coast. The missile later was identified to be a Russian-made shoulder-fired projectile, directly impacts the helicopter, killing two of the crew and causing the pilot to ditch the aircraft in the water beyond the North Korean boundary. Also, following an official condemnation of the attack, the ROK Division sits put on high alert. President Lee announces the closing of all border crossings, including seizing any southerners from entering the industrial zone at Kaesong. Inside reports suggest that President Obama was not consulted before the southern reaction.

December 2016: In a shocking move reminiscent of Korean politics in the Cold War period, ROK President Lee Myung-bak announces that the scheduled presidential election is to be indefinitely postponed due to national security concerns. Citing the attack on the American helicopter and ongoing inspections into the North's nuclear capabilities, Lee announces that a change in national leadership could jeopardize relations with the DPRK, allowing the north to take advantage of a weak new government.

November 2016: America elects a moderate Republican, former businessman as president and further boosts congressional Republican majorities who promise to focus on a tough foreign policy and rebuilding the American military from its time in Iraq and Afghanistan.

May 2017: Appearing to continue on the track to economic pragmatism, Moscow hosts a prominent delegation of North Korean economic officials and dignitaries, marking President Vladimir Putin's reengagement in Asian affairs. Western press sources are quick to speculate about the members of the delegations, while several of Kim Jong-il's closest advisors attend, his son and prospective heir does not.

November 2017: The IAEA offers its latest assessment of the program at Yongbyon after a year of relatively uninterrupted inspections. While the inspectors offer cautious optimism in that no new enrichment operations have been conducted for at least 2 years, there remains cause for alarm. The inspectors report that there are discrepancies between DPRK production records and the radiation levels observed in IAEA tests, suggesting that some nuclear material is unaccounted for at the known sites.

January 2018: After several intelligence reports from late leadership of North Korea officially announce people and the world that Kim dead. The 77-year-old leader but incapacitated for the past had fasted from public memory thousands of North Koreans state funeral in Pyongyang, by his relatively unknown heir.

2012 • 2013 • 2015 • 2016 • 2017 • 2018 •

MOLECULAR FLEXIBILITY
CONSTRUCT/DECONSTRUCT

The Intervention @ the 38th Parallel project envisions a shift in North Korea in the 21st century that would allow for the construction of dynamic modern architecture, and proposes a building for the demilitarized zone at Imjingang Bay and Kaesong. The land is unscathed, despite being close to development, because of its past as the demilitarized zone, and as such has abundant wildlife. Due to the uninhabited DMZ, this area has flourished with wildlife; it is here that the Intervention @ the 38th Parallel will become a catalyst for intelligent growth.

A deployable architecture system of self-replication, 3D printers and multiple manufacturing scales would enable people to create new architectural possibilities and leave behind the concrete Communist-blocs. Rail and crane infrastructure is created in a circle around the zone, and within that space skyscrapers are developed around the outer

[LE]SKYSCRAPERS

WORLD — ASIA — KOREA — IMJINGANG BAY

0492

REFUGEE ZONE

INDUSTRIAL ZONE

PORT

URBAN FABRIC

RAISED PLATFORMS

RAILWAY

MASTER PLAN

DMZ

HIGH-SPEED TRANSIT

POPULATION DENSITY

AGRICULTURE

WATER BODIES

2020 · 2021 · 2022 · 2023 · 2024 ·

Envisioning a change in the 21st century within North Korea (DPRK), the immense cultural disparities and introduction to the modern world should be an empowering transition filled with the power of each individual in the collective growth. This sudden shift in the DPRK will be empowering to architecture, by having a sudden area and population flourish in the opportunity to take advantage of rapid architecture and digital manufacturing.

On the west coast of the 38th parallel is Imjingang Bay, and shortly inland is Kaesong. This is one of few areas in the world where wild animals thrive while humans experience plight, there are few places in the world that the equilibrium of man and nature are proportionate to nature. Due to the uninhabited DMZ this area has flourished with wildlife despite its close proximity to development; it is here that the Intervention at the 38th Parallel will become a catalyst for intelligent growth.

This intelligent growth of Kaesong and Imjingang Bay will be able to spread throughout the DPRK to create a structure that spans across the DMZ. A deployable architecture system of self replication 3d printers and multiple manufacturing scales enables people to create new architectural possibility and context and leave behind the concrete communist-blocs. A CNC rail and crane infrastructure enables a broad swatch of land to be utilized while still preserving the natural DMZ. Customized files and various scales will lead to continual architectural progression and allow for a structure that can grow with the status of the settlement. Whether it is a refugee tower or a skyscraper, unplanned growth is matched by an immediate response of organization and serendipitous urban planning through the intelligent infrastructure.

The responsibilities of every mega-structure have differences in what they must do to achieve the correct solution. In order for the mega-structure to thrive it must adopt and be controlled by changing time, population, and economic times. The needs for a fallen North Korea will change over time and at a hectic pace. The mega-structure must not only allow intervention in the status-quo of now, but to facilitate an immediate change that can only be replicated in the technological world of connected people.

ring. As the outer ring fills, a new ring located tightly by the outer ring is formed, and so on as the settlement continues to grow inward. This helps preserve the natural beauty of the zone instead of sprawling development across the entire swath.

The mega structure development will have specific zones for the marina (which will have ports for shipping and receiving goods), a manufacturing and distribution zone (which will house the rail yard and the station for the high speed rail system), a refugee zone (which will house residences and all necessary amenities, such as schools and hospitals, for the structure's new residents), an international city zone (to house a university and all urban amenities needed within a city, such as residential and commercial spaces), an architecture manufacturing zone (with 3D printing

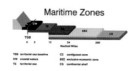

Maritime Zones

TSB territorial sea baseline   CZ contiguous zone
CW coastal waters   EEZ exclusive economic zone
TS territorial sea   CS continental shelf

DEPLOY[ABLE] CITIES

PROGRESSION OF N
ALONG THE DMZ A
2025-2060

KAESO

MEMBER HUB   CONNECTION BOLTS   ORIENTATION   FOOTING CONNECTION   MODULE CONNECTION   MULTIPLICITY   SINGULARITY

ANCHOR HUB   MEMBER   STEM CELL CONFIGURED   FOOTING ANCHOR   MODULE ANCHOR   CELL SCALING   MULTIPLICITY

STEM CELL CONSTRUCTION   CELL FAMILY

Part 5

Program & Function Outline

Part 1 Marina Zone	Part 2 Manufacturing/Distribution Zone		Part 3 Refuge/Integration Zone	Part 4 International City Zone	Part 5 Architecture Manufacturing Zone	Part 6 Extending Beyond
		Security Office(Explosion Proof) 30,000sm	Immediate Settlement 12,000,000sm	City Settlement 2,500,000sm	3D Printing 230,000sm	Generators
		Camera Rooms	Customs/Security	Apartment Housing	3D Modelling Office	Nuclear Reactor Generator
Shipping Port 1,600,000sm	Rail Yard (Shipping) 3,700,000sm	Firearms Storage	Processing	Office Buildings	Engineering Office	Solar Field Collector
Loading/Unloading Docks	Loading/Unloading	Customs/Security	Medical Facilities	Retail/Entertainment	Design Development Office	Wave Energy Converter
Fuelling Station	Customs/Security	Detaining Facility	Quarantine	Post Office/Banking	3D Printing Facility	Wind Turbine Field
Dry Docks/Maintenance Facility	Food and Beverage	Questioning and Interrogation	Food and Beverage	Parks and Recreation	Quality Control	
Customs/Security		Break room	Occupations Office	Medical Facilities	Printer Maintenance Garage	Mobile Printer
Food and Beverage	High Speed Rail Station(Passenger) 600,000sm	Locker room	Supplies Storage	Cultural Arts and History Museum	Supplies Storage	Operations Room
	Customs/Security		Trauma Counselling Centre	Parliament Hall	Break Room	Engine Room
Passenger Port 400,000sm	Food and Beverage	Public Functions 100,000sm	Temporary Housing	Tram System	Locker Room	Nuclear Reactor
Customs/Security	Baggage Claim	Lodging				3D Printing Facility
Food and Beverage	Check in/Ticketing	Food and Beverage	Primary Settlement 7,000,000sm	Unified Korea University 900,000sm	Assembly 600,000sm	Printer Maintenance
Baggage Claim	Waiting Lounge	Retail/Entertainment	School Systems K-12	University Campus	Engineering Office	Supplies Storage
Check in/Ticketing		Post Office/Banking	21st Century Integration Program	Education Buildings	Parts Assembly Facility	Parts Assembly Facility
Waiting Lounge	Storage Facilities 600,000sm		Trauma Counselling Centre	Dormitories	Quality Control	Quality Control
Parking	Security		Medical Facilities	Cafeteria		Construction Zone
	Goods Storage		Food and Beverage	Athletic Fields	Packaging 600,000sm	Equipment Storage
	Vehicular Equipment Storage		Retail/Entertainment	Recreation Centre		Equipment Maintenance
	Vehicular Equipment Maintenance		Post Office/Banking		Shipping/Receiving 1,200,000sm	Worker Accommodations
			Parks and Recreation			Cafeteria
			Occupations Office			Medical Clinic
			Apartment Housing			

facilities) and an "extending beyond" zone (with energy generators and mobile printers to expand the city as needed).

The responsibilities of every mega structure differences in what they must do to achieve the correct solution. In order for the mega-structure to thrive it must adopt and be controlled by changing time, population, and economic times. The needs for a fallen North Korea will change over time and at a hectic pace. The mega structure must not only allow intervention in the status-quo of now, but to facilitate an immediate change that can only be replicated in the technological world of connected people.

0492

IMJINGANG BAY
(NEUTRAL WATERS)

REFUGEE AND DMZ

HIGH-SPEED PASSENGER TRAIN TERMINAL, RAIL YARD AND GOODS DISTRIBUTION

INTERNATIONAL CITY

LOADING DOCKS IN THE MARINA

MARINA

MONUMENT OF CIVILIZATION

Lin Yu-Ta

3RD PLACE - 2012

Taiwan

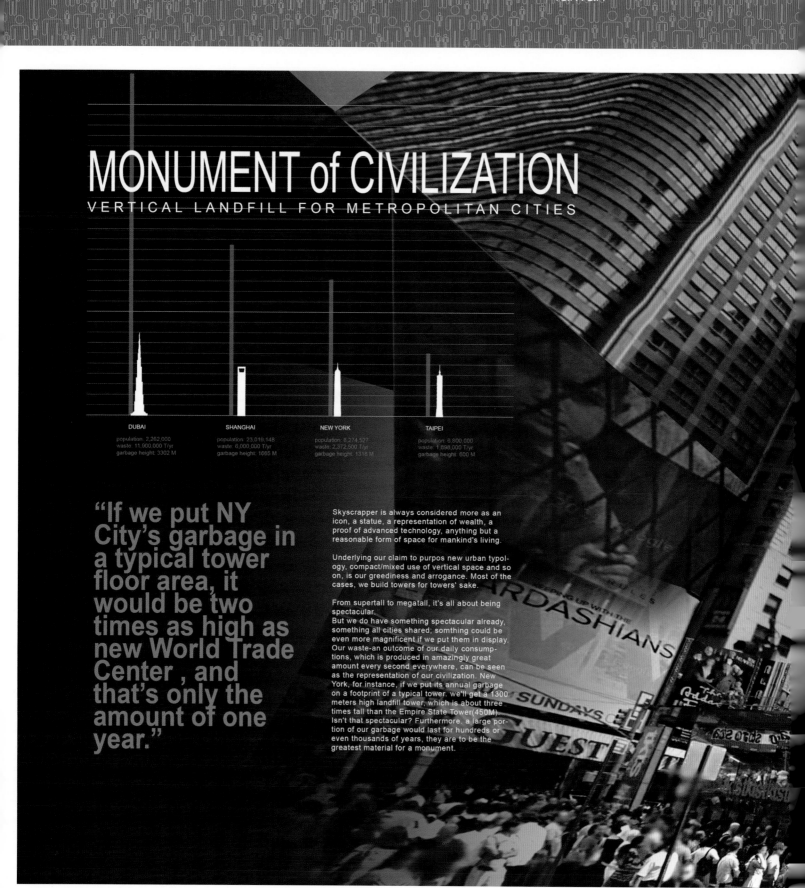

MONUMENT of CIVILIZATION
VERTICAL LANDFILL FOR METROPOLITAN CITIES

DUBAI
population: 2,262,000
waste: 11,900,000 T/yr
garbage height: 3302 M

SHANGHAI
population: 23,019,148
waste: 6,000,000 T/yr
garbage height: 1665 M

NEW YORK
population: 8,274,527
waste: 2,372,500 T/yr
garbage height: 1318 M

TAIPEI
population: 6,800,000
waste: 1,898,000 T/yr
garbage height: 600 M

"If we put NY City's garbage in a typical tower floor area, it would be two times as high as new World Trade Center , and that's only the amount of one year."

Skyscrapper is always considered more as an icon, a statue, a representation of wealth, a proof of advanced technology, anything but a reasonable form of space for mankind's living.

Underlying our claim to purpos new urban typology, compact/mixed use of vertical space and so on, is our greediness and arrogance. Most of the cases, we build towers for towers' sake.

From supertall to megatall, it's all about being spectacular.
But we do have something spectacular already, something all cities shared; somthing could be even more magnificent if we put them in display. Our waste-an outcome of our daily consumptions, which is produced in amazingly great amount every second everywhere, can be seen as the representation of our civilization. New York, for instance, if we put its annual garbage on a footprint of a typical tower. we'll get a 1300 meters high landfill tower, which is about three times tall than the Empire State Tower(450M). Isn't that spectacular? Furthermore. a large portion of our garbage would last for hundreds or even thousands of years, they are to be the greatest material for a monument.

Skyscrapers are meant to wow, to impress. But other things within cities are also impressive. New York, for instance: If we put its annual garbage on a area of a typical tower footprint, we will have a 1,300 meter high landfill tower, which is about as three times tall as the Empire State Building (450 meters). Skyscrapers are always considered more of just an icon but as a statue or representation of wealth and a proof of advanced technology. It is all about being spectacular. On the other hand landfills take up lots of space in metropolitan areas. Our waste, an outcome of our daily consumption, can be seen as the representation of our civilization.

As landfill possibilities surrounding growing metropolises disappear and cities fight waste management issues, the power of trash needs to be reconsidered. The accumulation of waste, for example, actually creates potential energy-

NEW YORK

recycle opportunities, such as when gas is emitted during decomposition. The Monument of Civilization proposal suggests locating trash vertically in a tower and using the energy generated from its decomposition to help power the surrounding city.

By locating the tower in the heart of the city, energy is provided in immediate proximity, and money is also saved in transportation costs when garbage no longer needs to be shipped out of town. It also able to serve there as a loud reminder of society's wasteful ways. The ever-growing Monument may evoke the citizens' introspection and somewhat lead to the entire city's waste-decreasing and better recycling. Seeing the tower as an "Earth-Friendliness Meter," the shorter the tower, the friendlier the city is, as that means less waste is made and more is recycled. Perhaps all

metropolitan cities would inverse the worldwide competition from being the tallest to being the shortest.

Underneath the structure lie recycling and wastewater processing facilities, gas and power stations, a temporary dump, and waste water tank. The tower consists of a garbage brick wall, gas transmission pipelines, and a solid-waste tank in the center.

Each city should have a garbage skyscraper to solve landfill shortage, to feed one's vanity of height, and to remark mankind's iconic civilization.

0546

DUBAI

SHANGHAI

TAIPEI

"Every city should has one garbage sky-scraper to solve landfill shortage, to feed one's vanity of height, and to remark mankind's icronic civilization."

BUCKY FULLER

Luis Vejo Fernández
Ricardo Martinez García
David Rodríguez Vicente

Spain

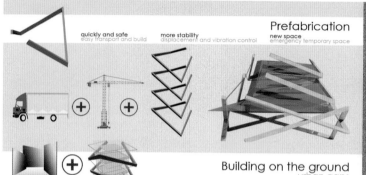

Prefabrication

quickly and safe
easy transport and build

more stability
displacement and vibration control

new space
emergency temporary space

Building on the ground
urban gaps

The construction system proposed can colonize large areas of land with a minimum land waste.

Can be a permanent or a temporary building depending of the needs.

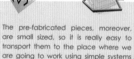

Building on other builds
ruins and skeletons

The pre-fabricated pieces, moreover, are small sized, so it is really easy to transport them to the place where we are going to work using simple systems like trucks, trains or even an helicopter in the most extreme situations.

It is not needed to wait for the pieces to get dry, so the assembly is very quick and easy, just like a "Mecanno" or a "Lego" play.

Building a green future
sustainable ideas

The building acts like an enormous solar chimney, so we are able to get renewable energy without need of the connection to the power supply. This is a auto-energy supplied building.

Can be associated with a building already built and use this as a building service

Solar chimney and old building.

Doubled-skin system.

Solar chimney
self-sufficient building

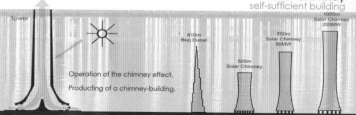

Tower

1000m
Solar Chimney
200MW

810m
Burj Dubai

750m
Solar Chimney
50MW

500m
Solar Chimney

Operation of the chimney effect.

Producting of a chimney-building.

Nowadays architecture has become to a crisis, not only in the economic issue, but also in its concept. The creation of new spaces has become so **DESTRUCTIVE** for our environment that we must look for **NEW WAYS** to occupy the space. Then is when the idea of the **SKYSCRAPER BECOMES USEFUL**, with these really tall buildings, we can have a great quantity of useful area, without occupying all the ground of our cities.

But these kinds of buildings are **TOO EXPENSIVE, TOO DIFFICULT** to be built. Companies waste a lot of time and money in those buildings, which seem to be reserved only for the wealthiest people on planet. Now, it is **TIME TO CHANGE** that idea about the skyscrapers.

We are proposing a new way to build, a new way to **UNDERSTAND THE STRUCTURE** of our buildings so we can take the most of the resources we can have, using the materials with intelligence, so they work the best they can do, for not wasting a great amount of material because of a bad design.

With an **EASY-TO-BUILD STRUCTURE**, people can get to build everywhere, so inhabitants are able to **COLONIZE** such an interesting place like **A RUIN** after an earthquake, or re-use an **OLD TOWN AREA**, so, expensive urban plans can be avoided. Thanks to its adaptability it can be use even in active zones of the town center, to **EXPAND** every kind of building (flats, offices, the city hall, etc).

Moreover, this skyscraper is designed to fully exploit the resources at our disposal. In the XXIst century, the ecology, and the **NEW SOURCES OF ENERGY** are an obligatory condition in every project. Renewable energies must be used more frequently so classic energies soon will become a thing of the old days. Specifically, we use the energy that the difference of temperature of the **AIR** gives us, using it to generate electricity with turbines in key points of the building.

BUCKY FULLER

Our project is also a tribute to Buckminster Fuller (who died 30 years ago from now), who designed and used strange and really **INNOVATIVE STRUCTURES** in their works, like the **TENSEGRITY** that we are going to use to create our skyscraper. In spite of Buckminster Fuller's fame, this kind of structures have fall into the obscurity although it is a structural system that has **PLENTY OF POSSIBILITIES**. It is in this point when we are going to take advantage of the great resistance of the steel, which works better with forces of traction, trying not to create compression forces, only in some **KEY POINTS** of the structure.

The point is to take the pieces to the place and mount the structure of the building using just one or two single cranes. After the structure is completed, we just have to put a "skin" around the levels and create the connections, stairs and lifts. So although this design can be used for many different issues, we can say that it is **ESPECIALLY USEFUL IN EXTREME CASES** like natural disasters, for example, to re-organize the main government structures in Haiti, after the disaster with the earthquake.

Bucky Fuller seeks to use pre-fabricated "tensegrity" structural components as a way of facilitating the quick and effective erection of environmentally savvy structures. A tensegrity structural component, like those advocated for by twentieth century architect Buckminster Fuller, is based on the notion of "tensional integrity," or "floating compression," which utilizes a set of isolated structural components in compression inside a net of continuous tension.

Each floor of a Bucky Fuller structure is comprised of one tensegrity module; these modules are stacked to a desired height and then in-filled with a concrete slab floor. The building acts like an enormous solar chimney, able to get renewable energy without the need of connection to the power supply. This is an auto-energy supplied building.

The point is to take the pieces to the place and mount the structure of the building using just one or two single

0628

cranes. After the structure is complete, only a skin is needed around the levels. Although this design can be used for many different contexts, it is especially useful in extreme cases like natural disasters for example to re-organize the main government structures.

A continuous, double-skinned facade draped between tensegrity modules creates a void running the entire height each structure that acts as both insulation and solar chimney. Through the stack effect, air which is taken in at the base of the building is propelled up through the facade and eventually released at the top of the structure, turning a wind mill on its way out, generating electricity. This allows for off-the grid power generation especially necessary during disaster situations.

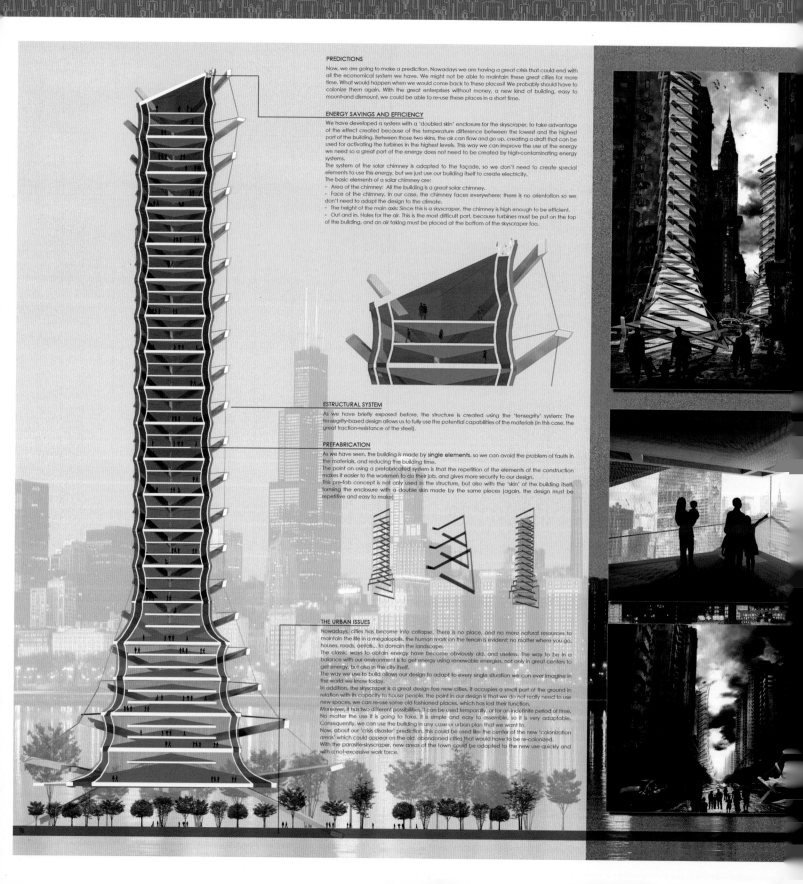

PREDICTIONS

Now, we are going to make a prediction. Nowadays we are having a great crisis that could end with all the economical system we have. We might not be able to maintain these great cities for more time. What would happen when we would come back to these places? We probably should have to colonize them again. With the great enterprises without money, a new kind of building, easy to mount-and dismount, we could be able to re-use these places in a short time.

ENERGY SAVINGS AND EFFICIENCY

We have developed a system with a 'doubled skin' enclosure for the skyscraper, to take advantage of the effect created because of the temperature difference between the lowest and the highest part of the building. Between those two skins, the air can flow and go up, creating a draft that can be used for activating the turbines in the highest levels. This way we can improve the use of the energy we need so a great part of the energy does not need to be created by high-contaminating energy systems.

The system of the solar chimney is adapted to the façade, so we don't need to create special elements to use this energy, but we just use our building itself to create electricity.

The basic elements of a solar chimney are:
- Area of the chimney: All the building is a great solar chimney.
- Face of the chimney: In our case, the chimney faces everywhere; there is no orientation so we don't need to adapt the design to the climate.
- The height of the main axis: Since this is a skyscraper, the chimney is high enough to be efficient.
- Out and in. Holes for the air. This is the most difficult part, because turbines must be put on the top of the building, and an air taking must be placed at the bottom of the skyscraper too.

ESTRUCTURAL SYSTEM

As we have briefly exposed before, the structure is created using the 'tensegrity' system: The tensegrity-based design allows us to fully use the potential capabilities of the materials (in this case, the great traction-resistance of the steel).

PREFABRICATION

As we have seen, the building is made by **single elements**, so we can avoid the problem of faults in the materials, and reducing the building time.

The point on using a prefabricated system is that the repetition of the elements of the construction makes it easier to the workmen to do their job, and gives more security to our design.

This pre-fab concept is not only used in the structure, but also with the 'skin' of the building itself, forming the enclosure with a double skin made by the same pieces (again, the design must be repetitive and easy to make)

THE URBAN ISSUES

Nowadays, cities has become into collapse. There is no place, and no more natural resources to maintain the life in a megalopolis, the human mark on the terrain is evident; no matter where you go, houses, roads, aerials... to domain the landscape.

The classic ways to obtain energy have become obviously old, and useless. The way to be in a balance with our environment is to get energy using renewable energies, not only in great centers to get energy, but also in the city itself.

The way we use to build allows our design to adapt to every single situation we can ever imagine in the world we know today.

In addition, the skyscraper is a great design foe new cities. It occupies a small part of the ground in relation with its capacity to house people, the point in our design is that we do not really need to use new spaces, we can re-use some old fashioned places, which has lost their function.

Moreover, it has two different possibilities. It can be used temporary, or for an indefinite period of time. No matter the use it is going to take, it is simple and easy to assemble, and it is very adaptable. Consequently, we can use the building in any case or urban plan that we want to.

Now, about our 'crisis disaster' prediction, this could be used like the center of the new 'colonization areas' which could appear on the old, abandoned cities that would have to be re-colonized.

With the parasite-skyscraper, new areas of the town could be adapted to the new use quickly and with a not-excessive work force.

These pre-fab components are theoretically small and modular enough that they cannot only be transferred easily, on trucks, trains or even helicopters, but can also be located anywhere in the world. Bucky Fuller structures can be deployed as permanent architectural forms within urban settings or can be utilized as temporary structures in disaster areas since it can be assembled easily. Bucky Fuller is very adaptable and could be used in any urban plan or to be used as the center of new colonization areas.

0628

GROWING SPACES 02

OCCUPY
MANHATTAN SKY

Xiaoben Dai
Li-Shung Yeung

Hong Kong

Occupy Manhattan Sky is a crowd-generated response to the Occupy Wall Street movement of 2011-2012 that takes the form of a metaphorical "skyscraper" above Manhattan. Occupy Manhattan Sky attempts to appropriate the skyscraper as a symbol for the 99 percent through its user-generated scheme. Through a special smartphone app, users are able to contribute to the "skyscraper." When users open this application, a virtual "string" is sent from their phone to the skyscraper, linking this particular user with everyone else who is contributing to the structure, displaying an image of the skyscraper on the phone's screen. The size and shape of the multi-faceted "building" created in the Manhattan sky is determined by the location, number, and movement of its users, constantly changing size, shape, and density of facets. This application system traces the movement of users, generating a three-dimensional cognitive

0631

OCCUPY MANHATTAN SKY

1%
the wealthiest U.S. citizens control 40% of the American wealth in 2011   99%

Amercian Skyscraper and Capitalism

In the 1870s, the Wall Street in New York was full of speculative people and tourists, and sooner became the "engine room of corporate capitalism" in America. That situation generated the first skyscrapers in business district. Skyscraper is a kind of American invention that can symbolize the cultural and economic predominance of the United States in the twentieth century. As architectural historian Carol Willis wrote in his book "Skyscraper Rivals", *"Skyscrapers are the ultimate architecture of capitalism. The first blueprint for every tall building is a balance sheet of estimated costs and returns."* Manhattan in New York City, which is a center of economic activity and capital of culture, cannot be imagined without skyscrapers. They are the icons of the city, stars of movies, symbols of corporate power, and the place where many New Yorkers report to work every morning.

In the late 2000s, the credit crunch happened in America. It was considered to be the worst financial crisis since the 1930s Great Depression. It resulted in the collapse of American financial system. In Sept 2011, the protest movement "Occupy Wall Street" began in New York City's Wall Street financial district. The protests are against social and economic inequality, high unemployment, greed, as well as corruption, and the undue influence of those financial corporations situated in the Manhattan skyscrapers. The protesters want more and better jobs, more equal distribution of income, bank reform, and a reduction of the influence of corporations on politics.

Sky-Skyscraper : Owned by 99% of People

The idea of "Sky-skyscraper" in Manhattan sky is generated in response to the "Occupy Wall Street". This is intended to design a memorial skyscraper that is owned and shared by the rest of the 99% of people: In May 2011, Joseph Stiglitz, a 2001 Nobel laureate and Columbia University economics professor, wrote an article for Vanity Fair and stated that the wealthiest 1% of U.S. citizens control 40% of the American wealth. Through the technology of augmented reality, all people are invited to get involved in the formation of building's characteristic with their smart phones and built-in GPS. The shape is varied according to the number of supporters who are opening the "Occupy Manhattan Sky" application in different locations. It's a virtual protest in response to the physical "Occupy Wall Street" in Manhattan.

Real Environment → Augmented Reality ←→ Augmented Virtuality ← Virtual Environment

image that acts as a visual registry of the activities of the city at any given moment.

Through the technology of augmented reality, all people are invited to get involved in the formation of the building's characteristic with their smart phones and built-in GPS. The shape is varied according to the number of supporters who are opening the Occupy Manhattan Sky application in different locations. It is a virtual protest in response to the physical "Occupy Wall Street" in Manhattan. This application system lets the traces of the movement supporters generate a three dimensional and spatial-temporal cognitive image as a structural registry of the activities of the city that is visible in the augmented reality of the environment. User can also upload the images or videos from their phones to the sky-skyscraper. This real-time data flow enhances the "here and now" experience of this virtual

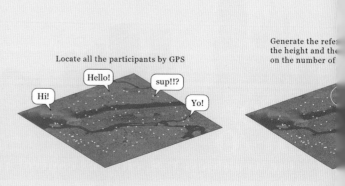

Locate all the participants by GPS

Generate the refe[...]
the height and the[...]
on the number of [...]

Augmented Reality

Once all the participants opened this application, they can see a virtual st[...]
from their smart phones connecting to the sky-skyscraper that locates the[...]
relation to other users' positions by the built-in GPS systems. Looking thr[...]
the screens, the users see the virtual and multi-faceted building that resp[...]
to the location, number and movement of its users, dynamically changin[...]
size, density of facets and its position in the sky.

"Rethinking Skyscrape[...]

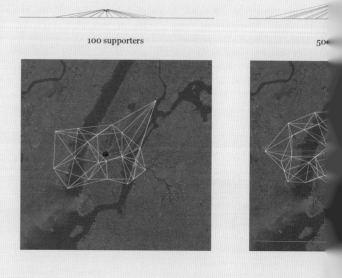

100 supporters   50[...]

constantly-changing mirror-like structure.

In this manner, Occupy Manhattan Sky utilizes a traditionally, capitalist-derived building typology, the skyscraper, to democratize its formal expression, doing so through the interaction among and between engaged users. This creates a real-time data flow that facilitates the temporal nature of the structure.

0631

OCCUPY MANHATTAN SKY

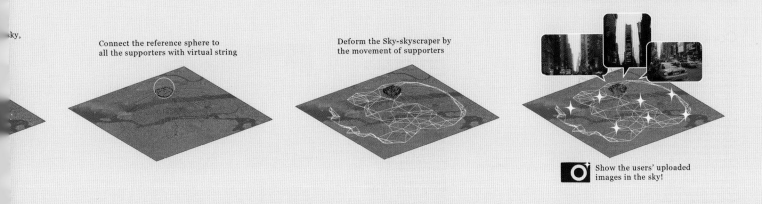

Connect the reference sphere to all the supporters with virtual string

Deform the Sky-skyscraper by the movement of supporters

Show the users' uploaded images in the sky!

...application system let the traces of the movement supporters generate a ...mensional and spatial-temporal cognitive image as a structural registry of ...activities of the city that is visible in the augmented reality of ...ronment. Users can also "upload" the images or videos from their phones ...e Sky-skyscraper. This real-time data flow enhances the "Here and Now" ...rience of this virtual constantly-changing mirror-like structure.

...e 99%"

1000 supporters

2000 supporters

5000 supporters

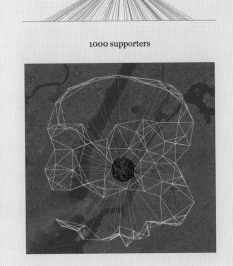

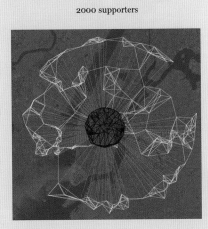

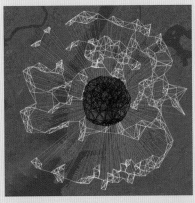

BRIDGE OF HOPE

Mohammed Adib
Ivan Arellano
Jordi Cunill
Maria Teresa Farre
Christian Koester
Davide Roncato

Spain

Bridge of Hope

bridge1. n . something that makes it easier to make a change from one situation to another

hōpe . n . to want something to happen or to be true, and usually have a good reason to think that it might.

Concept

A once united region, rich in minerals, has been split due to political decisions that are jeopardising the world peace on a daily basis. Arabs and Jews lived and worked together on the shores of the Dead Sea pre 1948, and the Palestine Potash Company employed both. Plans for expansion were drawn up and implemented in the 1934 south shore factory inauguration. In 1948 and due to subsequent quibbles and wars the Dead Sea was divided and segregated. Our wish is to build a symbolic bridge to reunite this region. The project would be built from both sides by the two parties to ultimately meet in the central part and create a settlement for both. At the same time the Dead Sea would be replenished, and in so doing would sink the first buildings from either side so as to make sure there is no return to the segregation. It is a symbolic gesture for those on both sides who wish to show the world that all can live in harmony together, and all that is needed is hope.

Process

The level is dropping by 1m a year. The World Economic Forum is funding a project on the Jordanian side to replenish the Dead Sea from the Red Sea by a connecting a pipeline (due to be completed in 2017). Our intention is to do the same from the Israeli side, replenishing from the Mediterranean. Both aqueducts would also generate electricity due to the 400m drop in level that is planned to desalinise the waters for irrigation and discharging the residual water into the Dead Sea, we also plan to create salt water pools (with normal salt levels) within the Dead Sea for fish farming and, other pools would be varied to offer the advantages of the minerals available; Salt, Potash (for fertilizers), Bromine (for fire retardants), sweet water (for hydroponic farming), Dunaliella bacteria (High CO_2 sequestration rate), Thalassotherapy, Asphalt, etc.

Amman

Jerusalem

1994 Treaty Line

1949 Armistice
Agreement Line

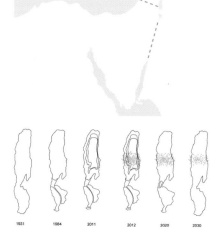

1931   1984   2011   2012   2020   2030

The Bridge of Hope is a symbolic structure that seeks to link the shores of the Dead Sea to promote peace between Jordan and Israel. Construction of the bridge would commence from both sides of the sea, ultimately meeting in the middle; there, a settlement for Arabs and Jews to live harmoniously is established.

The water level of the Dead Sea is dropping by one meter per year, and plans are currently underway by the Jordanians to replenish the water levels by connecting it, via pipelines, with the Red Sea. In addition to the bridge's construction, this project also proposes the creation of aqueducts from Israel's side to help replenish the sea with water from the Mediterranean. These aqueducts would generate electricity as the water flow drops 400 meters; this electricity is used to desalinate the water, making it useable for irrigation purposes (residual water is discharged into

0826

the Dead Sea).

Salt-water pools (with normal salt levels) are created within the Dead Sea for fish farming, and other pools are also created to cultivate mineral baths for a variety of uses (potash is used for fertilizer, bromine for fire retardants, fresh water for hydroponic farming, *Dunaliella* bacteria for its high CO_2 sequestration rate, etc.).

The houses within the bridge settlement are adaptations of traditional Middle Eastern "wind catcher chimney" house designs. These will differ, though, in that all sides of the structures will offer shaded areas and openings of varied sizes that lead to green terraces and water pool terraces. These openings allow for fresh airflow, which creates cool breezes to cool the homes in this warm environment.

Bridge of Hope

Architecture

Although the climate may seem extreme, the living conditions are quite favourable; low humidity, high oxygen content, no pollen (no allergies), weakened ultraviolet radiation, mineral rich mud baths, treatment conditions (Psoriasis, Rhino sinusitis, Osteoarthritis, etc.), etc. Due to the dry air (the body of water also limits the high temperatures), the aim of the architectural designs is to exploit the wind catcher chimney design of a traditional Middle Eastern house, but through all the sides, creating shaded areas and openings of varied sizes with green terraces and water pool terraces and fresh air is forced through the buildings creating a cool breeze. On the other hand, as approximately 7 million tons of water evaporates each day, we plan to recreate the water cycle within the buildings to collect the evaporated sweet water that would drip to the gardened terraces. The difference in temperature from the average air temperature and the lower stratus of salt water (at only 15m deep) is in excess of 20ºC; this difference would be used to generate the chilled water needed to condense the vapour.

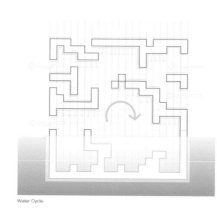

Water Cycle

Dunaliella Bacteria — Mud Bath — Potash — Local Stone — Salt — Hydroponic Culture

As approximately 7 million tons of water evaporates each day, a water cycle within the buildings will be established to create fresh water from condensation; this will help irrigate the gardened terraces. The condensation is created when ocean water is brought from a depth of 15 meters to the surface; when the salt water meets the warm air, the temperature difference (which is 20 degrees Celsius or more) creates vapor, and the molecules regroup without the salt, creating fresh water.

0826

FED-SCRAPER

Jon Bailey
Erick Katzenstein
Chad Porter

United States

dc limits

Never before in the country's history has the U.S. government owned more enclosed space in Washington, D.C. than it does today. The increased need for space for government facilities, and the lack of available land surrounding the capital, has resulted in a sprawl of agency offices. Some designers have suggested erecting massive skyscrapers at the National Mall to accommodate this needed space; the Fed-Scraper design vehemently makes up for this need, however. Instead, it proposes installing massive structures underground so the city can reclaim its land as offices move below.

This design is opposed to grand edifices, which break apart the find meshwork needed for a city to thrive. The solution to these mega structures is not a building reaching ever-higher into the atmosphere. This would pull apart

0832

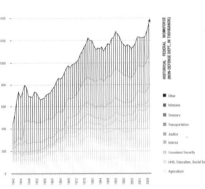

FED-SCRAPER

AND THE AMAZING TRANSFORMATION OF THE NATIONAL MALL: A FULLY FUNCTIONAL SELF-CONTAINED FEDERAL CITY.

That government transforms the way we occupy and inhabit space is nowhere more geodetically relevant than in the United States capitol of Washington DC, where limits have reached capacity in both physical space and organizational structure. Never before has the government owned more enclosed space within the U.S. than in the present. Following September 11th, the increase in subsidiary agencies has led to an explosive acquisition of government land. This growth has led to exponential sprawl reaching outward into the neighboring states in search for suitable living spaces.

The National Mall is one of the largest open spaces still in existence within Washington DC. Since its inception by Pierre L'Enfant in 1791, a continual source of speculative design projects has aimed at creating a picturesque foreground for the federal edifices that surround it.

Our design is opposed to these grand edifices which break apart the fine meshwork needed for a city to thrive. The solution to these mega structures is not a building reaching ever-higher into the atmosphere. This would pull apart the connections we have with the ground and further disconnect the government from the city. Rather, our proposal intends to dig into the earth, burying the program beneath whilst activating the ground plane.

In this canyon, walls become the physical limits of unrivaled growth. DC is given back in large swaths of land to the people, where previous federal land within is returned to the citizens of the city to re-inhabit. It is thus our intention, in reaction to the vertical limits imposed on the district, that the canyon becomes a central location for federal government offices, imposing limits on the size of the physical federal growth rates. This new juxtaposition of governmental program located beneath the ground plane creates a unique opportunity of oversight from the people above to the federal program within.

As if sedentary rock formations were revealed by the cutting away of ground at the National Mall, striated monolithic masses of federal programs are stretched within the void. As the masses are stretched within the canyon, transparent voids are opened around the below-grade infrastructure intersecting the site, acting simultaneously as both light-well and visibly transparent surfaces. Likened to the layering of matter, federal program either settles to the bottom or rises to the top. Utilizing the tensile structural capacity of steel, skewers in conversation with the programmatic arrangement float the buildings mass within the canyon. As the mass hovers above the canyon floor, an additional layer of outdoor experience is created. Accessible from the mall above, garden-like terraces wind down the canyon wall creating multiple layers of habitable space along the vertical surfaces.

parti: displace big block federal buildings, restore ground plane and submerge government

site

the connections we have with the ground and further disconnect the government from the city. Rather, this proposal intends to dig into the earth, burying the program beneath whilst activating the ground plane.

A canyon is created in the National Mall, and long rectangular tubes housing stretches of offices are attached to the canyon walls. Steel skewers support the separate agency structures against the earthen walls; the offices housing high-security agencies are located deep within the canyon, while the lowest-security offices are at the top. The long office structures are constructed from series of trusses that are covered in mesh. Garden-like terraces wind down the walls between structures.

Earth is also cleared away from under the office sites and filled in with water to create a large reservoir. Above

FED-SCRAPER

The inherent wetness in the low-lying area of the National Mall is exacerbated by the reopening of the Washington Canal as the ground level begins to flood. In addition to the naturally seeping ground water, the Capitol reflecting pool spills over the East canyon wall to create a waterfall which cascades down into the water below. Using Abraham Stroock's invention of a synthetic root system which transports water through evapotransporative techniques, ganglia-like ribbons dip down from the roof surface and into the reservoir below. Water is passively transported throughout these fibers, allowing for a thick vegetative growth to take hold.

Rather than rewriting the historic L'Enfant plan, this project seeks to work within the bounds. In addition to the acknowledgment of the city's limits, this project seeks a commentary on the future trajectory of growth within a city, with explicit attention toward the federal growth and spatial-composition within the confines of Washington DC.

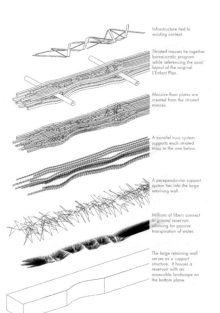

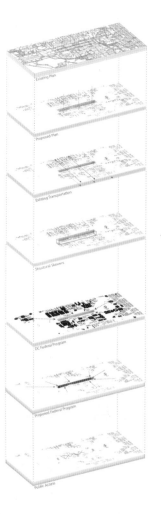

Infrastructure tied to existing context.

Striated masses tie together bureaucratic program while referencing the axial layout of the original L'Enfant Plan.

Massive floor plates are created from the striated masses.

A parallel truss system supports each striated mass to the one below.

A perpendicular support system ties into the large retaining wall.

Millions of fibers connect to ground reservoir, allowing for passive transpiration of water.

The large retaining wall serves as a support structure. It houses a reservoir with an accessible landscape on the bottom plane.

HANGING GARDENS | CANAL WALL | TRUSS + MESH FACAD

ground, the inherent wetness of the low-lying areas of the National Mall is exacerbated by the reopening of the Washington Canal, when these areas begin to flood. The excessive water mixes with the Capitol's reflecting pool, and the water spills over the eastern canyon wall, creating a waterfall. A synthetic root system is installed to transport water through evapo-transporative techniques, causing ganglia-like ribbons to run down the walls of the canyon from its top opening into the reservoir below. Water is passively transported throughout these fibers, allowing thick vegetative growth to develop.

0832

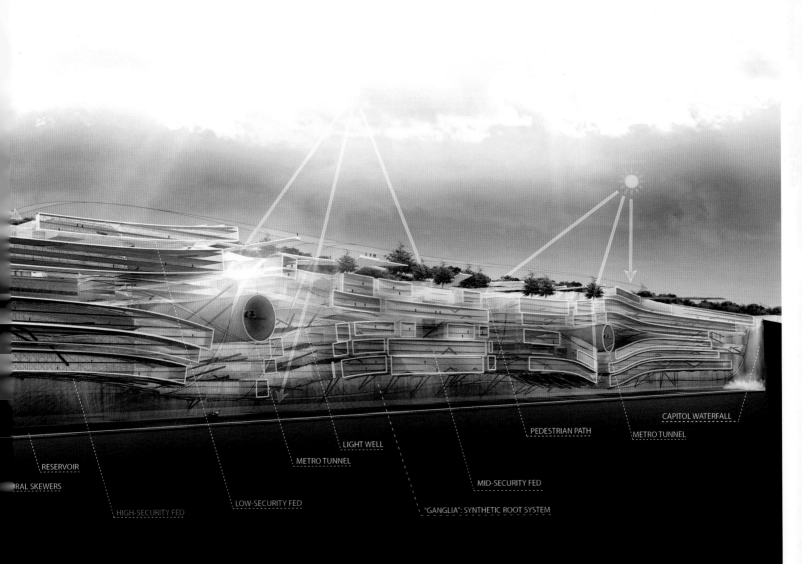

CAPITOL WATERFALL

PEDESTRIAN PATH

METRO TUNNEL

LIGHT WELL

METRO TUNNEL

MID-SECURITY FED

RESERVOIR

RAL SKEWERS

LOW-SECURITY FED

HIGH-SECURITY FED

"GANGLIA": SYNTHETIC ROOT SYSTEM

TOWER
OF BABEL

Maciej Nisztuk

Poland

TOWER O

In an era where mega structures threaten to strip man's needs and the humanity of architecture from new buildings and the field as a whole, the "Tower of Babel" seeks to do the opposite, existing as a living monument to its creator and their aspirations. The building is perpetually "under construction" as the needs and wants of its creator evolve, allowing the monument to experiment with and showcase many architectural trends.

The skyscraper is a mutation of the Palace of Culture and Science, an enormous, landmark structure built in 1955 in the destroyed center of Warsaw, Poland (which was still ravaged from WWII). Although it is the most recognizable symbol of Warsaw, it is a controversial building, as it symbolizes, to many, Soviet domination and the enslavement of the Polish nation. A typical communist monument, it ignored the local architectural vernacular and good urban

BABEL

0900-1

planning, and instead was built as a monolith to tower over the rest of the city.

Despite this, the designer of the Tower of Babel defends the Palace. It is a monument of idea, and a monument of its creators. Today's architectural monuments are driven by money, not people, and symbolize the culture's worship as such. This capitalist approach to architecture creates a "dystopia," says the designer. The Tower of Babel is therefore meant to glorify the old use of monuments to honor people and social ideas. It is a "maze of glued-together architectural blocks which are not finished, incomplete or damaged." This commentary reveals that though past monuments may have glorified controversial regimes or figureheads, at least they had soul, and purpose; modern monuments are about nothing but the monument itself, and the designer protests this reality by leaving the structure

TOWER OF BABEL

In the mercantile world, where money and economy is power, architecture became a product, which can be used in a good way to sell human aspirations. The more spectacular the better. Architecture no longer meets the needs of human living, it becomes a monument to money, prestige, a formal vision, somewhere, leaving behind its subject - human being. This dangerous trend leads to rejection of human as a fundament of architecture. Humanity is being alienated in architecture. Architecture is created only for architecture. Anonymous cold and unfriendly buildings with overwhelming scale.

This skyscraper is the ever-living monument of its creators and their aspirations. Skyscraper as an endless tale, monument which is still under construction. Building lives its own life, constantly evolving. Is an accumulation of various trends in architecture. Truly tower of Babel.

Skyscraper is basically a mutation of the Palace of Culture and Science, which was established in 1955 in destroyed center of Warsaw (Poland). The building was built in area which was earlier densely built-up by downtown buildings, destroyed during World War 2. The main author was a Soviet architect Lev Rudniew working with a team of Polish architects.

The project continues intentions of architects of this building to create a building - monument, the carrier of the Communist idea. Among the inhabitants of Warsaw object arouses many emotions. Although it is the most recognizable symbol of Warsaw as well as some sort of landmark, by its enormity, is a controversial building. It is a symbol of Soviet domination and enslavement of the Polish nation. It also totally misses the terms of local architecture and urban planning. Does not fit the scale and linkage with the surrounding buildings, urban layout and culture of the city. It is a monument of IDEA. A monument of its creators. Hypertrophy of form over content that dominates over the Warsaw. Political and cultural realities have changed, but concept to create monuments in architecture still remains. Ideas have changed but the rules of creation the architecture still remains the same.

This project sees the skyscraper as something in constant construction. The building is maze of glued together architectural blocks which are not finished, incomplete or damaged. Building is a response to capitalist approach to architecture. It reveals dystopia which can be create by modern approach to architecture

Location: Europe - Poland - Warsaw

Function mutation/disintegration

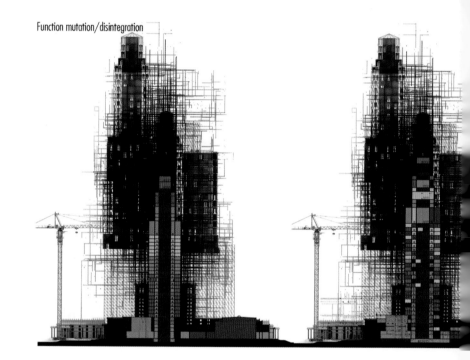

Elevations

raw, without purpose or completion.

Architecture no longer meets the needs of human living. It becomes a monument to money, prestige, a formal vision, somewhere leaving behind its subject, human beings. This project sees the skyscraper as something in constant construction. It reveals the dystopia that can be created by a modern approach to architecture.

0900-2

SCRAP SKYSCRAPER

Thiago Augustus Prenholato Alves
João Gabriel Kuster Cordeiro
Guilherme De Macedo
Rafael Santos Ferraz
Rodolfo Parolin Hardy
Giovanni Medeiros

Brazil

With the goal of recycling the city's trash for something useful and meaningful, the Scrap Skyscraper seeks to create a building will have a big impact, reaching the population socially, environmentally and functionally. The proposition is to break the traditional rules of construction by reusing as many elements as possible in their current state, combining them in a high-end software capable to catalogue and pre-dispose what will be built.

The main idea is about being a cultural landmark in changing the mindset of people where the future is the use of garbage. Nowadays people usually do not bother with the garbage they generate. They see it as a problem of others. Changing this thinking is crucial to change the course of evolution of the planet to a more sustainable path.

The project takes place at São Paulo, Brazil, the largest city in the south hemisphere by population, which

0905

UPCYCLING FOR SOCIAL ENHANCEMENT

a cultural landmark in changing the mindset of people, where the future is the the waste we generate has value both as an agent of social change and as tion. Nowadays people usually do not bother with the garbage they gener- rs. Changing this thinking is crucial to change the course of evolution of the

es of a specific city, in this case São Paulo, beginning a transition point that ality for the population by the use of the trash that its inhabitants generate.

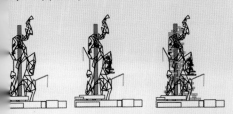

ongside the rivers Tietê and Pinheiros, those rivers will be used as water- the city to the upcycling centers. Using the rivers as waterways to transport n the city, enabling garbage trucks travel over shorter distances, and lever- of upcycling, that receives more material. In the basement of the building, e River, there is an upcycling and recycling center, giving rise to the building ategic location which enhances the transport of waste through the city. The rk on the bottom of the building, as a factory, recycling, cleaning and select- experts in the field. This material will be used on the building's construction tivity of the own workers. The opportunity for a social revolution that give- to learn a trade and have a place to live.

g, it focuses towards the reduction of processes that transform the material, ate that it were found.

CITY PANEL

The city of São Paulo has three alarming concerns: urban mobility, high levels of pollution and social inequality. However, these issues are intrinsically linked. The difficulty in improving urban mobility has to do with the excess of cars, whose fleet increases thousand vehicles per day, plus the limited and outdated public transportation line. This excess of cars brings high levels of pollution, especially in the air, attached to the disregard of the population about the garbage they generate, that degrades the city and its rivers. The rivers, polluted nowadays, are the reason of the location of the city, were left without any care and had its potencial to be navigable wasted. So, we are back to the mobility issues. Social inequality is present among the problems related to mobility and pollution, people living in slums, with no chance of social integration.

In São Paulo only 1% of the garbage is recycled. Still nowadays is cheaper to dispose the city's trash in a dump than to recycle it, so, the problem is about a society focused on price, they do not analyze that the whole trash issue is deeper and beyond the ambiental factor it grows as a social agravator.

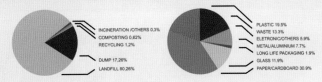

INCINERATION /OTHERS 0.3%
COMPOSTING 0,62%
RECYCLING 1,2%
DUMP 17,26%
LANDFILL 80,26%

PLASTIC 19.5%
WASTE 13.3%
ELETRONIC/OTHERS 5.9%
METAL/ALUMINIUM 7.7%
LONG LIFE PACKAGING 1.9%
GLASS 11.9%
PAPER/CARDBOARD 30.9%

generates 17,000 tons of garbage per day of which only 1% is recycled. Another two important facts to note are the bad use of the rivers that circle the city that used to be clean and nowadays are polluted and the general mindset of the residents of this metropolis, that still today do not care about recycling manners.

The buildings of the Scrap Skyscraper will be at the banks of Tiete River and Pinheiro River, and each building will receive the population's trash transported by the waterways. This way all the city's garbage can be organized and used at its best, being cleaned, catalogued and reused. The Scrap Skyscraper will have dwellings at its body and a kind of factory in its bottom that will focus on selecting and reusing trash.

The tower will provide module housing for São Paulo's homeless population and jobs in the factory. Experts will

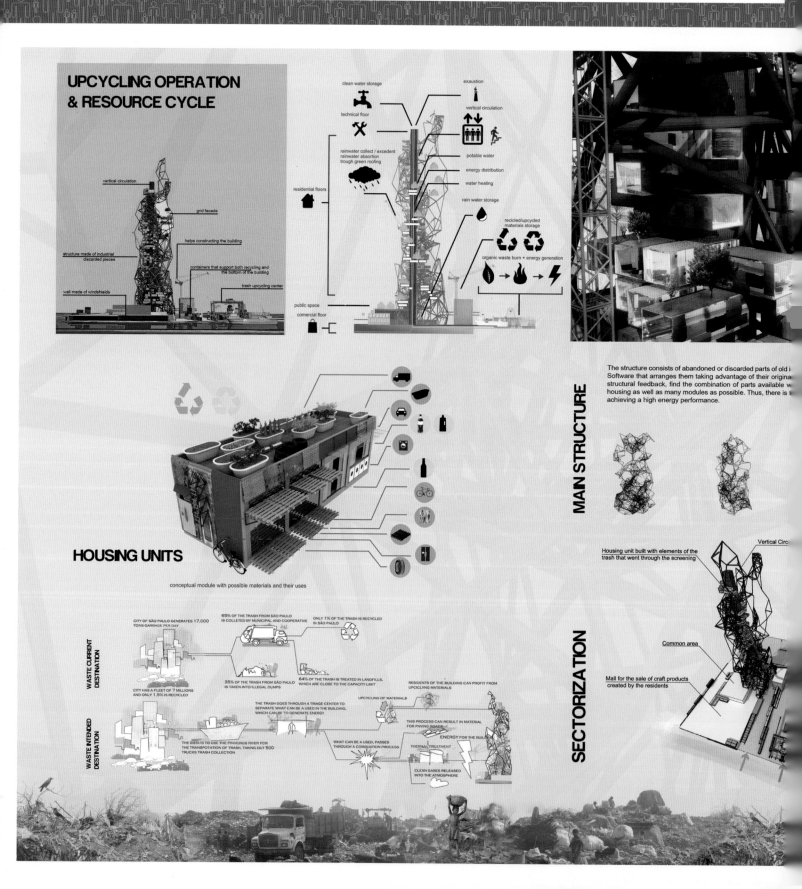

UPCYCLING OPERATION & RESOURCE CYCLE

HOUSING UNITS

conceptual module with possible materials and their uses

MAIN STRUCTURE

SECTORIZATION

WASTE CURRENT DESTINATION

WASTE INTENDED DESTINATION

train and guide the inhabitants in how to explore their own creativity and improve each shelter. These shelters will be made of up-cycled materials like windshields, doors of cars and refrigerators, and all sorts of material collected; each unit will remain singular depending on the available components. Likewise, there will not be any replicas of dwellings because of the variable components they are comprised of. The Scrap Skyscraper will stand as a landmark that can change the social consciousness of waste, showing the possible gain of social enhancement through up-cycling.

0905

...e is cataloged and then feed the ...sed on genetic algorithms with ...hat best exploits the verticality, ...est cost of transformation, thus

...aste not used for manufacture ...ed for the energy production of ...ng.

...acture of the building components ...e trash able for upcycling

...of trash

SPINELESS SKYSCRAPER

Weimeng Lu
Jia Wan
Ning Wei

China

SPINAL M

Spineless Skyscraper an experimental design that approaches on structural innovation of high-rise buildings. Located as a commercial tower in Manhattan, New York, the building's aim is to create a new structural language for skyscrapers both meaningful and buildable to the current society.

While the building's façade is not designed to be dramatically unique, its spineless nature creates a visibly different system on the exterior. As there are no central cores in this super high-rise building, the forms and functions under the skin of tower demonstrate a distinct contrast with the towers nearby. The skyscraper's historically unchanged structural mode, "core+frame," is redefined by using columns and a complex of inter-bracing elements which provides an equally strong structure against loads and shear forces as traditional commercial skyscrapers.

0925

Spineless skyscraper is an experimental design that approaches on structural innovation of super high-rise buildings. It is a commercial tower which locates in Manhattan, New York. With the context of one of world's densest skylines, the building's aim is to create a totally new structural language for skyscrapers which is both meaningful and buildable to the current society. At the same time, it drastically improves the architectural quality from the traditional skyscraper's mode. The exterior form of the building is not designed to be dramatically unique. However, as the title reveals, it does not have a "spine": there are no central cores in this super high-rise building. This eventually creates a whole new system in the interior, the forms and functions under the skin of tower demonstrate a distinct contrast with the towers nearby. During the whole design process, we deeply question skyscraper "mode", a series of studies on high-rises have been done in order to create a simple but effective solution. Looking back to the history, since the very first tower, skyscraper's structural mode has been remained basically unchanged. It is commonly known as the "Core+Frame" system, the central core bears the major structural role; it also serves the rest of the spaces in the building as a servant space. However, it results fixed and limited spaces, especially for commercial buildings. We are here to break the ice.

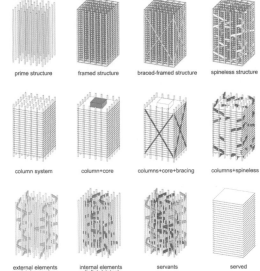

prime structure · framed structure · braced-framed structure · spineless structure

column system · column+core · columns+core+bracing · columns+spineless

external elements (staircases) · internal elements (toilets/piping) · servants · served

SPINELESS
TRANSFORMING STRUCTURE AND WORKPLACE

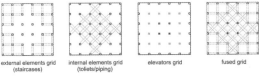

external elements grid (staircases) · internal elements grid (toliets/piping) · elevators grid · fused grid

SPATIAL COMPOSITION

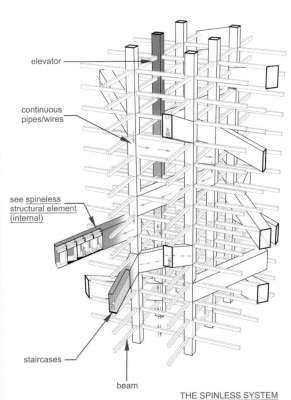

elevator

continuous pipes/wires

see spineless structural element (internal)

staircases

beam

THE SPINLESS SYSTEM

CROSS-SECTION

SPINELESS MODE

Meanwhile, each structural element contains functional roles including circulation, piping and bathrooms. They evenly distribute loads throughout the whole interior spaces, satisfying occupiers' needs. As a result of the new system, spaces on each floor could be seen as a free, open plan. There are no specially defined spaces at all, thus no "inside/outside" hierarchy can be found. Renters could freely arrange their own offices layout with a great flexibility, maximizing their creativity and allowing the spaces to quickly adapt to workers' changing needs over time.

The new system also produces a series of environmental benefits. Due to a lack of interior walls, sunlight can distribute more efficiently in the building. The coreless interior also makes cross ventilation possible in each level of a skyscraper, which is passive and enormously reduces the needs of mechanical ventilation system. The toilets contain

SPINELESS
TRANSFORMING STRUCTURE AND WORKPLACE

For making a change, the entire structure of Spineless Skyscraper is simply formed by columns and a complex of inter-bracing elements, which provides a equally strong structure against loads and shear forces as traditional skyscrapers. Meanwhile, each structural element contains functional roles including circulation, piping and bathrooms. They evenly distribute throughout the whole interior spaces, which satisfy occupiers' needs. As a result of the new system, spaces on each floor could be seen as a free, open plan. There are no specially defined spaces at all, no "inside/outside" hierarchy could be found. Renters could freely arrange their own offices layout with a great flexibility, this maximizes their creativity and allows the spaces to quickly adapt to workers' changing needs over time. The new system also produces a series of environmental benefits. Due to there are no interior walls, sunlight can distribute more efficiently in the building. The coreless interior also makes cross ventilation possible in each level of a skyscraper, which is passive and enormously reduces the needs of mechanical ventilation system. Even the toilets contain a non-water flush technology incorporating with their structural diagonality. After all, a more open and freer environment contributes to a better psychological condition for workers, which helps them achieve a better productivity. In summary, the spineless skyscraper is a "revolutionary work place with an innovative structure"

spinal
BASIC PLAN

spineless

spinal   spineless
HORIZONTAL CIRCULATION

spinal   spineless
INSIDE/OUTSIDE

random floor A   random floor B
PLAN VAIRATION

spinal   spineless
VERTICAL CIRCULATION

floor height X1   floor height X2
SPINELESS VARIATION

spinal   spineless
SILHOUTTE

distributed daylight

cross ventilation

non-hierarchical/free

SPINELESS'S S

L

p

vacum pump

non-water flush technology along with their structural "diagonality", as a more open environment contributes to a better psychological condition for workers, helping them achieve better productivity. After all, a more open and free environment contributes to a better psychological condition for workers, which helps them achieve better productivity. In summary, the Spineless Skyscraper is a revolutionary work place with an innovative structure.

0925

T(INTERNAL)

power room

bathrooms

fire elevator

t requires no water, using
flush waste down

SKYSCRAPER OF LIBERATION

Yikai Lin
Xiaoliang Lu

United States

DISTRICT 3 - SKYSCRAPER OF LIBERATION

····· 1949 Armistice "Green Line"

DISTRICT 1
▬▬▬ Areas Controlled by Palestinian

DISTRICT 2
▬▬▬ Areas Colonized by Israel

DISTRICT 3
─── Constructed West Bank Barrier
---- Under Construction West Bank Barrier
▬▬▬ Constructed Skyscraper of Liberation
☐ Aricultural Gate & Military Gate
  [Potential Skyscraper of Liberation Site]
○ Checkpoint
  [Potential Skyscraper of Liberation Site]

West Bank

West Jersalem

ISRAEL

Bethlehem

This skyscraper explores the relationship between conflict and border regions. Borders of two politically, religiously, and ethnically different nations are most likely the site of war. Consequently, citizens of these two parts are the major victims of conflicts. Since the era of weapons began, vast walls were used to defend territories. Until now, those immense walls are constructed to isolate conflict between two parts. However, does the construction of walls really reduce the hostility of two separated parts? In contrary, walls obstruct mutual understanding and intensify the discrepancy. The "good" component becomes irresistible and the "bad" part is hopelessness. The wall is a guilty instrument of despair.

In the border of Israel and Palestine, there are three districts: one is the area colonized by Israel, the other is

controlled by Palestine and the third one is hosted by the line/wall itself. This small strip exists in a legal and sovereign limbo—potentially an extra-territorial zone. It is a space of future liberation as the construction of the West Bank barrier isolates Palestinians and Israelis' lives. In this project, instead of a solid wall, the skyscraper is the materialization of the borderline and the transformation of a wall. It is no longer an isolated area, but a shared space. Both Israelis and Palestinians who look forward to peace and cooperation contribute to the area of District 3. It is administered by the United Nations and takes place around military gates and checkpoints. Only non-violent Israelis and Palestinians have right to utilize this district.

The discrepancies of culture mark the different appearances of Israelis and Palestinians. Destroying the opponent's

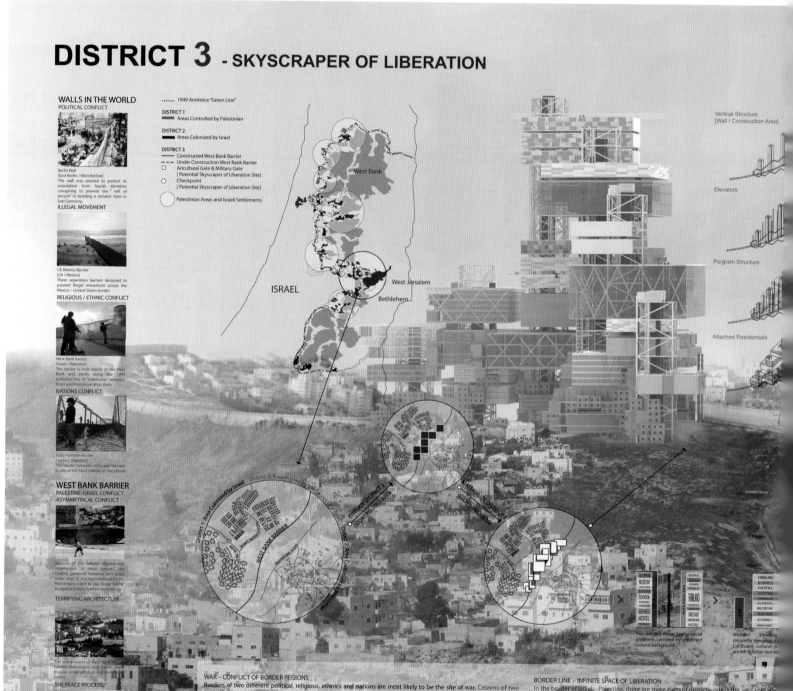

DISTRICT 3 - SKYSCRAPER OF LIBERATION

WALLS IN THE WORLD
POLITICAL CONFLICT

Berlin Wall
[East Berlin / West Berlin]
The wall was erected to protect its population from fascist elements conspiring to prevent the " will of people" in building a socialist state in East Germany.
ILLEGAL MOVEMENT

US-Mexico Border
[US / Mexico]
These separation barriers designed to prevent illegal movement across the Mexico – United States border.
RELIGIOUS / ETHNIC CONFLICT

West Bank barrier
[Israel / Palestine]
The barrier is built mainly in the West Bank and partly along the 1949 Armistice line for "Green Line" between Israel and Palestinian West Bank.
NATIONS CONFLICT

India-Pakistan Border
[India / Pakistan]
The border between India and Pakistan is one of the most volatile on the planet.

WEST BANK BARRIER
PALESTINE-ISRAEL CONFLICT
ASYMMETRICAL CONFLICT

Because of the history, religion and intervention of other nations , the conflict between Palestine and Israel never stop. In this asymmetrical battle, Palestinians resort to use 'body bombs' to against Israel's warfare technology.

TERRIFYING ARCHITECTURE

The construction of West Bank inculcate hostility Palestinians and Israelis from mutual understanding and con...
THE PEACE PROCESS

Palestinian and Israeli citizens are the major victims of this conflict. People are hoping the peace between these two parts could be come true.

········ 1949 Armistice "Green Line"
DISTRICT 1
████ Areas Controlled by Palestinian
DISTRICT 2
████ Areas Colonized by Israel
DISTRICT 3
——— Constructed West Bank Barrier
- - - Under Construction West Bank Barrier
▢ Aricultural Gate & Military Gate
[Potential Skyscraper of Liberation Site]
◯ Checkpoint
[Potential Skyscraper of Liberation Site]
◯ Palestinian Areas and Israeli Settlements

West Bank

ISRAEL

West Jerusalem

Bethlehem

Vertical Structure
[Wall / Construction Area]

Elevators

Porgram Structure

Attached Residentials

WAR – CONFLICT OF BORDER REGIONS
Borders of two different political, religious, ethnics and nations are most likely to be the site of war. Citizens of two parts are the major victims of conflicts. They are willing to have peaceful lives.

WALL – TERRIFYING ARCHITECTURE
Since the era of cold weapons, gigantic walls were used to defend territories. Until now, those immense walls are constructed to isolate conflict between two parts. Such as Berlin Wall between East Berlin and West Berlin, Korean Wall between North Korea and South Korea, US-Mexico Border between US and Mexico, Melilla Border Fence between Morocco and Spanish, Pakistan-Iran wall between Pakistan and Iran, Belfast Peace Line between Catholic and Protestant neighborhoods, West Bank Barrier between Israel and Palestine, Cyprus Wall between Greek Cypriot and Turkish Cypriot and India – Pakistan Border between India and Pakistan. However, the construction of walls really reduces the hostility of two separated parts? To the contrary, Walls obstruct mutual understanding and intensify the discrepancy. The good part becomes irresistible and the bad part is hopelessness. The wall is a "guilty instrument of despair".

BORDER LINE – INFINITE SPACE OF LIBERATION
In the border of Israel – Palestine, there are three parts of districts: one is the area colonize... tine and the third one is hosted by the line/wall itself. This small trip exists in a legal ar... territorial zone. It is a space of liberation. To this project, instead of solid wall, the skyscra... and the transformation of wall. It is no longer an isolated area. It is a share space. The are... and Palestinians who look forward to peace and cooperation. It is administered by the U... Palestinians have right to utilize this district.

CULTURE – ATTRACTION OR DISTRACTION OF CONFLICT
The discrepancies of culture mark the different appearances of Israelis and Palestinians. D... diminution of the enemy's forces. They are inculcated with hostility to alien culture and r... double edged. Complementary differences are capable of shaping a win – win situation wh... The District 3 is as an assembly where Israelis and Palestinians can negotiate, cooperate w...

culture is the strategy of diminution of the enemy's forces. They are inculcated with hostility to alien culture and race. However, the differences of culture are double edged. Complementary differences are capable of shaping a win-win situation, which is able to distract the attention of conflict. District 3 is an assembly where Israelis and Palestinians can negotiate, cooperate with each other, and represent themselves.

0954

BUSINESS
It is as a assembly for Palestinian and Israeli to negotiate and exchange views.

SPORTS STADIUM
Sports is the symbol of peace and friendship.

SCHOOL
The education institudes of Israel is better than Palestine. Many Palestinian attend Israeli school, but their are forced to learn Israel religion. In here, Palestinian and Israeli have equal right to learn knowledge.

FARMERS' MARKET
Agriculture is the main income of Palestine. Olive is the most important crop. Palestine can have a good deal in this market.

MUSEUM
It is the best place to present Palestine and Israel culture and history. It offers both side people to understand and tolerate the differences of each other.

THEATER
Palestine and Israel have their own famous artists performers, but they only perform in their own theaters. In here, both artists can present their art under the same roof.

ZOO
The warfare causes insufficient funds of Palestine zoo. It is a natural education place for young age Palestinian and

Tourism is Israel's main source of foreign exchange income.

Palestinian Area | The district 3 is as an assembly where Israeli and Palestinian can negotiate, cooperate with each other and represent themselves. | Israeli Area

BURJ SANA'A

Benjamin Albrecht
Margaret Hewitt

Germany/United States

01 BURJ / SANA'A
an innovative community of mud and water

SITE

Sana'a is a city that is undergoing extreme transformation- It is the third fasts growing city in the world. In current day the population of Sana'a has reached over two million people giving it the title mega-city as well as historic city. The population and development is happening at such a fast pace that is has become quite uncontrolled and unplanned. This factor is creating much concern for the cities inhabitants as well as anyone who knows the history and culture of Sana'a. The strong presence of Islamic faith in the city also drove it to have an interesting architectural feel, with 103 mosques, 14 hammams and over 6000 houses built before the 11th century. The spatial characteristics of the Sana'a create an experience totally unique to any other city. As a result a keen sense as to how people and water move through the structure is the focus - creating complex spatial transitions and overlaps between the structure and the modular elements.

URBANIZATION

The sudden globalization/urbanization in certain areas of the city can be witnessed visually and experientially through the lack open public spaces and the new developments. This accelerated growth is eroding at the city's character. Since the city is located in a valley, geographically horizontal growth [sprawl] is not possible. Instead of developing in the horizontal or vertical dimension strictly this project proposes a basis for growth through the development in a third dimension [both horizontal and vertical] floating above the city. The project introduces a new layer/element to the city, one of extreme height and large scale. In Sana'a one of the greatest traditions is the mud house- a structure built up from densely packed earth, adorned with geometric shapes on the exterior surface. But the maximum height for the mud house is limited, and does not allow for much growth in the vertical direction.

PROPOSAL

Therefore the proposal is not something occurring on the inhabited ground level of the city - it is removed from the city below through its height providing another level to the city much higher than the existing. Sana'a's is already one of the highest capitals in the world, sitting at an altitude of 7500 feet, this new structural tower will provide not only a new way of developing the city vertically, but will provide a new lens on which to view the city, from above.

PROGRAM

The design revolves around four programmatic elements; residential, markets, public space [gardens], and water filtration plant. The proposed infrastructural towers will occur at the main arteries surrounding the city, freeway intersections. The towers consist of a lightweight structure devised from a three dimensional grid serving as the starting point for the overall design of the primary structural wall. From here the secondary structure grows out morphing and deforming itself due to the insertion of the pod [partially enclosed areas for gardens/ public space]. The three main vertical towers function as an elevator for transporting clean water for community [mud house] building as well as human consumption. The pods serve as the main programmed elements while the rest of the infrastructure is open for development to happen as needed.

FUTURE

In time a network of these filtering towers can be created around the city, existing simultaneously in different locations yet connected visually and programmatically. The formal aesthetics will vary with each tower due to its location. The construction of the towers could change over time with the introduction of new technologies and materials, while the mud houses construction will remain, creating a contrast of past and present.

A new development model is introduced to the city.

Sana'a, Yemen is the third fastest growing city in the world. The population and development is growing at such a fast pace that it has become quite uncontrolled and unplanned. This factor is creating much concern for the city's inhabitants as well as anyone who knows the history and culture of Sana'a. The strong presence of Islamic faith in the city also drove it to feature an interesting architectural feel. As a result, a keen sense as to how people and water move through this tower is the focus; creating complex spatial transitions and overlaps between the structure and the modular elements are important.

The sudden globalization in certain areas of the city can be witnessed visually and experientially through the lack of open public spaces and the new developments. This accelerated growth is eroding at the city's character. Since the

city is located in a valley, geographically horizontal growth sprawl is not possible. Instead of strictly developing in the horizontal or vertical dimension, this project proposes a basis for growth through the development in a third dimension, floating above the city. The project introduces a new element to the city, one of extreme height and large scale.

The proposal is not something occurring on the inhabited ground level of the city—it is removed from the city below through its height providing another level to the city much higher than the existing. The design revolves around four programmatic elements: residential, markets, public space (gardens), and water filtration plant. The proposed infrastructural towers will occur at the main arteries surrounding the city, freeway intersections. The towers consist of a lightweight structure devised from a three dimensional grid serving as the starting point for the overall design of the

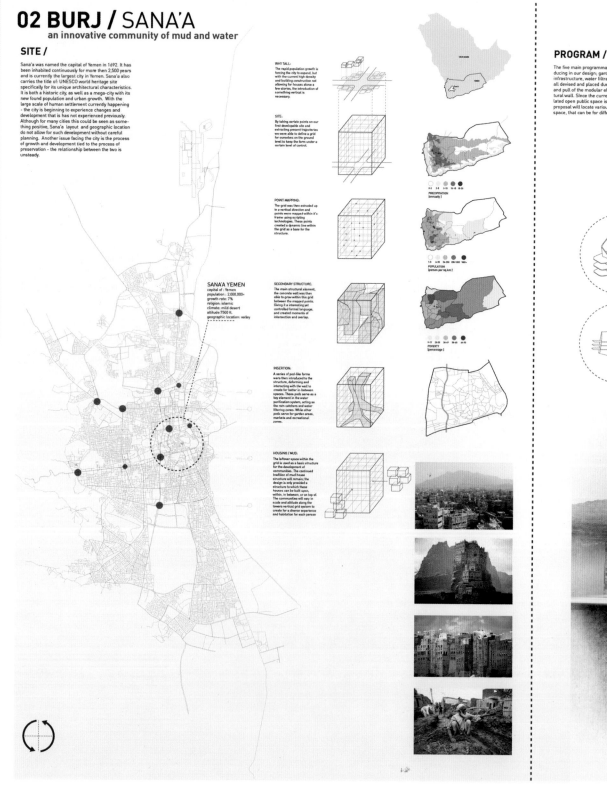

02 BURJ / SANA'A
an innovative community of mud and water

SITE /

Sana'a was named the capital of Yemen in 1692. It has been inhabited continuously for more then 2,500 years and is currently the largest city in Yemen. Sana'a also carries the title of: UNESCO world heritage site specifically for its unique architectural characteristics. It is both a historic city, as well as a mega-city with its new found population and urban growth. With the large scale of human settlement currently happening - the city is beginning to experience changes and development that is has not experienced previously. Although for many cities this could be seen as something positive, Sana'a layout and geographic location do not allow for such development without careful planning. Another issue facing the city is the process of growth and development tied to the process of preservation - the relationship between the two is unsteady.

SANA'A YEMEN
capital of : Yemen
population : 2,000,000+
growth rate: 7%
religion: islamic
climate: mild desert
altitude: 7500 ft.
geographic location: valley

WHY TALL:
The rapid population growth is forcing the city to expand, but with the current high density and building construction not allowing for houses above a few stories, the introduction of something vertical is necessary.

SITE:
By taking certain points on our first developable site and extracting present trajectories we were able to define a grid for ourselves on the ground level to keep the form under a certain level of control.

POINT MAPPING:
The grid was then extruded up in a vertical direction and points were mapped within it's frame using scripting technologies. These points created a dynamic line within the grid as a base for the structure.

SECONDARY STRUCTURE:
The main structural element, the concrete wall was then able to grow within this grid between the mapped points. Giving it a interesting yet controlled formal language, and created moments of intersection and overlap.

INSERTION:
A series of pod-like forms were then introduced to the structure, deforming and interacting with the wall to create for better in-between spaces. These pods serve as a key element in the water purification system, acting as the rain catchers and water filtering zones. While other pods serve for garden areas, markets and recreational zones.

HOUSING / MUD:
The leftover space within the grid is used as a basic structure for the development of communities. The continued tradition of mud house structure will remain; the design is only provided a structure to which these houses can be built upon within, in between, or on top of. The communities will vary in scale and altitude along the towers vertical grid system to create for a diverse experience and habitation for each person.

PRECIPITATION (annually)

POPULATION (person per sq.km)

POVERTY (percentage)

PROGRAM /

The five main programmatic elements we are introducing in our design; gardens, public space, housing infrastructure, water filtration, and market space are all devised and placed due to the insertion and push and pull of the modular elements against the structural wall. Since the current city is so densely populated open public space is not found often - the proposal will locate various zones for open public space, that can be for different recreational uses.

03

04

primary structural wall. From here the secondary structure grows out morphing and deforming itself due to the insertion of the pod (partially enclosed areas for gardens/ public space). The three main vertical towers function as an elevator for transporting clean water for the community (mud house) building as well as human consumption. The pods serve as the main programmed elements while the rest of the infrastructure is open for development to happen as needed.

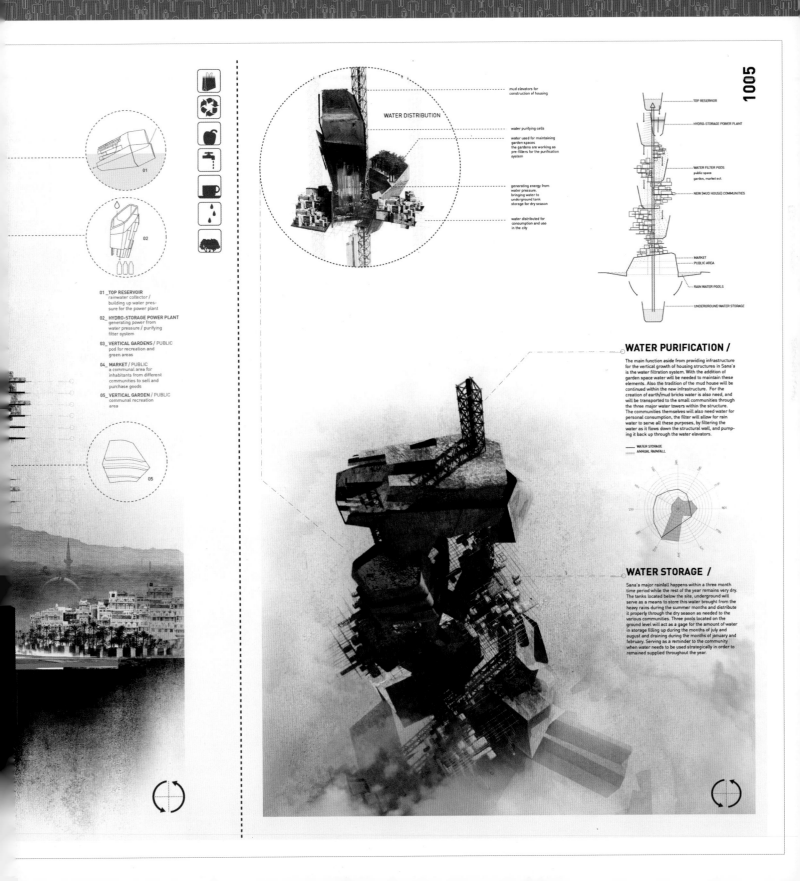

01 _TOP RESERVOIR /
rainwater collector /
building up water pres-
sure for the power plant

02 _HYDRO-STORAGE POWER PLANT /
generating power from
water pressure / purifying
filter system

03 _VERTICAL GARDENS / PUBLIC
pod for recreation and
green areas

04 _MARKET / PUBLIC
a communal area for
inhabitants from different
communities to sell and
purchase goods

05 _VERTICAL GARDEN / PUBLIC
communal recreation
area

1005

WATER DISTRIBUTION

mud elevators for
construction of housing

water purifying cells

water used for maintaining
garden spaces
the gardens are working as
pre-filters for the purification
system

generating energy from
water pressure,
bringing water to
underground tank
storage for dry season

water distributed for
consumption and use
in the city

TOP RESERVOIR

HYDRO-STORAGE POWER PLANT

WATER FILTER PODS
public space
garden, market ect.

NEW (MUD HOUSE) COMMUNITIES

MARKET
PUBLIC AREA

RAIN WATER POOLS

UNDERGROUND WATER STORAGE

WATER PURIFICATION /

The main function aside from providing infrastructure
for the vertical growth of housing structures in Sana'a
is the water filtration system. With the addition of
garden space water will be needed to maintain these
elements. Also the tradition of the mud house will be
continued within the new infrastructure. For the
creation of earth/mud bricks water is also need, and
will be transported to the small communities through
the three major water towers within the structure.
The communities themselves will also need water for
personal consumption, the filter will allow for rain
water to serve all these purposes, by filtering the
water as it flows down the structural wall, and pumping it back up through the water elevators.

WATER STORAGE
ANNUAL RAINFALL

WATER STORAGE /

Sana'a major rainfall happens within a three month
time period while the rest of the year remains very dry.
The tanks located below the site, underground will
serve as a means to store this water brought from the
heavy rains during the summer months and distribute
it properly through the dry season as needed to the
various communities. Three pools located on the
ground level will act as a gage for the amount of water
in storage filling up during the months of july and
august and draining during the months of january and
february. Serving as a reminder to the community
when water needs to be used strategically in order to
remained supplied throughout the year.

HUTONG MANIFESTO

Sara Bernardi
Riccardo Ferrari

Italy

SIHEYUAN
THE TRADITIONAL CHINESE COURTYARD HOUSE

CONTINUOS CLUSTERS OF SIHEYUAN
DEFINE THE HUTONGS URBAN TISSUE

HUTONG MANIFESTO RISE DIAGRAM

SIHEYUAN - COURTYARD HOUSE
SCHEMATIC PLAN

THE HUTONGS URBAN TISSUE

The Hutong Manifesto was designed to focus the world's attention to the cultural, architectural and social loss of the traditional old Beijing Hutong's neighborhood and challenge the fast urbanization and the recent city growth process.

The old city of Beijing was shaped on the Ancient typology of *Siheyuan*, the traditional Chinese Courtyard House; a continuous cluster of *Siheyuans* defined the unique urban tissue of the old Hutong neighborhood. The city landscape was shaped by this peculiar "urban fabric," in which the uniqueness of the spatial organization reflects the social and cultural roots of the inhabitants. This strong community life grown around the courtyards and the rows of common spaces led to a distinctive micro-urbanism, which could still be seen if Hutong areas remained untouched.

The spaces of *Siheyuan* have proven very adaptable to changes during different periods of history. Since

HUTONG MANIFESTO

1021

Hutong Manifesto aim to focus the world's attention to the cultural, architectural and social loss of the traditional old Beijing Hutong's neighborhood.

Hutong Manifesto aim to issue a challenge to the fast urbanization and the recent city growth process.

Hutong Manifesto imagines to encroach on the contemporary city field, and by filling the gaps of the modern Beijing Business District, to force the new city Icons to an exchange reaction with the old cultural and social heritage references.
Hutong Manifesto imagines to spread on the CBD area the rich and unique Hutong's urban tissue, but the challenge of this new peculiar "Hutong's microurbanism" goes even further in challenging the contemporary city vertically, in an attempt to launch his message to the entire city.

The Hutong's urban tissue spread out, and his impetus towards the sky is not a desire for revenge against the new city Icons, instead is a Manifesto of the richness and the uniqueness of the chinese cultural heritage that could still be saved from destruction.

Hutong Manifesto will stand above the tallest tower of Beijing to let people see from the bottom the ancient shape of the city, and to let people climb up to be able to see in-between the contemporary urban growth, the ancient urban singns.

THE VIEW POINTS TO THE CITY ARE SHAPED TO SHOW THE HERITAGE'S LOSS

AND THE URGENT NEED TO SAVE THE UNIQUE HUTONG'S NEIGHBORHOOD

HOUSE TO THE NEW HUTONG' URBAN TISSUE TILL THE RISE TO THE SKY

THE VERTICAL GLASS SPINE AND THE VIEW POINTS SYSTEM

HUTONG MANIFESTO TOWER 500 M
THE TOWER'S RISE TO THE SKY
WILL NOT STOP UNTIL THE HUTONG'S
CUTURAL HERITAGE WILL NOT BE SAVED

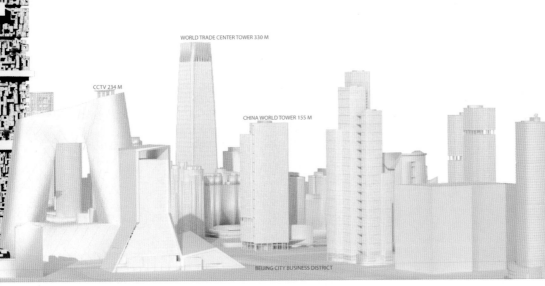

WORLD TRADE CENTER TOWER 330 M

CCTV 234 M

CHINA WORLD TOWER 155 M

BEIJING CITY BUSINESS DISTRICT

BEIJING SKYLINE

THE HUTONG'S URBAN TISSUE

1949, following the strategy of redistribution of dwellings, spaces that were originally occupied by one family were assigned to several nuclei. The wooden frame structure and the brick partitions, through simple rearrangements and constructions of new rooms, made it possible to adapt the buildings to a new lifestyle. That is the reason for the current denser and apparently "irregular" Hutong layout.

Many of Beijing's Hutong neighborhoods have been recently destroyed by the rapid urbanization, forcing the urban scale to a drastic increase. But what has been destroyed together with the urban layout is the strong relation and equilibrium between social and physical aspects of the urban environment, the relation between people and their habitat. For that reason Hutong Manifesto is not trying to replicate an ancient architectural typology, but is willing to

THE HUTONG'S URBAN TISSUE

bring back the identity of the city, and to preserve the special social and cultural environment that is still alive in this distinctive "micro-urbanism" typology.

The project would spread on the CBD area, the rich, unique Hutong urban tissue, but this new peculiar "Hutong micro-urbanism" goes even further to challenge the contemporary city vertically, in an attempt to launch the message to the entire city. The Hutong Manifesto will stand above the tallest tower of Beijing to let people see from the bottom the ancient shape of the city and to let people climb up to be able to see through the contemporary urban growth the ancient urban signs needed to be preserved.

HUTONG MANIFESTO 1021

VIEW POINTS TO THE CITY

FORBIDDEN CITY

HUTONG MANIFESTO SITE
BEIJING CBD

SECOND RING ROAD

THIRD RING ROAD

BEIJING CITY DIAGRAM

BEIJING CITY BUSINESS DISTRICT

CCTV 234 M

HUTONG MANIFESTO TOWER 500 M

WORLD TRADE CENTER TOWER 330 M

CHINA WORLD TOWER 155 M

HUTONGS TISSUE SPREAD

THIRD RING ROAD

PARK HYATT TOWER

THE NEW HUTONGS TISSUE SPREAD

HUTONG MANIFESTO MASTERPLAN

REHAB TOWER

Katsuya Arai
Akiko Suzuki

United States

ReHAB Tower
Rethinking Urban Structure

ReHAB Tower removes the urban environment from the surface of the earth, allowing the natural systems of the earth to replenish and rehabilitate itself.

GLOBAL ISSUE:

Approximately 3% of the earth's land mass is occupied by urban landscape. However small this proportion is, it is this 3% that consumes 3/4 of the world's energy, emits 3/4 of all green house gas emissions in the world, and consumes over half of the earth's fresh water supply. Today, about half of the human race lives in cities, and it is projected that by 2050, about 70% of the world's population will reside in urban areas. At the same time, population growth is occurring at an accumulating rate, and there is expected to be an increase in the world's population by about two billion between 2012 and 2050. This demonstrates the urgent need to reevaluate the urban situation, as the imbalance of supply and demand grows in severity.

It is apparent that humans are misusing the environment and the limited resources that exist. For instance, this can be read from the recent trends in global warming and climate change. According to the earth's surface temperature analysis conducted by NASA, There has been a large increase in the annual mean temperature of the world since the late 1900s. Human productivity is threatening natural ecosystems, inducing anomalies in climate and increasing the severity of natural catastrophes. Perhaps by reconsidering the 3% that cities occupy, there could be a way that the natural systems may recover and rehabilitate the earth.

CURRENT URBAN CONDITION:

The chosen site is New York City for being the densest urban environment in the United States and for being the symbol of commerce and power throughout the world. New York City sets the standard for progress. By today's standards, Manhattan is dense, but from another perspective, Manhattan is sprawl which has entirely replaced the natural systems of the island. ReHAB Tower on the island of Manhattan creates a provocative vision of a new urban life, and has the potential of being the initiator for change.

PROPOSAL:

ReHAB Tower erects horizontal urban life into a vertical organization. This configuration reduces the physical footprint on the earth, minimizing the amount of exposed hard surfaces, runoff, and pollution. Currently, 30% of energy needs are dedicated to transportation. By condensing all functions and programs of the city into a vertical orientation, these energy requirements may be minimized.

In this proposal, the core tower houses vegetation and agriculture, feeding into the residential shell that spirals around it. The main city functions, such as commerce and industry, are located below ground, at the base of the tower. Transportation to areas beyond the city also happens below ground, hidden from visibility. The expanse of land which used to be occupied by a sprawling city will be restored to naturally governed landscape. By removing city activity from the exposed surface, the earth may rehabilitate itself, replenishing its resources, and once again be maintained by the natural laws of the ecosystem.

This is ReHAB Tower.

Current urban expansion trend

- ⬛ urban footprint
- ⬚ peripheral urban influence
- 🌱 vegetation

Population (billions)

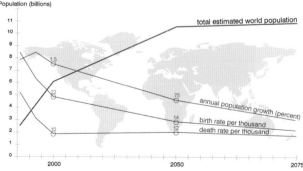

total estimated world population

annual population growth (percent)

birth rate per thousand
death rate per thousand

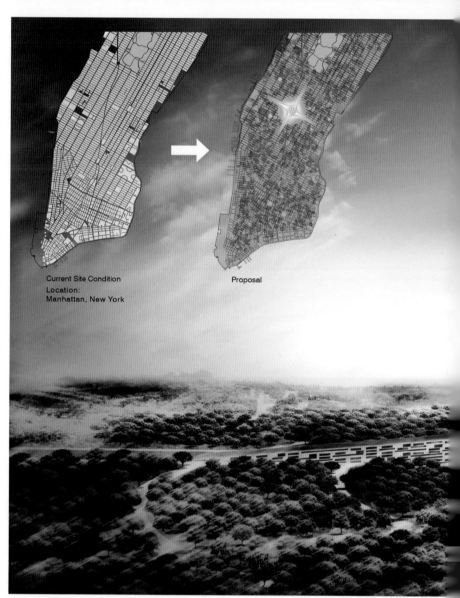

Current Site Condition
Location:
Manhattan, New York

Proposal

CONCEPT:

Through urbanization, hardscape has become the dominating surface material. ReHAB Tower inverts this scenario, restoring the vegetative landscape on the earth's surface and relocating what is man-made underneath it.

Current city condition

FLIP

Proposal

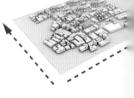

Current residential conditio

Approximately 3% of the earth's land mass is occupied by urban landscape. However small this proportion is, it is this 3% that consumes 3/4 of the world's energy, emits 3/4 of all green house gas emissions in the world, and consumes over half of the earth's fresh water supply. Today, about half of the human race lives in cities. It is projected that by 2050, about 70% of the people will reside in urban areas. By reconsidering the 3% that cities occupy, there could be a way that natural systems may recover and rehabilitate the earth.

The chosen site is New York City for being the densest urban environment in the United States and for being the symbol of commerce and power throughout the world. New York City sets the standard for

1084

Plan drawing

Agriculture

Residential

Proposal: vertical housing/agriculture

Front elevation

Section Perspective

progress. By today's standards, Manhattan is dense, but from another perspective, Manhattan is sprawl, which has entirely replaced the natural systems of the island. This tower located in Manhattan creates a provocative vision of a new urban life, and has the potential of being the initiator for change.

The tower erects horizontal urban life into a vertical organization. This configuration reduces the physical footprint on the earth, minimizing the amount of exposed hard surfaces, runoff, and pollution. Currently, 30% of energy needs are dedicated to transportation. By condensing all functions and programs of the city into a vertical orientation, these energy requirements may be minimized.

ReHAB Tower
Rethinking Urban Structure

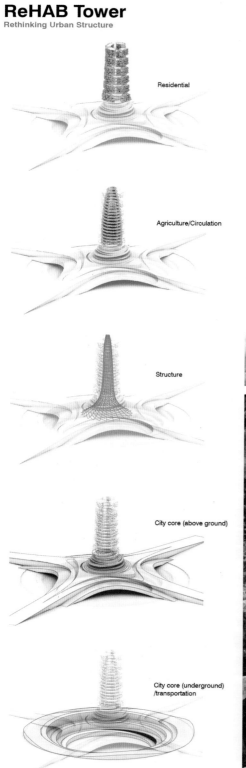

Residential

Agriculture/Circulation

Structure

City core (above ground)

City core (underground)
/transportation

In this proposal, the core tower houses agriculture, feeding into the residential shell that spirals around it. The main city functions, such as commerce, are located below ground, at the base of the tower. Transportation to areas beyond the city also happens below ground, hidden from visibility. The expanse of land that used to be occupied by a sprawling city will be restored to naturally governed landscape. Through urbanization, hardscape has become the dominating surface material. ReHAB Tower inverts this scenario, restoring the vegetative landscape on the earth's surface and relocating what is man-made underneath it. By removing city activity from the exposed surface, the earth may rehabilitate itself, replenishing its resources.

1084

City core:
All the city functions (transportation, commericial district, business district) are embedded under the structure to maximize the green and agricultural space.

Residential / Agriculture

Agriculture/ City core

City core

City core

Train station

SYMBIOCITY

Khem Aikwanich
Nigel Westbrook

Australia/Thailand

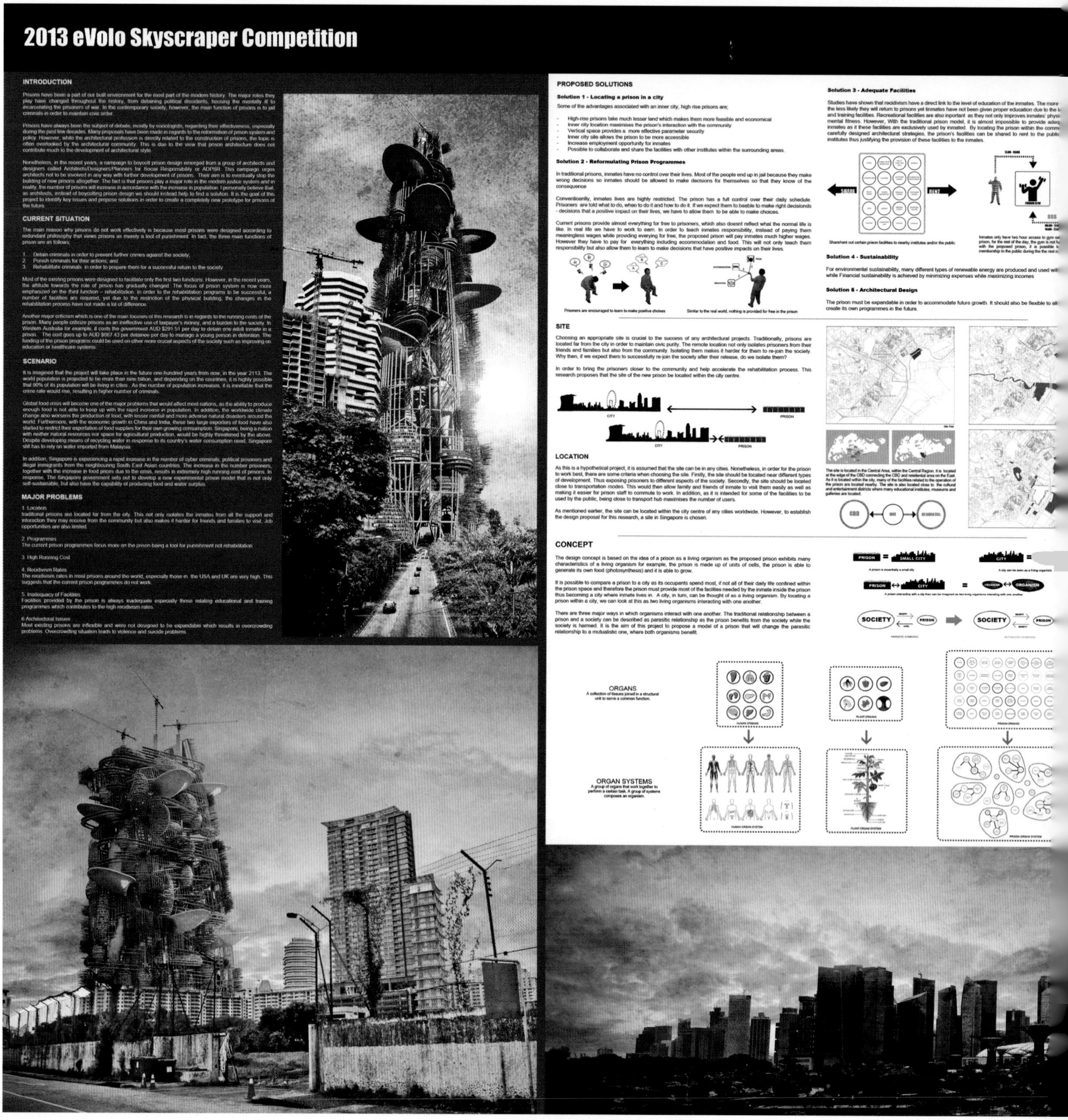

2013 eVolo Skyscraper Competition

INTRODUCTION

Prisons have been a part of our built environment for the most part of the modern history. The major roles they play have changed throughout the history, from detaining political dissidents, housing the mentally ill to incarcerating the prisoners of war. In the contemporary society, however, the main function of prisons is to jail criminals in order to maintain civic order.

Prisons have always been the subject of debate, mostly by sociologists, regarding their effectiveness, especially during the past few decades. Many proposals have been made in regards to the reformation of prison system and policy. However, while the architectural profession is directly related to the construction of prisons, the topic is often overlooked by the architectural community. This is due to the view that prison architecture does not contribute much to the development of architectural style.

Nonetheless, in the recent years, a campaign to boycott prison design emerged from a group of architects and designers called Architects/Designers/Planners for Social Responsibility or ADPSR. This campaign urges architects not to be involved in any way with further development of prisons. Their aim is to eventually stop the building of new prisons altogether. The fact is that prisons play a major role in the modern justice system and in reality, the number of prisons will increase in accordance with the increase in population. I personally believe that, as architects, instead of boycotting prison design we should instead help to find a solution. It is the goal of this project to identify key issues and propose solutions in order to create a completely new prototype for prisons of the future.

CURRENT SITUATION

The main reason why prisons do not work effectively is because most prisons were designed according to redundant philosophy that views prisons as merely a tool of punishment. In fact, the three main functions of prison are as follows;

1. Detain criminals in order to prevent further crimes against the society;
2. Punish criminals for their actions; and
3. Rehabilitate criminals in order to prepare them for a successful return to the society

Most of the existing prisons were designed to facilitate only the first two functions. However, in the recent years, the attitude towards the role of prison has gradually changed. The focus of prison system is now more emphasized on the third function – rehabilitation. In order to the rehabilitation programs to be successful, a number of facilities are required, yet due to the restriction of the physical building, the changes in the rehabilitation process have not made a lot of difference.

Another major criticism which is one of the main focuses of this research is in regards to the running costs of the prison. Many people criticize prisons as an ineffective use of taxpayer's money, and a burden to the society. In Western Australia for example, it costs the government AUD $291.51 per day to detain one adult inmate in a prison. The cost goes up to AUD $867.43 per detainee per day to manage a young person in detention. The funding of the prison programs could be used on other more crucial aspects of the society such as improving on education or healthcare systems.

SCENARIO

It is imagined that the project will take place in the future one-hundred years from now, in the year 2113. The world population is projected to be more than nine billion, and depending on the countries, it is highly possible that 90% of its population will be living in cities. As the number of population increases, it is inevitable that the crime rate would rise, resulting in higher number of criminals.

Global food crisis will become one of the major problems that would affect most nations, as the ability to produce enough food is not able to keep up with the rapid increase in population. In addition, the worldwide climate change also worsens the production of food, with lesser rainfall and more adverse natural disasters around the world. Furthermore, with the economic growth in China and India, these two large exporters of food have also started to restrict their exportation of food supplies for their own growing consumption. Singapore, being a nation with neither natural resources nor space for agricultural production, would be highly threatened by the above. Despite developing means of recycling water in response to its country's water consumption need, Singapore still has to rely on water imported from Malaysia.

In addition, Singapore is experiencing a rapid increase in the number of cyber criminals, political prisoners and illegal immigrants from the neighbouring South East Asian countries. The increase in the number prisoners, together with the increase in food plays due to the crisis, results in extremely high running cost of prisons. In response, the Singapore government sets out to develop a new experimental prison model that is not only self-sustainable, but also have the capability of producing food and water surplus.

MAJOR PROBLEMS

1. Location
traditional prisons are located far from the city. This not only isolates the inmates from all the support and interaction they may receive from the community but also makes it harder for friends and families to visit. Job opportunities are also limited.

2. Programmes
The current prison programmes focus more on the prison being a tool for punishment not rehabilitation.

3. High Running Cost

4. Recidivism Rates
The recidivism rates in most prisons around the world, especially those in the USA and UK are very high. This suggests that the current prison programmes do not work.

5. Inadequacy of Facilities
Facilities provided by the prison is always inadequate especially those relating educational and training programmes which contributes to the high recidivism rates.

6 Architectural Issues
Most existing prisons are inflexible and were not designed to be expandable which results in overcrowding problems. Overcrowding situation leads to violence and suicide problems.

PROPOSED SOLUTIONS

Solution 1 - Locating a prison in a city

Some of the advantages associated with an inner city, high rise prisons are;

- High-rise prisons take much lesser land which makes them more feasible and economical
- Inner city location maximises the prison's interaction with the community
- Vertical space provides a more effective parameter security
- Inner city site allows the prison to be more accessible
- Increase employment opportunity for inmates
- Possible to collaborate and share the facilities with other institutes within the surrounding areas.

Solution 2 - Reformulating Prison Programmes

In traditional prisons, inmates have no control over their lives. Most of the people end up in jail because they make wrong decisions so inmates should be allowed to make decisions for themselves so that they know of the consequence

Conventionally, inmates lives are highly restricted. The prison has a full control over their daily schedule. Prisoners are told what to do, when to do it and how to do it. If we expect them to beable to make right decisionds - decisions that a positive impact on their lives, we have to allow them to be able to make choices.

Current prisons provide almost everything free to prisoners, which also doesnt reflect what the normal life is like. In real life we have to work to earn. In order to teach inmates responsibility, instead of paying them meaningless wages while providing everying for free, the proposed prison will pay inmates much higher wages. However they have to pay for everything including accommodation and food. This will not only teach them responsibility but also allow them to learn to make decisions that have positive impacts on their lives.

Prisoners are encouraged to learn to make positive choices | Similar to the real world, nothing is provided for free in the prison

SITE

Choosing an appropriate site is crucial to the success of any architectural projects. Traditionally, prisons are located far from the city in order to maintain civic purity. The remote location not only isolates prisoners from their friends and families but also from the community. Isolating them makes it harder for them to re-join the society. Why then, if we expect them to successfully re-join the society after their release, do we isolate them?

In order to bring the prisoners closer to the community and help accelerate the rehabilitation process. This research proposes that the site of the new prison be located within the city centre.

CITY | PRISON

CITY | PRISON

LOCATION

As this is a hypothetical project, it is assumed that the site can be in any cities. Nonetheless, in order for the prison to work best, there are some criteria when choosing the site. Firstly, the site should be located near different types of development. Thus exposing prisoners to different aspects of the society. Secondly, the site should be located close to transportation modes. This would then allow family and friends of inmate to visit them easily as well as making it easier for prison staff to commute to work. In addition, as it is intended for some of the facilities to be used by the public, being close to transport hub maximises the number of users.

As mentioned earlier, the site can be located within the city centre of any cities worldwide. However, to establish the design proposal for this research, a site in Singapore is chosen.

CBD | SITE | RESIDENTIAL

CONCEPT

The design concept is based on the idea of a prison as a living organism as the proposed prison exhibits many characteristics of a living organism for example, the prison is made up of units of cells, the prison is able to generate its own food (photosynthesis) and it is able to grow.

It is possible to compare a prison to a city as its occupants spend most, if not all of their daily life confined within the prison space and therefore the prison must provide most of the facilities needed by the inmate inside the prison thus becoming a city where inmate lives in. A city, in turn, can be thought of as a living organism. By locating a prison within a city, we can look at this as two living organisms interacting with one another.

There are three major ways in which organisms interact with one another. The traditional relationship between a prison and a society can be described as parasitic relationship as the prison benefits from the society while the society is harmed. It is the aim of this project to propose a model of a prison that will change the parasitic relationship to a mutualistic one, where both organisms benefit.

PRISON = SMALL CITY | CITY =
A prison is essentially a small city | A city can be seen as a living organism

PRISON = CITY | ORGANISM
A prison interacting with a city then can be imagined as two living organisms interacting with one another

SOCIETY → PRISON → SOCIETY ⇄ PRISON
PARASITIC SYMBIOSIS | MUTUALISTIC SYMBIOSIS

ORGANS
A collection of tissues joined in a structural unit to serve a common function.

HUMAN ORGANS | PLANT ORGANS | PRISON ORGANS

ORGAN SYSTEMS
A group of organs that work together to perform a certain task. A group of systems composes an organism.

HUMAN ORGAN SYSTEM | PLANT ORGAN SYSTEM | PRISON ORGAN SYSTEM

Solution 3 - Adequate Facilities

Studies have shown that recidivism have a direct link to the level of education of the inmates. The more educated, the less likely they will return to prisons yet inmates have not been given proper education due to the lack of facilities and training facilities. Recreational facilities are also important as they not only improves inmates' physical and mental fitness. However, With the traditional prison model, it is almost impossible to provide adequate facilities for inmates as if these facilities are exclusively used by inmated. By locating the prison within the community and carefully designed architectural strategies, the prison's facilities can be shared to rent to the public and other institutes thus justifying the provision of these facilities to the inmates.

SHARE | RENT

Inmates only have two hour access to gym each day for the rest of the day, the gym is not for use with the proposed prison, it is possible to rent membership to the public during the the rest of the day.

Solution 4 - Sustainability

For environmental sustainability, many different types of renewable energy are produced and used within the prison while Financial sustainability is achieved by minimizing expenses while maximizing incomes.

Solution 5 - Architectural Design

The prison must be expandable in order to accommodate future growth. It should also be flexible to site create its own programmes in the future.

  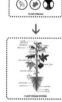

The site is located in the Central Area, within the Central Region. It is located at the edge of the CBD connecting the CBD and residential area on the East. As it is located within the city, many of the facilities related to the operation of the prison are located nearby. The site is also located close to the cultural and entertainment districts where many educational institutes, museums and galleries are located.

Despite the increase in numbers, studies show that the current prison system is not only ineffective, but also unsustainable. The reason why prisons do not work efficiently is because they were designed according to a philosophy that prisons are a tool for punishment. This project aims to focus more on their rehabilitative role.

Symbiocity is a proposal for prisons, to transform the parasitic symbiosis that exists between a traditional prison and a community, where the community is harmed while the prison is benefitted, into mutualistic symbiosis, where both the community and prison benefit one another. Traditionally, prisons are located far from the city. This not only isolates the inmates from support from the community, but also makes it harder

SYMBIOCITY 0022
AN EXPERIMANTAL PROTOTYPE FOR PRISONS OF THE FUTURE

CIRCULATION

Living organisms of certain complexity develop different networks or systems to carry out specific tasks. Plants have networks of Xylem and Phloem to transport different types of nutrients. In human, circulatory system supply oxygen rich blood throughout the body while channelling oxygen depleted blood back to the lung. The circulatory system circulate these two different blood types to all organs within the body without mixing them up. As the prison is used by the public as well as by inmates, there is a need to separate both user groups physically while maintaining visual contact. A circulation model based on different networks in a body is used to control different group of users.

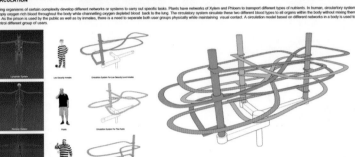

ACCESS AND SECURITY

Each circulation system pass through different buildings to provide access to specific groups of users at specific time. This increases the level of control and security thus allowing many different user groups to share the same facilities effectively. The circulation systems also provide full visual connection while restricting physical contact. Technology such as biometric management system where microchip imbeded in the prisoners' bodies determine whether or not they have an access to the specific buildings increase the efficiency while reducing labor cost.

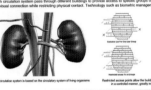

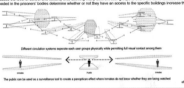

STRUCTURE

As the concept of the prison is based on the idea of a prison as a living organism, the structural system is also inspired by structure of living organisms. The structural system of the prison represents the skeletal system and the body the structure of organs. As it is one of the aims of the project to allow the prison to be flexible and expandable, some form of modular system is required.

Voronoi structure is a form of structural optimization based on Voronoi diagram which is a mathematical tessellation method. The voronoi diagram can be found in many areas of in the field of science and technology. Recently, it has also been explored in the architectural field as a experimental structural system.

The voronoi structure allows the building to expand organically into any shapes as the structural system is free from the restriction of the conventional post and beam structure. It also allows higher level of flexibility in terms of interior planning.

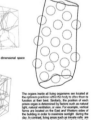

The Shape of The Prison

The structure when combined with super strong and light material such as carbon nanotube, offers many possibilities, allow the building to grow into any forms according to the requirement.

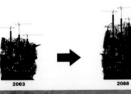

2063 → 2088 → 2113 → 21XX

for friends and families to visit. This project suggests building within the city center to prevent inmates from feeling too isolated and to help them re-join society.

Another problem is regarding sustainability, financially and environmentally. Prisons are not self-sufficient and are seen as a waste of taxes. It has to minimize its expenses while maximizing income. For example, inmates will produce food in vertical farms with livestock. The prison can rent out prison facilities to the public, solving the issue of high recidivism rates as a result of inadequate facilities for inmates. In traditional prisons, facilities are used only by inmates. By locating the prison within a city, it is possible to

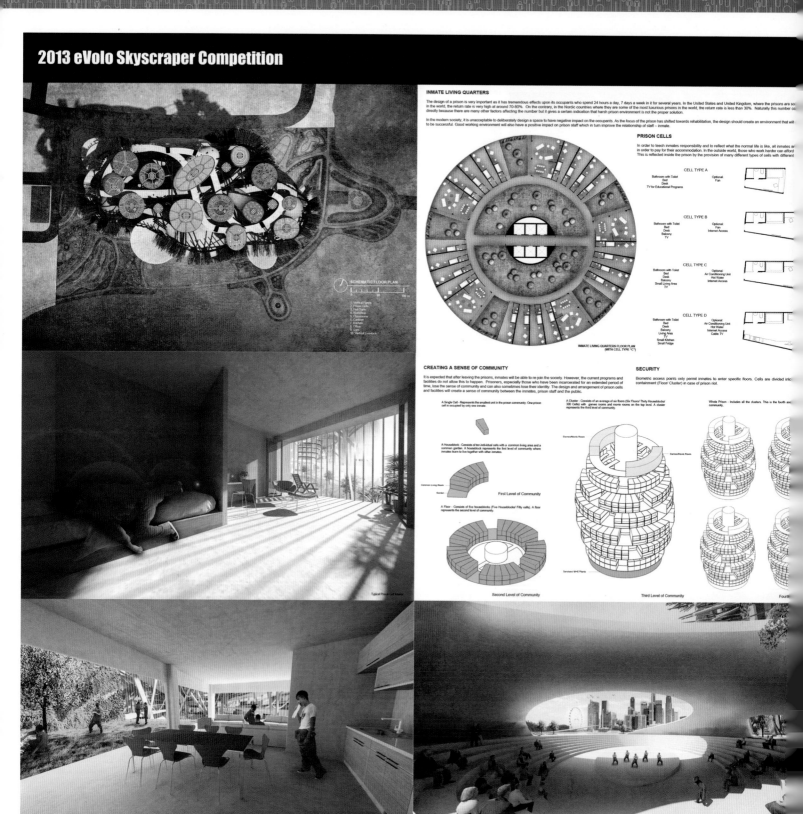

2013 eVolo Skyscraper Competition

rent out facilities thus justifying the provision cost. Inmates are usually allowed no more than two hours of gym access daily and therefore, for the rest of the day, the gym is not utilized. Through carefully designed circulation and security systems, it is possible to sell gym membership to the public to generate income.

As for environmental sustainability, besides harnessing renewable energies such as wind, solar and wave energy, hydroelectric turbines are used to harness gravity water flow within the prison. Also, due to a large number of users, piezoelectric generators are used to generate power by movement of the users. Finally, human waste, livestock waste and raw garbage are used to generate biogas from on-site facilities.

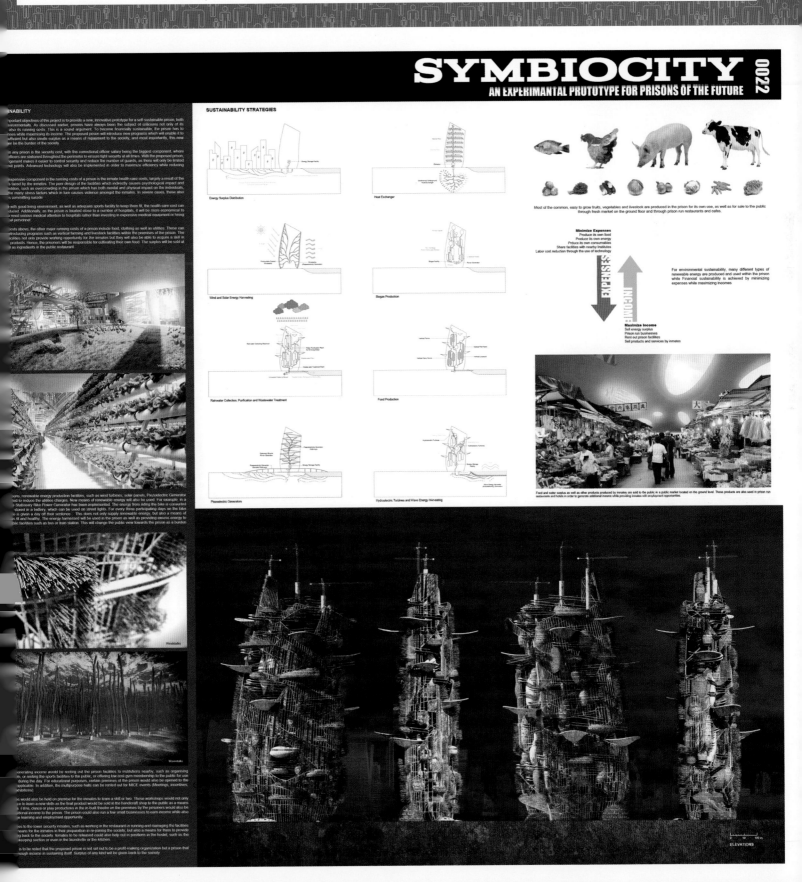

SYMBIOCITY 0022
AN EXPERIMANTAL PRUTUTYPE FOR PRISONS OF THE FUTURE

SUSTAINABILITY STRATEGIES

Energy Surplus Distribution

Heat Exchanger

Wind and Solar Energy Harvesting

Biogas Production

Rainwater Collection, Purification and Wastewater Treatment

Food Production

Piezoelectric Generators

Hydroelectric Turbines and Wave Energy Harvesting

Most of the common, easy to grow fruits, vegetables and livestock are produced in the prison for its own use, as well as for sale to the public through fresh market on the ground floor and through prison run restaurants and cafes.

Minimize Expenses
Produce its own food
Produce its own energy
Produce its own consumables
Share facilities with nearby institutes
Labor cost reduction through the use of technology

For environmental sustainability, many different types of renewable energy are produced and used within the prison while Financial sustainability is achieved by minimizing expenses while maximizing incomes

Maximize Income
Sell energy surplus
Prison run businesses
Rent out prison facilities
Sell products and services by inmates

Food and water surplus as well as other products produced by inmates are sold to the public in a public market located on the ground level. These products are also used in prison run restaurants and hotels in order to generate additional income while providing inmates with employment opportunities.

ELEVATIONS

NEW MAKOKO

Jelte Ten Holt
Shiran Alec Sooriya-Arachchi

Netherlands/
United Arab Emirates

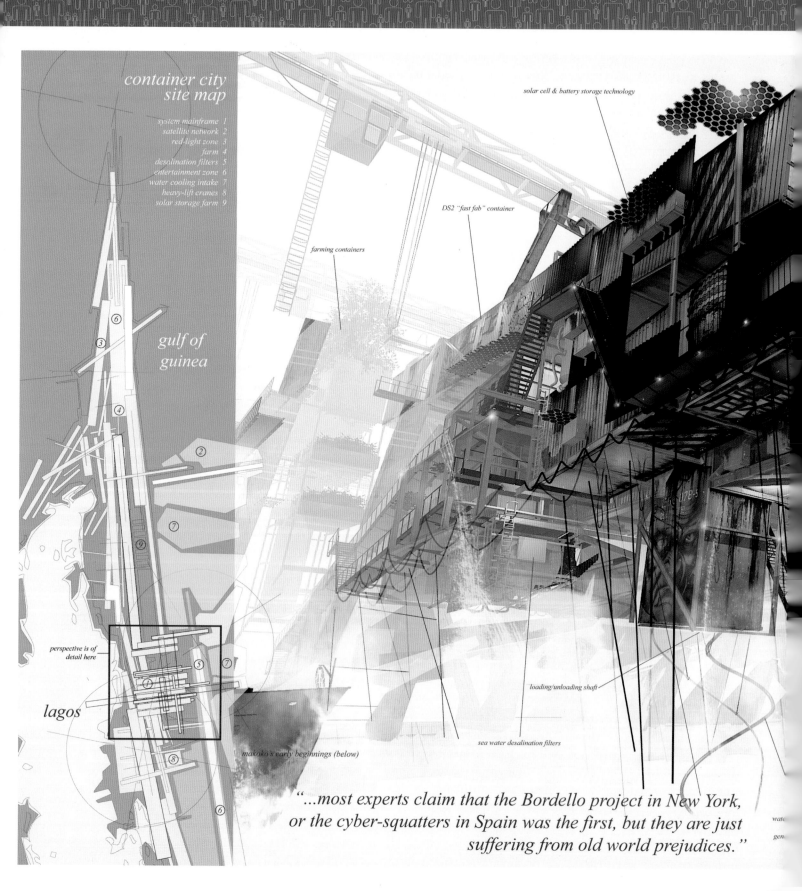

container city
site map

system mainframe 1
satellite network 2
red-light zone 3
farm 4
desalination filters 5
entertainment zone 6
water cooling intake 7
heavy-lift cranes 8
solar storage farm 9

gulf of
guinea

solar cell & battery storage technology

DS2 "fast fab" container

farming containers

perspective is of
detail here

lagos

makoko's early beginnings (below)

loading/unloading shaft

sea water desalination filters

"...most experts claim that the Bordello project in New York,
or the cyber-squatters in Spain was the first, but they are just
suffering from old world prejudices."

This project is located in Makoko, a settlement in the city of Lagos, Nigeria, which is one of the fastest growing cities in the world. According to the project's designers, Makoko is a slum built above an open sewer system (formerly a lagoon) that is made of illegally logged trees, debris and any material residents can find. There are no amenities, schools, or government facilities; "people work hard and die young," the designers say. But they are positive, entrepreneurial, adaptive, and self-reliant, and it is these people who have inspired New Makoko, the Container City.

Though top-down development and urban planning has attempted to get rid of Makoko many times, the slum still thrives. To help the residents safeguard themselves from displacement and also to provide better living conditions for them, the design has created a horizontal skyscraper that holds modular units, allowing it to change according to

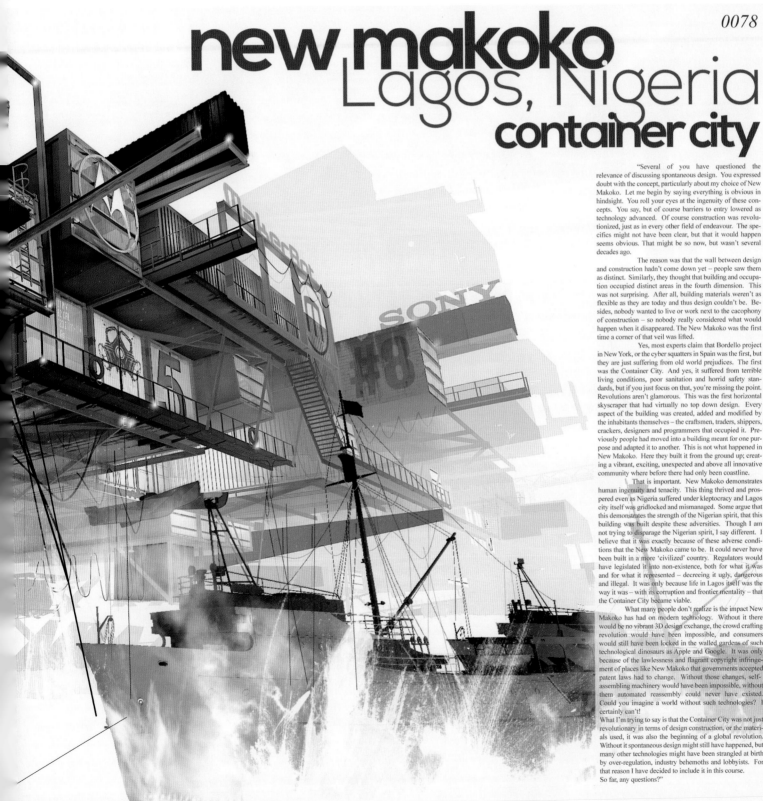

new makoko
Lagos, Nigeria
container city

0078

"Several of you have questioned the relevance of discussing spontaneous design. You expressed doubt with the concept, particularly about my choice of New Makoko. Let me begin by saying everything is obvious in hindsight. You roll your eyes at the ingenuity of these concepts. You say, but of course barriers to entry lowered as technology advanced. Of course construction was revolutionized, just as in every other field of endeavour. The specifics might not have been clear, but that it would happen seems obvious. That might be so now, but wasn't several decades ago.

The reason was that the wall between design and construction hadn't come down yet – people saw them as distinct. Similarly, they thought that building and occupation occupied distinct areas in the fourth dimension. This was not surprising. After all, building materials weren't as flexible as they are today and thus design couldn't be. Besides, nobody wanted to live or work next to the cacophony of construction – so nobody really considered what would happen when it disappeared. The New Makoko was the first time a corner of that veil was lifted.

Yes, most experts claim that Bordello project in New York, or the cyber squatters in Spain was the first, but they are just suffering from old world prejudices. The first was the Container City. And yes, it suffered from terrible living conditions, poor sanitation and horrid safety standards, but if you just focus on that, you're missing the point. Revolutions aren't glamorous. This was the first horizontal skyscraper that had virtually no top down design. Every aspect of the building was created, added and modified by the inhabitants themselves – the craftsmen, traders, shippers, crackers, designers and programmers that occupied it. Previously people had moved into a building meant for one purpose and adapted it to another. This is not what happened in New Makoko. Here they built it from the ground up; creating a vibrant, exciting, unexpected and above all innovative community where before there had only been coastline.

That is important. New Makoko demonstrates human ingenuity and tenacity. This thing thrived and prospered even as Nigeria suffered under kleptocracy and Lagos city itself was gridlocked and mismanaged. Some argue that this demonstrates the strength of the Nigerian spirit, that this building was built despite these adversities. Though I am not trying to disparage the Nigerian spirit, I say different. I believe that it was exactly because of these adverse conditions that the New Makoko came to be. It could never have been built in a more 'civilized' country. Regulators would have legislated it into non-existence, both for what it was and for what it represented – decreeing it ugly, dangerous and illegal. It was only because life in Lagos itself was the way it was – with its corruption and frontier mentality – that the Container City became viable.

What many people don't realize is the impact New Makoko has had on modern technology. Without it there would be no vibrant 3D design exchange, the crowd crafting revolution would have been impossible, and consumers would still have been locked in the walled gardens of such technological dinosaurs as Apple and Google. It was only because of the lawlessness and flagrant copyright infringement of places like New Makoko that governments accepted patent laws had to change. Without those changes, self-assembling machinery would have been impossible, without them automated reassembly could never have existed. Could you imagine a world without such technologies? I certainly can't!

What I'm trying to say is that the Container City was not just revolutionary in terms of design construction, or the materials used, it was also the beginning of a global revolution. Without it spontaneous design might still have happened, but many other technologies might have been strangled at birth by over-regulation, industry behemoths and lobbyists. For that reason I have decided to include it in this course. So far, any questions?"

fluctuating population numbers and economic evolution.

Raised above the sewer system by stilts, New Makoko is a series of stacked, snug container units. Some are residences, others are businesses; everything needed for a functioning society is present within the modules. There are farms, manufacturing centers, entertainment and red light districts, and any other use one could imagine.

Desalination filters are harnessed to the bottom of the development to provide fresh drinking water, and infrastructure to help move the units, such as cranes and loading and unloading shafts, are permanently located to keep the city readily adaptable. Additionally, the units can tap into a network-wide cooling system, and solar cells help provide power throughout the structure.

Gloop tanks:
Manufacturing techniques allow the construction of almost any product from base components (e.g. electronic, food, plant, ceramic). Base components consist of minerals, chemicals, biological and hybrid materials suspended in a nanobot reagent. Anything constructed can be destroyed and recycled at minimal loss of base materials.

Coin system:
The BOSS Inc. mission statement included an 'access for all' clause. To this end coin payment options were also included for those users without smart devices. Using coin payment allowed users to avoid registration of their electronic signatures. Though 97% of individuals had a smart device, only 42% used the smart device payment option.

Installation and Maintenance:
Because early 3D printers were 'dumb' they could not self-assemble, self-replicate or self-maintain. This was problematic, as many printing materials were hazardous to humans. Builders and fixers had to employ hazmat suits. The iconic suits of these 'Hazmen' became part of fashion.

Dumb Printing:
The BOSS DS2 is a 'dumb printer'. Dumb printers manufacture products as is, mistakes and all. Boss Inc. maintains smart printing requires too much processing power. An added - unmentioned - benefit is that dumb printers place responsibility for what is printed with the user, not the manufacturer. In New Makoko nearly all mass produced printers were dumb.

Fast Fab:
Many fast food principles were applied to the early 3D printing container. This included low pricing, quality and overheads, ease of use, market penetration, limited facilities, comfort and vandal resistant furniture, and press-button cleaning. The industry became the 'fast fab' industry, while the verb became 'to fab'.

solar cell & battery storage technology

" Circular manufacturing created the possibility to reuse base m *while 3D printing allowed for a departure from mass production into th* *of individualization and adap*

The designers imagine that New Makoko is the hub of new technological innovations, with containers serving as hosts to manufacturing endeavors such as "gloop tanks," which manufacture products from existing waste, and special 3D printer centers. This industry helps the new society further safeguard itself from top-down destruction as its economic grows and distinguishes itself through the manufacture of unique products.

0078

new makoko
Lagos, Nigeria
the DS2 'fast fab' printing container by Boss Inc.

"Let's discuss why the Container City was the birthplace of all these new technologies. Before New Makoko industry had two big problems. First, it wasn't naturally adaptive; factories were good at making what they were making, but the implementation of innovation required extensive retooling, making it expensive. Second, processes were incredibly wasteful, with the acquisition of a technology's newest incarnation requiring that the previous version be discarded. The result was a mass-produced throwaway society, where the purpose of production was apparently – except for the momentary blip of individual ownership – to fill landfills.

The dual technologies of circular manufacture and 3D printing solved both these problems. Circular manufacturing created the possibility to reuse base materials – consisting of easily transformable molecules suspended in a nanobot reagent – with very limited waste, while 3D printing allowed for a departure from mass production into the realm of individualization and adaptation.

Though these technologies went through several incarnations, they eventually congealed in New Makoko into what we nowadays call 'fast fab' printing kiosks.

Let me be clear, this was hardly the first attempt to install such technology, but due to general resistance previous attempts were stillborn. Unsurprisingly, really, since these technologies were incredibly disruptive. For example, they pushed code online, with designs only turned into a physical product at the point of purchase, thereby undermining shipping; the profits of assembly line manufacture were squeezed, forcing the closing of plants and the laying off of workers; and the ability of individual designers to knock off products made by large conglomerates, and the difficulty of persecuting such loosely connected networks, reduced the profitability of patent-protected innovation.

The reason that fast fab kiosks were built in Nigeria was that the country was the state of its government. Money trumped all regulations and legislation, and 3D printing was profitable. Besides, the largest interest group in Nigeria was a balooning middle class, with a great thirst for western gadgets at non-western prices. Catering to them meant allowing printing kiosks.

A law was adopted whereby any industrial building structure built over the Nigerian coastline & it's economic zone was not subject to Nigerian patent and copyright laws. After that New Makoko grew almost organically into a coast hugging horizontal skyscraper. This law – which turned New Makoko into one of the only places where the 3D design could legally be stored – turned New Makoko into a storehouse of the world's 3D designs, which were offered free of charge to the world at large. Though this might sound altruistic, it wasn't. The designers of New Makoko benefited tremendously, as they used those very designs to manufacture the knock off products that the Nigerian populace so desired.

Of course, eventually through the application of international pressure, the laws surrounding Nigerian patents were reversed. By this time, however, the structure had grown so large in status and size that the constant need to bribe police and suffer the occasional police raid could not undermine it. In this case the decentralization of the building, something previously considered disadvantageous, became advantageous, as it could not be crippled by one single act.

Instead, the building became a victim of its own success. After spending two decades trying to dismantle New Makoko, the international community finally came to accept the Container City and her implications. It became clear that open source design could be profitable, even for the designer, and patent laws were changed to be less restrictive. As the technologically fuelled social upheaval quieted down the world slowly inched towards a more New Makokoian model. New Makoko – which was still cramped, uncomfortable, dangerous and unsanitary – suddenly lost its reason for existence. The designers and crafters moved out of the cramped hotboxes and into a world that now accepted them. Their places within the Container City were taken by less savoury characters. From there it didn't take long for the population to turn against it. The government moved quickly and – 24 years after it was built – the supporting structure was blown up and she became a new habitat for fish. In other words, acceptance managed in a few years, what resistance hadn't managed in two decades. A delicious irony, to be sure, though it did cost us one of the most unique buildings of the 21st century."

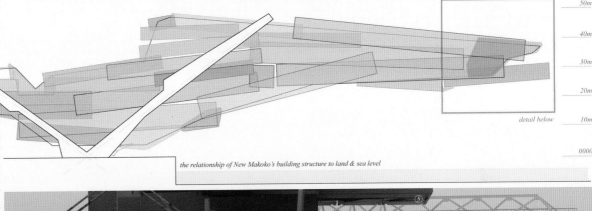

the relationship of New Makoko's building structure to land & sea level

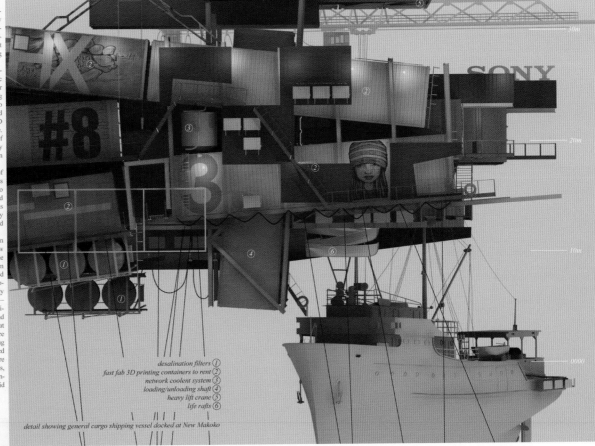

desalination filters ①
fast fab 3D printing containers to rent ②
network coolent system ③
loading/unloading shaft ④
heavy lift crane ⑤
life rafts ⑥

detail showing general cargo shipping vessel docked at New Makoko

ONE HOME FOR ALL THE HOMELESS

Karabaševic Andela
Sudžum Vladislav

Serbia

ONE HOME for all the HOMELESS

This project proposes one massive porous wall-like structure to house all the homeless people on our planet. It spreads continuously through the cities, fields and waters, only facilitating bare living necessities, and significantly increasing life quality in general, and therefore the overall rate of productivity.

If it is human nature to ignore what is difficult to process, this is a way to put the problem of homelessness out in the open. Even if the people are invisible to our eyes, the structure would still remain, and with its monumentality, it would pose as a daily reminder to the ignorant society of the problem it actually resolves.

The concept behind this project is a simple one: This is a project that proposes constructing a single, massive, porous, wall-like structure to house all the homeless people on the planet. This structure is not located in one city; instead, it snakes around the world, providing housing to the millions without it. It would also provide humane living situations to the billions that live without access to basic amenities such as clean water and electricity. Whereas the skyscraper has traditionally been the symbol of wealth, power, and technology, built for the wealthiest members of society, this reinterpretation creates a skyscraper that promotes spreading wealth for the good of all, and making a cared-for populace the new symbol of power and progress.

If it is human nature to ignore what is difficult to process, this is a way to put the problem of homelessness out in

0126

the open. Even if the people are invisible to our eyes, the structure would still remain, and with its monumentality, it would pose as a daily reminder to the ignorant society of the problem it actually resolves.

Cities can afford to have this skyscraper run through their acreage because it is located on a minimal amount of land; instead, the one to two-meter thick wall is tall, taking up airspace. The skyscraper is a wall of infrastructure, a vertical field of voids, that gives the homeless places to sleep, bathe, cook, store their belongings—a permanent home of their own.

The design follows three basic rules. The first is that the whole structure is dimensioned according to a diagram of its future usage that would predetermine it roughly. The second condition reserves the accessibility of the points of

Over 2.6 billion people around the world do not have access to adequate sanitation, while around 100 million have no housing whatsoever. These are all just assumptions, while the real numbers are much worse, and impossible to track. An unimaginable percentage of our society struggles to survive and doesn't even have a remote possibility to experience more of their life, and yet we remain indifferent, presumably secured and untouchable.

A skyscraper is a symbol of a nation's power, wealth and technological progress. It is designed and built for the wealthy leaders. This project proposes an opposite situation. The same progress and wealth is promoted by resolving one of the major problems it has caused to our society. To give part of the sky to the poor.

By diminishing its own flaws, the city becomes even stronger.

Instead of trying to reach the highest point on the sky, one single point!, the cities will compete in areas of their sky they are willing to give up in order to improve their society. This wall would become a new indicator of a city's power. Every city gets a certain length of the wall.

The longer the wall, the greater the city.

/typical floor

the structure to depend only on their users and the way they adapt it for themselves. Lastly, the boundary between the wall and the sky is undefined and in the end is irrelevant. In the beginning it is entirely empty and incomplete.

The raw concrete wall is empty, aside from infrastructure such as water and electricity, and is adaptable according to the desires of its inhabitants. Where and how residents access the upper levels from the floor is up to them to decide and devise; similarly, if they begin to build on its top, and take the structure further into the sky, they can. It is envisioned as a structure that has no horizontal beginning or end, as it circles the globe entirely. Vertically, and in terms of adaptability, the sky is literally the limit.

0126

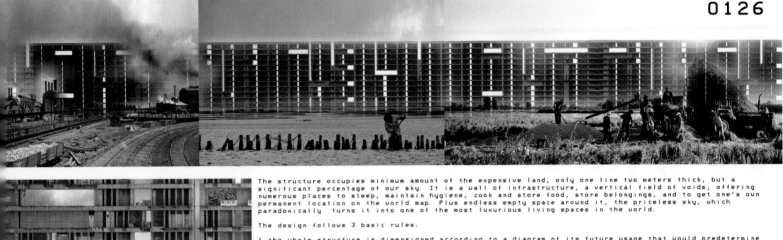

The structure occupies minimum amount of the expensive land, only one line two meters thick, but a significant percentage of our sky. It is a wall of infrastructure, a vertical field of voids, offering numerous places to sleep, maintain hygiene, cook and store food, store belongings, and to get one's own permanent location on the world map. Plus endless empty space around it, the priceless sky, which paradoxically turns it into one of the most luxurious living spaces in the world.

The design follows 3 basic rules:

1 the whole structure is dimensioned according to a diagram of its future usage that would predetermine it roughly,
2 the accessibility of the points of the structure depends only on their users, and the way they adapt it for themselves,
3 the boundary between the wall and the sky is undefined and in the end irrelevant.

In the beginning it is entirely empty and incomplete. Only raw concrete mass and the infrastructure inside it. Than as it is being occupied it starts to form its unique identity, that solely depends on its user.

  /occupying the wall. diagrams/

With no beginning nor the end, people all around the world are gathered into one single structure. Unlike Superstudio's Continuous Monument of 1969, which it was inspired with, it is not about globalization and loss of identity, it is about nourishing millions of identities that have yet to develop.

/section segments/

/diagram of use. segments/

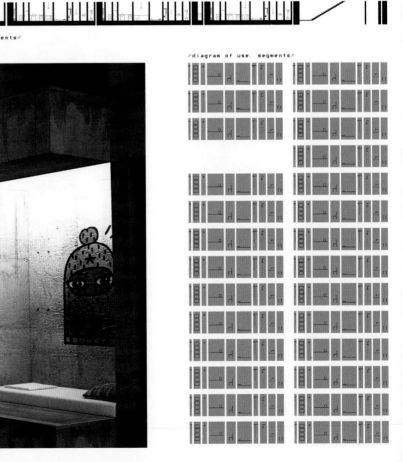

FROM WARFARE TO REBIRTH

Li Siqi
Yang Xin
Nan Yuchuan

China

This project is located in a post-war scenario. Iraq is a country in which the wounds of the war have been deeply carved on its cities, country, land, and people. This post-war effect creates an opportunity to rethink new strategies for how deeply destroyed a country such as Iraq can recover its economy, infrastructure, and city life.

Iraq has a considerable amount of abandoned armored vehicles and ammunition as result of the war, with great potential to provide adequate steel for quite a few temporary housing complexes. At the same time the ammunition waste left behind such as bombs contain enough energy to support the operation of construction machinery. The project goal its to transfer energy and material of wartime into the supplier for reconstruction. Therefore it will utilize the energy of abandoned ammunition to generate electricity, and use the armored vehicles as sources of building

m WARFARE to REBIRTH

ental resource regenerator in Iraq

0242

CASE

On December 14th 2011, U.S. President Barack Obama announced the end of the war in Iraq. U.S. army began to withdraw its troops, but the wounds of the war have been deeply carved on this land. With cities gravely destroyed and numerous population losing their home or even lives, Iraq is in desperate need of infrastructure to recover its life and production. However, the war has consumed massive resources and blown up numerous power stations, leaving a severe deficiency in both energy and material, which has tied the reconstruction to an impasse.

HOMELESS CHILD | ARMOR AND WEAPON | SCARS OF THE IRAQ

WAR energy- RECONSTRUCTION energy

The war has left within Iraq considerable amount of armored vehicles and ammunition.
The energy stored in a bomb may support the operation of certain machine for hours. The armor of a tank is potential to provide adequate steel for several temporary houses. We hope to transfer such energy and material in wartime into the supplier for reconstruction.
Therefore we try to utilize the energy of ammunition to generate electricity, and use the armored vehicles as sources of building materials needed for reconstruction.

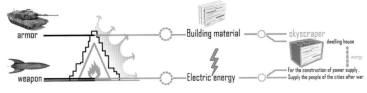

armor — Building material — skyscraper
dwelling house
weapon — Electric energy — For the construction of power supply.
Supply the people of the cities after war.

CONCEPT

The tower has a triple identity: energy transformer, housing complex and monument.

ENERGY TRANSFORMER:
The thermoelectric conversion device at the core of the tower transfers the chemical energy of the ammunition into heat and then electricity, which is to support the development of the city instead of consuming coal-oil based traditional energy. A factory to disassemble the armored vehicles is located on the base of the tower, whose product will provide recycled steel to construct the tower, and may further support the development of other constructions.

HOUSING COMPLEX:
The housing is arranged along the surface of the tower, constructed with recycled steel that is produced at the base of the tower. The energy conversion core of the tower will guarantee the electricity consummation of the housing.

MONUMENT:
The tower is constructed on the debris of Baghdad after bombing. Therefore, the building itself is like a new Babel commemorating the rebirth of the city, boosting up the spirit of people to build for their new life.

BUILDING CYCLE

The development of the tower is a dynamic process.
In the first phase, the tower is a bare framework with an inflaming core, with heated thermoelectric conversion going on. As the recycled steel made from armor being installed in the upper part of the tower, the inflaming core is gradually isolated and enclosed, thus leave the outer part of the building suitable for housing. In the final stage, the whole tower is filled with "armor housing blocks", and turning into a vivid city of Hanging Gardens.

materials needed for reconstruction.

The tower is constructed on the debris of Baghdad after bombing. Therefore, the building itself will be a new Babel tower commemorating the rebirth of the city, boosting up the spirit of people to build for their new life.

The tower will work as a thermoelectric conversion device, the core of the tower transfers the chemical energy of the ammunition into heat and then electricity, disassembling the armored vehicles in factories located on the base of the tower. All recycled steel produced will be used for constructing the tower.

Housing is arranged along the surface of the tower, constructed using recycled steel. The energy conversion core of the tower will guarantee the electricity consummation.

PHASE 1

- A mottled and sparking monument tower
- Combust and generate power once an hour, recalling the memory of people like a clock
- Utilize excess ammunition to generate power for the reconstruction in Iraq
- Utilize excess armored vehicles to provide building material for the reconstruction in Iraq

PHASE 2

- The tower will undergo a bottom-up transformation
- The steel made from the armored vehicles will gradually fill in the framework of the tower, forming suitable space for dwelling and other activities
- The core of the tower keeps combust on time, generating the power to supply the construction.

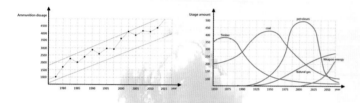

The construction strategies will be faced in phases; at first the tower is a bare framework with an inflaming core, with heated thermoelectric conversion going on. As the recycled steel made from armor is being installed in the upper part of the tower, the inflaming core is gradually isolated and enclosed, thus leave the outer part of the building suitable for housing. In the final phase, the whole tower is filled with "armor housing blocks" and turned into a vivid city of hanging gardens.

...lly cools down.
...g Gardens are thus formed.
...ng for the homeless left by the war.
...cess from war to peace.

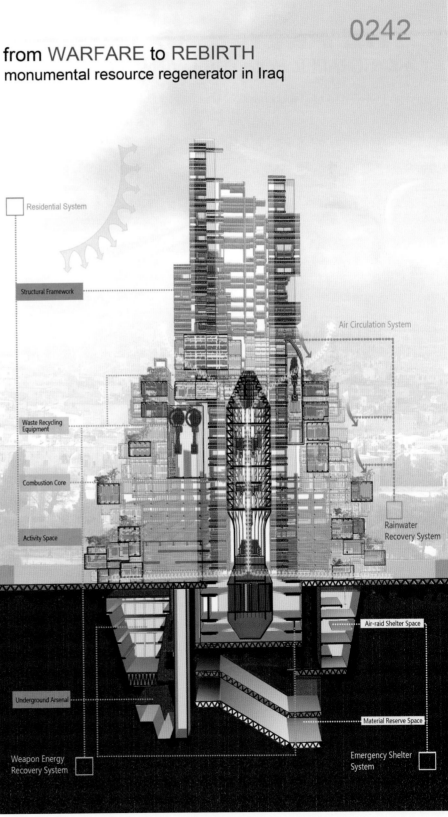

0242

from WARFARE to REBIRTH
monumental resource regenerator in Iraq

Residential System

Structural Framework

Air Circulation System

Waste Recycling Equipment

Combustion Core

Rainwater Recovery System

Activity Space

Air-raid Shelter Space

Underground Arsenal

Material Reserve Space

Weapon Energy Recovery System

Emergency Shelter System

THE PROMISED LAND

Xie Rui
Li Xiaodi
Yin Xiaoxiang
Chen Yao
Xiao Yunfeng

China

THE PROMISED LAND
SKYSCRAPER FOR THE LIVING AND THE DEAD

The LORD had said to Abram,
"Leave your country, your people and your father's household and
go to the land I will show you."

————— Genesis 12:1

The rising of sea level is one of the most dramatic crises that modern cities have had to face in the last few decades. It is estimated that sea level will rise of more than 500mm by the end of this century. At that time, 600 million people will lose their homeland with 3000 cities sinking into the water, since 2/3 of the world's population is settled in the coastal areas.

The Promised Land is conceived as humans' final homeland, a self-sustainable city on submerged places, shaped as a massive cross rising over the water level. The building works as a modular self-assembly system. Prefabricated girders and columns made of reinforced concrete are fixed on the ground as founding, and then the prefabricated floors are placed in order to sustain the different programmatic modules.

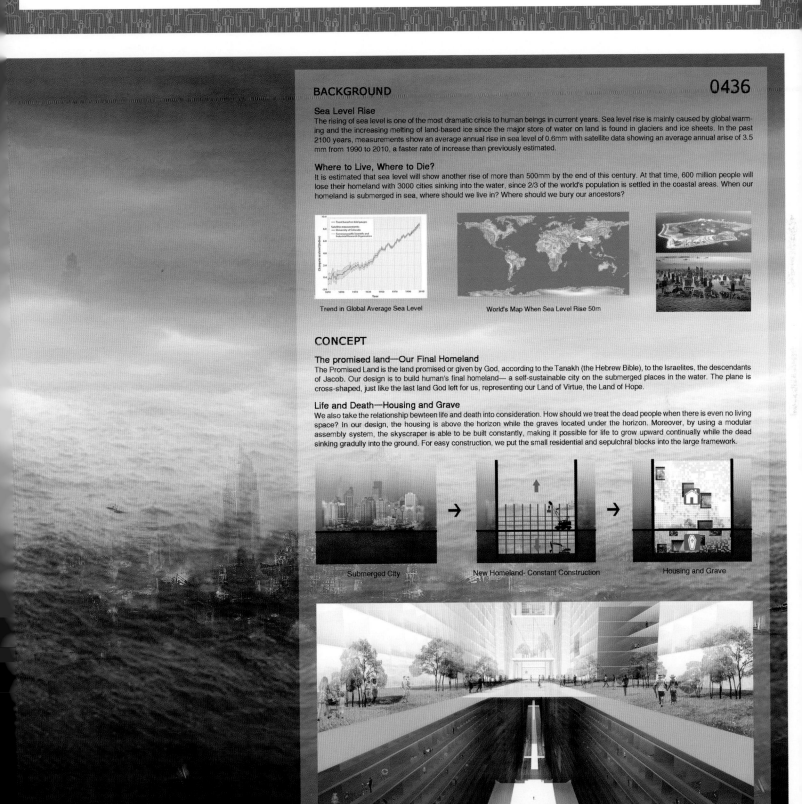

BACKGROUND

0436

Sea Level Rise

The rising of sea level is one of the most dramatic crisis to human beings in current years. Sea level rise is mainly caused by global warming and the increasing melting of land-based ice since the major store of water on land is found in glaciers and ice sheets. In the past 2100 years, measurements show an average annual rise in sea level of 0.6mm with satellite data showing an average annual arise of 3.5 mm from 1990 to 2010, a faster rate of increase than previously estimated.

Where to Live, Where to Die?

It is estimated that sea level will show another rise of more than 500mm by the end of this century. At that time, 600 million people will lose their homeland with 3000 cities sinking into the water, since 2/3 of the world's population is settled in the coastal areas. When our homeland is submerged in sea, where should we live in? Where should we bury our ancestors?

Trend in Global Average Sea Level

World's Map When Sea Level Rise 50m

CONCEPT

The promised land—Our Final Homeland

The Promised Land is the land promised or given by God, according to the Tanakh (the Hebrew Bible), to the Israelites, the descendants of Jacob. Our design is to build human's final homeland— a self-sustainable city on the submerged places in the water. The plane is cross-shaped, just like the last land God left for us, representing our Land of Virtue, the Land of Hope.

Life and Death—Housing and Grave

We also take the relationship bewteen life and death into consideration. How should we treat the dead people when there is even no living space? In our design, the housing is above the horizon while the graves located under the horizon. Moreover, by using a modular assembly system, the skyscraper is able to be built constantly, making it possible for life to grow upward continually while the dead sinking gradually into the ground. For easy construction, we put the small residential and sepulchral blocks into the large framework.

Submerged City

New Homeland- Constant Construction

Housing and Grave

By using a modular assembly system, the skyscraper is able to be rebuilt constantly, making it possible to develop upper programs continually.

Each block is designed in different sizes according to the program that will hold, making it flexible to adapt different functions and meet different requirements. The smaller blocks are housings cells while the bigger blocks are public spaces, such as shops, schools, hospitals, recreational spaces, etc. Housing will be located on the upper layers just above the horizon while the graves will located under the horizon. The relationship between life and death is taken into consideration. Moreover, with this modular system, the skyscraper is able to allow life to continually grow upward while the departed will gradually be sinking into the ground below. For easy construction, the design places small residential

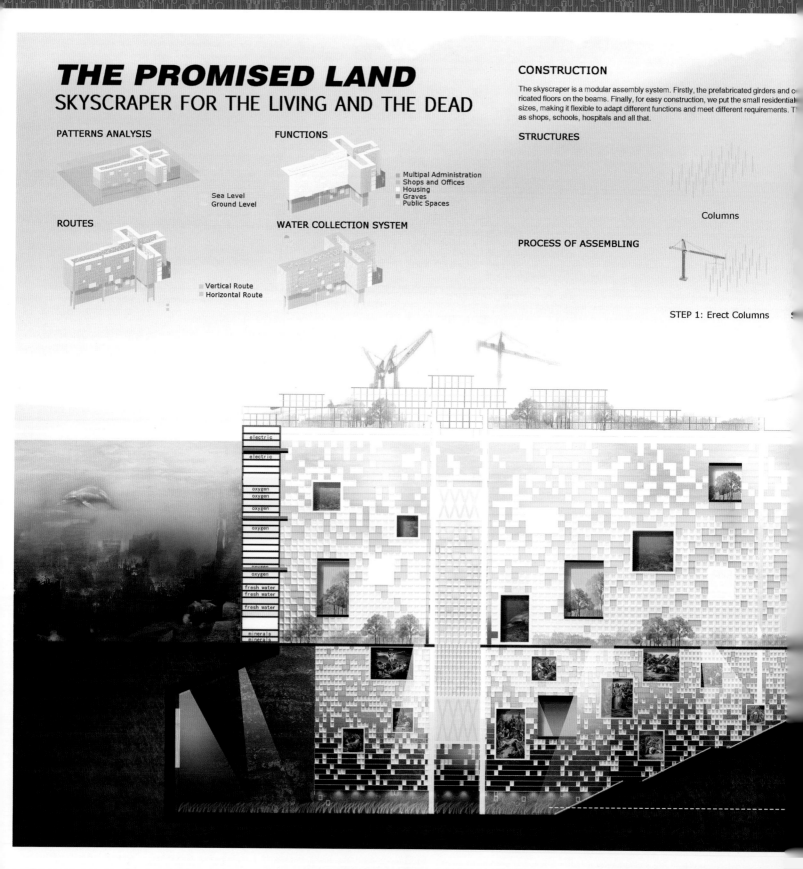

THE PROMISED LAND
SKYSCRAPER FOR THE LIVING AND THE DEAD

PATTERNS ANALYSIS

Sea Level
Ground Level

ROUTES

Vertical Route
Horizontal Route

FUNCTIONS

Multipal Administration
Shops and Offices
Housing
Graves
Public Spaces

WATER COLLECTION SYSTEM

CONSTRUCTION

The skyscraper is a modular assembly system. Firstly, the prefabricated girders and c ricated floors on the beams. Finally, for easy construction, we put the small residentia sizes, making it flexible to adapt different functions and meet different requirements. T as shops, schools, hospitals and all that.

STRUCTURES

Columns

PROCESS OF ASSEMBLING

STEP 1: Erect Columns

electric
electric
oxygen
oxygen
oxygen
oxygen
oxygen
oxygen
fresh water
fresh water
fresh water
minerals
minerals

and sepulchral blocks into the large framework.

The building is conceived applying the principle of water tank floatation system that steel ships use. When the water rises in an emergency, the tank can be closed against the waves of the sea, only let in as much water as it requires. The building will stand as a symbol for families to pay respect to those who die during the years.

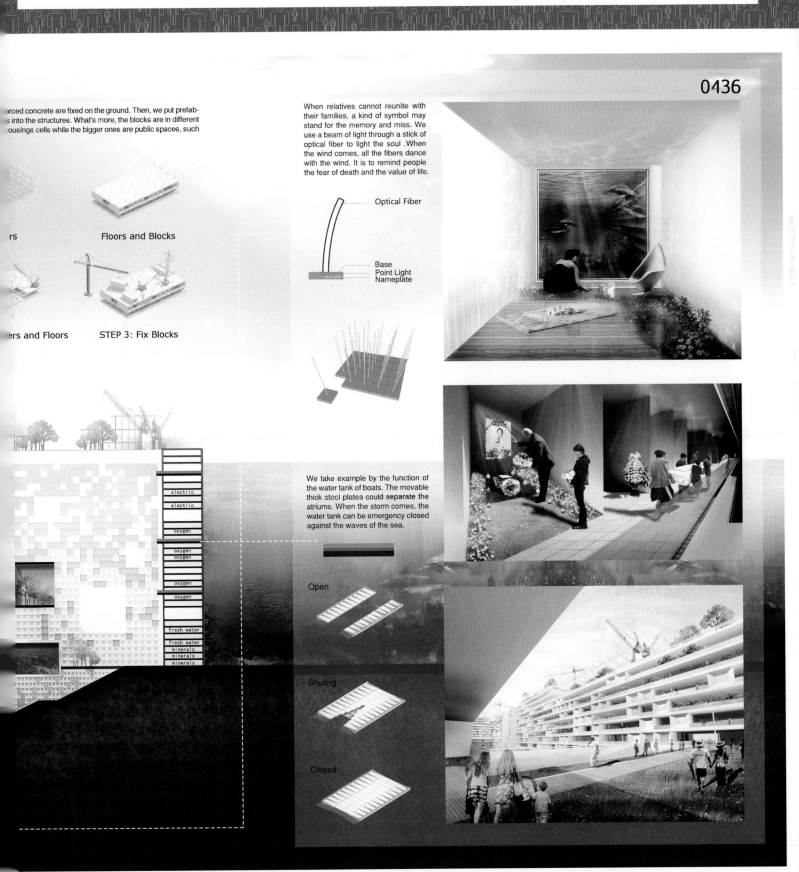

0436

...rced concrete are fixed on the ground. Then, we put prefab-... into the structures. What's more, the blocks are in different ...ousings cells while the bigger ones are public spaces, such

Floors and Blocks

...rs and Floors   STEP 3: Fix Blocks

When relatives cannot reunite with their families, a kind of symbol may stand for the memory and miss. We use a beam of light through a stick of optical fiber to light the soul .When the wind comes, all the fibers dance with the wind. It is to remind people the fear of death and the value of life.

Optical Fiber

Base
Point Light
Nameplate

We take example by the function of the water tank of boats. The movable thick steel plates could separate the atriums. When the storm comes, the water tank can be emergency closed against the waves of the sea.

Open

Shuting

Closed

electric
electric
oxygen
oxygen
oxygen
oxygen
oxygen
fresh water
fresh water
minerals
minerals
minerals

INVISIBLE WALL

Hong Ji Hye
Lee Han Sol

Republic of Korea

INVISIBLE WALL

" He let his mind drift as he stared at the city, half slum, half paradise.
How could a place be so ugly and violent, yet beautiful at the same time? "

-Chris Abani-

How do you imagine a future city?

The Intergovernmental Panel on Climate Change (IPCC)'s report has led us into "scientific consensus" on the danger of global warming (Davis, 2006), and we directly feel the impact of it with heat wave, heavy snow, flood, and etc. In addition to that, inevitable threats we face today are the "urban poverty" and "slumification of the city". The earth's urbanization is an ongoing process and by year 2050, the population of the cities will be increased up to 10 billion (Lutz, Sanderson, and Scherbor, 1997 as cited in Davis, 2006). If this is the case, and "if megacities are the brightest stars in the urban firmament, three-quarters of the burden of population growth will be borne by faintly visible second-tier and smaller urban areas." (UN-Habitat, 2003 as cited in Davis, 2006, p21).

In the city, while the rich and the poor adjoin each other, there exists an invisible wall between them. It is a common picture that the poor are crammed into the slum, like in an ant tunnel, while the rich enjoy extra spaces, such as gardens and the vacant lots. < INVISIBLE WALL > is the visualization of the obvious but invisible wall between the two, the one only for the rich and the other for the poor. It is also the symbol of the violence toward the poor who are driven out to the suburbs. At the same time, with the concept of "collapse of the wall", < INVISIBLE WALL > is designed as a desire for the collapse of the violence toward the poor.

Lastly, it is also designed as their new place to live.

The recent global exodus from rural to urban areas at an alarming rate has left cities around the world with inexistent urban design and services for a large part of their population. Just in China, 500 million people have migrated to urban areas in the last decade. Dreams of finding a better way of life in the city are shattered by an infrastructure incapable of accommodating a massive number of new inhabitants.

Slums at the periphery of these cities have sprawled in every continent. They are characterized by informal housing, commerce, and road structure. The lack of infrastructure, including energy, potable water, and drainage are some of the most important problems to solve.

The "collapse of the wall" is not only a symbol of the reality that isolates the slums but also a foundation of the

0523

BACKGROUND

The earth's urbanization and the city's slumification

We do not find a slum, a habitat for the poor, only in the Third World. There is a considerable overlap between the two categories, the urban poor and the Third World's slum resident. However, if it is based on the poverty line of the countries, the population of the urban poor is more than half of that all over the world. In addition, in the past, as the farmers moved into the city, the number of urban residents increased, and the income and the developmental gap between the rural and the urban was the problem (Guldin, 2001 as cited in Davis, 2006). However, in the present day, the rural itself has become urbanized; as a result, the residents in the rural places automatically became the urban residents. Recently, China has urbanized at the unprecedented speed in human history, and the official statistics in 1993 indicated that the 43% of the places were urban. Since 1978, the places where they were officially titled 'urban' have rapidly increased from 193 to 640 places.

However, the real problem was that the places where they absorbed the increased urban residents were not the metropolis, but the small and medium- sized cities (Guldin, 2001 as cited in Davis, 2006). 'Shanghai Economic District', established in 1983, was the world's largest government led developmental area, which includes the Shanghai metropolis and five adjacent provinces. The population in this area is approaching the total population of the US. For the next 100 years, the urban will be expanded greatly but unnaturally. Thus, in the history of the evolution of urban, the size and the population will soon be reached their peak. Therefore, the urban will experience a massive slumification.

CONCEPT

'The invisible wall exposed.' / 'Collapse of the wall.'

Our team tried to show a stark contrast of the gap between the rich and the poor that will reach its peak in the megalopolis, by visualizing the invisible wall between the areas of the rich and the poor. At the same time, we designed < INVISIBLE WALL > based on the concept of breaking down of the wall. We tried to reveal the reality of the aggressive development which is only for the upper class. Also, we depicted the urban poor who enjoy less accommodation and public service as a result of this, but to be evicted to the outer suburbs without any alternatives.

SCENARIO

The 'collapse of the wall' is not only the symbol of the reality that isolates the slums, but also a foundation of the life that can fulfil the urban poor's fundamental elements of life. The slum, which is the territory for the poor who are thrown out to the outer suburbs, should accommodate more population due to the rapid increase of the urban population. Since the city cannot accommodate the surging population, the poor who used to live in a flat land had to move to the steep hill slope where there is no urban infrastructure available. Those urban poor cannot help but being surrounded by trash and exposed to various climate or natural catastrophe such as a landslide. < INVISIBLE WALL > will provide public services, accommodation, and eventually set up a new base for the incessantly increasing urban poor.

Reference
Davis, M. (2007). Planet of Slums. (J. A. Kim, Trans.). London and New York: Verso. (Original work published 2006)

life that can fulfill the urban poor's fundamental elements of life. The slum, which is the territory for the poor who are thrown out to the outer suburbs, should accommodate more population due to the rapid increase of the urban population.

Since the city cannot accommodate the surging population, the poor who used to live in a flat land had to move to the steep hillside slope where there is no urban infrastructure available. Those urban poor cannot help but be surrounded by trash and be exposed to various climate or natural catastrophes such as landslides. The Invisible Wall project will provide public services, accommodations, and eventually set up a new base for the incessantly increasing urban poor.

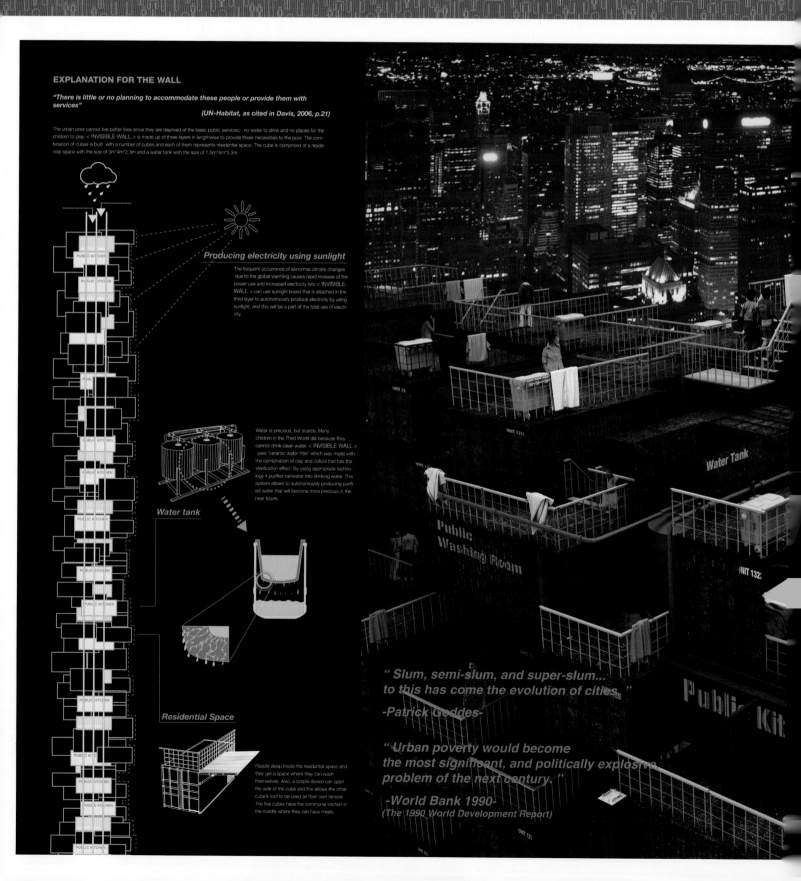

EXPLANATION FOR THE WALL

"There is little or no planning to accommodate these people or provide them with services"

(UN-Habitat, as cited in Davis, 2006, p.21)

The urban poor cannot live better lives since they are deprived of the basic public services; no water to drink and no places for the children to play. < INVISIBLE WALL > is made up of three layers in lengthwise to provide these necessities to the poor. The combination of cubes is built with a number of cubes and each of them represents residential space. The cube is comprised of a residential space with the size of 3m*4m*2.3m and a water tank with the size of 1.5m*4m*2.3m.

Producing electricity using sunlight

The frequent occurrence of abnormal climate changes due to the global warming causes rapid increase of the power use and increased electricity bills.< INVISIBLE-WALL > can use sunlight board that is attached in the third layer to autonomously produce electricity by using sunlight, and this will be a part of the total use of electricity.

Water is precious, but scarce. Many children in the Third World die because they cannot drink clean water. < INVISIBLE WALL > uses 'ceramic water filter' which was made with the combination of clay and colloid that has the sterilization effect. By using appropriate technology it purifies rainwater into drinking water. This system allows to autonomously producing purified water that will become more precious in the near future.

Water tank

Residential Space

People sleep inside the residential space and they get a space where they can wash themselves. Also, a simple device can open the side of the cube and this allows the other cube's roof to be used as their own terrace. The five cubes have the communal kitchen in the middle where they can have meals.

" Slum, semi-slum, and super-slum...
to this has come the evolution of cities. "
-Patrick Geddes-

"Urban poverty would become
the most significant, and politically explosive
problem of the next century. "

-World Bank 1990-
(The 1990 World Development Report)

The Invisible Wall is a project that seeks to blur the boundary between slums and well-urbanized parts of these cities. The project consists of three layers lengthwise to provide basic public services. It is an agglomeration of modular cubes defined as residential units and water tanks. The residential unit is a simple open space for sleeping and bathing while the roofs are used as terraces for recreational activities. Every five units there are insertions of program-specific units that serve the entire community including kitchens, solar plants, and water tanks, among others.

Davis, M. (2007). Planet of Slums. (J. A. Kim, Trans.). London and New York: Verso. (Original work published 2006)

Reference

HANGING TOWER

Dagang Qu

China

THE HANGING TOWER IN THE MOUNTAINS
HELPING THE POOR GET RID OF POVERTY

This project imagines the possibility of designing a hanging city within the mountains of China. The Chinese mountain range is a very populated region of the country and unfortunately, the majority of its inhabitants live below the poverty level. Millions of Chinese are poor, most of them living in the mountainous Sichuan area where traffic is unobstructed, and there is no television or radio. Because mountainous villages are scattered, children go to school with hardships. One elementary school being available to serve several villages is common. Here, poverty breaks their dreams and changes their lives. Instead of migrating to urban areas in hope of a better life this project seeks to create 21st century cities in their own habitat.

Skyscrapers along the transportation system in the mountains grow out in order to protect the original ecosystem

0761

Background:

According to the United Nations survey, in developing countries poverty population grow from 1 billion to the current 1.3 billion in 1990. These people have less than $1 income everyday per person . In developing countries 80 million people completely are unable to enjoy medical treatment service, 840 million are suffering from malnutrition, 260 million people are unable to go to school. At present, African population is 630 million, about half of them suffer from hunger. In the 1980 s, the developing countries have 100 million children strayed in the streets. Poverty is still the theme of the today's world.

"I'm hungry, I'm cold ,and I hope I can go to school."

"I hope my children can leave mountains and get rid of pover,."

"Today is my birthday,I can eat noodles, This is my best meal this year.I'm so happy"

"......But I am so hungry ......"

".......I hope you can go to school,but we are too poor.I am so sorry,my grandson......"

There are a lot of areas of the world that people are suffering from the disaster of survival, they are lack of necessary education, basic medical and health conditions, and even lack of food and drinking water needed for survival.A great part of the proportion of the population in extreme poverty live in mountains, because there are no roads or unobstructed roads , both information and material resources is very difficult to reach. Life here is difficult, even if they have the resources or product,which is difficult to carry out. So no roads,no wealth.No food,no education.No education,no future.So we must solve the problem.

China, for example,millions of people are in poor, most of them live in Sichuan mountainous area, traffic is unobstructed, there is no TV or radio. People have to carry water drink outside,buying things through walking for many hours to the nearby bigger villages. Because mountainous villages are scattered, children go to school very inconveniently, these places don't board school,because of less development. So,that in several villages there is only one elementary school is very common. Here, poverty breaks their dreams and changes their lives,The pressure of life has been written on their faces.

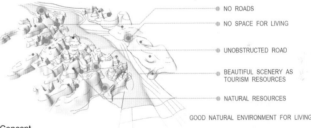

- NO ROADS
- NO SPACE FOR LIVING
- UNOBSTRUCTED ROAD
- BEAUTIFUL SCENERY AS TOURISM RESOURCES
- NATURAL RESOURCES

GOOD NATURAL ENVIRONMENT FOR LIVING

Concept

No way, no wealth. The key we solve the problem is road. Traffic brings wealth.We can use skyscrapers to solve the traffic problem, we use the relationship between the city and traffic to solve the problem of the area of transportation and construction. We use the soft structure of the traffic network.The city will develop with the development of the traffic network.Skyscrapers along the transportation system in mountains grow out,In order to protect the original ecosystem of valleys.we take the methods that skyscrapers are hung suspension in the traffic system,This method makes the nature and cities harmony.We can create a lot of wealth opportunities and create a different eco-city.

small city or town   middle city   big city

The traffic convenience condition determines the size of the city, the ity traffic condition is more convenient,the city is bigger. so,traffic in the mountains for the region also has the similar effects. So we adopt advanced transportation system drive mountainous area economy to solve the mountain people's poverty there.

Create traffic system to solve the problems of poverty caused by unobstructed traffic

Traffic system forms the Vertical stress system of skyscrapers.

Vertical stress system provide skyscrapers growth space

MORE SPACE

LESS SPACE

NO HARM TO VALLEYS

THE SKYSCRAPER GROWTH PATTERN

Significance

The development mode not only in order to solve the traffic problems, it can make people in the mountainous area out of poverty and access to education, medical and health resources. The mountain area is more than 10% of the earth's land area,where there is a large number of people living. In the global population rapidly growing today,that we solve such regional problems is of great significance. To maintain world peace is also very useful. It also can provide a huge amount of space for the future population. Even that in the future people moved to other planet is also significant, for example the moon is the mountains.

of the valleys. The design takes the method that skyscrapers are hung, suspended in the traffic system. This method makes the nature and cities exist harmoniously. This can create a different eco-city. The traffic convenience condition determines the size of the city. So the project adopts an advanced transportation system driving the mountainous area's economy to solve the mountain people's poverty there.

The main question is, how to create a new city without affecting the natural environment? The idea is to minimize its contact with the natural terrain. The first phase would establish a structural network of roads that will connect and support the city to the mountains. From there, hanging cylinders, as inverted skyscrapers, will create the city.

Each building would be equipped with sustainable assets such as wind turbines and photovoltaic cells for energy

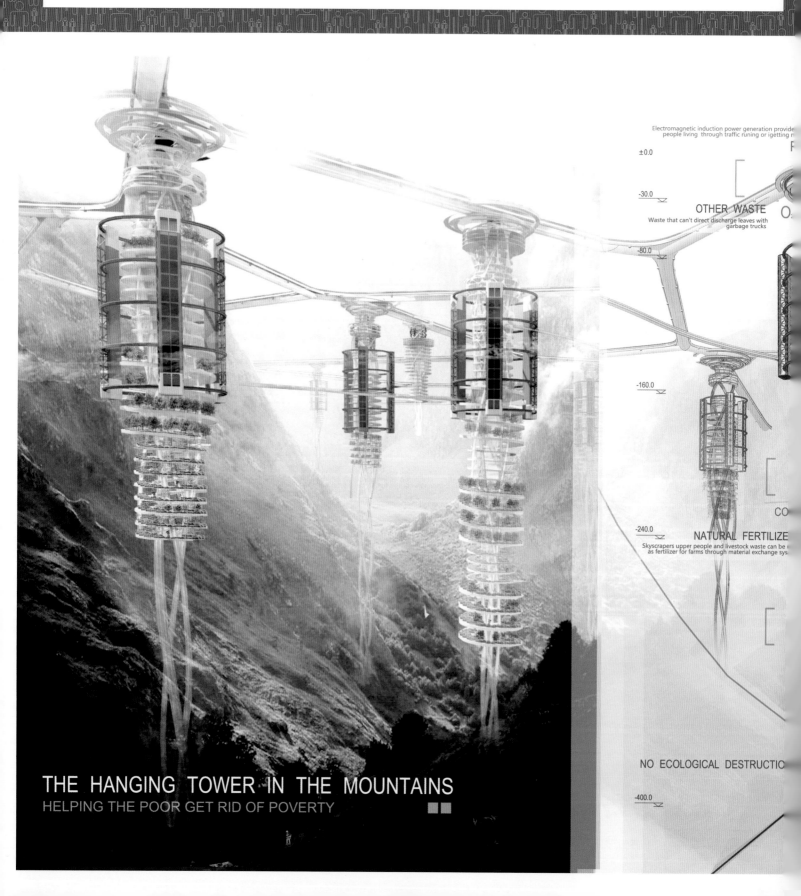

Electromagnetic induction power generation provide
people living through traffic runing or igetting r

±0.0

-30.0

OTHER WASTE
Waste that can't direct discharge leaves with
garbage trucks

-80.0

-160.0

-240.0   NATURAL FERTILIZE
Skyscrapers upper people and livestock waste can be
as fertilizer for farms through material exchange sys

NO ECOLOGICAL DESTRUCTIO

-400.0

THE HANGING TOWER IN THE MOUNTAINS
HELPING THE POOR GET RID OF POVERTY

generation and water collection and recycling systems. Also, each tower would be a mixed-use structure with defined zones for housing, commerce, culture, and recreational activities. Farming will be available in the closest mountain range to minimize food transportation. The idea is to create a self-sustaining city that will alleviate poverty in the region and serve as an example of architecture in harmony with nature.

0761

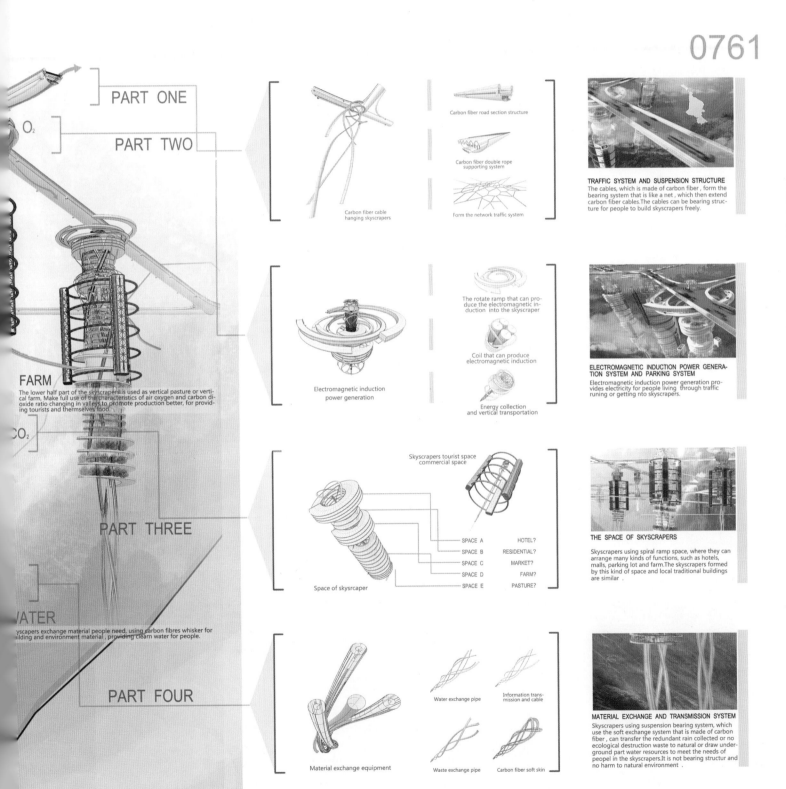

PART ONE

PART TWO

Carbon fiber road section structure

Carbon fiber double rope supporting system

Carbon fiber cable hanging skyscrapers

Form the network traffic system

TRAFFIC SYSTEM AND SUSPENSION STRUCTURE
The cables, which is made of carbon fiber , form the bearing system that is like a net , which then extend carbon fiber cables.The cables can be bearing structure for people to build skyscrapers freely.

O₂

FARM
The lower half part of the skyscrapers is used as vertical pasture or vertical farm, Make full use of the characteristics of air oxygen and carbon dioxide ratio changing in valleys to promote production better, for providing tourists and themselves food.

The rotate ramp that can produce the electromagnetic induction into the skyscraper

Coil that can produce electromagnetic induction

Electromagnetic induction power generation

Energy collection and vertical transportation

ELECTROMAGNETIC INDUCTION POWER GENERATION SYSTEM AND PARKING SYSTEM
Electromagnetic induction power generation provides electricity for people living through traffic runing or getting nto skyscrapers.

CO₂

Skyscrapers tourist space commercial space

PART THREE

Space of skysrcaper

SPACE A	HOTEL?
SPACE B	RESIDENTIAL?
SPACE C	MARKET?
SPACE D	FARM?
SPACE E	PASTURE?

THE SPACE OF SKYSCRAPERS
Skyscrapers using spiral ramp space, where they can arrange many kinds of functions, such as hotels, malls, parking lot and farm.The skyscrapers formed by this kind of space and local traditional buildings are similar .

WATER
...yscapers exchange material people need, using carbon fibres whisker for ...ilding and environment material , providing clearn water for people.

PART FOUR

Material exchange equipment

Water exchange pipe

Information transmission and cable

Waste exchange pipe

Carbon fiber soft skin

MATERIAL EXCHANGE AND TRANSMISSION SYSTEM
Skyscrapers using suspension bearing system, which use the soft exchange system that is made of carbon fiber , can transfer the redundant rain collected or no ecological destruction waste to natural or draw underground part water resources to meet the needs of peopel in the skyscrapers.It is not bearing structur and no harm to natural environment .

SYMBIOSIS CITY

Nguyen Ba Duc

Vietnam

During the last few decades, the speed of urbanization in developing countries has been so rapid that urban planning has played a secondary role in regards to progress. The majority of these cities lack the necessary infrastructure for their inhabitants.

Urbanization is causing more countrymen to move to the city causing many complications, socially, economically, and culturally. The cities become disorderly and lack consolidation.

The Symbiosis City is a proposal for a unified city where urban and rural areas could coexist. The main idea is borrowed from the mangrove, trees supported by a complex network of thin roots that allow for water and vegetation to flow freely on the ground. The trees are perceived to be floating in the air supported by hundreds of filaments.

0830

SYMBIOSIS CITY

Strength of connection

Ideas

Urbanization in developing countries takes place very quickly. The number of countryman move to the City rising day by day causing a lot of complicated in social, economic and cultural. The City become disorder, lack of consolidated.....

"SYMBIOSIS CITY " as one model of united City between urban and rural areas; it's both rehabilitate "Dead Cities" and raise ability of firm connection between human and nature.

The new city has been planned as a development in phases; the first one will be focused on the construction of network of superstructures above ground supported by stilts. Stage two includes clearing existing residential areas and reconstructing a terrestrial ecosystem such as a forest, natural canal, etc. in order to organize the development of cultivation and breeding. The idea is that eventually the rest of the city will be transferred to this new structure while the ground will be retaken by nature and used for agriculture and outdoor recreational activities.

The strength of the connection that will between created by this project will be evident as the network works to link the elements together. Rural and urban areas develop homogeneously in a closed circle, minimizing excess elements, which caused substantial impacts on global climate change. The scope of application of this design is that it could be

future

New urban structure: the whole city is an integrated and sustainable b

solution

This process starts from the small urban then spread over the world

exiting

disaster in VIETNAM   disaster in BRASIL   disaster INDONESIA
Traditional urban structures worldwide are helpless when confronted

applied on the existing city or on the new lands.

The future holds this design as a new urban structure to keep the typology of a whole city in an integrated and sustainable building.

Symbiosis City will serve as a model of a city uniting urban and rural areas; it is both to rehabilitate "dead cities" and to raise the ability to foster a firm connection between humankind and nature.

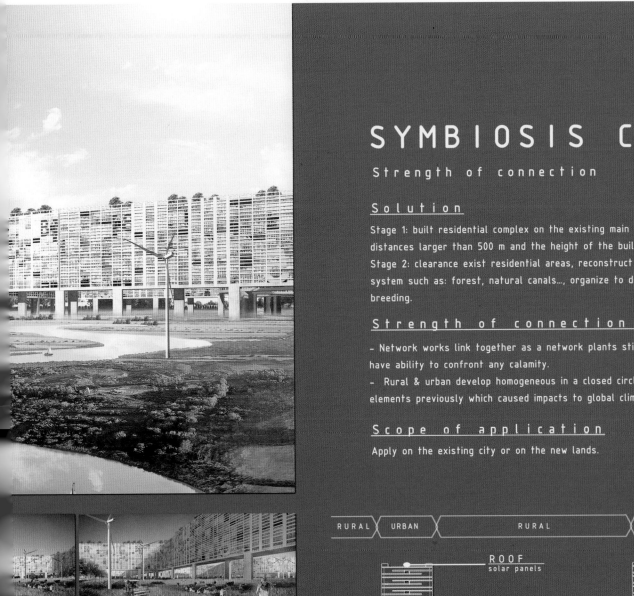

0830

SYMBIOSIS CITY

Strength of connection

Solution

Stage 1: built residential complex on the existing main roads with distances larger than 500 m and the height of the building is free.
Stage 2: clearance exist residential areas, reconstruct terrestrial eco-system such as: forest, natural canals..., organize to develop cultivate & breeding.

Strength of connection

- Network works link together as a network plants stick on the ground, have ability to confront any calamity.
- Rural & urban develop homogeneous in a closed circle, minimize excess elements previously which caused impacts to global climate change.

Scope of application

Apply on the existing city or on the new lands.

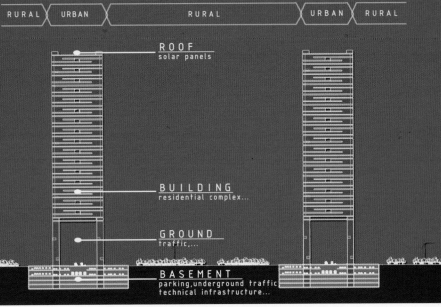

RURAL | URBAN | RURAL | URBAN | RURAL

ROOF
solar panels

BUILDING
residential complex...

GROUND
traffic,...

BASEMENT
parking,underground traffic
technical infrastructure...

...ster in JAPAN   Flooding in Iowa, 2008
...e calamity

photo by www.boston.com   AP Photo Jeff

TOWER OF ETERNITY

Keith L. Chung
Korn Kunalungkarn

Netherlands

Tower of Eternity : Beginning or End?

Monument as continuous transformation of precedents

abstract

Once, the Pyramid in Egypt was intended for the dead; the Coliseum in Rome was a place for those who were fighting for their lives; the Borobudur in Indonesia was a place to worship the forever Buddha. Nevertheless, all these iconic architecture around the world have become tourist attraction, where kiosk and market were setup next to the historical monument. This hints that we've collectively embraced a new ideology, an ideology where we prioritize economic values over all other values. Ironically, beside several important dates in a year (monument would actually become relevant in these occasions), it seems as if the monument, its space, its context and its purpose have become completely extraneous in our society. As if the monument could no longer be commemorated and revealed any form of human civilization or spiritual enlightenment. As if the monument was no longer the remembrance of the cultural and historical heritages, but just the mere architectural artifact that apprehends built-object (as public space for market and commercial opportunities, ensuring economic power at the center of society. For us, the challenge lies within; how monument can restores its nostalgic identity and serves as central, dious memorial ornament within the contemporary environment?

Class A/B Average family income above R$ 4,800.00
Classes C : Average family income between R$ 1,115.00 and R$1,800.00
Social Classes D : Average family income between R$804.00 e R$ 1,115.00
Social Classes E : Average family income below R$804.00

Sao Paulo

In Sao Paulo, there is a natural need of cemetery space, not simple because of the favelas or the notorious gangs, but due to the rapid growth of urban population and the short life expectancy of inhabitants. Our proposal is arranged, deliberated, segregated and regulated in order to be conveniently sustained, marketed and secured, in ways that direct to the unique cultural and social context that differ from the fundamental characteristics of any cemetery space. Since our society could no longer eradicate capitalist consumption and social inequality, this continuous monument offers lower class citizens to rest in peace in the bottom half of the tower with affordable price. Upper class citizens will be rested in peace in the top half of the tower with luxury views over the city. And since our society embraces styles, iconicity and technology, the tower allows future residents to insert their modern, parametric, sustainable or highly decorated tombstone / coffin to the façade as a cladding system. It's an inexorable rebellion.

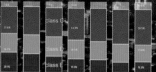

social inequality map - red is country with high social inequality

social class structure

Concept

Monument is made of sizes and powers; continuous monument is made of eternity and posterity. Every moment of our existence is a constant celebration of human civilization. Time has been suppressed, reprisal and paradox is needed to restore the primitive meaning of monument.

This continuous monument delicately mirrors such potential promoting the city, community and inhabitants to distinguish and quantify the forgotten sentimental qualities, motivating the general public to an experience of the metaphysics of presence that emerges with daily life. The monument as a catalyst bridges the gap between the residents and the city, solidifying a complex and yet diverse interrelations between subjects (life) and objects (dead) that become a new heroic social proposition; gradually unifying all societal domains through a central immense entity. From individual and collective memories and experiences, wills and projections, this monument will awake all citizens to provoke, repel and prevent any contamination (social inequality, poverty and capitalist consumption) that will infiltrate our society and physical environment.

core + circulation   structure system   graves as infill   platforms

As if the monument was no longer the remembrance of the cultural and historical heritages, The Tower of Eternity sets to resolve how the monument can restore its nostalgic identity and serve as a continuous memorial ornament within the contemporary environment.

In Sao Paulo, there is a natural need of cemetery space due to the rapid growth of urban population and the short life expectancy of inhabitants. Since society can no longer eradicate capitalist consumption and social inequality, this continuous monument designed by offers lower class citizens to rest in peace in the bottom half of the tower with an affordable price. Upper-class citizens will rest in peace in the top half of the tower with luxury views over the city. An inexorable rebellion, the tower allows future residents to insert their modern, parametric, sustainable or highly

1038

"continuous monument is made of eternity and posterity..."

The monumental started from one single tower as a symbol of death, and constantly growth follow by the death of people in the city. By the time past, the monument reflects a sense of time while people keeps infill the tower with coffins. The cemetery did not intended only for the deads, also reveal a social segregation in our society...

2150   2100   2080   2050   2030 2020 2013

+1260.00 m

upper-class

+700.00 m

middle-class

+500.00 m

lower/middle-class

+200.00 m

lower class

decorated coffin to the façade as a cladding system.

The system uses a simple structure to provide space for coffins to infill the gap and create a possibility for further expansion. For circulation, the core and ramps are intended to transport coffins and people around the tower, and support all of the sub-structure in its entirety.

This continuous monument delicately mirrors such potential, promoting the city, community, and inhabitants to distinguish and quantify the forgotten sentimental qualities, motivating the general public to an experience of the metaphysics of presence that emerges with daily life.

The monument as a catalyst bridges the gap between the residents and the city, solidifying a complex and yet

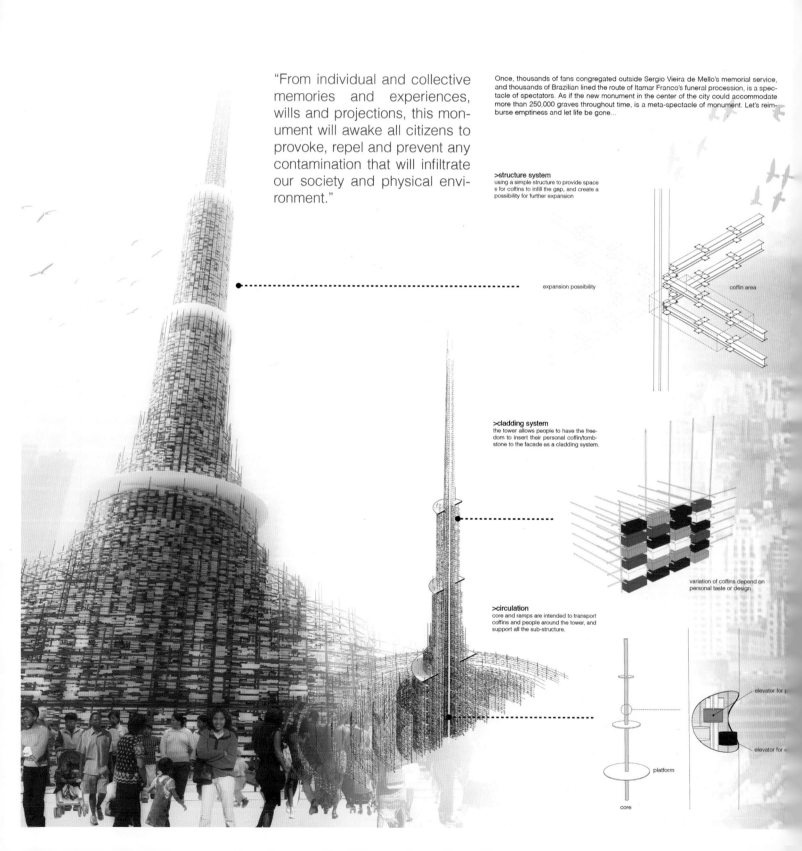

"From individual and collective memories and experiences, wills and projections, this monument will awake all citizens to provoke, repel and prevent any contamination that will infiltrate our society and physical environment."

Once, thousands of fans congregated outside Sergio Vieira de Mello's memorial service, and thousands of Brazilian lined the route of Itamar Franco's funeral procession, is a spectacle of spectators. As if the new monument in the center of the city could accommodate more than 250,000 graves throughout time, is a meta-spectacle of monument. Let's reimburse emptiness and let life be gone...

>structure system
using a simple structure to provide spaces for coffins to infill the gap, and create a possibility for further expansion

expansion possibility

coffin area

>cladding system
the tower allows people to have the freedom to insert their personal coffin/tombstone to the facade as a cladding system.

variation of coffins depend on personal taste or design

>circulation
core and ramps are intended to transport coffins and people around the tower, and support all the sub-structure.

elevator for

elevator for

platform

core

diverse interrelation between subjects (life) and objects (dead) that become a new heroic social proposition: gradually unifying all societal domains through a central immense entity.

From individual and collective memories and experiences, wills and projections, this monument will awake all citizens to provoke, repel, and prevent any contamination (social inequality, poverty and capitalist consumption) that will infiltrate our society and physical environment.

1038

TOWER TO THE HEAVEN

Li Ke
Yao Lifu
Du Xinchi

China

421

Dreaming to reach out to God is a rather common phenomenon throughout the history of mankind. For most, heaven is the preferred destination after death. The skyscraper takes the form of living space for people, varying from office buildings to residential buildings, but there is no skyscraper built for the people who are not with us any longer in the current world. Furthermore the dream of rising after death commonly is preferred by us instead of dropping into the earth.

On the other hand, the cemetery, one of the most important public spaces for the deceased and their relatives and friends, should be respected as the center of such activity. People gather from all over the world for their ancestors. The tomb, especially the modern cemetery, in any religion, is the space for people to reach their own god

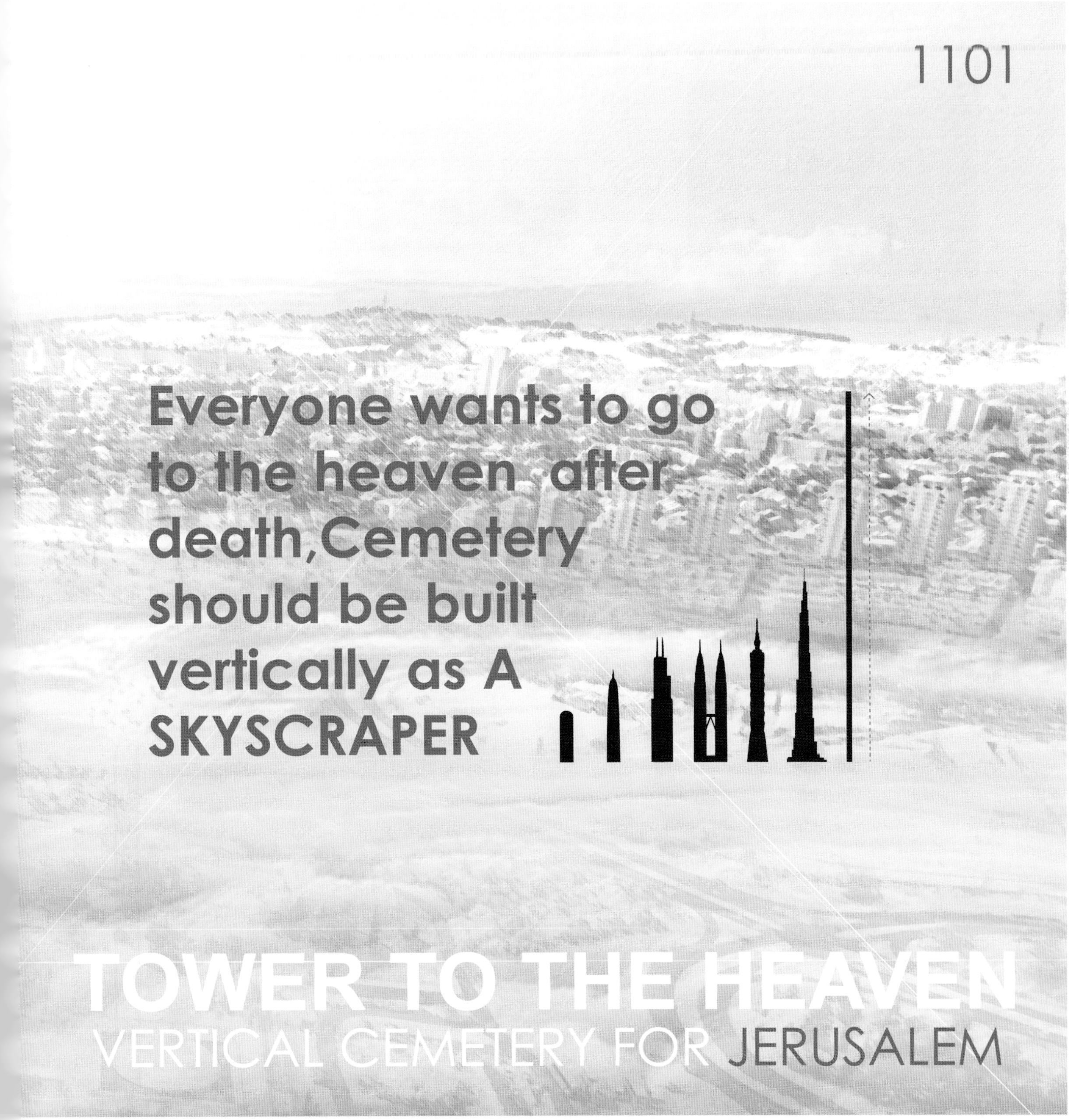

1101

Everyone wants to go to the heaven after death,Cemetery should be built vertically as A SKYSCRAPER

TOWER TO THE HEAVEN
VERTICAL CEMETERY FOR JERUSALEM

in the afterlife.

With the rapid increase of the world population, land is both becoming scarce for the living and the dead. In the Tower to the Heavens, the traditional cemetery was redesigned from spreading over the ground to vertically integrating numerous tombs in a single skyscraper. Thus, this design brings our beloved departed ones all closer to our "God" and saves space while maintaining the respect the dead deserve.

The Tower to Heavens consists of three parts, the envelope, the central core, and the top roof. A porous envelope encloses the skyscraper. In the windows lies the bone ash of dead people and marked with names and years. Also, every tomb is underneath a tree.

A /Concept

Dream to reach out the God is rather common phenomenon through the history of mankind. Everyone want to go the Heaven after death. Skyscraper as the form of living space for people alive, varied from office buildings to residential buildings. There is no skyscraper built for the people who are not LIVING in the current world. What's more, for the dreams of everyone, Rising, is preferred by us when talking about the way we would go after death, instead of Droping.

On the other hand, cemetery, as one of the most important public space for the soul gone and their relatives and friends, should be respected as the center of the activity. People gathered from all over the world for their ancestor. So, we present the design of a skyscraper of cetemery for dead people.

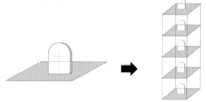

Tomb, especially the modern cemetery, in any religon, is the space for people to reach their own god after their life. Considering the fact that with the rising of the population of the world, land that could be used is getting less for not only the people alive, but also for the people gone. The traditional cetemery should change from the form of spreading over the ground to vertical to integrating numerous tomb in a single skyscraper.

B /Pattern

On the top roof, the pattern which was made up of mor Jerusalem

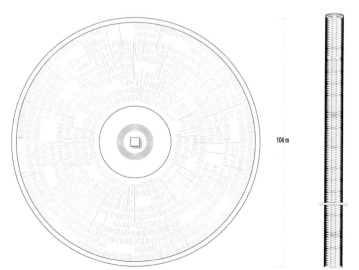

104 m

The central core consists of an elevator that transports people from the ground to the roof, and the stairs by which people walk on around the core, watching the tomb and the view from the tower. The rooftop is the space for gathering people and holding activities such as funerals and memorial services; its patter was made to symbolize the vivid pilgrimage activity to the city of Jerusalem.

1101

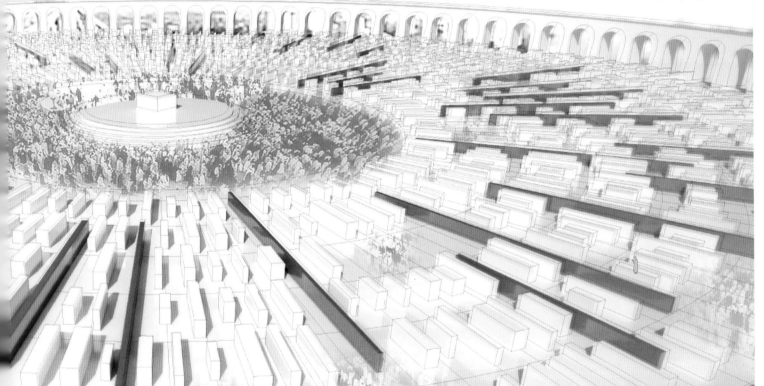

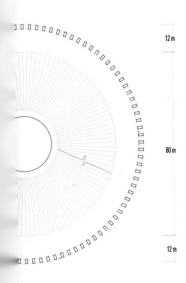

...s the activity of Pilgrimage in

12 m

80 m

12 m

C / Architecture

Considering the construction of the skyscraper, we made the building consist of three parts, the envelope, the central core, the top roof.

/1. The envelop
The skyscraper is wrapped by the envelope part which is porous. In the windows lies the bone ash of dead people and marked with names and years. What's more, every "tomb" is underneath a tree.

/2. Central Core
The central core consists of the elevator which could transport people from the ground to the roof, and the stairs by which people could walk on around the core, watching the tomb and the view outside the tower

/3. Top Roof
The top roof is the space for gathering people and holding activities such as funerals and memorial service

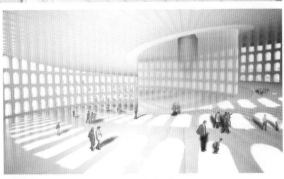

JACK SMITH
1942-2010

We have reached an era in which the advancement in computational tools and new materials has allowed architects and designers to imagine and build very complex geometries. In the last few years the evolution of architectural form has moved faster than in centuries and a new trend of architectural innovation is pushing the boundaries of design into what we call morphotectonic aesthetics. In this group of projects, form finding is the outcome of an analysis of information through mathematical systems. The results are fascinating buildings that respond to internal and external stimuli with the use of dynamic structures.

A few of the projects in this chapter include: a skyscraper designed to absorb noise and transform it into energy, a new type of inhabitable scaffolding that attaches to existing buildings to provide new living space and other secondary programs, and a linear city conceived along the coast of France that serves as a barrier to rising sea levels.

Other submissions investigate and replicate natural aggregation systems, such as cellular growth, with the intention of maximizing views, solar exposure, and energy conservation. The results include voronoi patterns that create a dialogue between the new buildings and the existing natural and urban conditions. Another example is the Quantum Skyscraper that mimics the growth of crystals and formulates an efficient pattern of program adjacencies and a novel structural system that not only responds to loads but also adapts to the building habitation changes over time.

Finally, Skinscape is a project that explores the possibility of creating building tissue between skyscrapers. The tissue not only attaches to the buildings, but also modifies them to allow for new programs – the evolution of the buildings and cities to satisfy new demands.

5 MORPHOTECTONIC AESTHETICS

IN THE LAST FEW YEARS THE EVOLUTION OF ARCHITECTURAL
FORM HAS MOVED FASTER THAN IN CENTURIES AND A
NEW TREND OF ARCHITECTURAL INNOVATION IS PUSHING
THE BOUNDARIES OF DESIGN INTO WHAT WE CALL
MORPHOTECTONIC AESTHETICS.

DOUBLE LIFE

Jieun Kim

France

The Site :
One Canada Square in Canary Wh...

The Existing Building

Analyses of One Canada Squre : people, act...

Concept : The 'double life' of users.

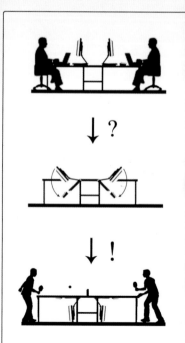

At 773 feet tall, the One Canada Square building in London's Canary Wharf is the tallest building in England, and the icon of the country's financial power. However, it is a cold building, of a classical typology and organized mass plan, one that has no purpose after business hours.

This designer imagines totally reinventing and rebranding the skyscraper as we think of it today, transforming it from simply an office tower to a building that would move from day to night seamlessly, allowing workers inside to benefit from a livelier environment and indeed, changing their behavior as the architecture of the building itself is changed and morphs to adapt to a more lax and playful environment after work hours when everyone is off duty for the day. This concept takes into account the double life of users as employees in the day and regular people just living

e site is a building called 'One Canada Square' in Canary Wharf in ndon. I will sum up in few words how this site is: Canary wharf is one of e most secure district in London, it is famous for the bancs.

The landscape is very horizontal and vertical; it makes me think of a matrice. A district which grew really fast since 1988 until nowadays. A cold place with a very organized mass plan. Buildings are very classical type.

0127

, founiture

What's the scale?
The building "one Canada Square" is the tallest skyscraper in England. The tower is the icon of the English finance power.

CN Tower
1.815ft

Petronas Tower
1.486ft

Eiffel Tower
984ft

One Canada Square
773ft

Intentions :
- to think again the office space;
- to change the behavior of the people who work there;

Spaces like the printer shop, the library, the meeting rooms and the leisure rooms are too formalize, too much normal in people daily lives.
I want to break all this linearity, the monotone's habits: telephone, fax, printer, meetings, work … etc..

Everything is already organized like a matrice and the goal is to transform these lives with the mechanisms I imagine, I want to tell another story about the site.

he light dig holes in the existent structure and e a bug invade the site to make its own house.

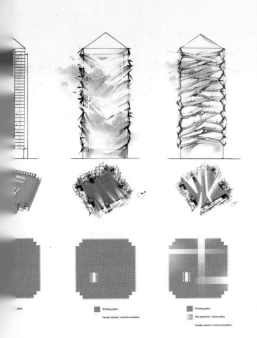

life at night.

The intentions of the designer are to rethink the office space and change the behavior of the people who work there. Spaces like the printer shop, the library, meeting rooms and leisure rooms are too formalized and normal in people's daily lives. This monotonous habit needs to be broken.

Everything is already organized like a matrix and the goal is to transform lives with mechanisms that will tell another story about the site. The mechanisms are interesting due to their movements, design and function. The goal is to change the aspect of the site. The building has a double life. By day people work as usual but when the office closes, the building starts to live on its own. All the little mechanisms start functioning and playing their movements.

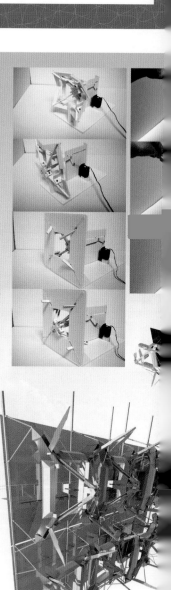

Research of Mechanisms

Different inside ambiances

Under the relax space (2) there is the organic office space(1).
The libray becomes the computers playground (3/5)
The lobby of the buiding(4)

Mechanisms are interesting for their their design and their function. Th change the aspect of the site and the the people who live in it, all that mechanisms. We can say 'the INPUT and OUTPUT the environm

Mechanisms are like the 'triggers' point for changements and transfo offices.The mechanism is plugg facades and interfere in people's life

As an example: Imagine, perhaps, if the furniture could serve a double purpose—if a desk could, with a few small folds, transform into a ping-pong table. By night, the library can become a "computer playground." Office space is transformed into relaxation space. The individual pieces inside the building, the furniture, the architectural elements, serve as "triggers" that are able to change function and effect a transformation in the building as a whole.

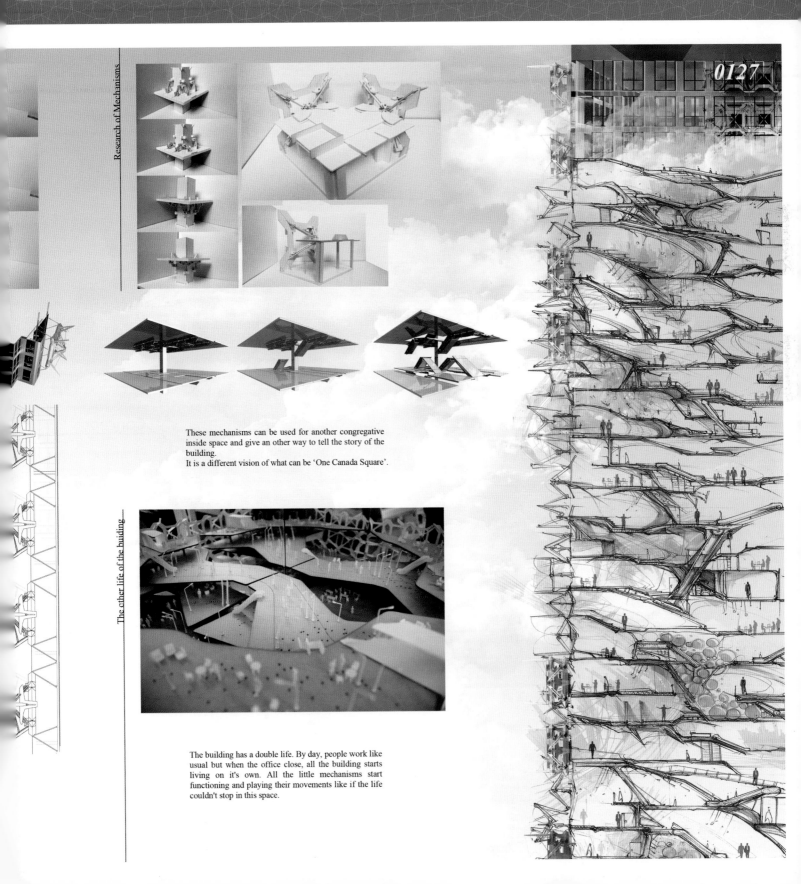

Research of Mechanisms

These mechanisms can be used for another congregative inside space and give an other way to tell the story of the building.
It is a different vision of what can be 'One Canada Square'.

The other life of the building

The building has a double life. By day, people work like usual but when the office close, all the building starts living on it's own. All the little mechanisms start functioning and playing their movements like if the life couldn't stop in this space.

BIOTOPE

Yuan-Cheng Wang

Taiwan

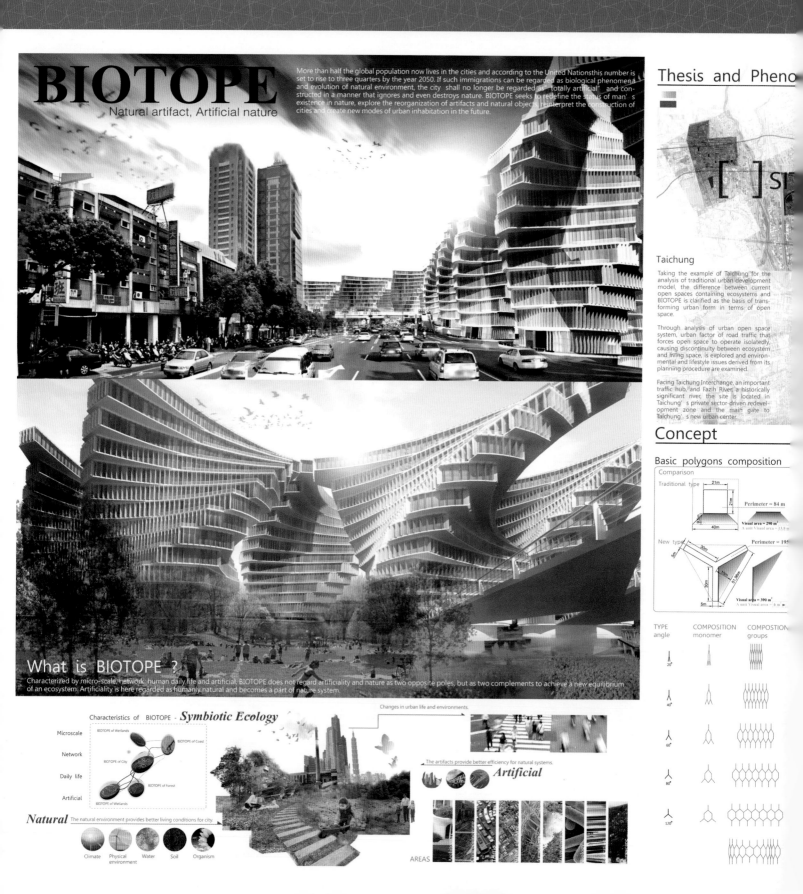

BIOTOPE
Natural artifact, Artificial nature

More than half the global population now lives in the cities and according to the United Nations this number is set to rise to three quarters by the year 2050. If such immigrations can be regarded as biological phenomena and evolution of natural environment, the city shall no longer be regarded as "totally artificial" and constructed in a manner that ignores and even destroys nature. BIOTOPE seeks to redefine the status of man's existence in nature, explore the reorganization of artifacts and natural objects, reinterpret the construction of cities and create new modes of urban inhabitation in the future.

Thesis and Pheno

[ ]s

Taichung

Taking the example of Taichung for the analysis of traditional urban development model, the difference between current open spaces containing ecosystems and BIOTOPE is clarified as the basis of transforming urban form in terms of open space.

Through analysis of urban open space system, urban factor of road traffic that forces open space to operate isolatedly, causing discontinuity between ecosystem and living space, is explored and environmental and lifestyle issues derived from its planning procedure are examined.

Facing Taichung Interchange, an important traffic hub, and Fazih River, a historically significant river, the site is located in Taichung's private sector-driven redevelopment zone and the main gate to Taichung's new urban center.

Concept

Basic polygons composition

Comparison

Traditional type — 21m — 21m — 40m
Perimeter = 84 m
Visual area = 290 m²
A unit Visual area = 13.8 m

New type — 30m — 5m — 57.58m — 30m — 5m
Perimeter = 195
Visual area = 390 m²
A unit Visual area = 6 m

TYPE angle	COMPOSITION monomer	COMPOSTION groups
20°		
40°		
60°		
80°		
120°		

What is BIOTOPE ?

Characterized by micro-scale, network, human daily life and artificial, BIOTOPE does not regard artificiality and nature as two opposite poles, but as two complements to achieve a new equilibrium of an ecosystem. Artificiality is here regarded as humanly natural and becomes a part of nature system.

Characteristics of BIOTOPE - *Symbiotic Ecology*

Microscale
Network
Daily life
Artificial

BIOTOPE of Wetlands
BIOTOPE of Coast
BIOTOPE of City
BIOTOPE of Forest
BIOTOPE of Wetlands

Changes in urban life and environments.

The artifacts provide better efficiency for natural systems.
Artificial

Natural The natural environment provides better living conditions for city

Climate | Physical environment | Water | Soil | Organism

AREAS

If three-quarters of the world's population will have migrated to live in cities by 2050, is it fair to keep referring to urban spaces as completely artificial environments? The Biotope skyscraper seeks to redefine the way a city is viewed, instead emphasizing migration as a biological phenomena, making urban life as natural an existence than one spent in a forest. In the Biotope, the built environment and the natural one complement each other, creating a new ecosystem for the future. Biotope seeks to redefine the status of man's existence in nature, explore the reorganization of artifacts and natural objects, reinterpret the construction of cities and create new modes of urban inhabitation in the future.

The Biotope is comprised of buildings stacked high with floors that are offset to create an overall appearance of structural twisting. The floors' positioning are inspired by the geometric theory of spiral phyllotaxis, which allows

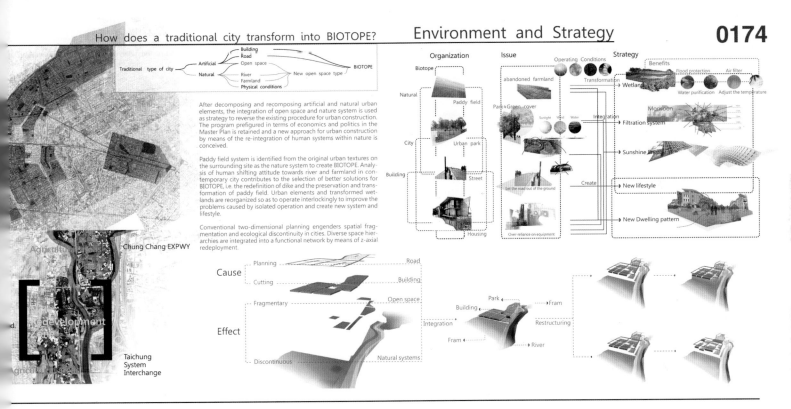

How does a traditional city transform into BIOTOPE?

Environment and Strategy

0174

After decomposing and recomposing artificial and natural urban elements, the integration of open space and nature system is used as strategy to reverse the existing procedure for urban construction. The program prefigured in terms of economics and politics in the Master Plan is retained and a new approach for urban construction by means of the re-integration of human systems within nature is conceived.

Paddy field system is identified from the original urban textures on the surrounding site as the nature system to create BIOTOPE. Analysis of human shifting attitude towards river and farmland in contemporary city contributes to the selection of better solutions for BIOTOPE, i.e. the redefinition of dike and the preservation and transformation of paddy field. Urban elements and transformed wetlands are reorganized so as to operate interlockingly to improve the problems caused by isolated operation and create new system and lifestyle.

Conventional two-dimensional planning engenders spatial fragmentation and ecological discontinuity in cities. Diverse space hierarchies are integrated into a functional network by means of z-axial redeployment.

Pattern evolution

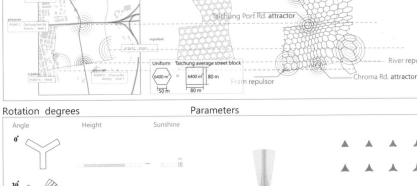

The most adaptable geometric prototype for both architectural spaces and open spaces is defined. Differentiation of positive and negative space yielded by various angle variations of prototype enables the creation of urban space diversity.

Analysis of influence of zoning-related activities on building types and living space configuration enables the hierarchical differentiation of rural/urban activity intensity and quality of life for the purpose of setting crucial parameters. Manipulation of radiolarian vector deformation with "attractor/repulsor" points in the grid.

On the principle of manipulating the proportional relationship between "architectural volume" and "open space", parametrically controlled generative prototypes will vary according to the adjusted parameters to create diverse urban spatial form to accommodate respective activities on the surrounding site.

Inspired by the geometric theory of spiral phyllotaxis, a mechanism that enables the building to expose its respective envelope surface of each floor to the same amount of sunlight by arranging the floors in such a manner that to what extent the lower will be shaded from light by the upper ones depends on their rotation angle and height is proposed. Different amount of sunlight required for diverse open spaces at different elevations and their respective functions will be defined by this means.

NEGATIVE space

Rotation degrees

Parameters

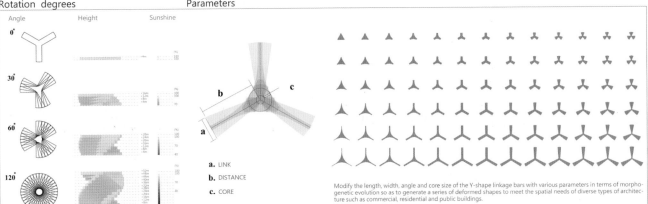

a. LINK
b. DISTANCE
c. CORE

Modify the length, width, angle and core size of the Y-shape linkage bars with various parameters in terms of morphogenetic evolution so as to generate a series of deformed shapes to meet the spatial needs of diverse types of architecture such as commercial, residential and public buildings.

a building's floor to both receive and also shade the floors below from sunlight throughout the day. Residential, commercial and public spaces are allotted for and mixed throughout each building.

Surrounding the massive structures, which are grouped closely to make a wall of twisting skyscrapers within a city, is ample green space that is used for recreation and for agricultural purposes. Instead of segregating land uses, the Biotope will combine them, having rice paddies abut buildings with roads adjacent, so as to keep people together despite varying uses and to keep urbanity green.

A paddy field system is identified from the original urban textures on the surrounding site as the nature system to create Biotope. Analysis of human shifting towards the river and farmland in contemporary times contributes to the

System Operation

Water system operation

Defensive line Section

4m

Watercourse filter system
2 years return period
rainfall 159mm /Day
level 112.58 m

Multi-functional constructed wetlands
10 years return period
rainfall 240mm /Day
level 113.71 m

Seasonal scenic wetlands
20 years return period
rainfall 348mm /Day
level 114.58 m

Urban park & urban detention ponds
100 years return period
rainfall 471mm /Day
level 116.73 m

Definition of four hierarchies of water system operation according to seasonal changes in Fazih River water level.

a. **Watercourse filter system** : watercourse change, aquatic plant filter bed system ;
b. **Multi-functional constructed wetlands** : water storage impoundment system that operates all year round, domestic sewage and river water purification ;
c. **Seasonal scenic wetlands** : wetlands respond to sudden storms and typhoon during the wet season, while they become verdant as stored water flows into multi-functional constructed wetlands during the dry season ;
d. **Urban park & urban detention ponds** : highest line of defense against the 100 year return period rainfall, which serves as urban park under ordinary circumstances.

The creation of a variety of types of open space and their respective novel utility under the circumstances of various hierarchies of operation. Illustration of water level variations that reflect various changes in rainfall.

Flood simulation

100 YEARS RETURN PERIOD
Total accumulated rainfall 471mm

20 YEARS RETURN PERIOD
Total accumulated rainfall 348mm

10 YEARS RETURN PERIOD
Total accumulated rainfall 240mm

2 YEARS RETURN PERIOD
Total accumulated rainfall 159mm

Water system

1st Defensive line
2nd Defensive line
3rd Defensive line

- Watercourse filter system
- Multi-functional constructed wetlands
- Seasonal scenic wetlands
- Urban park & urban detention ponds

Sediment pool
Watercourse
1st High-density planting
Junior School playground
Open Water Wetlands
Riverside Park
Seasonal scenic wetlands
2st High-density planting
Riverside Park
Ecological Pond
Elementary School playground
Metro Park
Landscape Pond

Building system

Height

Business & Office
Residential & Commercial
High-rise residential
Low-rise residential
Public space

Public space
Low-rise residential
High-rise residential
Residential & Commercial
Business & Office
High-rise residential
Public space
Low-rise residential

Architectural Det

Orienta
Orienta
Surface
Windo

Disposition of core system, building types and road system. Differentiation of various building types in BIOTOPE and definition of connected levels and rotation angles according to various functions of diverse generative prototypes. Categories of space-related activities corresponding to diverse architectural units.

BIOTOPE MASTERPLAN Section
water system, traffic system and architectural system are integrated into a network.

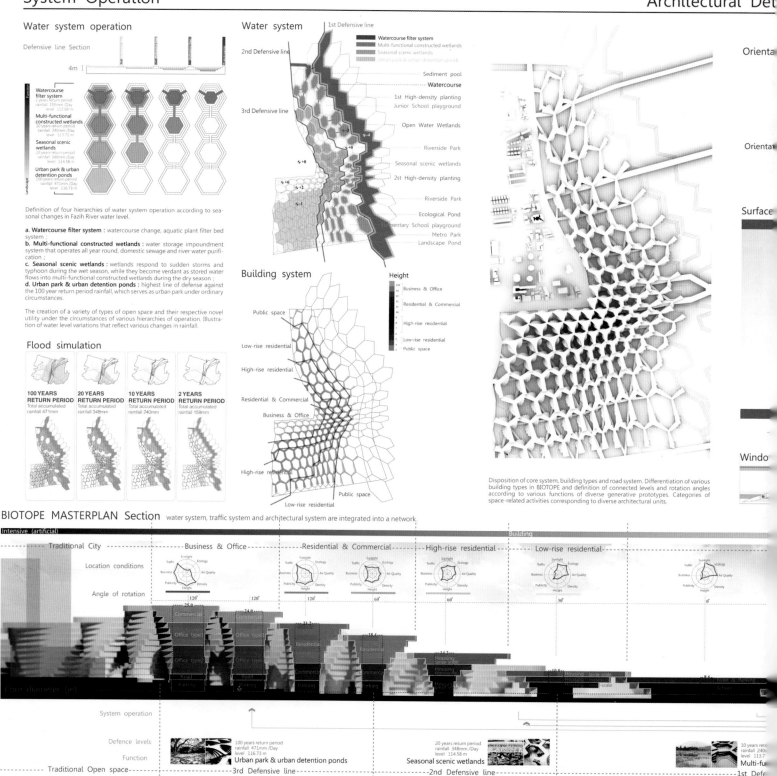

Intensive (artificial)

Traditional City — Business & Office — Residential & Commercial — High-rise residential — Low-rise residential

Building
Location conditions
Angle of rotation
Core diameter (m)
System operation
Defence levels
Function

100 years return period
rainfall 471mm /Day
level 116.73 m
Urban park & urban detention ponds

20 years return period
rainfall 348mm /Day
level 114.58 m
Seasonal scenic wetlands

10 years return period
rainfall 240mm /Day
level 113.7
Multi-fu

Traditional Open space — 3rd Defensive line — 2nd Defensive line — 1st Defe

Landscape
Orientation

selection of better solutions for Biotope including the redefinition of the dike and the preservation and transformation of the paddy field. Urban elements and transformed wetlands are reorganized so as to operate by interlocking to improve the problems cause by isolated operation and create a new system and lifestyle.

The complex of skyscrapers has an intricate water filtration system that helps safeguard the city against flooding. By utilizing park detention ponds, scenic wetlands, multi-functional constructed wetlands and a watercourse filter system, the layout of Biotope's natural spaces will help the city absorb water and clean it for reuse.

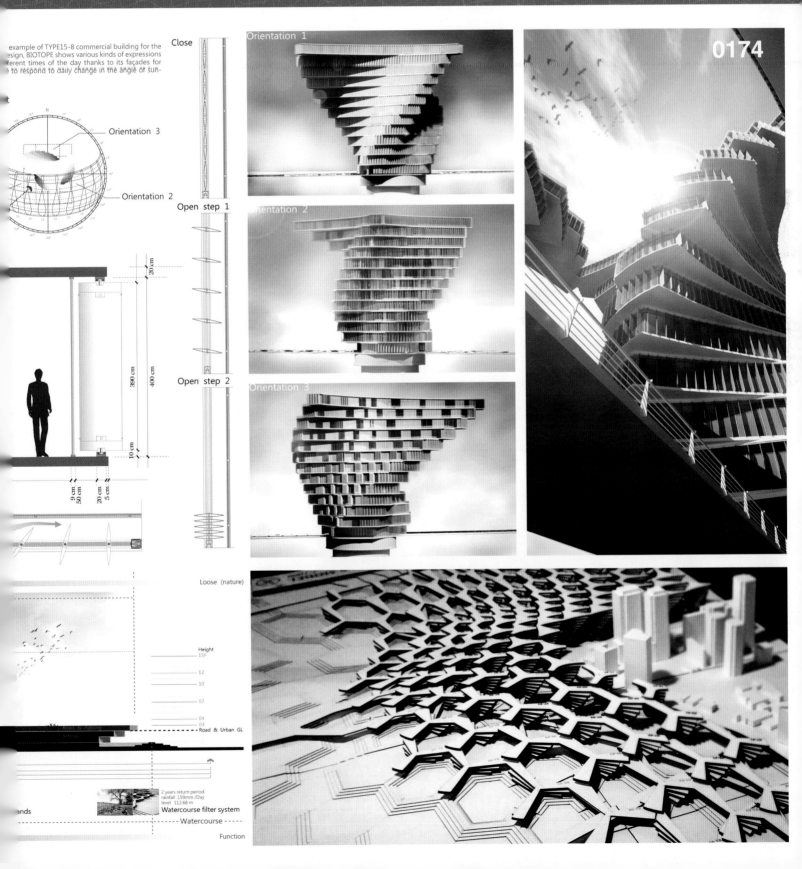

example of TYPE15-8 commercial building for the
esign, BIOTOPE shows various kinds of expressions
ferent times of the day thanks to its façades for
to respond to daily change in the angle of sun-

Orientation 3

Orientation 2

Close

Open step 1

Open step 2

20 cm

380 cm   400 cm

10 cm

9 cm
50 cm
20 cm
5 cm

Orientation 1

Orientation 2

Orientation 3

0174

Loose (nature)

Height
15F

12

10

07

04
03
Road & Urban GL

2 years return period
rainfall 159mm /Day
level 112.68 m
Watercourse filter system

Watercourse

Function

URBAN NOMADIC SCAFFOLDING

Volha Olya Piskun

Belarus

Globalization has led to increased levels of migrant construction workers.... = **potential** for architecture

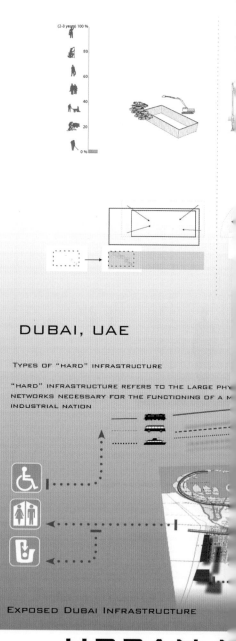

DUBAI, UAE

TYPES OF "HARD" INFRASTRUCTURE

"HARD" INFRASTRUCTURE REFERS TO THE LARGE PHY
NETWORKS NECESSARY FOR THE FUNCTIONING OF A M
INDUSTRIAL NATION

EXPOSED DUBAI INFRASTRUCTURE

URBAN N

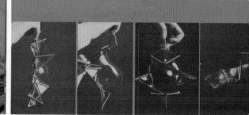

Globalization has led to an explosion of migrant workers across the world, and in Dubai migrant construction workers constitute 50% of the working class. To accommodate this ever-growing population, the designer of Urban Nomadic Scaffolding proposes rethinking stationary urban infrastructure to cater to this new migrant population in expanding and recently urbanized areas such as Dubai.

This project argues for the reprogramming of urban construction infrastructure based on a localized response to nomadic networks of workers in Dubai. However, all expatriates in Dubai, even those born in Dubai, are on short-term, renewable visas, living in overcrowded conditions. This project explores the potential for architecture to accommodate the flexible and ephemeral nature of nomadic populations in newly urbanized areas such as the UAE.

0370

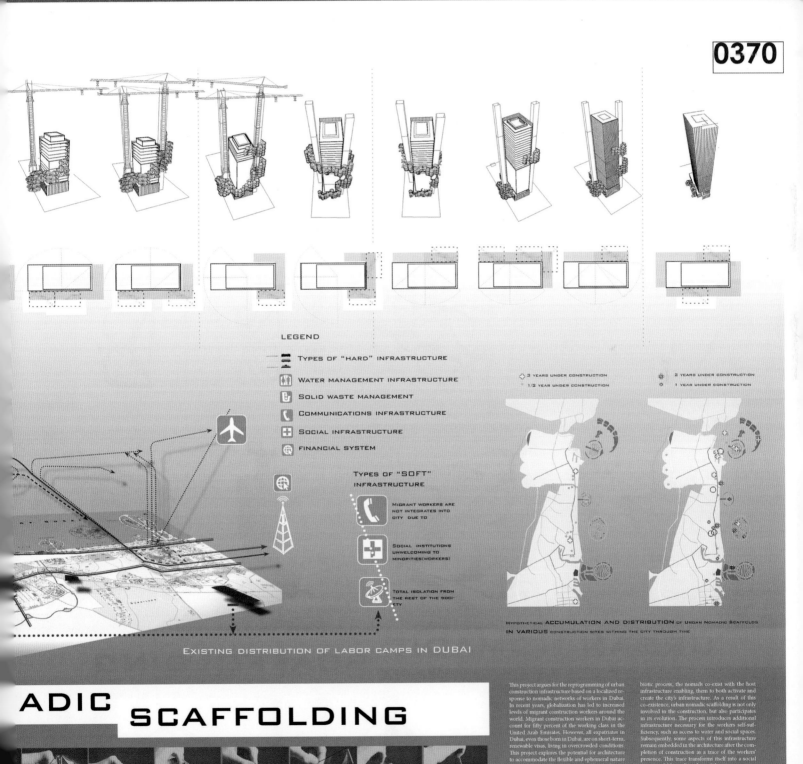

LEGEND

≡ TYPES OF "HARD" INFRASTRUCTURE

WATER MANAGEMENT INFRASTRUCTURE

SOLID WASTE MANAGEMENT

COMMUNICATIONS INFRASTRUCTURE

SOCIAL INFRASTRUCTURE

FINANCIAL SYSTEM

TYPES OF "SOFT" INFRASTRUCTURE

MIGRANT WORKERS ARE NOT INTEGRATES INTO CITY DUE TO

SOCIAL INSTITUTIONS UNWELCOMING TO MINORITIES (WORKERS)

TOTAL ISOLATION FROM THE REST OF THE SOCIETY

3 YEARS UNDER CONSTRUCTION
1/2 YEAR UNDER CONSTRUCTION

2 YEARS UNDER CONSTRUCTION
1 YEAR UNDER CONSTRUCTION

EXISTING DISTRIBUTION OF LABOR CAMPS IN DUBAI

HYPOTHETICAL ACCUMULATION AND DISTRIBUTION OF URBAN NOMADIC SCAFFLDS IN VARIOUS CONSTRUCTION SITES WITHIN THE CITY THROUGH TIME

ADIC SCAFFOLDING

This project argues for the reprogramming of urban construction infrastructure based on a localized response to nomadic networks of workers in Dubai. In recent years, globalization has led to increased levels of migrant construction workers around the world. Migrant construction workers in Dubai account for fifty percent of the working class in the United Arab Emirates. However, all expatriates in Dubai, even those born in Dubai, are on short-term, renewable visas, living in overcrowded conditions. This project explores the potential for architecture to accommodate the flexible and ephemeral nature of nomadic populations in newly urbanized areas such as the UAE.

The process of generating urban nomadic scaffolding creates a symbiosis between the nomadic construction workers and the infrastructure required in the process of building construction, as a social and spatial urban experience. Within this symbiotic process, the nomads co-exist with the host infrastructure enabling them to both activate and create the city's infrastructure. As a result of this co-existence, urban nomadic scaffolding is not only involved in the construction, but also participates in its evolution. The process introduces additional infrastructure necessary for the workers self-sufficiency, such as access to water and social spaces. Subsequently, some aspects of this infrastructure remain embedded in the architecture after the completion of construction as a trace of the workers' presence. This trace transforms itself into a social space available to all workers of the city.

The process of generating urban nomadic scaffolding creates a symbiosis between the nomadic construction workers and the infrastructure required in the process of building construction, as a social and spatial urban experience. Within this symbiotic process, the nomads co-exist with the host infrastructure enabling them to both activate and create the city's infrastructure.

As a result of this co-existence, urban nomadic scaffolding is not only involved in the construction, but also participates in its evolution. The process introduces additional infrastructure necessary for the workers self-sufficiency such as access to water and social spaces. Subsequently, some aspects of this infrastructure remain embedded in the architecture after the completion of construction as a trace of the workers' presence. This trace transforms itself

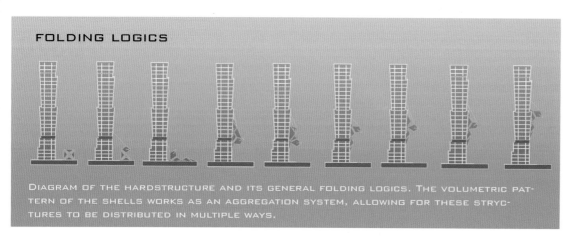

FOLDING LOGICS

DIAGRAM OF THE HARDSTRUCTURE AND ITS GENERAL FOLDING LOGICS. THE VOLUMETRIC PATTERN OF THE SHELLS WORKS AS AN AGGREGATION SYSTEM, ALLOWING FOR THESE STRYCTURES TO BE DISTRIBUTED IN MULTIPLE WAYS.

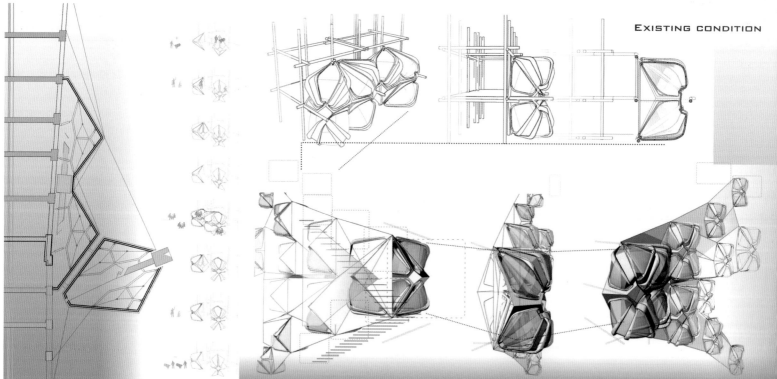

EXISTING CONDITION

URBAN NOMADIC SCAFFOLDING

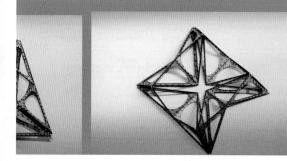
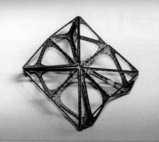
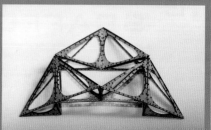

into a social space available to all workers of the city.

The buildings consist of minimal "hard structure," or skeletal bones that allow the skyscraper to stand. Basically towers with open floors, or "scaffolding," these skyscrapers can be adapted, floor-by-floor, to any use the inhabitants see fit. If one floor is to become a residence, access to electricity and water can be added if necessary, for example. The floors can be adapted in any way possible to ensure self-sufficiency. Globular mobile floors can also be added to the side and moved up and down to hold other programs, such as entertainment venues or public spaces.

By providing adaptable infrastructure, any number of vertical and horizontal, public and private uses can be created within these structures.

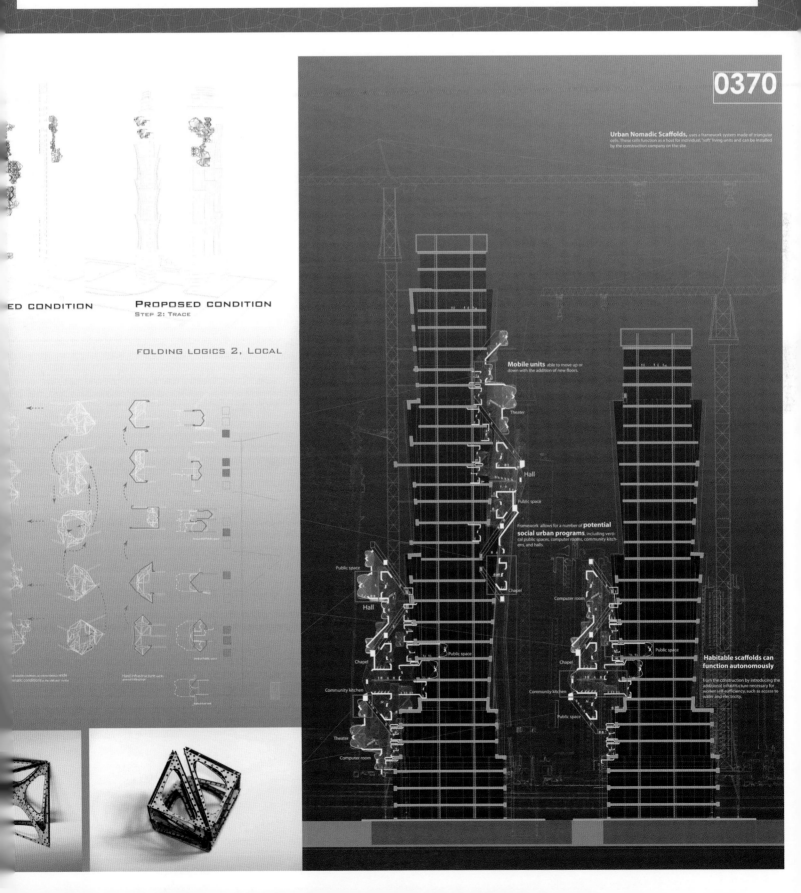

ED CONDITION   PROPOSED CONDITION
                      STEP 2: TRACE

FOLDING LOGICS 2, LOCAL

0370

Urban Nomadic Scaffolds, uses a framework system made of triangular cells. These cells function as a host for individual "soft" living units and can be installed by the construction company on the site.

Mobile units able to move up or down with the addition of new floors.

Theater

Hall

Public space

Framework allows for a number of **potential social urban programs**, including vertical public spaces, computer rooms, community kitchens, and halls.

Public space

Hall

Chapel

Public space

Chapel

Community kitchen

Theater

Computer room

Computer room

Chapel

Community kitchen

Public space

Public space

Habitable scaffolds can function autonomously

from the construction by introducing the additional infrastructure necessary for worker self-sufficiency, such as access to water and electricity.

NOISE REDUCTION TOWER

Radu Andrei
Mihail Simona Elena
Cojan Mihaela

Romania

SILEN

Noise pollution is a factor inherent in living and working situations that can completely disrupt a person's life. Unwanted sound can damage physiological and psychological health: it can cause annoyance and aggression, hypertension, high stress levels, tinnitus, hearing loss, sleep disturbances, and other harmful effects. By using several strategies in the construction of a skyscraper to reduce noise that can enter the structure, a residential building can be erected that can provide rest and relief from the chaotic urban environment even in the middle of the biggest city.

The skyscraper itself is comprised of two parts: a green urban platform and a residential tower, which are joined by a public area that also features commercial development. A sound-absorbent mesh is used to cover the platform, and the public area of the tower is made of similar sound absorbing materials; these feature spherical resonators that

0373

MUST BE HEARD

oise pollution still underestimated

is Noise Pollution

ne word noise comes from the Latin word us, meaning seasickness. Sound that is ed or disrupts one's quality of life is d noise. When there is lot of noise in nvironment, it is termed as noise ion. Sound becomes undesirable when it bs the normal activities such as g, sleeping, and during conversations. ISE POLLUTION IS EXCESSIVE, ASING HUMAN, animal or machine-created nmental noise that disrupts the ty or balance of human or animal life. rban planning may give rise to noise ion, since side-by-side industrial and ntial buildings can result in noise ion in the residential area.

e European Environment Agency (EEA) aunched the most comprehensive map of exposure to date, revealing the extent ich European citizens are exposed to ive acoustic pollution. The NOISE Observation and Information Service rope) database provides, at the click mouse, a picture of the numbers of exposed to noise generated by air, nd road traffic across Europe and in rge urban agglomerations.
ISE IS UBIQUITOUS BUT ITS ROLE AS A KEY F POLLUTION WITH SERIOUS HUMAN HEALTH UENCES IS STILL UNDERESTIMATED. ged exposure to even low levels of can trigger hypertension and disrupt A first glance at Europe's noise re map is far from soothing: it is ted than half of the population in areas with more than 250,000 tants endure levels above 55 dB(A) (the EU benchmark for an average 24-hour) as a result of ambient road noise.

Health Effects

Noise health effects are both health and behavioral in nature. This unwanted sound can damage physiological and psychological health. NOISE POLLUTION CAN CAUSE annoyance and aggression, HYPERTENSION, high stress levels, tinnitus, hearing loss, SLEEP DISTURBANCES, and other harmful effects.
Furthermore, stress and hypertension are the leading causes to health problems, whereas tinnitus can lead to forgetfulness, SEVERE DEPRESSION AND AT TIMES PANIC ATTACKS. Chronic exposure to noise may cause noise-induced hearing loss.
High noise levels can contribute to cardiovascular effects and exposure to moderately high levels during a single eight hour period causes a statistical rise in blood pressure of five to ten points and an increase in stress and vasoconstriction leading to the increased blood pressure noted above as well as to increased incidence of coronary artery disease.

Man-Made Noise May Be Altering Earth's Ecology

Bernie Krause listens to nature for a living. The 69-year-old is a field recording scientist.
Krause has a word for the pristine acoustics of nature: biophony. It's what the world sounds like in the absence of humans. But in 40 percent of the locations where Krause has recorded over the past 40 years, human-generated noise has infiltrated the wilderness.This isn't just a matter of aesthetics. "It's getting harder and harder to find places that aren't contaminated." The contamination of biophony may soon become a serious environmental issue.

Example of EEA noise exposure map Bucharest, Romania

In a biophony, animals divide up the acoustic spectrum so they don't interfere with one another's voices. It looks like the musical score for an orchestra, with each instrument in its place. No two species are using the same frequency. That's part of how they coexist so well. When they issue mating calls or all-important warning cries, they aren't masked by the noises of other animals.
But what happens when man-made noise — anthrophony — intrudes on the natural symphony? Maybe it's the low rumble of nearby construction or the high whine of a turboprop. Either way, it interferes with a segment of the spectrum already in use, and suddenly some animal can't make itself heard. The information flow in the jungle is compromised. IT DOESN'T TAKE MUCH TO DISRUPT A SOUNDSCAPE.
So how do you quiet an increasingly cacophonous world? Perhaps we should be developing not just clean tech but "quiet" tech, industrial machinery designed to run as silently as possible. More regulations could help, too. Cities have long had noise ordinances; wilderness areas could benefit from tighter protections as well.
Some of this is just about educating ourselves. We all recognize ecological tragedies by sight — when we see pictures of clear-cut areas, say, or melting Arctic ice shelves. NOW WE NEED TO LEARN TO LISTEN TO THE EARTH, too.

Sound Absorbtion

Conventionally speaking, acoustical materials are those materials designed and used for the purpose of absorbing sound that might otherwise be reflected.
SOUND ABSORPTION IS DEFINED, AS THE INCIDENT SOUND THAT STRIKES A MATERIAL THAT IS NOT REFLECTED BACK. An open window is an excellent absorber since the sounds passing through the open window are not reflected back but makes a poor sound barrier. Painted concrete block is a good sound barrier but will reflect about 97% if the incident sound striking it.
The sound absorbing characteristics of acoustical materials vary significantly with frequency. In general low frequency sounds are very difficult to absorb because of their long wavelength. Incorporating an air space behind an acoustical ceiling or wall panel often serves to improve low frequency performance.
When a sound source ceases in a space the sound waves will continue to reflect off the hard wall, floor and ceiling surfaces until it loses enough energy and dies out. The prolongation of the reflected sound is known as reverberation. Reverberation Time (RT) is defined as the number of seconds it takes for the reverberant sound energy to die down to one millionth (or 60dB) of it's original value from the instant that the sound signal ceases. Reverberation is dependent only on the volume of a space and the acoustically absorptive quality of the rooms finishes. Hard surfaced rooms will have a longer reverberation time than rooms finished with sound absorbing materials.
THE IMMEDIATE EFFECT OF MULTIPLE REFLECTIONS IS AN INCREASE IN THE SOUND INTENSITY CAUSED BY THE REFLECTIONS. A listener will hear the direct sound arriving at the ear along with all of the multiple reflections. Thus the combined loudness of the direct sound and the reflected sound will be greater than the direct sound alone.
There are three basic categories of sound absorbers: **porous materials** commonly formed of matted or spun fibers; **panel (membrane) absorbers** having an impervious surface mounted over an airspace; and **resonators** created by holes or slots connected to an enclosed volume of trapped air.

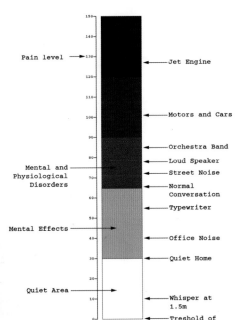

dB(A)
Examples of sound and their effects

Pain level → Jet Engine
→ Motors and Cars
→ Orchestra Band
→ Loud Speaker
Mental and Physiological Disorders → Street Noise
→ Normal Conversation
→ Typewriter
Mental Effects → Office Noise
→ Quiet Home
Quiet Area →
→ Whisper at 1.5m
→ Treshold of Audibility

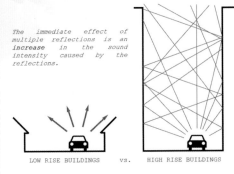

The immediate effect of multiple reflections is an **increase** in the sound intensity caused by the reflections.

LOW RISE BUILDINGS vs. HIGH RISE BUILDINGS

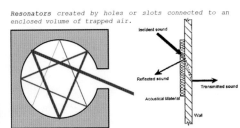

Resonators created by holes or slots connected to an enclosed volume of trapped air.

Incident sound
Reflected sound
Transmitted sound
Acoustical Material
Wall

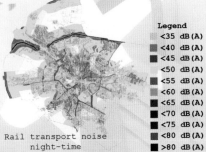

t noise -time

Street noise night-time

transport noise day-time

Rail transport noise night-time

Legend

	<35 dB(A)
	<40 dB(A)
	<45 dB(A)
	<50 dB(A)
	<55 dB(A)
	<60 dB(A)
	<65 dB(A)
	<70 dB(A)
	<75 dB(A)
	<80 dB(A)
	>80 dB(A)

sponge up the excessive acoustic pollution.

The main concept of the building is to absorb the noise created by the city and in doing so emphasizing the idea of the residential and public retreat. The mesh used to cover the platform and the public area of the tower is made up of fonoabsorbant materials with spherical resonators that manage to sponge up all the excessive acoustic pollution. The height of the tower as well as the level to which the sound absorbent mesh wrapped around it are dictated by the level of noise reflected from the neighboring buildings. The platform becomes a green public urban escape at street level, thanks to the multitude of resonators present at this plane. Once the noise reaches a certain acoustic comfort level, the residential modules start bursting forth from the tower's structural web.

The MAIN CONCEPT of the building is to ABSORB THE NOISE created by the city and in doing so EMPHASIZING THE IDEEA OF THE RESIDENTIAL AND PUBLIC RETREAT.

Around the world, cities are having to "think smart" to deal with GROWING URBANISATION. Available statistics show that more than half of the world's 7 billion people live in urban areas, crowded into 3% of the earth's land area. The proportion of the world's population living in urban areas, which was less than 5% in 1800 increased to 47% in 2000 and is expected to reach 65% in 2030. More than 90% of future population growth will be concentrated in cities in developing countries.

In Africa and Asia urbanization is still considerably lower (40%), both are expected to be 54% urban by 2025.

Although urbanization is the driving force for modernization, economic growth and development, there is increasing concern about the effects of expanding cities, principally on human health, livelihoods and the environment. Traffic congestion and noise pollution are major environmental impacts of large cities.

As a city grows, the need for space (land) grows and therefore highrise living becomes a necesity. The idea of having a RURAL RETREAT away from the cluster, constant noise and chaotic murmur of the city is APPEALING TO EVERYONE, BUT IMPOSSIBLE FOR MANY.

Combining all this factors the concept of somehow bringing such an oasis within the city becomes more and more feasible.

One of the main factors that must be taken into consideration is noise pollution. This modern plaque must be eliminated in order to create a space for tranquility in the heart of the city.

Therefore the main focus of this project is to provide a new way of living in the centre of the city, by dealing with the problem of sound polution.

The skyscaper proposal consists of TWO MAJOR PARTS: a URBAN PLATFORM and a RESIDENTIAL TOWER adjoint by a comercial and public area.

The MAIN CONCEPT of the building is to ABSORB THE NOISE created by the city and in doing so EMPHASIZING THE IDEEA OF THE RESIDENTIAL AND PUBLIC RETREAT.

THE MESH used to cover the platform and the area of the tower is made up of FONOA MATERIALS WITH SPHERIC RESONATORS, that ma sponge up all the excessive acoustic pollutio THE HIGHT OF THE TOWER as well as the level the sound absorbant mesh wrapped around it is BY THE LEVEL OF NOISE REFLECTED FROM THE NEIG BUILDINGS. The platform becomes a green publ escape at street level, thanks to the mult resonators present at this plain.

Once the noise reaches a certain acoustic com residential modules start bursting forth f towers structural web.

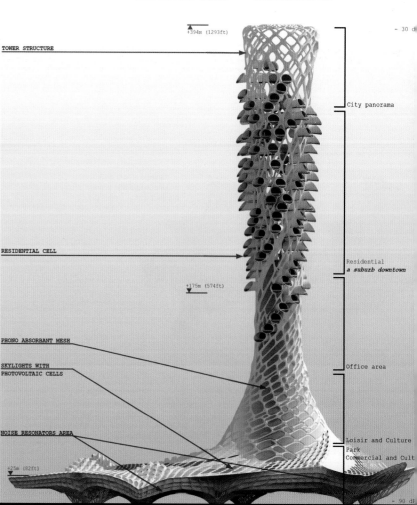

+394m (1293ft) — 30 d

TOWER STRUCTURE

City panorama

RESIDENTIAL CELL

+175m (574ft)

Residential
a suburb downtown

PHONO ABSORBANT MESH

SKYLIGHTS WITH
PHOTOVOLTAIC CELLS

Office area

NOISE RESONATORS AREA

+25m (82ft)

Loisir and Culture
Park
Commercial and Cult

— 90 d

These preventative measures, plus the building's height, are dictated by the location: The noisier the neighborhood, the higher and better insulated the skyscraper will be. This soundproof structural shell is outfitted with residential, office, and commercial cells to create clusters of programmatic uses.

Though negating urban noise pollution is the main focus of the structure, it also utilizes other sustainable elements in its construction, such as skylights with photovoltaic cells.

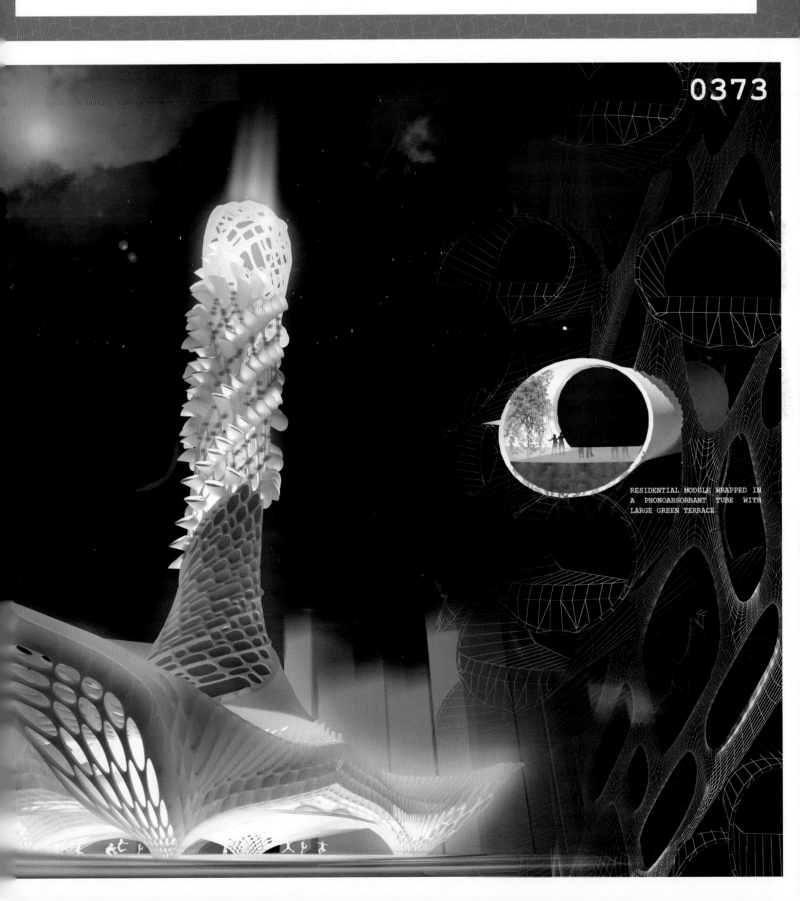

0373

RESIDENTIAL MODULE WRAPPED IN A PHONOABSORBANT TUBE WITH LARGE GREEN TERRACE

TEHRAN TOWER

Alireza Esfandiari
Nima Dehghani
Alireza Esfandiari
Mahdi Kamboozia
Mohammad Ashkbar Sefat

Iran

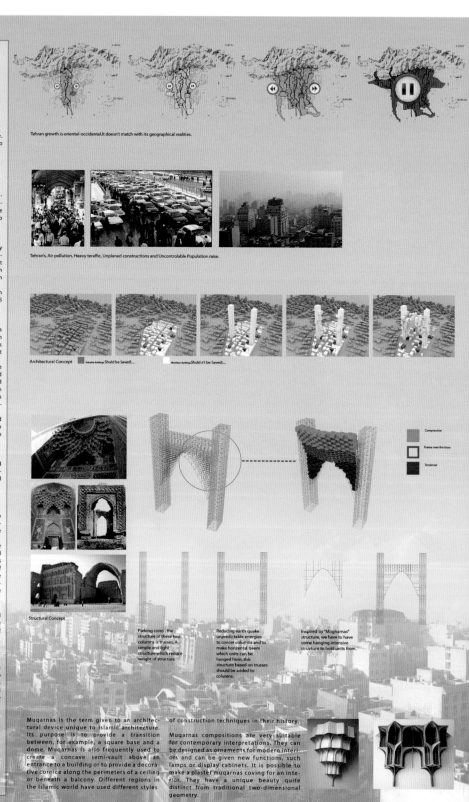

TEHRAN TOWER
Residential-cultural

City concept

Tehran introduction:
-Tehran is the capital of Iran and Tehran Province. With an estimated population of 8,429,807.it is also Iran's largest urban area and city.
-Urban area: 730 km2 (281.9 sq. mi)
-Elevation: 1,200 m (3,900 ft.)
-Density :10,327.6/km2 (26,748.3/sq. mi

-Tehran features a semi-arid, continental climate
-Tehran's climate is largely defined by its geographic location, with the towering Alborz Mountains to its north and the central desert to the south.it has 7 valley in the direction of north to south.

Tehran Problems:
Tehran suffers from severe air pollution and the city is often covered by smog , making breathing difficult and causing widespread pulmonary illnesses. It is estimated that about 27 people die each day from pollution-related diseases .and it cause more than 1000 million dollar damage to the city.
Every day 12 million useful hours of people in Tehran is wasted in traffic jams which results to 15 million dollars of defect to the country economy

why?
Not considering the earthquake faults, Tehran has been grown up in an unlimited way. With attention to the empty areas around Tehran, this growth has been done in a vertical way along the east and west axis.
According to the Tehran master plan ,buildings are allowed to build just 60 percent of their field because of this the speed of extension in west and east axes has grown up (the Tehran master plan which was proposed with victor Gruen ,a famous American architect ,did not coordinated with its geographical and social realities.)
this unscheduled and unplanned growth had resulted to the long daily working transportation from east to west and provoked to the air pollution and traffic jam.

Our proposal:
Stopping west to east growth of Tehran, and instead of it we propose north to south organization. Evacuating the faults, decreasing the planer density and exchanging the horizontal density to vertical

Architectural concept:

Our main idea in this project is to increasing the vertical density and decreasing the horizontal density to develop the green lands and retaining the most important buildings of the site.
Our method is to build the parking first to service the city and then omitting the old buildings and replacing them with new ones in our tower .in this level we keep the valuable buildings and instead of old buildings we will grow plants. And we estimate that after 5 years a tower will be ready to use completely while the incorrect buildings will be destroyed and instead of them green lands will be gifted to the city
This tower will supply about 1200 houses and occupy just 1200 m2 of the ground area whereas the same usual tower will destroy more than 30000 m2 of the ground to be built.

Structural concept:

Our idea is to use "Muqarnas" as a structural concept. "Muqarnas" is a traditional term .in order to build it they made a vault and hanged its basic parts with the tail horse hair and then they assembled other parts.it is a combination of vault and cable system .

Tehran growth is oriental-occidental.It doesn't match with its geographical realities.

Tehran's, Air pollution, Heavy teraffic, Unplaned constructions and Uncontrolable Population raise.

Architectural Concept — Valuable Buildings Shuld be Saved!... — Wortless Buildings Shuld n't be Saved!...

Structural Concept

Compressive
Frame over the truss
Tensional

Parking cores : the structure of these two columns is trusses. A simple and light structure which reduce weight of structure.

Reducing earth quake unpredictable energies to concet columns and to make horizental beem which units can be hanged from, this structure based on trusses should be added to columns.

Inspired by "Moqharnas" structure, we have to have some hanging intensive struvture to hold units from.

Muqarnas is the term given to an architectural device unique to Islamic architecture. Its purpose is to provide a transition between, for example, a square base and a dome. Muqarnas is also frequently used to create a concave semi-vault above an entrance to a building or to provide a decorative cornice along the perimeters of a ceiling or beneath a balcony. Different regions in the Islamic world have used different styles of construction techniques in their history.
Muqarnas compositions are very suitable for contemporary interpretations. They can be designed as ornaments for modern interiors and can be given new functions, such lamps or display cabinets. It is possible to make a plaster muqarnas coving for an interior. They have a unique beauty quite distinct from traditional two-dimensional geometry.

Tehran, Iran's largest city and its capital, is plagued by extreme air pollution, 80% of which is caused by auto traffic. Amongst its 8.5 million residents, it is estimated that 27 people die daily from pollution-related diseases, showing the tangible and deadly dangers that result from the traffic caused by urban sprawl. To combat this reality, the designers of the Tehran Tower propose building up, locating massive skyscrapers within Tehran to house masses of residents centrally.

Demolishing unimportant old buildings will create space both for the two legs of the large tower, which is connected above ground to create a wide building expanse, and for green space that will make the urban expanse as a whole more livable. By designing a tower with two legs that connect above ground, precious land is saved from

0415

development: the skyscraper occupies just 1,200 square meters of land versus the 30,000 square meters a typical tower would need for development. Each tower provides 1,200 housing units.

The overall shape for the tower is inspired by muqarnas, traditional Iranian vault and cable systems. Like concave vaults between two pillars, the residential units will hang en masse from the two sturdy legs of this structure. The legs are composed of trusses with parking cores at the bottom. (Cars park up the legs until the building convenes in the middle.) This helps keep them lightweight, and the structure as a whole flexible in the case of earthquakes.

The proposal also plants to stop west to east growth of the city of Tehran and instead begin a north to south organization, evacuating the earthquake faults in the area, decreating the planar density and exchanging the horizontal

density for a vertical one.

On the top of the structure, a solid floor is laid atop the hanging cells to create a green rooftop expanse to be enjoyed by residents. The tall height of the garden and the prefab residential cells help protect them from the noise pollution of the city, and subtle structural design elements provide shading to units in the summer to protect them from the harsh sun.

0415

First of all we construct the parking cores .these will service to the town and help to reduce the traffic and solves the big problem of lacking parking areas .after that the prefabricated unites will be installed.

Our project proposes a central garden above the tower which acts as a place for people in order to form social interactions .different activities like feeding birds and kite making are defined there.

Our tower is a combination of prefabricated units .they are shifted from each other in order to create roofs which act as a personal garden for units .these roofs also form the green façade of the project.

INVERTICITY

Ihnil Kim
Pannisa Praneeprachachon

United States

Our urban worlds, say the designers of Inverticity, are defined by cubes, structures that either impede pedestrians' paths or lure them in.

Looking to shake up this typical typology, the designers have envisioned locating a squat, truncated tetrahedron-shaped structure in the middle of dense Philadelphia. Not only is the shape unconventional, but the location of its interior tries to challenge the norm as well: Sky lobbies sit at the top of the building and small units are aggregated as legs for the structure that house private dwellings. In the middle are the more public programs, such as hotel units, a gym and public circulation. This arrangement brings people up from the ground and distributes them downwards, instead of the typical bottom-to-top public area distribution of skyscrapers. "The act of replicating the "ground level" experience

0418

Our world is massively constructed by different sizes of cubes. These cubes orient users to either flow around the mass or draws them in to its space. Our perspective of the world at "eye level" is blocked by these so called buildings. It has been our perception towards buildings that there is nothing wrong with what we see or not see. What we have forgotten is what it existed before all these buildings. The INVERTICITY is located in core of Philadelphia where it is densely built with tall massive buildings where people can't appreciate and experience. This is a study of giving the users a different experience of not just building but understanding what each person can see through the ground horizon level which we with "eye level" can see and understand a different typology of city without going into its mass.

The INVERTICITY challenges the urban typology of a skyscraper by inverting the programmatic convention of ground as public entity. With sky lobbies on the very top of the building, small units are aggregated as legs that house private dwellings, which then expand and intertwine to form more public programs, such as hotel units, gym, and public circulation. The transformation from individual modules to larger nesting geometry reflects the new programmatic arrangement that brings people up from the ground and distribute them downwards. The act of replicating the "ground level" experience on the top floor changes how the city and its urban nuances are perceived.

The geometry of a truncated tetrahedron lends itself to modularity that in turns increases efficiency in fabrication yet still produces variations in aggregation. The triangular and hexagonal faces that compose this geometry allows for change of direction and orientation and, as a result, affects the overall formation of the modules. The differences in each mode of aggregation produce unique typologies for different programmatic functions. The users are able to experience not only the aggregation as one big mass but also a singular unit with recognizable and familiar geometric forms. The modules are designed to facilitate future development as the city starts to change its culture as a response to current economy, demographics, and exchange. The modules can be easily added up to existing building or start where buildings have been demolished without disturbing their existence. We can visualize the method as a utilitarian city, yet the variety of its formal aggregation provides an opportunity for individuality. The new ground for viewing and inhabiting the urbanscape can simply stem from one geometry.

INVERTICITY

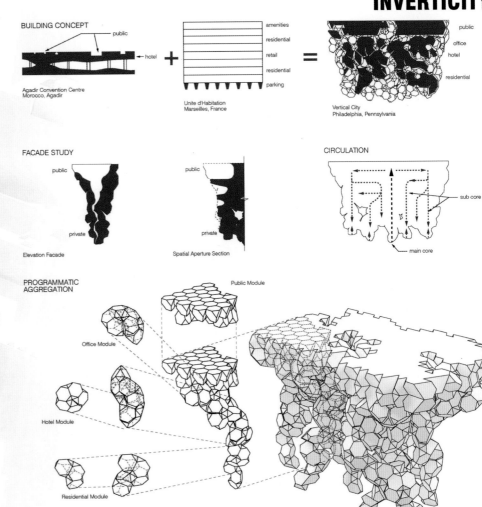

BUILDING CONCEPT

Agadir Convention Centre
Morocco, Agadir

amenities
residential
retail
residential
parking

Unite d'Habitation
Marseilles, France

public
office
hotel
residential

Vertical City
Philadelphia, Pennsylvania

FACADE STUDY

public   public
private   private

Elevation Facade   Spatial Aperture Section

CIRCULATION

sub core
main core

PROGRAMMATIC AGGREGATION

Public Module
Office Module
Hotel Module
Residential Module

on the top floor changes how the city and its urban nuances are perceived," the designers say.

Inverticity challenges the urban typology of a skyscraper by inverting the programmatic convention of ground as public entity. With sky lobbies on the very top of the building, small units are aggregated as legs that house private dwellings, which then expand and intertwine to form more public programs, such as hotel units, gym, and public circulation. The transformation from individual modules to larger nesting geometry reflects the new programmatic arrangement that brings people up from the ground and distributes them downwards. The act of replicating the ground level experience on the top floor changes how the city and its urban nuances are perceived.

The legs are thick but in no way uniformly shaped; as they rise taller, the legs merge towards each other, creating

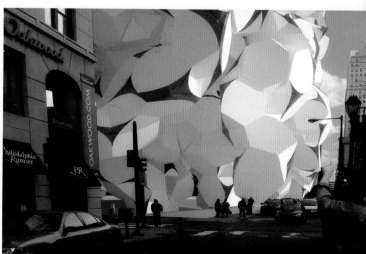

a more solid mass of building for its middle and top. The triangular and hexagonal forms that comprise the structure create modules, allowing the building to be flexible: as it needs to grow, more modules are added to the structure. While the uses within the building are utilitarian, the complex geometric shapes created through the module groupings give the structure a unique individuality.

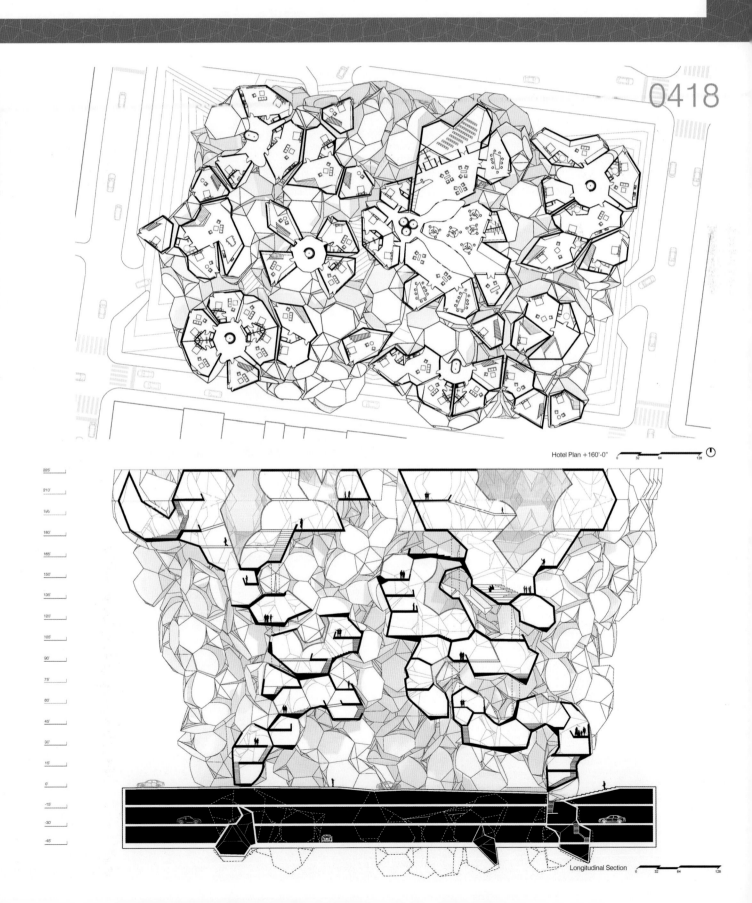

0418

Hotel Plan +160'-0"   0   32   64   128

Longitudinal Section   0   32   64   128

TUBULAR URBANISM

Toshiki Hirano

United States

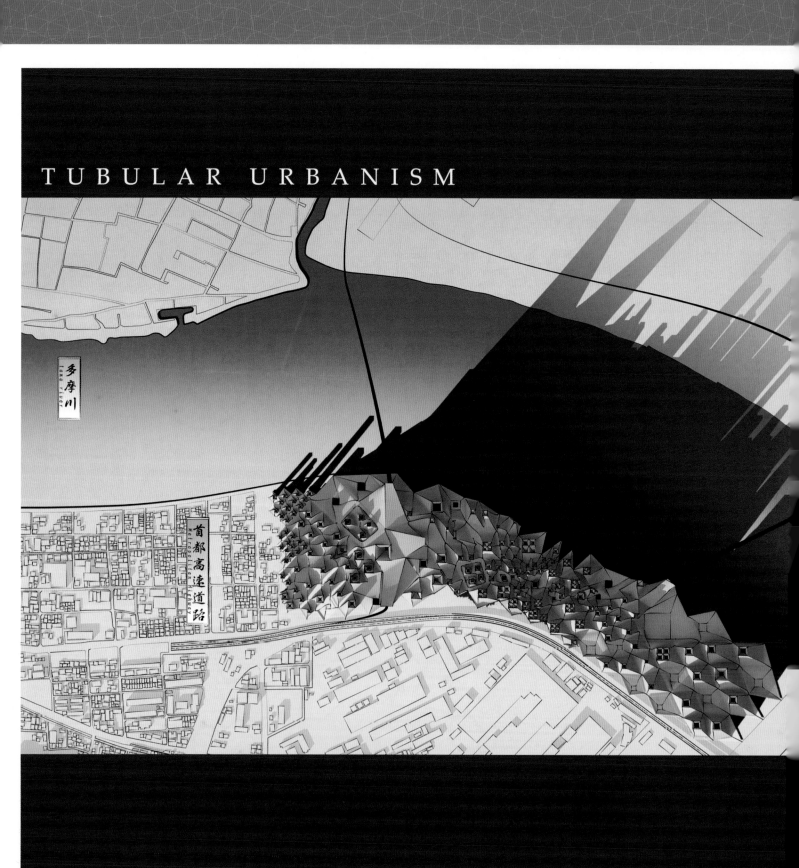

Centralized urban areas like Tokyo have been interested in subdividing the location and centers of business, culture, and governance for some time. Tubular Urbanism is a one such potential scheme for the decentralization of Tokyo, taking the idea of a fish market and converting it to a wholesale urban planning strategy. Taking Japanese Metabolist architecture as an inspiration,

Tubular Urbanism looks to create a richly diverse architectural scheme out of a singular, repeating typology. This is analogous to the three different kinds of meat typically harvested from tuna fish in Japan. In this model, like in the tuna, each programmatic component is distinctly different from the others, but contributes and is derived from the same homogenous whole.

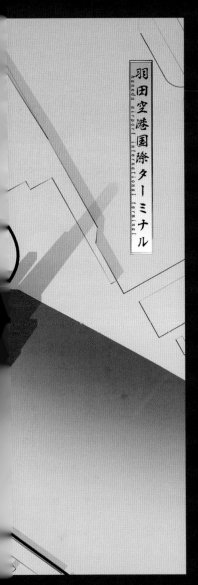

0563

Autonomous micro city

Being one of the few metropolises in the world which is still growing in population, and also having been a capitol city for more than 400 years, over-centralization of economy, industry, and culture in Tokyo reaches a certain point where it needs to find a way to decentralize its functions to reduce a risk of a possible disaster, which is estimated to have 4000 billion dollars damage. Tokyo needs a new urban model.

One solution can be dividing its functions into several autonomous micro-cities. Many of large scale redevelopment in Roppongi, such as Roppongi Hills and Tokyo Midtown can be defined as autonomous micro-cities. However, as Shohei Shigematsu of OMANY criticizes them by comparing to a Bento box, those redevelopments lack of identities and thus accelerate the generalization of the city.

This project is an experiment to seek a potential of the autonomous micro city by inserting a singular program in its core - fish market.

Tubular system

One of the characteristics of tubular form is a capability of connecting one space to the other while maintaining an implication of a division between each space.

In this project, this form enables fish market function to coexist with other urban programs, and creates an interaction between each other.

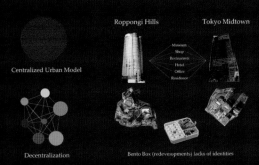

Centralized Urban Model

Roppongi Hills   Tokyo Midtown

Museum
Shop
Restaurants
Hotel
Office
Residence

Decentralization

Bento Box (redevelopments) lacks of identities

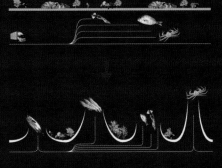

People can see, hear, or even smell activities inside the fish market through a hole of each tube.

One of the characteristics of tubular form is a capability of connecting one space to the other while maintaining an implication of a division between each space. In this project this form enables fish market functions to coexist with other urban programs and creates an interaction between each other.

Each capsule is fixed in its function as a habitation unit and plugged into a core. Metabolism treats a unit as a closed system that lacks flexibility and each of the units needs to be connected to another hierarchy system. As an alternative to Metabolism, this project seeks a potential of the open-ended system of tuna fish that creates different qualities out of a single system.

Here, an autonomous micro city is created through the development of this singular program, the fish market,

TUBULAR URBANISM

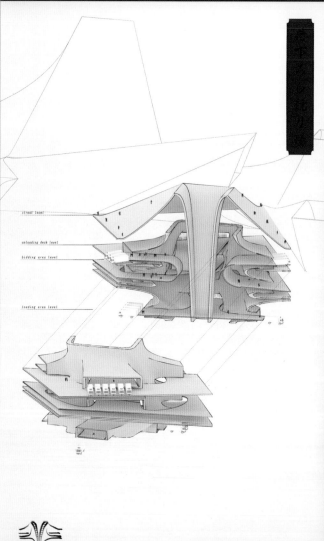

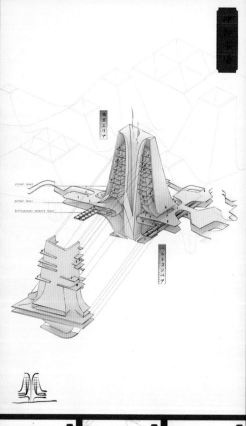

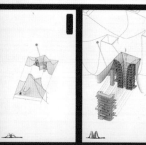

Tuna fish VS. Metabo

Japanese people distinguish a meat
Chu-toro, and Akami, and put a signific
However, these three parts are fundame
all consist of same three ingredient
differences in ratio(changes of comp
dramatic differences in their tastes.
Kurokawa is fixed in its function as a
core. Metabolism treats a unit as an clo
each of the units needs to be connected
As an alternative to Metabolism, this
ended system of tuna fish that create
system. Each tubular unit is made out
tubes growing downward. By changin
the unit adapts to various functions
wholesale market, office...etc. This city

Unit typology

Single housing unit   Collective housing unit   Unloading and

and is manifested in a variety of architectural expressions, each of which is based on particular use or function. The repeating unit in this micro city is a tube that is itself made of many other tubes that grow down towards the bay, tubes that grow up towards the sky, and floor slabs that connect and span between these two kinds of tubes. A functioning, autonomous city is created when these three forms are manipulated and interchanged.

0563

three parts: Toro,
e on each of them.
the sense that they
lean tissue. Only
ngredients create
Nakagin Tower by
nd plugged into a
acks flexibility and
hierarchy system.
ential of the open
es out of a single
pward ,slabs, and
of three elements,
s single housing,

Office, Temporary housing unit

Metabolism
"Monofunctional, Closed system"

VS

Tuna Fish
"Multifunctional, Opened system"

Ootoro

Chutoro

Akami

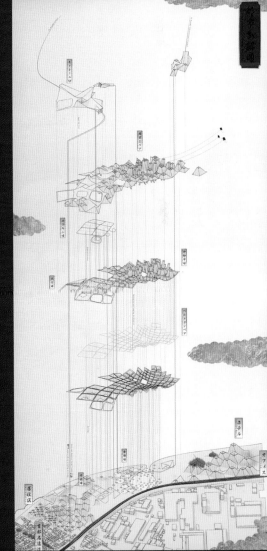

DOOMSDAY GREEN

Rajat Ghosh
Nafees Raees Ahmed Khan
Arun Mohan

India

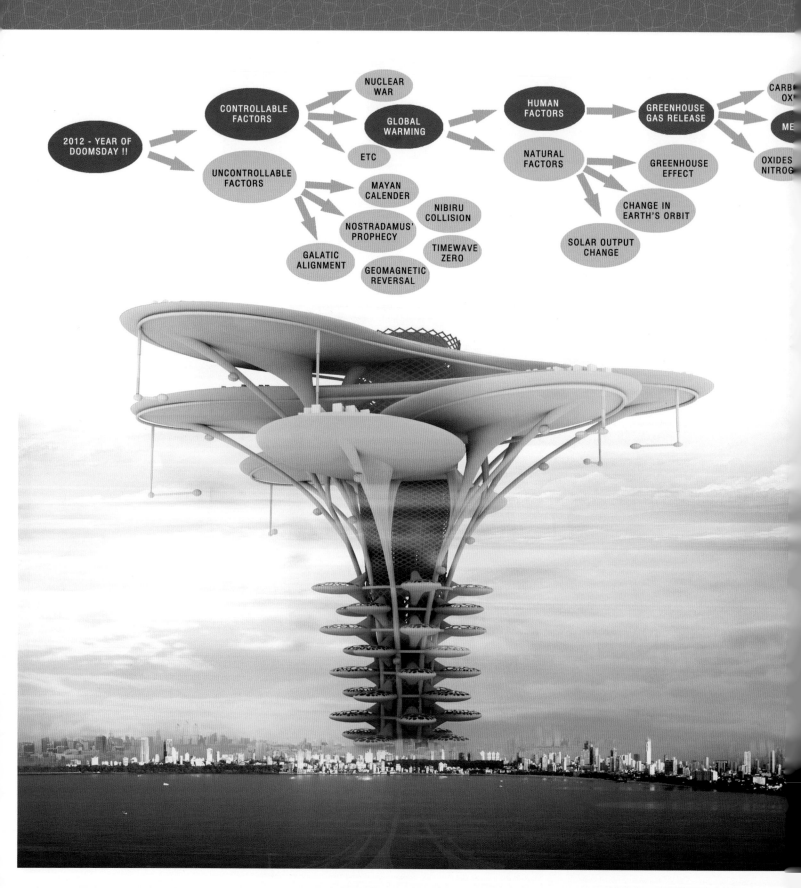

Doomsday Green is proposal for curbing anthropogenic climate change through the development of a vertical "suburb," an agricultural and waste management skyscraper. Choosing to focus on a doomsday-related aspect, specifically methane production as a potential source for human-caused global climate change, that can be potentially stalled or reversed, this proposal seeks to utilize methane as a productive natural resource.

The structure takes in citywide waste from the sewer system and through a series of vertically stacked farms arrayed around a central core, treats and purifies the methane gas expelled through agricultural processes. This gas rises through the structure and is eventually used to generate electricity to power a miniature suburb located atop the structure.

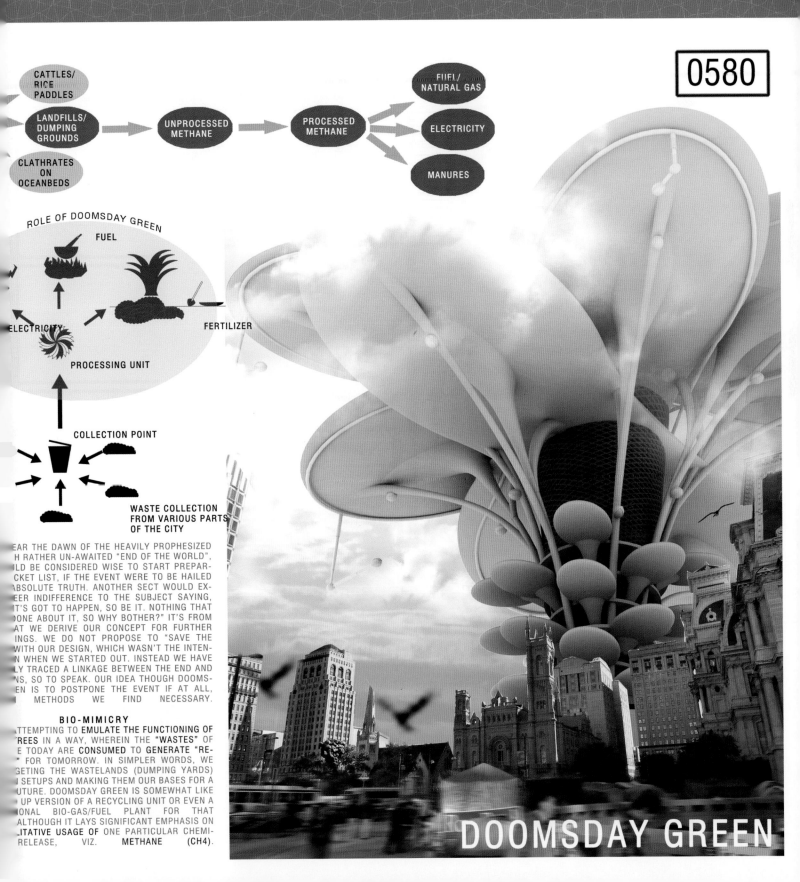

0580

CATTLES/ RICE PADDLES

LANDFILLS/ DUMPING GROUNDS → UNPROCESSED METHANE → PROCESSED METHANE → FUEL/ NATURAL GAS

CLATHRATES ON OCEANBEDS

ELECTRICITY

MANURES

ROLE OF DOOMSDAY GREEN

FUEL

ELECTRICITY

FERTILIZER

PROCESSING UNIT

COLLECTION POINT

WASTE COLLECTION FROM VARIOUS PARTS OF THE CITY

EAR THE DAWN OF THE HEAVILY PROPHESIZED H RATHER UN-AWAITED "END OF THE WORLD", LD BE CONSIDERED WISE TO START PREPAR-CKET LIST, IF THE EVENT WERE TO BE HAILED BSOLUTE TRUTH. ANOTHER SECT WOULD EX-ER INDIFFERENCE TO THE SUBJECT SAYING, T'S GOT TO HAPPEN, SO BE IT. NOTHING THAT ONE ABOUT IT, SO WHY BOTHER?" IT'S FROM AT WE DERIVE OUR CONCEPT FOR FURTHER INGS. WE DO NOT PROPOSE TO "SAVE THE WITH OUR DESIGN, WHICH WASN'T THE INTEN-N WHEN WE STARTED OUT. INSTEAD WE HAVE LY TRACED A LINKAGE BETWEEN THE END AND NS, SO TO SPEAK. OUR IDEA THOUGH DOOMS-EN IS TO POSTPONE THE EVENT IF AT ALL, METHODS WE FIND NECESSARY.

BIO-MIMICRY
TTEMPTING TO EMULATE THE FUNCTIONING OF REES IN A WAY, WHEREIN THE "WASTES" OF E TODAY ARE CONSUMED TO GENERATE "RE-" FOR TOMORROW. IN SIMPLER WORDS, WE GETING THE WASTELANDS (DUMPING YARDS) SETUPS AND MAKING THEM OUR BASES FOR A UTURE. DOOMSDAY GREEN IS SOMEWHAT LIKE UP VERSION OF A RECYCLING UNIT OR EVEN A IONAL BIO-GAS/FUEL PLANT FOR THAT ALTHOUGH IT LAYS SIGNIFICANT EMPHASIS ON ITATIVE USAGE OF ONE PARTICULAR CHEMI-RELEASE,   VIZ.   METHANE   (CH4).

DOOMSDAY GREEN

This design attempts to emulate the functioning of plants and trees in a way wherein the "wastes" of daily life are consumed to generate "resources" for tomorrow. In simpler terms, it targets the wastelands of urban setups and makes them the basis for a better future. Doomsday Green is like a scaled up version of a recycling unit of even a conventional biogas plant, although it lays significant emphasis on the qualitative usage of one particular chemical release, methane.

The role of Doomsday Green is to locate the collection point of waste and process what it resources it collects to produce electricity, fuel, fertilizer, and more.

Doomsday Green is modeled after the structural morphology of a tree, with a wide canopy at the top, populated

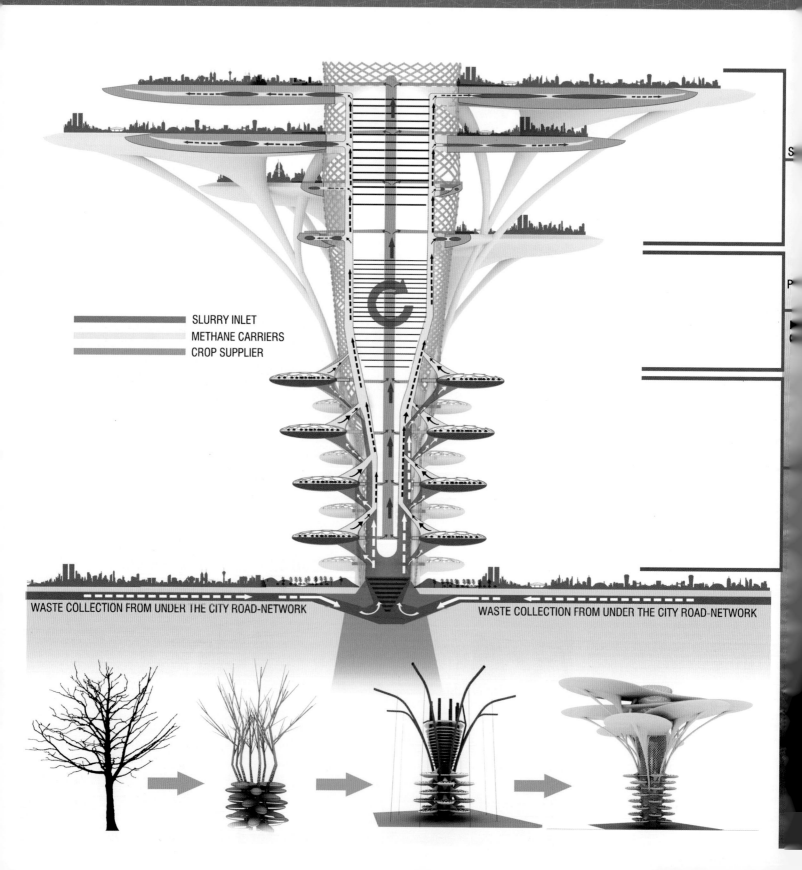

SLURRY INLET
METHANE CARRIERS
CROP SUPPLIER

WASTE COLLECTION FROM UNDER THE CITY ROAD-NETWORK   WASTE COLLECTION FROM UNDER THE CITY ROAD-NETWORK

by the fully functioning suburb, a central truck, through which the methane gas is purified, and with roots, which bring in the raw sewage. This biomimetic approach is present both in the formal expression of Doomsday Green, as well as in the programmatic scheme for the structure. The building proposes to create a closed loop of waste, natural materials, and outputs. It is anticipated that Doomsday Green can be adapted to any urban setting by simply plugging into an existing sewage system.

UNDERGROUND WASTE COLLECTION CHANNELS RUNNING BELOW THE ENTIRE CITY ROAD NETWORK

POSSIBLE SITE FOR "DOOMSDAY GREEN"

METHANE FROM MUNICIPAL SOLID WASTE LANDFILLS CH4 IS A HYDROCARBON AND THE PRIMARY COMPONENT OF NATURAL GAS. IT IS ALSO A POTENT GREEN HOUSE GAS WITH A GLOBAL WARMING POTENTIAL MORE THAN 20 TIMES THAT OF CO2. MUNICIPAL SOLID WASTE LANDFILLS ARE THE SECOND LARGEST SOURCE OF MAN-MADE CH4 EMISSIONS IN THE UNITED STATES, ACCOUNTING FOR ABOUT 23% OF THE COUNTRY'S CH4 EMISSIONS IN 2006. DESPITE ITS POTENCY AS A GREEN HOUSE GAS, CH4 HAS A RELATIVELY SHORT ATMOSPHERIC LIFETIME OF 9-14 YEARS, MEANING PROJECTS THAT CAPTURE CH4 FROM LANDFILLS OFFER A SIGNIFICANT OPPORTUNITY TO MITIGATE ATMOSPHERIC CONCENTRATIONS OF CH4
SOURCE:U.S.EPA,2008B .

METHANE IS USED IN INDUSTRIAL CHEMICAL PROCESSES AND MAY BE TRANSPORTED AS A REFRIGERATED LIQUID (LIQUEFIED NATURAL GAS, OR LNG). WHILE LEAKS FROM A REFRIGERATED LIQUID CONTAINER ARE INITIALLY HEAVIER THAN AIR DUE TO THE INCREASED DENSITY OF THE COLD GAS, THE GAS AT AMBIENT TEMPERATURE IS LIGHTER THAN AIR. GAS PIPELINES DISTRIBUTE LARGE AMOUNTS OF NATURAL GAS, OF WHICH METHANE IS THE PRINCIPAL COMPONENT.
- FUEL/NATURAL GAS
- ELECTRICITY
- CHEMICAL FEEDSTOCK
- POTENTIAL ROCKET FUEL

0580

DOOMSDAY GREEN

VERTICAL GROUND

Nassim Es-Haghi
George Kontalonis
Jared Ramsdell
Rana Zureikat

Greece/Jordan/
United Kingdom/United States

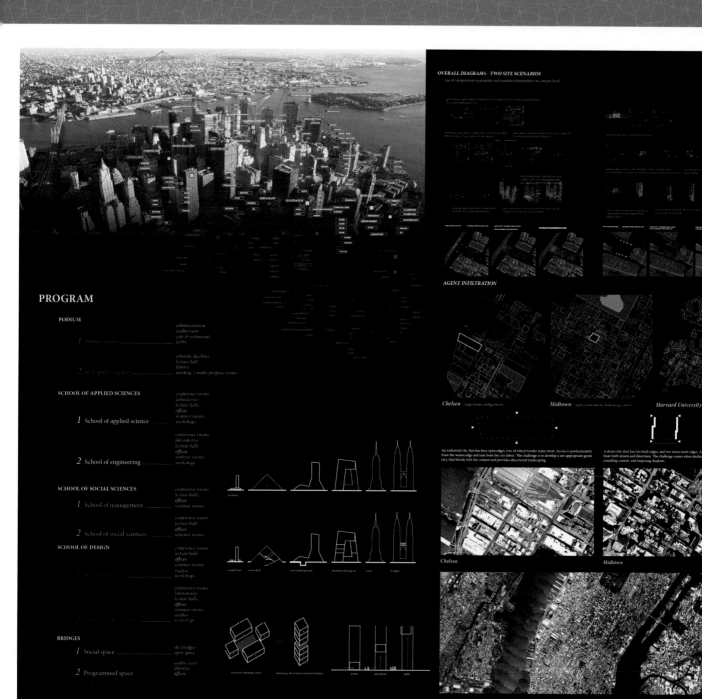

PROGRAM

PODIUM

1 public space
- administration
- auditorium
- cafe & restaurant
- lobby

2 non-public space
- athletic facilities
- lecture hall
- library
- meeting / multi-purpose rooms

SCHOOL OF APPLIED SCIENCES

1 School of applied science
- conference rooms
- laboratories
- lecture halls
- offices
- seminar rooms
- workshops

2 School of engineering
- conference rooms
- laboratories
- lecture halls
- offices
- seminar rooms
- workshops

SCHOOL OF SOCIAL SCIENCES

1 School of management
- conference rooms
- lecture halls
- offices
- seminar rooms

2 School of social sciences
- conference rooms
- lecture halls
- offices
- seminar rooms

SCHOOL OF DESIGN

1 School of design
- conference rooms
- lecture halls
- offices
- seminar rooms
- studios
- workshops

2 School of architecture
- conference rooms
- laboratories
- lecture halls
- offices
- seminar rooms
- studios
- workshops

BRIDGES

1 Social space
- sky bridges
- open space

2 Programmed space
- multi-stories
- libraries
- offices

OVERALL DIAGRAMS - TWO SITE SCENARIOS

AGENT INFILTRATION

Chelsea large linear configuration *Midtown* tight constraints & challenging context *Harvard University* traditional campus

Chelsea

Midtown

SITE INVESTIGATIONS - NEW YORK CITY

auditorium event space restaurant library research studio event space workshop computer lab connections

The Vertical Ground project re-examines the norm for the organization of college campuses. Students today want proximity to the culture, activities, and networks available in urban settings, but typical campuses are horizontally oriented and require large swaths of land for development, which are increasingly rare in desirable urban areas. By orienting a college campus vertically instead, colleges can locate in dense areas and perhaps even better facilitate social communication amongst students and faculty.

20,000 students are located on a campus complex that is comprised of several towers that occupy a small city footprint, and are connected at varying heights by sky bridges. By spacing programmatic needs properly throughout the towers, the vertically orientated campuses can give students both space for privacy and opportunities for dynamic

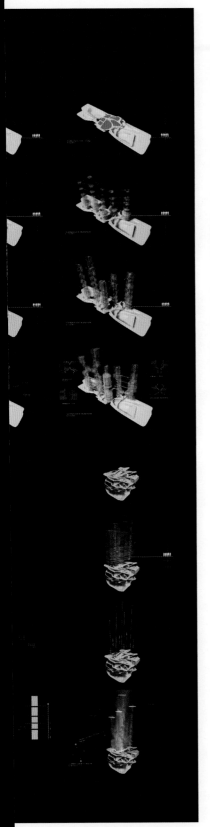

0788

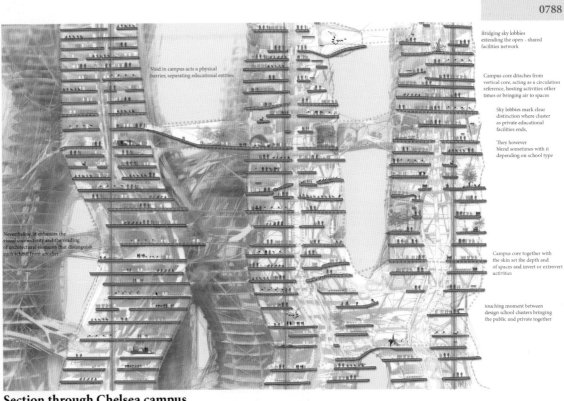

Void in campus acts a physical barrier, separating educational entities.

Nevertheless, it enhances the visual connectivity and the reading of architectural elements that distinguish each school from another

Bridging sky lobbies extending the open - shared facilities network

Campus core ditaches from vertical core, acting as a circulation reference, hosting activities other times or bringing air to spaces

Sky lobbies mark clear distinction where cluster as private educational facilities ends,

They however blend sometimes with it depending on school type

Campus core together with the skin set the depth and of spaces and invert or extrovert activities

touching moment between design school clusters bringing the public and private together

Section through Chelsea campus

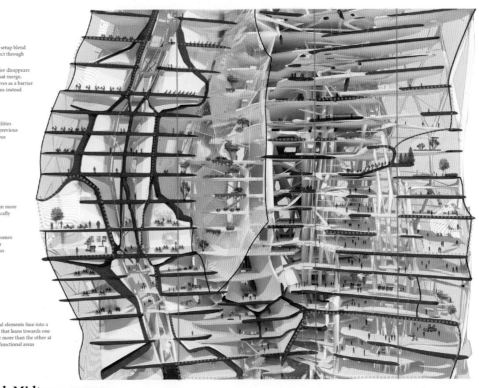

Sky lobbies in a confined setup blend with functions and connect through the body of schools

External skin barrier disappears between schools that merge, Campus core behaves as a barrier separating functions instead

Parts of major shared facilities are pushed to utilize the previous outdoor volume on campus

Open shared facilities gain more volume and expand vertically

This outdoor voulme becomes central and important for navigation though campus and ventilation

Structural elements fuse into a gradient that leans towards one language more than the other at distinct functional areas

Section through Midtown campus

interactions with others. The campus tower typology is composed of series of clustered departments and open spaces that are located amongst the college's three schools: Applied Sciences, Design, and Social Sciences.

The sky lobbies are bridged, extending the open, shared facilities network. The campus core detaches from the vertical core, acting as a circulation reference, hosting activities other times or bringing air spaces. Sky lobbies mark clear distinction where clusters of private educational facilities end. They however blend sometimes with it, depending on the school type.

The designers imagined two test sites for campuses within Manhattan, transforming the typical sprawling land model of a campus to one that is a super block. Lighting conditions and restrictions at ground level and in relation to

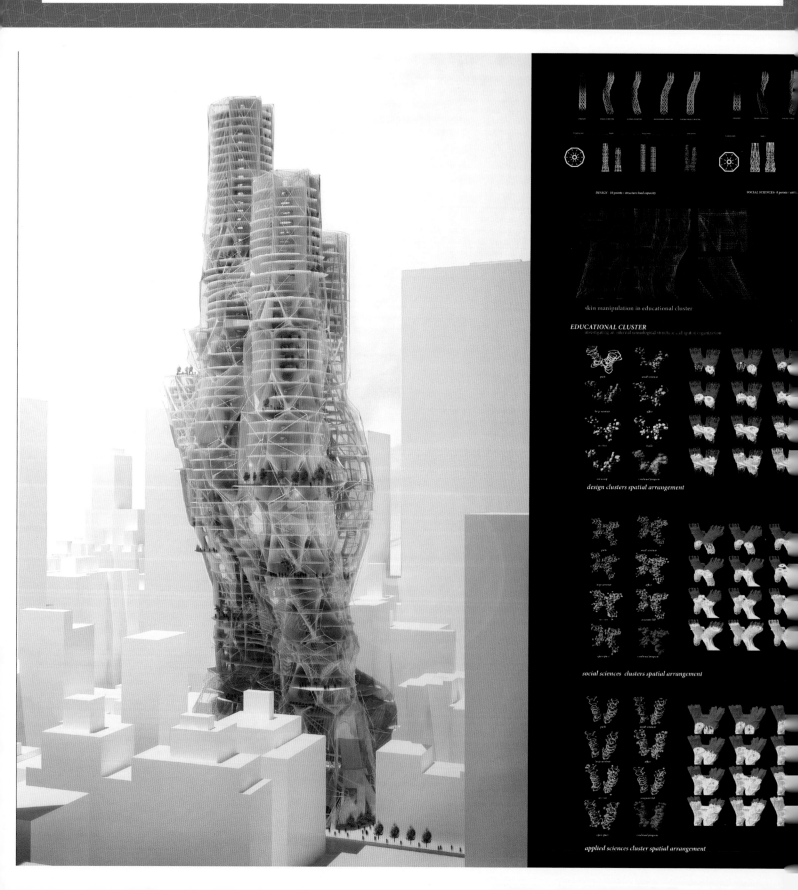

skin manipulation in educational cluster

EDUCATIONAL CLUSTER
investigating an internal technological structure and spatial organization

design clusters spatial arrangement

social sciences clusters spatial arrangement

applied sciences cluster spatial arrangement

other nearby buildings present new issues with which vertical campuses need to adapt. Neighborhood restrictions also pose interesting issues: Due to building requirements, a campus in New York's Chelsea neighborhood would look different than one built in Midtown, for example, as Midtown would allow for construction with taller tower heights. This might give a Chelsea campus difficulties should it ever need to expand, but despite these issues, the designers contend that orienting a campus vertically allows for more programmatic flexibility and opportunities for dynamic interaction than a campus plan that requires an open expanse of land.

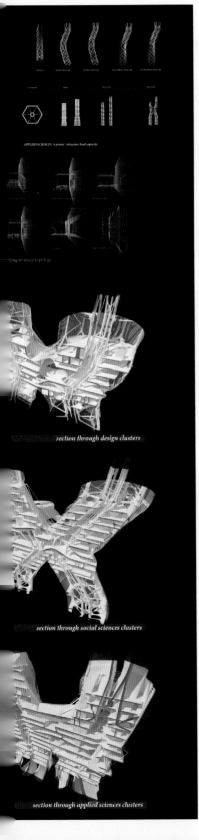

section through design clusters

section through social sciences clusters

section through applied sciences clusters

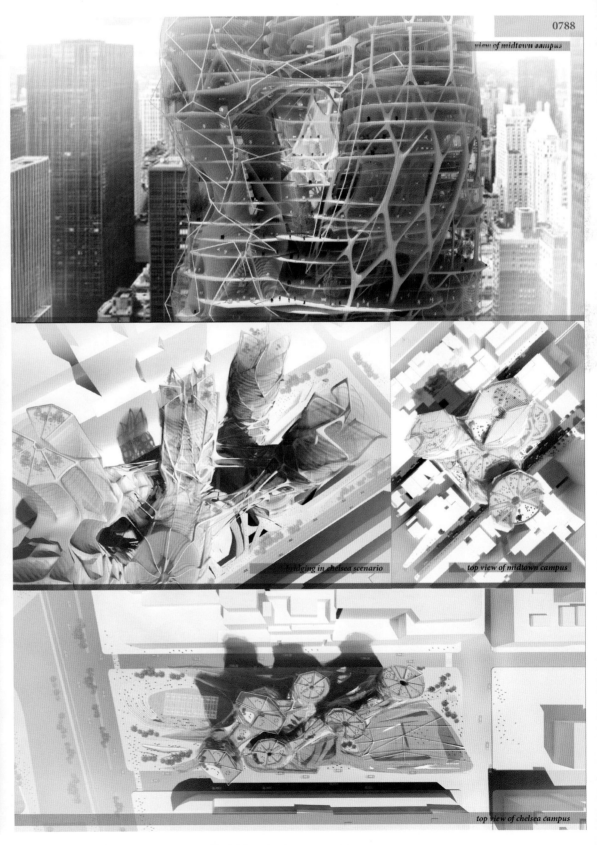

0788

view of midtown campus

bridging in chelsea scenario

top view of midtown campus

top view of chelsea campus

RADIO TOWER II

Cruz Crawford

United States

[Radio Tower II] Hong Kong, 2041
Symbiotic set of ecolocially and infrastructurally optimized systems

[Description]

The emergent population in the coming century will have tremendous effects on spatial cultural relationships. Global migrations into city centers will require updated mechanisms of social exchange which can effectively respond the flux in population densities. In particular it is at the spaces in the urban fabric where the heaviest density of intersections occur (highway interchanges, train and bus stations, and harbors) that we can start to reevaluate as moments of potential for successful cultural and social exchange which can be derived from an efficient infrastructural metabolism. Through linking infrastructural and social ecologies into a broader network of energy and information flow, the relationship of the urban condition to complex flows of forces (informational and resourceful) is redefined as a symbiotic set of systems; ecologically and tectonically optimized for performance.

The *Radio tower II* is a mixed-use infrastructural node within the city center of Hong Kong which attempts to effectively synthesize immense volumes of resources and social forces as well as natural potential energy into one confluent stream of social cohesion. From this stream of urban activity, a new network of social and economic exchange evolves through the intelligent capture and redistribution of embedded potential energy.

radiolarian   residential block

Built upon an existing major transportation node within Hong Kong, the first reaction of the Radio Tower II is an intentional distortion of the ground plane based on existing incoming force vectors in three dimensions to allow for a more fluid yet flexible network for the delivery of people and resources. The ground plane is unfolded into a non-Cartesian grid of synthesized flow lines, optimized for the movement and distribution of forces.

existing site

A network of programmatic adjacencies generates a more efficient model of urban activity. Freight and commerce is delivered to its prospective locations underground while incoming passengers and goods are delivered to the core of the ground station , which is interested by several major markets. These vectors float through a field of columnar tubes which serves simultaneously as scaffolding for the transverse infrastructural elements as well as foundation points of the vertical network of resources to the mixed use program above and the central energy plant below.

From the base of the tubes, non-orthogonal axis rise upward to form a network of interconnected program. The business district sits vertically adjacent to the market while three residential towers fragment into a community interconnected by a comprehensive network.

The nodal conditions of the vertical network serve as scaled versions of the larger central plant at the base of the tower. They effectively regulate and distribute resources within the program masses they relate to while simultaneously acting as a regulator for the greater system. In turn, these doubly serve as civic and social spaces, coupling typically hidden infrastructure systems of a city with the urban public spaces

Radio tower II is a mixed-use infrastructural node within the city center of Hong Kong which attempts to effectively synthesize immense volumes of resources and social forces as well as natural potential energy into one confluent stream of social cohesion. From this stream of urban activity, a new network of social and economic exchange evolves through the intelligent capture and redistribution of embedded potential energy.

    Built upon an existing major transportation node within Hong Kong, the first reaction of the Radio Tower II is an intentional distortion of the ground plane based on existing incoming force vectors in three dimensions to allow for a more fluid yet flexible network for the delivery of people and resources. The ground plane is

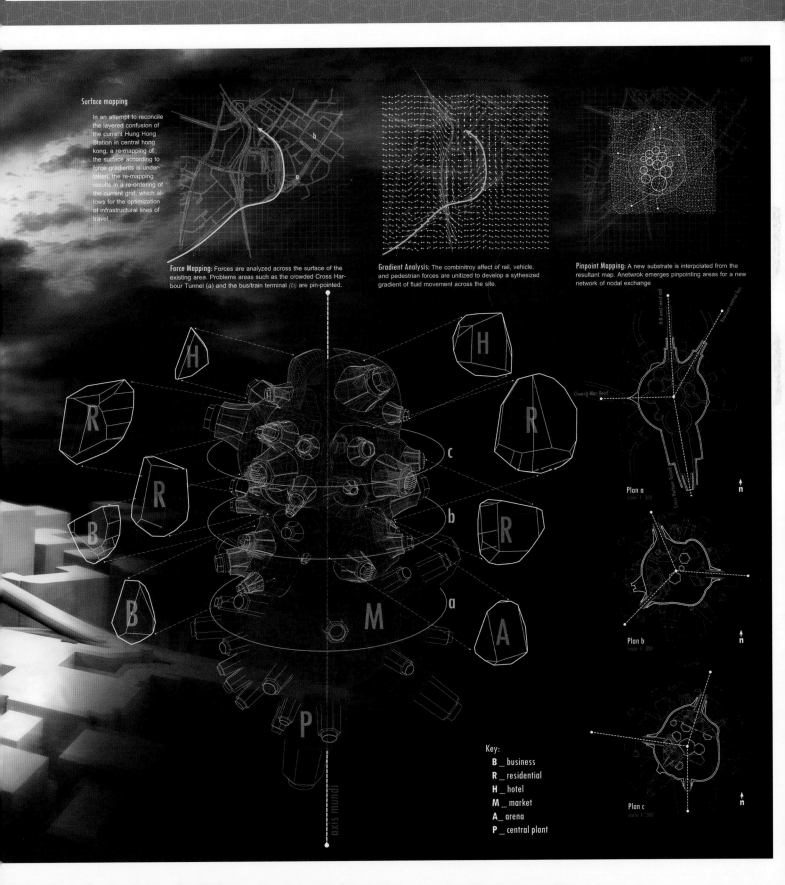

Surface mapping

In an attempt to reconcile the layered confusion of the current Hung Hong Station in central hong kong, a re-mapping of the surface according to force gradients is undertaken. the re-mapping results in a re-ordering of the current grid, which allows for the optimization of infrastructural lines of travel.

Force Mapping: Forces are analyzed across the surface of the existing area. Problems areas such as the crowded Cross Harbour Tunnel (a) and the bus/train terminal (b) are pin-pointed.

Gradient Analysis: The combinitroy affect of rail, vehicle, and pedestrian forces are unitized to develop a sythesized gradient of fluid movement across the site.

Pinpoint Mapping: A new substrate is interpolated from the resultant map. Anetwrok emerges pinpointing areas for a new network of nodal exchange

Plan a
scale 1 : 300

Plan b
scale 1 : 300

Plan c
scale 1 : 300

axis mundi

Key:
B _ business
R _ residential
H _ hotel
M _ market
A _ arena
P _ central plant

unfolded into a non-Cartesian grid of synthesized flow lines, optimized for the movement and distribution of forces. A network of programmatic adjacencies generates a more efficient model of urban activity. Freight and commerce is delivered to its prospective locations underground while incoming passengers and goods are delivered to the core of the ground station, which is interested by several major markets.

These vectors float through a field of columnar tubes, which serves simultaneously as scaffolding for the transverse infrastructural elements as well as foundation points of the vertical network of resources to the mixed-use program above and the central energy plant below. From the base of the tubes, a non-orthogonal

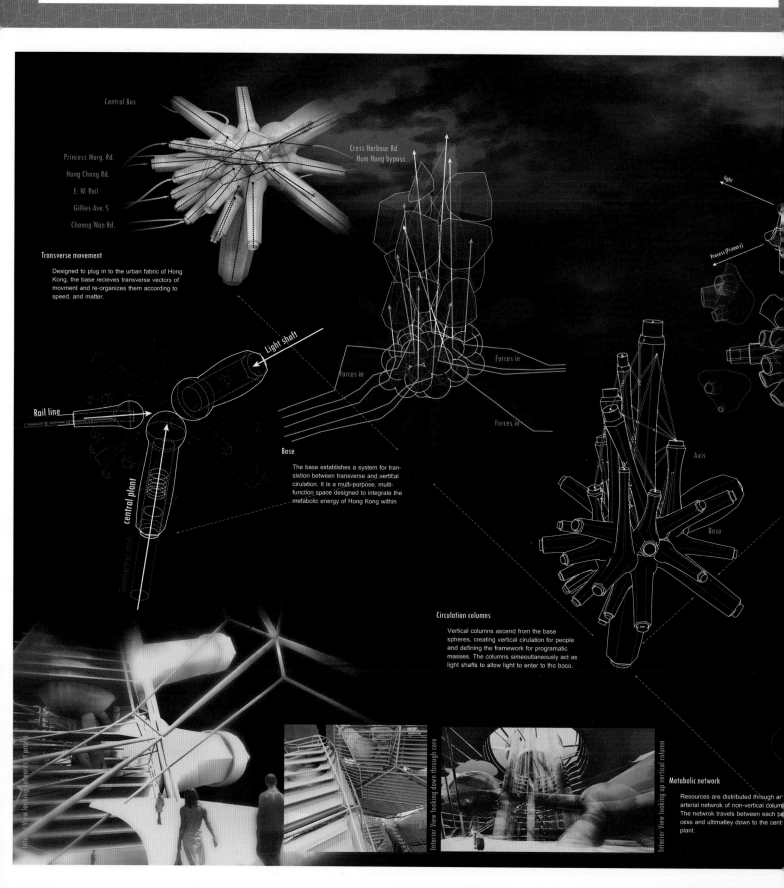

Transverse movement

Designed to plug in to the urban fabric of Hong Kong, the base recieves transverse vectors of movment and re-organizes them according to speed, and matter.

Central Bus

Princess Marg. Rd.

Hong Chong Rd.

E. W. Rail

Gillies Ave. S

Cheong Wan Rd.

Cross Harbour Rd
Hum Hong bypass

Light shaft

Rail line

central plant

light

Process (Primary)

Forces in

Forces in

Forces in

Axis

Base

Base

The base establishes a system for transistion between transverse and vertical cirulation. It is a multi-purpose, multi-function space designed to integrate the metabolic energy of Hong Kong within

Circulation columns

Vertical columns ascend from the base spheres, creating vertical cirulation for people and defining the framework for programatic masses. The columns simeoultaneously act as light shafts to allow light to enter to the base.

Interior View looking down through core

Interior View looking up vertical column

Metabolic network

Resources are distributed through an arterial netwrok of non-vertical colum. The network travels between each process and ultimatley down to the central plant.

axis rises upward to form a network of interconnected program. The business district sits vertically adjacent to the market while three residential towers fragment into a community interconnected by a comprehensive network.

The nodal conditions of the vertical network serve as scaled versions of the larger central plant at the base of the tower. They effectively regulate and distribute resources within the program masses they relate to while simultaneously acting as a regulator for the greater system. In turn, these doubly serve as civic and social spaces, coupling typically hidden infrastructure systems of a city with the urban public spaces.

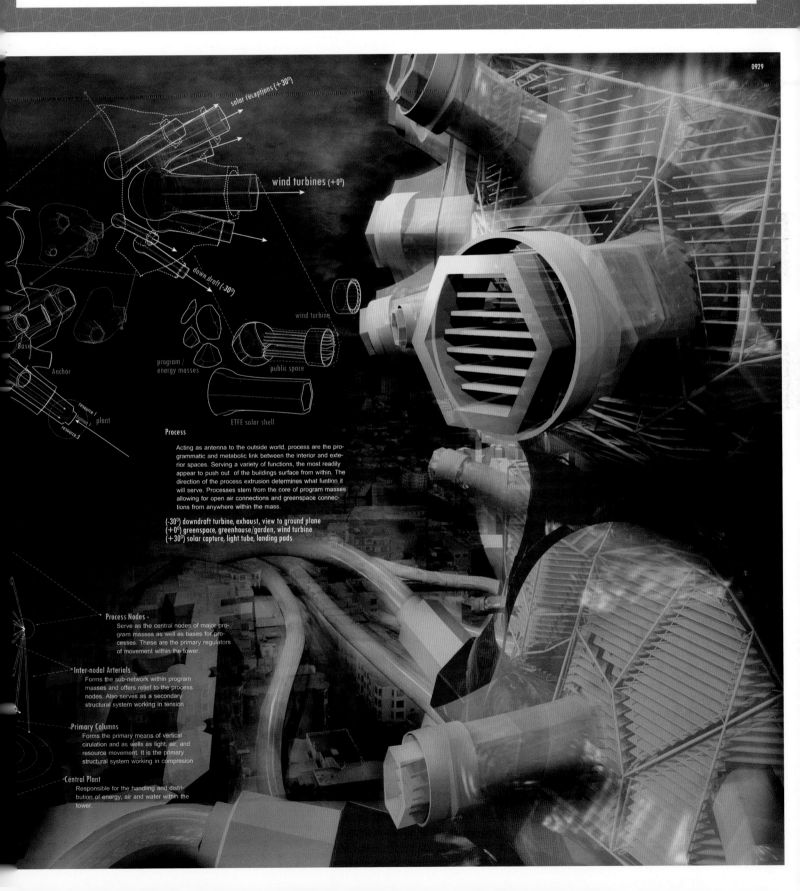

0929

solar receptions (+30°)

wind turbines (+0°)

down draft (-30°)

wind turbine

Base

Anchor

program /
energy masses

public space

resource 1

tunnel 1 plant

resource 3

ETFE solar shell

Process

Acting as antenna to the outside world, process are the programmatic and metabolic link between the interior and exterior spaces. Serving a variety of functions, the most readily appear to push out of the buildings surface from within. The direction of the process extrusion determines what funtion it will serve. Processes stem from the core of program masses allowing for open air connections and greenspace connections from anywhere within the mass.

(-30°) downdraft turbine, exhaust, view to ground plane
(+0°) greenspace, greenhouse/garden, wind turbine
(+30°) solar capture, light tube, landing pads

Process Nodes -
Serve as the central nodes of major program masses as well as bases for processes. These are the primary regulators of movement within the tower.

Inter-nodal Arterials
Forms the sub-network within program masses and offers relief to the process nodes. Also serves as a secondary structural system working in tension

Primary Columns
Forms the primary means of vertical cirulation and as wells as light, air, and resource movement. It is the primary structural system working in compression

Central Plant
Responsible for the handling and distribution of energy, air and water within the tower.

NEW URBANISM

Dongyul Kim
Youngbum Kim

United States

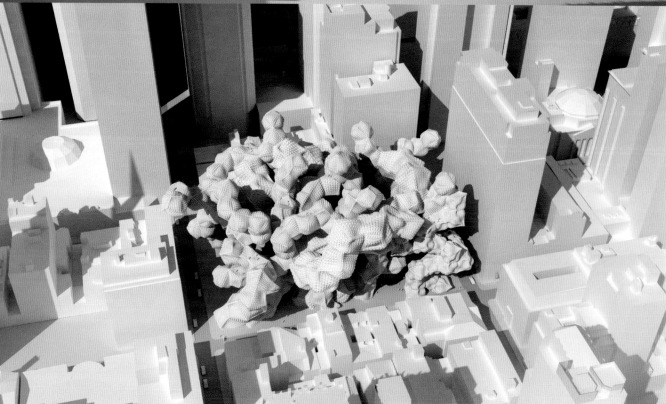

NEW URBANIS

CONCEPT DIAGRAM

Numerous aggregated figures within
the city fabric generate a new groun
for the city. Once a prototypical form
aggregation has been created, this
logic of aggregation can be applied
a different block of the city fabric.

AGENT BASED ALGORIT

By using Processing which is a prog
Java Script, we can trace and expre
people, cars, and infrastructures as
They create paths and spaces while

PLAN DIAGRAM

In Hilberseimer's thesis in which an architectural object is seen from the viewpoint of the economy of the metropolis, architecture formulates the relationship between elementary cells of inhabitation and the urban organism as a whole. Numerous aggregated figures within the city fabric generate a new ground for the city. The project is about designing an urban block and transforming its current program. Once a prototypical form of aggregation has been created, this formal logic of aggregation can be applied to a different block of the city fabric. The pattern thus created can be considered a new model of urbanization.

A site research conducted using Agent-based algorithm provides leads for the formulation of an

0982

...gated figuration

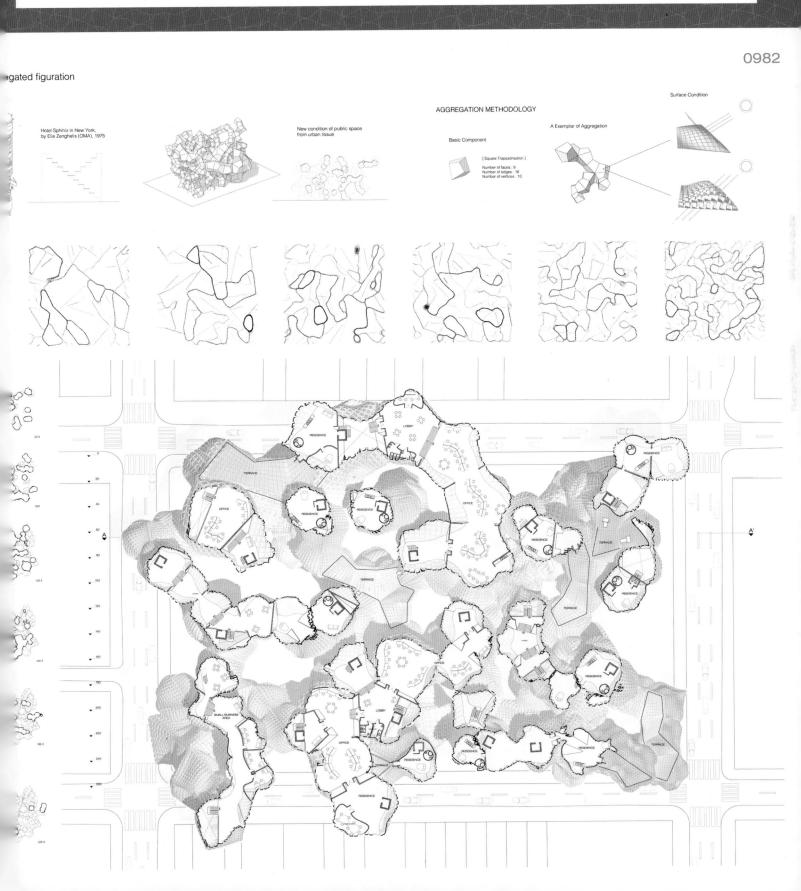

Hotel Sphinix in New York,
by Elia Zenghelis (OMA), 1975

New condition of public space
from urban tissue

AGGREGATION METHODOLOGY

Basic Component

[Square Trapezohedron]
Number of faces : 8
Number of edges : 16
Number of vertices : 10

A Exemplar of Aggregation

Surface Condition

aggregated figure. The agents representing human trajectories in the site organize themselves to create spatial entities that connect to the site program. The original programs at the site include a shopping center, offices, parking lots, storage, and housing. Several options of swarm intelligence with different porosities are derived. The best option which carries optimized spatial quality and is best suited to the programs is selected and developed.

    As each cell has a distinct microclimate, the folding structure facade treatment technique is introduced to respond to the specific microclimate, which is influenced by the sunlight. The facade structure swells for

MASSING STRATEGY / SWARM

SECTION

SECTION DIAGRAM

more sunlight exposure and flattens to block any direct sunlight. The programs determine the ideal amount of light. For example, when offices do not require a lot of lighting, the facade becomes flattened to block it.

This facade treatment brings a visual effect to the overall geometry by transforming a regulated aggregation of a "trapezohedron" into an organic shape just by applying the facade system on the basic geometry. Even though the edges of the basic geometry are still intact, the outer cell facade dismantles the cell boundaries. By doing so, the overall geometry overcomes the initial swarm intelligence form and combines individual cells into one system.

0982

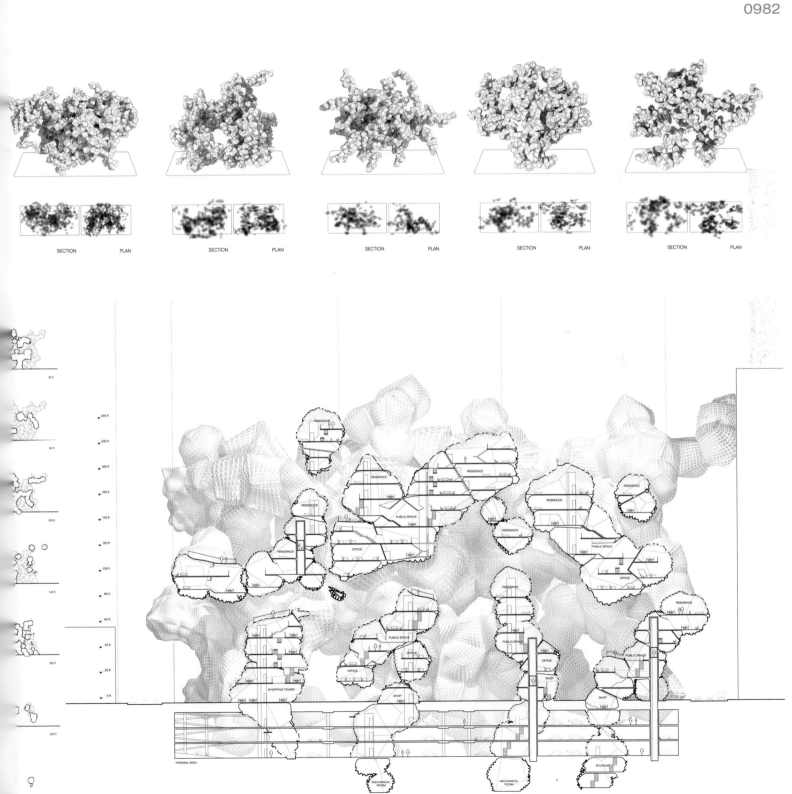

SECTION   PLAN   SECTION   PLAN   SECTION   PLAN   SECTION   PLAN   SECTION   PLAN

DNAGRICULTURE

Tristan McGuire

United States

UPPER FIELDS

1a. passive irrigation
1b. psyllium fields
1c. metal louvers
1d. graduate labs
1e. lecture halls

2 MIDDLE FIELDS

2a. undergraduate labs
2b. reclaimed irrigation
2c. elevator
2d. public restaurant/bar

3 HOUSING

3a. student housing
3b. visiting faculty housing
3c. gate to fields
3d. student gardens

4 PARK/GROUND

4a. school administration
4b. water reclamation

ELEVATION

SECTION

Urban growth over the past half century in Los Angeles has been an unstoppable concrete clotting of human density, pollution and activity. As we sprawl and cast the interior of this mega-city solid, the rural lands that nourish us are pushed farther and farther out of sight and out of mind. The average Los Angeleno suffers from malnourishment of information pertaining to the crops that provide not only his food but also his pharmaceuticals and other organic byproducts. Kept at such a distance the integrity of these products is sacrificed as it risks corruption by agricultural conglomerates that remain unchecked by their clients.

DNAgriculture seeks to regain lost proximity between consumer and producer with the introduction of

DNAGRICULTURE 1086
VERTICAL FARM & BIOTECHNOLOGY SCHOOL

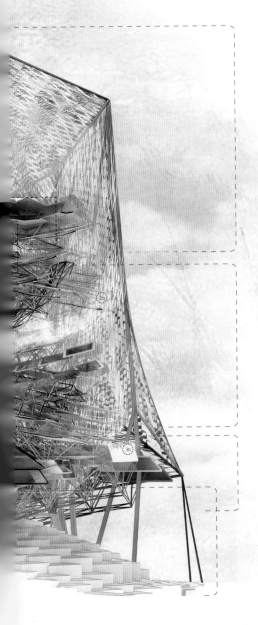

TOP FIELDS AND PASSIVE IRRIGATION SYSTEM

a vertical farm and biotechnology school in the heart of downtown Los Angeles. The school focuses on pharmaceutical crops and therefore relies on communities of fields, labs and classrooms to grow, harvest and study such crops. The project creates a live/study community that combines mid-rise housing with a vertical life in the fields and labs of the school.

Each diamond-shaped field is equipped to detect various indicators of plant productivity—carbon dioxide consumption, physical growth, etc.—and converts such data into a numeric output that informs architectural response in the dynamic skin system. The double skin is composed of an impermeable glass interior and

1086
DNAGRICULTURE

fall semester begins.

few plants remain after harvest.

louvers remain inactive.

fall.

seeds are planted.

louvers begin to activate as soil levels vary.

open louvers encourage solar heat gain.

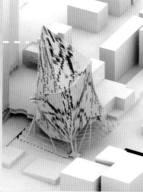

spring semester.

seeds germinate and plant growth increases rapidly.

louver DNA causes them to flutter at various intervals, creating randomized field effects.

summer semester.

as the growing season ends and plants are harvested, louver activity calms.

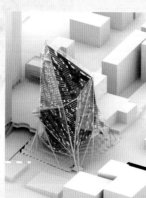

VARIOUS FIELD EFFECTS GIVEN BY DNA EXPRESSION

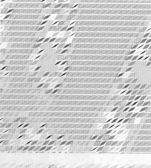

PASSIVE IRRIGATION SYSTEM

HOUSING   CIRCULATION   WORK   LIVE

STANDARD TOWER TYPOLOGY   ANGLE FLOORS FOR LIGHT GAIN

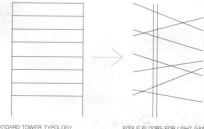

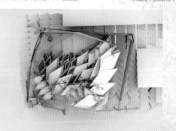

STUDENT HOUSING   MIDDLE F

USE OF PUBLIC PARK LEVEL

DNAgriculture

Urban growth ov
been an unstoppa
pollution and activ
this mega-city sc
pushed farther a
common Los Ang
mation pertaining
but also his phar
Kept at such a di
sacrificed as it ri
conglomerates th
clients

DNAgriculture se
sumer and produ
and biotechnolog
les. The school fo
fore relies on co
grow, harvest ar
live/study comm
vertical life in the

Each diamond-sh
indicators of plar
growth, spore cc
numeric output t
dynamic skin sys
impermeable glas
louvers on the e
directly by this n
unique set of alg
movement. Accele
organic activity i
resulting in ever-
visual abstraction
cycles inside. Wh
merging patterns
posed of the sim
closer investigati
louver, louver to
effect to passer
thrust the archit
maceutical crop
dynamic abstrac

a swarm of triangular metal louvers on the exterior whose reactions are controlled directly by numeric input. Each louver is assigned a unique set of algorithmic DNA that converts input into movement. Accelerations, decelerations and stagnations in organic activity instigate different responses in the louvers resulting in ever-changing visual field effects, serving as a visual abstraction that connects gazers with the plants' life cycles inside. What appears as a series of morphing and merging patterns from a mile away reveals itself to be composed of the simple opening and closing of louvers upon closer investigation. A layering of dialogues is created: plant to louver, louver to field effect, louver to pedestrian, and field effect to passer-by.

POST-SUSTAINABLE
TIMBERSCRAPER

Alex Kaiser
Magnus Larsson

United Kingdom

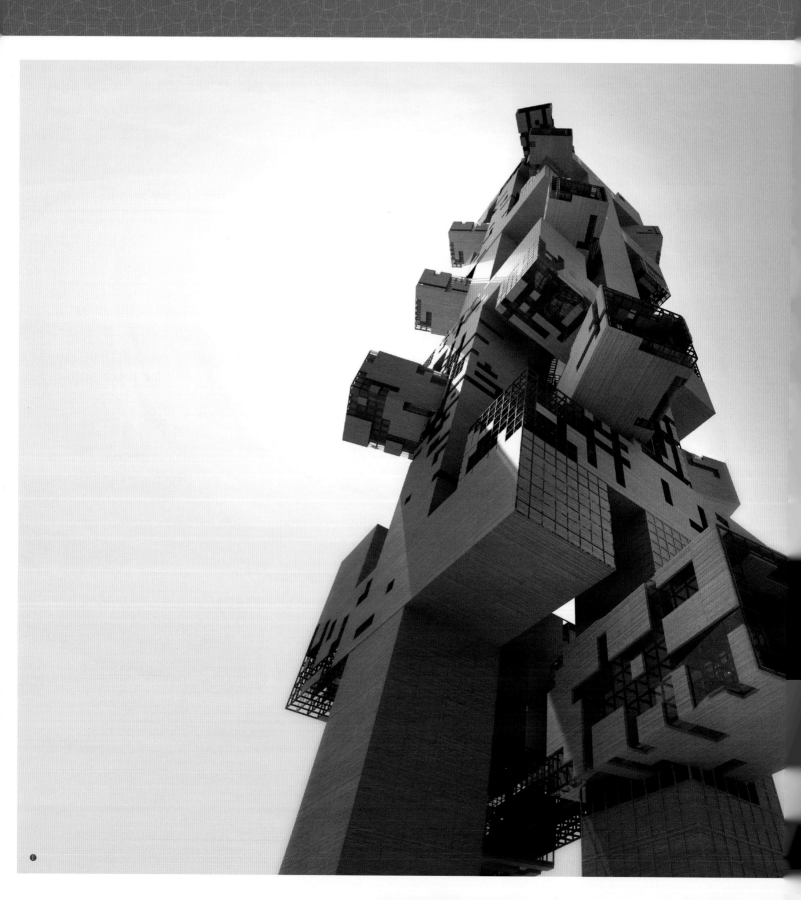

Harvard economist Edward Glaeser argues that where land is scarce, density becomes vital. Cities that cannot build out must build up. The resulting metropolises should be pinnacle achievements in the history of architecture. Yet the resulting urban centers, based on capitalist doctrines of hyper-density, are often, in the words of Rem Koolhaas, well on their way to "a grotesque saturation point of total extrusion."

The Post-Sustainable Timberscraper offers an alternative to these grotesque extrusions. A radical redefinition of the densely stacked logic of contemporary urban typologies, this skyscraper is based on the notion of low-density living. This reasoning acknowledges the need for vertical extrusions while arguing that

PARTICIPATION NUMBER 1090

POST-SUSTAINABLE TIMBERSCRAPER

The world population has experienced continuous growth since 1350; according to current projections the planet will support between 7.5 and 10.5 billion people by 2050.

This is a good thing.

Not only does this mean there will be more intelligence in the world, more beautiful innovations, more valuable human capital, culture, education, laughter, more heartbreaking works of staggering genius.[1] There will also be more and more people living in larger and larger cities. Emotional and intellectual playgrounds built on complexity and diversity, cities are humanity's most successful invention for delivering prosperity and progress.

The young and the poor don't go to the countryside to make their fortunes. They go to cities. This migration towards metropolitan cores intensifies the urban experience but not, crucially, the heedless burning of fossil fuels. As David Owen points out,[2] in comparison with the rest of the USA, New York City is "a model of environmental responsibility".

Since the 96m tall Latting Observatory went up in 1853, New York has given birth to 12 buildings that were the tallest in the world at the time of their completion. Most of them sought to maximise livable space through an "exploatation of congestion".[3] This won't come as a surprise to Harvard economist Edward Glaeser, who argues that where land is scarce, density becomes vital. Cities that cannot build out must build up.[4] The resulting conurbations should be pinnacle achievements in the history of architecture. And yet the resulting urban centres, based on capitalist doctrines of hyper-density, are too often, in the words of Rem Koolhaas, well on their way to "a grotesque saturation point of total extrusion".[5]

The Post-sustainable Timberscraper offers an alternative to these grotesque extrusions. A radical redefinition of the densely-stacked logic of contemporary urban typologies, this skyscraper is based on the notion of low-density living. This reasoning acknowledges the need for vertical extrusions while arguing that many downfalls of the contemporary metropolitan condition, in particular in a non-western context – overcrowding, environmental stress, social inequalities, lack of light and air, food security, diseases – could be overcome through the controlled use of spatial redundancy.

This term, which we borrow from the world of data compression,[6] is used here in two ways. By stacking prefabricated timber units, we achieve compression in the time and effort it takes to construct the building. And by shifting those units across the entire height of the skyscraper, we create de facto redundant spaces; bodies without organs; volumes without walls and floors; strategic perforations in the city fabric. This innovative internal logic is based on a programmatic reconsideration of what it means (or should mean) to live in a skyscraper: smaller contained interior spaces are matched by exterior spaces that offer framed views of the streetscape below, with vertical volumes acting as supporting storage capacities; bridges in the sky allow for chance meetings on the 14th or 21st floor; at pavement level, the street is given back to the city's inhabitants; while on the roof, a restaurant offers the public stunning views of the inner circuits of that great computer for human interactions that is the metropolis.

It is a new model born from a set of values that could be called post sustainable: the obvious-yet-rare insight that we need to readjust our environmental strategy globally to focus on continual improvement rather than mere sustainability. When the Brundtland Commission of the United Nations declared, in 1987, that "sustainable development is development that meets the needs of the present without compromising the ability of future generations to meet their own needs," it laid the foundation for a focus on the capacity to endure rather than the capacity to excel. We firmly believe it to be the responsibility of architects – who design for an exceptionally energy-intensive sector (75 per cent of global energy consumption is produced by buildings and transportation[7]) – to embrace the challenge of drawing up speculative trajectories aimed at reversing this fallacy. We are not calling for less passive houses, but questioning why we can't have more active houses.

How is this skyscraper post sustainable? How is it active? First and foremost through its radical materiality. Of all existing materials, humans use water (by volume) the most. But in second place, at more than 17 billion tons consumed each year, comes concrete, usually made with Portland cement. As of 2006, about 7.5 billion cubic meters of concrete are made each year—more than one cubic meter for every person on Earth.[8] The cement industry is one of two primary producers of carbon dioxide. Building skyscrapers, as we have seen, is sustainable. Since trees absorb CO2 as they grow, timber skyscrapers are post sustainable in that they employ a material that can achieve a negative carbon footprint. Add to this the higher pace of the (less energy-intensive) construction and the avoidance of additional insulation (wood has the best thermal insulation of any mainstream construction material, 350 times better than steel), and it becomes clear that this is a building capable of excelling rather than merely enduring.

Developers build what the market demands where it demands it. But at times (the frisbee, the electric guitar, the iPad) the market needs to be shown what it didn't know it wanted. We have chosen to place the Post-sustainable Timberscraper in London, UK, next to the world's tallest timber residential building, the Stadthaus, which reaches a mere nine stories into the sky. While the Stadthaus is a towering achievement today, there is nothing to say that a much taller wood structure, at the scale of the one we're presenting here, would not be achievable (beyond the 25-storey mark, p-delta effects become significant due to the relatively low modulus of elasticity of timber compared to steel or concrete).

England, one of the three most densely populated countries in the world, where 90% of the population live in cities, is of course the birthplace of industrialism, which in turn gave birth to the modernism that produced the manhattanist architecture of the world's corporate skyscrapers, tired monuments of a failed city ideal. In the 21st century, people no longer have to congregate in flat-packed, cramped spaces. They can live in a building as light and airy as the clouds flying through it. They can live in a Post-sustainable Timberscraper.

A
Worm's eye view: central shaft

B
Living unit interior

C
Shared bridge connection

D
Perspective (night)

E
Perspective (day)

[1] A phrase stolen, of course, from the title of Dave Eggers debut novel "A Heartbreaking Work of Staggering Genius" (Simon & Schuster, 2000)

[2] David Owen, "Green Manhattan: Everywhere Should be More like New York" (The New Yorker, October 18, 2004), p. 111

[3] Rem Koolhaas, "Delirious New York" (The Monacelli Press, 1994), p. 10

[4] Edward Glaeser, "Triumph of the city: how our greatest invention makes us richer, smarter, greener, healthier, and happier" (Penguin Press, 2011)

[5] Koolhaas, ibid, p. 89

[6] Spatial redundancy refers to the duplication of elements within a structure, such as repeated pixel values in a still image. Compression of data is based on the exploitation of spatial redundancy.

[7] Rogers Stirk Harbour + Partners website, http://www.rsh-p.com/theory/energy

[8] United States Geographic Service, "Minerals commodity summary – cement – 2007"

downfalls of the contemporary metropolitan condition, in particular in a non-western context—overcrowding, social inequalities, diseases—could be overcome through intelligent stacking of prefabricated timber units.

By shifting those units across the height of the skyscraper, strategic perforations in the city fabric are created. This internal logic is based on a programmatic reconsideration of what it should mean to live in a skyscraper: smaller contained interior spaces are matched by exterior spaces while vertical volumes act as supporting storage capacities; bridges in the sky allow for chance meetings; the street is given back to the city's inhabitants; at the top, a restaurant offers the public stunning views of the metropolis below.

01_RECLAIM THE STREET

The timberscraper is lifted off the ground to welcome pedestrians into its shaded footprint, where street life is born anew.

02_STACKED STRUCTURE

Pre-fabricated modules arrive as tightly controlled yet flexible units that can easily – and quickly – be stacked on site.

03_RADICAL MATERIALITY

Environmentally and socially responsible construction from engineered timber supports a post-sustainable urbanism.

04_CHINESE PUZZLE

All living units are interlinked in a manner similar to that of a Chinese puzzle, so as to better merge different programmes.

STACKING LOGIC

The nine initial volumes are stacked into a low-density module with five living units.

MODULE VOLUMES — T STACKING — BRIDGE INSERTION — FINISHED MODULE — SECOND MODULE

LIVING UNITS

Individually unique units are interlocked into novel programmatic configurations.

It is a new model born from a set of values that could be called post sustainable: the obvious-yet-rare insight that we need to readjust our environmental strategy to focus on continual improvement rather than mere sustainability. How is this skyscraper post sustainable? First and foremost is its radical materiality that makes it so. Since trees absorb carbon dioxide as they grow, timber skyscrapers are post sustainable in that they employ a material that can achieve a negative carbon footprint. Add to this the much higher speed of the less energy-intensive construction and the avoidance of additional insulation (wood has excellent thermal insulation), and it seems reasonable to assume that this design can excel rather than merely endure.

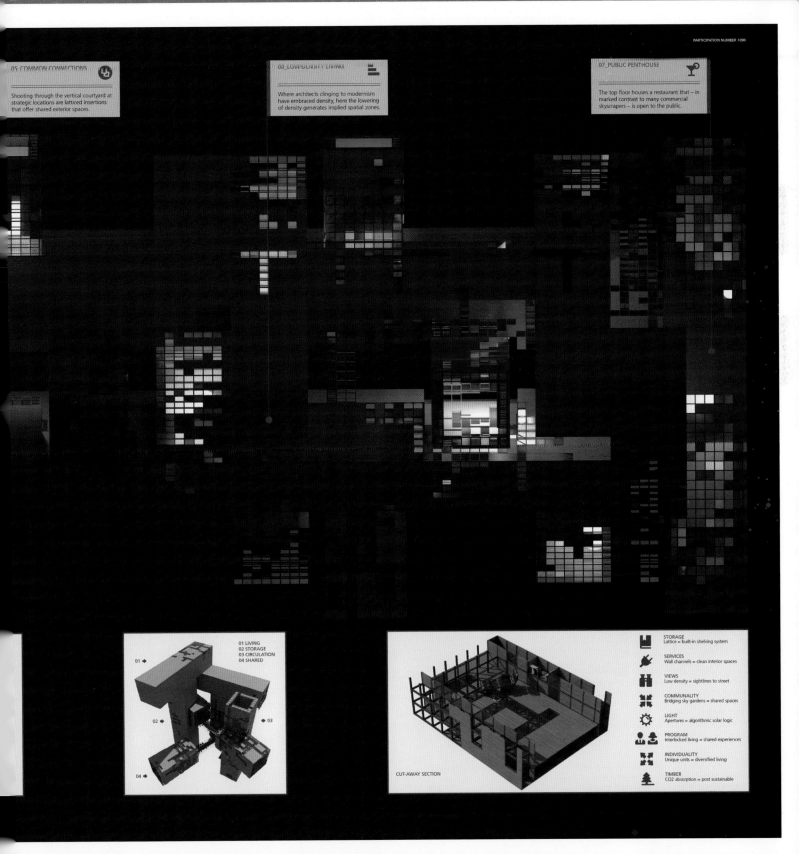

PARTICIPATION NUMBER 1090

05_COMMON CONNECTIONS
Shooting through the vertical courtyard at strategic locations are latticed insertions that offer shared exterior spaces.

03_LOW-DENSITY LIVING
Where architects clinging to modernism have embraced density, here the lowering of density generates implied spatial zones.

07_PUBLIC PENTHOUSE
The top floor houses a restaurant that – in marked contrast to many commercial skyscrapers – is open to the public.

01 LIVING
02 STORAGE
03 CIRCULATION
04 SHARED

01
02
03
04

CUT-AWAY SECTION

STORAGE
Lattice = built-in shelving system

SERVICES
Wall channels = clean interior spaces

VIEWS
Low density = sightlines to street

COMMUNALITY
Bridging sky gardens = shared spaces

LIGHT
Apertures = algorithmic solar logic

PROGRAM
Interlocked living = shared experiences

INDIVIDUALITY
Unique units = diversified living

TIMBER
CO2 absorption = post sustainable

THE LINEAR COASTAL CITY

Manuel Galipeau

Canada

LINEAR COASTAL CITY
ANTI-EROSION & SELF-SUFFICIENT SKYSCRAPER

DISAPPEARING CITY

Bonifacio, the southernmost commune of Corsica, France, is a citadel city located atop vertical limestone cliffs, hanging 230 feet above the sea below. Its 2870 inhabitants live either around the fjord-like harbor or in the historic UNESCO Heritage City. While most of Corsica's landmass is granite, Bonifacio's cliffs are regrettably made of limestone, a soft stone extremely vulnerable to erosion. The Bonifacio cliff endures dual erosion: wind above and sea below. The windstorms prevent vegetation to settle in causing the limestone to be exposed and more vulnerable to further climatic effects.

The sea digs its way through the bottom of the cliffs by constantly subjecting them to the beating of its pounding waves. Since the erosion caused by the sea is stronger than the one inflected by the wind, the Bonifacio cliffs appear to leave the Upper City dangling in mid-air.

Rising sea levels caused by Global Warming and persistent erosion will eventually throw Bonifacio out to sea.

CITY ON THE RISE

Each year, over 2 million visitors travel to Corsica and over 4 million visit the neighboring island of Sardinia. Bonifacio alone attracts more than 500 000 tourists, making it a prime international destination.

Due to a shortage of local accommodations, visitors can spend a limited amount of time admiring the views of Bonifacio. The gap between Bonifacio's international appeal and its capacity to lodge even a small fraction of its visitors is an overlooked opportunity.

CITY ON THE CLIFF

The Linear Coastal City proposal aims to reduce the erosion of Bonifacio's limestone cliffs, maximize the city's hosting capacity while limiting interference with the city's current state.

Having reached its current maximum density, Bonifacio offers a unique topography. Its two miles of 230 feet limestone cliffs can be optimized as coveted vertical real-estate. A Linear Coastal Skyscraper can be deployed along the cliffs as demand for lodging rises.

A physical barrier between the limestone cliff and the natural elements, the Linear Coastal Skyscraper will act as a wind deterrent and a wave breaker. The Bonifacio cliffs would then be sealed against nature's destructive power assuring the longevity of this historical city.

The Linear Coastal Skyscraper, built as a thin transparent overlay, allows the cliffs' natural beauty to be enjoyed from the sea and from within its "Hanging Villas". By "Living on the Cliff", visitors will benefit from breathtaking Mediterranean views, proximity to a unique historical city, direct access to the sea while never appearing in the locals' direct view.

This vertical skyscraper doesn't seek to be a mono-functional unit but rather a socially porous network of public and private entities. "Hanging" villas, restaurants and shops will be scattered throughout the linear resort and will be linked by endless suspended public paths, staircases and vertical elevators.

SELF-SUFFICIENT CITY

By using the kinetic power of the regular periodic waves, the Linear Coastal City will harvest the energy it needs through wave turbines spread at its base. The constant movement of the waves will compress and decompress an air chamber which will activate an electricity-producing turbine. The "Hanging City" will act as its own power-plant rendering it completely independent from the city grid and able to share its surplus with the neighboring areas. The once destructive wave will become a limitless supply of positive energy.

REFLECTIONS

Can a strategic urban intervention reconcile the international lodging demand without transforming this peaceful time-defying city into an overcrowded urban sprawl? If the city of Bonifacio taps into this great economical potential, what will become of the locals?

Can an architectural addition save the limestone cliffs of Bonifacio and eternalize the historical city? Could this model be adapted to similar cliffs from around the world?

Bonifacio, a commune of Corsica, France, is a citadel city located atop limestone cliffs, hanging 230 feet above the sea. While most of Corsica's landmass is granite, Bonifacio's cliffs are made of limestone, a soft stone vulnerable to erosion. The cliff endures erosion from wind and sea. The sea digs its way through the bottom of the cliffs by constantly subjecting them to the beating of its pounding waves. Since the erosion caused by the sea is stronger than the one inflected by the wind, Bonifacio's cliffs appear to leave the upper city dangling in mid-air.

Rising sea levels from global warming leading to erosion will throw Bonifacio out to sea. Each year, over

1104

2 million visitors visit Corsica; Bonifacio alone attracts more than 500,000 tourists. Due to a shortage of local accommodations, visitors can only spend a limited amount of time admiring the views of Bonifacio and roaming its streets. The gap between Bonifacio's international appeal and its capacity to lodge even a small fraction of its visitors is an overlooked opportunity. The Linear Coastal City proposal aims to reduce the erosion of Bonifacio's limestone cliffs, maximizing the city's hosting capacity.

Having reached its current maximum density, Bonifacio offers a unique topography. Its two miles of 230 feet limestone cliffs can be optimized as coveted vertical real estate. A Linear Coastal Skyscraper can

be deployed along the cliffs as demand for lodging rises. A physical barrier between the cliff and natural elements, the Linear Coastal Skyscraper will act as a wind deterrent and a wave breaker. The Bonifacio cliffs would then be sealed against nature's destructive power assuring the longevity of this city.

The Linear Coastal Skyscraper, built as a thin transparent overlay, allows the cliffs' natural beauty to be enjoyed. It does not seek to be a mono-functional unit but rather a socially porous network of public and private entities. Hanging villas, restaurants, and shops will be scattered throughout the resort, linked by endless suspended public paths, staircases, and elevators.

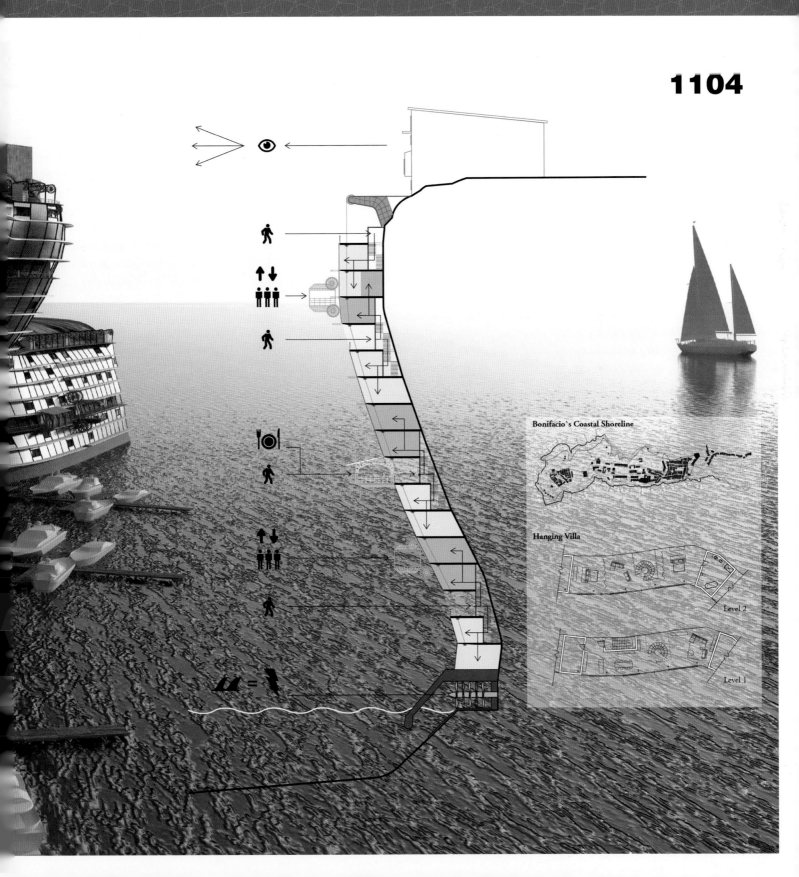

1104

Bonifacio's Coastal Shoreline

Hanging Villa

Level 2

Level 1

THE RACK

Ludovic Martial
Jean-Baptiste Nicolas

France

In this world, personal universe is without border. Personal universe is becoming a common jar where everyone is invited to discover other mentalities, other cultures and other countries in other ways of life. The contemporary world through economic and social transformations is changing the perception of urban life.

In this world everyone builds, interprets, and lives in his own universe. How could architecture give a response to these features? This would be achieved with a city, a territory, networks, poles, and projects.

This temporal perspective is not only a linear time when events follow each other but also a more complex time in which virtual dimensions get involved, allowing information to overlap. A time when

THE RACK
modular mixed-use skyscraper

The contemporary world, through economic and social transformation, is changing the perception of urban life. In this context where are current any more neither symbol, nor metaphors, nor dominion of the space on the time, nor of time on the space, in this world where cut themselves the usual marks, the cultures and the modes, everyone builds, interprets and lives his universe.

In this world, personal universe is without border. Personal universe is becoming a common jar where everyone is invited to discover other mentalities, other cultures, other countries in brief other ways of life.

How could architecture give a response to these new features?

A city, a territory, networks, poles, projects. To seize the urban, urbanistic, geographical or still economic, social and cultural data which define our project, it is necessary to put in perspective, in particular by the test of time.

This temporal perspective is not only a linear time when events follow each other ; but also a more complex time in which virtual dimension get involved, allowing information overlapping, their simultaneity and their combination. A time when everything is immediate and integrated : physical, digital, human, past, present and future data.

This project, The Rack, suggest hiring a reflection on the new modes of living, the architectural and urban consequences of the setting-up of a new structure sheltering places of meeting the needs life and in the requirements of the user of the contemporary city.

The Rack is in connection with the problem of new existing connections between the housing environment, the work and the leisure activities in a context of a 24 hours a day city.

The Rack configuration for high dense-city

The Rack configuration for medium dense-city

The Rack configuration for low dense-city

1

everything is immediate and integrated includes physical, digital, human, past, present, and future data.

This project, The Rack, suggests hiring a reflection on the new modes of living, the architectural and urban consequences of the setting up of a new structure sheltering places of meeting the needs of life and in the requirements of the user of the contemporary city.

The Rack is a modular, mixed-use skyscraper that responds to the modern world's changing urban spaces. Modern technology, globalization and personal freedom have allowed individuals to achieve their destinies like never before; this skyscraper responds to that freedom.

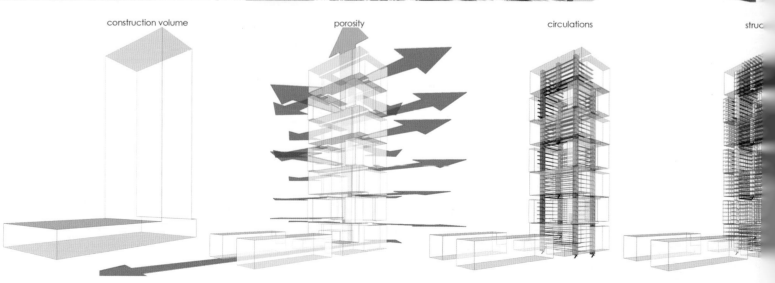

construction volume   porosity   circulations   struc

The Rack holds public and private spaces, with ample residential units. Public sky gardens are interspersed throughout the structure. The structure aims to connect housing, work and leisure activities in the context of a city that is alive 24 hours a day.

THE RACK
modular mixed-use skyscraper

public equipment

public sky garden

public sky garden

public equipment

public equipment
public sky garden

public sky garden

public garden

public equipment
public garden

public equipment

public garden

public facilities
(in the tower participate to the structure)

overview public gardens

housing

private exterior areas

FORMAL ATTIRE

Caroline Dieden
Brian Henry

United States

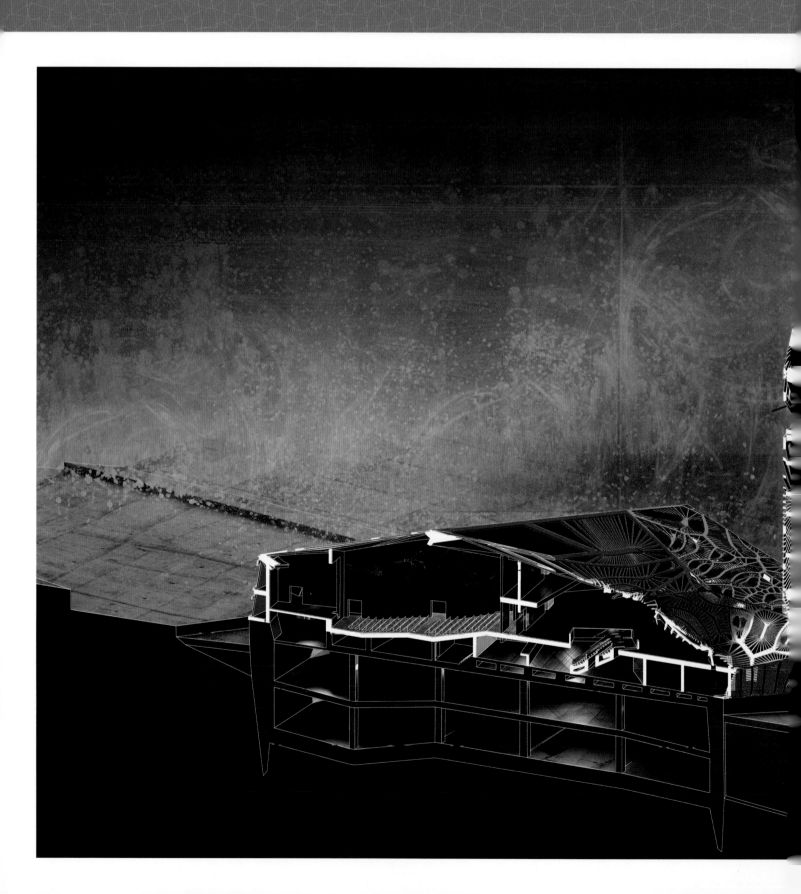

Formal Attire attempts to initiate a kind of elegant tension between each of its autonomous elements or ideas. The scripted pattern of the skin system intelligently maneuvers between the realms of overwhelming complexity and precise organization.

  The tension of this contrast, derived by the calculated use of two different mathematical logics, the sinus and the voronoi, gives the pattern an organic quality of aggregated cells. In addition to this subtle, but apparent opposition, is the dialogue between surface and volume. The pattern's relationship to the volume is one of actively directing its generated form to intelligently follow and address the seam or edge of the

FORMAL ATTIRE   1153

Formal Attire attempts to initiate a kind of elegant tension between each of its autonomous elements or ideas. The scripted pattern of the skin system intelligently maneuvers between the realms of overwhelming complexity and precise organization. The tension of this contrast, derived by the calculated use of two different mathematical logics: the sinus and the voronoi, gives the pattern an organic quality of aggregated cells. In addition to this subtle, but apparent opposition is the dialogue between surface and volume. The pattern's relationship to the volume is one of actively directing its generated form to intelligently follow and address the seam or edge of the volume. Furthering this dialogue, the volume still obviously a separate entity of the skin, interior organizations begin to be affected by a secondary layer of structure intruding into the space. A polite intrusion that creates a spatial agenda for the interior and relates back to the formal characteristics of the pattern. An elegant agitation is generated in the relationship between mass and skin in that this tertiary layer directly affects interior organizations without compromising the volumetric form. An agitation that is enhanced by the careful use and exploration of material qualities: finishes, light, shadow, reflections, and color. The black-on-black palette contradictorily begins to both reduce the vivid separation of skin and mass, but also actually re-activates the difference by enforcing comparisons of strictly textural material qualities. These delicate relationships allow this project to differentiate itself from being simply a surface/volume problem; and does so in a way that is somewhat unexpected, elegant, and subtle. Activating again a common discussion, but without overwhelming disturbance, forced integration of systems, or drastic bodily deformations.

Left: Axonometric section
Top right: Pattern language studies
Mid right: Interior render study
Bottom right: Cut paper model pattern study

volume.

Furthering this dialogue, the volume still obviously a separate entity of the skin, interior organizations begin to be affected by a secondary layer of structure intruding into the space. It is polite intrusion that creates a spatial agenda for the interior and relates back to the formal characteristics of the pattern. An elegant agitation is generated in the relationship between mass and skin in that this tertiary layer directly affects interior organizations without compromising the volumetric form. It is an agitation that is enhanced by the careful use and exploration of material qualities: finishes, light, shadow, reflections, and color. The black

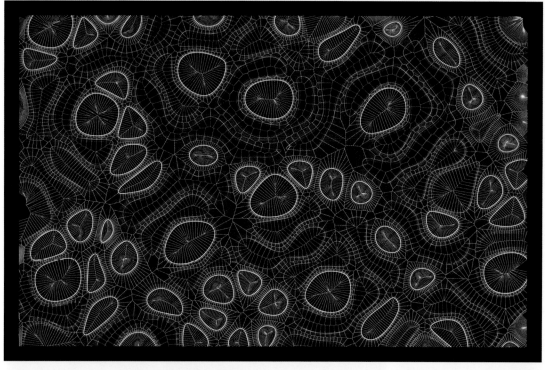

Top left: Scripted drawing study

Bottom left: Exterior render

Top middle: Scripting procedure method

Bottom middle: First floor plan

Top right: 11th floor plan

Mid right: Enclosure system analysis

Bottom right: Structural system analysis

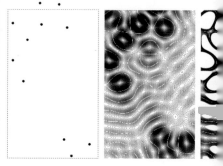

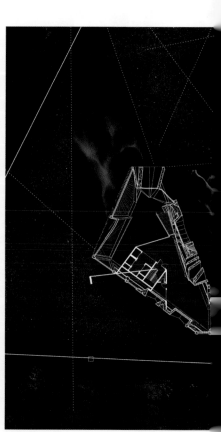

on-black palette contradictorily begins to both reduce the vivid separation of skin and mass, but also actually re-activates the difference by enforcing comparisons of strictly textural material qualities.

These delicate relationships allow this project to differentiate itself from being simply a surface/volume problem and so does in a way that is somewhat unexpected, elegant, and subtle. It activates again a common discussion, but without overwhelming disturbance, forced integration of systems, or drastic bodily deformations.

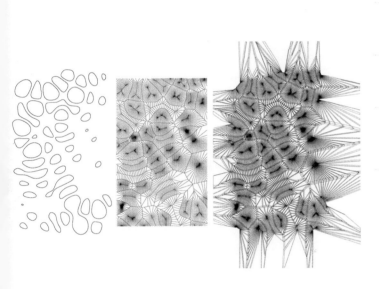

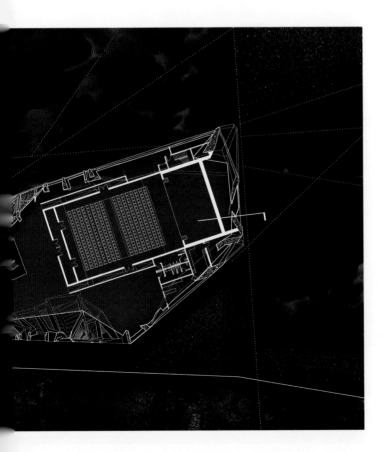

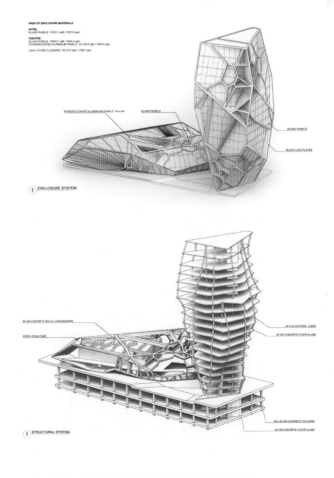

PAKSAN

Mahdiar Ghaffarian

Canada

THE PASKAN

INTRODUCTION.PASKAN

Dance in the aboriginal culture of Calgary is a way to trigger or to celebrate an event and Paskan as a self-generative infrastructural system triggers life in the city and celebrates the new alive system as an urban feature.

The name "Paskan" -Which in Blackfoot language means "dance"- was chosen according to the characteristics of the building and history of the site located in the east village, where Calgary, its native history and culture was formed. A dance in the east of Calgary's downtown, a moment of capture, a point where all the flows gather, a skyscraper based on the notion of system based relations.

PROBLEM+ Urban ISSUE

Socially, culturally and even environmentally speaking, Calgary is not an alive city to the level that its capacities demand. The city is spreading all around and is losing focus, there is no visible role and impact of cultural flow in town, and the environment is not understood/ respected in a comprehensive and useful way at architecture or urban scale. All the aforementioned issues cause a lot of urban, traffic, economic, cultural and ecological problems.

Also according to the seasonal changes and the weather condition city is totally dead during at least six months of the year and there is no activity happening on the surface of the city regardless to all the potentials.

CONCEPT +ARCHITECTURE

"Design is a manifestation of the forces that are driving it." The forces in this project come from all the sources around, visible or invisible, physical or none-physical, such as; power flow, water flow, Garbage, waste water, the flow of data, people flows, surrounding buildings, public motions, economy, culture, nature, structure, ecology, function, program, vision, ideas, demands, future, and so on.

"Our task is to move from dualism to pluralism and from there to advance to philosophy of coexistence."

Capturing all these flows and forces as in nature and biological forms, the building comes to existence and starts his life in a synergetic relation with all the factors.

To solve this problem this city needs a new system, a new world created by architecture. The proposal is a system based design of a living form with the integration of all the architectural and urban aspects, a system of connection through the whole city, a cluster of structures that are providing a new active world around them that will bring the city back to life. This is not a matter of 'a building in a city' or 'a city in a building' but it is the idea of 'a city in building in a city'.

SKYSCRAPER, SYSTEM

This project is a multi-use skyscraper, designed according to the demands and desires of the space, the visual impacts, the functions, structural concerns, sustainable considerations, concept of 'arcology', responsive architecture, agility in design, self-generative system and creating a living form in the city.

The idea is to build a structural frame in certain locations in the city, where this new system is more likely to emerge, then based on the needs of the society they start emerging through three different phases. Each phase starts with a giant base that generates all the factors required for living and growing, and then continues to form the occupiable upper multi-use portion.

The circulation is working through three connection stations located at each base, designed to distribute the circulation load and services, working as three city squares. At each of these connection stations a sky lobby is integrated on top, where a garden oriented to a certain target is serving users by providing a natural landscape.

PARTI - FLOW - SYSTEM
It was tend to build a base in order to capture the various flows and provide a field for them to go up and ascend while twisting around and blending into each other in a way that they work as a synergetic system, not as parts but as a whole functioning as a union. The interesting point is the fact that you can tell apart all the start points easily when it seems impossible to differentiate different flows in the middle or end points at the top, there is no way to relate end points to start points, they all just look like a whole.

CITY PLAN ANALYSIS/POTENTIAL BLOCKS

BASE STRUCTURE

FLOWS/FORCES

Instead of proposing the construction of a single skyscraper within a city, or a city within a skyscraper, the Paskan towers suggest the implementation of an infrastructure system that can better connect and revitalize the city as a whole. The word "paskan," to the aboriginal tribes that lived in Calgary, Canada, meant "dance," and dance was used to organically trigger an event. The skyscraper adopts this namesake symbolically as a self-generating infrastructure system that triggers new life within a city.

Paskan skyscrapers are strategically located throughout the city, and are built in three phases. The first phase is the construction of a base that holds all the supplies and processes needed to construct the rest

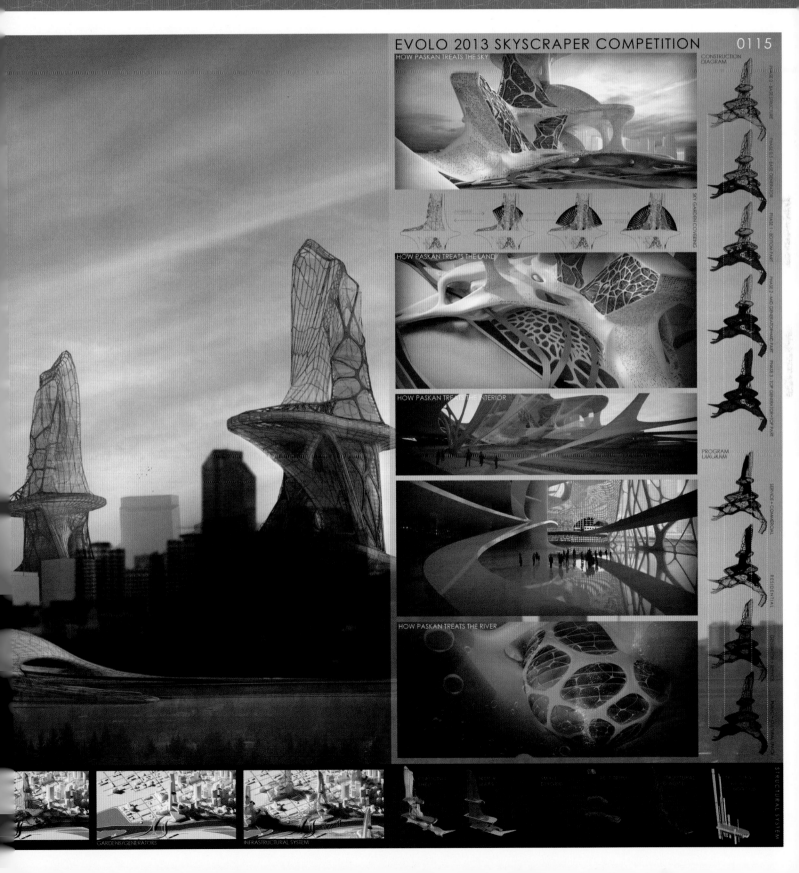

of the structure. With the exception of their base, these towers, therefore, are self-generating and self-sustaining. In addition to being self-creating factories, the bases of these structures also hold circulation systems that connect them to the other Paskan structures across the city.

The towers are then completed in two more phases, as a middle section and top section are built. Energy generators are located in all three levels of the Paskan tower. Photovoltaic panels, wind turbines and windbreaker walls provide the energy itself; also on the structure's surface are water collectors.

The towers grow in an "organic" shape and actually feature vegetation on their surface in the form of sky

SECTIONAL DIAGRAM - THE SYSTEM

gardens. In the winter, sky domes cover these gardens to allow for their use as greenhouses.

Ultimately, these structures exist to aid the city's growth in whatever capacity it may need; within the Paskan itself, its use is also flexible, with no initial plans dictating how people use the structure, and moveable walls being featured throughout. Whether it is needed to generate energy for the city, grow food for residents, allow for better transfer of information or data across town, or myriad possible other uses, the Paskan can generate itself into whatever form its operators need for the good of the city.

EVOLO 2013   0115

RESPONSIVE/ENVIRONMENTAL SYSTEM

Paskan is not only an organic shape, but it is a living form based on its functions, sustainability and agility. It has been designed in a way that responds to all different type of factors around and all the aspects of the site to fit in and blend into the context. Flexible plans and a system of moveable walls, responds to the needs and functions of the interior. The reaction of the building to seasons is obvious through the sky gardens, with a system of movable sliding domes that cover parts of the sky gardens to let people use it as a greenhouse during the winter; the building is changing by seasons in order to provide a better living condition inside. Paskan also reacts to the sun, wind and the water...

...The gardens are capturing rain water and providing a container for storing and using the water for secondary uses in the building. The orientation and the large penetrations in the form are addressing the force of the sun; also the use of integrated photovoltaic panels in the glazing system will provide a significant portion of the energy. In each connection level there is a station for providing and distributing power, data and water for the portion of the building above. Based on the wind analysis the form of the building was refined in order the meet the aerodynamic requirements and to locate the spots with the highest capacity for capturing wind in order to install micro wind turbines. The whole cladding system is a faceted shell of panels with flexible windows responding to the interior and functional forces while considering the environment and sun path. The sum of these two forces will result as a live pattern of size changing windows covering the Paskan.

494

PHOBIA SKYSCRAPER

2ND PLACE - 2013

Elodie Godo
Darius Maïkoff

France

Question of density and future of the cityscape cannot be avoided today.

The swarm cities are growing (3 out of 5 person is an urban citizen by 2050) and world population is over 7 billion human beings since 2011. Our proposition consists in a hyperdensity manipulated by the levers of one of the most popular phenomena of our urban age : Phobia.

00 .Paris is facing an urban sprawl. The mediatised 2005 suburbs riots showed clear disparities in term of genius loci between center and outskirts : local activities, perspectives for the future, identity, economical viability. No mans lands spread at the cost of agriculture with a pollution expansion, for an investor-suggested-standardised-happiness :« my house, my car, my backyard».
Clear ambition is to invite individuals into participating consciously and unconsciously in the creation of hyperdensity.

The project echoes with the remnant of the circle railway line, the Petite Ceinture, which tastes of forbiding, abandon and borderline activities.On this site, palpable reclaim of the industrial wasteland is operated by nature. Viewpoints over and under the city, coupled to the loss of perpetual advertisement place one in a position of spectator .Confrontation between two worlds evoke the phobias founders of our towns : darkness, wildlife, loneliness, uselessness.

01.Phobia plays with a duality between psychic and physical domains ; a physical reaction is induced by a phobogenic object. Its perception involves a psychological suffering which is released by actions : avoiding , confonting or adopting the phobogenic object, reactions awoken again by a new encounter.
This buckled system may apply to city selfproposition, as far as the population has an efficient organs leading to perception.

02.Electronical items in our daily life and sensors, harvest billions of informations . Statistics coupled to interpolation and comparison gave birth to Big Data analysis. This method uses parallel use of simple calculator to answer quickly to queries. Unpredictable results suggest new trends and solutions ,provided hypothesis are well displayed.

03.Application
Sample : Nucleus : population of a geographical area.
Several in the tower, each, constituted around a void, core.
Data collection : vocabulary used / noise of the city / production / consumption
Data synthesis : consumption_ production / self development_domination

Adjustments : unbalanced couples defined above, on a local (nucleus) and global (city+ tower) basis, weighed by distance and exchange rate between nuclei.

Derivated data : mixity(diversity), demography, velocity.

Range of Actions :
1 developpment
2 stagnation
3 regression
4 scission
applied to every field (programs)

Output :
proposal of a topographic and programmatic hypothesis, ; submitted to the population which choose as individuals to follow or not the scheme. The newbuild land is a new open playground.

04.The tower is constituted of single prefabricated structure units. Two slabs define a volume,hollow building allowed to be redistributed as will .Enveloppe is constituted of reclaimed industrial products at individual discretion. Piling up of the single volumes allow them to have common irrigation systems.Their rotation opens outdoor places or artificial lands.
The piling around the voids- centers of nucleus defines a new public space, a new basilicum and constitute a higher order of shellstructures.

05.Nuclei centers are equiped with displays giving feedbacks of informations, considering the status of the society, the occupancy and programm of the tower. Outer nuclei accumulate water to serve as counterweigh or use their orientation to concentrate solar power.

06.The system is open to evolutions : its parts survive abandonment and reuse ; as crisis explode or resolves, opportunities are offered to its inhabitants, which can choose to contest, amend or live with it.

EVERY BLACK CLOUD HAS A SILVER LINING

Phobia

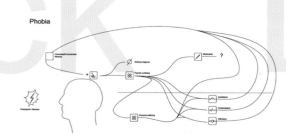

Program

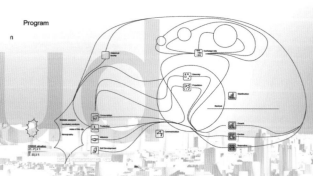

CONFRONTATION

STRUCTURE

WASTE = RAW MATERIA

NATURE RESILIENC

The Phobia Skyscraper is a new form of modular suburban residential development for Paris, France. It is located over the "Petite Ceinture", a former industrial site with excellent views of the city and an extensive transportation network. The project echoes with the remnant of the circle railway line, the Petite Ceinture, which tastes of forbidding, abandon and borderline activities. On this site, reclamation of the industrial wasteland is operated by nature. Viewpoints over and under the city, coupled to the loss of perpetual advertisement place one in a position of spectator. Confrontation between two worlds evokes the phobias of darkness, wildlife, loneliness, and uselessness.

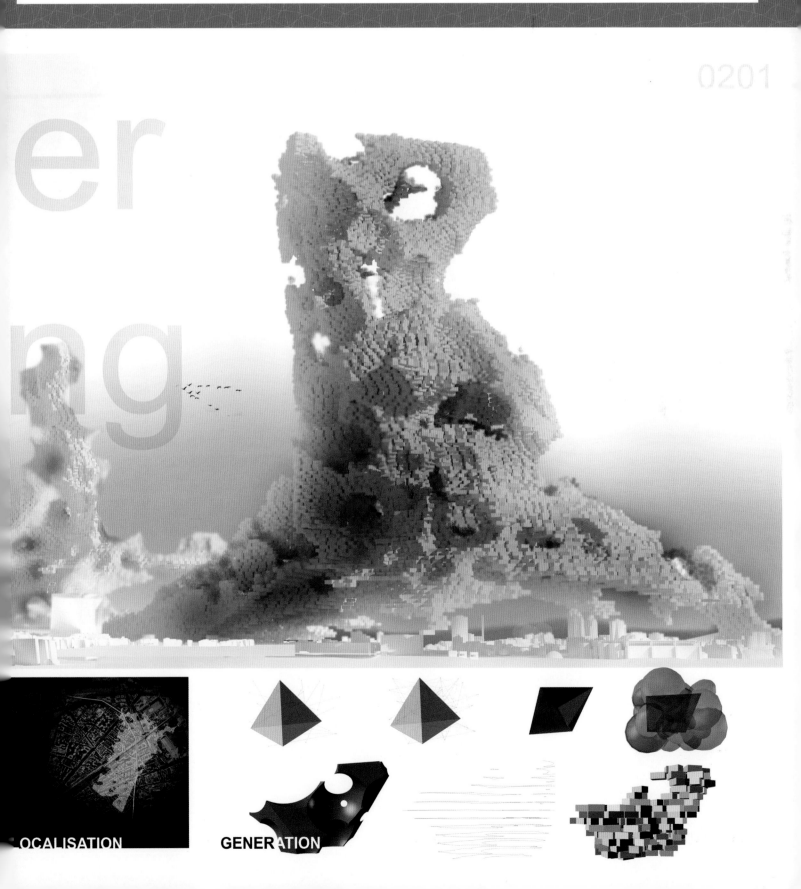

LOCALISATION   GENERATION

Phobia plays with a duality between psychic and physical domains; a physical reaction is induced by a "phobogenic" object. Its perception involves a psychological suffering which is released by actions: avoiding, confronting or adopting the phobogenic object.

Two main ground slabs and an empty tower structure constructed of recycled industrial materials hold prefabricated units that are stacked to utilize the same plumbing system but rotated to open to outdoor spaces. The units are grouped around outdoor common green spaces.

These common areas, or "nuclei centers," are also equipped with displays that provide real-time

- Shop
- Industry
- Culture
- Housing
- Nature

CONSTRUCTION

STABILISATION

DESERTIFICATION

BASE UN

feedback for residents on societal issues within the community, occupancy rates of the structure, and messages. It is also equipped with water-collection equipment and solar power panels.

Despite its solid skeleton, the Phobia skyscraper and its modular units are designed to evolve as society itself evolves. As its materials are the byproducts of abandonment and recycling, the building itself could go out of use or perhaps once more be revitalized, depending on the desires and needs of its residents. The system is open to evolution: its parts survive abandonment and reuse. As crises explode or become resolved, opportunities are offered to its inhabitants, which can choose to contest, amend, or live with it.

TUVALU IN 2050

Tang Shengquan
Huang Yaojun

China

Tuvalu in 2050
DISARSTER · DEVELOPING · DEVELOPED

Poor countries are the vulnerable group in the world.They do not have much respect.And when they are facing some disasters that they cannot solve ,they seldom get generated help immediately.Like Tuvalu,even the it will submerge under the ocean and has already sent the SOS to the world to ask for help ---immigrating the whole country. NO one answers except New Sealand,who only promises to give them an unequil treatment when they immigrate. So such design wants to focus on how to solve the disaster and development problem of Tuvalu.We think the disaster is a kind of energy which is too rich in a time.As we know ,if a country has enough electricity power, it can build it own industry system ,which is the base of a independent developed country.So if we can find a way to translate the energy of disaster to use ,many poor countries can have the condition to build its own industry system.This design take Tuvalu for an example to create a specific way for it..

STRATEGY

STEP ONE
As phosphorus is the only one of the mine resources of Tuvalu.So we design such mode of the development of the country that digging as much mine as possible for exporting ,which is to gather enough money to have next step of development plan.

STEP TWO
As the sea level is growing, we use concrete to fulfill the tube of mine to form the base of the skyscraper.And we move some soil that has submerged under the water to protect the formal naure system can continue exist.

Formal Nature System grows along the moved soiled

the hole of mine

2025

STEP THREE
When 2025 has come ,the main part for residents has finished.And still increase the height of the building to build a tall and thin building ,since we can gather more wind power in the top.

residental houses

the hole become the area of subway

2030

BASICALLY DONE
In this time ,wind power becomes the most useful an rich energy for Tuvalu .By ha enough energy , Tuvalu can form its own industry ,then fishing , farming and build a sophisticated economy system.

2015   DIGGING

2035

Tuvalu its a poor island that is submerging under the ocean. The country has already sent an S.O.S. to the world asking for help.

Tuvalu sinking is a reality in a non-far future; when this happens their people will face an extreme immigration. But immigrating the whole country to a new region is not the best answer. The solution is simple: build a skyscraper that is higher than the sea level. This will help Tuvalu have continuity in the region.

The strategy of construction starts by digging material from the soil using mining technics to exploit as much material as the complex need, then the void of material excavation will be filled with concrete to create

0320

Background

Because of global warming, sea level rise, many low-lying countries and cities now has always faced with the danger of submerged by the sea. Tuvalu is a country, is located in the south Pacific, the nine ring of coral islands, the highest elevation of the site is only 4.5 meters. Due to the topography is extremely low, rising temperatures and sea levels poses a serious threat to tuvalu, make this country is faced with the plight of abandoned.

South Pacific

Tuvalu

Site

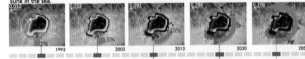

From 1993 years so far 19 years, tuvalu sea level rose a total of 9.15 cm, according to the digital prediction, fifty years later, sea level will rise 37.6 centimeters, this means that tuvalu at least 60% of the land will be completely sunk in the sea.

1993   2003   2013   2030   2050

National pressure

As sea levels rise slowly, after many years, the island will completely sunk in the sea; So long before, tuvalu is ready to the immigration.

Analysis

Tuvalu major industry

Fishery
Exporting
Transportation
Tourist trade
Crop farming

On average, Tuvalu national major industry in recent years, with the development of the rise in sea level falling.

Sustainable energy

Water Nuder Solar Tidel Wind Ocean

Wind and solar energy inTuvalu sustainable energy occupies a large proportion.And cosidering the continuity, wind power is the best.

GDP growth rate

1 New Zealand
2 Palau
3 Tuvalu

Neighboring developing countries GDP value comparison .

CURRENT SITUATION

Though the datas ,condition and analysis ,we know that Tuvalu is a poor and often suffer from the hurrican disaster. It does not have its own farming system and industry system.And currently it is facing a serious disaster that can destroy the whole country----the rising sea level will submerge Tuvalu under the water .As the member of vulnerable group in the world ,they do not have the ability to solve such problem.

CHARACTERISTIC

If nobody would give Tuvalu a generous hand,we have to solve such problem all by ourselves.The best way to figure out the method is to realize what we have now ,and what is the contry's characteristic.We can find out that ,in Tuvalu, the resources of phosphorus is abundant.It still can be mine for many decades.In the mean time,if we define hurricanes as a kind of energy.Tuvalu has enough energy.

METHODE

To solve the problem of increasing sea level is simple.Build a new country higher than the sea level.Then what we need to know is to find such technic and enough money to do it. And we know ,building an industry system is a good way to make a country rich.And forming urban industry system ,it needs energy.Then how to translate the disasters into energy that we can use is the key.

...PMENT SCOPE

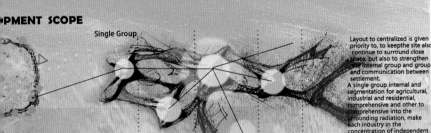

Single Group

Industrial   Agricultural   Comprehensive   Fishery
...ps Settlement

Layout to centralized is given priority to, to keepthe site also continue to surround close space, but also to strengthen the internal group and group and communication between settlement.
A single group internal and segmentation for agricultural, industrial and residential, comprehensive and other to comprehensive into the surrounding radiation, make each industry in the concentration of independent development and at the same time also can mutual penetration.

PROGRAM RESULT

Formation of the four dimension to form a group, in the vertical and lateral through traffic space to strengthen the relationship between each other and at the same time, they formed a original ecological system; Agricultural region in the middle, through their own photosynthesis generated gas reached around the mass produced gas a purification, and at the same time also can photosynthesis collected materials. So by the formation of the green ecological building system can realize zero discharge effect, a certain degree of slow down the greenhouse effect.

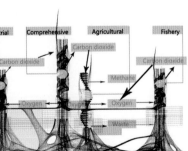

Industrial   Comprehensive   Agricultural   Fishery
Carbon dioxide   Carbon dioxide   Carbon dioxide
Methane
Oxygen   Oxygen   Oxygen
Waste

the founding for the skyscraper construction.

The tower is composed of habitable spaces in the middle and a wind power system in the top of the spine spiral. As the spiral works as a wind power generator it also will be covered by natural vegetation, which will be change according to the season. So the facade and the skin of the building will face different colors and textures trough the year.

There will be different applied programs for each tower such as Industrial, agricultural, housing, fishery, recreational, etc. Each program will determine the height and characteristics of the tower, as well as the

Tuvalu in 2050
DISARSTER · DEVELOPING · DEVELOPED

relation and connection to the contiguous tower.

The plan is to create a sustainable chain, composed by a series of skyscrapers connected to each other, generating resources and habitable spaces for Tuvalu community, in order to maintain and promote the development of the region.

The towers will be connected to each other by horizontal green bridges; this will function as the organic system of the complex, creating through photosynthesis enough oxygen for sustainable life.

SASTER IS MORE THAN A TREATEN

0320

ricane is the main disaster that people in tuvalu do not like .In the current day , some times when ricanes come ,most of the country that people are living in can submerged .Such situation affect normal life of the residents seriously.But if we try to see such thing in another angle,we can find easily that hurricane is a rich kind of energy .A lot of hurricanes means a lot of energy.Instead of ding it ,why we do not try to use it,because the development of a country can not practice without energy. a more , if we do can exploit such energy ,which is abundant in tuvalu, may be it can be one of biggest energy exporting countres,and then tuvalu has been developed.

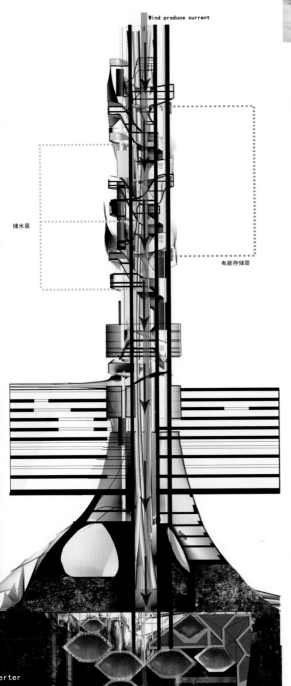

Wind produce current

储水层

电能存储层

-rter

strong wind

in the top of each building ,the most fragile part we design a fan to protect the whole building ,while collecting energy.

such fans surround the top part .when the wind pulls the fans, the wind will move along the surface of the fans . And finally the orientation of the wind will totally change .By reducing the amount of wind that can affect the bulding , such affect decreases.

As the fans are moved by the wind, we can translate it into electricity energy.

the small fans connects the near part of the building which contain the traslation equipment and store the energy in anothor form of .

on the big fans ,there are also manysmall fans,which can make suchtraslationmore efficient.

there are also some glass ball on the big fans ,which can provide more oxygen for the near people .Becase we think a development contains the increasing of people's life.

in the glass ball ,there is some plants.Such balls can purify the air

see from outside

spring   fall   winter

symbol of the country

since there are many such ball on the skin of the fans and the color of the plants in the glass ball can change as weather has change , then the surface of the fans can change color. And because the fans is the main part of the skin of the buildings .When people visit Tuvalu or pass by ,no matter by air or by boat , the first thing gets into their eyes is the skin.Maybe every time they visit ,Tuvalu the color will be different.Such secial fisrst impression will easily become the symbol of Tuvalu.Then the image of Tuvalu before hat poor and undeveloped will totally changes into interesting ,funny and developed.

Vegetation transplantation. The formal nature system will continue exist and the variety of creature can be protected.The residents still can enjoy the formal environment of Tuvalu.

1. From the top of the skyscraper wind generates current

2. Train cutting magnetic induction line movement, produce directional current

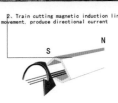

N

S

502

QUANTUM SKYSCRAPER

Ivan Maltsev
Artem Melnik

Russia

```
quantum_skyscraper
```

The form of this skyscraper is a growing crystal, a structure characterized by the inconstancy and regularity of its elements. The external crystal structure of the building is mobile and can be transformed depending on the configuration of the plan and the conditions of research, to flow into one another forming a transition between the other units.

The height of the units ranges from 130 to 180 m. At its full height, in the center of Multipurpose Research Complex (MNC), is a static rod. It is a quantum safe energy source, which will produce energy in the required quantity. The center of quantum computing, greenhouses, walking tracks and, aeration blocks

0791

are placed in immediate proximity.

The external crystal structure of the building is mobile and can be transformed depending on the configuration of the plan and the conditions of research, to flow into one another, forming a transition between the other MNCs. Transparent gateways for people access to the building are located at different heights while the ground floors are occupied by technical units, air purification, and transportation compartments—10% of the total area. The research part is the largest part of the building, different laboratories, lecture halls, and areas for meditation are located here taking up 65%. The information section

Multipurpose research complex MRC

130.000   Facade

Structure MRC

"It was almost evening. The wanderer was walking across the plain heading towards the hills covered with frosty grass and light fog hiding the silhouettes of trees and bushes. The fresh wind was bringing the voices of birds and the sounds of leaves from far away, almost like in his childhood. The wanderer easily recognized this place, this landscape. Rising slowly, step by step, these places became recognizable and swept memories, here he was born and raised. Gradually the panorama of the endless living plains opened to his view. The wanderer`s eye stopped on the unusual for these places forms, numerous winding paths leading to them. They were huge buildings or giant migrating animals that stopped here for a while to settle. Slowly approaching the silhouettes the wanderer noticed that the building was really alive, it was slowly and easily changing its crystalline structure ... "

We think about our impact on the environment more and more often. Man's need for natural and energy resources increases, this leads to the disruption of the balance between the desire (need) and nature`s ability to restore them. We think about it, because our actions "now" can seriously affect the lives of future generations, their thinking and dreams of the future. There is a great number of scenarios for unravelling of the plot of the future. And, in most scenarios the "energy" factor plays a vital role. Thus, many questions concerning energy production and storage arise.

We think that people will have more opportunities to return to balance and move to a new "energy" level without any influences. The latest and safe (for nature and man) power generation and accumulation technologies, transport, the AI (artificial intelligence) and medicine will be the determining factor in technological development of society in the future. For example, new discoveries in physics will help compensate for the lack of energy and use new sources (safe ones), open and use new materials with fundamentally new physical properties that can be used everywhere. All this will give birth to a new aesthetic revolution in the minds of people and, of course, architects and designers.

In our view, all these factors will affect the appearance of multi-functional research facilities (MNCs), which will hold all sorts of research for our future. These will be high-tech systems, in which the results of research and energy, matter and space will look like wizardry or magic.

MNCs will be easily placed in different conditions, as all their parts will be made of super-strong and ultra-light materials with unique, at times fantastic properties. The properties of color, transparency, heat, strain, weight, etc. in the envelope (structure) elements of the building will be changeable (or will change in standalone mode).

Probably the new scheme of new bearing materials will independently adapt to the environment, changing the overall image or building plan. Overlapping plans will be made of very strong and at the same time light materials changing the configuration of the plan. Superconductors will provide using gravitational platforms inside the building for movement of people in a variety of ways instead of elevators. Super-light materials in the building will create nearly invisible flexible membranes and set a unique micro-climate for any type of laboratory or research.

The form of a skyscraper is a growing crystal. Its structure is characterized by inconstancy and at the same time the order, regularity, structuredness of elements. Height units ranges from 130 to 180 m. The full height in the center of MCS is a static rod - a quantum safe energy source, which will produce energy in the required quantity, change and accumulate it, thus making the building autonomous. The center of quantum computing, some greenhouses, walking tracks and aeration blocks are placed in immediate proximity.

The external crystal structure of the building is mobile and can be transformed depending on the configuration of the plan and the conditions of research, to flow into one another, forming a transition between the other MNCs. Transparent gateways for people`s access to the building are located at different heights. The ground floors are occupied by technical units, air purification and transportation compartments - 10% of the total area. The research part is the largest part of the building, different laboratories, lecture halls, areas for meditation are located here taking up 65%. Information part takes 4-5 floors and comprises a media center, a cafe, a conference room - 25%.

Floors are made of super-light and ductile material capable change their configuration depending on the requirements and structure of foreign shell. Move between floors possible by means of gravitational platforms through the atrium.

91.000

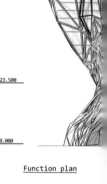

The outer shell of transparent material, able to change the color assignments, transparency, strain (stress), the masses. This will change the location of points in the structure space depending on the influence external (wind pressure, shade, landscape) and internal (condition survey) area.

23.500

Unique materials will allow the carrier structure to become mobile and to adapt under the surrounding landscape features (slopes, rivers, high peaks, etc.). Due to the mobility of construction will be easy to carry earthquake floods or hurricanes.

0.000

Function plan

"Heart" of the building - a static rod who is the "supervisors" of all transformation of carrying and protecting parts of the building. Carries a counterweight in areas of high seismicity. Here are the quantum computing center of the generation and accumulation of energy, communication systems and aeration.

Concept sketchers

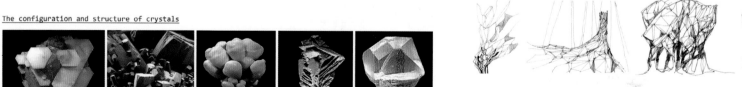

The configuration and structure of crystals

Growth patterns, step 15 m

takes 4-5 floors and comprises a media center, a cafe, and a conference room, the remaining 25% of the area.

The new scheme of new bearing materials will independently adapt to the environment changing the overall image and building plan. Overlapping plans will be made of very strong yet light materials changing the configuration of the plan. Superconductors will provide using gravitational platforms inside the building for movement of people in a variety of ways instead of elevators. Super-light materials in the building will create nearly invisible flexible membranes and set a unique microclimate for any type of laboratory or research.

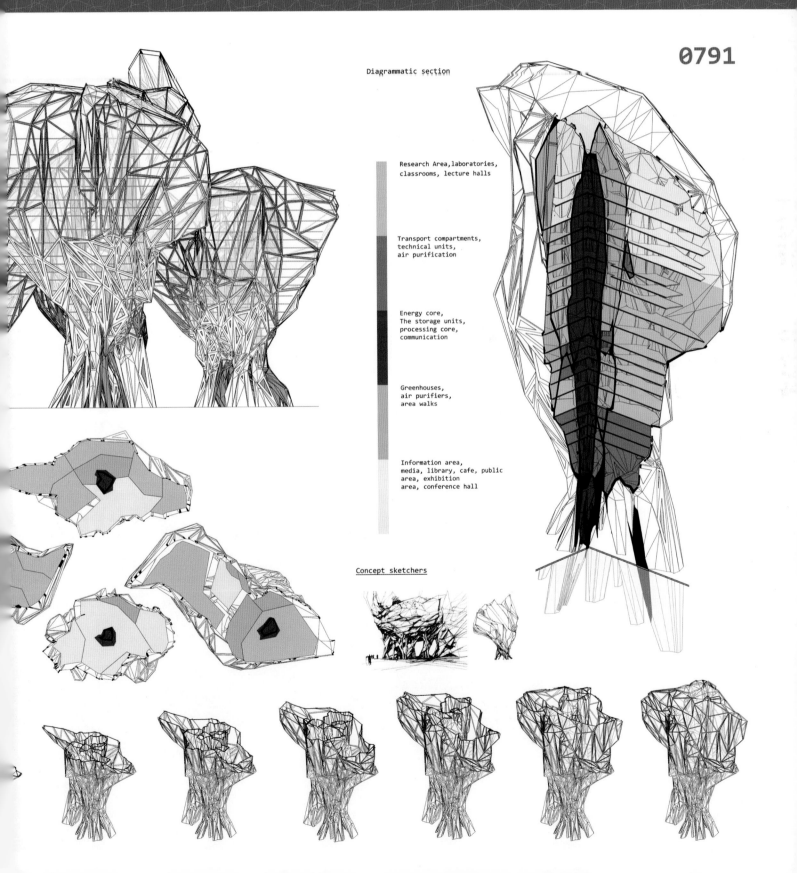

0791

Diagrammatic section

Research Area, laboratories, classrooms, lecture halls

Transport compartments, technical units, air purification

Energy core, The storage units, processing core, communication

Greenhouses, air purifiers, area walks

Information area, media, library, cafe, public area, exhibition area, conference hall

Concept sketchers

ANOTHER BRICK IN THE WALL

Michael Hara

United States

The costly and horrific wars the United States wages are decided not by generals on the battle field nor by ordinary citizens and families, but rather are voted upon and enacted by individuals mostly protected from the scars of war: members of Congress and the United States government. The majority of these individuals have never born the horror of combat themselves.

    The casualties of war thus come to these individuals not as the tragic stories of fathers, mothers, sons, or daughters; but rather as the quantified numeric of data. As Joseph Stalin once proclaimed: "One death is a tragedy; one million deaths is a statistic." This sentiment illustrates a disturbing reality: that when tragedy

0817

creeps beyond the comprehension of one's personal immediacy, it begins to lose its humanity.

This project is located on a vacant triangular lot immediately adjacent to the U.S. Capitol in Washington D.C. The monument consists of two towers, one each for the wars in Afghanistan and Iraq. The towers are themselves simple constructs: an interior consisting of a structural steel truss and stair that winds to the top of the ever-growing memorial, and a monolithic exterior wall made of carved marble blocks. Each block is representative of a single soldier lost in the war. An integrated crane at the top of each structure ensures that the towers continue their upward climb, raising and setting a stone for every fallen soldier. The towers

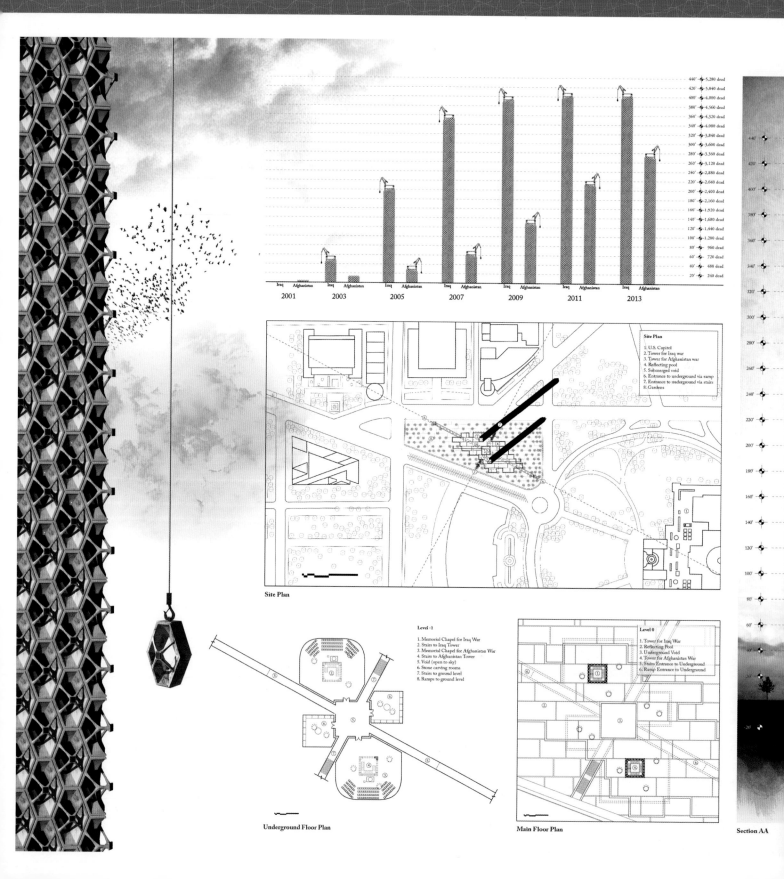

Site Plan

1. U.S. Capitol
2. Tower for Iraq war
3. Tower for Afghanistan war
4. Reflecting pool
5. Submerged void
6. Entrance to underground via ramp
7. Entrance to underground via stairs
8. Gardens

Level -1

1. Memorial Chapel for Iraq War
2. Stairs to Iraq Tower
3. Memorial Chapel for Afghanistan War
4. Stairs to Afghanistan Tower
5. Void (open to sky)
6. Stone carving rooms
7. Stairs to ground level
8. Ramps to ground level

Level 0

1. Tower for Iraq war
2. Reflecting Pool
3. Underground Void
4. Tower for Afghanistan war
5. Stairs Entrance to Underground
6. Ramp Entrance to Underground

Underground Floor Plan

Main Floor Plan

Section AA

began their ascent at the beginning of the war, each with the laying of a single stone. As the carnage of war continues, the towers, too, continue to rise.

The modules are carved, on site, from a single block of marble. The exterior of each stone is adorned with a copper nameplate, bearing the inscription of the individual's name, rank, birth and death. The outward facing half of the stone is skeletal, bare, and morose. The inside of each stone bears the same inscription, and also has a small integrated planter, creating on the interior of each tower a wall of red flowers. At night the tower is internally illuminated, creating a shimmering perforated pillar form against the night sky.

0817

SKINSCAPE

Haejun Jung
Karam Kim
Jaegeun Lim
Woongyeun Park

United States

S K I N S C A P E

Introduction

In our society, there are issues of increasing counteracted space due to many reasons. One reason could be the movement of the tenant whom are willing to move in newer buildings. This situation occurs a lot from straggled buildings. Furthermore, when the buildings were built at the certain period, the spaces were required more spaces due to industrial propensity at that time. However, in these days, many industries do not require huge spaces to produce what the company need. The function of the spaces was changing based on those circumstances. Therefore, the idea of our project was to explore the solution of the conditions where problem occurred.

Design inspiration

As a starting point of our design, the project which we called 'Skinscape' was inspired from the idea of modification on the architecture which affected by the natural environmental situations. For example, the Angkor Wat was built in 12th century and as time goes the structure was interrupted by the nature which is Banyan tree. The trees were growing inside and outside of the temple as weaves through the buildings. As the tree was almost embedded into the architecture, experts decided not to eliminate the vegetation because it will cause collapse of the building and it has beauty of the vegetation itself. At this point, we could think about this as relationships between two completely different elements which became a symbiotic relation to each other. Also, the form has two different characteristics of linear quality and organic figures that were blended each other.

Idea of applying to the Design

Therefore, the consideration of our project was to solve increasing rates of vacancy situations in the old buildings by applying the idea of symbiotic relations between formal skyscrapers and the Skinscape. In order to decrease rates of vacancy, the existing space where it encountered to new structure needs to transform and redesign the space. However, the purpose of having organic form is to translate the extension of the existing building's textures and the functionality. By the action of creating the elements that are out scaled of the existing building, we wanted to represent the results of emphasizing the growth of the spaces just like looking into convex glasses. Therefore, it is almost to reinterpreting the optical illusions and it can also represent in our concept. Also, the new mass was based on the grid system. The skyscraper's verticality conditions are transitioning to horizontality and that action results to create new vertexes which is diversity of the curves. While the curves generates, the mass becomes bundle and create 'Skinscapes'.

The Skinscape project was inspired from the idea that the natural environment modifies architecture as time passes by and in some instances nature even reclaims it. For example, Banyan trees now cover the Angkor Wat Temple in Cambodia built in 12th century. Experts have decided not to remove the trees because they now serve as part of the structural system; building and nature have become one. At this point we can think about this as a relationship between two completely different elements brought together to house a symbiotic relation to each other.

    The consideration of this project was to solve the increase rate of vacancy situations in old buildings by

0 8 3 9

applying the idea of symbiotic relations between formal skyscrapers and Skinscape. In order to decrease rates of vacancy, the existing space, where it encountered new structure, needs to transform and be redesigned. However, the purpose of having an organic form is to translate the extension of the existing building's textures and functionality. By the action of creating the elements that are out scaled of the existing building, the results of emphasizing the growth of the spaces was to be presented. The new mass was based on the grid system; the skyscraper's verticality conditions transition to horizontality and that action results in creating new vertexes for diversity of the curves.

Furthermore, there is most common way to create expanded spaces such as renovation etc. However, our design is reinforcing the existing conditions of skyscrapers and creates connections between old buildings and new buildings. The direction of expanded spaces can be vertical or horizontal depends on the situation where new action is occured. Also, the project was formed as to differentiate formal building envelopes. It is similar with infill architecture but different. However, the terminology of the 'SKINSCAPE' can describe as the building skin grows within blocks of the city and that growth create spaces that are extended from formal existing buildings. Therefore, the actions of connecting those buildings are creating 'SKINSCAPE'. The important aspect of this project is that the newer version of the buildings should not cover the existing building completely and should not have feelings of overpowering and controlling the formal architecture.

The expansion of the spaces is created as the tim horizontal conditions, the city itself turns from v the existing space and create another activity sp means the newer mass and formal mass are ble using existing skin and structure of the formal tecture and modern architecture, we could disc characteristics of verticality. It also created city s space and the inner space without disconnectio

This project explores the possibility of creating a building tissue between skyscrapers. The form has two different characteristics of linear quality and organic figures that were blended together. This tissue not only adds unto the buildings but also modifies them to allow for new programs. The idea is that buildings need to evolve with time because their initial design intentions and programs morph with time. Vacant space become active and a new hybrid emerges from the integration of two distinct buildings.

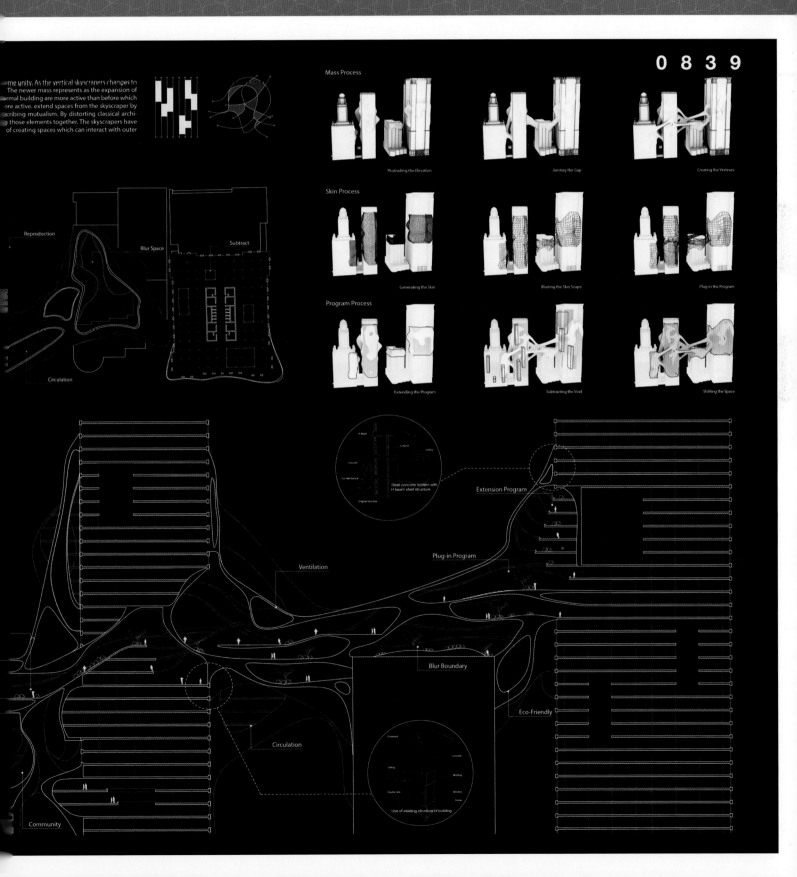

HETEROGENEOUS TOWER

Joe Balin
Kate Hanson
Alejandra Martin Laguna
Taylor McGrady
Gabriel Morales-Olivares
Marco Ulloa
Juan Carlos Zepeda

United States

TURBULENCE
// THE HETEROGENEOUS TOWER

Altering the typological fabric of the contemporary skyscraper, our research leads beyond two modernist strongholds: homogeneity and delimitation. Through the study of differentiation (as opposed to mere variety) and complex adaptive computational processes, heterogeneity becomes inherent in the process. Diffuse edges bound by discontinuous surfaces increase the resolution of the architectural fabric that can be physically manifested with fabrication technologies like contour crafting or 3D printing. As such, our research has updated these conditions based on "behaviors" of society in the pursuit after the same symbiotic relationship that exists between contemporary society and emergent technologies, from which "institutional" hybrids such as facebook, google, hackerspace, occupy, etc. have emerged. Those information processes as patterns of organization allow for the architectural articulation of differentiated behaviors, spatial heterogeneities and material composites. Computation was used not as a mere form-finding or emergent inspiration, but rather as a technique of integration of large amounts of data.

Within this complex adaptive system we hold agency over the performative output within architecture. The successful assembling of an ecology of agents satisfy their critical design goals such as differentiation within the layers of fabric. This counteracts modernist visions of repetition, rigidity, segregation, and flatness, which has not been addressed since Mies's first model of monotonous floor slabs. In rethinking this framework, the typical assemblage has been replaced by a field of n-dimensions. This organization of space and material has increased the spatial resolution, complexity, and information - thus abdicating the reductionist "bigness-from-size" via a "kit-of-parts." The notion of turbulence was used to create a specific type of heterogeneity that shows the first glimpses of designing for discontinuity. A clear point of departure localized within the larger system enabled the recognition of one specific kind of pattern even within another pattern, generating a shock-wave-like mediation of the two. Turbulence has also acted as a force to disturb the typical "still" medium with a substrate that reacts and changes. The coupling of patterning conditions and proto-programmatic qualities (larger, smaller, deeper, wider) demonstrates the ability to adapt to specific design requirements. Furthermore, the application of peaks and valleys leads to different appropriation techniques, culminating in a diffuse layer that adapts to specific conditions.

The diffusion of limits approaches edges that do not work as clean-cut delimitation of interior and exterior, but rather as discontinuous surfaces that are the overall average of the previous step. This removes the necessity of special host-conditions by thinking of the skyscraper condition as a whole. A contingent new process recalculates the complex potentials that the nature of larger-sized programmatic aggregates hold. Shying away from the spectacle of the silhouette, interior/exterior experiences are not defined by a definite enclosure. Instead, internal mechanisms of material differentiation speak of the distribution of other systems - structure, light, air, and vegetation. Natural cooling and vertical circulation are thus present without the addition of external technologies.

cross-section over tower and plaza

The Heterogeneous Tower integrates the study of two modernist strongholds: homogeneity and delimitation. The process of differentiation results in a variety of complex adaptive computational patterns and discontinuous surfaces that increase the resolution of the architecture, but ultimately produce heterogeneous results. Conditions were created, based on the same recent "behaviors" of society analogous to Facebook, Google, Hackerspace, Occupy, etc. in order to link these information processes as patterns of organization that will allow for the architectural articulation of differentiated behaviors via spatial heterogeneities and material composites. Computation was utilized as a technique of integration of large

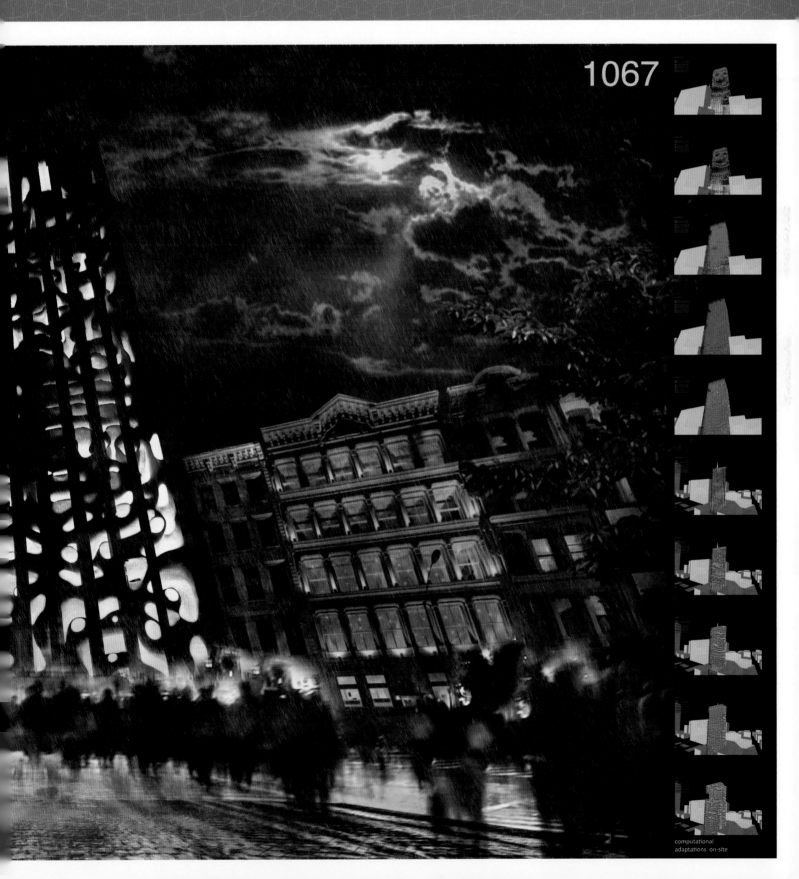

1067

computational
adaptations on-site

sets of data, allowing for the performance qualities of the architecture to be articulated. Differentiation within the layers of fabric has resulted in the integration of n-dimensions as an organization of space and material, abdicating the reductionist mindset as a "knit of parts."

An average infield site in San Francisco was chosen to test the overall strategy because of both the social and physical contexts of the city. The process of symbiosis towards the site is the emergence of the interaction of the forces of neighboring structures that converge as turbulence in the viscous medium of articulated space as the initial condition for differentiation and diffusion. Proportions of the pattern are loosely

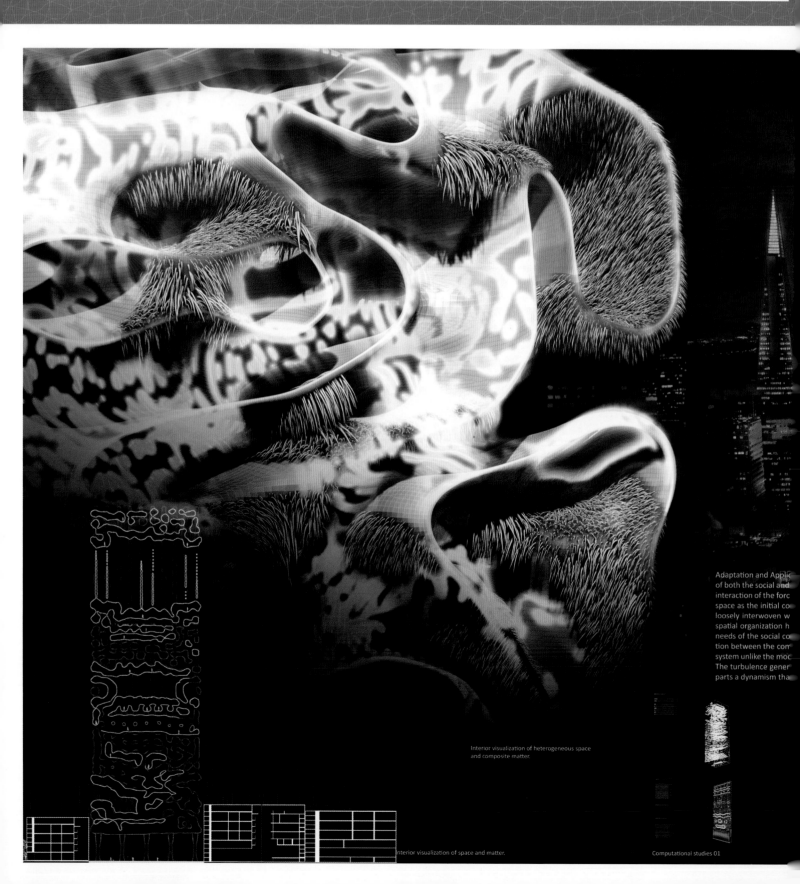

Adaptation and Applic
of both the social and
interaction of the forc
space as the initial co
loosely interwoven w
spatial organization h
needs of the social co
tion between the com
system unlike the moc
The turbulence gener
parts a dynamism tha

Interior visualization of heterogeneous space
and composite matter.

Interior visualization of space and matter.

Computational studies 01

interwoven with those of the context. The possibilities of utilization within the proposed heterogeneous spatial organization have clearer definitions, such as an auditorium, but other areas are left to be defined by the needs of the social complex that takes over. Achieving such constructs further demonstrates control via a mutation between the computation, the designer, and host-conditions. The symbiosis of form and function is an open system unlike the modernist vision where furniture and partitions are requisites of a successful spatial composition. The turbulence generated through the aggregation contrasts with the static nature of the existing facades and imparts a dynamism that reflects the socio-technical diversity of the cityscape.

1067

LIGHT   AIR FLOW   CIRCULATION   VEGETATION   INTERIOR/EXTERIOR

ite in San Francisco was chosen to test our overall strategy because
y. The process of symbiosis towards the site is the emergence of the
es that converge as turbulence in the viscous medium of articulated
tion and diffusion in our vessel. The proportions of the pattern are
The possibilities of utilization within the proposed heterogeneous
ich as an auditorium, but other areas are left to be defined by the
Achieving such constructs further demonstrates control via a muta-
and the host-conditions. The symbiosis of form-function is an open
ure and partitions are requisites of a successful spatial composition.
tion contrasts with the static nature of the existing facades and im-
al diversity of the cityscape.

Wall section

DISAPPEARED TSUNAMI

Jung Jinho
Jung Jongdae

France

Disappeared Tsunami

Today, The world are wearing serious damage to the unexpected natural disasters.
We understand that the Tsunami is always important risk factor should be prepared.
Our team start this project from a question how we avoid this huge movement of the Earth.
Of course, we know that we can't protect 100% the city and peoples from the tsunami.
Therefore, the goal is to be minimized risks with the efforts we can do as much as possible.
Technically, this proposal would be impossible the scale of the architecture current. However,
we look forward to applying this idea with more reasonable project, or would be realized in
the near future. Therefore, we want to defend the city and people from the Tsunami.
We think that this is the goal of Skyscrapper competition of value as well

A tsunami is a series of water waves caused by the
a large volume of a body of water, typically an ocean
volcanic eruptions and other underwater explosions
underwater nuclear devices), landslides, glacier calv
other disturbances above or below water all have the
Tsunami waves do not resemble normal sea waves,
Rather than appearing as a breaking wave, a tsunami
rising tide, and for this reason they are often referre
Tsunamis generally consist of a series of waves with
arriving in a so-called "wave train". Wave heights of
events. Although the impact of tsunamis is limited to
can be enormous and they can affect entire ocean b
among the deadliest natural disasters in human hist
14 countries bordering the Indian Ocean.

Today, the world has seen the serious damage unexpected natural disasters can cause and understand that the tsunami is an important risk factor to consider. Disappeared Tsunami begins with the problem of how to avoid such huge movements of the earth. Since it is acknowledged that it is impossible to protect the entire city and its people from the tsunami, the project's primary objective is to minimize risks as much as possible.

As much as 80% of tsunamis arise on the Pacific Rim, including the western slope of the Kuril-Kamchatka Trench, causing the metropolis of the Pacific coast to be a primary subject in this project. Since gravity exists everywhere on Earth, the gravity of the tsunami defense system was further studied and

1105

ZONE OF RISK OF TSUNAMI

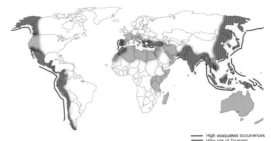

As many as 80% of the Tsunami arise on the Pacific Rim, including the western slope of the Kuril–Kamchatka Trench, Metropolis of the pacific coast will be an important subject of this project.

— High seaquakes occurrences
▓ Hing risk of Tsunami
▓ Moderate risk of Tsunamis

THE MOST DESTRUCTIVE TSUNAMIS OF LAST 50 YEARS

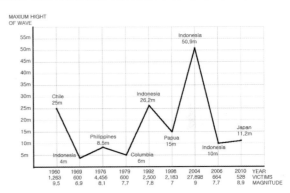

	1960	1969	1976	1979	1992	1998	2004	2006	2010	YEAR
	1,263	600	4,456	600	2,500	2,183	27,898	664	528	VICTIMS
	9.5	6.9	8.1	7.7	7.8	7	9	7.7	8.9	MAGNITUDE

IDEA CONCEPT (OVERFLOW SYSTEM OF THE WATERTANK)

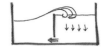

The gravity exists anywhere in the Earth. And we use this power in our life. Our team want to apply the gravity of the Tsunami defense system. For example, there is one big water tank which is divided two part. And we open the bottom of the blockage so, the water is going to be moved freely through this opening. In this case, if you push water to the other side by hand, what is going to happen? Of course, the gravity will return the original side until equilibrium of the water surface which is the additional water can be through the opening to the bottom . That's how we are called the overflow system.

APPLICATION IN THE PROJECT

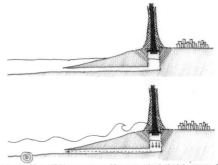

Overflow system does not need any artificial power or energy. It is a permanent and natural phenomenon of the Earth. Tsunami, we stand against this huge movement of our planet with another giant force of the gravity. In front of a coastal city, we will install a band of mega pit in front of a coastal city. The bottom of the pit is a large number of grand pipe which can be connected with the sea.

Due to the Tsunami, if the water level of the pit rises higher than the level of the sea, the gravity will return the amount of added water through the discharge pipe like the water tank above.

As a result, the project can be the drainage itself of the Tsunami and will be protect a city and people who located on the rear side.

applied to an overflow system. For example, if there is one big water tank which is divided into two parts and the bottom of the tank is blocked, water will move freely through this opening. In this case, if water is pushed to the other side by hand, the gravity will return the original side that is open until equilibrium of the water surface is reached, which is dependent on the additional water coming through the opening at the bottom.

An overflow system does not need any artificial power or energy. It is a permanent and natural phenomenon of the Earth. During a tsunami, we stand against two opposing forces of gravity. In front of a coastal city, a band of mega pit would be installed. The bottom of the pit contains a large amount of grand

Tower form research

Behavior agents : 50   Target height : 300   Starting Position = SP

SP 10 X 10   SP 50 X 50   SP 100 X 100   SP 150 X 150   SP 200 X 200

Prototype of panel

Type A / Evacuation panel

Type B / Transformative open panel

Type C / Convex panel

Type D / Plane panel

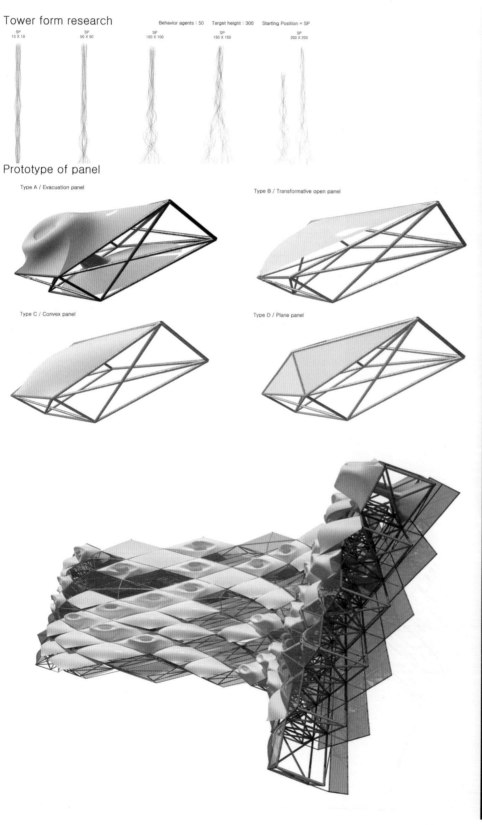

Change from disaster to event

Huge amount of water become waterfall. And people can see actual view of the water can go back to the sea. It will be amazing spectacle, it will be also the evidence of human wisdom which overcome the disaster. Tsunami, this is no longer fearful disaster.

It can be changed from a disaster to an event.

pipe which can be connected with the sea. Due to the tsunami, if the water level of the pit rises higher than the level of the sea, the gravity will return the amount of added water through the discharge pipe like the water tank above. As a result, the project can be drained itself of the tsunami and will protect a city and people who are located on the rear side. Consequently, this huge amount of water will become a waterfall. It will be an amazing spectacle, and could no longer be viewed as a fearful disaster; it can transform from a disaster to a magnificent event.

1105

Bending tower / Evacuation

Bending tower

Evacuation system
between main support structure
against tsunami

Overflow tsunami

THE IDEAS COVERED IN THIS CHAPTER ARE AN INVESTIGATION ON THE ROLE OF THE SKYSCRAPER IN THE OVERALL FUNCTIONALITY OF CITIES. WE HAVE REACHED A PERIOD DEFINED BY MASSIVE STRUCTURES THAT OPERATE SIMILARLY TO CITIES. THE CONSTANT QUESTION HAS ALWAYS BEEN HOW TO INTEGRATE THESE STRUCTURES TO EXISTING CONDITIONS.

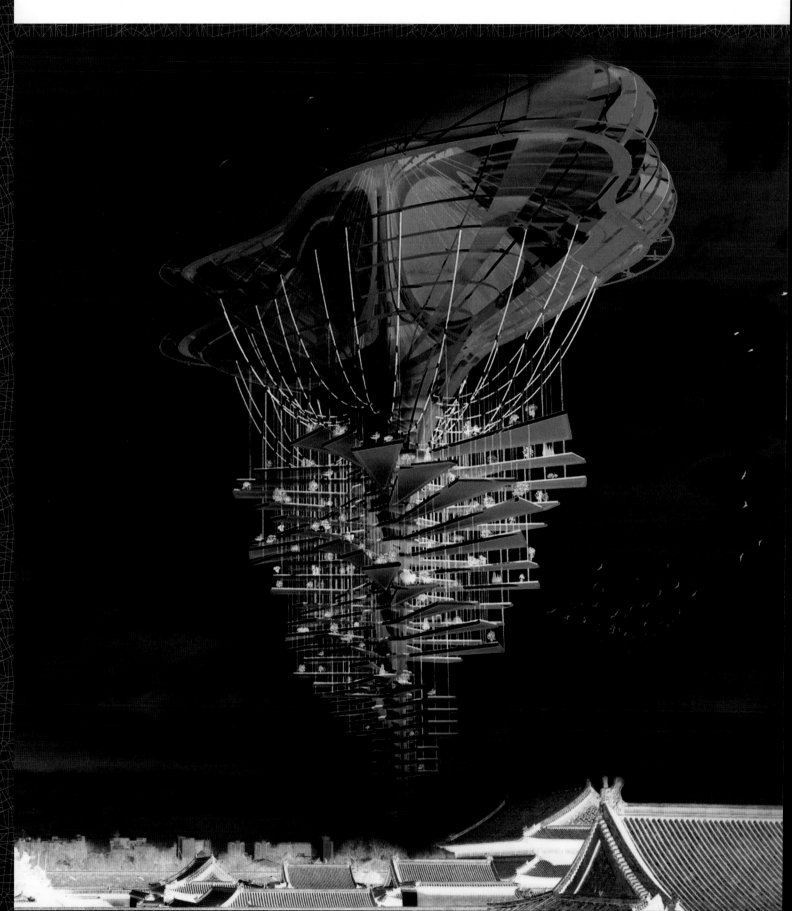

The ideas covered in this chapter are an investigation on the role of the skyscraper in the overall functionality of cities. We have reached a period defined by massive structures that operate similarly to cities. The constant question has always been how to integrate these structures to existing conditions, not only to provide new infrastructure but also to redefine the existing one. These are proposals that range from super-tall skyscrapers to inhabitable bridges and even the conception of entirely new metropolis; there is an understanding that in only 30 years more than 70% of the World's population will live in an urban development.

Instead of designing settlements that follow traditional design layouts, there is a new exploration at every design level, from new materials research to the study of natural cellular aggregations and their logic of integration and growth.

Other submissions research digital tools, including Augmented Reality developments in which digital components enhance the users experience of space and their consumption of information. Linear cities are another interesting approach to connect two settlements with a third one that serves as an inhabitable link – an urban design approach similar to Roadtown conceived by Edgar Chambless in 1910 to connect Washington D.C. to Baltimore with rail lines at subterranean levels and row-houses above.

Finally, the use of psycho-mathematical information to conceive new inhabitable areas where form is the product of emotions is explored by other projects. The transformation of this information into architecture is done by programmed robots, which use the new information to build these structures.

524

SMARTSCRAPER

Bastien Papetti
Adrien Piebourg

France

GET THE SMARTSCRAPER

How to live vertically? Climb higher and higher does not seem to change the way we live. Most people wish to live in individuals houses. So we have to be interested by the pavilion. But the problems is now well established: sprawl, lack of diversity and density, ghetto, poverty of an architectural uniformity etc.. Our question is: How to involve everyone to live at home with the qualities that implies, and living together, as in the heart of the city?

Now let's found where the tower's history started. This goes back to Elisha Otis, who was the inventor of what we call now the Elevator. This began the conquest of the sky and generate projects competing for prowess and sizes. What could be the lift of the twentieth? Within the house, he would like to be a remote control to move from one floor to another, but also from one program to another.

The function of living would be challenged in the object. The house become as smart as the Smartphone, and incorporates multiple applications. One application per floor. The elevator is for house that Internet is for phone. A necessary parameter! Now you can "zap" your life spatially. Imagine yourself in your room, put on your slippers, go in your elevator, and zap! You will be almost instantaneous in your living room, your garage, your favorite bar or business place, the park where you go jogging!

The new tower is born, or rather, what is the first cell. We must now find the idea of "Tower". It's going to go through the quantity. This lonely cell is only anecdotal, but multiplied and intensified, it marks its existence. It is now clearly identifiable as an "object".
The idea of Tower is inseparable from the idea of city, so we have now an object in the city who looks like a city. Perceptions are distorted. The object in the city became literally the "city object".

How to live vertically? Building higher and higher does not seem to change the way we live. Most people wish to live in single-family residences, but the problem is the lack of diversity and density. How to have the benefits of suburbia combined with the intensity of living in the city?

The history of the skyscrapers goes back to Elisha Otis, who invented the elevator in the 19th century. This invention promoted the conquest of the sky with projects competing for prowess and size. What would happen if within a house the elevator were to be used as a remote control to move from one floor to another, from one program to another?

0067

This new object would challenge the function of living. The house becomes smart and incorporates multiple applications, one application per floor. The elevator is for the house what that Internet is for a smartphone—a necessary parameter. Now one can "zap" his or her life spatially. One can zap from the living room, to the garage, to a favorite to the park.

In the future our communication systems will be miniaturized. Computers, cars, and phones will become more compact and their applications will increase. Similarly, the tower here is compacted; compressed, it does not look like a tower but we have the feel of it. Generally, programs are typically overlapped by stratum

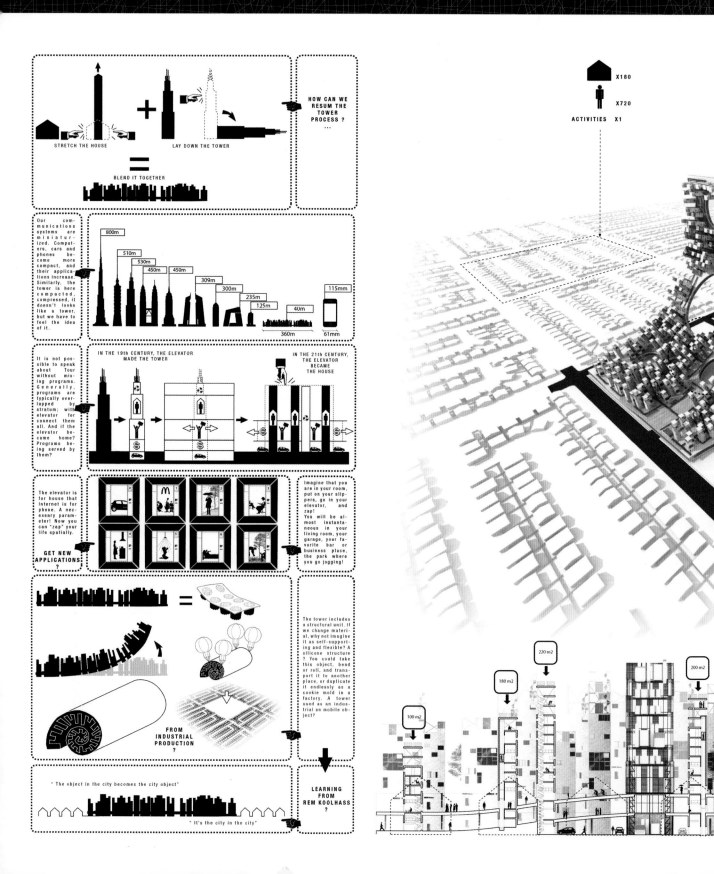

STRETCH THE HOUSE + LAY DOWN THE TOWER = BLEND IT TOGETHER

HOW CAN WE RESUM THE TOWER PROCESS ? ...

Our communications systems are miniaturized. Computers, cars and phones become more compact, and their applications increase. Similarly, the tower is here compacted, compressed, it doesn't looks like a tower, but we have to feel the idea of it.

800m 510m 530m 450m 450m 309m 300m 235m 125m 40m 360m 115mm 61mm

It is not possible to speak about Tour without mixing programs. Generally, programs are typically overlapped by stratum; with elevator for connect them all. And if the elevator became home? Programs being served by them?

IN THE 19th CENTURY, THE ELEVATOR MADE THE TOWER

IN THE 21th CENTURY, THE ELEVATOR BECAME THE HOUSE

The elevator is for house that Internet is for phone. A necessary parameter! Now you can "zap" your life spatially.

GET NEW APPLICATIONS ?

Imagine that you are in your room, put on your slippers, go in your elevator, and zap! You will be almost instantaneous in your living room, your garage, your favorite bar or business place, the park where you go jogging!

=

The tower includes a structural unit. If we change material, why not imagine it as self-supporting and flexible? A silicone structure? You could take this object, bend or roll, and transport it to another place, or duplicate it endlessly as a cookie mold in a factory. A tower used as an industrial an mobile object?

FROM INDUSTRIAL PRODUCTION ?

" The object in the city becomes the city object"

" It's the city in the city"

LEARNING FROM REM KOOLHASS ?

X180 X720 ACTIVITIES X1

100 m2 180 m2 220 m2 200 m2 160 m2

with an elevator to connect them all. The elevator is the key.

The new tower is born, or rather, the first cell. We must now find the idea of "tower." This cell is only anecdotal, but multiplied and intensified, it marks its existence. It is now clearly identifiable as an object. The idea of "tower" is inseparable from the idea of city, so we would have an object in the city, which looks like a city, distorting perception.

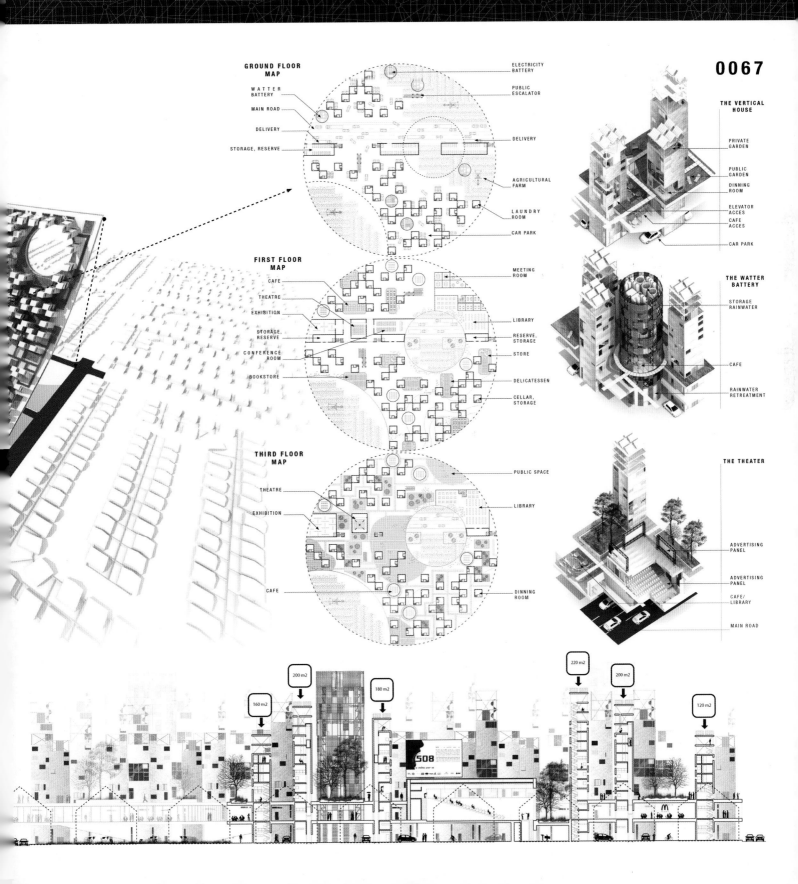

GROUND FLOOR MAP

WATTER BATTERY — MAIN ROAD — DELIVERY — STORAGE, RESERVE — ELECTRICITY BATTERY — PUBLIC ESCALATOR — DELIVERY — AGRICULTURAL FARM — LAUNDRY ROOM — CAR PARK

FIRST FLOOR MAP

CAFE — THEATRE — EXHIBITION — STORAGE, RESERVE — CONFERENCE ROOM — BOOKSTORE — MEETING ROOM — LIBRARY — RESERVE, STORAGE — STORE — DELICATESSEN — CELLAR, STORAGE

THIRD FLOOR MAP

THEATRE — EXHIBITION — CAFE — PUBLIC SPACE — LIBRARY — DINNING ROOM

0067

THE VERTICAL HOUSE

PRIVATE GARDEN — PUBLIC GARDEN — DINNING ROOM — ELEVATOR ACCES — CAFE ACCES — CAR PARK

THE WATTER BATTERY

STORAGE RAINWATER — CAFE — RAINWATER RETREATMENT

THE THEATER

ADVERTISING PANEL — ADVERTISING PANEL — CAFE/ LIBRARY — MAIN ROAD

160 m2   200 m2   180 m2   220 m2   200 m2   120 m2

508

SOCIAL EQUILIBRIUM

Kim Hong Chur
Kwak Naekyung
Lee Byoung Wook

Republic of Korea

Social Equilibrium

Issue

1. Disappear Old Urban Fabric

The city of Seoul has been filled with products of fast-growing industrialism without mediating process. Therefore, its history accumulated over 600 years was replaced with maximized land use, and as a result the identity of Seoul has been still disappearing.

1960' Seoul

2000' Seoul

2. Economical Needs

Concentration of urban area is considered as efficient use of land, minimizing cost for building infrastructure and environment, and skyscraper has emerged as a symbol of urban planning.

3. Coexistence

The goal of my team is not only producing financial profits of concentration of urban area but also preserving urban identity of the old city.

How to coexist = 4D Urban Planning

Physical and cultural concentration can be created when the old city can embrace the high density required for a new urban planning. We bended the existed urban ground for reorganizing the city that will be extended vertically by proposing new urban planning that contains the old urban infrastructure. The new building called cityscraper will be created on this vertical ground and floats above the old city without destroying the identity of old city.
It means that 4d urban planning will facilitate accumulating urban memories.

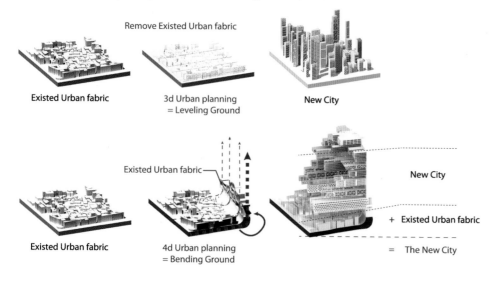

Remove Existed Urban fabric

Existed Urban fabric

3d Urban planning = Leveling Ground

New City

Existed Urban fabric

Existed Urban fabric

4d Urban planning = Bending Ground

New City

+ Existed Urban fabric

= The New City

Vision

4 dimensional urban planning is possible through converting existing skyscraper into vertical urban planning. It will make more compact city at the same time preserving its urban identity by accumulating historical layers. This hyper-reality that looks like a rotated city maximizes possibility of close relationship between the old and new. The new city provides greenery and public space to the old city.
The buildings in the new city will stand as landmarks that create new cultural layer to its urbanscape.

Industrialism of the 19th and 20th centuries replaced much of Seoul, Korea's historic core, with old structures replaced with skyscrapers in the name of density and efficiency. Seoul has been filled with products of fast-growing industrialism without mediating process. The Social Equilibrium plan seeks to still maximize financial gain from land use, but to do so in a way that restores the identity and 600 year history of Seoul.

Concentration of urban area is considered as efficient use of land, minimizing cost of building infrastructure and environment, and skyscraper has emerged as a symbol of urban planning. The goal of this

design is not only producing financial profits of urban area but also preserving the urban identity of this city.

The Social Equilibrium plan "bends the ground"; infrastructure is laid alongside the historic part of the city that allows "cityscrapers" to be built vertically. They are vertical on this new plane—to those within the old city, these new buildings extend horizontally over existing historic structures, allowing for new, dense growth but sparing the urban fabric. The designers call this bending of space "4-dimensional urban planning."

The buildings that extend horizontally in 2D space over the existing part of Seoul are also stacked vertically. In each building, the bottom floors are used as commercial and community spaces. Above it are

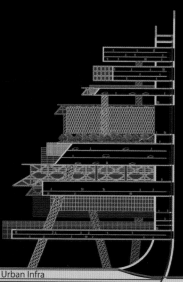

Resident

Parkinglot

Hotel & Office

Parkinglot

Commercial & Community

Urban Infra

Program

Each program is separated by parking layer considering the shortage of parking space in the old city. It also provides parking for additional programs in the future. Performing arts halls, community centers and galleries are located near the urban ground adding to urban diversity. Hotels and offices are located in the middle floors, and residential area is placed on the top floors.

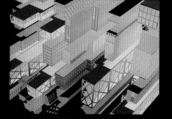

Structure

Urbanscaper extends horizontally and supported by main cores connected to the old city. Parking area structured with trusses acts as thick slab in urban scale and is secondary supported by each cores.

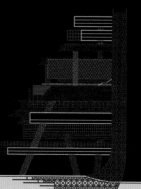

Green Layer

The new city provides green that the existing could not offer. It resolves solutions to issues and public use o

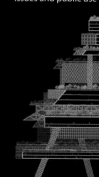

floors for parking, and above those are floors with a hotel and offices. Next comes another parking lot, and finally at the top are levels for private residences. The ample parking space that separates each program within the building makes up for the lack of available parking in the old city. The buildings have green spaces on roofs and scattered throughout the levels along exteriors, providing more green space than traditional vertical skyscrapers are able to provide.

This vision of a rotated city allows for harmony between the old and the new, allowing for compactness while also preserving the historic layers of the already-built city.

ST. PETERSBURG MEGA BRIDGE

Igor Korobitsyn

Russia

EVOLO
2012
SKYSCRAPER COMPETITION

SCHEME OF TRANSPORT COMMUNICATIONS AND SPATIAL STRUCTURES

185.0m

3

4

3

3

3

1

2

185.0M

000.0m

1

160.0M

185.0M

650.0m

-75.0m

2

cut floors

This project proposes the construction of a monolith at sea as an attempt to stop the growth of St. Petersburg, Russia's urban area, preserving what is there and taking new residents and development to a nearby but separate location. The location of this project is over a large body of water formed by Peter and Paul Fortress, the Palace Embankment and Exchange arrow of Vasilyevsky Island.

Working with existing city infrastructure, especially a historical one, can cause negative reactions from citizens. However, the "invasion" is needed for at least one main purpose—to stop the growth of the urban area.

0238

THE SOUTH-EAST FACADE

Location of the project is part of the city of St.Petersburg, a large water area, formed by Peter and Paul Fortress, the Palace Embankment and Exchange arrow of Vasilyevsky island. Doing works in the existing city infrastructure, and especially in the historical part, always cause a negative reaction from society. However, the "invasion" is needed at least for one purpose - to stop the growth of the urban area. From the vast uncomfortable surface of the northern city (permanently needed to be deconstructed), - move to the civilized multilayer work.

This project is the embodiment of an extensive three - dimensional system, which is open for further development. Four high-rise cmplexes, growing out of the water surface. They are connected to each other with curved froms dynamics of giant bridge spatial structures.Bridges spanned between the shaft and the structures of communication. The space takes on a new scale, the clash of old and new exacerbates the feeling of a whole, is not only visually but also physically.

Residential Complex at 50-120 thousand inhabitants (depending one the needs) is regarded as a complete autonomous organizm built into the infrastructure of the city. The dwellings are placed as the continuous terraces with embrasure formed as transparent strctures. Communication of the fifty-floor building with the surface, underground and water transportation ways bylifting, monorail and suspended trasport systems is three-dimensional. Under water space is used for parking cars and boats and technical equipment storage as well. Huge top floor of the plane fnd the vertical walls can be used for renewable energy systems.

953.0m

1 docking of transport communiccations

2 parking of cars and boats
technical premises equipment

3 atriums

4 residential floors

The design calls for four high-rise complexes, which are connected via a giant curving bridge, to be built rising out of the water off the shore of St. Petersburg. The enormous complex is stark, almost brutalist; this design creates not only a new scale of development but brings about a clash of old and new that leads to a feeling of wholeness for the city, visually and physically.

The structure's residential complex can house between 50,000 and 150,000 people. It is constructed to be autonomous, self-sustaining and therefore not an additional burden to the existing infrastructure of the city. Living quarters share continuous terraces that are separated with transparent divides.

EVOLO
2012
SKYSCRAPER COMPETITION

Underwater portions of the facility are used for parking cars and boats, and also for storage of technical equipment. The cars can be moved up and down via lifts; the complex also has a monorail and 3D suspended transport systems. On the massive top level of the 50-level structure, vertical walls cover the surface and hold within them renewable energy systems.

0238

TRE NORTH-EASTERN FACADE

SCHEME OF THE SPATIAL STRUCTURE OF CONSTRUCTIONS

883.0M

FRAGMENT OF THE GENERAL PLAN

TUNDRA CENTER

Pavel Sipkin

Russia

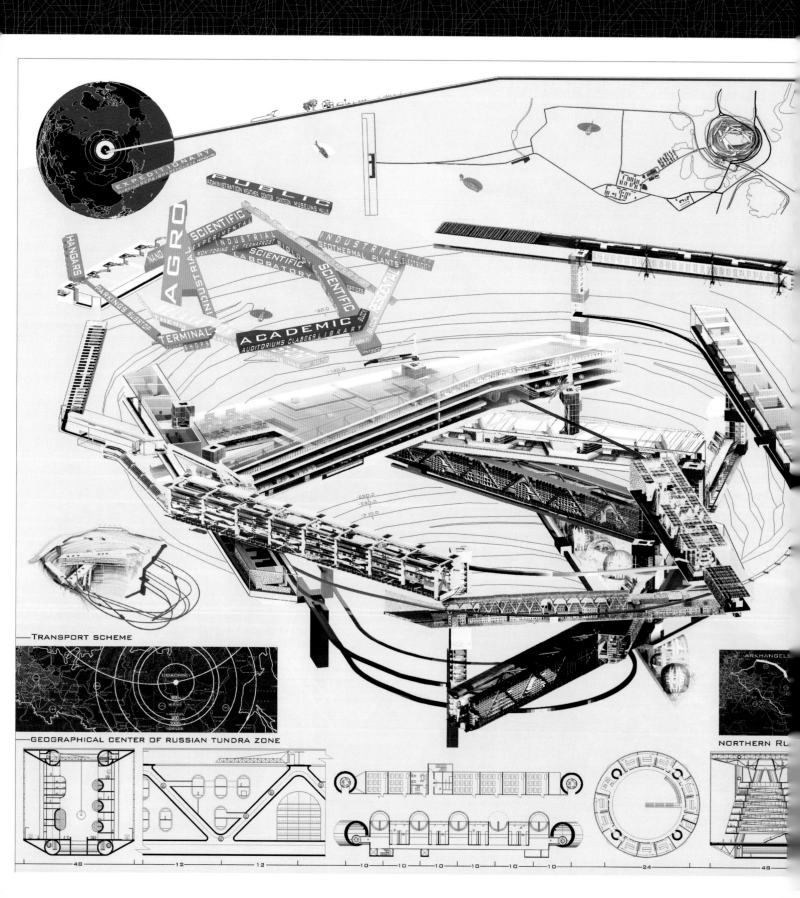

TRANSPORT SCHEME

GEOGRAPHICAL CENTER OF RUSSIAN TUNDRA ZONE

NORTHERN RU

Tundra City is located in the exhausted diamond mine "Lucky" which is the geographical center of the entire Russian Tundra, the last point of urbanization of the Russian North.

    The tundra is an unexplored region, which hardly anyone wants to visit. It is associated with a "hole" due to poor living conditions. The Russian government has paid attention to the prospect and huge potential benefits of developing the region to the whole the country. This has been facilitated by the existing geopolitical threat posed by the rapidly development of China, India, and other countries.

    Tundra City is a launching pad to address the problems of the region: population, development of

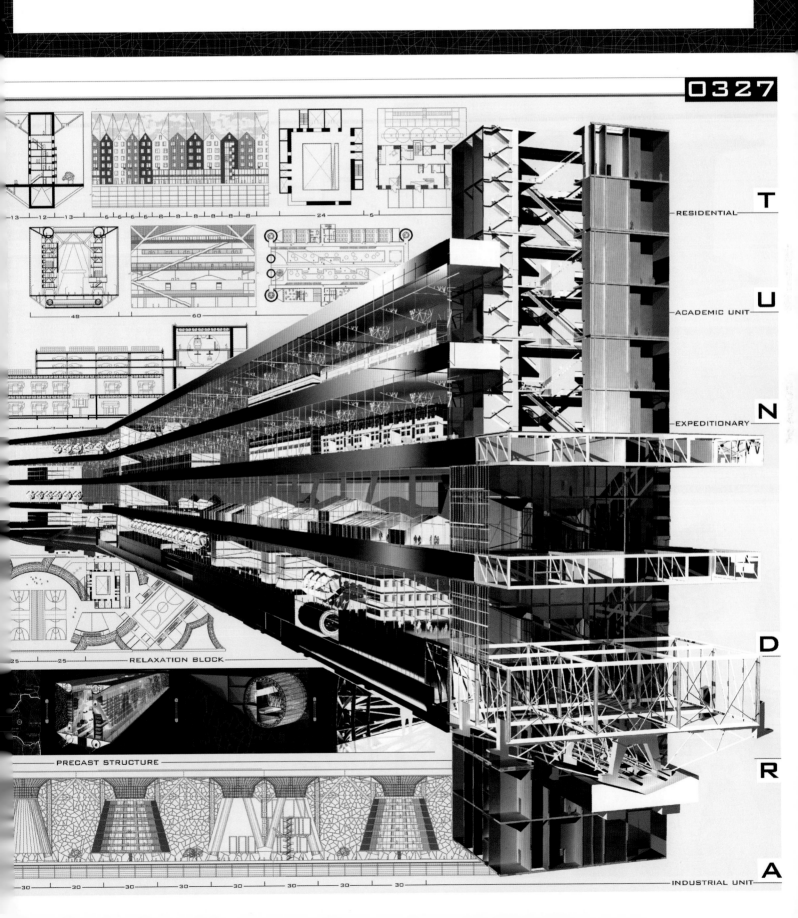

0327

RESIDENTIAL

ACADEMIC UNIT

EXPEDITIONARY

RELAXATION BLOCK

PRECAST STRUCTURE

INDUSTRIAL UNIT

T U N D R A

538

infrastructure, creation of new industry, agriculture, science, and culture.

Tundra City is a new ark, which will gather people together for a new life, new qualified scientists and workers will grow, who will put the Yakut ideas into practice. The tradition of the Yakut people is dominated by the heart, "olonkho." The center (a symbolic heart) is built of 11 modules—logs, including the following areas: scientific, social, agro-industrial, residential, relaxation, hospitality, educational, and industrial.

Two blocks (expedition and station) are located on the surface; the rest of the program is located underneath. A central skeleton supports spatial structures while residential unit are built around an "H"

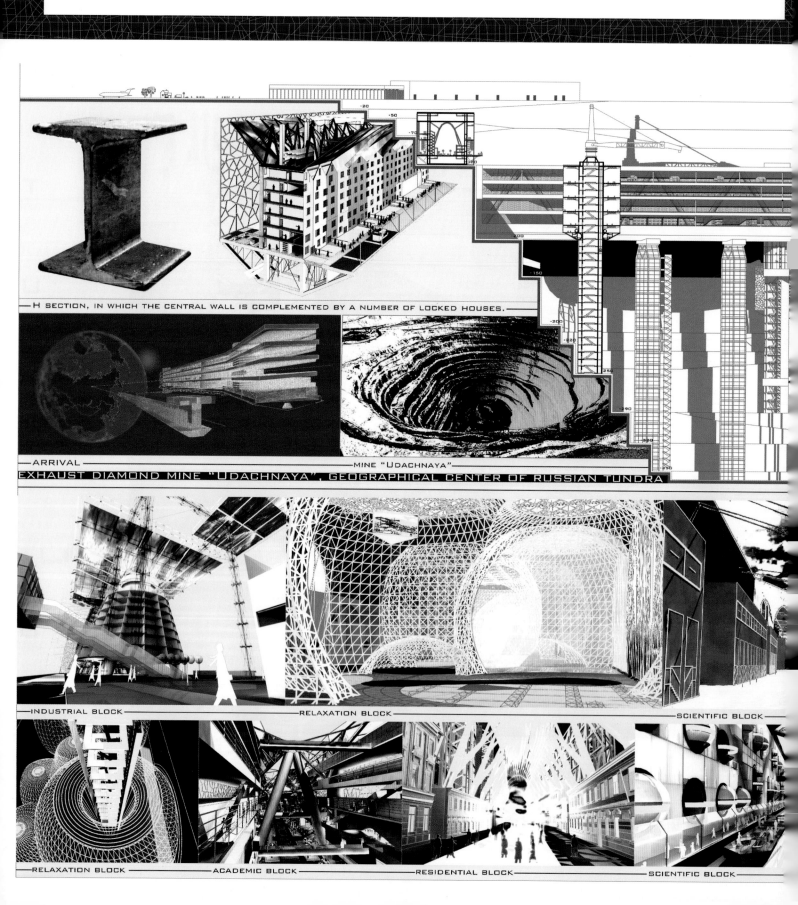

— H SECTION, IN WHICH THE CENTRAL WALL IS COMPLEMENTED BY A NUMBER OF LOCKED HOUSES. —

— ARRIVAL —   — MINE "UDACHNAYA" —

EXHAUST DIAMOND MINE "UDACHNAYA", GEOGRAPHICAL CENTER OF RUSSIAN TUNDRA

— INDUSTRIAL BLOCK —   — RELAXATION BLOCK —   — SCIENTIFIC BLOCK —

— RELAXATION BLOCK —   — ACADEMIC BLOCK —   — RESIDENTIAL BLOCK —   — SCIENTIFIC BLOCK —

section, in which the central wall is complemented by a number of locked houses. Academic (scientific) units are built of space trusses. The agro-industrial unit consists of a structure of massive floors, fixed on the central bearing wall.

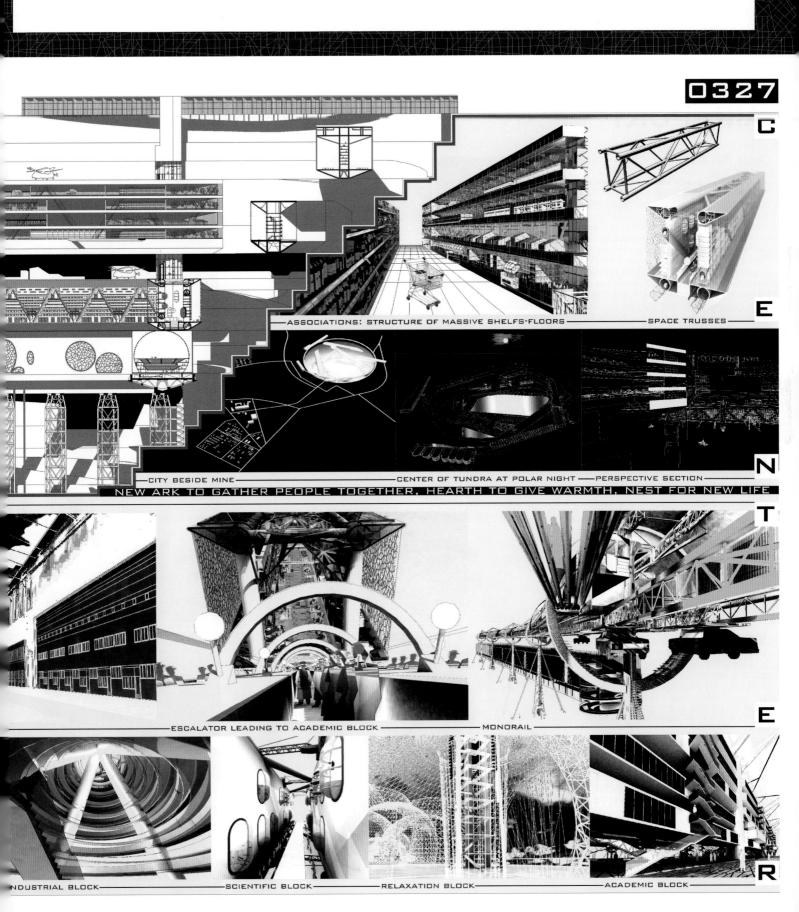

0327

C

ASSOCIATIONS: STRUCTURE OF MASSIVE SHELFS-FLOORS   SPACE TRUSSES

E

CITY BESIDE MINE   CENTER OF TUNDRA AT POLAR NIGHT   PERSPECTIVE SECTION

N

NEW ARK TO GATHER PEOPLE TOGETHER, HEARTH TO GIVE WARMTH, NEST FOR NEW LIFE

T

ESCALATOR LEADING TO ACADEMIC BLOCK   MONORAIL

E

INDUSTRIAL BLOCK   SCIENTIFIC BLOCK   RELAXATION BLOCK   ACADEMIC BLOCK

R

540

AIR@PORT

ZhiYong Hong
XueTing Zhang

China

AIR@PORT —PART I

Before 1900, the entrance of a city is the physical wall and gate.

1900-1980 , The train station had taken the role of city gate for about 100 years.

since 1980, The airport has become the most important gateway to a city.

With the rapid development of modern aerial transportation, the world transportation entered into an "epoch of aviation". On the other hand, we are facing a serious shortage of airport capacity. According to the survey, until 2020, 97% of Chinese airports will be rebuild. But meanwhile, we were surprised to find out that there are serious contradictions between the airport and urban development.

Before 1900 The gate

1900-1980 Train station

Since 1980 Air Port

? What's next ?

WHY

Firstly, Airport will take a huge amount of urban land. And because of the safety requirement of the flight, there is strict restriction of building height in a wide area, which is a enormous waste of land and also result in a huge distance between airport and downtown (for example, the capital airport of Beijing all together with its air restriction area have occupied 1800km2 urban land, but meanwhile, the FAR/floor area ratio/ is unbelievably low, just less than 0.6).

Adverse effects,

1, It is an enormous waste of urban land.

2,Significantly increasing the flow of traffic to connect airport and downtown, and reduce the time advantage of air travel.

3, Greatly reducing the value of the urban land in a wide area.

Thus, along with the growing of airport and the city, the conflict between them will become more and more serious. In some cases of city development, they have to remove the old airport and build a new one in farther suburbs, which undoubtedly is a great waste of resource.

Waste of urbsn land

increase the pressure of city center

WHAT

In our proposal, we raise the airport 450m up to the air, and integrate it with functions such as hotel, office, exhibition, conference and commercial to build an Air City. At the sometime, the air city takes the role of the city landmark and integrated into the urban center park system to create a dynamic city center, which is an effective way of saving urban land.

As the airport is in the air, there is no building height restriction. The airport city center will give a wonderful stimulating effect on the surrounding area, to lead the steady development of the entire district.

Our proposal can effectively disperse the pressure of the city center, and stimulate the development of underdeveloped region. At the same time, due to the formation of a fully functional city center, it will greatly reduce the traffic flow between the airport and the original city center. Finally, we can find a more harmonious way of urban development.

Traditional Air Port System

AIR@PORT System

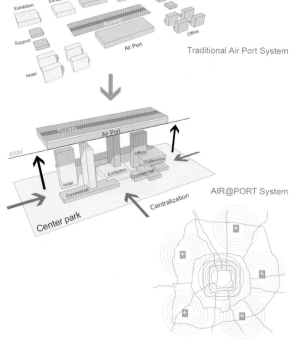

Disperse the pressure of city center

97 percent of Chinese airports will need to be rebuilt by 2020, according to a recent survey, causing huge implications for cost and land use issues; the city of Beijing is currently planning the construction of a second airport. There are quite a few adverse effects to traditional airports. First off, they are an enormous waste of urban land. They significantly increase the flow of traffic to connect airport and downtown which reduces the time advantage of air travel. Also they greatly reduce the value of urban land surrounding them. Thus, along with the growth of airports and the city, the conflict between them will soon become more and more serious. In some cases of city development, they have to remove the old airport and building a new

0328

one in farther suburbs, which undoubtedly is a great waste of resources.

The designers of the Air@Port propose avoiding using precious land for new airports by constructing one that is positioned 450 meters in the air. The airport sits atop the bases of dozens of thin towers that mushroom out at the top with wide platforms that all connect to support the runways and airport facilities on top.

Locating an airport city so high in the air has many immediate benefits. Being so high up will mean that there will not be height restrictions on the buildings erected on the platform, which will allow for great

AIR@PORT
—PART II

HOW
We try to give some explanations about the feasibility and advantages of our proposal.

Site
Key factors for a plane to take off are the wind speed and the ground speed of the aircraft. The wind speed at 450 meters above ground is a times the wind speed on the ground, which means the length of the airport runway in the air can be effectively reduced compared to the si on the ground.

Traffic
The airport will have a huge flow of people at any minutes, so we have to think about a new system of vertical transportation--Air Bus. As th system is always in a balance state of the force of gravity on both sides, so we only need very little power to get a strong passenger carrying ca At the same time, it can be effectively integrated with the subway and the automobile system.

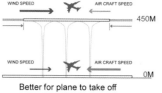

Better for plane to take off

balance state of Air_Bus system

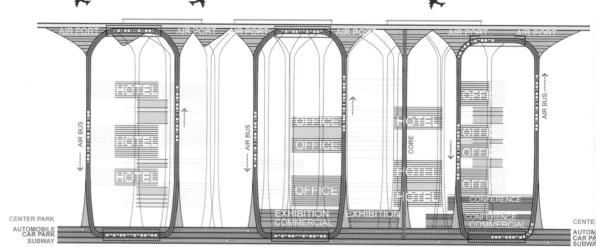

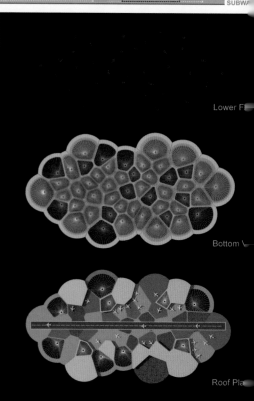

stimulation and creativity in the resulting development. Also, because wind speed is higher 450 meters in the air than it is at sea level, the length of the runway can be effectively reduced, saving space.

Vertical airbuses will transport visitors from the ground (or underground, if they are arriving via subway) up the stems of the tall structures. In addition to air transport facilities, this air city will also include a hotel and commercial, conference and office spaces; these areas are located in the towers beneath the airport. Passengers can stop anywhere on the airbus ride to access these other programs.

0328

ING 2ND AIR PORT

ays Beijing are
to have the
ital air port.We
see what can

ound
part of Beijing
ell developed,
it is not far
rom the city
ccording to the
on map of
ark system,we
read the short-
ablic park of
ijing.

Center Park System

Air@Port+stimulating effect

Beijing 2050

544

ANTS AND ELEPHANT

Qiu Tian

China

Ants and Elephant

This project is located in Beijing, the capital of China. With high speed developing, Beijing has become a huge city in these decades. It has massive population, massive traffic and massive large-scale skyscrapers. To get more land to built skyscrapers, under the public land ownership system, government pulled down old houses like Hutong, over huge areas. Then they changed these ants-scale areas into elephant-scale duplicated skyscrapers. They sacrificed organic humanity spaces to get convenient functional city in highest speed. Under the modern skin, only unimaginative elephant-scaled building left to citizen.

Louis Kahn said that a city is the place where a small boy, as he walks through it, may see something that will tell him what he wants to do for his whole life. It is so hard to image this story could happen in today's Beijing.

Almost all skyscrapers in Beijing are symbolized as power, royalty, wealthy etc. Although one big city needs that kind of appearance, it is not a kind building for common people.

In this project, we attempt to propose a neutral skyscraper which can compatible with pedestrian and driving, humanity and mechanize, casual and formal, democracy and autocracy.

"Ants and Elephant" is constituted by two parts to fill these gaps. It is a 210 cubic meters cube constructed by 8 high buildings and one big roof. On ground level, it is set as elephant-scale for city operates effectively. It is also seem clean enough to be a modern city according to official esthetics. Function contains working offices and commercial amusement systems. At roof ground, it is covered by ants-scale houses for citizen live. The part of ants-scale is full of zigzag ramps and small voids randomly where people enjoy their daily communication then get back old humanity city life they have lost. This kind of community provides a sense of joy and richness in everyday life, and become a place to make people proud of their community.

This skyscraper can be a new type of Soho, it can satisfy both people and big city's demand.

People are tiny, but sometimes they need looks significant, we need both ants and elephant.

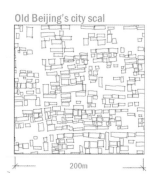

Old Beijing's city scal

New Beijing's city scal

200m   200m

They like and need the scale like ants.

They like and need the scale like elephants.

proposal ants scale for daily life.

proposal elephant scale for office use and city beauty.

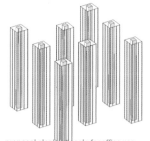

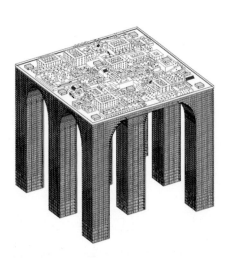

Locate in Beijing, China

In the crowded city of Beijing, the state-controlled real estate system has seen drastic changes as the population has continued to grow. Human-scale sized developments such as Hutong have been demolished to make way for massive skyscrapers, changing the whole feel of the city.

Skyscrapers in Beijing symbolize wealth, power, and status; although a city needs to make symbolic shows of grandeur through "elephant" sized development, the majority of citizens benefit from organic, "ant"-scale buildings that are accessible to common people.

This project proposes a "neutral" skyscraper that is compatible for both pedestrians and drivers, rich and

0465

poor, humans and machines, democracy and autocracy.

The "Ants and Elephant" structure comes in two parts. The 210 cubic meter cube holds eight buildings that are joined by one large roof. On the ground level, it appeases the government's desire to build massive structures, as it is bulky, and also a modern, clean design, all strategies to appease government builders. This "elephant" part of the building holds office and commercial areas.

On the roof, the structure it is developed on the "ant" level, and holds residences. The living units are connected by zigzagging ramps and areas for people to mingle and communicate, hearkening to the

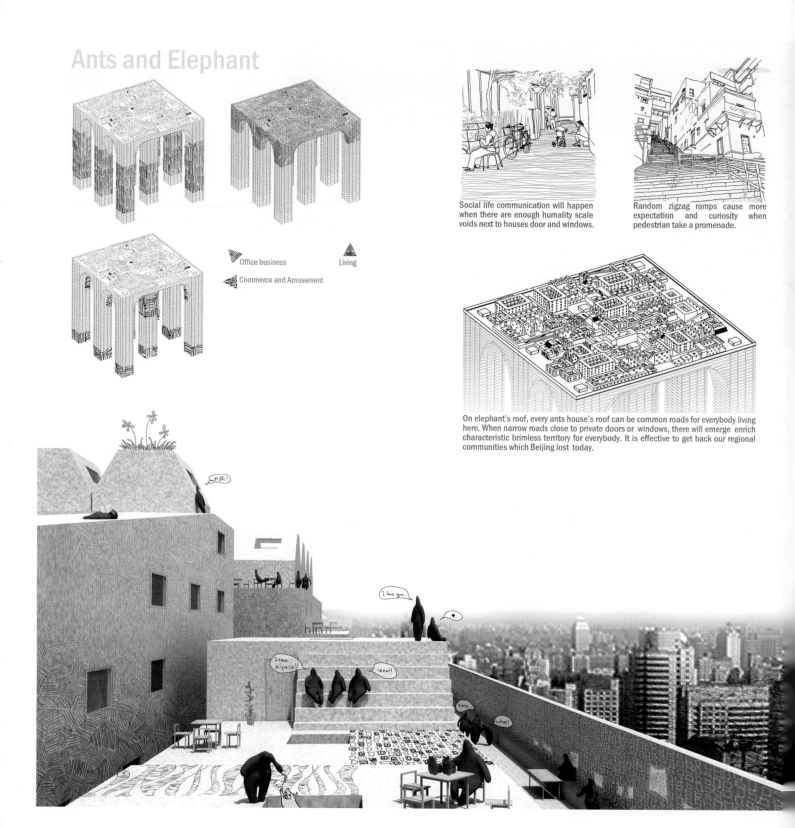

Ants and Elephant

Office business

Commerce and Amusement

Living

Social life communication will happen when there are enough humality scale voids next to houses door and windows.

Random zigzag ramps cause more expectation and curiosity when pedestrian take a promenade.

On elephant's roof, every ants house's roof can be common roads for everybody living here. When narrow roads close to private doors or windows, there will emerge enrich characteristic brimless territory for everybody. It is effective to get back our regional communities which Beijing lost today.

amenities of human-scale development of years past. Such interaction is necessary to help people enjoy the richness of everyday life, the designer says, and to allow people to take pride in their community. This skyscraper can be a new type of Soho, as it can satisfy both people's and the big city's demands.

0465

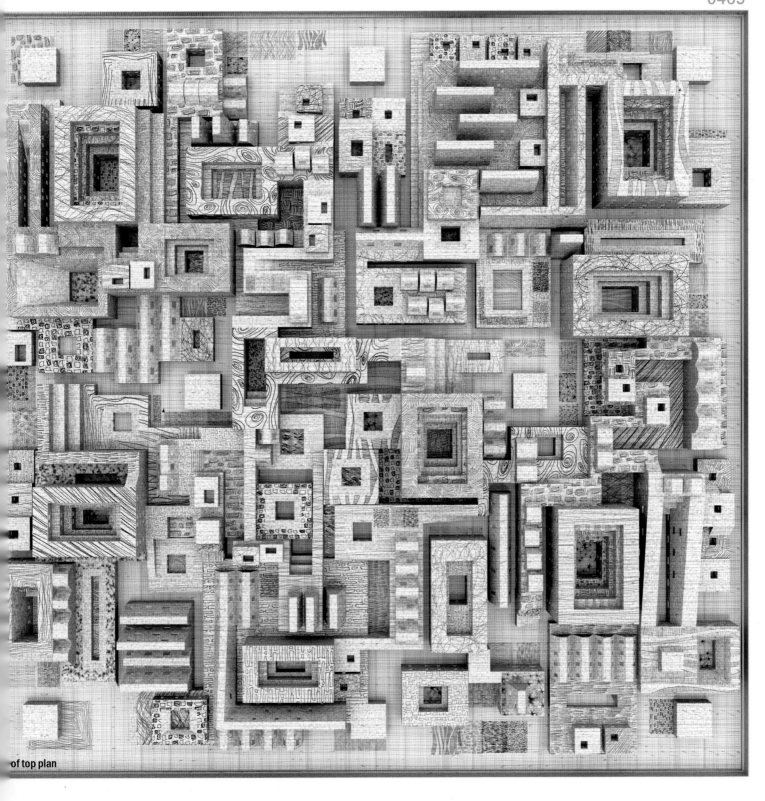

of top plan

BRIDGE FOR A COMMUNE

JongUk Lee

Republic of Korea

THE BRIDGE FOR A COMMUNE

INTRO

IT IS WELL KNOWN THAT URBAN ENVIRONMENT IS GETTING WORSE BY CONTINUOUS RISE OF DENSITY. RISING LAND PRICES AND CONTINUED DENSE URBAN DEVELOPMENT MAKE THE EXPANSION OF SPACE THAT CAN CREATE HIGH PROFIT, AND CONSEQUENTLY REDUCE THE AMOUNT OF GREEN SPACE, LIVING AREA AND SPACE FOR FOOD PRODUCTION AND INCREASE PROBLEMS OF SPATIAL SEPARATION OF INNER/OUTER CITY.

IN ADDITION, THE CONCENTRATION OF THE POPULATION DISABLED THE RESIDENTS TO DIRECTLY PARTICIPATE IN POLITICS AND POLICY DECISIONS THAT CAN HAVE DECISIVE EFFECT ON THEIR LIFE.

ACCORDINGLY, TO BE FREE FROM THESE PROBLEMS, NEW REQUIREMENTS FOR NEW TERRITORY AND COMMUNITIES ARE NOW LOOMING LARGER THAN EVER BEFORE.

NEW TERRITORY

THE NEW TERRITORY WILL BE LOCATED ABOVE THE RIVER – THE LAST SPACE OF NON-PROPRIETARY RIGHT. A STATE CAN BUILD A NEW FORM OF BRIDGE INFRASTRUCTURE THAT CAN BE USED AS THE BASIC FRAMEWORK FOR CONSTRUCTION OF HABITATATION, COMMUNITY SPACE AND FARMLAND. AFTER THE COMPLETION OF INFRASTRUCTURE CONSTRUCTION, THE PEOPLE BUILD HABITATION AND FARMS – THE NOVEL URBAN SPACE FOR NEW LIFE.

FINALLY, THE BRIDGE IS EQUIPPED WITH LIVING SPACE, FARMS, EXCHANGE SPACE FOR THE RESIDENTS, SPACE FOR POLITICAL PARTICIPATION AND ECOLOGIC SEWAGE DISPOSAL FACILITIES FOR SELF PURIFICATION. AND ALSO, EACH PROGRAMS ARE PLACED ON THE APPROPRIATE PLACE FOR MAXIMUM PERFORMANCE OF THE FUNCTION - ON, IN UNDER THE BRIDGE.

ON : FARMLAND
IN : AGORA (PUBLIC SPACE FOR A COMMUNE)
UNDER : HABITATION

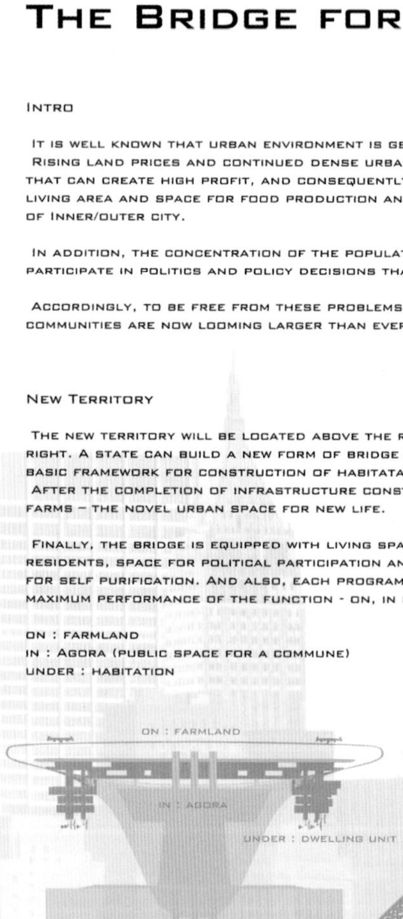

ON : FARMLAND
IN : AGORA
UNDER : DWELLING UNIT

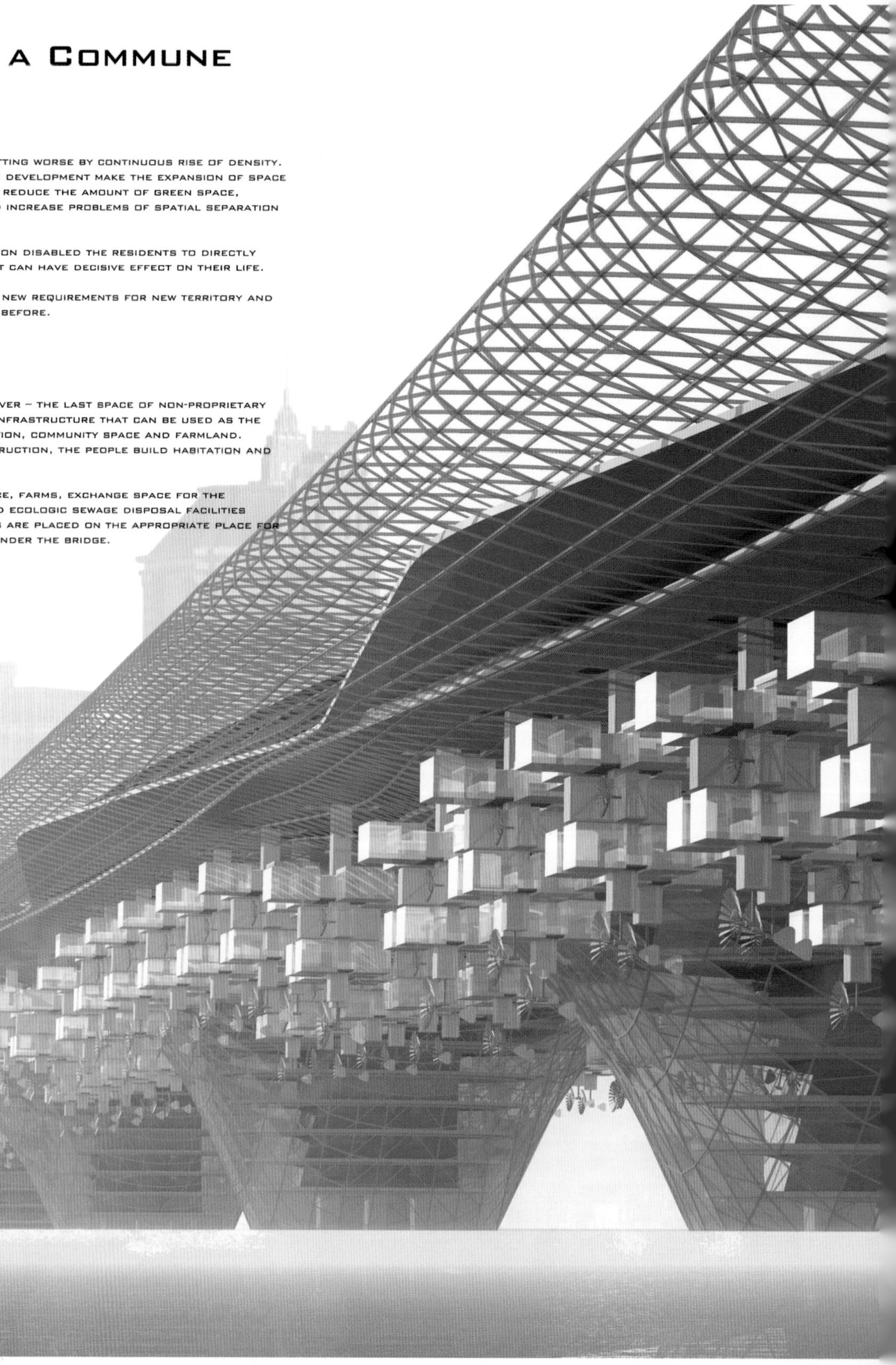

So many problems shape life in big cities these days: pollution, disenfranchisement, high real estate prices, scant green space, and lack of local space for agriculture. To be free of these problems, new territories must emerge that have regulations to fix such issues.

The proposed new territory will be built on unregulated space, over a river. It will take the form of a bridge, but will exist as a sort of mega-bridge that can hold residences, community space and farmland (as well as an exchange space for the residents, space for political participation and ecologic sewage disposal facilities). The bridge will provide a new urban space for new life.

The farm is located on the top of the bridge so as to receive ample sunlight. The area is 196,000 square meters, making a grain crop of almost 980 tons possible. (This is the amount of consumption for 9,800 people per year.) The farm will also include a large ranch for livestock.

Inside the pier of the bridge, there are various programs such as a public gathering space, a political participation space, a market space, a small production space and office space. Collectively, this interior area is dubbed the "Agora." There are five Agoras total within the bridge, each 42,000 square meters large and able to accommodate 6,000 people. At the bottom of each Agora are ecologic wastewater purification

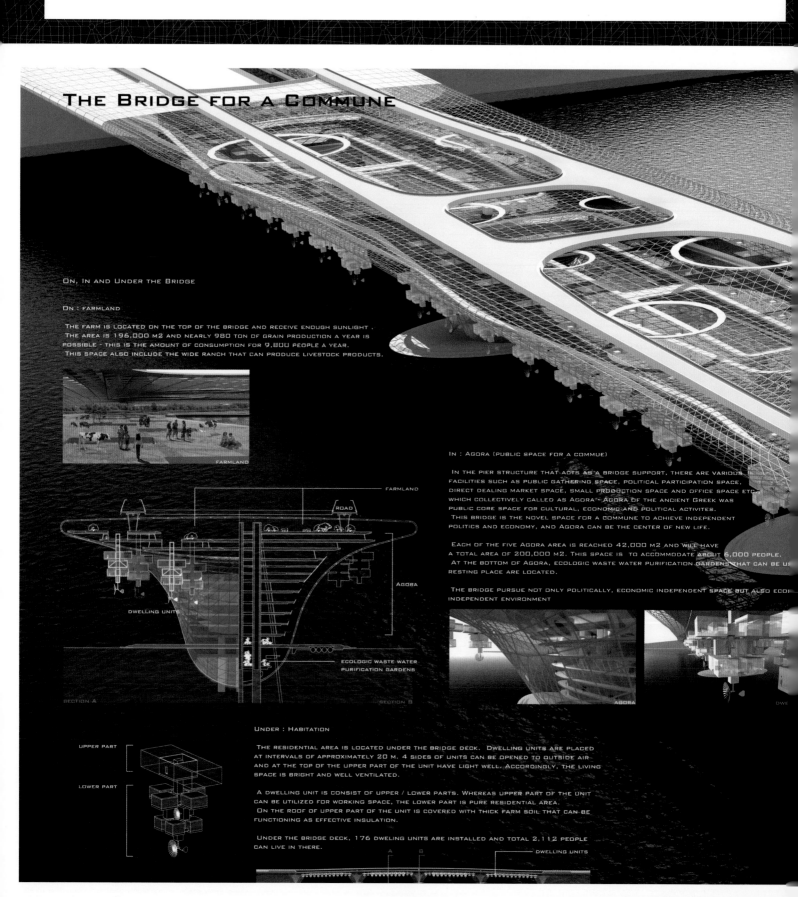

THE BRIDGE FOR A COMMUNE

ON, IN AND UNDER THE BRIDGE

ON : FARMLAND

THE FARM IS LOCATED ON THE TOP OF THE BRIDGE AND RECEIVE ENOUGH SUNLIGHT .
THE AREA IS 196,000 M2 AND NEARLY 980 TON OF GRAIN PRODUCTION A YEAR IS
POSSIBLE - THIS IS THE AMOUNT OF CONSUMPTION FOR 9,800 PEOPLE A YEAR.
THIS SPACE ALSO INCLUDE THE WIDE RANCH THAT CAN PRODUCE LIVESTOCK PRODUCTS.

FARMLAND

FARMLAND

ROAD

AGORA

DWELLING UNITS

ECOLOGIC WASTE WATER
PURIFICATION GARDENS

SECTION A

SECTION B

AGORA

IN : AGORA (PUBLIC SPACE FOR A COMMUE)

IN THE PIER STRUCTURE THAT ACTS AS A BRIDGE SUPPORT, THERE ARE VARIOUS
FACILITIES SUCH AS PUBLIC GATHERING SPACE, POLITICAL PARTICIPATION SPACE,
DIRECT DEALING MARKET SPACE, SMALL PRODUCTION SPACE AND OFFICE SPACE ETC.
WHICH COLLECTIVELY CALLED AS AGORA . AGORA OF THE ANCIENT GREEK WAS
PUBLIC CORE SPACE FOR CULTURAL, ECONOMIC AND POLITICAL ACTIVITES.
THIS BRIDGE IS THE NOVEL SPACE FOR A COMMUNE TO ACHIEVE INDEPENDENT
POLITICS AND ECONOMY, AND AGORA CAN BE THE CENTER OF NEW LIFE.

EACH OF THE FIVE AGORA AREA IS REACHED 42,000 M2 AND WILL HAVE
A TOTAL AREA OF 200,000 M2. THIS SPACE IS TO ACCOMMODATE ABOUT 6,000 PEOPLE.
AT THE BOTTOM OF AGORA, ECOLOGIC WASTE WATER PURIFICATION GARDENS THAT CAN BE U
RESTING PLACE ARE LOCATED.

THE BRIDGE PURSUE NOT ONLY POLITICALLY, ECONOMIC INDEPENDENT SPACE BUT ALSO ECOL
INDEPENDENT ENVIRONMENT

UNDER : HABITATION

UPPER PART

LOWER PART

THE RESIDENTIAL AREA IS LOCATED UNDER THE BRIDGE DECK. DWELLING UNITS ARE PLACED
AT INTERVALS OF APPROXIMATELY 20 M. 4 SIDES OF UNITS CAN BE OPENED TO OUTSIDE AIR
AND AT THE TOP OF THE UPPER PART OF THE UNIT HAVE LIGHT WELL. ACCORDINGLY, THE LIVING
SPACE IS BRIGHT AND WELL VENTILATED.

A DWELLING UNIT IS CONSIST OF UPPER / LOWER PARTS. WHEREAS UPPER PART OF THE UNIT
CAN BE UTILIZED FOR WORKING SPACE, THE LOWER PART IS PURE RESIDENTIAL AREA.
ON THE ROOF OF UPPER PART OF THE UNIT IS COVERED WITH THICK FARM SOIL THAT CAN BE
FUNCTIONING AS EFFECTIVE INSULATION.

UNDER THE BRIDGE DECK, 176 DWELING UNITS ARE INSTALLED AND TOTAL 2,112 PEOPLE
CAN LIVE IN THERE.

DWELLING UNITS

gardens that double as relaxation areas for residents.

Residents of the bridge territory live underneath its surface. Units are spaced 20 meters from each other and can open on all four sides and on the top for ventilation and sunlight. Each unit is two floors, the upper used as office space and the lower for living and sleeping. The roofs of the units are covered with thick soil as insulation. There are 176 units total, providing shelter for up to 2,112 people.

□478

Conclusion

THE BRIDGE FOR A COMMUNE IS THE INNOVATIVE FORM OF PUBLIC INFRASTRUCTURE THAT BE CONSTRUCTED BY CLEAR DIVISION OF ROLES AND ACTIVE PARTICAPATION OF THE STATE AND THE PEOPLE, AND IT PROVIDE NOVEL LIFE-STYLE TO IMPROVE THE QUALITY OF LIFE IN THE CITY CENTER.

VILLAGE IN THE ARCH

Misook Jung
Dongwon Kim
Jinsoo Yim

France

Village in the Arch

This project would play a role of landmark as a new urban gate being located in the border of Paris and La Défense and reinforces the traditional city expansion axe as visual and perceptual medium between the Triumphal Arch and the Grande Arch. This suggestion shows unique symbolism can be connoted through ties with other cultural programs within historical cities by location.

Paris is characterized by the historical monuments such as Louvre, the Triumphal Arch (La Arc de Triomphe) and the Grand Arch (La Grande Arche). The historical landmark of these historical cities not only shows social demands and values by each era and but are indicators which represent the developmental stage of cities.

Under these circumstances, this projects aims to suggest potentials of vertical development through combinations with existing contexts within historical cities and shape assumption. It is a suggestion to solve architectural problems such as lack of community, monotonous residential space, vulnerable accessibility, etc. emerging as the problems of existing tower-type housing and urban problems such as architectural types based on location, etc.

Horizontal villages forming groups of one or multi-story houses are transformed into vertical villages by being lifted up for the necessity of density. In this process, diverse combinations of unit forms diversified residential spaces by creating primitive and agreeable terrace gardens. Also, objects in organic shapes which play a role of air garden ware inserted in primitive shapes to secure community spaces of residents. This is to express clouds in metaphorically. Also, wind generators installed in places inside supply energy required to each space including air gardens.

This series of processes can re-interpret meaning of land within historical cities and have strong symbolism within residences or cities like monuments which involve publicness through architectural process of existing contexts and would show creation of new residential space gets possible within them.

Existing Village   Uplift Village   Fo

Circula

Structu

Bridge

Seine

Housin

Platfor

Sky Ga

Wind T

The Village in the Arch would serve as a new city gateway for Paris, located at the city's border with La Défense. By connecting with the L'Arc de Triomphe and the Grande Arche, the Village in the Arch reinforces the traditional city expansion axial and connects the city's rich history to the future.

Under these circumstances, this project aims to suggest potentials of vertical development through combinations with existing contexts within historical cities. It is a suggestion to solve architectural problems such as lack of community, monotonous residential space, etc. emerging as the problems of existing tower-type housing and urban problems such as architectural types based on location, etc.

Insert Form Atypical _ Sky Garden

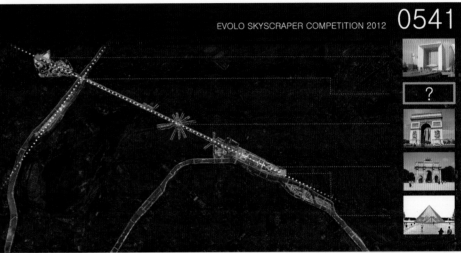

EVOLO SKYSCRAPER COMPETITION 2012 0541

The structure is a large wheel that locates steppes of a vertical village in the outer ring. Imagine a residential tower bent: then connect several together, and one would have a wheel of apartments. The residential units are surrounded and topped with green space, dubbed by the designers as "air gardens."

Inside of the wheel, a curving, free form support comprised of walls holds several wind generators, which are able to provide energy needed to power the residential units. More green spaces, including clusters of trees, are placed within this middle section, atop the structural walls.

This project invigorates the isolated islands in the Seine River, which are underutilized due to lack of

It is true that most of islands around Seine River excluding Cite Island are not utilized positively due to difficult accessibility from outside. It is hard to find vigorous activities although this site also has significance as a cross pint of two urban contexts, city expansion axial line and Seine River which are the most important in Paris. Under these circumstances, this project achieves invigoration in the isolated area by inserting new type of monument in axial line.

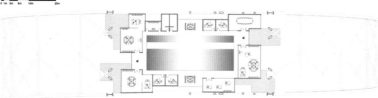

29th FLOOR PLAN

21th FLO

accessibility, by inserting new type of monument in axial line, which is another perk. It is hard to find vigorous activities although this site also has significance as a cross point of two urban contexts, city expansion, axial line, and the Seine River, which are very important to the city of Paris. Under these circumstances, this project achieves invigoration in the isolated area by inserting this new type of monument in axial line.

The design is basic, but that is not the real point of the structure. This series of processes can re-interpret meaning of land within historical cities and have strong symbolism. The public nature of monuments is examined anew as residential space is located within the arch.

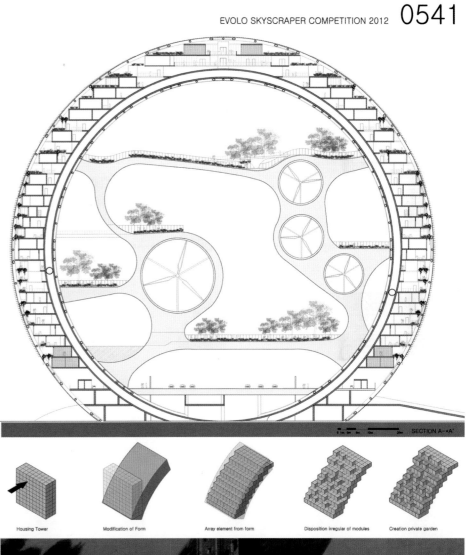

EVOLO SKYSCRAPER COMPETITION 2012 **0541**

SECTION A-·A'

Housing Tower | Modification of Form | Array element from form | Disposition irregular of modules | Creation private garden

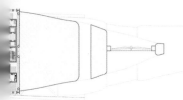

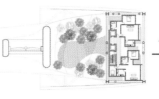

12th FLOOR PLAN

1st FLOOR PLAN

URBAN FOREST

Shim Hunyong
Kang Jiho

Republic of Korea

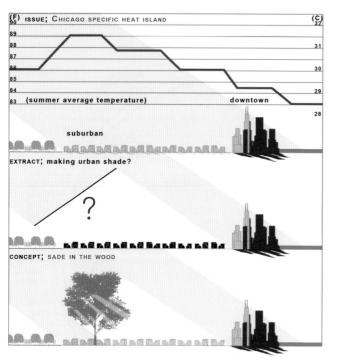

ISSUE; CHICAGO SPECIFIC HEAT ISLAND

(summer average temperature)   downtown

suburban

EXTRACT; making urban shade?

?

CONCEPT; SADE IN THE WOOD

PROLOGUE

Among the world's major cities Chicago is a leading city. But, present Chicago needs a leap to the 2nd generation. Obviously this 2nd generation city needs to solve the problems of the present Chicago's problem. We suggest this city of Chicago's 2nd generation.

ISSUE

The city of Chicago has a "Heat Problem". The heat wave in 1995 led to approximately 750 deaths in Chicago over five days. Urban heat island raised nighttime temperatures by more than 3.6°F(2°C). It had also driven to 13 heat-related deaths in 2011. The average temperature in the summer of 2011 was above 85°F(30°C), the highest was 100°F(37.8°C) and the sensible temperature was 116°F(46.7°C). These days Chicago exhibits a heat island effect, larger in the surrounding suburban area than in urban area. This can be explained by the following three factors.

1. A recent rapid development in the suburbs brings an increased active population, air pollution and heat generated by rising energy usage in the area.
2. Lake Michigan cools off Chicago's downtown area.
3. Shadows form from Chicago Loop and its skyscraper over the whole city, as they block out the sunlight from reaching the surface.

EXTRACTION; Urban Shade?

We focused on the idea that shadows can be a function with reducing the effect of heat island in the suburbs.

However, space under the shadow blocking the sun completely makes the atmosphere cold and dark, and is not suitable for people as "outside". The other side of the shadow, meanwhile, has too much sunlight and is a cause of heat island effect pulling people inside the building.

CONCEPT; Shade in the woods

The trees provide shade with their branches and leaves, and they don't totally block the sun. Shade created by the trees attract people during the hotter periods of the year.

People love shade of the trees.

They enjoy staying cool and breezy outdoors rather than sitting indoors with air conditioning. Shade also can be one solution for increasing surface temperature and heat island effect.

We suggest a design of skyscraper that will build the next generation of Chicago.

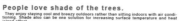

EFFECT

HOT
HOTTER
People go inside
Vicious circle
Air conditioning heat
Thermal storage
Car exhaust gas

Air conditioning heat
Thermal storage
Car exhaust gas

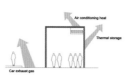

HOT
COOL
Urban forest
Virtuous circle
Reduction of
- Air conditioning
- Thermal storage
- Exhaust gas
People go outside

- The expected effect by making 'Forest Shading' at the suburban of Chicago.

By casting a shadow at the hot outside space the quantity of the thermal storage will be reduced. The building's concrete and road's asphalt absorbs heat at the day and it gives off at night. So by reducing the heat itself its absolute quantity will be reduced. The form of the shading will not block the sun completely. Its shape will be like a shade of a forest. This 'Urban Forest' will draw people outside and reduce the heat formed by air-conditioning and make more lively city. It will cut the vicious circle formed by the human's inside-oriented activity.

DESIGN STRATEGY

I, SRTRUT; main structure
vertical lift and the service duct

II, BRANCH; 2nd main structure
diagonal lift and the duct

III, TWIG; substructure
reinforces the building
and make shading.

IV, LEAF;
shading performance

1 unit; funtional shading module
(25 m X 60 m)

• summer highest sun altitude

210 m

By considering city's unit (60 X 100 m) and the highest solar altitude of summer (60-70 angle) the height of the forest face is 210m

80 - 100 m

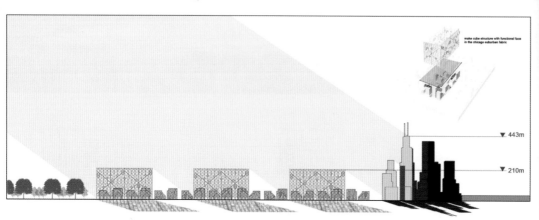

make cube structure with functional face
in the chicago suburban fabric

▼ 443m

▼ 210m

Urban Forest attempts to solve Chicago's urban heat island effect through the creation of a 2nd generation of skyscrapers modeled after the geometry and functions of a tree. These massive tree-like structures, climbing up to 210 meters and spanning many city blocks, filter and absorb light and create shadows across the city, lowering ambient temperature throughout the urban area. These structures are located away from the city center, in suburban areas where the heat island effect is more pronounced due to the sheer number of cars on highways, large expanses of asphalt pavement, and low building height present throughout. Urban Forest seeks to create large, shade-giving structures similar to the skyscrapers of

2nd generation sky scraper of Chicago; URBAN FOREST
0609

downtown Chicago, in the suburbs.

Constructed as four elements, strut, branch, twig, and leaf, Urban Forest is an architectural formalization of the tree itself. "Struts" act as the main, vertical structural component, housing a service core and vertical lift. "Branches" provide lateral support, and house diagonal lifts and necessary ductwork. The "twig" substructure re enforces the building and provides the actual shading mechanism. "Leaves" provide a second level of shading. Embedded within this tree matrix are several inhabitable "cubes." Management and Observation cubes contain offices for Urban Forest managers. Public cubes house either public space,

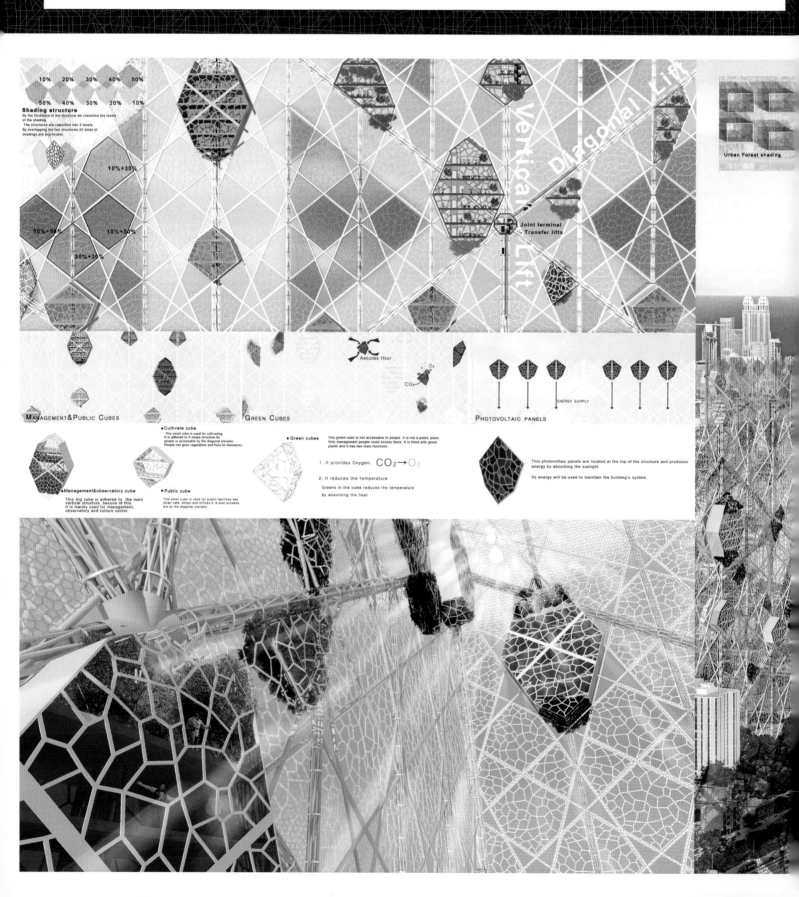

small retail, or office spaces. Cultivate cubes contain community gardens. Green cubes are inaccessible to the public, and house trees and greenery utilized exclusively for their shading potential.

By casting a shadow at the hot outside space, the amount of thermal storage will be reduced. The building's concrete and road's asphalt absorb heat in the day and release it at night. By reducing the heat itself, its absolute quantity will be reduced. The shading will not block the sun completely. Its shape will be like a shade of a forest. Urban Forest will draw people outside and reduce heat formed by air-conditioning and a make more lively city. It will cut the vicious cycle formed by human's inside-oriented activity.

0609

nd generation sky scraper of Chicago, URBAN FOREST

MASS SKYSCRAPER

Hock Beng Gan

Malaysia

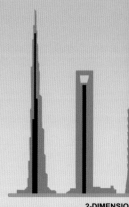

MOLECULAR **MASS** SUPPORT
ARCHITECTURE SKYSCRAPER STRUCTURE

2-DIMENSION

The MASS (Modern Architecture Support Structure) Skyscraper is envisioned to be like a tree, with a sturdy trunk permanently supporting branches where leaves, or in this case, modular apartments, can come and go as seasons shift. It is an acknowledgement that nature is the ultimate adaptor, and that organic processes hold the answers to even the most advanced human endeavors—in this case, totally portable housing units for a globalized, mobile world.

The support structures, built of building blocks called "Cor," are shaped as pyramids, making them extremely stable. The modular units attach to the support structures, and are themselves totally adaptable;

MASS SKYSCRAPER = MA MOLECULAR ARCHITECTURE + SS SUPPORT STRUCTURE

0780

The support structure is thought of as a tree trunk. A permanent element.

The leaves, flowers and fruits are referred to as the dwelling, possessing temporary elements which fall down and are renewed according to the needs of the moment.

The dwelling can change and evolve within this support structure.

While the support structure, remains intact.

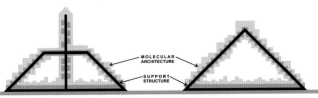

MOLECULAR ARCHITECTURE

SUPPORT STRUCTURE

3-DIMENSIONAL MASS SKYSCRAPERS

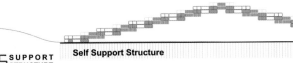

Self Support Structure

SS SUPPORT STRUCTURE

- Transformation of spherical space into support structure.
- Setting us free from ground with unlimited span in the air.
- Utilizing a tensegrity structure - continuous tension, discontinuous compression.
- Creating new possibilities for skyscrapers of tomorrow.

Cor is the basic building block. When Cor units are organized and arranged together in a way that renders the making up of a whole, this unified physical outcome is referred to as the support structure. he master form of the 3-Dimensional pyramidal skyscrapers.

In a pyramid formation, the transmission of forces occurs in two directions, longitudinally and latitudinally. Apart from that, there are also ring forces. The occurring forces are divided between the two load components according to the form of the pyramid. An internal balance of forces occur dividing them in such a way that equilibrium is obtained. The stress condition in the pyramid is spatial and is not in a plane. This is what makes a pyramid structure extremely strong compared to other geometrical formations.

In addition to such a self-supporting structure, a complementary yet completely independent auxiliary support structure can be introduced to further secure the whole. Tensegrity, termed as tension-integrity is a structure which has continuous tension and discontinuous compression. By having a compression pole at 1 or 4 corners of the arrangement which supports the volumetric modules by tensioned cables throughout the structure, the arrangement forms a continuous structure like a bucket or motor wheel. By introducing compression poles to take all the compressive load, and continuous tensional cable throughout the structure, tensegrity structure is formed.

Hence, the concept of function and structure are correlated. It exists in a strict geometrical order. It also allows further evolution and transformation into a more sophisticated shape if required.

Tensigrity & Core Support

3D Circulation with Lift Shaft, Pathway and Staircases

- kitchen
- staircase
- courtyard
- bathroom

Architecturalization of Support Structure

Extension and Transformation

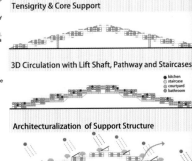

Sustainable Strategies Prototypes

staircase insertion   courtyard insertion   kitchen / bathroom insertion

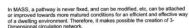

MA MOLECULAR ARCHITECTURE

There are two lessons to be learned from the combination of molecules in nature. The first is that molecules always combine in a diverging manner. And the second is that during each process of divergent combination, there arise new possibilities of function. We call this the emergent function.

Molecular architecture is a new paradigm of human habitation, inspired directly by nature. Through diverging design process, the function of a molecular dwelling can be achieved by simple insertion of various units such as the kitchen, bathroom and courtyard. For example, by inserting kitchen units, the emergent function of a dining space is produced.

There is never a need to conceive a building plan in advance. The mere additions of various functional units allow the function of a dwelling to emerge, evolving from simple insertion. In essence, the whole exercise allows free combinations of units to form different dwellings to suit individual lifestyles. It also allows constant renewal from time to time without any significant disturbance to a neighboring unit. In all aspects, it is similar to the molecular switch in nature.

In MASS, a pathway is never fixed, and can be modified, etc, can be attached or improved towards more matured conditions for an efficient and effective way of a dwelling environment. Therefore, it makes possible the creation of 3-Dimensional circulation network.

Change is in fact part of the design. And this change is done through a simple process by the mere switching of independent units within the overall configuration. Hence, one does not have to live in a dwelling built with predetermined, rigidly set functions. In MASS, the function of a unit, a neighbourhood or a zone can be cultivated and adapted to the needs of the occupants, whenever and wherever required. The habitation is therefore sustainable, no matter how the community and the environment grows and alters.

All these changes can only be possible with the essence of architecture being ingrained in a divergent process.

With the same model , same structure and same construction, the Cor can produce millions and millions of configurations, each of which is of high level of design and function in architecture and high level of form and organization in structure.

the units have no set design or building plan. Instead, residents insert whatever service units they desire: kitchens, bathrooms or courtyards, for example. This approach to unit creation allows each living space to be completely customizable for the individuals living inside, and also allows for future changes to be easily achieved, as units can simply have services replaced or added anew whenever the owners see fit.

This adaptability allows for the creation of skyscrapers that can grow old without becoming obsolete. Also, the designers stress the importance that in a MASS Skyscraper, a pathway is never fixed; they can always be modified, allowing for new positioning of units as efficiency or comfort dictates. Therefore, it

MOLECULAR MASS SUPPORT
ARCHITECTURE STRUCTURE
SKYSCRAPER

makes possible the creation of three-dimensional circulation network.

The essence of this project is that its function is inherent within. This intangible characteristic is inbuilt to be in effect as long as the tangible structure exists. This beauty is not set in artificially for human aesthetic purposes but is organically observed as a manifestation of nature's workings. Instead of envisioning a MASS Skyscraper as a single, massive tower, the designers imagined an area full of MASS Skyscrapers, located in such close proximity that the branches of the different trees seem to blend into one mass. Because the Cor can be arranged into millions of configurations, no MASS Skyscraper will truly be the same.

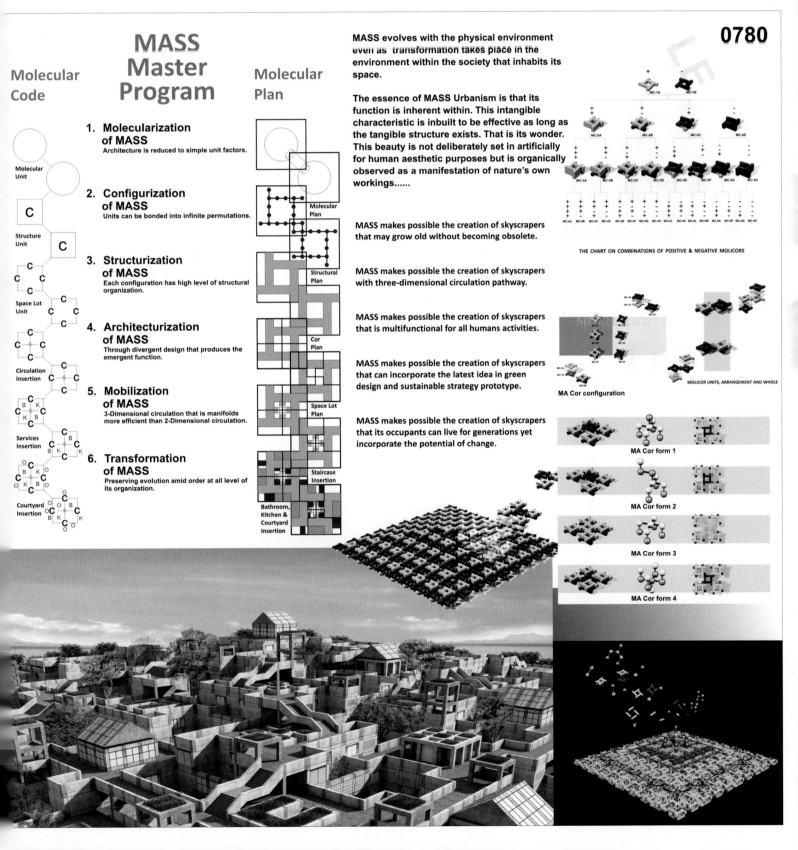

MASS Master Program

0780

Molecular Code

Molecular Plan

Molecular Unit

Structure Unit

Space Lot Unit

Circulation Insertion

Services Insertion

Courtyard Insertion

1. **Molecularization of MASS**
   Architecture is reduced to simple unit factors.

2. **Configurization of MASS**
   Units can be bonded into infinite permutations.

3. **Structurization of MASS**
   Each configuration has high level of structural organization.

4. **Architecturization of MASS**
   Through divergent design that produces the emergent function.

5. **Mobilization of MASS**
   3-Dimensional circulation that is manifolds more efficient than 2-Dimensional circulation.

6. **Transformation of MASS**
   Preserving evolution amid order at all level of its organization.

Molecular Plan

Structural Plan

Cor Plan

Space Lot Plan

Staircase Insertion

Bathroom, Kitchen & Courtyard Insertion

MASS evolves with the physical environment even as transformation takes place in the environment within the society that inhabits its space.

The essence of MASS Urbanism is that its function is inherent within. This intangible characteristic is inbuilt to be effective as long as the tangible structure exists. That is its wonder. This beauty is not deliberately set in artificially for human aesthetic purposes but is organically observed as a manifestation of nature's own workings......

MASS makes possible the creation of skyscrapers that may grow old without becoming obsolete.

MASS makes possible the creation of skyscrapers with three-dimensional circulation pathway.

MASS makes possible the creation of skyscrapers that is multifunctional for all humans activities.

MASS makes possible the creation of skyscrapers that can incorporate the latest idea in green design and sustainable strategy prototype.

MASS makes possible the creation of skyscrapers that its occupants can live for generations yet incorporate the potential of change.

THE CHART ON COMBINATIONS OF POSITIVE & NEGATIVE MOLICORS

MOLICOR UNITS, ARRANGEMENT AND WHOLE

MA Cor configuration

MA Cor form 1

MA Cor form 2

MA Cor form 3

MA Cor form 4

THE GRID WALL

Dante Giovanni Borgo Lopez

Netherlands

2025 will commemorate the 50th anniversary of Mao's death. Is Mao's ideology still deeply embedded on Chinese way of city making? The Grid Wall city model aims to recapture Mao's urban principles on city making, materializing them it into a 12 km by 12 km skyscraper system of clusters.

Standing over the first 2nd and 3rd ring and surrounding the historical city center, this model operates as a group of semi autonomous 3 km x 3 km clusters that all together work as a major entity of modern production and living space for 10.4 million people. Housing, working, common areas, parking, and commerce are integrated in the program of each one of these units providing the inhabitants with everything

1134
THE GRID WALL
50 years after Mao

2025 will commemorate the 50th anniversary of Mao's death, five decades of China opened to the rest of the world and capitalism but is Mao's ideology still deeply embedded on Chinese way of thinking and city making?

As the same way as it is in Chinese culture and society, Beijing's urban growth it is the physical representation of its own history. Different social and political periods the city has passed through are printed ring after ring on its urban fabric, as expansive scars or visible marks. Starting from the Dynasties era to Mao's dictatorship and afterwards from Mao's dead to the "open door" policy at the beginning of the 70's, all of these archetypes of Chinese power have a specific and representative typology both in the urban configuration and the housing units.

Without any doubt the most representative of all these archetypes was the Danwei. Infinitely repeated within the 2nd to the 4th ring of Beijing, the Danwei imported from Russia at the beginning of the 50's, was the urban archetype of Mao who made from it his apparatus of control, governance and management of the city and the society. These series of multi-housing walled clusters arranged in an orthogonal city grid worked mostly as autonomous entities, the plots were own by all kind of industries where the workers not only worked but lived in. The inhabitants didn't have almost any need to go out of the cluster, to cross the wall; schools for the kids, commerce and sport facilities were also part of the complex, till the point that in a lot of cases people were even only allowed to marry with neighbors from the same Danwei. Each one of these units played a specific role or activity and production within the city context and the quality of life of its inhabitants was directly related with the money their Danwei was producing for the government. In this context Mao extended his power and control through these repetitive and adaptable device of governance managing and controlling the whole city and therefore the whole society.

Almost 10 million new citizens are expected for the coming 15 years in Beijing, and the city is expanding in a brutal speed of development and urbanization, where some sort of cannibal urbanism is taking place. How is it possible to address the spatial needs of such an enormous amount of people within the city and stopping the horizontal expansion of the city with the less footprint possible, preventing the urban sprawl to the outskirts but giving them the same qualities that they are looking for and that they are only capable to found in the suburbs life style with more livable, green and leisure space per capita?

Beijing's urban growth

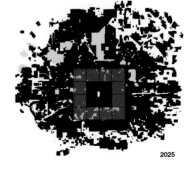

they need. As the same way as the Danwei did, every cluster works a specialized modern machine of production facilitating in this way the management and control of the production, the city and the inhabitants.

Due to the fact that the whole grid is standing over pilotis, the urban footprint is a very small one compared to the dimension of this project. This urban prototype will also offer parking spaces for 3.7 million cars, one per family and more working and shopping space per capita. The housing program is located in the lower and upper part of each cluster of the grid; meanwhile the public program and production is in the in-between space of these ones.

The Production Cluster

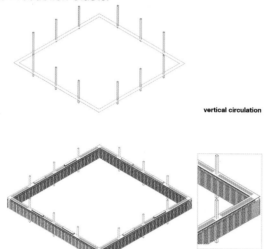

vertical circulation

650,000 sqm of production
400,000 parking spaces
130,000 sqm of green space

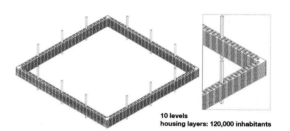

10 levels
housing layers: 120,000 inhabitants

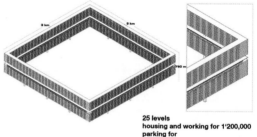

25 levels
housing and working for 1'200,000
parking for

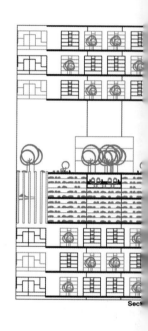

Sect

Proposal

If 50 years after his dead Mao were still alive, how it will be his ideology on making city translated in the context of Beijing in 2025 and what kind of form it would take his apparatus of governance and management, the Danwei?

The Grid Wall city model is aiming to recapture Mao's urban principles on city making materliazing them it into a skyscraper system of clusters. Standing over the first 2nd and 3rd ring and surrounding the historical city center, this model operates as a group of semi autonomous 3 x 3 km clusters that all together works as a major entity of production. Housing, production, common areas, parking and commerce are integrated in the program of each one of these units providing the inhabitants pretty much with everything they need. As the same way as the Danwei did, every cluster works a specialized modern machine of production facilitating in this way the management and control of the production, the city and the inhabitants.

Composed by 12 clusters with a population of 1'200,000 people each one of them The Grid Wall city model provides within its 12x 12 km large and its 750 mts tall housing for 10.4 mil¬lion people giving to each one of them 30 sqm per capita which is more than the current one in Beijing and more than twice as cities such as Tokyo or Hong Kong. At the same time it will also provide 20.1 sqm of green space per capita which is as well twice of the current average of the city. Due to the fact the whole grid is standing over pilotis the urban footprint is a very small one compared to the dimension of the project. This urban prototype will also offer parking space for 3.7 million cars, one per family and more working and shopping space per capita. The housing program is located in the lower and upper part of each cluster of the grid; meanwhile the public program and production is in the in-between space of these ones.

The transport system within The Grid Wall has different speeds and stages. In the housing areas the transit is only for pedestrians or bikes and the largest distance between a house and a vertical circulation hub is 400 mts. Subway and buses are located in the in-between space as well all the public, production program and parking is, making also possible to use private transportation to travel to different clusters.

The Grid Wall

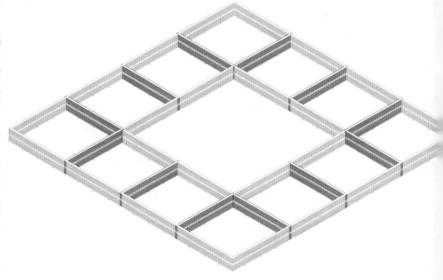

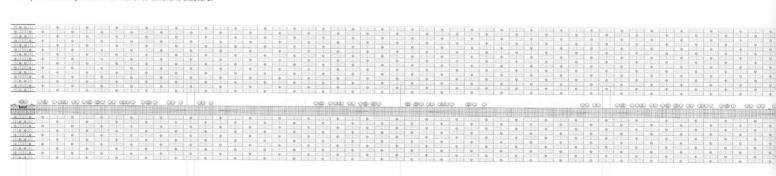

These series of multi-housing walled clusters arranged in an orthogonal city grid worked mostly as autonomous entities. The plots were owned by all kinds of industries where the workers not only worked but also lived in. The inhabitants did not have almost any need to go out of the cluster, to cross the wall; schools for the kids, commerce and sport facilities were also part of the complex. Each one of these units played a specific role or activity and production within the city context and the quality of life of its inhabitants was directly related with the money their Danwei was producing for the government. In this context Mao extended his power and control through these repetitive and adaptable devices of governance managing.

1134

MUTATING SKY CITY

Kim Duk Hwan

Republic of Korea

1: High rise > Anti rise   2: Typical public domain > New public domain   3: Monolithic> Porous   4: Solid> Adj

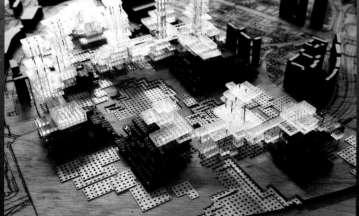

Rules as Theoretical Base

This project is making adaptable system for the unpredictable city conditions.
It started by looking at the typical high rise towers. The black part of the picture 1, is the sillouette of high r
And I made an opposite approach with the white part so to make the new form of skyscraper, what I calle
rise'. So I focused on many ideas that breaking the general notions of skyscrapers.

I looked at how skyscrapers actually work. And what I wanted to propose is shifting the public domain into
position of the skyscraper(picture 2). I thought that the typical typology of towers' public domain at the b
usually come up with the isolation of individual towers. For that I propose a new public realm in the sky wh
better accessibility and can provide even environment regarding the height.
Then I looked again into a individual skyscraper and saw that it was solid and monolithic. If I break down th
I could improve the problems of shading, by getting more lights into the deep part of the building. And a
repetative plans can be varied(picture 3).
Rules are completed by making adjustable, scattered structures(picture 4: compare to the gigantic type o
structure)on the regular grid, which guide the position of columns. Scattered structures can make it poss
adapt more easy on diverse city context. It can be put anywhere undisturbed.

Consequently, various activities are possible on the freed ground. And we can have the sky community whic
bines several towers. You can see the result plan based on those rules at the left image.

And that rigid, regular grid on the ground was the starting point of making a system for adapting city.

Concept

I focused on these grids which is quite rigid, I imagined a forest of columns on that
grid. Then I tried to mutate it that could become a new form of structure.

Here we have a forest of columns on regular grid as a base structure. And then gr
or just release. By changing the rules in little actions, we can extract many different t
spaces.

Consider the structure as a framework in order to put in the programs. The spaces
made up inside of the structure depending on the use of it. The cores can be gener
the 'grab' action and huge voids can be made by 'split' action to put in the structure fo
activities. Indivisual units can also be put in place where it is needed to be. And the h
structures can be extended or reduced to control the view from the points.

This simple logic can generate diverse types of spaces. An example image at the botto
can see that how the column forests are inhabited. Also, there are various forms like
like a river crossing through the structures, intersecting public spaces. Literally, colum
tate itself to adapt on the conditions of surroundings and beneath.

Column Forest   Grab   Split

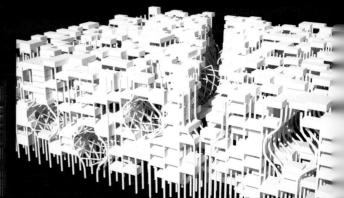

Mutating Sky City questions the traditional form and use of a skyscraper and, by inverting it, seeks to create a city grid of completely adaptable structures that will improve the urban activity within. This project makes an adaptable system for unpredictable city conditions.

The designer of this project started by considering a black and white drawing of a city skyline, and by flipping it upside down and inverting the colors, imagined that the empty spaces could instead be the buildings. By rethinking the solid, monolithic norm of skyscrapers, the designer decided to base the Mutating Sky City on an idea of a city of structural columns, which are located at regular points on a grid. From these

0088

Mutating Sky city
A System for unpredictable city

columns, buildings emerge as connecting units are constructed to link them. This makes the city and its buildings completely adaptable. They can be changed and adjusted as needed and it also creates a more porous landscape, allowing more sunlight in.

A goal of this urban form is to abandon the ground, essentially, where skyscrapers are accessed individually, making them isolated. By lifting the public domain into the sky, where people are all connected through these connected units held by the columns, the streetscape is freed from activity, allowing for a reimagining of uses that could occur in this new open space.

Structural Plan

Columns adjusting to the site condition   Grabbed columns making insi

The structure serves as framework for programs to be inserted into. The spaces can be made up inside the structure based on their uses. The cores can be generated by the "grab" action and huge voids can be made by "split" action to put into the structure for public activities.

The designer imagines the new urban grid as taking over a typical Asian city mega block. The columns are inserted into the ground in a square, leaving a large empty square space in the middle. As the needs of the city's residents and entities are established, buildings are constructed above ground between the columns. The space on the ground is therefore left open, and can be used as public space for residents.

0088

Contextualizing

Finally, I wanted to show this abstact model into the context of site. The site is a typical mega block of asian city. I free the center of the land as a inner court yard, structures fit in around. Technically, The columns are on the infinite grid, and that grid is modified and selected to fit in the site. So the columns take place of that modified grid. After that, columns start to mutate. Freed area could become a park, could be used for various events. And structures around it mutate itself according to the programs and other connecting roads through the site. Circulations are made around the inner side of the plan.

The basic rules for breaking typical problems of skyscrapers(Problems of repetitive plans, lack of lights in deep inside of the buildings, isolation of each towers and bad accessibility from the top of the building to its public area)can also be seen in these images. Indivisual units are put porously around the public area. Public activities can be held in higher position that is trying to invert the typical position of private and public. They became more accessible from the higher part of the towers. The inside view, there are various kind of activities available in public space, and the individual units are around it.

By using this system, we can generate not only a skyscraper but also a new form of adapting city which responds to the uncountable cases of urban context.

Top View

Inside view of public space

Formation Logic

Inner circulation spaces inserted

Individual units and structures placed

COEXISTENCE

Jaehoon Oh

Republic of Korea

Suburban living has become a desirable option for aging retirees in Asia. While populations who migrate out to the suburbs often go to return to a more traditional lifestyle that offers tranquil settings, better access to natural environments and the opportunity to be self-sufficient, these same people often come back to the city, not realizing how much they had come to rely on the advantages afforded by urban settings.

This project proposes marrying the best of urban and rural lifestyles to appeal to this older demographic. It is done with the construction of a skyscraper within the city that towers far above the rest of the skyline. Residential living spaces are located at the base of the skyscraper, for those who seek to be within the city,

0100

EXISTING SITUATION

An increasing number of Asia's retiree population is heading to the suburbs. As the quality of life and average income of the retiree population has improved, an increasing proportion of this population has started to desire a tranquil suburban lifestyle; an opportunity to immerse into nature; and the enjoyment of being self-sufficient. This trend of 'returning to tradition' seems to be a good answer for common urban issues such as overpopulation or environmental pollutions. Despite this trend, a fairly big portion of these retirees end up coming back to the city. They soon realize the difficulties of leaving their comfort zone and the conveniences which science and technology has brought to their everyday live. Nonetheless, these retirees still dream of the quiet and modest suburban lifestyle.

CONCEPT

The project suggest the best alternative where both rural and urban lives can coexist. Individual household can freely move from traditional space to industrial space and vice versa by utilizing vertical transportation. This vertical transportation enables the targeted retirees to enjoy a more traditional and rural lifestyle without feeling isolated or detached.

Why vertical?

The traditional town on the higher level allows residents to not only build their own community with shared interest for living in tradition but also enjoy stunning panorama of the city from the above. Furthermore, any feeling of isolation and detachment can be completely avoided by easy access to the ground level via vertical transportation. Additionally, the vicinity to the city facilitates prolongation of employment, helping the residents be more financially stable.

and also at the top of the skyscraper, for those who seek tranquility. Between the two levels is a column that supports the weight of the top level.

The top level mimics a rural lifestyle; those who locate their residences on the top of this skyscraper create their own traditional town in the sky, and are able to enjoy tranquility without feeling isolated. A "return to tradition" is a theme prevalent in this project, and this idea is possible on the top floor, where residents can orient their community as they please and live a traditional farming lifestyle.

There are two advantageous aspects to this set-up for residents. First, because of their proximity to

the city, aging residents who seek to live on the tranquil floor but need to earn a city dweller's wage can still descend to the city and continue working if needed. Second, those who live on the top can grow and harvest their own crops, and then have immediate buyers on the ground level. This provides city-dwellers with fresh food, and eliminates transportation costs for the farmers.

If residents change their mind as to whether they want to live within the city on the ground floor or in the suburbs at the top, they are able to easily move. Each unit is modular, and vertical transporters can move modules from top to bottom. Once reaching their new level, horizontal transporters fit modules into place.

0100

Historical Value

Expeditiously advancing technology, repetitive schedules and routines have set today's urban population afar from their own history and traditions, making them grow ignorant and oblivious. By physically placing such traditional community on higher level, "returning to tradition" will become the symbol for nobleness, thus more desired and appreciated. This will be the first step towards returning to the traditional values of 'cooperation' and 'living within nature'.

Vertical Farm

Crops harvested from the traditional residential areas on the top level can add novel value to the economy. These crops are directly delivered markets on ground level by simply transporting the goods on trolly hoists built on the exterior of the building and ultimately presented to consumers.

A Right beneath the residential areas of both the ground level and the uppermost level lies a 'horizontal transporter'. This 'horizontal transporter' quickly transports residential areas across each level.

B Next to the column bearing the main load, lies a 'vertical transporter' which catches the incoming modules from the 'horizontal transporter' and then transports them between each level.

C At the outermost parts of the building are elevators that convey crops harvested from the traditional residential area to the ground level. At the ground level, fresh crops are quickly sent to the market for awaiting consumers.

continuous context with surroundings

576

LINEAR SKYSCRAPER

Jon Andoni Iparragirre Apraiz
Julen Quevedo Corral
Xabier Arranz Díez
Ubay Calle Garcia

Spain

 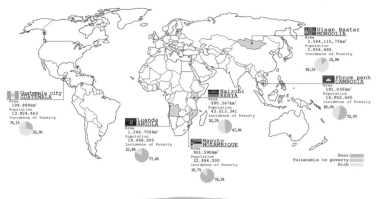 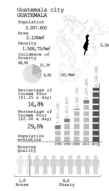 

Globalization and the widespread migration of countryside residents into the capital cities of some of the world's poorest countries has led to unmitigated suburban sprawl that often manifests itself more as ghetto wasteland than simply unattractive, homogenous development. Growing cities that do not have the money to properly fund rapid expansion often must compromise their unique cultural offerings and architectural vernacular in pursuit of constructing areas of housing to accommodate these swelling populations.

This project seeks to help a capital city provide proper, livable infrastructure for its new residents without sacrificing its identity. Though the concept could be deliverable in any number of cities, this project

■0141

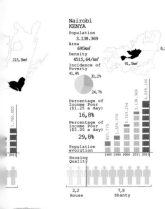 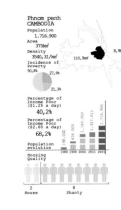 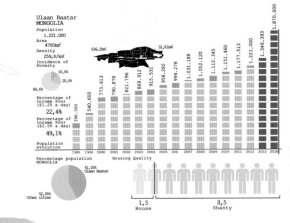 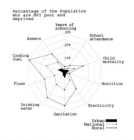

Nairobi KENYA
Population 3.138.369
Area 695km²
Density 4515,64/km²
Incidence of Poverty 41,4%
Percentage of Income Poor ($1.25 a day) 16,8%
Percentage of Income Poor ($2.00 a day) 29,8%
Population evolution
Housing Quality
2,2 House — 7,8 Shanty

Phnom penh CAMBODIA
Population 1.716.900
Area 375km²
Density 3540,31/km²
Incidence of Poverty 50,8%
Percentage of Income Poor ($1.25 a day) 40,2%
Percentage of Income Poor ($2.00 a day) 68,2%
Population evolution
Housing Quality
2 House — 8 Shanty

Ulaan Baatar MONGOLIA
Population 1.221.000
Area 4700km²
Density 259,8/km²
Incidence of Poverty 10,8%
Percentage of Income Poor ($1.25 a day) 22,4%
Percentage of Income Poor ($2.00 a day) 49,1%
Population evolution
Percentage population MONGOLIA
41,55% Ulaan Baatar
52,45% Other cities
Housing Quality
1,5 House — 8,5 Shanty

Percentage of the Population who are MPI poor and deprived

The Mongolian traditional lifestyle has always been associated with nomadism (Yurt). Today this way has become an unviable option because it can't compete against the international market.

Annually since the decade of the eighties Ulaan Baatar population increases by 50,000 new residents who are forced to sedentary.

■ REDUCE DISTANCES, SAVE CITY

The world goes too fast despite its people. Globalization, masked in a neoliberal financial system has pushed citizens all over the world to a rootless lifestyle, losing all connection with nature and their origins. Wherever you go, cities have the same desire; expansion, growth... but not all of them are capable of such thing.

The capital is the heart of a country and a big part of its state revenues is directed to its progress and comfort, trying to make it an attractive home. The moment a city is born, its demographic rate increases steadily; this should be anticipated and cities must be prepared for it.

Guatemala City, Luanda, Maputo, Nairobi Phnom Penh and Ulaan Baatar are some of the main city capitals in undeveloped countries that have failed to solve the problem of overpopulation. The huge suburbs that surround these cities and many times grow bigger than the city itself are a clear of this failure.

The moment this uncontrolled expansion reaches a considerable size, distance becomes the biggest issue. Water, food, sewers, light, education, and job opportunities and everything that makes a person live with dignity.

focuses on Ulan Bator, the capital of Mongolia, where 85 percent of the city's people live in the capital's impoverished, sprawling outskirts. However, with so many Mongolians having descended from nomadic tribes who lived in Yurt tents, this modern development pattern is detrimental not just in the undesirable nature of living conditions but because it is a complete departure from traditions held in the country.

This project proposes the construction of a thin skyscraper that is longer than it is tall that serves as infrastructure, and indeed is a stacked series of platforms that allow families to construct and live in yurts but enjoy modern amenities at the same time. The 100 meter-tall structure has renewable energy sources that

residents can tap into, such as solar panels and wind turbines, as well as water collection and distribution capabilities and shared green spaces. Families locate their yurts along the long platforms, with shared amenities interspersed. The structures, instead of being horizontally straight, periodically angle, creating a zigzag shape, allowing sunshine to reach more areas of the platform levels.

Such a development offers the services of modern architecture without imposing it on a city, while simultaneously presenting an option for urban growth that does not require construction of the sprawl that eats land and people's time as they struggle to commute to work while living in affordable areas.

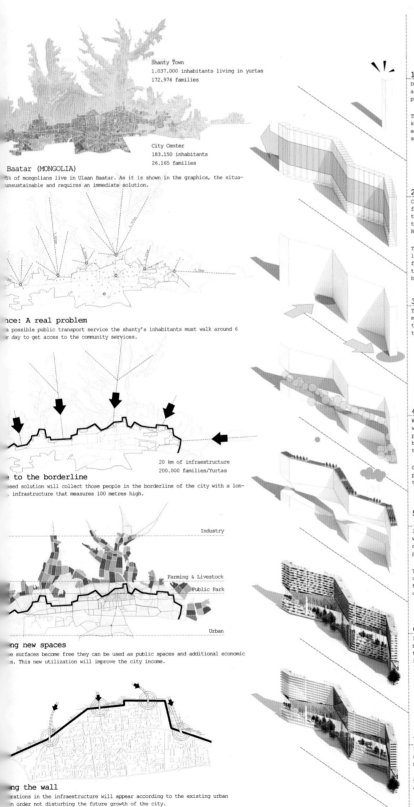

Shanty Town
1.037.000 inhabitants living in yurtas
172.974 families

City Center
183.150 inhabitants
26.165 families

Baatar (MONGOLIA)
5% of mongolians live in Ulaan Baatar. As it is shown in the graphics, the situa-
unsustainable and requires an immediate solution.

nce: A real problem
a possible public transport service the shanty's inhabitants must walk around 6
r day to get acces to the community services.

20 km of infraestructure
200.000 families/Yurtas

e to the borderline
sed solution will collect those people in the borderline of the city with a lon-
infrastructure that measures 100 metres high.

Industry

Farming & Livestock
Public Park

Urban

ng new spaces
e surfaces become free they can be used as public spaces and additional economic
s. This new utilization will improve the city income.

ng the wall
rations in the infrastructure will appear according to the existing urban
n order not disturbing the future growth of the city.

1. ORDINARY SKYCRAPER

Due to the nature of the contest, a conventional skyscraper interpretation is performed.

That condition invite us thinking about an estructure that escapes from existing urban scale in this place.

2. LINEAL SKYCRAPER

City demand requires a larger surface. It is decided to multiply the building as necessary along the northern borderline of Ulaan Baatar.

The addition of volumes becomes a lineal skyscraper. Despite conforming an slender vertical section the result is an horizontal building.

3. URBAN CONECTION

The infraestructure and the city must live together. To reach this, the building acquires all the urban conditions.

4. PUBLIC SPACE

What height can be reached without losing contact with the public space? This question has been discussed since the birth of the skyscrapers.

Give the third dimension to public space is a must for this type of megalomaniacs building.

5. ENERGY/WATER/SOSTENIBILITY

330.000 m² of rooftops offer water and energy to a large number of inhabitants through passive and active systems.

This way the building becomes a community equipment not only for the poor people but for all the city inhabitants.

6. RESULT 2015

In a short time the global problem can be solved because only the estructure and the basic urban installations are needed.

7. 2040 ESTIMATE

If necessary, a part of the structure could be used as community equipments.

The proposal becomes a safe investment for the city.

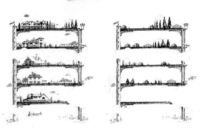

■0141

DELIRIOUS NY/ DELIRIOUS ULAAN BAATAR
The theorem of 1909 is useful a century later in Ulaan Baatar: the skyscraper understood as an utopian device for producing an unlimited number of virgin placements in a single metropolitan location.

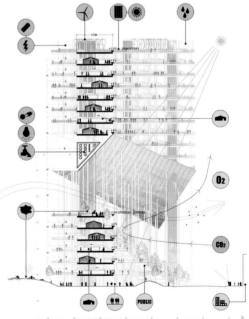

O₂

CO₂

PUBLIC

■ REDUCE DISTANCES, SAVE CITY

Ulan Bator, Mongolia's capital is one of the clearest examples. With 1.221.000 people living in it, 85% of them live in this kind of ghettos. However, vernacular lifestyle has been maintained thanks to the nomad ancestors who invented the Yurt, an ephemeral construction that responded to the local climatic conditions.

As it's been previously exposed, distance gains a special relevance thanks to this urbanization process, making life harder for the people living in the suburbs.

Architecture can solve some of these issues by reinterpreting its conventional meaning. We must study the real needs of a problem in order to propose an adequate solution. If the Yurt covers already some of the basic needs people have, the building must be a complement to it that, at the same time, can solve the problems related to distance.

This is a proposal to offer (not impose) modern architecture at the service of the vernacular's lifestyle respecting and maintaining their old traditions as far as we can and reducing distances to save Ulaan Baatar.

CUBE SOCIETY

Folcher Julien
Wang Mi

Australia

Nowadays metropolises like Chengdu develop horizontaly, the vertical growth of high rise building is just an extension of the private property on the ground level. The city doesn't gain any qualities in this third dimension. This project proposes to extend and complexify the city grid into this new territory. This additional dimension must be a continuity of the second and gives an alternative in a dense urban environment with an increasing property value.

Is Chengdu going to be a duplicate of Beijing or Shanghai after the fierce urbanization in China? Are there qualities that can make the new city "a different place"?
How to interpret the essence of the unique lifestyle of Chengdu and combine it with a model of centralized organization, to enable its vernacular culture to survive within a large scale and highly densified new urban environment?

Cube society is a three-dimensional superstructure network organized in a horizontal, vertical and diagonal street grid that offers short connection paths and higher urban density with better local communications, less social isolation, and higher number of neighbor interactions. This projects seeks to create a hyper-cube, where residents can occupy a building site on 3 dimensions.

In order to make the project not just a generic mixed use building, all the programs need to interact with each other through some interface spaces. These will increase the potential link between activities by making them spatially and functionally interdependent. The approach is to take the original spaces from the existing city fabric as these interface elements; they are considered to be the most characteristic places in Chengdu. Such spaces are proven to work well under the local climate and cultural conditions, people are familiar with them and they are part of the city lifestyle.

How can a rapidly growing city redefine how a city is built? How can the parameters of verticality or horizontality, which have always defined development, be surpassed?

The Cube Society is a three-dimensional superstructure network, or a "hyper-cube," as the designers have dubbed it, organized with a horizontal, vertical and diagonal street grid. By adding a third dimension of development that residents can utilize, shorter connection paths are created between locations, which makes high urban density more efficient and social, as it fosters better communication amongst neighbors.

This improved ability for communication can only be fully realized, though, if the programmatic uses

0161

of the cubes that are directly connected are beneficial to one another. Therefore, to avoid a generic, mixed-use development, the Cube Society must locate different but related uses close to one another to foster collaboration. Housing for the elderly, for example, could be directly linked to businesses, health care, nonprofit groups and recreational facilities that serve elderly clients. Cube Societies and the uses they host within, though, are meant to speak to the unique local culture of the cities they are built in, and such increased interaction amongst organizations and uses housed within will help maintain and grow the individual attributes that are special to that city.

The project focuses on exploring interactions between indoor and outdoor spaces and how the distribution of programs drives circulation.

Unlike the common podium and private towers typology in China, these interface spaces assemble different elements into one urban area and increases interactions between programs, they make the project a much more efficient hybrid organization with local characters instead of some generic mixed use buildings.

The complimentarity and proximity of the functions allows greater interaction between different groups of users. During their journey, the visitors will pass varied urban elements along their route, and will have a new spacial experience. Compare to connecting destinations in a linear way, this kind of journey will bring a sense of serendipity into the city and therefore add more interest to the urban environment.

Cube Society proposes more density than most existing developments in China, and at the same time provides more public spaces and accessibility It allows the joyfull lifestyle of Chengdu to breathe and live within this urban superstructure This hybrid project combines modern efficiency and the unique local culture; it introduces a new typology that cultivates difference through the coexistence of multiple types through hybridization and to develop a strategy for maximizing the intensity between local, metropolitan and global conditions. We think it will provide an alternative approach to the future Chinese urbanization process.

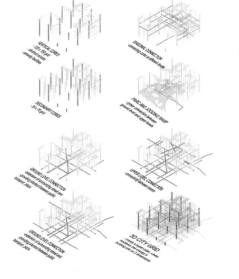

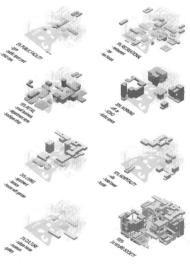

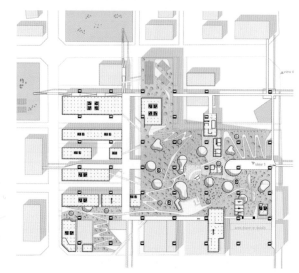

In total, 24 percent of the space within the cube will be residential, 10 percent is for tourist hospitality, 3 percent is for cultural uses (such as museums and galleries), 9 percent is for recreation, 5 percent holds public facilities such as gyms, 19 percent is retail and 30 percent is office and other work space. Green space within and surrounding the Cube Society is prevalent, and the streets and plazas are designed to further foster positive interaction amongst people, a necessity since housing within the Cube Society increases density within the structure. Cafes and wide, tree-lined streets hold opportunities for people to eat and relax together, display art, hold outdoor classes and even participate in impromptu social gatherings.

CRATER SCRAPER

Minzhao Guo
Xinmin Li
Lixiang Miao
Xiaomia Xiao

China

Crater Scraper
Healing the Earth's Wound

As a planet in solar system, the Earth has been existing for 4.6 billion years. However, there are some threatening factors in the solar system even though it seems to be a calm and stable system.

65 million years ago, when dinosaurs ruled the Earth, an asteroid hit the earth. The climate changed rapidly and dinosaurs were not able to adapt the abrupt climate change, which led to the extinction of them. This is just one of the major disasters since the Earth's existence. Numerous asteroids, comets, meteorites are floating in the universe. During the last 4.6 billion years of history, the Earth daily faced the threat of meteorite impact.

The film 《2012》 led to the thinking of the human disaster, destruction and rebirth. If the Earth is again hit by asteroids, and environment of the Earth's surface would been destroyed to devastated, how humans can carry out the post-disaster reconstruction? Will the form of human settlement be changed because of the impact?

The concept of this program is to heal the earth's wounds. Craters will be filled with giant framed building to form communities. Large and small craters on Earth will form different crater community settlements.

Usually, the city skyline is gradually increased from surrounding to the middle, our building is also in line with this point. Mesh-shaped building has more convenient transportation. By contacting the surrounding ground at the top, people can be conveniently transferred to the building bottom through vertical transportation.

Community space mode is similar to the garden city model. The mesh-shaped construction enclosure variety kinds of space, containing the core spirit of the community, Central Park, the green space, the water system, market, stadium, etc.

Building types along the direction from center to the surrounding are business, office, commercial, recreational and residential. Their distribution and size is formed according to the laws of human activities.

The program would like to unify Genius Loci and architectural space; ground and underground; artificial and natural; disaster and memory elements in order to create a harmonious social life state

Before humans appeared on the Earth, meteorites from space begin to hit the Earth.
After billions of years of earth-shaking changes, scientists still believe that it is possible to identify the meteorite impact ground.
The big ball leaves a big hole on the earth. There are over 170 such kind of holes on Earth today according to the American geologist's statistics.
The holes are located in every continent, even on the seabed.

The Crater Scraper project is an imagined solution for the healing of the Earth's surface as the planet suffers the impact of major asteroid strikes. Asteroid craters could be filled in with built settlements, holding communities of different sizes depending on the size of the crater.

As cities historically form at a core and extend peripherally, Crater Scrapers too have a central core that connects the settlement as a whole vertically and horizontally.

The crater is filled with towers and structures that are covered by a roof system that has large holes, causing the built community, from an aerial view, to resemble mesh. Imagining that top-down view, each

0171

cylindrical opening of the mesh holds a type of development that is needed for the community to function, from residences to shops and offices to hospitals to recreational spaces. The community as a whole is developed with the garden city model in mind, featuring a central park located at the core and open green spaces interspersed throughout.

The roof allows for sunlight to stream in thanks to the holes, but it also holds vegetation on its solid structure, which allows for water capture. The water that falls onto the roof surface is redirected so that it falls into the crater community on the edges of the actual crater, creating a water curtain, and is also partially

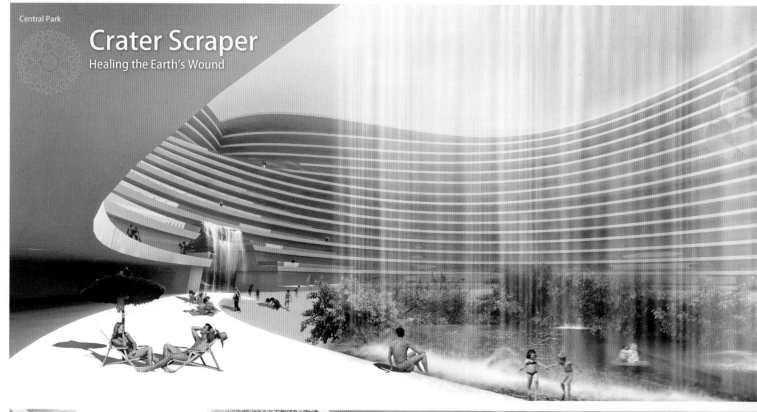

Central Park

Crater Scraper
Healing the Earth's Wound

Residential District

directed into the central park to create a beautiful waterfall.

The roof consists of three systems: road, greening and water. As a whole, the net-building system constituted by a number of high-se buildings which have independent vertical transportation systems, has an obvious advantage than the ordinary transportation system as well as the structure system.

The concept as a whole is to unify opposites: ground and underground, artificial and natural, disaster and rebirth, to create a utopian reality in the aftermath of the disaster of an asteroid strike.

Mirror City

In traditional urban traffic system, the car is on the ground and people lives upon the transportation system.

In this case, we design two transportation systems: roof and ground transit system. The top is designed for quick transportations while the under system is designed for walking .People can easily get accsess to anywhere with choice of freedom.

Evolution

Density
The traditional town is consist of high-rise buildings with high density in the central area and low buildings of high density off the egde.

Links
The distribution of the mass is between the state of connection and seperation.One space interactive with another leads to the change of the space property.

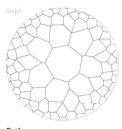

Path
The density of central district road network is low , while the surrounding road consist of the high density network.

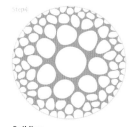

Building
Center area is ocupied with public buildings of large scale .Buildings on edge for living are small scale.

Compound

The central area is public area .The yard near the edge is more private compared with the one in the central area.

System Structure

The roof consists of three systems: road, greening and water. Greening and water provide ecological landscape, and also can play a role in cooling insulation and rainwater collection. Water can form a water curtain and double glazing to generate the micro-climate. And landscape waterfall formed in central landscape area.

As a whole, the net-building system constituted by a number of high-rise buildings, which have independent vertical transportation system, has an obvious advantage than the ordinary transportation system as well as the structure system.

We set different public active node based on the community function. In this way ,it can create the system of commercial space and landscape stroll system.

Link Analysis

Weak connections among buildings and ground floor traffic is limited

Every floor is a part of the traffic system

Transportation
Traditional traffic between isolated buildings is not convenient.The corridor links can provide an convenient way for people to get access to each building.

Every building is isolated and not strong engoub

Structure systems work together

Structure
By linking the isolated buildings ,it can make the building as one mega-structure mass. It can provide a stronger support to resist the disaster.

Sustainable Strategy

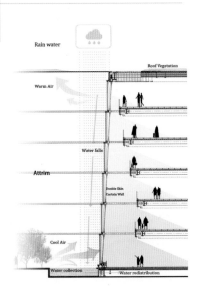

Rain water

Roof Vegetation

Warm Air

Water falls

Attrim

Double Skin Curtain Wall

Cool Air

Water collection   Water redistribution

System

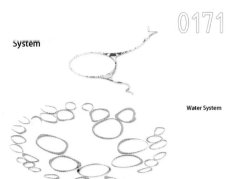

Water System

Roof Garden

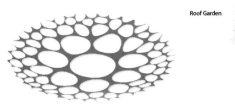

Vehicle Transportation

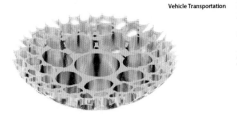

Floor Plan

Vertical Transportation

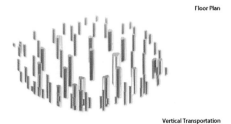

Facade System

Ground Eco-System

0171

LIGHT PARK

Yiming Chen
Ting Xu

3RD PLACE - 2013

China

Light Park

City Issue

In the context of high-speed urban development in Beijing, this capital city of China aims to become an international one. High-efficiency plays an important role in urban development undoubtedly. Wide roads come along and became the necessities for the city. Under the circumstances of huge-scale of road network, the city cannot afford the traffic capacity anymore. Urban development directly impacts the lifestyle of the residents. The numbers of population and vehicles are rising rapidly on parallel lines, the government had to make a move in creating new regulations to limit the growth of the number of vehicles.

Pollution has also become a big problem within the development of the city. The large number of buildings and roads occupy public green space. Excessive vehicle congestion caused serious air pollution. This will in no doubt effect the health and safety of the city and its residents. For the purpose of efficiency, urban space forced the city to demolish ancient architectures. The expanding of urbanization oppressed residents' living space. People spend a lot of time on the road everyday, but they are not enjoying it. In the meanwhile, they have to endure the poor environment. On the long run, people have to become accustomed to pursuit the efficiency and material, and forget life itself. This phenomenon will trigger a series of social problems.

Concept

When the skyscraper gets to be replaced by open public green space, it will effectively solve the problem for the lacking of urban greening. But there is no space to construct a large number of Vertical Parks in Beijing. As a solution, we need an object that possess a detachment of urban space and improve the capacity of urban space, combined with airship technology, which will in return be effective. Airship technology has broad development space on the volume and load capacity. When both volumes increase large enough and structure rationally, it can overhang a vertical park and move over the city.

Setting up the ground transportation station will share a lot of urban transport tasks. Profiting from the huge part of the airship translucent surface, it can be effectively combined with solar energy and rainwater collection, and utilization technology. With the combination of non-polluting, low energy consumption, low noise, shadow-free system, and mobile Park, it will optimize the urban air. Light Park is an urban transportation revolution. Using park as the transportation deck, the moving process will become comfortable and healthy. Traffic congestion and unhealthy problems will be resolved in the end. More importantly, it will benefit the residents, regulates them to pay more attention to their life in a way.

The rapid increase of population within the major cities around the world has led to poor development and serious urban design problems, including the lack of infrastructure, housing, and recreational areas. In Beijing, a large portion of the historic center has been demolished.

One way to make scarce green and recreation space available to residents of this crowded city is a skyscraper that floats above the land, taking new development to the sky. The Light Park stays afloat thanks to a large, mushroom cap-like helium-filled balloon at its top, and solar-powered propellers directly below. Programmatic platforms that host parks, sports fields, green houses, restaurants, and other uses are

0208

suspended from the top of the structure by reinforced steel cables; the platforms fan in different directions around the spherical vessel to balance its weight. These slabs are also staggered to allow for maximum exposure to sunlight on each level.

With the combination of non-polluting, low energy consumption, low noise, shadow-free system, and mobile park, it will optimize the urban air. Light Park is an urban transportation revolution. Using the park as the transportation deck, the moving process will become comfortable and healthy. Traffic congestion and unhealthy problems will be resolved in the end.

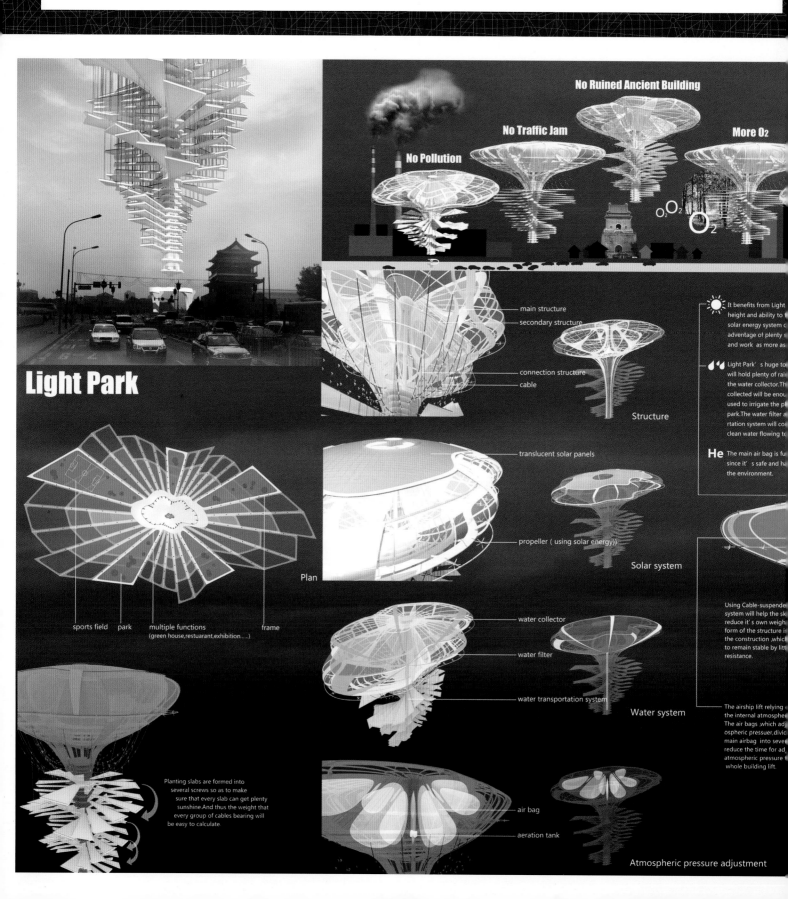

No Pollution   No Traffic Jam   No Ruined Ancient Building   More O₂

Light Park

sports field   park   multiple functions (green house,restuarant,exhibition......)   frame

Plan

main structure
secondary structure
connection structure
cable

Structure

translucent solar panels

propeller (using solar energy))

Solar system

water collector

water filter

water transportation system

Water system

Planting slabs are formed into several screws so as to make sure that every slab can get plenty sunshine.And thus the weight that every group of cables bearing will be easy to calculate.

air bag
aeration tank

Atmospheric pressure adjustment

It benefits from Light ... height and ability to ... solar energy system ... adventage of plenty s... and work as more as ...

Light Park's huge to... will hold plenty of rai... the water collector.Th... collected will be enou... used to irrigate the pl... park.The water filter a... rtation system will co... clean water flowing to

He The main air bag is fu... since it's safe and ha... the environment.

Using Cable-suspende... system will help the sk... reduce it's own weigh... form of the structure i... the construction ,which... to remain stable by litt... resistance.

The airship lift relying ... the internal atmosphe... The air bags ,which ad... ospheric pressuer,divic... main airbag into sever... reduce the time for ad... atmospheric pressure ... whole building lift.

Translucent solar panels cover the top of the vessel to power the uses below, and water collectors, also located at the top, direct precipitation towards filters that, after cleaning the water, send it throughout the structure.

Though it does not completely solve Beijing's serious traffic and crowding problems, the Light Park can return valuable green space to the public, and also help mitigate the pollutions that come with increased development; with parks and plants floating in the sky above the city, the air is partially cleaned.

THE VERTICAL COUNTRY

Sergiy Prokofyev
Olga Prokofyeva

Ukraine

YOU ARE PASS UNDER
THE TERRITORY OF
THE FREE STATE

TERRITORY OF THE
SECOND WORLD

THE V

one

PRE

two

FU

two sep
Distan

The term of c
third appeared i
countries of the
Alliance. The c
Warsaw Agreement
countries of the
in the cold war
fication was of

At the beginn
has changed some
At present the
with the high st
developing, that
second world.

Modern society conceptions divide the global territories as countries of first and third world. This proposal focuses on the inequality between this two social layer, understanding that the social and economical development gap has been increasing in the last decades. Lacking of a second world country population, the proposal aims to create a new territory of reconciliation were new countries will arise.

 The second world territory should become a social bridge for equality; the new country should be located at the border of the developed and developing countries. As far as there is no free territory between them, the new country will be horizontal as a mega-story above existing territories, related to the ground only

AL COUNTRY OF THE SECOND WORLD

0237-1

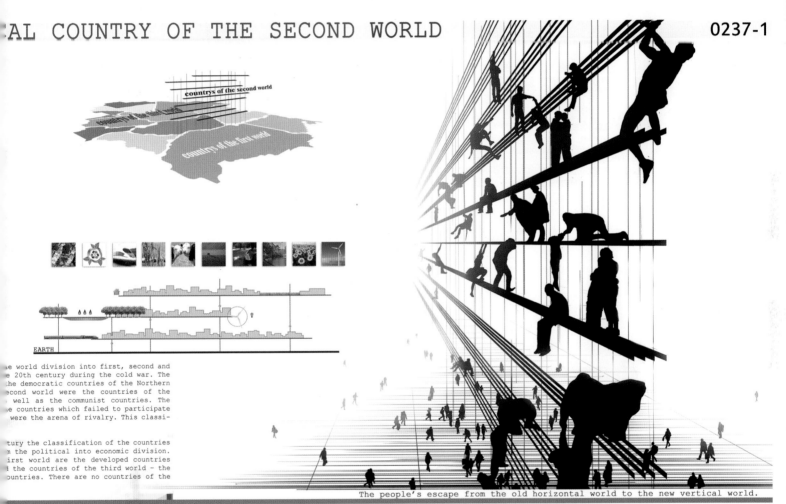

The people's escape from the old horizontal world to the new vertical world.

e world division into first, second and
e 20th century during the cold war. The
he democratic countries of the Northern
econd world were the countries of the
 well as the communist countries. The
e countries which failed to participate
 were the arena of rivalry. This classi-

tury the classification of the countries
n the political into economic division.
irst world are the developed countries
 the countries of the third world - the
ountries. There are no countries of the

The development dynamics of the countries of the first world and the conservatism of those of the third world more and more increase the time distance between the two worlds. With every decade this distance will be only increasing. Two different worlds will exist on one terrestrial globe. The developed countries will cut them- selves off with the help of new borders, and the hatred and oppo- sition will grow up in the countries of the third world.

 The necessity in creating the new countries of reconciliation will arise. They were the countries of the so-called buffer zone where the people from the 1st and 3rd worlds will be able to get freely and voluntarily. Thereby the Second World will again come into existence, but in the new aspect.

 However the modern world does not have any territory to creation of the new country. There are the unpopulated territories, but they are unfit for the habitation. The new country, to our mind, should be located at the border of the developed and developing countries. As far as there is no free territory between them, the new country should be vertical touching the ground only with the supports.

 The colonization of such a country will be realized according to the free principle. All the volunteers who are tired of the po- litical wars or infringement of the liberties in their countries may settle the vertical country free of politics. The main aim of the countries of the Second World will be the reconciliation of the different nations of the world, as well as learning of their histo- ry and culture.

 Stretching along the borders of the states the length of such a country may be over 300 km, and its width may vary between 200-300 m. Its height will be about 500 m. The horizontal surfaces will be located one over another.

The new vertical world has all the functional components of the ordinary country. Each horizontal surface is a city with buildings, parks, transport. All the cities are different by size. The elec- trical trains move in the horizontal direction to long distance. The vertical communication is performed with the help of lifts. The lift bar has the threading and at the same time it is the vertical support element of the common structure. The movements of the lift cabin up and down are performed by the principle of bolt twisting and untwisting at the expense of the mobile mechanism. At that the part where people are situated remain immovable. This principle of raising is less power-consuming than the classical lift, which allows saving the economy for the whole country. The bars by which the lifts move are also the supports of the horizontal surfaces. Their ultra strength and their big quantity allow supporting the whole country.

The cargo lifting of the new territory is provided at the expense of the trains energy which are connected to the vertical mechanism, which acts based on the principle of the scissors. The trains are meeting raising the goods up and are separating lowering it down.

The wind power stations provide the required energy. The accumula- tion, purification, processing and storage of the water provide the water requirements of the state. The agriculture will satisfy the food needs of the population.

The newly appeared Second World will connect the two rest world like a thin thread without allowing them to separate one from an- other. And maybe even help to bring them together.

by the vertical implantation and structural support.

The proposal conceives each country as a horizontal city block; in it there will be parks, buildings, public transportation, recreational spaces, and housing. It aims to generate a sustainable system of energy and food production as well as new and innovate strategies for waste recycling.

The electrical trains move in the horizontal direction to long distance. The vertical communication is performed with the help of lifts. The lift bar has the threading and at the same time it is the vertical support element of the common structure. The up and down movements of the lift cabin are performed by the

principle of bolt twisting and untwisting at the expense of the mobile mechanism.

The colonization of such a country will be realized according to the free principle. All volunteers who are tired of political wars or infringement of their liberties in their respective countries may settle in the Vertical Country free politics. The new vertical world has all the functional components of any ordinary country. Each horizontal surface is a city with buildings, parks and transportation. The main aim of the countries of the Second World will be the reconciliation of the different nations of the world, as well as learning of their history and culture.

0237-2

WALLSCRAPER

Gabriel Ioan Mihalea

Romania

UNIFYING WALL . WALL[WORLD]SCRAPER

LOCATION : PLANET EARTH
OBJECTIVES : UNIFYING PEOPLE - ONE SHELTER FOR ALL
TYPOLOGY : WALL[WORLD]SCRAPER
LENGTH : 11800KM
POPULATION : 10,000,000,000 SOULS
AGE : "REMOTE FUTURE"

...STORY...
A WALL usually separates: objects, rooms, activity spaces, apartments, offices and even...people. A WALL succeeded once to split a nation (The Berlin WALL), another WALL defe create a shelter for them.

BACKGROUND [][]
I was thinking about this idea of connecting people all around the globe; is it possible? I've started to analyze the possibility of linking individuals > families > cities >

CONCEPT \//\
I chosen the WALL as an ironic and sarcastic element but yet a strong and efficient tool to sustain my idea. I imagine a WALL structure all around the globe, where every nati with the next one, forming a continuous space and where mobility is ensured by public transportation (airplanes and trains).

TYPOLOGY _|
Rather then expending our habitats vertically, trying to touch the sky and segregate individuals in layers, why not expend our living structures horizontally, connecting indi

"QUOTE"
A WALL usually separates...but this WALL unifies.

DESERT   HILLSIDE   SAVANNA

A wall usually separates but the Wallscraper unifies. A wall is conceived as an architectonical element that separates spaces and activities.

But what if we ask the question in a different way, not to apply the concept of a wall as a separative element, but instead as an element that brings together individuals as an unifying architectonical system to create a shelter and connecting people all around the globe.

The project analyzes the possibility of linking individuals, families, cities, and countries to each other for equal and fair opportunities (from Africa to America) in a continuous and unique shelter structure for all of us

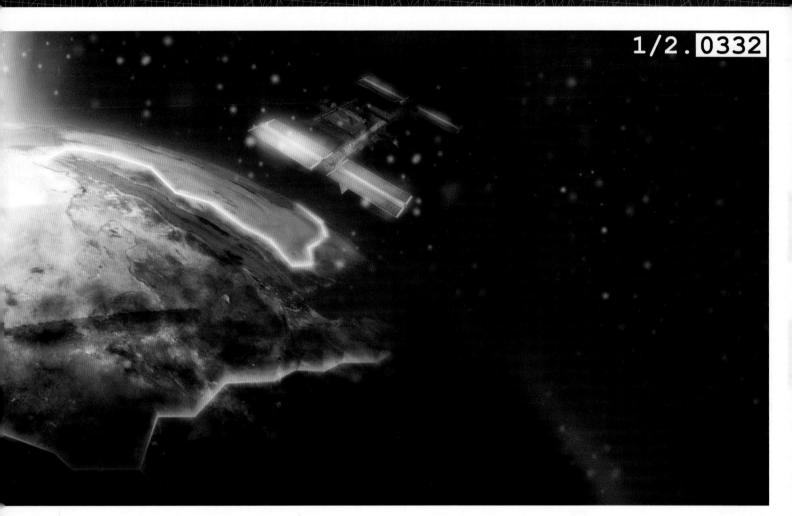

1/2.0332

Great WALL of China) and became one of the world wonders. It is possible for a WALL to unify?! and not to separate or defend; but instead to bring together individuals, to

other. For equal and fair opportunities offered to all of us (from Africa to America)...a continuous and unique shelter/a structure for all of us to live in.

lace. A linear and continuous monument modulated in segments - which can sustain up to 2000 individuals each, plus their day-by-day activities. Each segment is connected

layer. Instead of building skyscrapers, I was thinking to build a WALLscraper...a WORLDscraper.

SOUTH POLE   GREENLAND

to live in.

Rather then expanding our habitats vertically, trying to touch the sky and segregate individuals in layers, the proposal expands our living structures horizontally connecting individuals on the same layer all together in a linear Wallscraper.

Program-wise, the Wallscraper is able to host a variety of spaces. A hierarchy is created; retail and transit are on the bottom while housing and cultural spaces are in the higher spaces. Airport terminals and the promenade are at the absolute top.

UNIFYING **WALL** . WALL [WORLD] SCRAPER

Regular Flights (to custom destinations)

Airplane Shuttle (stops in each country)

Ⓛ   Ⓛ   Ⓛ   Ⓛ   Ⓛ   Ⓛ   Ⓛ

Local Train (stops at each hub, including border hubs)

Ⓡ

Regional Train (stops only at border hubs)

Border Hub ⫶ State Customs

PROMENADE
LOISIR / AIRPORT TERMINALS
CULTURE/ENTERTAINMENT
HOUSING
WORKING
COMMERCIAL/URBAN SPINE
TRANSIT HUB
RETAIL & LOUNGES
TECHNICAL & STORAGE

The wall will provide a strong and efficient architectonical structure to sustain human interaction all around the globe. A linear and continuous monument modulated in segments with each one able to sustain up to 2000 individuals each, plus their daily activities. Each segment is connected with the next one, forming a continuous space.

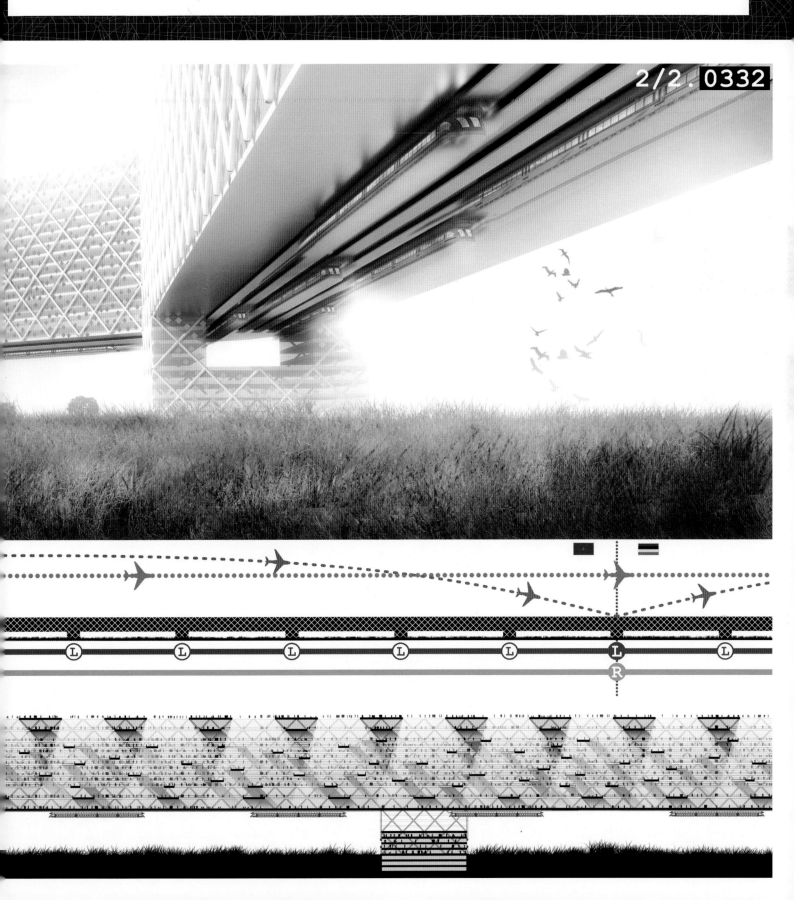

2/2.0332

INFINITECITY

Giuseppe Mecca

Italy

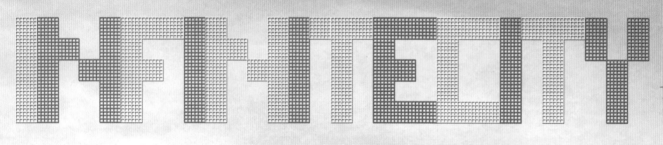

Human history is characterized by the birth, the growth and death of many civilizations during the centuries. The legacy is the existence of big towns all around the world that every civilization left to us.

The current metropolitan areas have been consolidated over time according to several reasons, like: political, cultural, economic, geographic, and environmental factors. People are concentrated in areas of the world where they can more easily satisfy their necessity.

All the big cities together compose a world not where more of 50% of population of the planet is living. The forecast is that this data will grow up to more than 75% in the 2050. At the same time the population of the planet will grow up of 25% during the next decades, especially in the developing countries of Asia. For these reasons, it will be necessary to expand the metropolitan areas to support the arrival of the people from the rural areas.

A rapid growth of towns could worsen the problems of urban planning. The urban sprawl has already shown problems during the last decades. It is related to the inapt use of land and to the limits of big scale infrastructures.

INFINITECITY is the the global linear city with a vertical growth around the equatorial zone of the planet.

Could it be the answer to the problems that the metropolitan areas are showing? Is it the alternative to the urban sprawl that characterizes the human life in cities all over the planet?

Could this kind of real global city pull down the geographical and cultural boundaries that limit social development and at the same time could it solve problems such as: transports, services, ecological and environmental issues ? Could it also limit the uncontrolled expansion to the external areas around the towns, the excessive concentration of central functions and the expulsion of the poorer classes from urban centers?

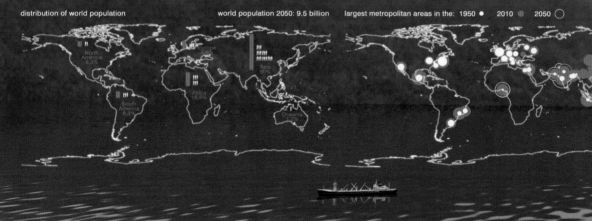

distribution of world population   world population 2050: 9.5 billion   largest metropolitan areas in the: 1950 ●   2010 ◐   2050 ○

Current metropolitan areas have been collapsing in the last years. More of 50% of world population is living now in cities. Studies show that this number will increase to more than 75% by 2050. At the same time, the population of the planet will grow by 25% during the next few decades, especially in the emerging countries such as China and India.

As the horizontal expansion of metropolitan areas as a solution has only created extreme urban sprawl, Infinitecity is proposed as a possible alternative to create an understandable morphological order.

The proposal stems from the fact that the extensions of the post-industrial cities of the 21st century have

0383

worsened traffic conditions, construction costs, levels of pollution, losing environmental and life quality. It may be a way to rethink what will be the real development of future metropolitan areas in which societies became more conscious about overpopulation.

Infinitecity stands as a global linear city of vertical growth located on the equatorial line of the earth. It contains within itself all the functions of a city without creating divisions between different layers. Services, transportation, residential, cultural, commercial, and productive areas are distributed both in height and along its linear development.

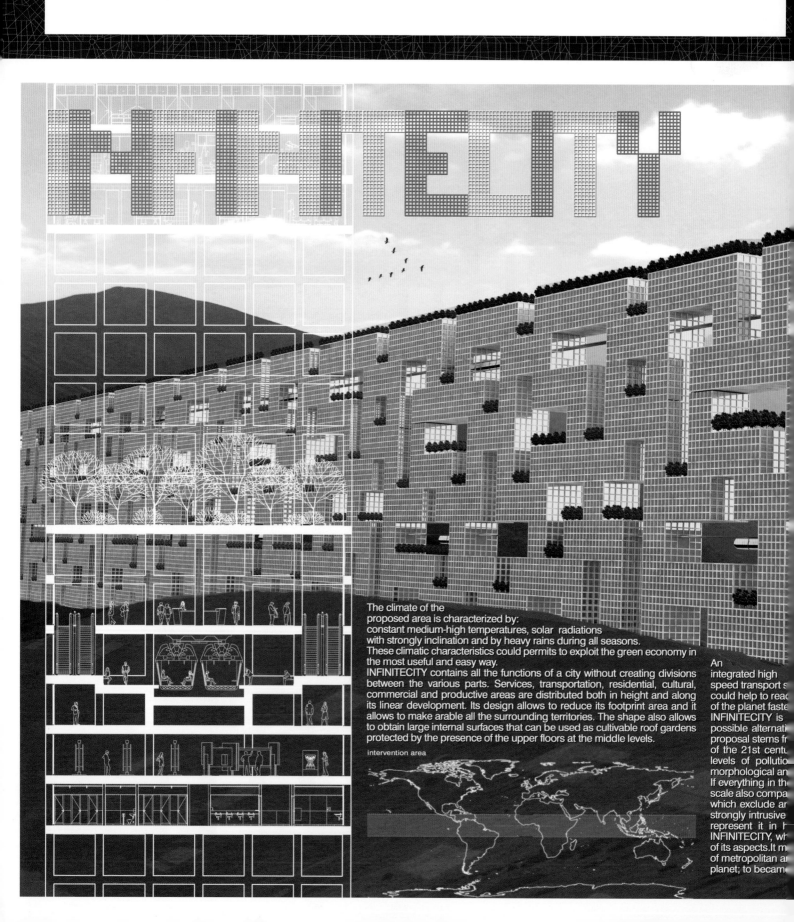

The climate of the
proposed area is characterized by:
constant medium-high temperatures, solar radiations
with strongly inclination and by heavy rains during all seasons.
These climatic characteristics could permits to exploit the green economy in the most useful and easy way.
INFINITECITY contains all the functions of a city without creating divisions between the various parts. Services, transportation, residential, cultural, commercial and productive areas are distributed both in height and along its linear development. Its design allows to reduce its footprint area and it allows to make usable all the surrounding territories. The shape also allows to obtain large internal surfaces that can be used as cultivable roof gardens protected by the presence of the upper floors at the middle levels.

intervention area

An
integrated high
speed transport s
could help to read
of the planet faste
INFINITECITY is
possible alternati
proposal stems fr
of the 21st centu
levels of pollutio
morphological an
If everything in the
scale also compa
which exclude ar
strongly intrusive
represent it in h
INFINITECITY, wh
of its aspects. It m
of metropolitan ar
planet; to became

Its design allows reducing its footprint area and it allows making all the surrounding territories arable. The shape also allows obtaining large internal surfaces that can be used as agricultural roof gardens protected by the presence of the upper floors at the middle levels.

luting ways.
a model or a project but just like a
erstandable morphological order. The
extensions of the post-industrial cities
traffic conditions, construction costs,
ons the good use of land and the
ality were lost.
has to be so big, so huge and out of
d of multiplication of the same element
erence - or using architectural shapes
xistent urban context - could be better
ng a global outsize city like a real
are strength and awareness in every
t on what will be the real development
decades according to the future of our
our destiny according to density.

604

PSYCHO

Viktor Kopeikin
Kobets Olena
Pavel Zabotin

Ukraine

PSYCHO- MATHEMATICAL MEGASTRUCTURE
MODERN VISION OF THE POST NONCLASSICAL DESIGN

The idea of post-neoclassical design model lies in creation of direction—the "society-architectural product."
Society constructs ambient space being directly the customer and creator of space. It is environmental
modeling due to the collective mind.

Form is the product of collective consciousness. Common consciousness will be able to create and
transform ambient space.

Conception of post-neoclassical design suggested in this project is based on analysis of developed
design models of previous generation. Classical (until modernism) and non-classical (after modernism)

0726

THE IDEA OF THE PROJECT LIES IN CREATION OF ARCHITECTURAL SPACE
IN THE SYSTEM OF EXISTING CITY BY READING PSYCHO-EMOTIONAL
BACKGROUND WITH APPLICATION OF INFORMATIONAL AND ANALYTICAL
TECHNOLOGIES. WHEREUPON "PSYCHO-MATHEMATICAL" SPACE OF THE
CITY IS FORMED.
FORM IS PRODUCT OF EMOTIONS.
THREE CONCEPTUAL LINED ARE:
1.   CITY AND FORM
2.   POST-NEOCLASSICAL DESIGN MODEL
3.   STRUCTURAL MODULE AS CONSEQUENCE OF RECYCLED SCRAP
1. CITY IS "MATERNAL" BACKGROUND FOR AN OBJECT, THE OBJECT IS
A NEW STAGE OF CITY DEVELOPMENT. FORM IS THE RESULT OF
PROCESSING OF "PSYCHO-EMOTIONAL BACKGROUND" OF THE CITY.
TRANSFORMATION OF PSYCHO-EMOTIONAL BACKGROUND INTO
MATHEMATICAL MODEL IS INFORMATION AND TECHNICAL TASK, WHICH
PRODUCT IS BUILDING OF MATERIAL (STRESSED OR ANY OTHER) FORM.
PROGRAMMED MECHANISMS (ROBOTS), WHICH TRANSFORM
"PSYCHO-MATHEMATICAL" INFORMATIONAL AND ANALYTICAL MATERIAL
INTO SPATIAL ARCHITECTURAL OBJECTS WITH THE HELP OF SENSORS
AND TRANSMITTERS ARE PHYSICAL BASIS FOR BUILDING NEW SPACE.
CONSTRUCTION OF NEW ARCHITECTURAL SPACE IS SPECIFIED BY THE
CITY ITSELF AND ITS INHABITANTS. ANY CHANGES INTO
"PSYCHO-EMOTIONAL BACKGROUND", "EMOTIONAL FRAMEWORK"
OF THE CITY DIRECTLY INFLUENCE SHAPING OF TOTALLY NEW SPATIAL
FRAMEWORK AND IMAGE.
2. CONCEPTION OF POST-NEOCLASSICAL DESIGN MODEL, SUGGESTED
IN THE PROJECT, IS BASED UPON ANALYSIS OF DEVELOPED DESIGN
MODEL OF PREVIOUS GENERATIONS. CLASSICAL (UNTIL MODERNISM)
AND NON-CLASSICAL (AFTER MODERNISM) DESIGN LINE WAS TAKEN AS
THE BASIS OF ANALYSIS:
1. CUSTOMER, 2. ARCHITECT, 3. OBJECT.

THE IDEA OF POST-NEOCLASSICAL DESIGN MODEL LIES IN CREATION OF
DIRECT CONNECTION "SOCIETY – ARCHITECTURAL PRODUCT". SOCIETY
CONSTRUCTS AMBIENT SPACE BEING DIRECTLY CUSTOMER AND CREATOR
OF THIS SPACE. IT'S ENVIRONMENT MODELING DUE TO COLLECTIVE
MIND. FORM IS THE PRODUCT OF COLLECTIVE CONSCIOUSNESS.
A NEW ARCHITECT OF THE FUTURE IS COMMON INTELLIGENCE, COMMON
CONSCIOUSNESS ABLE TO CREATE AND TRANSFORM AMBIENT SPACE
LIKE ORGANISM.

design ideals were taken as the basis of analysis of three embodiments: the customer, the architect, and the object.

The main idea of this project lies in the creation of novel architectural space within an existing urban fabric by using psycho-mathematical information to conceive new inhabitable areas where form is the product of emotions. The transformation of this information into architecture is done by programmed robots, which use the new information to build structures.

The new areas are specified and designed by the emotions of the inhabitants as the collective

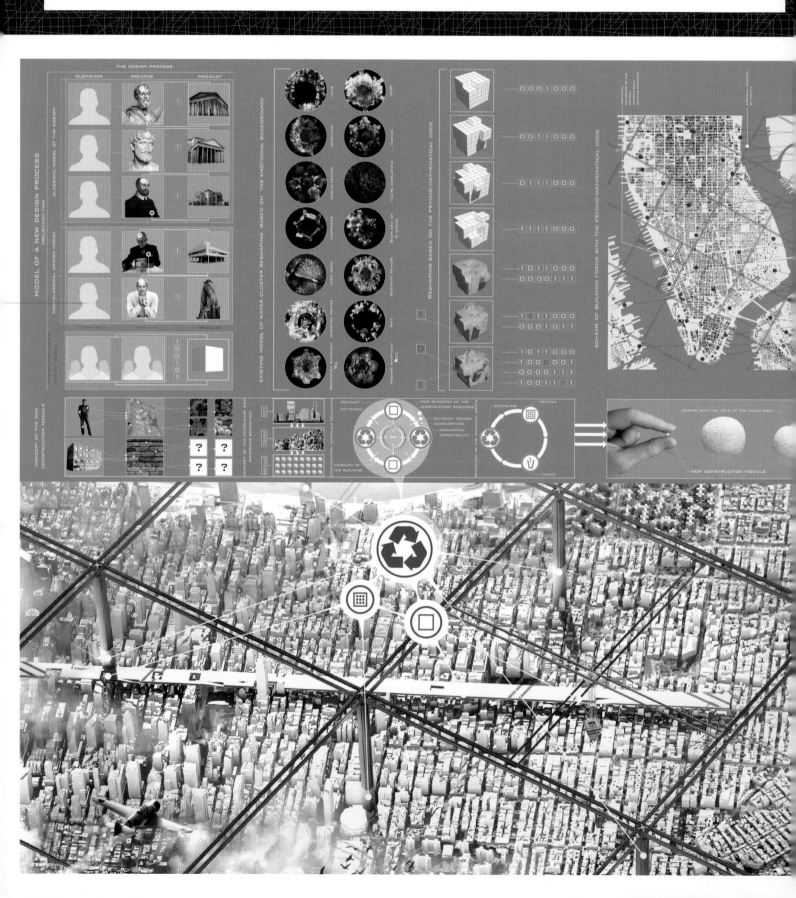

consciousness; the architect of the future is common intelligence.

The project presented here is not the final product. In turn, it is the conceptual idea of creating form by the analysis of a collective consciousness. It is aimed at the symbiosis of architecture, society, and emotions as the future of design.

TOWER+

Aghigh Etehadroodi
Ali Danesh Ali Maleki
Armin Mottaghi Raad

Iran

Tower+

A Gamified Life in a Residential Tower

This 57-floor Dynamic Tower is proposed to be built in Tehran; the capital of Iran. The dynamic structure along with the private social networking -which consists of each individual resident of this tower- lead to a self-organized system which would update slowly and progressively in a participatory manner by engaging these system components -residents- in order to achieve a better level.

The self-organizing characteristics of this system are derived from the behavior of each individuals residing in the tower, who would then become a member of the aforementioned private social network -by purchasing, renting or even constructing a single housing unit in one of the cells of the tower- as part of a small community, which is the virtual model/aspect of the tower. This would in fact make them participate in an online inner-circle game that would soon become an integral part of their lives as a resident in the tower.

Self-organization is a process where some form of global order or coordination arises out of the local interactions between the components of an initially disordered system. This process is spontaneous: it is not directed or controlled by any agent or subsystem inside or outside of the system; however, the laws followed by the process and its initial conditions may have been chosen or caused by an agent.*

Birds flocking   Gosper's Glider Gun

The premise behind this project is to create a dynamic skyscraper that transforms according to a social network game played by the residents. The tower consists of a fixed core and wireframe where mobile units will be able to rotate its position around it and move up and down.

The units will move according to points achieved in the game. The more points one has, the better placement his or her unit will have in the tower. Having gained more points, residents of each housing unit can improve the conditions of their unit by moving it to a more desirable position in terms of natural lighting, view, height, etc. Conversely, by earning negative scores, their unit will be transferred to a less pleasant

0782

610

location.

This 57-floor dynamic tower is proposed to be built in Tehran, Iran. The dynamic structure along with the private social networking will lead to a self-organized system, which would update in a participatory manner. The game would soon become an integral part of the residents' life. The self-organizing characteristics of this system are derived from the behavior of each individual residing in the tower who then become a member of the social network by purchasing or renting a single housing unit.

In this private social network, residents of each housing unit have a defined share of voting to support

Tower+
A Gamified Life in a Residential Tower

The appearance and the behavior of this buil of buildings such as multi-storey car parks, th and the Dynamic Tower in Dubai. In order t to another, the tower employs the structu to a cylindrical Rubik pattern. Therefore, apa the core -along with the whole storey, similar to the units are also capable of moving vertically. by the performance of the social network data which

In this private social network, residents of each of voting to support or refuse certain behaviors of face-to-face communication, the active parti the network can inform the residents of any p

Therefore, each resident can be optimistic by participating in social welfare activities, the complex, and to refrain from any action wh

Having gained more points, residents of the conditions of their unit -by moving it to a m natural lighting, view, height, etc.. Also b is transferred to a less pleasant location.

The idea of the tower is originated from Ga greater functionality by using Augmented re -whilst encouraging residents to respect the rig shifting of units, we would have a dynamic tower

This concept is only applicable if we take int context of Iran. Although Iran is a count to the most modern technologies, appropriate b

For those who have traveled to Iran, the gene public rights of even the simplest of social obeying traffic laws and the hygiene of the city

The online social networking and social games this has provided a deeper connection between

*Reference: wikipedia.org

Service Core   Fixed Middle Corridor and Structure   Movable Outer Structure   Movable Unit

or refuse certain behaviors of other units' residents. Thus as well as face-to-face communication, the active participation and social awareness in the network can inform the residents of any positive or negative activities.

Therefore, each resident can be optimistic about gaining points and rankings by participating in social welfare activities, providing useful propositions for the complex, and to refrain from any action which is contrary to the public rights.

to the architecture
omplex in Chicago
its from one point
a pattern similar
each unit around
nic Tower in Dubai-
ents are influenced
e residents' behavior.

ve a defined share
nts. Thus as well as
cial awareness in
ve activities.

ints and rankings
ul propositions for
o the public rights.

unit can improve
osition- in terms of
ve scores, their unit

ch would achieve
nification concept
th slow and steady
ously transforming.

the current social
ple have access
cial life is hindered.

behavior regarding
standing in line,
is quite noticeable.

y young adults and
wer and its context.

An automated (car) parking system (APS) is a mechanical system designed to minimize the area and/or volume required for parking cars. Like a multi-story parking garage, an APS provides parking for cars on multiple levels stacked vertically to maximize the number of parking spaces while minimizing land usage. *

Marina City is a mixed-use residential/commercial building complex occupying an entire city block on State Street in Chicago, Illinois.*

420-metre, 80-floor moving skyscraper in Dubai, designed by architect David Fisher. Each floor will be able to rotate independently. This will result in a constantly changing shape of the tower. *

A cylinder shaped puzzle/toy similar to the Rubik Cube which can be solved by circular and vertical movements of colored pieces.

social network sites as web-based services that allow individuals to construct a public or semi-public profile within a bounded system, articulate a list of other users with whom they share a connection, and view and traverse their list of connections and those made by others within the system. The nature and nomenclature of these connections may vary from site to site. *

Gamification is the use of game-thinking and game mechanics in non-game contexts in order to engage users and solve problems.*

Augmented reality (AR) is a live, direct or indirect, view of a physical, real-world environment whose elements are augmented by computer-generated sensory input such as sound, video, graphics or GPS data.*

0782

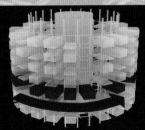

Rotation of a Unit around the core in beginning level

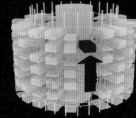

Shifting of the Unit in an Unfilled Column Up or Down

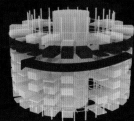

Rotation of a Unit around the core in destination level

PANGEA SKYSCRAPER

Mohammed I. Al Hajajreh
Tamim N. Al Tamimi
Rami O. Shatat
Ma'en Zeyadeh

Jordan

Pangea skyscraper

The Pangea Skyscraper is a 21st century exploration of an inhabitable bridge. The project seeks to eliminate the use of existing natural terrain to create new urban areas. Instead, the proposal bridges across a straight between two mountain ranges.

The structure is designed as a soft arch from which hanging skyscrapers are attached. The structure is 5 kilometers long and 150 meters wide with 116 skyscrapers of variable heights ranging from 40 to 200 meters high. Each multi-use building measure 20 x 20 meters in plan and is equipped with solar panels and wind turbines. The main loads of the body is supported on the main structure, designed as an arc shape

Review

Continued urban expansion and the demand for land and people trying to get close with each other to facilitate various aspects of life, other reasons like the infrastructure requirement, speed of transportation and delivery, finding commercial and service centers, for that was the use of high-rises buildings.

But that situation created a group of problems and with the high density of population and the increase of users in each city make the number of high building increases as well, so each city get their skyscrapers as the need the want.

The rising up was not enough they get back and expand horizontally which means the need for more lands but that won't be a problem unless the lands were used as green lands, and it would be worst if the country suffer from lack of green lands.

Concept

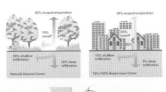

The most important thing in our skyscraper was how to solve the buildings extension without make any effect on the green lands, if we notice any building will be construct needs an area of land and that mean to eliminate the old use of it, so we rise the land up and lat the buildings go down and so we keep the origin lands and create another one above it. And by this way we decrease the surface runoff of rainwater caused by urbanization.

The other part was to connect any two close parts of separated lands not just by a bridge or ferry but with another city so we can have a cultural, economical and political connection.

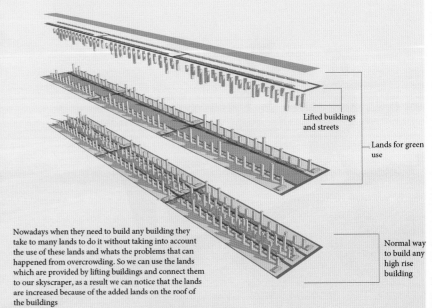

Lifted buildings and streets

Lands for green use

Normal way to build any high rise building

Nowadays when they need to build any building they take to many lands to do it without taking into account the use of these lands and whats the problems that can happened from overcrowding. So we can use the lands which are provided by lifting buildings and connect them to our skyscraper, as a result we can notice that the lands are increased because of the added lands on the roof of the buildings

Buildings extend over green lands

Saving green lands and keep the buildings extension

...ity of terrai

Connecting two separated lands

Urban contact

...ountains winds

Winds used to produce energy

Energy consumed by skyscraper users

to be more effective in supporting. The buildings are connected with the main structure so their loads are moved up. The supporting elements used to make the main structure are made more efficient.

The most important thing in this design was how to solve the building's extension without having a significant impact on the green lands. The other consideration was to connect any two close parts of separated land not just by bridge but also with another city in order to foster cultural, economical, and political connections.

The arch also contains the necessary infrastructure for the hanging city such as transportation roads,

Pangea skyscraper

Escape stairs and elevators are the only way to escape from any danger located in the building, but we can evacuate by jumping from the building using a parachute and landing in the water below

The needed time to evacuate from the skyscraper is less than any other , where all the buildings need 15 minuts to be evacuated,else skyscraper needs at least 1 hour and 15 minuts.

Escape Plan

Air ventelation

The air is restored by outside winds which ventilate the bod of skyscraper by the difference of air pressure. The filtration air which produced by automobiles are made by a 8m widt of green strip which extended beside of the street

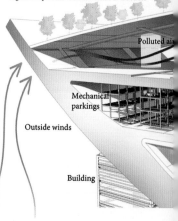

Polluted air

Mechanical parkings

Outside winds

Building

water cisterns, power plants, recreational and cultural areas, and farmlands.

Being a self-sufficient city it does not require any supplies from the mainland; on the contrary, the surplus energy and products are given away to support the nearby communities. It could be said that the bridge city could become an independent nation.

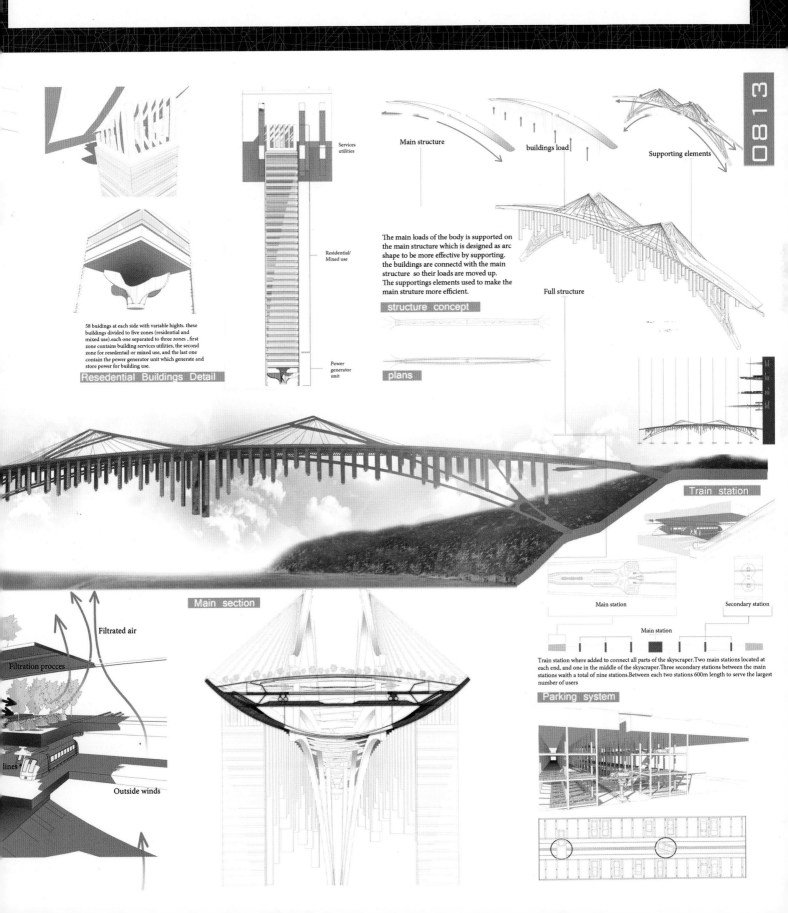

0813

Main structure

buildings load

Supporting elements

The main loads of the body is supported on the main structure which is designed as arc shape to be more effective by supporting. the buildings are connectd with the main structure so their loads are moved up. The supportings elements used to make the main struture more efficient.

structure concept

Full structure

plans

Services utilities

Residential/ Mixed use

Power generator unit

58 buidings at each side with variable hights. these buildings divided to five zones (residential and mixed use).each one separated to three zones , first zone contains building services utilities, the second zone for resedentail or mixed use, and the last one contain the power generator unit which generate and store power for building use.

Resedential Buildings Detail

Train station

Main station

Secondary station

Main station

Train station where added to connect all parts of the skyscraper.Two main stations located at each end, and one in the middle of the skyscraper.Three secondary stations between the main stations waith a total of nine stations.Between each two stations 600m length to serve the largest number of users

Filtrated air

Filtration procces

lines

Outside winds

Main section

Parking system

SPHERA

Sebastiano Maccarrone
Santi Musmeci

China

SPHERA THE EARTH'S REGENERATION

2050 PREVISION

The report from the Organisation for Economic Cooperation and Development, Environmental Outlook to 2050: The consequences of inaction, presents the latest projections of socio-economic trends over the next four decades, and their implications for four key areas of concern: climate change, biodiversity, water and the health impacts of environmental pollution. Despite the recent recession, the global economy is projected to nearly quadruple by 2050. Rising living standards will be accompanied by ever growing demands for energy, food and natural resources and more pollution.

Urban air pollution is set to become the top environmental cause of mortality worldwide by 2050, ahead of dirty water and lack of sanitation. The number of premature deaths from exposure to particulate air pollutants leading to respiratory failure could double from current levels to 3.6 million every year globally, with most occurring in China and India.

2150 VISION

By 2100 it will be extremely unhealthy to live in megacity areas and people will migrate to the countryside seeking cleaner air, food and water.

By 2150 megacities like Beijing, Jakarta, New York and London will be abandoned ghost cities and automated bulldozers will be sent to demolish buildings and infrastructures, saving only sited of historical value.

By recycling the demolished material, the bulldozers start the construction of **SPHERA**.

SPHERA is a new type of living environment, where the citizens of the world will live during the **"earth's regeneration"**, by using innovative and sustainable energies. At the same time, the purpose of SPHERA is to build an entirely new civilization, where people will try to redesign their culture and generate a sustainable society by creating a global-resource based economy that enables all people to reach their highest potential, a society that protects and preserves its environment. All people, regardless of political views, social customs and religion, ultimately require the same resources, such as clean air and water, arable land, medical care and relevant education. The human race is a single family and the earth is home to us all. It is simply not possible to separate ourselves from our fellow human beings anymore and coexistence is a necessity.

Each SPHERA-Unit provides all the sustenance needs of a human being and can hold 4 million inhabitants. SPHERA is divided into different areas from bottom to top: goods production area, research area, educational area, mixed use and residential area.

Included in the idea of self-sufficiency is the automatization of the production, distribution and disposal lines, thereby allowing SPHERA's inhabitants to develop their diversity and explore their individuality. As they are freed of boring and frustrating jobs they are allowed to follow their creative instinct instead of being slaves to the monthly pay-check, because there's "No social stability without individual stability".

SPHERA Construction

The construction is divided in 3 phases:

Core: Connected to the ground with storage tanks of water, energies, goods, this is the heart of SPHERA. It works like a distribution network for energies, supplies and transportations. The residential area is located in its top part.

Floor plates and buildings: Thanks to the production area in the bottom part of the core, the construction of SPHERA is totally automated. Green areas and buildings are designed to generate a friendly and healthy environment according to a grid following the transportation system

Shield: While the second phase is in process, the shield starts to grow all around the shape. SPHERA's shield is an automated screen that controls lighting, temperature and air quality due to APA (air polluted abatement) equipment that can purify the air coming inside.

The screen connected with the core can harvest, purify and store rainwater, generating energy during this process by water turbin.es In this shell there are also wind turbines, solar panels and air filters.

SPHERA Connections

All SPHERA Units are connected to each other by a high-speed transportation track that can quickly connect cities all over the world, thus creating a new global society.

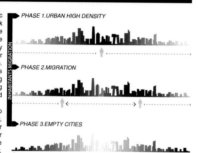
PHASE 1.URBAN HIGH DENSITY
PHASE 2.MIGRATION
PHASE 3.EMPTY CITIES

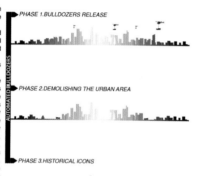
PHASE 1.BULLDOZERS RELEASE
PHASE 2.DEMOLISHING THE URBAN AREA
PHASE 3.HISTORICAL ICONS

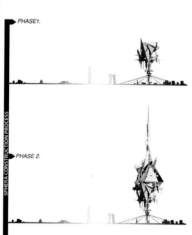
PHASE1.

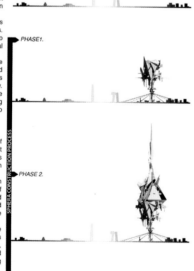
PHASE 2.
PHASE 3.

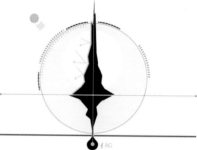

Renwable Energies: Solar energy
A solar panels system produce energy that is stored in the underground accumulator and sun-shading structures rotates around the shield following the sun rotation, controlling in this way the lighting inside SPHERA. The Core is covered by a reflecting material that reflect the light from top to down.

Renwable Energies: Rain water
Rainwater harvesting accumulate and stored the rainwater collected from small cuts in the shield surface. on the way to the tank the water go through a purify system and turbines generating cleaning water and energy

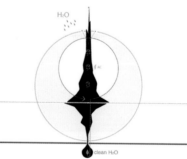

CO_2
NOx
SOx
$PM>5$
$PM>10$
+ APA
O_2
O_2
CO_2

Renwable Energies: Wind
The shield protect SPHERA from the polluted air generatir air through APA (air pollution abatement).The clean air is produced from the indoor space but is also produced outside. In this way all the SPHERA Units around the contribute to its renovation. Wind turbines around th generate electricity that is stored in the accumulator locate underground

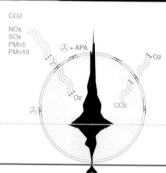

O_2 O_2

Renwable Energies: Natural ventilation
Filtered openings in the shield generate the chimne stimulated also by the green system that convert carbon di oxygen.

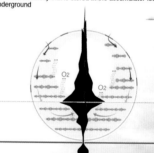

FUNCTIONS DISTRIBUTION

RECYCLE SYSTEM 5%

ENERGY SYSTEM 10%

FOOD PRODUCTION 20%

GOODS PRODUCTIO

By 2100 it will be extremely unhealthy to live in megacity areas and people will migrate to the countryside seeking cleaner air, food and water. By 2150 megacities like Beijing, Jakarta, New York, and London will be abandoned ghost cities and automated bulldozers will be sent to demolish buildings and infrastructures, saving only sites of historical value. By recycling the demolished material, the bulldozers start the construction of Sphera.

The construction of Sphera is divided into three phases. Firstly connected to the ground with storage tanks of water, energies, and goods is the heart of Sphera. It works like a distribution network for energy and

1027

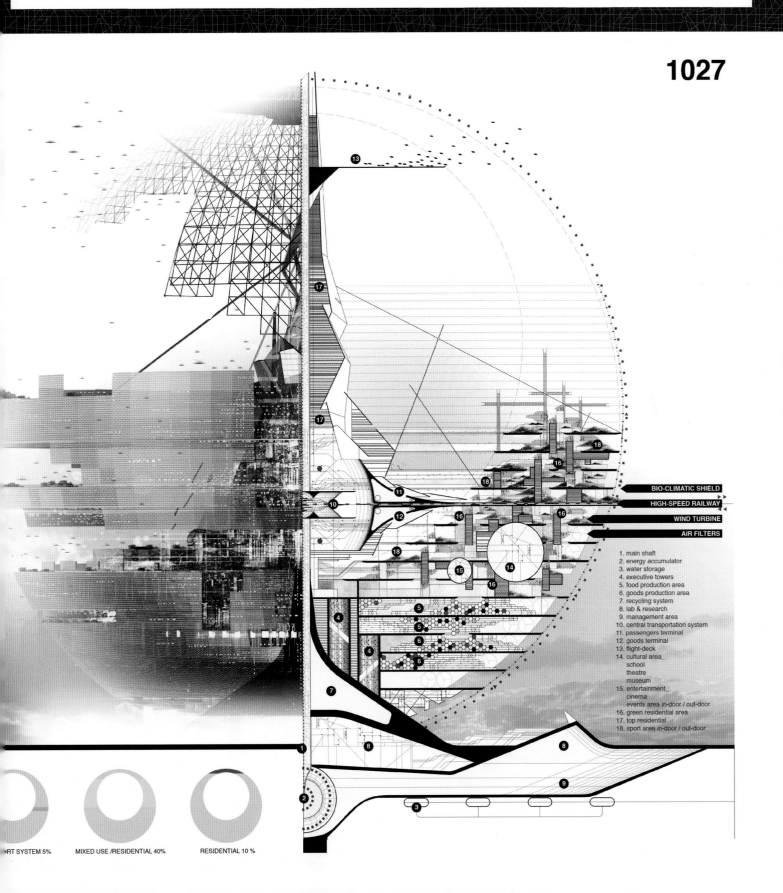

BIO-CLIMATIC SHIELD
HIGH-SPEED RAILWAY
WIND TURBINE
AIR FILTERS

1. main shaft
2. energy accumulator
3. water storage
4. executive towers
5. food production area
6. goods production area
7. recycling system
8. lab & research
9. management area
10. central transportation system
11. passengers terminal
12. goods terminal
13. flight-deck
14. cultural area_
    school
    theatre
    museum
15. entertainment_
    cinema
    events area in-door / out-door
16. green residential area
17. top residential
18. sport area in-door / out-door

RT SYSTEM 5%   MIXED USE /RESIDENTIAL 40%   RESIDENTIAL 10 %

supplies. The residential area is located in its top part. Next come the floor plates and buildings. Thanks to the production area in the bottom part of the core, the construction of Sphera is totally automated. Green areas and buildings are designed to generate a healthy environment according to a grid following the transportation system. While the second phase is in process, the shield starts to grow all around the shape. Sphera's shield is an automated screen that controls lighting, temperature and air quality.

Sphera is a new type of living environment, where the citizens of the world will live during the "earth's regeneration," by using innovative and sustainable energies. At the same time, the purpose of Sphera is to

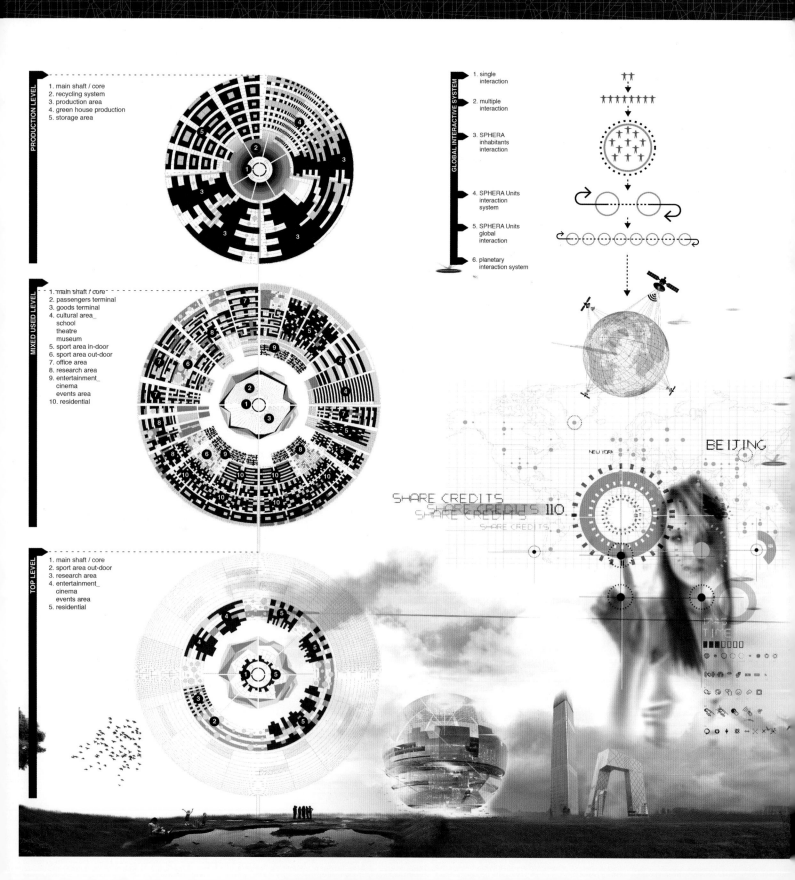

PRODUCTION LEVEL
1. main shaft / core
2. recycling system
3. production area
4. green house production
5. storage area

MIXED USED LEVEL
1. main shaft / core
2. passengers terminal
3. goods terminal
4. cultural area_
   school
   theatre
   museum
5. sport area in-door
6. sport area out-door
7. office area
8. research area
9. entertainment_
   cinema
   events area
10. residential

TOP LEVEL
1. main shaft / core
2. sport area out-door
3. research area
4. entertainment_
   cinema
   events area
5. residential

GLOBAL INTERACTIVE SYSTEM
1. single interaction
2. multiple interaction
3. SPHERA inhabitants interaction
4. SPHERA Units interaction system
5. SPHERA Units global interaction
6. planetary interaction system

SHARE CREDITS

SHARE CREDITS 110

SHARE CREDITS

NEW YORK

BEIJING

build an entirely new civilization, where people will try to redesign their culture and generate a sustainable society by creating a global-resource based economy that enables all people to reach their highest potential, a society that protects and preserves its environment.

Each Sphera provides all the sustenance needs of a human being and can hold 4 million inhabitants. Sphera is divided into different areas from bottom to top: goods production, research, educational, mixed use, and residential. Included in the idea of self-sufficiency is the automatization of the production, distribution and disposal lines, and thereby allowing Spehra's inhabitants to explore their individuality.

1027

SPHERA THE EARTH'S REGENERATION

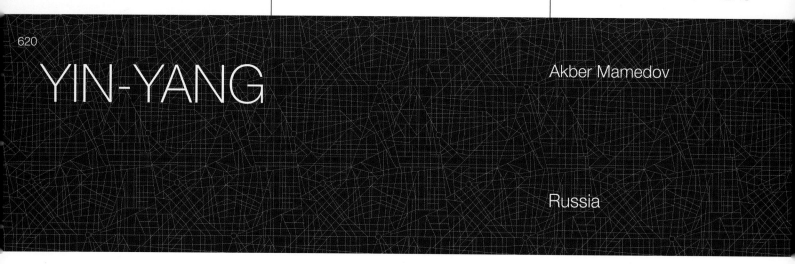

YIN-YANG

Akber Mamedov

Russia

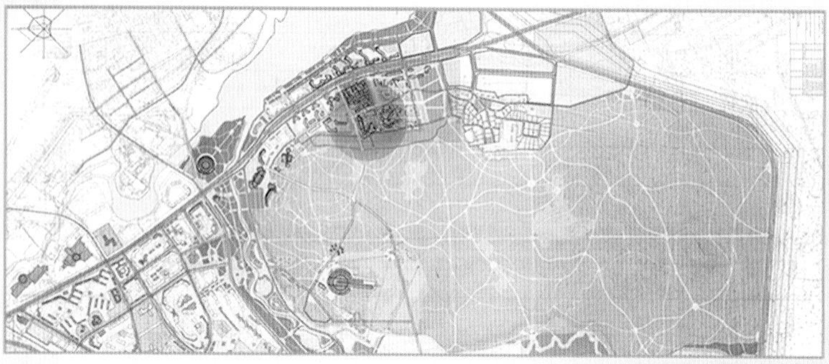

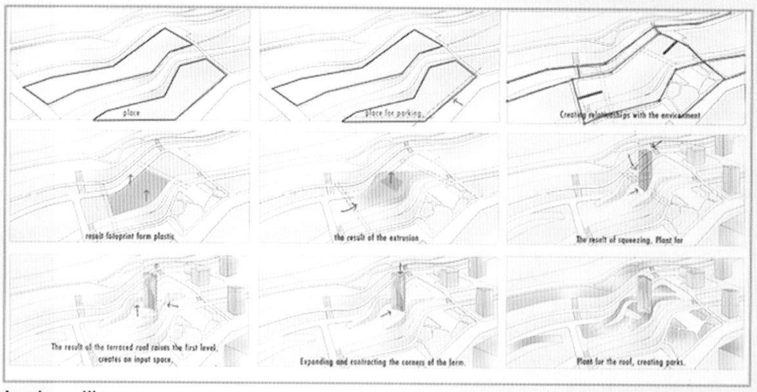

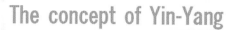

The concept of Yin-Yang

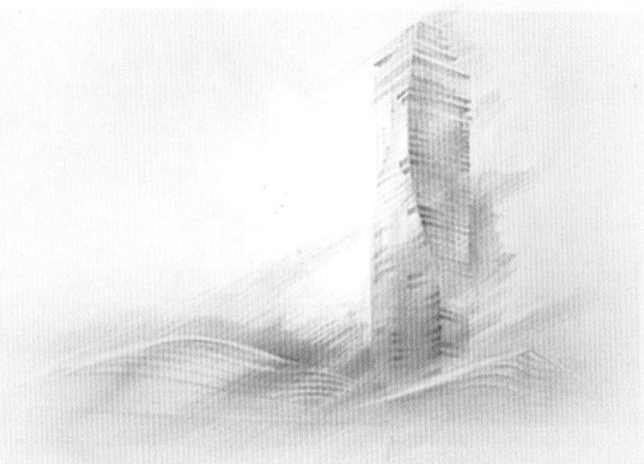

An urban setting.
Land area of 20 hectares of design, is located in the city of Yekaterinburg,(Russia) in the immediate vicinity of the highway.
Object Design - Multi-storey residential / public house (**The concept of Yin-Yang**)
At the heart of the neighborhood is planning concept of a continuum of transport and pedestrian connection with the existing building and the city center, at the expense extension of streets. Building plot located in close proximity to neighborhoods with historical buildings. In the south-west by the borders urban waterfront.
Creating a courtyard spaces with opening the park area allows you to organize visual communication with the external environment. Distinctive features of area is the presence of the river, visual connections with dominant urban center, proximity of the park and a few blocks from the historical buildings. The concept of creating a residential area, providing comfortable accommodation, reflected in the design of building, which includes residential, commercial residential houses, as well as public buildings. To this end, at the site are planned: a hotel, park and beach areas.
Constructive solution.
Frame system (Svjaseva). In terms of the purpose of the building, the most promising option is framed, with beamless slabs. Irregular column grid with variable step. This type of structural system allows you to transform, change, typical layout of the apartments. Stairs and walls elevator assembly in conjunction with the discs overlap, form the barrel stiffness and provide the spatial stability of the building framework.
Space - planning solution.
The architectural composition of the house built from the foundations of nature and man. Man as a complex structure has various microorganisms, nature and relief help to create the plastic form. (See details in pictures)
The main building is divided into two functional parts, assuming public offices, shops and residential part. The upper part of the flats using an alternative source of energy. Due to wind and solar energy building begins to live independently.
On the roof of organized green space with heavy soil for planting dwarf trees and shrubs.
Technical and economic indicators.
Built-up area - 12500 m2.
Building volume - 45000 m3.
Guest parking - 45 seats.
Total number of apartments: 140.
The total number of leased premises 3400 m2

The concept of Yin-Yang is a multi-story residential building located at the heart of a neighborhood in the city of Yekaterinburg that seeks to achieve a continuum of transport and pedestrian connection with the existing building and city center at the expense of extending streets.

Bordered in the southwest by an urban waterfront, the project contains several courtyard spaces that open up the park and allow for the organization of visual communication with the external environment. Such connections include places such as the river, the urban center, historical buildings, and different parts of the park itself.

1072-1

The concept is creating a residential area, providing comfortable accommodations reflected in the design of the building. The objective of designing a multi-story residential and public house enforces this concept of Yin-Yang.

A frame system made of beamless slabs interacts with an irregular column grid with varied steps, allowing for various apartment layouts and spatial stability among overlapping discs. This type of structural system allows one to transform the typical layout of the apartments. Stairs and elevator assembly in conjunction with the discs overlap, forming the barrel's stiffness and provide the spatial stability of the

residential floor

alternative energy source
technical floor

public floor

Stair lift unit

building framework.

The main building is divided into two functional parts, assuming public offices, shops and the residential part. The upper part of the flats uses an alternative source of energy. With wind and solar energy the building begins to live independently.

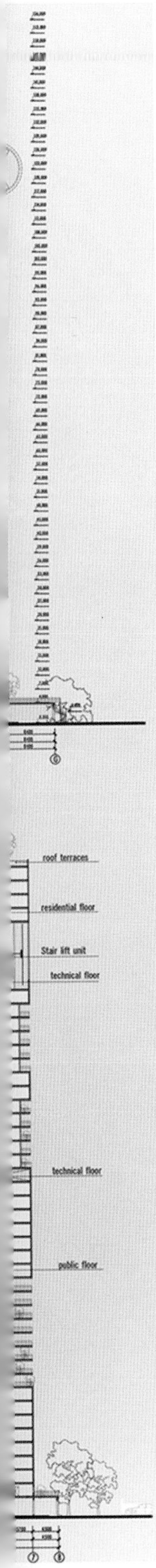

The concept of Yin-Yang

1072-2

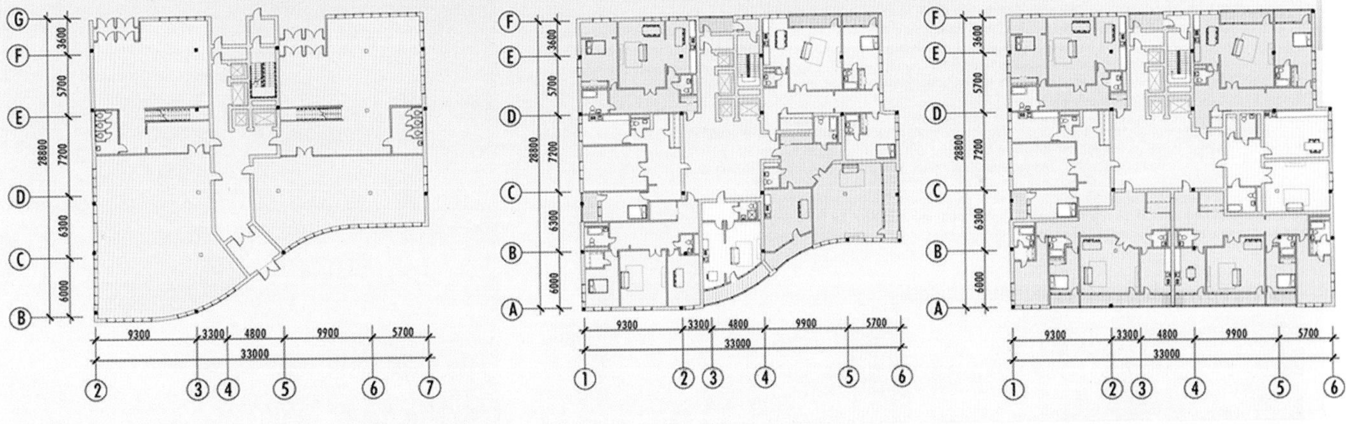

REHABILITATION TOWER

Min Gun Ho
Kim Seung Il
Ahn Byung Woo

Republic of Korea

REHABILITATION TOWER
SALVATION FROM THE CAGE

A big city is indiscriminately expanding under closed eyes to human ethical beliefs. Basically the city is supposed to play a role of proving an opportunity to people of starting to live a life. But city is not able to embrace all the people and become eventually the foundations of 'survival' rather than 'livelihoods for the people'. City is limited in terms of the area, but the population of city is increasing day by day. The large cities they gathered has shown saturation of the resident population beyond the capacity. In order to accept these people, the more high-rise building, the narrower and more selfish society becomes. Basically the narrower environment of home gives a direct hit on external elements as well as social atmosphere and a personal nature, meaning a worrying that people may be affected by losing control of human life elements and reason.

But now it's no longer enough to have high-rise apartments in the city that is already saturated. Without a handful of space, high-rise residential buildings cause several adverse effects such as fever phenomenon caused by less eco-friendly design, building-causing monroe effect, accumulation of pollutants, and other adverse effects of degrading the quality of life.

All of building are becoming high-rise buildings, it is not desired vision of mankind. Human life become persecution as they are. Not only to accommodate the growing population, the situation creates adverse effects far from desire for coexistence of nature and human nature. It is time to give a reinterpretation to high-rise that improves the quality of life of residents.

The shadow of high-rise residential building in Hong Kong

Hong Kong is a large gap between the rich and the poor country in the world. In general, Hong Kong's high-rise housing is being supplied to the general populace, but the growing population requires the government to supply directly from a high-rise built. In one apartment of 66m2 apartment so called 'cage apartment' behind the colorful city of Hong Kong and the poor, about 20 people are living. Then the poor in these apartments, are witnessed to live in high-rise flat separating a small space of cage with a rod of iron like that of animals.

Hong Kong's high-rise is associated with serious national problem with this cage apartment. With each passing day, the number of high-rise apartments are rapidly aging and thus resulting problems of urban beauty and hygiene. Because there's serious gap between the rich and the poor and Hong Kong's soaring home values, the disadvantaged and poor have lived in a small room in a small house, even by splitting the flat a little more than their 'cage'.

High-rise apartment is affected by the heat island phenomenon and error of the high-rise design and the higher the temperature and humidity within the building with mold walls causing disease is rampant, drugs and poverty-stricken people are living in the building. In order to prevent population overcrowding phenomenon and provide them to the general populace, poor construction of the low-level apartments was conducted and its lifetime is limited. This situation will worsen as time goes by as the building is old, unsanitary and dirty concrete facade with its exposure to pollutants (actually now just as often witnessed in Hong Kong). Life of the lower middle class in this gorgeous city is hell. At least of urban residential character would have to be in the city.

Conditions Graph of Hong Kong

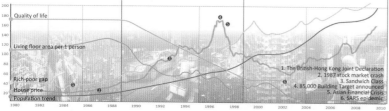

1. The British-Hong Kong Joint Declaration
2. 1987 stock market crash
3. Sandwich Class
4. 85,000 Building Target announced
5. Asian Financial Crisis
6. SARS epidemic

Rehabilitation Tower proposes a direction to solve the problems of city centering on Hong Kong. Firstly, Hong Kong has a serious wealth gap problem between the rich and the poor, and its lower middle class people cannot afford expensive land in the country. Hong Kong's strict market economy and high housing prices have driven the poor into small houses, small rooms, small cages with a rod of iron.

The main point is the use of underdeveloped buildings. High-rise apartments in Hong Kong are exposed to environmental pollutants and have a limited lifespan. Together, the high-rise buildings form a new single building; this will be a renovation strategy of re-birth of those abandoned buildings and thus a new lifetime

1112

is reassigned. Old, poorly used high-rise buildings are expected to bring substantiality to the city. Also, functional aspects must be able to accommodate a lot of people, and thus the existing cage apartment moves away from the negative elements into the new space to be born.

The solution proposed in Rehabilitation Tower is to create as many voids as possible throughout the city by relocating Hong Kong's existing underdeveloped buildings into one single building and give more open space to the city. With 90 degree grade or built up horizontally laid, three-dimensional space can be created. The escape from the negative elements of a "cage apartment" and three-dimensional space configurations

The cage is transformed to a converted and creation of vertical space

Above problems arise as high-rise buildings without a handful of free are elected. These dense low quality of the high-rise buildings need aggressive gesture. Overcrowding the city needs free space as the green space. But our solution is to provide Hong Kong, under the current City Planned Act in a broader perspective. Breather city of open space is to be created voids throughout the city as the existing outdated buildings moved into a single skyscraper.

But now it's no longer enough to have high-rise apartments in the city that is already saturated. Without a handful of space, high-rise residential buildings cause several adverse effects such as fever phenomenon caused by less eco-friendly design, building-causing monroe effect, accumulation of pollutants, and other adverse effects of degrading the quality of life.

Recycling of whole building to renewable city

Our main point in this part is the use of the underdeveloped buildings . As discussed earlier, the high-rise apartments in Hong Kong are exposed to environmental pollutants and have a limited lifespan. Together the high-rise buildings into a new single building, this will be a renovation strategy of re-birth of these abandoned and thus a new lifetime is reassigned. Old poorly used high-rise buildings is expected to bring substantiality of the city in terms of macroscopic urban of the city itself.

High-density city by High rise buildings — Selecting the cramped and lagged buildings

Grant green space — Move out of targets to empty space for urban breathing

Regeneration of city — Stacking the building to skyscraper by freeing, give comfort

Recycle of stable reinforced concrete structures

Reinforced concrete structures are maintained as most of the buildings in Hong Kong are concrete structures. These are the same materials and thus it is available as a single building construction. Material properties as a semi-permanent reinforced concrete of the city, but a bad environment has left it a non-permanent disposal to be neglected, if indeed wasted, it's actually waste of national economics. It has an environmental significance of recycling of the non-permanent buildings to a semi-permanent life.

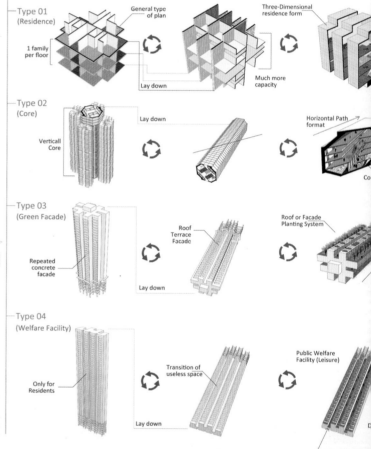

Type 01 (Residence)
- 1 family per floor
- General type of plan
- Lay down
- Three-Dimensional residence form
- Much more capacity

Type 02 (Core)
- Verticall Core
- Lay down
- Horizontal Path format

Type 03 (Green Facade)
- Repeated concrete facade
- Roof Terrace Facade
- Lay down
- Roof or Facade Planting System

Type 04 (Welfare Facility)
- Only for Residents
- Transition of useless space
- Lay down
- Public Welfare Facility (Leisure)

such as usual slab-to-wall and a standing wall-to-slabs allows people living in the building to create a multilateral community. Connecting space with an upper and lower element between buildings is used for a required space in a projected high-rise or the city.

m to a vertical space
he of monotonous building

not buildings existing vertical
ts of Hong Kong's 'cages' liter-
return to the rod of steel the
valls, separated by a little more
lat space, which can accommo-
pace in the poor gather in Hong
nake a living. A good point, all
can never find. Also functional
ust be able to accommodate a
ole, and thus the existing cage
t moves away from the nega-
ents into the new space to be

ing slabs as walls, slabs and
wall directed by three-dimen-
ice allowing for the multilateral
y residents as well as their re-
s with a layer of three-dimen-
nfiguration. The change pro-
fare facilities to the people
he cage and general amenities
dents from various angles. The
these programs has resulted in
private space separated with
ed wire cage apartment. Simi-
e corresponding saturated for
ng population, the high-rise
hat improves the quality of life
nts and contributes to the com-
fe.

No More Demolition!

ed and association of space
the buildings

ng high-rise buildings in Hong
pical type of overlap of these
apartment, an element that
e to create a space inside a
s well as another space associ-
veen buildings in the heart of
s buildings can go up and their
can have a wide variety of
development of space for the
ty is to be created. Although it
ed randomly, but a new fea-
e high-rise that you can con-
cultivate a comfortable life is
and semi-public space is pro-
sidents living in such a space
he newly created space and it
as an open space to the urban.
tocking a building, but contrib-
ban society by bringing a sys-
d reliable structure function to
ildings even with apparently
looks.

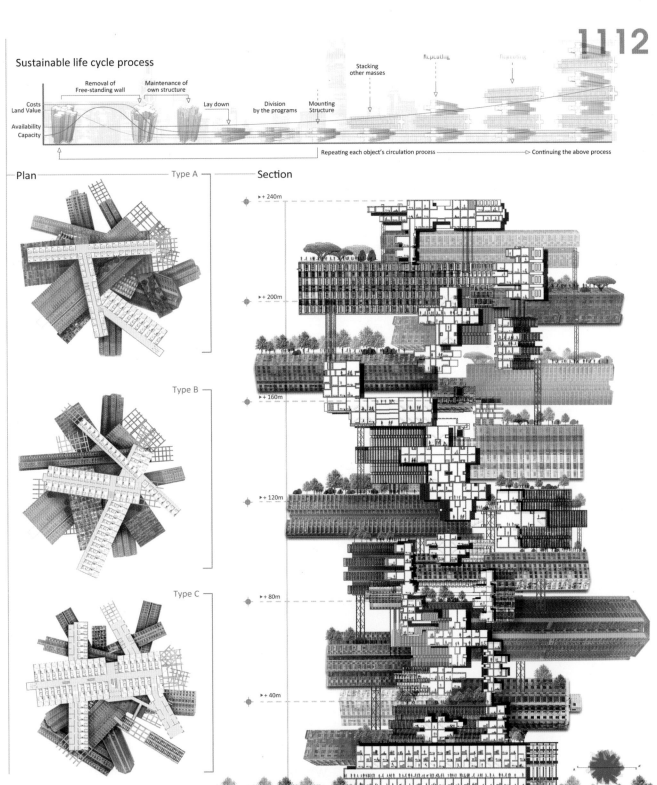

1112

Sustainable life cycle process

Costs / Land Value
Availability / Capacity

Removal of Free-standing wall
Maintenance of own structure
Lay down
Division by the programs
Mounting Structure
Stacking other masses
Repeating
Repeating

Repeating each object's circulation process　　▷ Continuing the above process

Plan　　　　　Type A　　　　Section

Type B

Type C

► + 240m
► + 200m
► + 160m
► + 120m
► + 80m
► + 40m

ISBN: 978-1-938740-05-3

Evolo, Inc.
6363 Wilshire Blvd. #311
Los Angeles, CA 90048

www.evolo.us